The Hindu Quest for the Perfection of Man

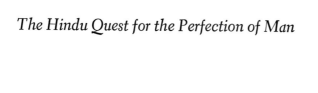

The Hindu Quest for

by TROY WILSON ORGAN

[T]he Perfection of Man

Ohio University ATHENS, OHIO

LIBRARY OF CONGRESS CATALOG NUMBER: 73–81450
SBN 8214—0066–5
MANUFACTURED IN THE UNITED STATES OF AMERICA

Contents

Foreword

A complete list of those who helped write this book would include persons ranging from the members of the 79th Congress who passed Public Law 584 (The Fulbright Act) to bearers Abdul, Kasi, and Babulal who sent me off each morning in India with shoes polished and body sustained with a warm breakfast. My indebtedness is here expressed to only a few, but it is symbolic of my gratitude to many.

What I owe to my "co-author" I shall intimate in the words of the *Mahābhārata:* "When one sets out for a strange land one's wife is one's trusted companion." Thanks are due to the U.S. Department of State and to the U.S. Educational Foundation in India for two research grants (1958–59, 1965–66), to Ohio University for the Distinguished Professor Award which made possible a third trip to India and for a Baker Award for study at the British Museum, to the Vice-Chancellor of Visva-Bharati University and the members of the Centre for Advanced Study in Philosophy for a Visiting Professorship (1968) and for the opportunity to present some of the material of this book in ten public lectures, to the members of the Śantiniketan *āśrama* for their patience in listening to a *mleccha* and for their suggestions, to librarians at the Indian National Library in Calcutta, at Śantiniketan, and at the Library of the British Museum, and to the many helpful people at The Ohio University Press.

I have borrowed ideas and phrases from three previously published articles of mine: "Two Forms of Tolerance," *The Visvabharati Quarterly,* Vol. 26, No. 2, Autumn 1960, pp. 162–169; "Hinduism as *Sādhana,*" *Ohio University Review,* Vol. 9, 1967, pp. 44–52; "The Self as Discovery and

Creation in Western and Indian Philosophy," *East-West Studies on the Problem of the Self*, edited by P. T. Raju and Alburey Castell, The Hague; Martinus Nijhoff, 1968, pp. 163–176. Permissions have been granted for reprinting from the following materials:

Deben Bhattacharya, trans. *Love Songs of Vidyapati.* (London: George Allen & Unwin, 1963); Charles E. Gover, trans. *The Folk Songs of Southern India.* (Madras: The South India Saiva Saddhanta Works Publishing Society, 1959); J. S. Hooper, trans. *Hymns of the Alvars.* (Calcutta: Association Press, 1920); Nicol Macnicol. *Psalms of Maratha Saints.* (London: Oxford University Press, 1919. Calcutta; Association Press, 1919); Swami Nikhilananda, ed. *Self Knowledge, An English Translation of Sankara-Charya's Atmabodha.* (New York: Ramakrishna-Vivekananda Center, 1946); Kishitimohan Sen. *Mediaeval Mysticism of India.* (London: Luzac & Co., 1936): Rabindranath Tagore. *Gitanjali.* (New York: Macmillan, 1916).

If a dedication is in order, it is to those who help us pass from the opening lines of Kipling's "A Ballad of East and West" to the next lines:

But there is neither East nor West, Border
nor Breed, nor Birth,
When two strong men stand face to face,
tho' they come from the ends of the earth!

Athens, Ohio
March 1970

TROY ORGAN

The Hindu Quest for the Perfection of Man

CHAPTER I

Hinduism as Quest

1. THE ESSENCE OF HINDUISM

An ancient prayer widely used in India petitions that the individual be led from illusion to reality, from ignorance to knowledge, and from mortality to immortality. This prayer contains salient features of Hinduism: concern for the life of man is the chief concern; the ideal life for man is a life of progressive development; man's life is capable of tremendous expansion; from present appearances he can move to reality; his state of ignorance can be overcome; he can be freed from time-bindedness; and he may appeal to universal powers for assistance. The absence of praise or adoration of the gods ought not to pass unnoticed.

> From the unreal lead me to the real!
> From darkness lead me to light!
> From death lead me to immortality! [1]

The student of philosophy and religion will be less likely to lose his bearings among the ramifications of the Hindu way of life and thought if he constantly comes back to this prayer as an expression of the fundamentals of Hinduism.

Four Sanskrit terms express different aspects of Hinduism: *mata,*

[1] *Bṛhad-Āraṇyaka Upaniṣad* 1. 3. 28. Robert Ernest Hume translation.

dharma, bhakti, and *mārga. Mata* means teachings or doctrines. The *mata* of a sect is its collection of opinions about god, the world, sin, man, etc. *Dharma* means duties, obligations, rules, and guides one should follow because of one's birth and status. *Dharma* in its simplest form means the essence of a thing, e.g., yellow color and malleability are the *dharma* of gold. When used with regard to man, *dharma* means what a man should do by reason of his nature as a man. *Bhakti* indicates the feeling of devotion toward an object of worship. *Mārga* is the path or way prescribed in order to reach a destination or to satisfy a desire. Originally *mārga* meant the track of wild animals; next it denoted the well-trodden path of animals, hence the proper path for the hunter to follow; and finally, the meaning was generalized to indicate any action that leads to the realization of a desired end.

Mata is the least important of the four terms, for there are no beliefs universally held in Hinduism. There is no common creed. There are no opinions required to be held in order to be a Hindu, unless it be the notion that man-the-less must become Man-the-More, that man is deity-*in-posse*: "O man, you are born for perfection," sang an ancient sage.[2] The absence of a common body of doctrine puzzles those Western scholars who study Hinduism assuming that it is a religion. Lyall failed to understand Hinduism when he described it as "the wandering beliefs of an intensely superstitious people." [3] Wilkins likewise erred when he observed, "My wonder is, considering their religious faiths and the character of the deities they worship, that they are not worse than they are." [4] These critics failed to understand Hinduism, as have many others, because they thought *mata* was the essence of Hinduism. This is a natural mistake for Christians to make because Christianity is a creedal religion: it stresses the objects of belief. "What must I *believe* in order to be saved?" is a uniquely Christian question.

Dharma expresses more of the nature of Hinduism than does *mata*. Hinduism in its social dimensions gives meaning and direction to duties of individuals covering almost every aspect of life. *Dharma* includes both the morally right and the ceremonially right. "What must I *do* in order to be saved?" is a basic Jewish and Hindu question. However, the concept of doing is far more moralistically limited in Judaism than in Hinduism; in other words, the *dharma* of Hinduism is incorporated into the *mārga*. Doing refers to the total disciplinary methods of training the will, rather than to the moral rightness or wrongness of single acts as measured by a fixed law.

[2] *Yajur Veda*. N. B. Sen, *Glorious Thoughts of the Vedas,* p. 128.
[3] Alfred C. Lyall, *Asiatic Studies*. Second Series, p. 291.
[4] W. J. Wilkins, *Modern Hinduism,* p. 146.

The place of *bhakti* or devotional love is as controversial in Hinduism as it is in Christianity and Islam. The orthodox within a faith suspect that the emotional component may become excessive, and that through absence of rational controls, emotion might lead to heterodoxy. On the other hand, the *bhakti* supporters hold that without emotion life becomes a dry husk of formal behavior and sterile ideas. Sufism in Islam, Hasidism in Judaism, Pietism in Christianity, and Tantrism in Hinduism and Buddhism are instances of *bhakti*. The question as to whether these movements are protest movements or permanent changes is controversial in most religions.

Mārga is central in Hinduism. Hinduism is a way or path to follow. It is a search for reality, for understanding, and for timelessness. The next four chapters of this book spell out the most important quests of Hinduism: reality, spirituality, integration, and liberation. Mahatma Gandhi caught the essence of Hinduism when, upon being asked to define the "Hindu Creed," he replied, "Search after Truth through non-violent means." [5] He often described himself as "a humble seeker after Truth." [6] Christianity stresses the *objects* of belief, and neglects the human quest; Hinduism stresses the *quest*, and neglects the objects of belief. Hence, Hindus sometimes claim that Christians, Muslims, Jews, and Buddhists are actually Hindus inasmuch as all are engaged in similar quests; sometimes Hindus swallow all religions into the great body of Hinduism, e.g., "Vedānta embraces all scriptures of the world." [7] Some Hindus have even been presumptuous enough to affirm that Hindus are also by nature good members of other religious groups, e.g., "The true Hindu is also a true Christian and a true Muslim." [8] But the usual pattern in Hindu thought is to acknowledge parallelism rather than identity: "The Christian is not to become a Hindu or a Buddhist, nor a Hindu or a Buddhist to become a Christian. But each must assimilate the spirit of the others and preserve his individuality and grow according to his own law of growth." [9] Christians in particular find identification, and even parallelism, unpleasant, since Christianity emphasizes differences in beliefs among religions. The Christian says, "Seek and ye shall *find*." But the Hindu says, "*Seek* and ye shall find." For him the quest for release or fulfillment is primary: the problems about the existence and nature of God are secondary. Hinduism is a process, not a result—a process of the Perfecting of Man.

[5] *Hindu Dharma*, p. 4.
[6] *Ibid.*, p. 14.
[7] Swami Adhedananda, *The Path of Realization*, p. 51.
[8] C. P. Ramaswami Aiyar, *Fundamentals of Hindu Faith and Culture*, p. 1.
[9] Swami Vivekananda, *The Complete Works of Swami Vivekānanda*, Vol. 1, p. 22.

2. WHY "HINDU" RATHER THAN "INDIAN"

The title *The Indian Quest for the Perfection of Man* might have greater appeal to many readers than *The Hindu Quest for the Perfection of Man,* but "Indian" includes 366,162,693 Hindus, 49,911,731 Muslims, 10,498,077 Christians, 7,846,074 Sikhs, 100,000 Parsis, and 30,000 Jews, according to the 1961 Census of India—which, by the way, did not provide for the Indians who prefer, as Nehru did, to be known as agnostics. This broader use of the term is in keeping with the Constitution of India which distinguishes between citizenship and religious preference. Articles 25 (1) and (2) read as follows: "Subject to public order, morality, and health and to the other provisions of this Part, all persons are equally entitled to freedom of conscience and the right freely to profess, practice and propagate religion. Nothing in this article shall affect the operation of any existing law or prevent the state from making any law—(a) regulating or restricting any economic, financial, political or other secular activity which may be associated with religious practice; (b) providing for social welfare and reform or the throwing open of Hindu religious institutions of a public character to all classes and sections of Hindus." The singling out of Hinduism for special clarification was anticipatory of troubles that would arise in the new democracy by reason of the caste practices of Hindus. Because of the different attitude toward religion in Pakistan, and because of the presence of almost 50,000,000 Muslims in India, the Central Government has during the years of independence emphasized that India is a secular state.[10]

Running through the writings of Radhakrishnan prior to his election to the presidency are found expressions of his recognition of the peculiarity of a secular nation with a spiritual foundation, e.g., "It may appear somewhat strange that our government should be a secular one while our culture is rooted in spiritual values."[11] Even more striking are his

[10] An interesting touchstone of India's political secularism is its legal attitude toward the slaughter of cattle. Muslims and Sikhs eat beef, and Hindus venerate cows. Therefore a law forbidding the slaughter of cows can scarcely be called secular. The Central Government solves the problem by having no laws on the subject, but it does not forbid the states from establishing such laws. Nehru saw the issue clearly: "Nehru's unequivocal opposition to a ban on cow slaughter was based on the contention that 'the agitation was motivated chiefly by sentimental and religious not economic considerations.' He also posed the question whether in a secular country the coercive power of the State should be used to impose upon all citizens the taboos of one section of the community." *The Pioneer*, November 6, 1966. Quoted by *India Briefing*, India Council of the Asia Society, January 1967, No. 14, p. 4.

[11] Foreword to S. Abid Husain, *The National Culture of India*. Second edition, p. vii.

doubts about the wisdom of Indian nationhood, e.g., "The living contiguity of Indian life is to be seen not in her political history, but in her cultural and social life. Political obsession has captured India since the battle of Plassey. To-day politics have absorbed life. The State is invading society, and the India of 'no nation,' as Rabindranath puts it, is struggling to become a 'nation' in the Western sense of the term, with all its defects and merits." [12] His reference to Tagore may have been to the poet's observation, "India's heart is in society, not in the state." [13] The tragedy of India-Pakistan relations is that while India is desperately trying to be a secular state, Pakistan persists in viewing all political matters within the context of a Muslim-controlled state. Pakistan's attack on India becomes a holy war, but India cannot respond in kind. If India is ever prodded into affirming that she is a Hindu state, then much is lost as far as India is concerned—and much is gained for Pakistan! Prime Minister Shastri saw this clearly. In his radio broadcast to the nation on September 3, 1965, he said, "There are no Hindus, no Muslims, no Christians, no Sikhs, but only Indians. I am confident that the people of this country who have given proof of their patriotism and commonsense on so many occasions in the past, will stand united as one man to defend their country. We must all be on guard against mischief-makers and agents who may try to instigate communal disturbances." [14] And on September 26 Shastri said in a speech at Ramlila Grounds, New Delhi, "The unique thing about our country is that we have Hindus, Muslims, Christians, Sikhs, Parsis and people of all other religions. We have temples and mosques, gurdwaras and churches. But we do not bring all this into politics. We are not working to make India a Hindu State or a Muslim State. This is the difference between India and Pakistan. Whereas Pakistan proclaims herself to be an Islamic State and uses religion as a political factor, we Indians have the freedom to follow whatever religion we may choose, to worship in any way we please. So far as politics is concerned, each one of us is as much an Indian as the other." [15]

Unfortunately some of the more zealous Hindus have been working contrary to these pragmatically desirable positions and have attempted to remind all Indians that the ideals and the strength of the nation stem from Vedic fountainheads, e.g., K. S. Ramaswami Sastri in *Hindu Cul-*

[12] Radhakrishnan, *The Heart of Hindusthan*, pp. 18–19.

[13] Quoted by B. G. Gokhale, *Indian Thought Through the Ages: A Study of Some Dominant Concepts*, p. 169.

[14] D. R. Mankekar, *Twenty-two Fateful Days*, p. 200. Cf. the observation of Max Weber that "the concept of the citizen has not existed outside the Occident." *The Protestant Ethic and the Spirit of Capitalism*. Translated by Talcott Parsons. New York: Charles Scribner's Sons, 1930, p. 23.

[15] D. R. Mankekar, *op. cit.*, p. 209.

ture and the Modern Age says, "My aim in this book is to show how India is the temple, nay, the goddess of our spiritual culture and how India and Hinduism are organically related as body and soul." [16] Such a claim handicaps India's efforts to convince the community of nations that she is unique in the practice of tolerance and brotherhood. Two fears stalk the Indian Government: the fear of communal riots among Hindus and Muslims, and the fear that states with a high percentage of Muslims, e.g., Hyderabad, might attempt to withdraw from the nation. India remembers that her greatest modern hero was martyred by a Hindu because he attempted to placate the Muslims. So India is spreading the word that she is not a *Hindu* nation, although her message is sometimes clouded by her actions, e.g., in 1965 when the Lok Sabha (House of the People) in New Delhi discussed the removal of the terms "Muslim" and "Hindu" from Aligarh Muslim University and Banaras Hindu University, the question of the removal of "Muslim" provoked little discussion while the question of the removal of "Hindu" provoked such a furor that the issue was not settled. Since this study examines the ways of thinking and acting which stem from literature rooted in the Hindu tradition and excludes the Jain, Buddhist, and Muslim traditions in India, we shall cooperate with the wishes of the Central Government of India by using the word "Hindu" rather than "Indian" except where we mean the citizenry of India. It is interesting to note that Radhakrishnan when he wrote his *Indian Philosophy* made a contrary decision: "It is necessary to give some justification for the title 'Indian Philosophy,' when we are discussing the philosophy of the Hindus as distinct from that of the other communities which have also their place in India. The most obvious reason is that of common usage. India even today is mainly Hindu." [17] Needless to say, *President* Radhakrishnan did not talk that way!

This study is an examination of the ideal claims of Hinduism, not the realization of these claims. The writings of sages, poets, and philosophers are the sources. Although this is a study of theory rather than practice, practices will be introduced as illustrative material. Two reasons can be given for the use of this material: the author's leanings to realism, empiricism, and pragmatism, and the constant claim of Indian intellectuals that theory and practice are not separated in Hinduism. But let it be clear at the beginning—this is not a sociological study. India is a fertile field for excellent specific sociological studies, but India also attracts general studies of dubious sociological value. There have been and there should be more careful scientific studies of the Santals, the

[16] Pp. 10–11.
[17] *Indian Philosophy*, Vol. 1, p. 56.

Anglo-Indian community, city slums, and villages. But India does not seem ripe for scientific public opinion polls, and certainly not for general studies of "Indian society." For example, the life of the Indian peasant in the village is a fascinating subject for novelists, short-story writers, journalists, and others who have no training in the methods of modern sociological research. Books written by such people have wide appeal among the reading public, but they easily give wrong impressions. Two recent books of this character are *Blossoms in the Dust* by Kusum Nair and *The Crisis of India* by Ronald Segal. More worthwhile are River's *The Todas*, Wisers' *Behind Mud Walls*, and Isaac's *India's Ex-Untouchables.*

3. HINDUISM AS PROMOTER OF NOBLE LIVES

Many Western visitors to India whose experiences of Hinduism are limited to sights such as the burning ghats of Banaras, goat sacrifices at Kalighat in Calcutta, *liṅga* shrines, and pilgrims at Puri are repelled by Hinduism. The early Christian missionaries, not penetrating the outer covering that had grown around Hinduism, sometimes brought back stories of the type found in Katherine Mayo's *Mother India.* William Carey was an exception, as can easily be seen by visiting the Carey Memorial Library at Serampore College. Still there is justice in accusing Hinduism of failing to develop a uniform high level of social life. Hunger, disease, illiteracy, and poverty are facts in India which cannot be ignored. "One of the most deplorable features of Hindu society is that while here and there we have individuals who possess religious culture of a very high degree, the average level of culture is very low," admits D. S. Sarma.[18] The Hindu culture of the few—the philosophers, artists, *ṛṣis* (seers), and poets—is a culture much to be admired. But for every Śaṅkara, or Kālidāsa, or Buddha, or Tagore there are thousands living in squalor, filth, and ignorance. This cannot be denied by even the most enthusiastic Indophile. The failure to improve the lot of the common man is a conspicuous weakness of Hinduism. But this should not blind critics to one of the great strengths of this culture—the fact that it has

[18] *Studies in the Renaissance of Hinduism in the Nineteenth and Twentieth Centuries,* p. 646. Amaury de Riencourt argues that whereas the French and the Chinese distrust individuality, the Germans and the Indians revel in self-experimentation: "China could boast thousands of poets, scholars and philosophers, but no outstanding personality remotely comparable to those of India—even in modern times when the colourful Roys, Keshabs, Rāmakrishnas, Vivekānandas, Gandhis and Nehrus have no equivalent among China's intellectual and political leaders, shadowy and slightly anonymous men like Sun Yat-sen, Hu Shih, Chiang Kai-shek and Mao Tse-tung." *The Soul of India,* pp. 260–261.

produced some of the noblest specimens of the human race. One of the first insights the Western world had of the potentiality of Hinduism for the creation of superior individuals came in 1893 when Swami Vivekananda visited the World's Columbian Exposition in Chicago to participate in the Parliament of Religions. The *New York Herald* said, "He is undoubtedly the greatest figure in the Parliament of Religions." The *Boston Evening Transcript* reported, "At the Parliament of Religions they used to keep Vivekananda until the end of the programme to make people stay till the end of the session. . . . The four thousand fanning people in the Hall of Columbus would sit smiling and expectant, waiting for an hour or two of other men's speeches, to listen to Vivekananda for fifteen minutes." During his visit to America, both Harvard and Columbia universities offered him full professorships.[19] If asked to select but one man to represent the highest Hinduism has produced, many would select Rabindranath Tagore (1861–1941), a Renaissance man in the twentieth century. He was a genius in many fields—poetry, short stories, music, choreography, painting, architecture, science, education, social service, and statesmanship. Three months before his death, though troubled by the war in Europe, he wrote an essay "Crisis in Civilization" in which he said, "I shall not commit the grievous sin of losing faith in Man." He closed the essay with a poem:

> The Great One comes,
> sending shivers across the dust of the earth.
> In the heavens sounds the trumpet,
> in the world of man drums of victory are heard,
> the Hour has arrived of the Great Birth.
> The gates of Night's fortress
> crumble into the dust—
> on the crest of awakening dawn
> assurance of a new life
> proclaims "Fear Not."
> The great sky resounds with hallelujahs of victory
> to the Coming of Man.[20]

4. HINDUISM AS RELIGION

One of the most persistent claims of Western observers, and even of Indians, is that India is a religion-obsessed or religion-possessed land.

[19] "Swami Vivekananda and America." A pamphlet published by United States Information Service, Sikandra Road, New Delhi, 1963, p. 9.

[20] Sisirkumar Ghose (editor), *Faith of a Poet: Selections from Rabindranath Tagore.* Bombay: Bhavan's Book University, 1964, p. 56.

Innovations will not be accepted in the "marketplace of ideas" unless they are shown somehow to be rooted in the spiritual heritage of India. "Did you ever see such a country? If you want to get up a gang of robbers, the leader will have to preach some sort of religion, then formulate some bogus metaphysics, and say that this method is the clearest and quickest way to get to God. Then he finds a following. Otherwise, not." [21] The first charge Indians bring against legislative decisions is that they are a violation of "our noble religious heritage." For example, when the West Bengal Cabinet sought in August of 1965 to save milk for infants and children by banning the making of sandish (a popular Bengali sweet), protestors paraded in the streets, petitions were signed, and letters were written to the editors of newspapers condemning this outrage against religious customs. "How can we celebrate holy days and festivals without sandish?" was the refrain. Some objectors even pointed out that the officer chiefly responsible for the ban was a member of the Brahmo Samaj, therefore not an orthodox Hindu, and therefore this was a case of religious persecution! But in spite of the omnipresence of religion in India, one can also argue that India is a land without religion, for Hindu India takes no cognizance of religion as an independent phenomenon as is done in the West with its conflicts between religion and science, Church and State, faith and reason. Hinduism as the expression and carrier of a great civilization is inseparable from philosophical speculation, literary activity, and artistic creation. It is inherent in customs regarding marriage, vocation, dining, and other activities of primary group relationships. It is not a decision problem for the individual. It is not something he may or may not possess. One of the Sanskrit terms for Hinduism—*Āryadharma*—means the traditional obligations which fall upon one by reason of his birth. "Religion" so defined is obviously universal and inescapable. These obligations may fall so lightly, and will fall so unquestionably, that many Hindus are almost unaware of their existence. The author recalls helping a Hindu friend register for graduate work in an American university. When he came to the blank marked "Religious Preference" he asked, "What do I put here? What is my religion?" On another occasion while talking in India with a young Hindu student, the author suggested that perhaps his vocational goals would be more easily reached if he did not marry. The student could not comprehend. The notion of not marrying was too foreign to him. Even though at the time he had no plans

[21] Swami Vivekananda, "An Unpublished Lecture" in *Vedānta for the Western World*. Edited by Christopher Isherwood, p. 228. Keshub Chunder Sen once said, "It has been justly said that the Hindus walk and sit religiously, eat and drink religiously, work and sleep religiously;—their social organism is interwoven with their religion." *Lectures in India*, Vol. 2, p. 396.

for marriage, and no great interest in the opposite sex, he replied spontaneously, "But you can't escape marriage! It's part of life." This young man was existentially verifying the view that Hinduism is a way of life and thought that has become second nature. He could have quoted from the *Laws of Manu:* "The man is not man alone, but his wife and children also." [22] Hinduism is "an anthropological process to which by a strange irony of fate, the name of 'religion' has been given." [23] Hinduism as thought is inseparable from communal and social life. Furthermore, theory and practice are inseparable in the sense that the one who knows the theory will necessarily be involved in the practice, but not everyone who is a practicing Hindu will be able to give a rationale for his acts. Also the "thought" in Hinduism will not always be theological thought. Among most Hindus it will be mythopoetic, metaphysical, and aesthetic. The villager will be more likely to explain his behavior in terms of legends and myths of village gods than by quotations from the Upaniṣads.

Is Hinduism a religion? The answer depends on what one means by religion. Religion in any culture is an expression of dissatisfaction with life as man finds it and of longing for better things. It is a lover's quarrel with life, a grumbling about the *status quo* accompanied by a search for a promised land. If men were fully satisfied with their earthly existence, religion would never have been created. The popular hypothesis that fear produces religion is much too simple. Other psychological motives are equally prominent, e.g., disintegration, loneliness, fragmentation, anxiety, hope. The dissatisfaction which stimulates the appearance of religion is not simply the desire for the good things of life, such as food, clothing, shelter, friends, and children, nor is it a quest for more security, power, or pleasure. It is an uneasiness about all things, even about the good things of life, a feeling that the most durable and rewarding enjoyments are alloyed with baser stuff, a recognition that one's house is founded on sand and one's gods have feet of clay, a haunting awareness of incompleteness, and a dream of a time and place in which these unnamable perturbations will be no more. The creative geniuses in religion are individuals in whom this restlessness becomes overpowering until they reach out in desperation to find that which will bring real or imagined improvement. The quest is often one of great anguish. Moses in the wilderness of Midian argues with his God that he is not the man to lead the Israelites out of Egypt; Jesus at the opening of his prophetic role goes into the desert "to be tempted of the devil" and at the close of his short life pleads that he be spared the torture of the cross; Siddhartha Gautama deserts his wife and home to search for enlightenment through the meth-

[22] 9.45.
[23] Govindā-Dāsa, *Hinduism*, p. 45.

ods of meditation and bodily punishment; Muhammad considers suicide as the way out of his torments during the two years between his first and his second visions. The life of a prophet is not a happy one. Yet not all is gloom, for the dissatisfaction is also a response to the belief that values latent in the cosmos can be appropriated for the improvement of man's existence.

Religion is a human phenomenon so diverse in its manifestations that scholars despair of forming a definition which will cover all its chameleonic appearances. When one considers how religions have varied from age to age, from country to country, and from person to person, one can sympathize with those who say "religion is utterly indefinable." [24] What are the common elements among the experiences of a savage cowering before an idol of mud, a Buddhist placing flowers on an altar, a Hindu bathing in a sacred river, a Shintoist climbing a mountain, a Quaker meditating in silence, a Roman Catholic kneeling at Mass, a Holy Roller shouting and thrashing about on the floor, and a Unitarian participating in a forum discussion?

Some scholars deny that there is any such thing as religion in general. They claim that there are religions, i.e., particular patterns of life and thought, and there are religious attitudes, i.e., particular responses to life experiences, but there is no abstraction known as religion. In similar fashion one could say there is no science in general; there is only chemistry, biology, physics, geology, etc. Yet common usage demands the generic words, religion and science, and even though agreement as to their exact meaning is unlikely, the words will probably remain.

Leuba in a volume now regarded as a classic in its field made a study of many definitions of religion.[25] He divided the definitions into three classes according to the point of view they represented: Intellectualistic, Affectivistic, and Voluntaristic. A definition may stress religion as action, e.g., "the recognition of all duties as divine commands," [26] or as emotion, e.g., "the feeling of absolute dependence," [27] or as thought, e.g., "the realm where all the riddles of the world are solved, all the contradictions of probing thought are unveiled." [28] Leuba's classification of the definitions of religion is a good delineation of the nature of religion: religion must give its devotees something to do, something to feel, and something

[24] Frederic Spiegelberg, *Living Religions of the World.* Englewood Cliffs, New Jersey: Prentice-Hall, 1956, p. 7.

[25] James H. Leuba, *A Psychological Study of Religion.* New York: The Macmillan Company, 1912, Chapter II and Appendix.

[26] Immanuel Kant, *Religion Within the Limits of Reason Alone.* Translated by T. M. Greene and H. H. Hudson. Chicago: Open Court Publishing Company, 1934, p. 142.

[27] Friedrich Schleiermacher, *Der Christliche Glaube,* Vol. 1, Chapter 15, Section 4.

[28] Georg W. F. Hegel, *Werke,* Vol. 11, p. 3.

to believe. Religion, like ethics, seeks the good; like art, seeks the beautiful; and, like science, seeks the true. But religion is not satisfied with the goodness of ethics, nor with the beauty of art, nor with the truth of science. It seeks a goodness, a beauty, and a truth transcending the noblest achievements of moralists, artists, and scientists. In the promised land is goodness better than moral goods, beauty more beautiful than artistic creations, and truth truer than scientific truths. This claim can be made only if religion contacts a reality more real than the realities of ethics, art, and science. And this *is* the claim of religion. Religion asserts that it places man in relationship to Ultimate Reality, the Reality which is the source of all realities and the criterion of all values.

When the emotional element of religion is emphasized there is danger that religion may become an art, and thus neglect the other two sides. George Santayana claimed religion is the highest art and as an art it should make no claim to truth. Religion so conceived is something to enjoy like a fragile flower or a sonata, but the more disciplined elements of thought and action are missing. W. E. Hocking declared religion to be the mother of all arts, a mother fully manifested in no one of her children. She has supplied many of the great themes in music, painting, poetry, and architecture. Others have asserted the independence of religion and art. Religion may use the arts as her servant, or she may neglect them, or she may condemn them. The arts likewise are independent of religion. For example, music may be used in religious worship, it may promote patriotism, it may be instrumental in psychotherapy, or it may be used to stimulate sexual passion, but music itself is none of these. The beauty religion seeks is a beauty that cannot be divorced from truth and reality, whereas art may seek the beautiful isolated from truth and reality.

In most religions the ethical element is so organically related it cannot be separated without destroying the religion. This fact has led to two divergent interpretations: some have claimed that morality is a product of religion, and others that religion is a type of morality. The element of truth in the first claim is that an ethic is usually dependent upon a particular metaphysical system; one's decision as to what is most worthwhile in life depends upon what one believes to be most real. Ethical systems which have been weak in metaphysical speculations usually appropriate a theory of reality and adapt it for their purposes, e.g., Epicureanism's use of atomism and Utilitarianism's use of naturalism. The second interpretation regards religion as emotionalized morality. Höffding held that morality creates values, but religion conserves values. A third interpretation could contend that religion and morality are independent elements of human experience. In Christianity one might derive this inference from Jesus' words that he who enters the Kingdom of God is he who does the will of God, not he who cries, "Lord, Lord." Those who do the will of God are the moralists; those who merely worship are the religionists. A non-religious ethic is far more conceivable than a non-moral religion. A religion without morality would be a truncated religion, one that might bring comfort to its followers but would place no demands upon their lives. The followers of such an aesthetic faith would in time cry for action.

A religion gives its followers something to believe. It seeks to convey true insights into the nature of reality as well as bring warmth of emotional experience and moral goodness. In its third aspect religion often runs counter to another element in human experience, whose business is entirely the discovery of the nature of the physical world, namely, the sciences. Many have claimed that there can be no conflict between religion and science, but that there can be, and often is, conflict between theology and science. The fallacy in this statement is the assumption that religion is an experience that does not include factual statements about the nature of the world. The broader conception is that religion must include thought as well as feeling and action. Therefore conflict between religion and science is possible, indeed probable.

There have been three principal efforts to resolve the conflict between religion and science in Western tradition. (1) Dogmatic scientists have claimed that science gives the true picture of the world; religion gives either a false or a factually meaningless view of the world. (2) Dogmatic religionists have countered with the claim that, because of its wider perspective, religion makes a full analysis of reality, whereas the sciences by limiting their methodology to the quantitatively measurable, the empirically testable, and the linguistically expressible cut themselves off from any aspects of reality which do not conform to their methodological prerequisites. (3) Others—both religionists and scientists—have attempted to allocate the subject matter, giving the area of facts to science and the area of values to religion.

Religion is solemn and serious in its relation to the Ultimate Reality. It is a travesty upon the term to speak of pipe-smoking or golf as a religion. Religion may be orientated about trivial objects, but the situation *in toto* is not trivial. A primitive man bowing before a rude idol is motivated by serious desires: victory in battle, escape from famine, fertility of crops, cure of disease, birth of a son, or life beyond death. The Christian communion service may be celebrated with bread and grape juice from the corner grocery, but it symbolizes the sacrificial death of Christ. Religion concerns itself with that which is regarded as the very heart and core of life.

Religion is social. Its emotion is expressed in sacrifices, rites, ceremonies, and prayers of groups; its action embodies human relationships, and its thought manifests itself in creeds, doctrines, and scriptures. Church, synagogue, mosque, and temple are not extraneous to religion. Religion may be what one does with his solitude, but the religious community determines what one will think and feel in solitude.

Religion is a serious and social human effort to think, to feel, and to act toward Ultimate Reality in ways which anticipate future melioration. Is Hinduism a religion? The answer is Yes, but only in the sense of religion so defined. For example, the term Ultimate Reality must not be assumed to be synonymous with a theistic conception of the universe. Indeed, this definition of religion is especially appropriate for Hinduism with its goal of the Perfection of Man in all dimensions of his being. Is Hinduism only a religion? The answer to this question is not easy, for Hinduism is far more than a cluster of events associated with temples, pilgrimages, worship, and the reading of scriptures. The separation of sacred and profane, of religious and non-religious, is foreign to Hinduism. The problem arises only when a Hindu is converted to Christianity, or to Islam, or even to Buddhism. What part of his old life must the convert give up because it is a part of Hindu religion, and what of his old life may he retain since it is a part of Hindu culture and not of Hindu religion *per se*? For example, is caste an element of Hindu religion or of Hindu culture? Caste is one of the conspicuous features of Hinduism which is manifestly in violation of the doctrine of equality found in Islam, Buddhism, and Christianity, yet caste not only remains among converts from Hinduism, but also tends to creep into the three communities when they live in contact with Hinduism. T. S. Wilkinson acknowledges, "The most outstanding feature of Indian society is its caste hierarchy. Caste is so much in the air that members of religious groups that otherwise denounce caste yet follow its proscriptions and prescriptions, consciously or unconsciously." [29] He continues in this article on the situation of the Christian Church in India to point out that "in certain cities of Northern India the caste ties and *biradari* (brotherhood) continue to remain a strong basis for community life among Christians converted from the Scheduled castes" [30] and also the educated Christians tend to form a new caste, "the 'Brahmins' of the Church." [31] Hutton not only admits that in India "Muslims do form a real caste," [32] but also he lists over a dozen of the Muslim castes.[33] B. R. Ambedkar in October 1956

[29] "Urban Community and the Church," *The United Church Review*, August 1964, p. 171.

[30] *Ibid.*, p. 173.

[31] *Loc. cit.*

[32] J. H. Hutton, *Caste in India*, p. 174.

[33] *Ibid.*, p. 306.

in an impressive ceremony at Nagpur led 300,000 of his followers—mostly Untouchables—into the Buddhist fold, and on the following day expressed his desire that all India become Buddhist.[34] Since he died a few weeks later, Ambedkar did not live to see the results of the mass conversion: the Untouchables instead of escaping the problems of caste discrimination through mass conversion to Buddhism, formed a neo-Buddhist subcaste within the Untouchables! In India one will find second and third generation Christians who remain vegetarians, who accept the doctrine of *karma* and reincarnation, and who observe some of the Hindu festivals and holy days. Obviously to become a Christian does not mean to cease being a Hindu! Hinduism is not easily classified as only a religion, or perhaps one should say, in view of the "religionless Christianity" intimated by Dietrich Bonhoeffer, that Christianity and Hinduism are not "religions" or "non-religions" in the same sense.

5. HINDUISM AS PHILOSOPHY

Hinduism is not philosophy in the Western sense. Although its reliance upon the Upaniṣads for themes and proofs looks suspiciously like medieval Scholasticism to Western eyes, such reliance has not prevented Indian thought from moving in a variety of directions. Its catholicity has resulted in unpleasant confrontations of philosophers East and West due to the proclivity of the Indians to playing a game of "Me Too" in which every idea that is proposed is countered with the observation that the Indians have the same idea, or that they got it first, or that they have a clearer conception of it, or that they have already seen through the errors of the idea. International congresses of philosophy should begin by reciting these lines from Radhakrishnan: "The question of the affiliation of ideas is a useless pursuit. To an unbiased mind, the coincidences will be an evidence of historical parallelism. Similar experiences engender in men's minds similar views." [35] At the close of the Second East-West Philosophers' Conference in Honolulu in 1949 a Chinese philosopher stated publicly that he was grateful for having attended the Conference to learn that any statement made about Indian philosophy can be both supported and refuted! Fraser and Edwards think Indians do not prize consistency: "Men are not and cannot be wholly consistent in their religious and moral systems, but in India the capacity for inconsistency is greater than elsewhere." [36] This touches on the value of tolerance, a

[34] Donald Eugene Smith, *India as a Secular State*, p. 167.
[35] *Indian Philosophy*, Vol. 1, p. 24.
[36] J. N. Fraser and J. F. Edwards, *The Life and Teachings of Tukārām*, p. 35.

value which Indians often claim is superbly manifested in their culture. While one would be hard pressed to find a philosophical position which has not been supported by someone in the long cultural history of India, and while with certain exceptions each view has been given a proper hearing, it would be a great mistake to dwell upon the multiform nature of Hindu philosophy and miss the common theme running through the systems. Indian music is a helpful analogue of Hindu philosophy. In classical Indian music the musicians start with a *rāga,* i.e., a melody composed of notes in a specific order and with specific emphases, and a *tāla,* i.e., an organized group of beats on which the rhythmic structure is based. *Rāga* corresponds approximately to scale in Western musical theory; *tāla* corresponds to measure. *Rāga* and *tāla* may be thought of as the warp of the music. The musicians are challenged to weave a woof consistent with the given melodic and rhythmic pattern. Whereas a concert of Western music is a re-creation of an original creation, a concert of Indian music is a creation within the imposed limits of *rāga* and *tāla. Rāga* and *tāla* constitute the invariable; the musicians supply the variable. The spectators are privileged to watch a cooperative and sometimes competitive effort to bring forth from the given *rāga* and *tāla* every conceivable variation. Indian music is far more than disciplined sound; it is a revealing of the pluralities within oneness. Rabindranath Tagore expressed this in his early play *Nature's Revenge,* and it became the keynote of his life: "the great is to be found in the small, the infinite within the bound of form, and the eternal freedom of the soul in love." [37] Tagore adds that *Nature's Revenge* "may be looked upon as an introduction to the whole of my future literary work: or, rather, this has been the subject on which all my writings have dwelt—the joy of attaining the Infinite within the finite." [38] Indian music and Tagore's poetry may be described as the manifold manifesting of the Cosmic Oneness. And so moves Hindu philosophy. A basic theme comes from *śruti,* the authoritatively revealed writings of the Hindus, and each philosophy is a variation on the theme. Thus there are within Vedānta the commentaries of Śaṅkara, Rāmānuja, Madhva, Nimbarka, Vallabha, and Bhedabheda on the *sūtras* of Bādarāyaṇa. Within all Indian philosophy, both orthodox and heterodox, there are variations on great ideas such as Brahman, *Ātman, ṛta, māyā, karma, saṁsāra,* and *līlā* which were originally set forth by the ancient *ṛṣis.* The manifold variations of these themes make ridiculous the efforts of those who attempt to capture Hindu philosophy within single capsule terms like "other-worldly," or "pessimistic," or "spiritual."

A second feature of Hindu philosophy is the centrality of metaphysics.

[37] *My Reminiscences,* p. 237.
[38] *Ibid.,* p. 238.

Radhakrishnan defines all philosophy as "a systematic study of the ultimate nature of reality" [39]—a definition rejected by most modern Western philosophers. To return to the analogy of music, we can say that the primary texts of Hinduism, the Vedas and the Upaniṣads, supply the *rāga* and the *tāla*. This is the speculative insight that Reality is the integration of values. Practically this means that man can live with confidence in the universe. The universe is not a great machine bent on destroying all man holds dear; rather the universe which has brought human consciousness into existence is pregnant with unrealized values transcending those now known to man. Man is not condemned to invent his own values; he can discover the values already latent in the world. Intellectually this metaphysical insight creates problems; for if the Real is absolutely One, then it cannot be known. Knowledge requires a knower outside the known. But man both East and West has not been willing to rest on irrationality if he can avoid it, especially when his ignorance concerns the ground of being. In both Eastern and Western traditions philosophers have concluded that if there is to be knowledge of the One, this knowledge must be in a dimension of "knowing" other than ordinary empirical or rational knowing. Plato in his *Seventh Epistle* says that the Good can be grasped only if there is a "leaping spark" to bridge the hiatus between man and the Good.[40] Plotinus says that the last step of the return of the soul to the One is bridged when the One reaches down after the soul can no longer reach up.[41] And in Hinduism the Advaita Vedāntists cry "*Neti! Neti!*" (Not this! Not this! or Inadequate! Inadequate!) to every suggestion of a human way out of the dilemma of knowing the Absolute One.

In the opinion of Hiriyanna, Hindu philosophy is primarily a philosophy of values, rather than a philosophy of reality: "One of the distinguishing features of Indian philosophy is that, as a consequence of the pragmatic view it takes of knowledge, it has, throughout its history, given the foremost place to values. Indeed, they form its central theme; and questions like those of 'being' and of 'knowing' come in only as a matter of course. It may, on this account, be described as essentially a philosophy of values." [42] To say that questions of being and knowing come in "only as a matter of course" suggests a secondary role for metaphysics and epistemology. Hiriyanna is overlooking the fact that in Hindu thought being and value are so integrated that one cannot be sought without the other. The very term for being—*sat*—is also a term for the good. Again

[39] *Reign of Religion in Contemporary Philosophy*, p. 1.
[40] 341 D.
[41] *Enneads* 5. 3. 17.
[42] M. Hiriyanna, *The Quest for Perfection*, p. 101.

there is a striking parallel to Plato's Form of the Good, the One that is both the source of all being and the source of all good.

A third distinguishing feature of Hindu philosophy is the recognition that it always includes a discipline, a *sādhana*. It is both a view and a way, a vision and a path. Since in India the *telos* of philosophy is to cope with the sufferings inherent in the human condition, rather than the satisfaction of wonder as Plato and Aristotle said, it is not at all surprising that Hindu philosophy prescribes techniques for the alleviation of suffering. A physician of the soul who merely identifies the malady is not a true physician. The human ideal according to Western philosophy is the man who loves wisdom and who has wisdom—the sage. In the Western tradition philosophers have been pressed again and again to shift their ground in order not to be forced to the admission that the scientist has displaced the philosopher. But in India the human ideal to which philosophy directs man is the Perfecting of Man. *Sādhana* is the unique factor in Hindu philosophy. If the day ever comes when this aspect of Hindu philosophy ceases to be virile, then Hindu philosophy will have sold itself out to the West. It will have become an informing, rather than a transforming philosophy. The nearest approach to *sādhana* in Western philosophy is to be found in ancient Stoicism. For example, Epictetus says that the first and most necessary topic of philosophy is the life of philosophy, the practical application of principles; the second is the demonstration of the principles; and the third is the clarification of the terms and processes.[43] The example given by Epictetus is that the philosopher should be concerned first and foremost with the life of truth, the avoidance of lying; secondly, he should give demonstrations of why one ought not to lie; and thirdly, he should give information as to the nature of demonstration, the meaning of truth and falsehood, and the principles of logical contradiction. Unfortunately, lamented Epictetus, the philosophers spend all their time on the third—that which A. N. Whitehead called the antiseptic aspects of philosophy—and entirely neglect the first.

Radhakrishnan says "In ancient India philosophy was not an auxiliary to any other science or art, but always held a prominent position of independence." [44] A statement like this is very misleading. In India philosophy has always had two aspects: the theoretical and the practical. In fact, a constant criticism of the philosophy of the West from the Indian point of view is that it is "intellectualistic" whereas Indian philosophy is "practical." The difference is that Indian philosophy starts with the practical urgency of dealing with the human problem of suffering. The human

[43] *The Enchiridion*, Section 51.
[44] *Indian Philosophy*, Vol. 2, p. 22.

condition is one of suffering, and philosophy is one of the techniques to do something about it. So philosophy in India has not "always held a prominent position of independence"; instead it has been engaged in for the purpose of dealing with suffering. Salvation, liberation, emancipation, or *mokṣa* has been its end. Radhakrishnan says that philosophy in the West has leaned for support on politics, or ethics, or theology, whereas "In India philosophy stood on its own legs, and all other studies looked to it for inspiration and support." [45] Three pages later Radhakrishnan modifies his position: "Though philosophy in India has not as a rule completely freed itself from the fascinations of religious speculations, yet the philosophical discussions have not been hampered by religious forms." [46] And on the next page the "independence" of philosophy is still further qualified: "Every doctrine is turned into a passionate conviction, stirring the heart of man and quickening his breath." [47] This overlooks the fact that Indian philosophy found its reason for existence not in itself, but in the existential fact of human suffering. *Sādhana* has two forms: philosophy and religion. There is a curious conflict in Nalini Kanta Brahma's excellent book, *Philosophy of Hindu Sādhanā.* In his preface Brahma says, "The theoretical side of Indian philosophy has been ably presented in the monumental works of Sir Sarbapalli Radhakrishnan and Dr. Surendra Nath Dasgupta. I have attempted in the following pages a presentation of the practical side of Hindu philosophy." [48] However, Radhakrishnan, in the foreword, identifies the book as a book on religion: "In 'Hindu Sadhana' Dr. Nalini Kanta Brahma contributes a highly interesting and important work to the literature of Hindu Thought and Religion." [49]

Man is *homo philosophicus,* the being ever in quest of understanding of his world and himself. If man has an essence, it is the activity of questing for understanding. He is philosophizing incarnate. The ambiguity of philosophy is therefore the ambiguity of man. Philosophical understanding means to know and to value. When philosophy leans to knowing, the result is science; and when philosophy leans to valuing, the result is religion. Man-the-philosopher is constantly in danger of slipping into man-the-scientist or man-the-religionist.

The ideal science is value-free pursuit of knowledge; the ideal religion is total commitment to values. Philosophy in the West is constantly becoming a science, either as a handmaiden for science in clarifying terms

[45] *Ibid.,* p. 23.
[46] *Ibid.,* p. 26.
[47] *Ibid.,* p. 27.
[48] P. xi. *Sādhanā* is Bengali; *sādhana* is Sanskrit.
[49] P. ix.

and methods, or as a super-science that attempts to discover or create relations among the separate sciences. In India, on the other hand, philosophy constantly slips into religion. In India the motive for philosophizing is not the satisfaction of wonder as it is in the West; instead it is the effort to deal with the sufferings and anxieties inherent in the life of man. In India philosophy tends to become a quest for salvation; in the West it becomes a quest for knowledge. But in either case the result is the same: the death of philosophy. If philosophy dies, then man ceases to be man, the being in quest of understanding. Today we see the end of the line for either the Western approach or the Indian approach. The two cannot go their separate ways. This does not mean that some sort of hybrid of Western and Indian must come into being. Rather within each tradition there must come an increasing awareness of other traditions, and a greater desire to work out in our times better ways of being human in the fullest sense of that term. Man must take on his own biological evolution and also his own ideological evolution. In the Indian tradition this is expressed as man becoming God; in the Western tradition it is expressed as man realizing his fullest potentialities. Perhaps these are but two ways of stating the same idea.

6. HINDUISM AS *Sādhana*

Hinduism is a religion, a philosophy, and a social system, but it is no one of these. Hinduism can be better understood as *sādhana* which takes the forms of religion, philosophy, and a social system. "It may be safely asserted that in India philosophy and religion are but the theoretical and practical aspects of one and the same attempt at realising (and not merely knowing) the highest end of life." [50] Brahma has correctly stated that philosophy and religion are two aspects of the attempt to realize the highest end of life, but he spoils his insight by the strangely un-Indian claim that philosophy is theory and religion is practice. G. R. Malkani gives a much more Indian (i.e., synthetic) definition, although he also illustrates the problem of trying to distinguish Hindu religion and philosophy: "Hinduism is . . . a religion that cannot be divorced from philosophy and is in fact the highest form of philosophy." [51] The word "*sādhana*" comes from "*sādha*" meaning to reach one's goal, to accomplish one's aim, to guide aright, to fulfill, to subdue, to gain power over, to bring about. *Sādhana* connotes the successful achieving of a desired end. The notions of activity, movement, change, process, struggle, and

[50] N. K. Brahma, *Philosophy of Hindu Sādhanā*, p. 7.
[51] A. R. Wadia, *Essays in Philosophy Presented in His Honour*, p. 186.

power are inherent in the concept. *Sādhana* is the instrument for the attainment of perfection (*siddhi*). *Sādhana* is the healing of the division between theory and practice. The means by which the end is attained is not specified by the term; hence, *sādhana* can be used in the contexts of science, of industry, of jurisprudence, of warfare, of persuasion, of instruction, of prayer, and even of magic. No matter how *siddhi* is reached, the means to *siddhi* is *sādhana.*

Hindu philosophers know very well the pure love of wisdom, the desire to know for its own sake. "*Jijñāsā*" is the term for this intellectual motivation. However, *jijñāsā* does not have the independent status that it has in the West; it is controlled by and subordinate to *mumukṣutva,* the desire for emancipation. Edgerton is very dogmatic on this point. He says, "Contrary to the opinion of H. Oldenberg, *Vorwissenschaftliche Wissenschaft* 3–8, who says it is 'rare' to find, before the Upaniṣads, a Vedic philosopher seeking 'to unfold a picture of things as they are for their own sake, out of the pure joy of perceiving and understanding,' but finds (as a 'genuine novelty') such 'true philosophers' in the authors of the Upaniṣads. In my opinion there never was such a figure in ancient India. Even the latest Classical Indian philosophers would have been amazed to hear this said of themselves. Purely abstract speculation would have seemed to them pointless and incomprehensible. Their aim is to point the way to human salvation." [52] All systems of Hindu philosophy start with the aim of freeing man from the sufferings inherent in the human condition. This position is succinctly stated in the Four Noble Truths of Buddhism: man's life necessarily involves suffering; the cleaving to life is the cause of suffering; a caused phenomenon can be eliminated; therefore, there is a remedy—the Eight-Fold Way. "For India, truth is not precious in itself; it becomes precious by virtue of its soteriological functions." [53] No knowledge has value unless it promotes either directly or indirectly the ultimate good of man. There is no higher knowledge than the knowledge that liberates man; no higher use can be found to which to put any knowledge. In the words of the *Śvetāśvatara Upaniṣad,* "That Eternal which rests in the self should be known. Truly there is nothing beyond this to be known." [54]

Such a view of the function of truth may seem strangely pragmatic, and so it is, but it is not American pragmatism. It is rooted in an intoxicating view of the nature of man as the necessary, finest, and ultimate

[52] Franklin Edgerton, *The Beginnings of Indian Philosophy,* p. 28, footnote 7. Medard Boss, Professor of Psychotherapy at Zurich University, suggests that Indian philosophies be called "elucidation therapies." *A Psychiatrist Discovers India,* p. 184.

[53] Mircea Eliade, *Yoga: Immortality and Freedom,* p. 4.

[54] 1. 12. Radhakrishnan translation.

evolutionary manifestation of Being: "There is no status that is superior to that of humanity." [55] The value of knowledge is its service to man's full development as Nature's finest fruit, not its correspondence to realities as measured by scientific methods. Indian philosophers complain against the Western views of philosophy as pure intellectuality: "A philosophy which is merely an enquiry into the ultimate nature of the spatio-temporal world of the nature of consciousness as such and is thus merely a philosophy of being is a truncated thing . . . . no philosophical theory can be wholly true unless it is based on and shaped by our deepest experiences involving active interaction between ourselves and the objective world. It should be a reflection of the whole of our life and not simply of a fraction of it." [56]

The philosopher is the seeker of wisdom; he is the one ever seeking and never claiming that he has found the goal of his search. Socrates set the pattern in the West when he announced his "wisdom" was his awareness of his non-wisdom. He was a *seeker* of truth, not a possessor of truth. His life was a life of *pursuit* of wisdom. The unexamined life, he said, is not fit for man. Philosophy remains a frustrating business until one grasps what the business is. An American mathematician and administrator confesses that he disliked formal philosophy for many years until he "became sensible enough to realize that it profoundly differs from science in that its interest and value do not depend upon its making progress in the solution of the problems with which it is concerned." [57] He is not quite correct in thinking that the value of philosophy does not depend upon its solution of problems. He should have said that in philosophy progress is not measured in the same manner in which it is measured in other disciplines. Sometimes a clarification of the problem may be extremely gratifying to the philosopher, although the clarification may not constitute a solution of the problem. Hindu philosophy may be disappointing if evaluated by concrete achievements and solutions of problems, but if evaluated as *sādhana* it proves to be a very important enterprise.

One of the interesting differences between Western philosophy and Hindu philosophy is in their impact on the life of ordinary men. In the West despite all that professional philosophers have done to interpret their function to the public, the common opinion is that philosophy is at best a luxury, at worst a triviality. In India there seems to be a differ-

[55] *Mahābhārata* 12.300. Quotations from the *Mahābhārata*, unless otherwise stated, are from the translation edited by Pratap Chandra Roy.

[56] L. C. Gupta, "Philosophy and Life," *Proceedings of the 28th Indian Philosophical Congress*, 1953, pp. 27–28.

[57] Warren Weaver, "Confessions of a Scientific-Humanist," *Saturday Review*, May 28, 1966, p. 13.

ent opinion, although the casual visitor may not notice it. The first impression a Western visitor to India has is being overwhelmed and horrified by the poverty of the masses. Cultural shock in India is largely economic shock. But if the visitor remains several months, if he roams beyond the usual tourist places, and if he is perceptive, he may get a second impression of India and her people. He discovers a peculiarly philosophical people. He may even become tantalized by what he finds. Among those who came, saw, and were conquered are Friedrich Max Müller, Charlie Andrews, Warren Hastings, Margaret Noble, Arthur Osborne, Paul Brunton, Annie Besant, John Woodroffe, Bhikshu Sangharakshita, and Anne Marshall. The list could be greatly extended, but this list is representative of the spread of the appeal, for it includes a scholar, a preacher, a judge, a governor, a social worker, a soldier, and a journalist. That which attracts the discerning visitor is the *questing* of the Hindus. Of course there is in India a questing for food, shelter, clothing, and security. This can be matched in the West. There is also the pathetic questing for alms—and many a Westerner even after visiting India thinks of it chiefly as a land of beggars. But there is a more abstract questing which can perhaps best be described as a questing for salvation. This is neither religion nor philosophy alone but *sādhana.* One might point out that this quest is not unknown in the West. The difference is that whereas in the West the quest for salvation is a secondary concern to be manifested only in the terminal years of life, in India this quest is lifelong. Salvation for the Hindu is a central concern, not a peripheral one. For the most part in the West such matters loom large in the life of the dispossessed, but in India salvation, however defined, is a necessity. The Hindu does not hold to the typical Western view that the quest is to be postponed as long as possible. Hence, a successful Calcutta businessman may be found at sunrise in the Maidan "seeking the eternal" through Yogic practices and meditation. A Chicago businessman takes an afternoon off to play golf, but it stretches the imagination to think of him as "seeking the eternal" in Grant Park at dawn!

Ramakrishna once said, "Man is always restless, always moving from place to place. Why? Because he is never satisfied, because nothing brings him permanent satisfaction; and this very fact that he is dissatisfied with his finite nature shows that it is not his natural condition. The fact that he has infinite ambition, that he has insatiable hunger for more and more, proves that he is infinite by nature, and that is why he is always dissatisfied with whatever is finite." [58] He added, "The contented man is no man; he is no more than a brute." [59] Man's uniqueness among living

[58] *Works,* Vol. 1, pp. 222–223.
[59] *Ibid.,* p. 224.

forms is that in him questing has risen to consciousness. He seeks food as all animals do, but he also is aware that he seeks food. In him passion is not merely passion, because he knows he is passionate; he senses, and he more than senses, because he is aware that he senses; he wills to live, but he is not at the mercy of his will to live, for being aware of his will to live he can bring it under submission to other values: patriotism, social service, vocation, brotherhood, art, science, religion, or romantic love.

Living forms have evolved man, and man now takes on his own evolution. He is more than his history. To predict human future on the basis of human past is to ignore an important fact about man: man makes his own history. Through memory and anticipation he may not be able to annihilate time, but he is able to overcome the tyranny of the present. Through public opinion polls, computer projections, probabilities studies, behavioral sciences, and genetic research he may not yet be able to write "instant history," but he is able to determine and evaluate events before they are part of his present experience. Man is essentially subject, not object. According to Hinduism, his future is to become fully what he is. He is to become fully subject, that is, the active agent in all forms of becoming—the knower, not the known—the willer, not the willed—the actor, not the acted upon. His being is his becoming. He is Being in his becoming. In him Reality manifests itself in a form unique, necessary, and complete.[60]

Man is the only being that has *sādhana* because he is the only being that has *siddhi* possibilities. He is the only being that can become divine. The gods are divine and cannot *become*—they *are*; the lower animals do not have desire for liberation (*mumukṣutva*), the first step in *sādhana*. Only man has the conscious urge to expand without limit. An interesting theme found in Indian literature is the gods' envy of man. In Kālidāsa's play, *Shakuntala,* King Dushyanta upon being told of divine jealousy of a sage's austerities, remarks, "I'm told the gods are nervous people." [61]

Another implication about the nature of man which follows from *sādhana* is that men differ in their capacities (*adhikāra*) for spiritual development. The doctrine of division of men according to capacities

[60] " 'Become in fact what you are by virtue of your individual nature': such is the call of non-cosmic personal love to every man, and in its going-out to him it is this image of his particular vocation, and not a standardized pattern of excellence, which is held up before him, as it were, as his own intrinsic ideal. For in the physical order of experience men may all be dispensable, more or less, according to their kind; but in the non-cosmic realm of the metaphysical order they may differ in value, yet are indispensable, one and all." Max Scheler, *The Nature of Sympathy*. Translated by Peter Heath. London: Routledge and Kegan Paul, 1954, p. 128.

[61] Act I. Lal translation. P. Lal, *Great Sanskrit Plays*, p. 19.

(*adhikārabhedavāda*) is that each aspirant differs in the level of achievement he has made in self-development; hence the training he is to undergo needs to be adjusted to his level of progress. There is an old saying in India that when the pupil (*śiṣya*) is ready, the spiritual guide (*guru*) will appear. This saying is often interpreted to mean that the young man is expected to search until he finds his *guru*, but the idea behind the saying is that pupil-readiness is everything. When the pupil is ready, the teacher will be found because it is the readiness of the pupil that determines the proper pupil-teacher relationship. When the young man is ready for instruction, almost any *guru* will do! The doctrine of *adhikārabhedavāda* will go a long way toward clarifying the "contradictions" found in Hindu scriptures. For example, in the *Bhagavad Gītā* Arjuna does not desire to go into battle because he does not wish to bring about the death of friends and relatives, especially of the saintly grandsire Bhīṣma. Kṛṣṇa argues with him from many points of view, and at the close of the *Gītā* [62] Arjuna is at last convinced and says to Kṛṣṇa, "I will follow your advice." The implication is that Arjuna had the capacity either to follow or to reject the advice of Kṛṣṇa. However, at the close of the *Mahābhārata* as Bhīṣma dies on the battlefield, Yudhiṣṭhira laments that he has been responsible for bringing about the death of Bhīṣma, "Beholding thy body covered with arrows and festering with bad sores, I fail to find, O hero, any peace of mind at the thought of the evils I have wrought." [63] Bhīṣma's comfort is: "Whatever is done is done under the influence of *Kāla* (time). I have said it before . . . that *Kāla* is the cause of all and that for this reason we . . . acting under the inspiration of *Kāla* do our appointed work, and therefore . . . do not deserve censure . . . in any way." [64] Is this a flat contradiction? Does the *Mahābhārata* teach both a doctrine of free will and a doctrine of fate? [65] The application of the doctrine of *adhikārabhedavāda* may help in reminding us that Hindu scriptures are *sādhana*-oriented, that the *sādhana* of Arjuna required that he at the stage of development he was in at the opening of the battle be strengthened by the view that he was acting freely and in accord with his caste responsibilities, and that the *sādhana* of Yudhiṣṭhira required that he at the stage of his development at the close of the battle be comforted by the view that he was caught in the net of *Kāla* and was therefore not morally accountable for the death of Bhīṣma. Just how far this type of interpretation should be exercised on the vast literature of Hinduism is hard to say, but at least the

[62] 18. 73.
[63] *Mahābhārata* 13. 1.
[64] *Ibid.*
[65] The *Bhagavad Gītā* is part of Book 6 of the *Mahābhārata*.

reader should be warned to expect some teachings for the neophyte, some for the adept, and some for the liberated. When Hinduism is thought of as *sādhana,* rather than *sādhana* as an expression of Hinduism, the Hindu scriptures begin to be seen as textbooks for pupils rather than as a source of proof texts to be used in controversies.

Hindu *sādhana* is comprehensive. In the long history of its development there is scarcely any aspect of life, however minute, which has not been regulated: the life of the individual from conception to cremation, daily life from the first waking moment to sleep postures, the activities of the lowest slave and of the king himself. *Sādhana* determines the length of the neem stick (the poor man's toothbrush), the kinds and quality of foods, the clothing to be worn, the distance one can travel, the hours to be spent in sleep, and the most intimate aspects of married life. But—and here is where Westerners become completely dumbfounded!—the Hindu who will have none of these regulations, who lives a life in violation of the rules, who even ridicules Hinduism, remains a Hindu. He may be shunned by Hindus, despised by his joint family, and ostracised by his caste council, but he cannot be made a *mleccha* (literally a foreigner or barbarian, one ignorant of the vernacular—originally used as a generic term to mean non-Aryan but it has taken on the meaning of non-Hindu, and still carries with it the connotation of disapproval). Some Hindus follow the rigid disciplines literally; others flout them entirely, or at least think they do! *Sādhana* may become so subtly a part of one's life that one is unaware of it. The author recalls sitting at the dining table with a young Hindu who remarked that while his father was a strict observer of the rules of Hinduism, he rejected Hinduism completely. A few minutes later when a fly flew into his glass of water, he carefully removed the fly with a spoon, gently placed it on the floor, and remarked, "It will be all right now." Hindu non-violence had become second nature.

Hindu *sādhana* is based fundamentally on actual experience. Observance of rules, acceptance of a creed, performance of rites, and/or obedience to codes of ethics cannot substitute for the living experience of God-realization, self-realization, *samādhi,* ecstasy, or however the experience may be designated. *Sādhana* knowledge is more than rational acquaintance with the truth. To know God is to experience God. The greater the intensity of the experience, the higher the man is believed to have attained spiritual growth. Mystics like Caitanya, Ramana Maharshi, and Ramakrishna were acclaimed as *sādhus*—even as incarnations of God—by their followers because of the quality of their experiences. The Bengali saint, Sitārāmdās Omkārnāth, is most revered by his followers during those months in which he is secluded in his mountain retreat wrapped in a constant state of *samādhi*. Because of the fact that Hindu religion and Hindu philosophy are manifestations of Hindu *sādhana* there has been no need for an existentialistic reform as has been the case in Christianity and Western philosophy. India has had many "Kierkegaards," but they are natural products of *sādhana,* not reformers radically changing the pattern of life within Hinduism.

Another feature of all forms of Hindu *sādhana* is its two phases, one negative, the other positive. Whatever be the form of *sādhana* there will be *vairāgya* (the state of not being possessed by passion) and *abhyāsa* (the repetition of action). Both aspects are clearly stated in the *Bhagavad Gītā:* "The Lord said: Doubtless, O mighty-armed, the mind is hard to curb and restless; but by exercise (*abhyāsa*), son of Kuntī, and absence of passion (*vairāgya*) it is captured." [66] *Vairāgya* does not mean the state of indifference to pleasure or pain praised by the Epicureans; it means being master of one's emotions rather than being mastered by them. "Discipline of passion" would be more correct than "absence of passion." Mysticism in all cultures has insisted that purgation is a necessary preliminary to the mystic state *per se.* Asceticism, properly understood, is an effort to provide a proper atmosphere in which the truly spiritual life can be lived; it is not self-mortification for its own sake. The repetition of an act or word is consistent with the Hindu belief that the desired state of liberation is to be attained gradually. *Sādhana* is controlled progress toward an ideal goal. The sudden conversion, so dearly loved by some evangelical sects in Christianity and archetypically found in the conversion of Saint Paul, is not usual in Hindu *sādhana,* although it is sometimes found, e.g., the conversion of Vivekananda.[67]

Another aspect found in almost all forms of *sādhana* is a distinction between the exoteric and the esoteric. In general the exoteric aspects are for the beginner; the esoteric for the advanced. During the ancient period of Hindu history the young boy would be given the exoteric instructions by his father and mother in the home until the time came for him to be sent to the family *guru.* During his years with his *guru* he would be taught the *upaniṣads,* i.e., the secret doctrines of his faith. Each form of *sādhana* has its *bahiraṅga* (exoteric) and its *antaraṅga* (esoteric) aspects. Sometimes the latter may be the secret meaning of the rites; sometimes it may be the rites themselves. The concept of exoteric and esoteric is preserved to this day in the Hindu temple, with its public areas and

[66] 6. 35. Edward J. Thomas translation.

[67] A distinction is sometimes made between *sadyo-mukti* (sudden release) and *krama-mukti* (gradual release).

the central room into which only Hindus may go. A non-Hindu is not allowed to go into the secret room containing the image or other sacred object, but often the attendant priest will allow a visitor to look into the room! At least one temple in India—the Lakshmi Temple in New Delhi—has no secret chamber, which causes some orthodox Hindus to say that it is not actually a temple, but rather a museum or showpiece for tourists.

Hindu *sādhana*, like all Indian cultural movements, is not easily placed chronologically. As Macdonell has said, "History is the one weak spot in Indian literature. It is, in fact, non-existent." [68] He gives two reasons for this fact about India's culture: the first, "early India wrote no history because it never made any," [69] is unkind and untrue, and the second, ". . . the Brahmans, whose task it would naturally have been to record great deeds, had early embraced the doctrine that all action and existence are a positive evil, and could therefore have felt but little inclination to chronicle historical events," [70] is true, but misleading. The belief that "all action and existence are a positive evil" was not always a belief of the Brahmins. Not enough recognition has been given to the fact that Hindus are great storytellers, and that their history is embodied largely in legends, fairy tales, and myths. This is not history as it is commonly known. No records were kept as they were in China. What the Hindus felt worth preserving was the meaning of events, not a record of when the events took place. They were a tradition-minded, but not a history-

[68] A. A. Macdonell, A *History of Sanskrit Literature*, p. 10. According to Amaury de Riencourt "the most remarkable trait of Indian psychology" is "a complete, instinctive indifference to history and the preservation of historical records." He adds, "If the history of the Indians is as shadowy as has already been pointed out on more than one occasion, it is largely because, of all the people on this earth, they were the least interested in history. The picture of India's historical development is as blurred as the development of the Indian soul is clear and sharply outlined. The key to an understanding of Indian Culture lies precisely in this total indifference toward history, toward the very process of *time*. Aryan India had no memory because she focused her attention on *eternity* not on time. Thus, the Indian world outlook developed in a direction diametrically opposed to China's, for instance." *The Soul of India*, pp. 9, 15. Nirad C. Chaudhuri reports in his autobiography that "there was nothing which came as a greater surprise to me, a student of history, than the disparagement of history by educated Indians of my class." *The Autobiography of an Unknown Indian*, p. 426. Chaudhuri also observes, "Historical conferences in India always remind me of séances." *The Continent of Circe*, p. 56. According to Dhan Gopal Mukherji, "Properly speaking India has no history. We as a race have no consciousness of it, for our history has been written mostly by foreigners—the Greeks, the Arabs and the Chinese. The consciousness of history as an asset of life and as an expression of our people, does not seem important to us. History is the record of man's relation to time, but the Hindu does not believe in time, and all our life, according to the Hindu's vision, is an illusion and something to be transcended." *Caste and Outcast*, pp. 74–75.

[69] A. A. Macdonell, A *History of Sanskrit Literature*, p. 11.

[70] *Loc. cit.*

minded, people. This is still largely true. K. M. Panikkar's popular little book, *A Survey of Indian History*, published on the day of India's independence from British rule (August 15, 1947), and written according to the author to meet "a growing demand for a history of India which would try and reconstruct the past in a way that would give us an idea of our heritage,"[71] contains not one chronological table. Indian history was first written by Westerners to understand the land and people over which they ruled. Such histories attempted to fit Indian history into a typical Western mold of Ancient, Medieval, and Modern—Modern begins with the British occupation!—and they also showed India as a nation molded by a series of foreign invasions, neglecting to report her continuous cultural and political background. In the writing of a cultural history of India the problem of finding a date for the origin of a movement is topped by the problem of fixing a date for the terminus of a movement, for, as has often been said, India is a land where nothing ever dies. The traditional morning prayer of the Hindu has been unchanged for three thousand years; the marriage ceremony is at least two thousand years old; and in Poona is a school for the training of priests to conduct Vedic sacrifices, even though none has been seriously performed for three thousand years.

The most definite dates in Indian history are the dates of empires: Maurya 325–183 B.C., Gupta A.D. 320–544, Muslim 1192–1370, Mogul 1565–1707, and British 1803–1947. A history of Hindu philosophy lends itself to a loose fourfold chronological division: (1) the Vedic Period when the Vedas and the Upaniṣads were written, (2) the Epic Period marked chiefly by the compiling of the *Rāmāyaṇa* and the *Mahābhārata*, (3) the Sūtra Period during which the meaning of the Upaniṣads was captured in aphoristic writings suitable for memorizing, and (4) the Period of Commentaries on the Sūtras. As for assigning dates to the periods, 600 B.C. can quite confidently be given as the end of the Vedic Period and the beginning of the Epic Period; the Period of Commentaries falls between the ninth and the sixteenth centuries A.D.; but any more precise dating would be rather arbitrary. The fourfold divisions themselves are very inadequate when one considers the religious movements, especially those since the tenth century, and also when one considers the many movements in South India.

A history of Hindu *sādhana* would be even more difficult than a history of Hindu philosophy or Hindu religion, since, as we have noted, *sādhana* denotes the Hindu questing which manifests itself both in philosophy

[71] P. viii.

and religion. Since orthodox Hindus claim that the Vedas are eternal, and since it is also the claim of many that all forms of *sādhana* appear in the Vedas, the conclusion is that all forms of *sādhana* have always existed. This solution to the problem of origination of *sādhana* is similar to Winternitz's suggestion in view of the conflicting claims of the arrival of the Indo-Aryans in India, "The right date is *x* to 500 B.C." [72] Not only does *sādhana* in general appear to be a very ancient element in Hindu culture, but also the various kinds of *sādhana* are found in the earliest Aryan culture in India, judging by the literature. At the beginning of this chapter reference was made to *mārga* (path, way) as one of the aspects of Hinduism. *Sādhana* denotes the wayfulness of human life to the attainment of ideal goals; *mārga* denotes the distinct ways to follow. *Mārgas* are the kinds of *sādhana.*

Aurobindo in *The Renaissance in India* points out three movements of creativity in India's cultural history: (1) an age of *spirit* in which the truth of existence was sought through an intuitive mind; (2) an age of the *intellect* with the rise of the philosophical schools and the attempt to establish ethical norms; (3) an age of *emotion* in which the passions were directed to the attainment of the highest goals. All of these, argues Aurobindo, had run their course by the time the British arrived, so that the British found a people in whom the vital energy had faded, free intellectual activity had ceased, and the old synthesis had been dispersed. The introduction of Western ways and ideas proved to be for many Indians the very stimulus they needed to reawaken lost enthusiasms.

Aurobindo's three creative movements correspond closely to the *mārgas.* The earliest *mārga* in Hindu cultural history consisted of petitionary sacrificial rites. Complicated sacrifices accompanied with hymns were addressed to the natural powers as deities who might be described as cases of arrested development. The goods sought through the sacrifices were the goods of this world: food, comfort, longevity, children, cure of diseases, and victory in battle. A prayer to a minor sun-god, Pushan, is representative of these petitions:

> Pushan, convey us over the road, remove the wicked (obstructor of the way). Son of the cloud, deity, go before us. If a wicked (adversary), Pushan, a robber, or one who delights in evil, points out to us (the way we ought not to go), do thou drive him from the road. . . . Lead us where there is abundant fodder; let there be no extreme heat by the way; Pushan, know how to protect us on this (journey). Be favourable to us, fill us (with abundance), give us (all good things), sharpen us (with vigour), fill our bellies; Pushan, know how to protect us on this (journey).

[72] Moriz Winternitz, *Geschichte der Indischen Litteratur,* p. 254.

> We do not censure Pushan, but praise him with hymns; we solicit the good-looking (Pushan) for riches.[73]

In time the sacrifice itself was more important than the being to whom the sacrifice was made. The act itself acted. Sacrifice became almost the sole obligation of man. The sacrifice was called *kriyā* (action) or *karma*. Sacerdotal rites were exercised to bring evil to enemies, to gain prosperity, to overcome obstacles. The power of the sacrifice became so great that even natural phenomena became dependent upon the rites. The sun could not rise without the priestly ritual. So it was not surprising that the priests who performed the sacrifices became rivals of the gods: "Verily, there are two kinds of gods; for the gods themselves assuredly are gods, and then the priests who have studied and teach Vedic lore are the human gods." [74]

The ancient hymns and directions for performance of sacrifices constitute the Vedas. They are said to be *śruti,* that is, revelatory. The word *śruti* means heard, since the sages are thought to have received them (or heard them) in a high state of spiritual intuition. Other works have been written on the Vedas and are said to be *smṛti* (remembered). These secondary materials are authoritative because they are derivative and explanatory of the *śruti* writings. A conflict regarding *smṛti* can always be settled within Hinduism by a quotation from a *śruti* writing. The more important of the *smṛti* writings are the *Gṛhya Sūtras,* the *Dharma Sūtras,* and the *Dharma Śāstras*—the last dealing with the ceremonies, rights, and duties of domestic life. The collection of rules and regulations of the sacrificial rites and of the ceremonial and moral aspects of the life of the people form the *karma mārga,* the way of action.

The earliest Vedas, or wisdom literature, of the Aryan people were the hymns of praise and petition to the nature gods. These are called *mantras.* From the *mantras* developed the *brāhmaṇas,* the directions for sacerdotal sacrifices. *Mantras* and *brāhmaṇas* together constitute the *karma kāṇḍa,* the work section of the Vedic literature. The other section, the knowledge section (*jñāna kāṇḍa*) consists of *āraṇyakas* (allegorical interpretations of the sacrifices) and *upaniṣads* (metaphysical interpretations of the sacrifices, hymns, and myths). The *sādhana* presented in the *jñāna kāṇḍa* is based on the primitive notion of the power of a name. To know the name is to get power over the object bearing the name. In *Atharva Veda* the author in a charm to gain hold of a public assembly

[73] *Ṛg Veda* 1. 42. 1–2, 8–10. H. H. Wilson translation. This translation, except where otherwise indicated, will be used throughout.

[74] *Śatapatha Brāhmaṇa* 2. 2. 2. 6. See Radhakrishnan, *Indian Philosophy,* Vol. 1, p. 126.

says, "We know your name, O Assembly!" [75] and again to cure sores a magician cries, "I have grasped the names of all of them." [76] At a much higher level the way of knowledge (*jñāna mārga*) transcends ignorance of one's finite existence by intellectually and existentially realizing the unlimited nature of one's true being.

A third *mārga* is found in the two great epics of India, the *Rāmāyaṇa* and the *Mahābhārata,* and in the Purāṇas. These writings are the result of a vast unwritten literature of pre-Aryan wandering minstrels called the *sūtas.* The sayings of the *sūtas* and the *ṛṣis* are the two sources of classical literature in Hinduism. The extant literature, although extensive, is but representative of a much larger oral literature. From *sūta* lore has come the epics and Purāṇas; from *ṛṣi* lore has come the Vedas and Upaniṣads. One of the reasons why the *Bhagavad Gītā* is so important in Hindu literature is that in it the pre-Aryan or non-Brahmanist ideas are combined with the Vedic ideas of the ancient Aryans. In the *sūta* lore there is another *mārga.* Whereas the *mārgas* derived from the *mantras* and the *brāhmaṇas* were sacrificial systems designed to persuade and to force the gods of natural phenomena to do what men wanted them to do, the *mārga* of epics and Purāṇas is a submission to the grace of a loving god in confidence that the god will bestow favors without petition. The tone is no longer one of pleading; now it is one of gratitude for blessings received and expected. Joyous confidence replaces anxious hope. This is the way of loving adoration (*bhakti mārga*).

The fourth *mārga* is associated with Patañjali (second century B.C.). This is known as the way of discipline (*yoga mārga*). Patañjali is often credited as the founder of *yoga,* the originator of the philosophical system of that name, and the author of the basic yogic text, the *Yoga Sūtras.* Actually he was neither founder nor originator, and he was more of an editor than an author of the *Yoga Sūtras.* The fundamental principle of *yoga,* the curbing of the physical in order to advance the spiritual, is found in Hindu literature centuries earlier than the *Yogas Sūtras.* In *Chāndogya Upaniṣad,* austerity is praised as a priestly virtue: "And austerity, almsgiving, uprightness, non-violence, truthfulness, these are the gifts of the priests." [77] In *Bṛhad-Āraṇyaka Upaniṣad,* the Creator fashioned the world by means of *yoga:* "He desired: 'Let me sacrifice again with a greater sacrifice.' He rested himself, he practised austerity. While he was thus rested and heated, fame and vigour went forth." [78] *Yoga mārga* remains in Hinduism to the present day as an important ingredient in

[75] 7. 12. 2.
[76] *Ibid.,* 6. 83. 2.
[77] 3. 17. 4. Radhakrishnan translation.
[78] 1. 2. 6. Radhakrishnan translation.

the Perfecting of Man. The intent is not to beat the body, but to make the body a perfect instrument of the spirit.

Closely related to *yoga mārga*—in fact, better described as a combination of *yoga mārga* and *bhakti mārga*—is the tantric *mārga*. Tantra emphasizes the love of man and woman as the ideal relationship of God and man. Tantra also makes much use of occultism in disciplining the hidden powers of human nature. Tantra *mārga* will be treated in this study as a type of *yoga mārga*.

There are therefore four *mārgas*: *jñāna*, *karma*, *bhakti*, and *yoga*. However, the thesis of this study is that the *mārgas* are not mutually exclusive. Whether one is a *jñānin*, or a *karmin*, or a *bhakta*, or a *yogi*, he will incorporate to some degree the features of the other *mārgas* in his own path to the Perfection of Man. Since each individual may select and adapt from the *mārgas* according to his preferences, there is a sense in which there are as many *mārgas* as there are individual personalities!

"No foreigner has ever adequately understood our land." [79] This is a surprising remark to come from one of the most scholarly Indian philosophers of the twentieth century, but certain qualifications will make it more acceptable. In a sense, no foreigner has ever understood any people as long as he must conceptualize their culture in his own categories; yet if he ever reached the state in which this was unnecessary, then he would no longer be a foreigner. Part of the difficulty with respect to Indian religion and philosophy is that they have been so often surveyed and examined within the context of the nature and function of Western philosophies and religions. This has been one of the problems of the East-West Philosophers' Conferences at the University of Hawaii.[80] Dasgupta's complaint against foreigners can be modified to read, "No one who attempts to understand one culture in the categories of another can attain the understanding of the one who has been reared in it." The contention of this study is that a Western man can best understand Hinduism if he examines it as *sādhana*, and if he does not try to fit it into the molds of Western philosophy and religion.

[79] Surendra Nath Dasgupta, *Hindu Mysticism*, p. 168.

[80] See Troy Organ, "What Is an Individual? Report of the Fourth East-West Philosophers' Conference," *International Philosophical Quarterly*, Vol. 5, No. 4, December 1965, pp. 666–676.

CHAPTER II
The Quest for Reality

1. THE PROMINENCE OF ONTOLOGY

The *Matsya Purāṇa* records a myth about a *ṛṣi* named Mārkandeya who had been endowed with unending life.[1] Mārkandeya is said to be living within the sleeping god, Viṣṇu, which is to be interpreted that he is within the area of created things. In the course of his wanderings within the god he falls through the parted lips of the sleeping deity and plunges into the "cosmic sea." His circumstances are now so different from his former estate that, instead of exploring his new environment or of comparing it with his accustomed surroundings, he asks himself which is the real world—the world within Viṣṇu, or the world of the "cosmic sea"? He sees no sun nor moon; he feels no wind nor rain. The familiar earth itself has vanished. He is unable to establish meaningful relationships with the new world. He asks himself if he had been dreaming and is now awake, or was he awake and is now dreaming. This myth is symbolic of the Hindu quest for reality. Hinduism is more than a metaphysical quest, i.e., a quest to determine the natures of different kinds of things; it is an ontological quest, that is, a quest for Being itself. What is meant by saying something is? What is the Is-ness of which individual existences partake? What is the Being which would remain were beings destroyed? The quest is an effort to cut through the entanglement of existences to find, if possible, a Reality which when known will make

[1] 167. 13–35. This Purāṇa is one of the largest of the eight Mahāpurāṇas. It is a conglomeration of advice on devotional subjects and domestic problems.

all things known. Through It "the unhearable becomes heard, the unperceivable becomes perceived, the unknowable becomes known." [2] These paradoxical-sounding statements are not necessarily paradoxical. Hindus are not as oxymoronic as Western scholars have sometimes imagined. The quest is for a Reality which will make known the real in the apparent, the noumenal in the phenomenal. Hinduism seeks a common ground, which may be indeterminate and unfathomable in itself, yet is still an explanatory device to put experienced pluralities into the framework of a manifested Oneness. The search is for a One which generates no antithesis, and therefore from which no higher synthesis can come. It is a One which fully satisfies the questing soul:

> Which having gained, it cannot dream
> Of any greater gain
> Than this true State, wherein once settled,
> It dwells, unshaken by the direst pain.[3]

We do not know why but we do know that the Babylonians were obsessed with attempts to predict the future by the study of the heavenly bodies, the Egyptians and Taoists with efforts to conquer death, the Hebrews with the search for moral law, and the Greeks with the creation of beauty. Hindu civilization has been, and is, in quest of reality. "What is the real which if known will make all things known?" has been one of the fundamental quests of the Hindus. Furthermore, the search has been directed not to the starry heavens but to the inner world of the human spirit.

Perhaps in his pursuit of Being the Hindu has been too indifferent to the concrete particular, at least Coomaraswamy has so charged: "In the realm of the practical, empirical and material life, India has been roused to a realisation of the fact that, in her devotion to the highest things, she has carried too far her indifference to the concrete." [4] If this is true—and it is difficult to deny the evidence—this is surely a mistaken interpretation of the meaning of Hindu ontology; for what is affirmed is that the manifold entities of common experience are exemplifications of a single Reality, not that they are unimportant. As we shall point out later, they are the necessary exemplifications of the Real, and hence share both reality and value with the Real. Radhakrishnan and Aurobindo have said this in many different ways. The fact that both have felt the necessity of affirming the significance of particulars and denying

[2] *Chāndogya Upaniṣad* 6. 1. 3. Radhakrishnan translation.
[3] *Bhagavad Gītā* 6. 22. F. T. Brooks translation.
[4] Ananda K. Coomaraswamy, *The Message of the East*, pp. 1–2.

the illusionism so often charged against Hinduism suggests that the charge is felt and needs to be refuted.

The quest for reality is not a part-time, halfhearted pursuit. Again and again in Hindu literature we read that it must be an overpowering search. One example is the legend of a would-be disciple who paid a visit to a *yogi* and asked that he be instructed. The *yogi*, suspecting that the man did not seek reality in a completely serious manner, paid no attention to the request, and continued in his meditation. Again the disciple asked to be taught; and again there was no reply. When the disciple asked a third time, the *yogi* arose and asked the disciple to follow. When they came to a river, the *yogi* walked into the water, the disciple following. Suddenly the *yogi* turned, seized the man, and held his head under the water. After a great struggle the man was released, and upon catching his breath asked, "Why did you do that?" "Why did you struggle so violently when your head was under the water?" asked the *yogi*. "Because I wanted air," replied the man. "Well," said the *yogi*, "When you want to know reality as you wanted to breathe air when I held your head under the water, come to me and I will teach you!"

The feeling of unreality is not an uncommon experience in the sanest of lives. In the midst of a highly emotional experience the question may arise, "Is this real?" One may even have the sensation of being an onlooker rather than a participant. Extremely joyous and extremely dangerous experiences are ones most likely to produce the feeling of irreality. The feeling is so common in war that soldiers are trained in such a manner that even in their first battle their behavior will be habitual. Sometimes brides feel a strange unreality in the happy emotions of their wedding day. Again people who have been lost in wooded areas report hallucinations and inability to recognize familiar landmarks. But some people never appear to have these feelings of unreality, and some, in the words of a comic-strip character, "merely dread each day as it comes!"

The Hindus seem to be prone to the feeling of unreality, and hence appear to raise the question of what is real more persistently than do other peoples. What is the reason for this phenomenon? Could it be the impact of climate? India has a short season for the planting, tilling, and harvesting of crops and then a long wait for the monsoon rains to provide the moisture for the next growing season. For at least six months of the year the farmer can sit under the shade of trees idly gazing out on his sun-baked fields or herding his cattle and goats along the dusty roadsides. Much of the life of the peasant seems to be spent waiting for rain. The days blend into each other with nothing unusual to mark them. The Hindus do not even break the week with a Sabbath. Such dreamy monotony of hot, parching days may account for the questions of what is real and what is not real, although the dangers of explaining human attitudes on the basis of climate are well known. Anthropogeography has run its course, and we do not intend to revive it here. The chief reason for avoiding accounting for propensities of thought on the basis of geographic conditions is that man has demonstrated over and over again an ability to adjust to conditions far beyond what one might have predicted. Again, were the Hindus by nature Berkleians who doubted the ability of sight, sound, touch, taste, and smell to convey the substance of things, and were there no stone-kicking Johnsons among the Hindus? No—this is not quite to the point, for the Hindus did not deny the realities of sense experience within the frame of reference of the senses. Their quest for reality was not an effort to deal with perceptual errors so much as an attempt to cope with the human experience of the passing of things. Within the ideal hundred-year span of life a man would experience a great deal of the transitoriness of things. It was the experience of passing away that caused the Hindu to ask "What is real?" And the question was not the simple one of the difference between an existing thing and a non-existing thing; it was a question of what does it mean when we say that something is. It was a question about Being in general, not a question of the existence of a thing here today and gone tomorrow.

Perhaps we cannot identify why the Hindus raised the ontological question so early and so persistently, but the fact is that they did. Edgerton says that two habits of thought exist alongside each other in traditional thinking, the "ordinary" and the "extraordinary." [5] The ordinary is the stuff of which history is made; these are events that can be located in space and time, that can be established by the public test, that can be predicted to repeat themselves under given conditions. The extraordinary deals with the abstract, the unpredictable, the unobservable. In Hinduism the extraordinary has always tended to drive out the ordinary. It was the extraordinary that was prized, and above all the knowledge of the meaning of Being *per se*. According to the Hebrew myth, when man was placed in the Garden of Eden with its tree of life and tree of the knowledge of good and evil, he was tempted and he yielded, tasting the fruit of the second tree. Had Adam been a Hindu, the case might have been different! Vamdeo Sastri, for example, has said, "Of the two trees that stood in your Garden of Eden we Hindus should have chosen the tree of life, which has been mystically understood to symbolize the wisdom which apprehends reality; whereas by eating of the food which gave discernment of good and evil, Adam fell down into the region of earthly pains and pleasures, of will and desire." [6]

[5] *Journal of American Oriental Society*, Vol. 57, 1942, pp. 151–156.
[6] Quoted by Lyall, *Asiatic Studies*. Second Series, p. 86.

Whereas the West has channeled human curiosity about the world into questions about origin, function, and usefulness, Hindus have persisted in asking the question of reality; and they have put the question not so much to the things in the universe as to the universe itself. It is a question about the possibility of existential error: what right does the experienced world have to claim to be a real world? Skepticism about the gods appeared early in the speculation of the Aryans. Although the best known instance of skepticism is skepticism about the omniscience of god, "This creation, whence it came into being, whether it was established, or whether not—he who is its overseer in the highest heavens, he verily knows, or perchance he knows it not," [7] a more remarkable instance of skepticism entertains the possibility that god himself does not exist: "The terrible one, of whom they ask, Where is he? and then even say of him, He is not at all." [8] The author recognizes the existence of such atheistic ideas, but he rejects them, and pleads with his hearers to recognize the existence of the god: "Believe in him! He, O folk, is Indra." [9]

The quest for reality assumes that reality can be known, and that when known will make all things known: "He who knows the thread (*sūtra*), O Kāpya, and that inner controller, indeed knows Brahman, he knows the worlds, he knows the gods, he knows the Vedas, he knows being, he knows the self, he knows everything." [10] A second assumption of the quest considerably modifies the first. It is that reality can be known only from within, for the Self is "the Real of the real": "From Him, indeed, who is in the soul (*ātman*) come forth all breathing creatures, all worlds, all the Vedas, all gods, all beings. The mystic meaning (*upaniṣad*) thereof is: The Real of the real." [11] The primary knowledge is therefore not discursive knowledge; it is direct knowing—if such can be called knowing. This knowing is subject-knowing-subject, not subject-knowing-object. Hindu *sādhana* seeks "the final grasp, not mere argumentative philosophy." [12] Much confusion about Hinduism would be overcome if the term "knowledge" were not forced to do double service, that is, to denote

[7] *Ṛg Veda* 10. 129. 7. Edgerton translation.
[8] *Ibid.*, 2. 12. 5. Edgerton translation.
[9] *Loc. cit.*
[10] *Bṛhad-Āraṇyaka Upaniṣad* 3. 7. 1. Radhakrishnan translation.
[11] *Maitrī Upaniṣad* 6. 32. Hume translation.
[12] Kalidas Bhattacharyya, *Alternative Standpoints in Philosophy*, p. 366. Bhattacharyya also says, "Philosophy is the understanding (or interpretation) *of* reality. The 'of'-relation here indicates as much a close unity as in the case of 'knowledge of object'; and as there, so here there is no mere Dualistic correspondence between Philosophy and reality. It is not true that on the one side there are alternative realities and on the other side alternative Philosophies as representations of these. Our common notion that Philosophy is an external reflection outside has to be given up once for all." *Ibid.*, p. 361.

the knowing appropriate to Being and the knowing appropriate to beings. Imagine the confusions if "seeing" were used to mean both eye-seeing-things-other-than-itself and eye-seeing-itself. Perhaps instead of dividing knowledge into direct and indirect knowledge, two species of a common genus, we should insist that all knowledge is indirect; the direct form is important, but it is not knowledge. Knowledge is a salute, not an embrace; a representation, not a presentation; a symbolization, not a reality; a universalizing, not a concretizing. To know is to translate the concrete, particular, specific, and unanalyzed into the abstract, universal, general, and analyzed. In a sense to know is to falsify. Known water is H_2O, or the universal solvent, or a substance that swells when it freezes, or the first principle of all things according to Thales; water thrown in the face by an enthusiastic Zen master is not known water, however arresting may be the experience of being on the receiving end of the water. Let us call this non-cognitive grasping of things insight—and keep it quite distinct from knowledge. Then we can rephrase the assumptions of the Hindu quest for reality: the quest for reality within Hinduism assumes that when *inner* reality is grasped by insight a basis is attained from which *external* reality may be *known.*

2. *Māyā*

The Upaniṣads contain a number of seminal ideas which, while not constituting in themselves a doctrine of *māyā* in the sense developed by Śaṅkara, do provide a basis for this doctrine. The earliest use of the term was to refer to the magic-working powers of the Vedic gods, particularly the power to disguise themselves in alternative forms, e.g., "Indra by his magic powers (*māyā*) goes about in many forms."[13] In the *Śvetāśvatara Upaniṣad* the *ṛṣi* speaks of the *māyin* (magician, sorcerer, juggler) who produces the world by his *māyā* (magical powers) out of the material cause:

> This whole world the illusion-maker (*māyin*) projects out of this [Brahma].
> And in it by illusion (*māyā*) the other is confined.
> Now one should know that Nature (*Prakṛti*) is illusion (*māyā*),
> And that the Mighty Lord (*maheśvara*) is the illusion-maker (*māyin*).[14]

Note that in the first quotation the god works his magic upon himself, while in the second he seems to operate on a substance outside himself.

[13] *Bṛhad-Āraṇyaka Upaniṣad* 2. 5. 19. Hume translation. This is probably a quotation from *Ṛg Veda* 6. 47. 18.

[14] 4. 9–10. Hume translation.

In neither case is the term *māyā* prejudicial; *māyā* is power to accomplish in a miraculous manner. There is no demerit in this conjuring, but other contexts do give an unfavorable slant. For example, the *Praśna Upaniṣad* states that in those who belong to the world of Brahmā the Creator "there is no crookedness and falsehood, nor trickery (*māyā*)." [15] *Māyā* here means the saying of one thing while doing another.

There are also references in the Upaniṣads to the veiling or hiding of reality. *Īśa Upaniṣad* reports that the face of truth is veiled with a golden disc,[16] and in *Chāndogya Upaniṣad* the *ṛṣi* teaches that just as all things made of clay are really clay, so all things made of the one Reality are really that Reality; the only difference is that different names are given to the things. The reality is hidden by the name. The distinction of real and unreal we have already noted in the ancient purificatory hymn: "From the unreal lead me to the real." [17]

There are many references in the Upaniṣads to the ignorance (*avidyā*) of man. *Māyā* and *avidyā* may be regarded as the same fact from two points of view: the magical power of the gods to create an illusion, and the inability of man to perceive the Real. The ignorant man is a blind man led about by another who is also blind.[18] Again ignorance is likened to a knot which must be untied in order to get to truth.[19] In another place the *ṛṣi* says in language anticipatory of Bacon that knowledge of what is happening is part of the power of the sacrifice; ignorance is impotence: "Knowledge and ignorance, however, are different. What, indeed, one performs with knowledge, faith and meditation, that, indeed, becomes more powerful." [20]

Perhaps the most interesting word that later developed into the doctrine of *māyā* was the word "*iva*" (as it were). *Iva* is used in the Upaniṣads to indicate the difference between things that are real and things which merely appear to be real. For example, in the *Bṛhad-Āraṇyaka Upaniṣad* a *ṛṣi* describing the state of dreaming says that the dreamer "now, as it were (*iva*), enjoying pleasure with women; now, as it were (*iva*), laughing and even beholding fearful sights." [21] Again the *ṛṣi* speaks of the self "seeming to think, seeming to move about," [22] which is interpreted by Śaṅkara to show that the soul is not an agent, it merely acts

[15] 1. 16. Hume translation.

[16] 15.

[17] *Bṛhad-Āraṇyaka Upaniṣad* 1. 3. 28. Hume translation.

[18] *Kaṭha Upaniṣad* 1. 2. 5; *Muṇḍaka Upaniṣad* 1. 2. 8; *Maitrī Upaniṣad* 7. 9.

[19] *Muṇḍaka Upaniṣad* 2. 1. 10.

[20] *Chāndogya Upaniṣad* 1. 1. 10. Radhakrishnan translation.

[21] 4. 3. 13. Hume translation.

[22] *Bṛhad-Āraṇyaka Upaniṣad* 4. 3. 7. Radhakrishnan translation. Hume translates this as "appearing to think, appearing to move about."

as if thinking, as if moving. Also in the *Bṛhad-Āraṇyaka Upaniṣad* reference is made to the appearance of duality in the world of sensations which hides the basic unity: "For where there is duality (*dvaita*), as it were (*iva*), there one sees another; there one smells another . . . hears . . . speaks to . . . thinks of . . . understands." [23]

The Upaniṣads hold that duality, plurality, time sequence, spatial co-existences, the subject-object relationship, and even causality are not marks of the highest Reality. The distinction between appearance and reality is made, but there is no indication that things that appear to be non-existent are non-existent: "The Upaniṣads support the doctrine of *māyā* only in the sense that there is an underlying reality containing all elements from the personal God to the telegraph post." [24] The Upaniṣads grant that man may be deceived, but they do not teach that the world is a play of shadows, an illusion, or an unreality.

It was Śaṅkara, the brilliant ninth-century A.D. founder of Advaita Vedāntism, who placed the quest for reality central in Hindu *sādhana* by marshaling Upaniṣadic insights on *māyā, avidyā,* and *iva* together with such conceptions as that of a dream world (*māyāmātram*) from Bādarāyaṇa's aphoristic summaries of Vedic teaching.[25] His teachings that the world is *māyā*—or the result of *māyā*, if one wishes to preserve the earlier connotations of magical power—have so captured the imagination of Hindus and non-Hindus that this doctrine is often thought to be the foremost teaching of Advaita Vedāntism. As a matter of fact, it is a derivative doctrine: only Brahman is real; the world is not identical with Brahman; so the world is not real as Brahman is real. To deny absolute reality to the world is not to affirm that the world is unreal or illusory.

Part of the problem resulting from Śaṅkara's analysis of the reality of the world results from his purist use of the terms *sat* (real) and *asat* (unreal). He takes these words in their absolute sense. "Real" means, for him, real for all time. Only Brahman can be real in that sense. The "existence" of Brahman is so different from all empirical existences that Brahman's "existence" may just as well be said to be "non-existence." "Unreal" means absolutely unreal, completely impossible. Even a mirage

[23] 2. 4. 14; 4. 5. 15. Hume translation.

[24] Radhakrishnan, *Indian Philosophy*, Vol. 1, p. 197.

[25] *The Brahma Sūtras* 3. 2. 3. This is the only place where the term *māyā* appears in *The Brahma Sūtras* (or *Vedānta Sūtras*). W. S. Urquhart has written, "Śaṅkara does not make any very direct appeal to the text of the *Vedānta Sūtras* in support of his doctrine of *māyā*. . . . In this avoidance he is probably wise, for the Sūtras do not support his conclusions very fully. They are in closer agreement with Rāmānuja's doctrine of the relation of God to the world, which is that God is the material cause of the world and that finite things have the reality of determinations of His essence." *Pantheism and the Value of Life with Special Reference to Indian Philosophy*, p. 206. See *The Brahma Sūtras* 1. 1. 2 and 1. 4. 23, 25 for instances of closeness to Rāmānuja.

on the desert is not unreal, for there must be conditions of light and heat for the mirage to appear. Śaṅkara's example of *asat* is the son of a barren woman. Furthermore, Śaṅkara speaks in context. The world is *sat* within the context of time, for it does exist as a phenomenon of time, but the world is also *asat* because it has no existence in the Absolute; or to state this in a manner more in keeping with Śaṅkara's intention, the world is not *sat* because it exists only in temporal limits, and the world is not *asat* because it does exist but only in temporal limits. The world is not utterly unreal, for it is rooted and grounded in Brahman, the Absolute Reality; the world is not ultimately real, for it passes away. As long as we are in the world, the world seems real; it is only when we are liberated from the fever of life, or when we catch glimpses of enlightenment while still within the world, that we experience the unreality of the world. The characteristic of non-classifiability as either *sat* or *asat* (*sadasadvilakṣaṇa*) is the uniqueness of the things of experience and of the experienced world; it is also the characteristic of *māyā* itself. For Śaṅkara the principle of world phenomenalism is itself a phenomenon, that is, it is not independent of Brahman. To regard the world as self-sufficient is to commit either the error of identifying temporal and eternal or the error of deriving the eternal from the temporal. To regard the world as an illusion is to withdraw all value from the world.

Māyā according to Śaṅkara is other than *sat* (absolute Being) and also other than *asat* (absolute non-Being). The world as *māyā* has a certain name (*nāma*) and existential reality (*rūpa*), but both the name and the what are conventional. Confusion arises if we fail to distinguish two types of *māyā* in Śaṅkara. The physical world is *māyā,* and the individual self is *māyā,* although they are not the same in their *māyā*-ness. The world's *māyā* is like that of a "snake" which upon closer examination is seen to be a rope. The "snake" was a case of mistaken identity; it was a rope that under certain conditions appeared to be a snake. The individual self's *māyā* is like that of a piece of paper seen as white, whereas it is in fact a piece of red paper seen at night by illumination from a red neon tube. The *māyā* in this case has to do with the reality or irreality of a certain sensed quality of the object, not with the existence or non-existence of the object. When Śaṅkara refers to the *māyā* of the world, he denotes the problem of the existence of the world; when he refers to the *māyā* of the self, he denotes the problem of the individuality of the self, not of the existence of the self. This is a crucial point, for if the *jīva* (individual soul) were false as the "snake" in the rope is false, then there would be nothing to be liberated. Liberation, for Śaṅkara, is the losing of the limiting adjuncts (*upādhis,* the mistaken notions that the self is in reality the individual) and the discovering that the *jīva, sub specie aeternitatis,* is Brahman.

The central affirmation in Śaṅkara's *māyā* doctrine is that the world is unreal apart from Brahman and real as grounded in Brahman. Śaṅkara does not write off the empirical world as an illusion; it is that which Reality makes us perceive.[26] Reality may also be manifested in ways far beyond the power of human minds to imagine. The Perfected Man will understand that the world in itself has no existence; it is only *māyā*. Rāmānuja says that only an insane person would take pleasure in an unreal play in an unreal world with unreal instruments.[27] Rāmānuja holds that the world is the expression of divine love and joy; it is far too precious to be disposed of, even by the Perfected Man. Gokhale has argued that Śaṅkara did teach that the world is essentially an illusion, offering as his strongest argument: "But if Śaṅkara did not really mean to ascribe the nature of illusion to the world of experience Rāmānuja's refutation of the theory of *Māyā* would be tantamount to setting up straw men only to knock them down." [28] According to Gokhale while Śaṅkara carried to a logical conclusion the concept of the world as an illusion which began with the breakup of the imperial polity after the disintegration of the Gupta empire, Rāmānuja preached again the reality of the world, and reversed the trend. Gokhale's assumption that Rāmānuja would not set up straw men only to knock them down makes one

[26] Radhakrishnan writes that for Śaṅkara "unreal the world is, illusory it is not." *Indian Philosophy,* Vol. 2, p. 583. A. C. Mukerji commenting on this statement says that Radhakrishnan would have stated this much better if he had said, "The world of plurality is perfectly real from the standpoint of finite experience; but when looked at from that of the Infinite experience, it is even less than a dream or illusion, and, as such, it has never existed in the past, does not exist at present, and will never exist in the future." *The Nature of the Self,* p. 287, footnote 29. K. C. Bhattacharyya contends, "The acosmism of Śaṅkara goes beyond both realism and idealism by reducing the world to absolute illusion, by interpreting the vanity of life as implying the denial of given reality." *Studies in Philosophy,* Vol. 1, p. 96. Bhattacharyya distinguishes three stages of *māyā:* (1) the implicitly real object which is grasped by uncritical thought, e.g., the snake in the rope believed to be real; (2) the unreal object which is grasped by critical thought, e.g., the belief that there is a snake is corrected by perception that what was thought to be a snake is a rope; (3) the "indescribable" which is grasped only by faith, e.g., the snake is contemplated not only as non-existent now but as non-existent even when it appeared to be perceived. According to Bhattacharyya, "Both Māyā and Brahman are taken to be incapable of being established by reason of any natural pramāṇa. . . . They are in fact to be accepted in faith and only interpreted by thought." *Ibid.,* p. 95. One wonders if in his interpretation of Śaṅkara's doctrine of *māyā* Bhattacharyya has taken sufficient notice of the fact that it is man living in the *māyā* world who identifies and interprets both *māyā* and Brahman.

[27] Quoted by Radhakrishnan, *The Brahma Sūtras,* pp. 348–349.

[28] B. G. Gokhale, *Indian Thought Through the Ages: A Study of Some Dominant Concepts,* p. 138.

wonder if Gokhale has read some of the extant writings of Rāmānuja. Anyone who constantly refers to Śaṅkara as "our opponent" and who offers as his first evaluation of Śaṅkara's conception of Brahman, "The entire theory rests on a fictitious foundation of altogether hollow and vicious arguments, incapable of being stated in definite logical alternatives. . . . The theory therefore must needs be rejected by all those who, through texts, perception, and the other means of knowledge—assisted by sound reasoning—have an insight into the true nature of things," [29] seems to be more anxious to refute an idea than to be certain the idea he refutes is one he completely understands. Rāmānuja, the man of feeling, was chiefly motivated by devotion to his god; the intellectualism of Śaṅkara seems to have infuriated him into almost irrational anger.[30] Instead of repudiating the doctrine of *māyā*, Rāmānuja missed a golden opportunity of pointing out that a theistic god being what he is, and man's power to know being what it is, divine revealing must necessarily be a veiling; so *māyā* is the revelation of divinity in human categories.

Māyā is Śaṅkara's alternative to the Sāṅkhya hypothesis of *prakṛti*, the independent material principle which activates the world to the realization of spirit. *Māyā*, while it is also a material principle, differs from *prakṛti* in that it is dependent upon Brahman; it does not participate in the reality of Brahman, and its products are not real as Brahman is real.

Perhaps of all the insights potentially productive of the conception of *māyā*, Śaṅkara makes most use of the term "*iva*." For example, he finds it helpful to give a metonymous meaning to ideas that do not easily fit into his own categories. *Vedānta Sūtra* 2. 3. 43 taken literally violates Śaṅkara's absolute monism, and gives the individual soul a separate existence contrary to Śaṅkara's notion that the individual soul is *māyā*: "The soul is part of the Lord." But in his commentary on the passage Śaṅkara is able to interpret the passage in such a way as to support rather than weaken his position: "By 'part' we mean 'a part as it were' (*iva*), since a being not composed of parts cannot have parts in the literal sense." [31]

Śaṅkara's doctrine of *māyā* has stimulated a controversy which sometimes loses sight of the fundamental notion of the theory, which is that anyone is deluded who thinks that reality is exhausted by the physical universe, individual selves, and the gods. Far more important than the

[29] *Vedānta Sūtras with the Commentary of Rāmānuga* 1. 1. 1. Translated by George Thibaut. *The Sacred Books of the East*, Vol. 48, p. 39.

[30] See Troy Organ, *The Self in Indian Philosophy*, pp. 116–121.

[31] *Vedānta Sūtras with the Commentary by Śaṅkarācārya*. Translated by George Thibaut. *The Sacred Books of the East*, Vol. 38, p. 61.

negative emphasis on the illusory character of our human experiences is the positive teaching that our lives are played on an earthly stage with a backdrop of infinity. The doctrine should encourage men with its assurance of reality, not discourage them with the notion of illusion.

The doctrine of *māyā* does not mean that man ought to renounce life. The good life for man is a life of fulfillment, not of sublation. *Tapas* (asceticism) does not imply a masochistic denial of the satisfaction of human desires. The Upaniṣads hold that life should be so rich and full that "Always performing works here one should wish to live a hundred years." [32] *Māyā* means that man should see behind the veil, not become caught in outward appearances, nor fail to redeem life by using it to realize the Self. "A philosophy of resignation, an ascetic code of ethics, and a temper of languid world-weariness are an insult to the Creator of the universe, a sin against ourselves and the world which has a claim on us." [33]

3. METHODS OF KNOWING

Since ignorance is a root cause of man's condition of bondage, much emphasis is placed within Hinduism on the methods of knowing (*pramāṇa*). Epistemology or theory of knowledge is not separated from ontology, metaphysics, religion, or ethics, because knowing is a means to assist man in guiding his life to integration, liberation from suffering, and existential enlightenment. Six methods of knowing have been distinguished by the various Hindu philosophical schools, although only the Advaita Vedāntists and the Bhāṭṭa Mīmāṁsists accept all six. These methods are ways of knowing *beings* rather than of knowing *Being*. By this we mean that the six might be used to know the realities of the world without ever raising the ontological question of Being itself; although for one who asks the ontological question, they serve as ways to discern the realities which are assumed to be manifestations of the Reality, and hence are instrumental in the quest for Absolute Reality. The six are perception (*pratyakṣa*), inference (*anumāna*), authority (*śabda*), analogy (*upamāna*), implication (*arthāpatti*), and negation (*anupalabdhi*).

Perception is the most important source of knowing the realities of man's world. It carries with it conclusive assurance: "When a man has once perceived the thing directly, his desires are at rest, and he does not

[32] *Īśā Upaniṣad* 2. Radhakrishnan translation.
[33] Radhakrishnan, *Indian Philosophy*, Vol. 1, p. 219.

seek for any other kind of knowledge." [34] The sense organs are the five external ones, plus the internal one, mind (*manas*). The external sense organs operate by means of the five elements, i.e., smell is by means of the element earth, taste by water, sight by light, touch by air, and sound by ether. A perception is determinate; it is so well defined that conviction is inherent in it. Secondly, a perception is unexpressible in words; one is never able to convey one's own perceptions to another person, although one can appeal to the other person and ask if he does not have perceptions so-and-so. The third claim, that perception is unerring, recognizes that while a perception is self-validating, error may enter in the interpretation of the perception. He who sees a "snake" does have a perception; the error is in attributing "snake" to the external object, the rope, that makes him see a "snake." Philosophers differ widely as to the nature of mind: some regard it as a condition of all perception; others think of mind as an independent perceiving agency. Those taking the second alternative contend that there are three kinds of perceptions: the ordinary sense perceptions, after-image perceptions, and direct awareness of the self.

The inferential way of knowing combines induction and deduction. Gautama, an early logician (third century B.C.), distinguished three kinds of inference: that which does not appeal to experience, that which does appeal to experience and also to argument, and that which appeals to experience but not to argument. The last is an inference "commonly seen," e.g., one sees a horned animal and infers that it has a tail. The early logicians also worked out a series of principles for determining cause-and-effect relations which are quite similar to J. S. Mill's methods of agreement and difference; however, the most interesting and illuminating aspect of the work of the logicians is the Indian syllogism. Far in advance of Western logicians they saw that the syllogism was a pedagogical device rather than a strictly logical apparatus, a method of convincing rather than a method of discovering. This is clearly indicated by their habit of presenting the conclusion first in the form of a thesis to be established. Thus the five-part syllogism—the usual form of the syllogism in Hindu philosophy—proceeds by these steps:

1. The thesis to be established.
2. The reason.
3. The example.
4. The application.
5. The conclusion, that is, the thesis established.

[34] Commentary on *Nyāya Sūtra* 1. 1. 3 from *Gautama's Nyāyasūtras with Vātsyāyaṇa's Bhāṣya.* Translated by Ganganatha Jha.

The thesis fixes the problem and limits the inquiry. The reason names the middle or vanishing term, the term in the argument which makes it possible to move from starting point to conclusion. The example actually contains two parts: the major premise or general statement, plus a familiar instance illustrating the general statement. The application points out that the example is exemplified in the case in question, and the conclusion restates the original thesis as now confirmed. An illustration of the five-part syllogism often given in the logical literature is this:

1. The thesis: "That mountain has fire."
2. The reason: "Because there is smoke on the mountain."
3. The example: "Anything that has smoke has fire, e.g., an oven."
4. The application: "That mountain has smoke which is invariably accompanied by fire."
5. The conclusion: "That mountain has fire."

Authority denotes both the revealed writings (*śruti*), which refer to the Vedas regarded as unqualifiedly authoritative within Hinduism, and the verbal testimony of a reliable person. Gautama made suggestions about the second form of authority which are markedly sensible: that the meaning of every word is due to convention, so care must be taken to know what meaning the word has for the speaker; that words should have duplicate meaning, so that the word when used by the speaker and the listener might be identical in denotation and connotation; that key words should be defined and repeated when necessary, and if synonymous words are to be used, their synonymity should be indicated; that the context in which words are used should always be taken into account, particularly the intention of the speaker.

Analogy is the means by which knowledge is attained from the similarity of a novel thing to another thing well known. Things alike in one respect are also alike in another respect: "If this medicine cured him when he had a fever, then it will cure me now that I have a fever"; "Goats have horns, and sheep are like goats, so sheep have horns." Western-trained minds tend to be suspicious of this way of knowing, regarding it more as a source of hypotheses than as a method of arriving at knowledge of the world. Analogy without verification and argument is more poetic than scientific.

The method of implication is also more a method of hypothesis-making than a method of establishing knowledge. Logically it can be described as supplying the missing premise in an enthymeme. The example given in the literature is that of a person who fasts by day, but who is gaining weight. By method of implication it is concluded that he is eating during the night.

Negation or non-cognition deals with what has been called negative facts. In *Through the Looking-Glass* the White King asks Alice to look along the road to see if two expected messengers are coming. Alice reports, "I see nobody on the road." To which the King replies, "I only wish I had such eyes. To be able to see Nobody! And at that distance too! Why, it's as much as I can do to see real people, by this light!" Had Alice been trained in Vedāntin epistemology she might have retorted, "I know that non-existence cannot be perceived through the senses. Non-existence, however, can be known by non-cognition. Positive perception is the source of knowledge about positive entities. So I know by the fact that I do not perceive the messengers along the road that the messengers are not now coming on the road." Again a Western-trained mind would doubt that negation is enough different from perception to be classified as a separate way of knowing.

Since knowing is a necessary ingredient in *sādhana,* there is an inherent pragmatism about Hindu epistemology. Knowing is essentially pragmatic when it is placed within the context of human salvation. The truth of an idea will, in the last analysis, be the extent to which the idea contributes to the existential enlightenment of the person, rather than its correspondence to realities within the space-time world. Hindu philosophy needs no William James to develop the thesis that the truth is that which works. Coping with suffering is the ultimate test of all knowledge in *sādhana.*

4. NON-PHILOSOPHICAL ASPECTS OF THE QUEST

Men are not perfected by merely changing their ontologies! The quest for reality is an exertion of the will which includes and transcends intellection. The wisdom that is sought is more than knowledge. The subject-object relationship of knowing is to be supplemented by a fuller and closer identity. For the Hindu the problem of reality is a problem of experiencing reality in man's total being—his mind, his feelings, his will, and his actions. "A mere thinker cannot understand the nature of reality. . . . We must become sensuous-intellectual-intuitional to know reality in its flesh and blood and not merely its skin and bones." [35] Furthermore, the Hindu does not proceed by solving first the ontological problems, then the problems of cosmology, and then psychology, before seeking the final liberation—a chronology of events suggested by Mahendranath Sircar in *The System of Vedāntic Thought and Culture.* Such a neat

[35] Radhakrishnan, *The Reign of Religion in Contemporary Philosophy,* pp. 434–435.

classification is foreign to the integrative *sādhana* of Hinduism. A more typical Indian synthesis of disciplines is indicated on the cover page of a scholarly Indian journal which states that it is "An International Quarterly of Philosophy, Psychology, Psychical Research, Religion, Mysticism, and Sociology." Such a mixing of methodologies and subject matters spells chaos to the Western mind, but the Hindu sees no difficulty; this simply exemplifies Hindu *sādhana* in Western terminology!

The non-philosophical aspects of the quest for reality are indicated in the Upaniṣadic suggestions for practical realizations of the Absolute. *Sādhana* requires a final grasp, not an argumented conclusion. There must be an effort and a program for entering into full Being. No doctrine in Hindu *sādhana* would be complete without offering to the aspirant a variety of techniques for implementing the insights into his life. Many of the dialogues in the Upaniṣads are long, monotonous, and tedious—at least to the Western reader. But their repetitiveness is part of the *sādhana*. For example, in the *Chāndogya Upaniṣad* Śvetaketu Āruṇeya returns to his parental home after twelve years of Vedic study with his *guru*, and is confronted with this question from his father: "Śvetaketu, my dear, since now you are conceited, think yourself learned, and are proud, did you also ask for that teaching whereby what has not been heard of becomes heard of, what has not been thought of becomes thought of, what has not been understood becomes understood?" [36] After some more explanation to clarify the question, Śvetaketu confesses that he has not received instruction concerning the key to all knowledge, and his father sets upon the process of instruction. Nine times over he concludes each illustrative instruction with "That is Reality, That is Ātman, That art thou, Śvetaketu." To set this aside as merely Oriental exaggeration and repetition is to miss the point entirely. If knowledge were the only end of instruction, one illustration plus a generalization should be adequate; but the end is to inculcate a habit of thinking, feeling, and acting which will incorporate all that is involved in the identity of the true Self and Reality. Such a discovery does not come by listening to a lecture. Repeated verbalization of a truth is universally recommended as a way to push truth past the door of the intellect into the inner being of rational creatures. Sometimes the repetition of words or sounds is designed to create an atmosphere of holiness. Both of these ends are sought by the use of chantings, litanies, credos, *mantras*, and even refrains to music.[37]

[36] *Chāndogya Upaniṣad* 6. 1. 3. Hume translation.

[37] Cf. Ronald Segal, *The Crisis of India*, pp. 153–154: "At first study the Indians appear to use language as a flourish rather than as a vehicle, with the object of producing an effect rather than conveying a belief or statement of fact. And this impression is confirmed by the custom of religious chanting, when crowds will mutter 'Ram! Ram!'

Man is unique among all living beings in that in him the questing for Reality rises to consciousness, but this does not mean that the questing is itself a consciously intellectual process. There are references in the Vedas and the Upaniṣads to the sensory aspects of the process. Hindus are not anti-empirical, as some have supposed, but they assume that the empirical is not the total experience; behind the empirical is the Reality which appears under the guise of the empirical. Physical forms in themselves are experienced as evidences of Brahman: "Fog, smoke, sun, wind, fire, fireflies, lightning, crystal moon, these are the preliminary forms which produce the manifestation of Brahman in Yoga." [38] The formed Brahman also appears as color: "The form of this person is like a saffron-coloured robe, like white wool, like the Indragopa insect, like a flame of fire, like a white lotus, like a sudden flash of lightning." [39] A continuation of the use of color is noticed in the brilliant reds, blues, and yellows in some of the temples of South India. For all mystics, the photist experience is peculiarly symbolic of divinity. *Śvetāśvatara Upaniṣad* 4. 18 reminds the Christian of the Revelation of John in which the Heavenly City has no sun because the light of the Redeemer is sufficient: "When there is no darkness, then there is neither day nor night, neither being nor non-being, only the auspicious one alone. That is the imperishable, the adorable light of Savitṛ and the ancient wisdom proceeded from that." [40]

Sound deserves a special treatment, for it is identified with Brahman early in the *Ṛg Veda*. *Vāc* (speech, sound), like Brahman, is an inexhaustible ocean. It is "infinite in the highest heaven"; [41] it is "beyond the heaven, beyond this earth." [42] The personalized *Vāc* says, "I also blow forth, (pervading everything) like the wind, taking to myself all the worlds. Beyond the heaven, beyond this earth, so great I have become in grandeur." [43] *Vāc* is a feminine designation for the Holy Word (*bṛh*, *brahman*). She is the magical power which must be manifested at each Vedic sacrifice. The *udgātar* priest is the one who chants from the *Sāma Veda* in order that the rite may accomplish its purpose. *Vāc* is the holy utterance, as distinguished from the common utterances of ordinary men. She is not mere sound, but the sound of Reality: "I am queen, gatherer of riches; very wise, the first of beings worthy of reverence. I am she

---

over and over again in a kind of verbal trance, by the daily repetition of sacred texts which very few understand, by the popularity of traditional songs in an archaic language, which are sung with a display of emotion that completely disguises their unintelligibility. It is a play on language as though it were a musical instrument, to make patterns of sound and establish a mood rather than a meaning."

[38] *Śvetāśvatara Upaniṣad* 2. 11. Radhakrishnan translation.

[39] *Bṛhad-Āraṇyaka Upaniṣad* 2. 3. 6. Radhakrishnan translation.

[40] Radhakrishnan translation.

[41] *Ṛg Veda* 1. 164. 41.

[42] *Ibid.*, 10. 125. 8.

[43] *Ibid.* Edgerton translation.

whom the gods have settled in various places; I have many stations and bestow boons on many."[44] A curious passage in the Upaniṣads states there is a sound of life which vanishes shortly before death: "It is the sound thereof that one hears by covering the ears thus. When one is about to depart from this life one does not hear this sound."[45] It is an interesting fact that in Hindu and Buddhist epistemological literature examples are usually auditory; claps of thunder and human cries displace the blue patches, the yellow flowers, and the tree growing unseen in the courtyard which appear in the pages of Western essays on philosophy of knowledge. The similarity between the Sanskrit *Vāc* and the Greek Logos is striking.

While it is extremely difficult to state the role of art in the five-thousand-year history of Hindu culture, art should be mentioned as one of the non-philosophical aspects of the quest for reality. In Hinduism, as in Christianity, art has been both an obedient handmaiden and a belligerent opponent. In the early Vedic times the artist expressed delight in the world rather than contributing to the serious quest for reality. *Rasa* is the Sanskrit term for emotional delight. Sixty-four arts were sometimes listed; among them were music, dancing, flower arrangement, cooking, embroidery, legerdemain, fencing, gardening, training fighting cocks, and clay modeling. Classical music is still enjoyed for pure sensory delight. In Indian sculpture may be found examples of the sheer joy of the artist. The figures of the shy cat, the reclining deer, and the monkey family in the Descent of the Ganges at Mahābalīpuram were quite obviously placed there for the delight of the spectator rather than for any religious or ethical message. This aspect of Indian art needs to be mentioned to counteract the view that Indian art is always dominated by religion. These humanistic protests against the religious domination of art remind one of the playful carvings on the misericords under the seats of the choir stalls in English cathedrals. Of course, much of the art of the Hindu temple is designed to keep mythologies alive among illiterate peoples. While some sculptures are so spiritualized that they would easily pass the most scrupulous Puritan test, others are so erotic that Westerners are shocked. Under the influence of the Sāṅkhya philosophy art was a deflection from reality, an escape from the natural world, whereas under the influence of Vedāntic philosophers art serves as a path to reality, calling attention to the universal in the form of the particular. In the divine life visualized by Aurobindo, art would have a central function: "The arts and the crafts would exist, not for any inferior mental or vital amusement, entertainment of leisure and relieving excitement or

[44] *Ibid.*, 10. 125. 3. Edgerton translation.
[45] *Bṛhad-Āraṇyaka Upaniṣad* 5. 9. 1; *Maitrī Upaniṣad* 2. 6. Radhakrishnan translation.

pleasure, but as expressions and means of the truth of the spirit and the beauty and delight of existence."[46] Aesthetics has not been a popular study in India. The exploration of art and the artist is a lacuna in Hindu philosophical literature. This seems strange in view of the huge part art has in Indian culture. Perhaps the explanation is that philosophers did not believe that visual art directly ministered to the perfection of human life or to the alleviation of suffering.

Palmistry, numerology, phrenology, dream analysis, and above all astrology have contributed to the Hindu feeling for reality. These magical arts continue to be prominent in prognostication and decision-making. The astrologer is consulted in selecting a spouse, and even in solving problems in business. According to *The Statesman* (Calcutta) two astrologers were brought from Calcutta to Delhi by some members of the Congress Party to assist in the selection of a Prime Minister to replace the deceased Shastri. When a science-oriented Westerner objects, he is apt to be reminded that this is another indication of the open-mindedness and tolerance of Indians, or he may be confronted with the argument that the possibility of the stars affecting human fortunes has not been disproven! Another telling blow is for the Indian to remind the Western scientist that by incorporating the supernatural and preternatural into his life he is not confronted with schizophrenic shock when he visits his house of worship.

The epistemologically centered Western intellectual fears committing an error in statement more than omitting a reality in his scheme of things. He, following the Greek pattern of thought, prefers the rational, the determinate, the measurable. He favors sharply defined boundaries in reasoning in empirical investigations. The Indian philosopher's fear of excluding a reality from his system tends—at least from the Western point of view—to promote preference for the fantastic, the vague, the shapeless. The typical Western philosopher would rather have precise knowledge of little than adumbrations of much; the ontologically centered Indian employs methodologies of sufficient scope to encompass all that is real. He practices the skeptics' admonition, "Better risk loss of truth than chance of error."[47]

5. THE NATURE OF REALITY

The Hindu quest for reality has not been a searching for a completely unknown; the Vedic Indians at a very early time had quite defi-

[46] *The Life Divine*, p. 944.
[47] William James, "The Will to Believe," Section 10.

nite ideas of the reality they sought. Our tendency to read profundities and subtleties into the predominantly magical formulae of the *Ṛg Veda* should not prevent us from noting the more obvious insights into the nature of reality presented in this amazing collection of hymns. The Vedics were convinced that in spite of the pluralities of their experiences a unity pervaded all beings. In one of the earliest monistic speculations Puruṣa, the cosmic person with "a thousand heads, a thousand eyes, and a thousand feet," is said to be greater than space and time.[48] He is the universe of present, past, and future; only one-fourth of Puruṣa is exhausted in all beings—three-fourths of him is in the unmanifested state, i.e., abides in the heavens. The conception of a Being of whom men can experience only one-fourth seems to have been a favorite image, for Holy Speech or Holy Sound (*Vāc*) is said to be a whole of which men can speak only one-quarter.[49] Another early speculation about a oneness behind worlds and gods is found in *Ṛg Veda* 3. 55. Each of the twenty-two stanzas of this hymn ends with the refrain "great and unequalled is the might of the gods." The might of the gods seems to be a unified strength of which each god reveals only a portion. This unity is still more obviously indicated in another passage: "They call it Indra, Mitra, Varuna, Agni; or it is the heavenly Sun-bird. That which is One the seers speak of in various terms: they call it Fire, Yama, Mātariśvan." [50] The *ṛṣis* for purposes of worship make into many forms that which is in fact only one.[51] The author of *Ṛg Veda* 3. 54. 8, referring only to created beings, says, "all moving and stationary beings rest upon one basis, whether animals, or birds, or creatures of various kinds." In another passage Vāc as personified sound says, "I spread through all beings. . . . I breathe forth like the wind, giving form to all created worlds; beyond the heaven, beyond this earth am I, so vast am I in greatness." [52] And the celebrated hymn, *Ṛg Veda* 10. 129, speculates that before there was any existence or non-existence there was "That One."

This insight into the oneness of reality was continued and developed by the later seers and philosophers. As the problems inherent in monism became apparent, philosophers and religionists offered dualistic modifications. Yet the conviction of the fundamental unity of the cosmos and of life has remained a hallmark of Hinduism.

A second presupposition about reality was that it is fundamentally and

[48] *Ṛg Veda* 10. 90.
[49] *Ibid.*, 1. 164. 45.
[50] *Ṛg Veda* 1. 164. 46. Edgerton translation.
[51] "The wise seers through their praise make into many forms the birth which is only one." *Ṛg Veda* 10. 114. 5.
[52] *Ibid.*, 10. 125. 7, 8.

basically pure being: "In the beginning . . . this world was just Being (*sat*), one only, without a second." [53] "All creatures here . . . have Being as their root, have Being as their abode, have Being as their support." [54] The concept of Being without any limitations or attributes is so ambivalent, so difficult to grasp, that the *ṛṣi* adds in the same stanza, "To be sure, some people say, 'In the beginning this world was just Non-being (*asat*), one only, without a second; from that Non-being Being was produced.'" The second opinion is found in *Chāndogya Upaniṣad*, "In the beginning this world was merely non-being" [55] and in *Taittirīya Upaniṣad*, "In the beginning, verily, this world was non-existent. Therefrom, verily, Being was produced." [56] The interpretation of such passages hinges upon whether *asat* is to be taken as absolute Non-Being or relative non-being, that is, as the complete absence of Being or the complete absence of beings. The absolute interpretation would run into the Parmenidean problem of deriving something from nothing. Furthermore, "non-existent" and "existent" seem in some passages to refer to two types of beings—perhaps material and spiritual, e.g., "The non-existent was not, the existent was not." [57] However, the chief significance of characterizing Reality as *sat* is that beings do not exist as fortuitous combinations of atoms coming together in one grouping and then in another, all equally meaningless. Our earthly home may be but one of millions upon which life and consciousness have appeared, but all beings are manifestations of Being. Each being has the dignity of witnessing to Being in a unique manner within its own mode of existence. The Absolute Being by reason of its Absoluteness cannot exist; only beings can exist, and Being is not a kind of being. If existence is a value—and Hinduism assumes that it is better to be than not to be—then beings contribute a value to the universe which Being cannot contribute directly. Being exists only through the beings which are its manifestation. Although some of the sects of Hinduism have regarded created beings as evidence of a loss of pristine unity, the view supported by the Upaniṣads is that the pluralization is the result of divine longing: "He desired, 'Would that I were many! Let me procreate myself!' He performed austerity. Having performed austerity he created this whole world, whatever there is here. Having created it, into it, indeed, he entered. . . . As the real, he became whatever there is here. That is what they call the real." [58]

[53] *Chāndogya Upaniṣad* 6. 2. 1. Hume translation.
[54] *Ibid.*, 6. 8. 6. Hume translation.
[55] 3. 19. 1. Hume translation.
[56] 2. 7. Hume translation.
[57] *Ṛg Veda* 10. 129. 1.
[58] *Taittirīya Upaniṣad* 2. 6. Hume translation.

The Reality sought by man is also said by Hinduism to be *cit*. This term has shifted from its earliest meaning of "the energy that creates the world" to "conscious force," and finally to consciousness itself. *Cit* is the foundation of being aware, as *sat* is the foundation of being existent. When the *Bṛhad-Āraṇyaka Upaniṣad* refers to "the seer of seeing," "the hearer of hearing," "the thinker of thinking," and "the understander of understanding," [59] it is designating the foundation of seeing, hearing, thinking, and understanding, and not a being that sees, hears, thinks, and understands. Man is the being in whom *cit* manifests itself in sensations and thoughts. Like all beings the center of man's being is in Being, and unlike any other being, man is aware of the place he has in the order of things. He is the being who can become awake (*buddha*). As Tillich has stated, "But out of the fertile soil of the earth a being was generated, who was able to find the key to the foundation of all being. That being was man." [60] But when Tillich's remarks are placed in the context in which he expressed them—the discovery of the way to release atomic energy—the Hindu can only in disgust observe that this is typical of the Western mind, and also how strange that the Christian philosopher-theologian who preferred the expression "the Ground of Being" to "God" should have stated that atomic energy rather than the Ground of Being is the key to the foundation of all beings. Reality according to Hindu *sādhana* is not blind energy to be used either for constructive or destructive purposes, nor a chance joining of particles of matter, nor a great machine grinding to its own destruction. Reality is foundational consciousness. All the works of the mind—literature, poetry, myth, legend, science, philosophy, and theology—are Reality at work in the space-time mode of existence. The more man enters into such creations and the more he is aware of his essence as a rational being, the richer is his perfection and the deeper his joy in his being. In such manifestations he fills a niche which only he can fill.

Man is still more significant because he is the only being who can enter into the *ānanda* dimension of Reality. *Ānanda* means bliss, joy, happiness. Reality is *sat, cit,* and *ānanda—Satcitānanda*. Being is joyousness, the foundation of joy. The black world-view of the Hellenes—"The best of all things is never to have been born on earth, never to see the rays of the burning sun. And once a man is born the best thing for him to do is to travel quickly to the gates of Death and lie at rest under a close-fitted coverlet of earth" [61]—is not for the Hindus. *Ānanda* means

[59] 3.4.2. Hume translation.

[60] Paul Tillich, *The Shaking of the Foundations*. New York: Charles Scribner's Sons, 1948, p. 4.

[61] *Theognis* 1.425.

that this is a world in which values are inherent. They are rooted in the Real. Reality is like that. Beings do exist. Mentation does arise. Values do appear. The good, the beautiful, and the true depend upon man for full exploitation, although even before the work of the hand and mind of man, Goodness, Beauty, and Truth (*Śivam, Sundaram, Satyam*) were in Reality. *Ānanda* is a repudiation of the subjective theory of value. Man lives, moves, and has his being in a universe saturated with value; therefore man can live out his life in confidence that the universe is value-in-itself—it is value conserving and value creating. He may live in joyous confidence, surrounded by the ocean of bliss (*ānanda*): "For truly, beings here are born from bliss, when born, they live by bliss and into bliss, when departing, they enter." [62]

When Reality is identified as *Satcitānanda,* the order is important. Being is the foundation of consciousness and values, and conscious beings (i.e., men) are necessary for the appearance of value at the level of beings. Man is the ultimate expression of Reality. In him the Oneness of Reality becomes individuated in unique personalities; in him the Being of Reality comes to the level of beings. Man shares with the lower animals, the plants, and possibly even rocks and stones the exemplification of Oneness and Being. In man the Consciousness of Reality manifests itself in sensation, external awareness, and self-knowledge; and some of these manifestations he shares with the animals. In man the Blissfulness of Reality becomes expressed in the joy of living, in creations of intellect and imagination, and in the consciousness of his existence. In man *Satcitānanda* appears as a quest for Oneness, for Being, for Consciousness, and for Values. In man Reality is real*ing.* Being is. Human *sādhana* is *Satcitānanda* pluralistically realizing the perfections latent within Itself. The quest for Reality is the quest for oneness in plurality, for stability in flux, for consciousness in matter, and for joy in existence. The faith of Hinduism is that *sat, cit,* and *ānanda* are the essence of the Real. The glory of man is that he is the only being who can release these potencies of Reality and creatively develop and enjoy them in time and space.

[62] *Taittirīya Upaniṣad* 3. 6. 1. Radhakrishnan translation.

CHAPTER III

The Quest for Spirituality

1. THE HINDU CONCEPTION OF SPIRITUALITY

"Spirituality is indeed the master-key of the Indian mind." [1] Spirituality is often praised by Indians as their unique contribution to human culture. Vivekananda made spirituality the battlecry for world domination: "Up, India, and conquer the world with your spirituality! . . . Spirituality must conquer the West. . . . We must go out, we must conquer the world through our spirituality and philosophy." [2] Naravane points out that many Indian writers regard India as "the eternal teacher in all things spiritual": "They look upon the development of Indian thought as though it had taken place in complete isolation from the rest of human civilisation." [3] The theme of spirituality is repeated over and over again both in the history of Hinduism and in Hindu India today with emphases ranging from Gandhi's anti-scientific, anti-urban, anti-materialistic theories expressed in the wearing of hand-spun, hand-woven clothing to Tagore's insistence that the scientific and materialistic achievements of the West are themselves spiritual. Nehru was one who

[1] Aurobindo, *The Renaissance in India*, p. 9.

[2] *The Complete Works of Swami Vivekānanda*, Vol. 3, pp. 276–277.

[3] V. S. Naravane, *Modern Indian Thought*, p. 2. Naravane continues, "A striking example is the manner in which Romain Rolland's work on Ramakrishna has been dealt with by the Indian editor. Although the author is lavish in his tribute to the ideas of Ramakrishna and Vivekananda, the editor considers it necessary to controvert in footnotes every single comment, however mild, which may be remotely regarded as critical." *Ibid.*, pp. 2–3.

rebelled against the theme of spirituality; he was convinced that the real struggle in India was between the spiritual culture represented by Hinduism and Islam and the scientific culture of Western civilization, and he did not hesitate to indicate his preference for the scientific.[4] Sometimes the spiritual was conceived in ascetic terms: "In the West they are trying to solve the problem of how much a man can possess, and we are trying to solve the problem on how little a man can live." [5] At other times matter has been given the highest dignity: "Matter is Sachchidananda represented to His own mental experience as a formal basis of objective knowledge, action and delight of existence," and hence "the sharp division which particular experience and long habit of mind have created between Spirit and Matter has no longer any fundamental reality." [6] In the life of the Hindu, spirituality may take the form of sanctifying or deifying a rock, a tree, a river, a tank, an animal, a man, etc. When the authorities of a temple at Kathiawar were unable to induce the Dheds, the outcaste people whose caste responsibility is the removal of carcasses, to drag the body of a cow from the temple courtyard, they buried the animal where it lay, set up a marble image over its grave, and worship it to this day.[7]

Spirituality in Hinduism is both a theory of reality and a criterion of values. The spiritual is the real; the spiritual is the valuable. As a theory of reality, spirituality must be dualistic, because spirit can be spirit only in contrast to that which is not spirit. Absolute Reality, having no opposing entity, cannot be spirit. The Upaniṣads, as we noted in the previous chapter, teach the *Satcitānanda* theory of reality but do not teach, at least not directly, a spiritual theory of reality. This is the contribution of the first Hindu philosophical system, the *Sāṅkhya*, a system that "goes radically and essentially beyond the teachings of the Upaniṣads." [8] The Sāṅkhya gives up completely the Upaniṣadic Absolute, although it would not be correct to affirm that the Sāṅkhya contradicts the teachings of the Upaniṣads since the seeds of metaphysical dualism are found there. One of the most interesting suggestions of dualism is found in *Bṛhad-Āraṇyaka Upaniṣad* 1.4. According to this cosmogonic myth there was in the beginning only the One, and the One, being personal, realized its state of oneness, and became lonely. His loneliness became manifested in two emotions, a rejoicing in his oneness because there was no one to make him afraid, and a lamenting in his oneness because there was no

[4] *An Autobiography*, p. 470.
[5] Vivekananda, *Works*, Vol. 3, p. 181.
[6] Aurobindo, *The Life Divine*, pp. 220, 221.
[7] Margaret Sinclair Stevenson, *Without the Pale*, p. 8.
[8] A. Berriedale Keith, *The Sāṁkhya System*, p. 8.

one to bring him delight. The absence of delight being dominant, the Cosmic Person made himself "as large as a woman and a man closely embraced," and then caused himself to fall into two parts. The reason for the split was that he might enjoy the delight of copulation, a relationship of two in an experience of oneness. The relationship, however, was also one of conflict; and in the account of the conflict we find the anticipations of the Sāṅkhya dualism of spirit and matter. The female part of the original One, now an independent entity, thought, "How can he unite with me after having produced me from himself?" This question, by the way, raises problems: if the antecedent of "he" is the male part of the original One, as it must be in order for there to be union with the female part, then how can it also be the case that the female was produced from "himself" (i.e., the male part)? Or can we infer that the male part is in some fashion the inheritor of the reality of the original One, whereas the female part is an unreality? Because of the doubts of the female part about the possibility of copulation under these circumstances, she attempted to hide herself, and thereby instituted a conflict which doubtlessly enhanced the delight of both: "She became a cow. He became a bull. . . . She became a mare, he a stallion. She became a female ass, he a male ass. . . . She became a she-goat, he a he-goat; she a ewe, he a ram." [9] Passages like these seem to have suggested to the Sāṅkhya philosophers the possibility of denying the One in order to develop the concept of spirit.

The Sāṅkhya concept of spirit (*puruṣa*) can be understood only in its relationship to the other reality in this metaphysical scheme, the concept of *prakṛti*. *Prakṛti* should be related to That One (*Tat Ekam*), "That One breathed without breath by inner power; than it verily there was nothing else further. Darkness there was, hidden by darkness, in the beginning: an undistinguishable ocean was This All," [10] and also to a nameless universal power (*māyā*), "Indra, multiform by his artifices, proceeds to his many worshippers." [11] *Śvetāśvatara* 4. 10a is especially intriguing in the Radhakrishnan translation because he wisely has transliterated rather than translated the key concepts: "know then that *prakṛti* is *māyā* and the wielder of *māyā* is the Great Lord." *Māyām tu prakṛtim viddhi, māyinaṁ tu maheśvaram.* "*Prakṛti*" is translated "matter" or "nature." It is an uncreated, undeveloped "stuff" which contains the possibilities of all things. *Prakṛti* can become anything. It is the indeterminate material cause which requires only the presence of a determinate efficient cause to initiate action and direction. *Prakṛti* has infinite potentialities,

[9] Hume translation.
[10] *Ṛg Veda* 10. 129. 2, 3. Edgerton translation.
[11] *Ibid.*, 6. 47. 18. See also *Bṛhad-Āraṇyaka Upaniṣad* 2. 6. 19.

none of which will be actualized save in the presence of an efficient cause. The efficient cause is spirit (*puruṣa*). *Puruṣa* initiates the evolutionary movement of *prakṛti* by being, rather than by doing; it is spectator only: "The Spirit exists as a witness without acting."[12] Since *puruṣa* is not associated with anything, it cannot enjoy happiness,[13] nor can it experience woe—these are experienced only by the beings produced from *prakṛti*.[14] Final release comes through the recognition of the fundamental distinction of *puruṣa* and *prakṛti*; "*Jīva* (the individual soul) in reality is that very Soul (Cosmic *Puruṣa*) which transcends *Prakṛti*. When he succeeds in knowing that Supreme Soul, he then becomes indefinable with the Supreme Soul. . . . They who behold this universe as many instead of seeing it as one and uniform are said to see it incorrectly. . . . They who know the Soul have no fear of returning to the world."[15] *Prakṛti*, whose reason for existence is the release of *puruṣa*, having fulfilled this unconscious purpose of its being, vanishes "as a dancer desists from dancing, having exhibited herself to the audience,"[16] and never again comes into the view of *puruṣa*.

The Sāṅkhya philosophy, while setting the pattern for Hindu beliefs and attitudes about spirit, bequeathed a number of problems: What is the relation of the plurality of spirits to the unity of the Cosmic Spirit? How can the notion of the inactivity of spirit be made compatible with the essential activity of man? Does *prakṛti* have no value or function other than that of releasing *puruṣa*? If enlightenment is a state beyond joy and sorrow, is it a state to be sought after? Attempts to answer these questions have produced the pluralities in Hindu *sādhana*.

The Sāṅkhya is a curious and important chapter in the history of the development of Hindu philosophy, for by setting forth a reasoned dualistic alternative to the monistic tendencies of the Upaniṣads it set the basic metaphysical problem for all succeeding Indian philosophers: How to account for spirit and matter in a consistent monism? Some students of Indian thought believe that no Indian system has satisfactorily met the challenge of Sāṅkhya. Schweitzer's interpretation of Indian thought in his volume, *Indian Thought and Its Development*, may be regarded as an illegitimate Sāṅkhya treatment of Absolute Reality. He believes that Hinduism from the time of the *Atharva Veda* to the renaissance movements of the nineteenth century has been marked by "world and life negation." Although he claims to find such an attitude toward the

[12] *Mahābhārata* 12. 194.
[13] *Ibid.*, 12. 222.
[14] *Ibid.*, 12. 304.
[15] *Ibid.*, 12. 207.
[16] *Sāṅkhya Kārikā* 59. S. S. Suryanarayana Sastri translation.

world and life in the *Ṛg Veda*,[17] he believes that it was the Brahmins who became obsessed with the notions that the secret of the universe is to be found in the sacrificial rites and that the real essence of things lies in "something immaterial and eternal which derives from the primal cause of the Immaterial, from the World-Soul, and that it participates in the World-Soul and returns to it."[18] Schweitzer's contention that the Brahman is a "World-Soul" and that it can also be called "the Immaterial" is a strange and erroneous confusion of the Upaniṣadic Absolute Being and the Sāṅkhya *puruṣa.* The Absolute of the Upaniṣads is, as we have seen, not spirit, but *Satcitānanda.* If Being is the Absolute, then it cannot be an *order* of reality, and there cannot be a "material world" outside of Being which can be denied. Furthermore, the Sāṅkhya philosophers disposed of the concept of the Absolute, since only thus could spirit exist, as spirit can exist only in a cosmos in which there is also that which is other than spirit.

Spirituality in Hinduism is both a theory of reality and a criterion of values. The Hindu quest for spirituality is a search for the spirit as contrasted to matter, and for the spiritual as contrasted to the material. Stated in this manner Hinduism appears to be a Gnosticism placing value only in the immaterial—and so it has been conceived; in fact, a cliché often thrown in the face of Western visitors to India is that Western peoples especially Americans are obsessed with the material, the physical, the monetary aspects of life. "Indians are spiritual-minded; Americans are material-minded"—how often this is heard in modern India. A Westerner who enters the arena on this touchy issue is likely to be misunderstood and condemned for treading on sacred ground.[19] Whatever spirituality may mean in practice—and one might argue that the Indian peasant who spends most of his day securing and preparing food can hardly be said to be spiritual-minded—in theory spirituality as a criterion of value means that the human body, physical life, and rational faculties are not ends in themselves but instruments for the realization of man's true ends; they are the *prakṛti* whose function is to assist *puruṣa.* Body and mind are the framework with which man can grow into his real self. The grossest animal functions and the subtlest mental endeavors have roles in the *sādhana* of man. The spiritual as a value category may be applied to any act or object that contributes to the Perfection of Man. When an Indian philosopher like Radhakrishnan pleads for a rebirth of

[17] Albert Schweitzer, *Indian Thought and Its Development*, p. 21.

[18] *Ibid.*, p. 29.

[19] See Troy Organ, "Spirituality—Indian and American," *The Philosophical Quarterly*, Amalnar, India, 1960, pp. 243–248 and the reply of Anima Sen Gupta, *Essays on Sāṁkhya and Other Systems of Indian Philosophy*, pp. 124–127.

spirituality, e.g., "A reborn living faith in spiritual values is the deepest need of our times," [20] he is not implying that there should be more writing of poetry, composing of music, giving to charities, or worshiping in temples; he is seeking a new dimension of the life man already lives.

Hindu spirituality has to do with man. Stated negatively, spirituality is the dissatisfaction of man with every possession and every attainment that he can call his. Spirituality is divine discontent. Stated positively, spirituality is the striving for realities and values which always elude man. Spirituality is self-transcendence. Anything is spiritual that advances man toward the Perfection which is the human ideal. The spiritual is a seeking; it is not a gift of nature. It is an ever-active pursuing of goals that tantalize in purity, remoteness, and joy. The spiritual is the Perfecting of Man, the Divinizing of Man; for in Hinduism the metaphysical-axiological principles of divinity and humanity tend to blend into one another. Hinduism deifies man and humanizes God. The spiritual man is the man in process toward the god-man. In India one often hears certain animals and plants described as "semi-divine," as though divinity were on a sliding scale so that a being might have more or less of the attribute—and such is the case in Hinduism; in fact, in this as in all discussions of Hindu ideas, caution must be taken not to set man in a class unrelated to other beings. Two of India's greatest scientists, Jagadish Chandra Bose and C. P. Raman, rooted their research in the Hindu conception of the uniformity of beings organic and inorganic, the former in the affective life of plants, and the latter in the biological growth of crystals. Nonetheless, we shall attempt to establish that man has at least one unique function which distinguishes him from crystals, from lower animals, and even from the gods—his *sādhana.*

A serious problem in the development of Hinduism has been the altering of the concept of spirit without losing the benefits of the concept as it was formulated by the Sāṅkhya philosophers. The Sāṅkhya concept is rich and helpful in its notion of a *telos* transcending the physical aspects of human life and the materiality of the world. But the hiatus of *prakṛti* and *puruṣa* is a serious flaw. If spirit is remote from matter, then the values inherent in each are also remote, and the spiritual becomes the non-material, the material the non-spiritual. The material world is then a world of disvalue, and the spiritual world a world of value. The interpreter who starts with this supposition about Hindu thought can find support for his thesis. How unfortunate that the pessimistic Schopenhauer was the first European to study the Upaniṣads! Schweitzer also, starting with the assumption that Hinduism is "world and life negation," which

[20] *Eastern Religions and Western Thought,* p. 114.

he defined as the position in which "man takes no interest whatever in any realisable purpose nor in the improvement of conditions in this world," [21] found world and life negation even in the *Ṛg Veda* although he admitted that it was not until the time of the *Atharva Veda* that the Brahmin priests theorized that the secret of the universe lies in sacrificial rites and the real essence of things lies in the immaterial and derives from the World Soul. According to Schweitzer, withdrawal from the world that one might return to the mystical World Soul was the heart of spirituality in Hinduism up to the middle of the last century. There is no denying that spirituality has been so interpreted and so implemented by some in India, but one purpose of this chapter is to make evident that only a narrow Sāṅkhya-like interpretation of spirit would regard the quest for spirituality as a "one-sided and inadequate" [22] withdrawal from this world and the full human life. The *Atharva Veda* itself is far from being a consistently Gnostic work; it also claims that the human body is the very home of the gods: "The impregnable citadel of the gods has eight circles, nine doors. In it is a golden treasure-chest, heavenly, enveloped in light." [23] The circles refer to the parts of the human body that touch the ground when fully prostrated before the gods—head, chest, hands, knees, and feet. Reference to the nine doors or openings of the body is commonly found in both Eastern and Western literature. The "golden treasure-chest" is the human head: "Verily that head of Atharvan is a treasure-chest of the gods." [24]

2. THE THIRD EYE OF ŚIVA

The god Śiva is commonly represented with a third eye in the middle of his forehead. This eye is an instrument of destruction; with it he once reduced to ashes Kāma, the god of love, who had inspired amorous desires in his wife while he was engaged in meditation. The third eye of Śiva is also the eye of the inward look. With two of his eyes he looks upon the external world, and with one eye he looks into the interior world. Śiva's third eye is a consant reminder to the Hindu that life cannot be lived well in the light of externalities; the world within must also be taken into account. The good life for man includes the inner vision.

[21] *Indian Thought and Its Development*, p. 7.
[22] *Ibid.*, p. 9.
[23] 10. 2. 31. Edgerton translation.
[24] *Ibid.*, 10. 2. 27. Edgerton translation. Atharvan is the ancestor of the priestly family for whom the *Atharva Veda* is named.

The foremost quest of the Hindu is the quest for reality, not an external reality that may be known discursively, but an inner reality to be known by direct insight. The self must relate itself to the Self. The relationship is a reciprocal one. The relating self is modified by the process of insight, and the Self related to is also modified. The process of self-knowing is both a real*ing* and a find*ing*. For man the quest of self-knowing is an inherent part of his being; for man *to be* is to quest. He is the self-knowing animal. Man is the being who is aware of himself. The lower animals exist—but man *knows* that he exists.[25] An animal is; man is and knows *that* he is; God is and knows both *that* he is and *what* he is. Man seeks to know *what* he is. He would be as God. God is Being whose essence is existence. Man is the contingent being that attempts to remove contigency from its being. Sartre calls this effort the desire of the for-itself to become in-itself-for-itself. He wrote: "Every human reality is a passion in which it projects losing itself so as to establish being and by the same stroke to constitute the In-itself which escapes contingency by being its own foundation, the *Ens causa sui* which religions call God." [26] Another way of stating this is to declare man the being who because of his self-awareness can exercise self-control and self-direction, and together with his scientific knowledge and technology can and must take over his own evolution as well as the creation of his social world, his political world, and even to some extent his physical world.

But he who can know can also forget. He who can will to know can also will not to know. Man can become committed to nescience as well as to science. The animal that can know himself can also prefer not to know himself. An individual can turn his back on the evolved ability of his species to know itself; he may choose to live at a level of life which places no premium on self-knowing. Eating, sleeping, working, and playing may complete the round of his days. For him self-knowing is an unrealized potentiality. One who may be aware of the self-knowing potential may choose to allow it to atrophy. A generation of men may so choose; and, if self-knowing is a Lamarckian modification—as well it may be—self-knowing may cease to be a human potential. Man, the self-knowing animal, is also man, the self-forgetting animal. Man can

[25] Śaṅkara says in his commentary on *Taittirīya Upaniṣad* 2. 1, "The Self or *ātman* is manifest most in man; he is indeed best equipped with intelligence. He utters what he knows, conceives it, knows what it is to be, knows this world and the next, and seeks to attain immortality through his mortal nature. Other living beings are aware only of hunger and thrist."

[26] Jean-Paul Sartre, *Being and Nothingness.* Translated by Hazel E. Barnes. New York: Philosophical Library, 1956, p. 615.

create the world of his dreams; he can also create the world of his nightmares. Man-the-creator is also man-the-destroyer.

The subject-object duality in self-knowing is poetically presented in the *Ṛg Veda*,[27] and is repeated in both the *Muṇḍaka Upaniṣad* and the *Śvetāśvatara Upaniṣad*: "Two birds associated together, and mutual friends, take refuge in the same tree: one of them eats the sweet fig; the other, abstaining from food, merely looks on." [28] The ancient commentator Sāyana explained that the two birds are the vital spirit and the supreme spirit. This interpretation is shared by Advaita Vedāntists, but the Viśiṣṭādvaita Vedānta philosophers tend to treat such passages as referring to a duality within the constitution of man. The tree is the human body; the bird that eats the fruit is the active self that enters fully into the experiences of physical life: eating, drinking, waking, sleeping, breeding, suffering, and dying. The bird that does not eat the fruit but merely watches the activity of the first bird is known as the passive self, the witnessing self (*sakṣin*). It refrains from entanglement in bodily acts. It contemplates the life of physical activity; it does not censure the active self, but when the active self compares its own helplessness with the quiet strength of the passive self it grieves and turns from its life of sorrow and bondage. This duality of the self appears predominantly in the *Kaṭha Upaniṣad*: "There are two selves that drink the fruit of Karma in the world of good deeds. Both are lodged in the secret place (of the heart), the chief seat of the Supreme." [29] Whenever the concept of duality of the self is introduced in the Upaniṣads reference is made to a tension between the selves. The lower or active self is so closely related to the body that "Whatever body he takes to himself, with that he becomes connected." [30] It brings difference to all it touches; it is the doer of the deeds which must be carried out to their fruition. Thus it is the carrier of *karma*. But the higher or passive self is the self that points the way to liberation.

The problem of self-knowing has been concisely and metaphorically stated by the contemporary existentialist author, Simone de Beauvoir: "It's easy to say 'I am I.' But who am I? Where find myself? I would have to be on the other side of every door, but when it's I who knock the other grows silent." [31] To know the self, the self must be on both

[27] 1. 163. 20.
[28] *Muṇḍaka Upaniṣad* 3. 1. 1; *Śvetāśvatara Upaniṣad* 4. 6. Nikhilananda translation.
[29] 1. 3. 1. Radhakrishnan translation.
[30] *Śvetāśvatara Upaniṣad* 5. 10. Hume translation.
[31] *The Mandarins*. Translated by Leonard M. Friedman. Cleveland and New York: The World Publishing Company, 1960, p. 43.

sides of the same door, but—alas—when the self knocks on the knower side of the door there is no one on the other side to open the door, and when there is a self on the known side of the door to open there is no self on the other side of the door to knock!

Man tries in two ways to overcome the epistemological dichotomy which is inherent in self-knowing. One way is to confine his knowing to objects of the world of the non-self. This way is to turn from self-knowledge as introverted, unsocial, abnormal, even perverted—a kind of intellectual masturbation. "None of us really wants to observe or know ourselves. Such observation is not natural to us," writes Otto Rank.[32] "I'm neither virgin nor priest enough to play with the inner life," says Antoine Roquentin, the hero of Sartre's *Nausea.*[33] The second effort to overcome the subject-object dichotomy is the way of the mystic. The scientist *avoids* the problem of self-knowing; the mystic *transcends* the problem by attempting a form of "knowing" in which knower and known are merged into a unit. There is no disputing that there are experiences in which the agent feels a unity with the object of his awareness, but when the epistemological object is the self a special problem arises, namely, is the self-as-object a discovery or a creation? Do I *find* myself? Or do I *form* myself? In the West philosophers have sought to avoid making contradictory statements about the self by attempting to limit the known self to the status of either a discovery or a creation. They have sought to know the self as an object in the order of things, e.g., Descartes said it is "a real thing, and really existent." They have also sought to avoid contradiction by denying thinghood altogether. The self, said Hume, is "a bundle or collection of different perceptions." One of Hume's better analogies is that of the theater. The self is a kind of theater where "perceptions successively make their appearance: pass, repass, glide away, and mingle in an infinite variety of postures and situations."[34] Hume, knowing that the fate of analogies is to be pushed too far, added that the self is not the theater as building, but only the theater as spectacle. Not a *thing,* we might say, but an every-changing array of color and sound. For Descartes the self is a discovered thing; for Hume the self is a created spectacle. The former view overobjectifies; the latter oversubjectifies. The former betrays the Unlimited; the latter betrays the Limited.

In India the conflict between self-as-discovery and self-as-creation may be avoided by the doctrine of *māyā.* From the Limited point of view the

[32] *Psychology and the Soul.* New York: A. S. Barnes and Company, 1950, p. 6.
[33] Norfolk, Conn.: New Directions Books, 1959, p. 18.
[34] *A Treatise of Human Nature,* Part 4, Section 6.

attainment of *mokṣa* is a creative achievement by which the finite self through proper techniques reaches an identity with the Supreme Reality. From the Unlimited point of view *mokṣa* is the removal of confining perspectives which prevent the self from an existential awareness of its true nature. *Mokṣa* from the second point of view is the transcendence of phenomenalism. The two interpretations do not conflict. A Hindu myth puts this as follows: a tiger cub once became lost from its mother and was adopted by a flock of sheep who reared the cub as though it were a sheep. One day a tiger attacked the flock and saw the timid cub bleating among the sheep. "What do you think you are?" asked the tiger. "I'm a sheep," replied the cub. The tiger took the cub to a pond of water and forced the cub to look into the water and to compare reflections. Then it pushed the nose of the tiger cub into the warm bloody carcass of a recently slain sheep. "Now what are you?" asked the tiger. "I'm a tiger," replied the cub.

Man as a self is a thing aspiring to Being. Man becomes what he is. His is-*ness* is his becoming. He is a becoming, not a Being. His "being" is becoming-*ness*. His is-*ness* is in process such that he never is with the finality of beast or god. He creatively discovers what he is, and he discovers creatively what he can become. The self is always infinitely more than it would be if it were only what it is.

The theory that man is a becoming is subject to qualification in the Advaita philosophy. According to these Vedāntic philosophers the self that becomes is the self considered from the Limited point of view, whereas from the Unlimited "point of view" the Self is Reality, and as Reality It is not subject to change of any sort—or more exactly, It as atemporal cannot be said to have either static qualities or dynamic qualities. The self-as-*jīva* is the Self-as-*Ātman* seen under the conditions of time and space. "Becoming," "change," "dynamic," and "progressive" are descriptions of temporal being. A twentieth-century Advaitin says that "progress is for the being that feels finitude and imperfection; it is for you and me, not for a God held to be perfect. . . . *For* the real there is no progress; but *in* the real there is progress and this is all that we as progressive creatures are concerned with." [35]

The self-as-object is both a discovery and a creation. Man *is* his becoming; his becoming is what he is. He is ever in process. Jaspers says

[35] S. S. Suryanarayana Sastri, "Advaita and the Concept of Progress" in *Collected Papers of Professor S. S. Suryanarayana Sastri*, p. 159. He also says, "The error of some Advaitins and of all their critics is in holding the worldly life to be essentially inconsistent with and opposed to self-realisation, while in truth it is a phase of that realisation. From the higher stage no doubt the lower will be called untrue and erroneous; that should not make us forget that it is the error which has led to the truth." *Ibid.*, p. 160.

he is "that creature which poses problems beyond his powers." [36] In the words of Nietzsche, man is "the animal that is not yet established." [37] And we might add he is the animal that is never established. Buber holds that man can be defined only in terms of his relations to all being.[38] These relations, says Buber, are his relations to the world of things, his relations to the world of individuals, and his relations to the world of Being—call it Absolute or God. Buber speculates that there might be a fourth relation—a very special one, i.e., man's relation to his self. Buber withdraws from this possibility because, as he says, this relation cannot be completed or perfected, but perhaps imperfection is part of the Perfection. Man is a great promise—a promise forever unfulfilled, but great in the complete persistence of his incompleteness.

3. INTELLECTUALITY

Hindu spirituality is rooted in man's ability to transcend limits. Although his body occupies but five or six cubic feet of space, a man is not confined to that bit of the spatial universe; and although his personal memory seldom extends over more than sixty-five or seventy years, he does not allow himself to be confined to these years. Through invented instruments of rapid transportation and communication he has weakened the constricting bonds of space and time, but his space-time transcendence is expressed in more fundamental ways, i.e., every idea expressed transcends time, every thought breaks the speed of light, every emotion defies quantitative measurement. Man's spirituality is revealed in his intellectual powers of communication, imagination, creation, memory, and argument. Every concept conveyed by physical gesture or by spoken word, or by written symbol, is a transcending of the self and an evidence of spirituality. Were man fully to realize the wonder of intellectual self-transcendence, the reading of a line from Homer or from the *Ṛg Veda* would send him into a state of ecstasy far surpassing an LSD trip.

No other people, not even the ancient Greeks, placed a higher value on knowledge. In Vedic times the knowledge sought was a magical name—a *mantra*—which would give the knower power over the object that bore the name. If the One and True Name of the All could be found, power would be attained over this life and the next, this world

[36] Karl Jaspers, *Reason and Existenz*. Translated by William Earle. New York: The Noonday Press, 1955, p. 50.
[37] Quoted by Martin Buber, *Between Man and Man*. Translated by Gregor Smith. London: The Fontana Library, 1961, p. 183.
[38] *Ibid.*, pp. 215–220.

and the next. Knowledge was power. The ancient Hindu did not seek knowledge for its own sake, but for the sake of that which could be attained by knowing. Long after the early magical conception of knowledge had weakened, the philosophers sought knowledge as a *mārga* to the realization of man's highest good. It was the means to the cessation of suffering. The extrinsic rather than the intrinsic values of knowing were the motivations. Research was applied, not pure. Unfortunately, these attitudes toward knowledge have in a measure been retained in modern India. Indian universities are plagued with the student attitude that courses and classes are instruments to assist "boning" for the examination; the university degree is prized chiefly as the necessary ticket to desirable positions, particularly in government service; the university professor is both honored as the magician who dispenses the Word and despised as one who does not cash in the Word for the prizes the student is seeking.

Even though sometimes credited with the discovery of the symbols of numbers and of the decimal system of notation, Indians place the higher value on emotional, rather than abstract thought, that is, on "not a mere conception of the nature of the universe but [on] its direct intuitive apprehension in which the thinker finds himself steeped in love and reverence for the object of his thought."[39] Western logicians, following the Aristotelian tradition of non-contradiction, are appalled by the Hindu thinking in terms of "this as well as that" (*sive . . . sive*) rather than in terms of "either . . . or" (*aut . . . aut*). While this type of thinking seems to Western logicians unbelievably sloppy, the Hindu believes that this form of reasoning is necessary because of the prodigious productivity of Nature. Ambiguity of knowledge is a sign of wealth of potentialities of the object. Change reveals the restless dynamics of the universal life-force. Rigid exactness suggests limited possibilities. This attitude toward Nature's pluralities is noted in the fact that in Sanskrit rather than using a single word with a fixed meaning, basic words are used over and over again, yet with different meanings, e.g., the word "*varṇa*" means both color and sound, "*khya*" is to say and also to see, "*vas*" means to dwell and to speed, and "*ṛj*" means to move and to stand still on reaching the goal.[40]

The movement of thought in Western thinking is from the known to the unknown-but-knowable. The known may be established by empirical

[39] S. Abid Husain, *The National Culture of India*, p. 20.

[40] See Betty Heimann, *Facets of Indian Thought*, pp. 154, 102. See also Hajime Nakamura, *Ways of Thinking of Eastern Peoples: India-China-Tibet-Japan*. Part I of this book is an important study of Indian thinking chiefly by analyzing the Indian use of language.

experience, or by revelation, or by taking-for-granted. The unknown is the as-yet-unknown. Western man generally entertains an assumption that unknowability is a temporary characteristic, that there is nothing that is completely and everlastingly unknowable. Of course, there are vast modifications of this confidence, especially in Existentialism, but still the generalization seems defensible that Western thinking in philosophy, in science both pure and applied, and even in religion has seldom comfortably settled in the notion that anything must be forever unknown to man. In India thought proceeds by radiations from a productive center, moving out in all directions and carrying its starting point with it. If the characteristic movement of thought in the West may be represented as a movement from A to B, then from B to C, and then from C to D, the movement of Indian thought may be described as a movement from A to AB, then from AB to C, and then from ABC to D. Gandhi once remarked that the difference between his view of action and Stalin's was that whereas Stalin thought the end justified the means, he (Gandhi) believed that the means and end must be of the same pattern. This remark is typically Indian. Dichotomies such as means-end, known-unknown, and subject-object, are foreign to the Hindu. The Indian movement of thought—A to AB, AB to ABC, etc.—merits another observation: opinions are not given up when debating with a person holding another point of view. Somehow and someway opinion A will be preserved although BCD and XYZ are added to it. Chinese call this face-saving; one Indian has called it the fixed attitude, and has characterized it as India's problem of problems.[41]

In India logic and psychology are not separated, hence discussions between a Westerner and an Indian may easily turn into expressions which to the Westerner seem to be *argumentum ad hominem*—and even downright insulting. Emotionally toned expressions such as "completely wrong," "absolutely right," and "no denying the fact" are found even in the professional philosophical journals. That which the Westerner would present as a hypothesis supported with evidence may appear in India as

[41] Madan Gopal, "India's Problem of Problems: The Fixed Attitude," *The Aryan Path*, Vol. 14, December 1943, pp. 539–543. Gopal closes his article with these words: "There is, however, a silver lining to the cloud. The one hope of India's salvation lies in her industrialisation, which, if history is any reliable guide, will bring about some vital changes, for it is incompatible with any social order based on a different system of production, as is India's. The history of Europe shows that it can be left to the machine to shatter the existing social fabric." The editor could not allow Gopal's thesis to go unchallenged. Therefore he added these comments at the head of the article: "We do not share the hopes Shri Madan Gopal pins upon the industrialisation of India. It might indeed, if it came, 'shatter the existing social fabric,' but it would shatter too how much besides that India can ill afford to lose! The remedy would be far worse than the disease. The proof? Society in the highly industrialised countries of the West!"

an unqualified affirmation supported by psychological certainty. But this is not to be taken as either bad manners or bad logic. In Indian speculation the burden of proof and evidence falls upon the opponent of the thesis, not on the proponent. A premium is placed on disproof and disconfirming evidence, rather than on proof and confirming evidence. The propounder of a thesis does not say, "This thesis I present for these reasons," rather he says, "This thesis I present. Now why do you think it is not true?" This pattern of thought becomes additionally puzzling to the Western mind when it is accompanied by a pragmatic attitude toward belief, reverential regard for tradition, resistance to change, fear of the novel, and deference to religious teachers and authorities.

Gurus and *ācāryas* (religious teachers) and *paṇḍitas* (secular teachers) are honored within Hinduism as men proficient in the quest for knowledge, and not necessarily as those who have acquired a vast store of items of information. The quest does not eventuate in fulfillment. The knowing activity is of greater value than the attainment of knowledge. The gods have a thousand names (*sahasra-nāma*) declares the Hindu, by which he means both there are many fitting names to take one to the gods and also, since *sahasra* is not literally one thousand but a symbol for an infinite number, the gods can never be fully known. Knowing is therefore a part of *sādhana* in Hinduism. Whereas the West has sought an intellectual theory of things, Hinduism has valued intellectuality as a path of realization, a way to the Perfecting of Man. Unfortunately, the higher knowledge has up to very recent years in India been an *upaniṣad*, a secret knowing. The great masses of people were privileged to support the learned Brahmins, who in proud exclusiveness kept the inherited wisdom within the Brahmin community, giving the masses only crumbs of learning. Higher knowledge was *ṛṣisanghajustam,* that which is possessed and cultivated only by *ṛṣis.*

4. TOLERANCE

Hinduism is often presented as the most tolerant of all religions and the most open-minded of all philosophies. The Buddha has been accepted as one of the earthly appearances of Viṣṇu; Ramakrishna chose to live as a Christian and as a Muslim as well as a Hindu; in the center of the temple of Śiva at Chidambaram Vaiṣṇavite priests worship at a shrine of Viṣṇu; and on the wall of the temple of Kesava in Belur this prayer may be found: "May Hari, the Lord of the three worlds, worshipped by the Śaivas as Śiva, by the Vedāntists as Brahman, by the Buddhists as the Buddha, by the logicians as the chief agent, by the Jains as the emancipated being, and by the ritualists as the principle of observance, grant our prayers." On the other hand there are evidences of intolerance. In Vedic times Vasishtha, the family priest of King Sudās, when displaced by Visvāmitra, a non-Brahmin, slew all the sons of Visvāmitra; in the second century B.C. the emperor Pushyamitra, the sixth in succession to Aśoka, issued a proclamation that whoever brought him the head of a Buddhist monk would receive a reward; about A.D. 600 Śaśānka, a king of Bengal, destroyed the holy Bodhi tree and dispersed the Buddhist order; and when Kuresh, a disciple of Rāmānuja, refused to embrace Śaivism his eyes were plucked out. In the face of such evidence how can Radhakrishnan say that "heresy-hunting, the favourite game of many religions, is singularly absent from Hinduism."? [42] One of the most curious instances of intolerance today is found among the swamis of the Ramakrishna-Vivekananda order. They are enlightened Hindu scholars who teach the importance of tolerance toward peoples of all faiths, and yet "a single critical comment on either Ramakrishna or Vivekananda is not acceptable to them." [43] Tolerance is not a simple spiritual value. A proper treatment requires careful analysis.

Nehru once observed that Indians are the least tolerant of all peoples in social forms and the most tolerant in the realm of ideas. The same distinction was made by John Stuart Mill when he divided liberty into "liberty of action" and "liberty of thought and expression." One may show tolerance to another in the area of manners, tastes, morals, and active pursuits in general, or one may show tolerance in the area of expression of ideas in speaking and writing. The second form of tolerance, tolerance of the expression of opinions, is the one which concerns us here.[44]

In the West, Voltaire's remark to an opponent is often cited as a classic example of tolerance of expression: "I do not agree with a word you say, but I'd defend with my life your right to say it." There are at least three interpretations of Voltaire's statement: (1) "I do not agree with a word you say, but go ahead and say it. However, do not expect me to listen. My mind is closed. I have reached the truth." (2) "I do not agree with a word you say, but go ahead and say it. What you are saying is a matter of complete indifference to me." (3) "I do not agree

[42] *The Hindu View of Life*, p. 37. Some of these items of Hindu intolerance, and many more, may be found in *A Modern Hindu View of Life* by Chuni Mukerji, a book written to correct what Mukerji believes to be the false impression of Hinduism in Radhakrishnan's *The Hindu View of Life*.

[43] V. S. Naravane, *Modern Indian Thought*, p. 19, footnote 19. See also the preface to A. C. Das, *A Modern Incarnation of God*.

[44] See Troy Organ, "Two Forms of Tolerance," *The Visvabharati Quarterly*, Vol. 26, No. 2, Autumn 1960, pp. 162–169.

with a word you say, but do keep on. I want to hear what you have to say. You may clarify my own thinking, and I might even change my views on the subject after I hear you." It is safe to suppose that Voltaire had the first interpretation in mind! Thomas Jefferson expressed the second interpretation in his *Notes on Virginia:* "It does me no injury for my neighbor to say there are twenty gods, or no god. It neither picks my pocket nor breaks my leg." These two forms of tolerance can be called sufferance. They allow the speaker to speak, but they indicate no desire to give him a personal hearing. This seems to be the tolerance defined in *Webster's International Dictionary:* "Consent or sanction that is not explicit but is implied by a lack of interference or the nonenforcement of a prohibition." It is passive or tacit permission. It is a *laissez-faire* attitude toward another's opinions. A person who is tolerant in this manner is not intolerant. He shows non-interference. His is a forbearance that may grow out of indifference, despair, or a tightly closed mind. It may be accompanied with the most confident dogmatism.

The third interpretation is active rather than passive; it springs from concern rather than from indifference or fixity of opinion; it is not a sterile letting alone but a creative search for truth and value. The justification for this form of tolerance has never been better stated than by Mill:

> If all mankind minus one were of one opinion and only one person were of the contrary opinion, mankind would be no more justified in silencing that one person, than he, if he had the power, would be justified in silencing mankind. Were an opinion a personal possession of no value except to the owner; if to be obstructed in the enjoyment of it were simply a private injury, it would make some difference whether the injury was inflicted only on a few persons or on many. But the peculiar evil of silencing the expression of an opinion is, that it is robbing the human race: posterity as well as the existing generation; those who dissent from the opinion, still more than those who hold it. If the opinion is right, they are deprived of the opportunity of exchanging error for truth; if wrong, they lose, what is almost as great a benefit, the clearer perception and livelier impression of truth, produced by its collision with error.[45]

Tolerance does not prevent one from taking a side; it means that everyone should have a fair opportunity to speak his mind—and that he will be listened to. But tolerance is not without limits. India and the West have learned that the Good, the Right, and the True will not always be sought by everyone in the marketplace of ideas, nor will they always win on the battlefields of discussion. Furthermore, the highest form of

[45] *On Liberty,* Chapter II, lines 30–42.

tolerance is possible only from a point of view; a man with no concern about the question at issue cannot be expected to show the third type of tolerance. Only those who care enough to have an opinion can be tolerant.

Tolerance then, can be analyzed into three forms: (1) Tolerance of dogmatism: "Speak! But I'll not change my view"; (2) Tolerance of indifference: "Speak! But the issue is unimportant to me"; (3) Tolerance of concern: "Speak! I wish to learn your opinion." With this background we can examine what sort of tolerance has been practiced in India.

Hindu tolerance is rooted in the notion of metaphysical plenitude. Reality cannot be capsuled in finite verbal structures, the totality of viewpoints does not represent the whole of Being. Hence to cut off an opinion may be a denial of part of the Real. A Hindu does not reject anything he can possibly absorb, nor declare to be false that which might have a modicum of truth. Any god a man chooses to worship is god—his deity (*iṣṭa-devatā*); any chosen form of worship or rejection of worship is a path (*mārga*); any chosen point of view is a philosophy (*darśana*). This accommodating spirit of Hinduism has produced "a heterogeneous mass of philosophies, religions, mythologies and magics." [46] Idealism, naturalism, monism, pluralism, dualism, theism, pantheism, atheism, animism, animatism, and fetishism are all "Hinduism." But sometimes even Radhakrishnan, who usually finds some way to defend the various ideas and practices of Hinduism, rebels: "Hinduism must learn to be less compromising and more emphatic in its denunciation of imperfect conceptions of God and cruder modes of worship. Hinduism fondly believed that truth would slowly work its way and lower conceptions would be themselves repudiated. . . . This has remained a pious hope." [47] And again: "I would sacrifice India herself on the altar not of freedom but of truth." [48]

Intellectual tolerance also is an expression of the Hindu way of thinking. The typical Hindu manner of thought is an exploration of possibilities rather than a reaching of conclusions. The Hindu specializes in hypothesis formation, and does not push a single hypothesis into the role of the solution of a problem. The *Bhagavad Gītā*, that gem of Hindu *sādhana*, remains a baffling and frustrating book for those who, unwilling to recognize its "curious many-sidedness, tolerance, or inconsistency—whichever one may choose to call it," [49] attempt to read it as a document with a single message. The Hindu must have everything

[46] Radhakrishnan, *Indian Philosophy*, Vol. 1, p. 92.
[47] *The Heart of Hindusthan*, pp. 87–88.
[48] Radhakrishnan, *The Religion We Need*, p. 32.
[49] Edgerton, *The Bhagavad Gita*. Harper Torchbooks, p. 179.

explained before he can live, and, since problems are so complex, he may still be trying to understand long after the time for action has passed. The Central Government of India is long on planning but somewhat short on carrying out the plans. The attitude is nicely expressed in the Indian novel *The Dark Dancer* by Balachandra Rajan. In the novel Krishnan has returned after ten years of study in England, and finds many problems in settling comfortably into the old grooves of Indian life. Kruger, his uncle, summarizes Krishnan's difficulties thus: ". . . like metaphysicians you simplify the issue. You think there are only two sides to any problem. In India there are at least five hundred." [50] The implication is that since there are so many sides to an issue, action ought to be postponed until all sides have been understood. The Upaniṣads conform to the ideal of tolerance; they contain hints, suggestions, guesses, and opinions so divergent that each school of thought may find in these books support for its own doctrines. No single system of thought is developed in them. Hence the Hindu philosophical systems and the *mārgas* can all be shown to be rooted in the Upaniṣads. It is not surprising therefore to find agnosticism in *smṛti* writings, e.g., Yudhiṣṭhira expresses this attitude explicitly when he says, "Argument leads to no certain conclusion, the *Śrutis* are different from one another; there is not even one Rishi whose opinion can be accepted by all; the truth about religion and duty is hid in caves." [51]

Some observers, even among the Hindus, have regarded this catholicity of belief and practice as an expression of a live-and-let-live philosophy, as toleration of indifference rather than toleration of concern.[52] The *Mahābhārata* may be quoted to support this view, e.g., the dying Bhīṣma says, "I neither praise nor blame the acts of others, viewing this variety in the world . . . to be like the variety observable in the sky. . . . I see no difference between a clod of earth, a piece of stone, and a lump of gold." [53] This is to be understood as the view of the man in the last stage of life, the stage of renunciation. For the man involved in the affairs of this world, Hindu tolerance is not merely an attitude of sufferance consciously chosen as a way of life and thought, instead it is an essential expression of the metaphysical view that despite the pluralistic phenomena of the world there is an underlying and basic unity. This will become clearer in later chapters. At this point it will suffice to indicate that conflicts have an aura of irreality when the universe is thought to be a unit. Today there is a greater diversity of religions in India than in

[50] P. 32.
[51] *Mahābhārata* 3. 311.
[52] E.g., C. P. Ramaswami Aiyar, *Fundamentals of Hindu Faith and Culture*, p. 61.
[53] *Mahābhārata* 12. 262.

any other country in the world, but one is hard pressed to decide whether this is the result of the tolerant attitude of Hinduism or whether this tolerant attitude is the result of the diversity of races and religions in India. Whatever be the cause, the fact remains that, notwithstanding exceptions such as those mentioned earlier in this section, Hinduism has allowed and still does allow a wide variety of ideas to be expressed as long as they can be interpreted as contributing to *sādhana*, e.g., the burning of widows is still occasionally defended as a meritorious act.[54] The words that close the *Ṛg Veda*—"Common be your intentions; common be the wishes of your hearts; common be your thoughts, so that there may be a thorough union among you"—refer to a common quest, not to a common creed.

5. HARMLESSNESS

"That mode of living which is founded upon a total harmlessness towards all creatures or in case of actual necessity upon a minimum of such harm, is the highest morality."[55] This is the noblest and clearest statement of the doctrine of harmlessness (*ahiṃsā*) in Hindu literature. Only twice has the principle been tried in India on a collective level: in the third century B.C. under the leadership of Emperor Aśoka, and in the twentieth century at the instigation of Gandhi as an instrument to free India from the British. Aśoka applied the principle with greater scrupulousness to animals than to man: "Here no animal shall be killed or sacrificed. . . . Formerly, several thousands of animals were slaughtered for soups in the kitchen of King Devānāmpriya Priyadarśin. But now, when this instruction on Dharma is being inscribed, only three animals are being killed: i.e., two peacocks and one deer; even this deer is not slaughtered regularly. In future, even these three lives shall not be slaughtered."[56] In Rock Edict 13, after stating that his men killed 100,000 and led 150,000 to captivity in Kalinga, Aśoka expressed the desire that "all beings should be left unhurt, should have self-control, have impartial treatment and should lead happy lives"—yet they are to remember that although the emperor is compassionate he still has power and willingness to punish them, and they ought therefore to "feel ashamed of their past conduct, and not be killed." The non-violence of Gandhi is under attack in India today. The India-Pakistan War of

[54] Basanta Kumar Chattopadhyaya, "Sahamaran or Sati," *The Mother*, Vol. 8, No. 8, April 1966, pp. 317–320.
[55] *Mahābhārata* 12. 262.
[56] Rock Edict 1.

September 1965 produced a wave of militarism: "It (the September conflict) rubbed into us certain vital facts of international life: that God is on the side of the legions; that the world respects only military strength; and that in such a world, Gandhian pacifism is entirely misplaced and misconstrued." [57] The statue of Mahatma Gandhi in the maidan of Calcutta was mutilated so often after its erection in 1958 that a policeman had to be posted each night to guard it, and it is still at the time of this writing (1968) protected by a scaleproof fence—the only statue so protected of the scores in the maidan, yet on the other hand, when the statue of Netaji Subhas Chandra Bose, "India's Greatest Revolutionary," was dedicated on December 23, 1965, over a million people turned out for the ceremonies, according to the report in *The Statesman.* Statements like "While in the West statesmen and soldiers claim men's devoted admiration and allegiance, in India we still venerate only saints and prophets like Sri Ramakrishna and Swami Vivekananda" [58] are controverted by facts. Yet it is premature to announce the death of *ahiṃsā* as a moral and spiritual value in Hinduism and in India. The wisdom of the *Mahābhārata* remains viable: if possible, practice total harmlessness; if not, keep necessary harm to the minimum.

The doctrine of *ahiṃsā* is not developed in the Upaniṣads. It probably originated among the Jains and the Buddhists, and was borrowed from them by the Hindus. The Vedic Indians had no scruples about the slaughter of animals; some of their sacrificial rites required the slaying of hundreds of animals—and probably human sacrifices were not unknown.[59] Some Hindus have supposed that *ahiṃsā* developed because there was an abundance of grain, milk, and butter, making meat consumption unnecessary.[60] This, of course, is only a necessary condition not a sufficient condition of *ahiṃsā*. In the absence of evidence we can only hypothesize that on the basis of what is known about the mentality

[57] D. R. Mankekar, *Twenty-two Fateful Days*, p. 166. Dr. Ambedkar once said that in opposition to Gandhi's principle of non-violence he recommended "Non-violence wherever possible; violence wherever necessary." Dhananjay Keer, *Dr. Ambedkar, Life and Mission*, p. 87.

[58] K. Sundararama Aiyar, *Dharma and Life*, p. 15.

[59] The following news item appeared in *The Statesman* (Calcutta) on July 9, 1965: "The arrival of a police party at a bridge under construction near Khulna in East Pakistan recently saved the life of a boy who was about to be sacrificed, according to a report by the Associated Press of Pakistan from Khulna, says Reuter. The police said the boy was about to be offered to the river goddess to pacify her and stop her obstructing the work on Patkelghata bridge in Satkhira. Police arrested the contractor and an accomplice for allegedly procuring the boy as a human sacrifice, adds the news agency."

[60] E.g., Suniti Kumar Chatterji, "Contributions from Different Language-Culture Groups," *The Cultural History of India*, Vol. 1, p. 86.

of early man the probability is that *ahiṃsā* arose out of notions of defilement and purity rather than out of any compassion for living creatures. The appalling lack of care for and even mistreatment of cows and dogs in India today is clear evidence that *ahiṃsā* is commonly detached from any feeling of compassion. *Ahiṃsā* is harmlessness, not helpfulness.

There are few references to *ahiṃsā* in the Upaniṣads. One is in the *Chāndogya Upaniṣad:* "Austerity, almsgiving, uprightness, non-violence, truthfulness—these are the gifts for the priests." [61] The meaning is that these are the right forms of conduct. Another is found in a list of the virtuous acts which will remove the necessity of returning to this life in another incarnation. The list makes reference to the person "who is harmless (*ahiṁsant*) toward all things elsewhere than at holy places (*tīrtha*)." [62] The exception is that animal sacrifices are not subject to the *ahiṃsā* principle.

In *Mahābhārata* 12. 272 *ahiṃsā* is extended to include animal sacrifices. The story is told of a Brahmin who lived as a forest recluse. He abstained from injuring any creature, and offered only roots and fruits to Viṣṇu. An antelope—which was in fact Dharma, the god of righteousness, appeared before the Brahmin informing him that the most meritorious sacrifice is an animal sacrifice, and offered himself as the sacrificial animal: "Thou wouldst be acting very improperly, if this sacrifice of thine were accomplished in such a manner as to be defective in *mantras* and other particulars of ritual. I, therefore, ask thee to slay and cut me in pieces for making libations therewith on thy sacrificial fire. Do this and becoming blameless ascend to heaven." When the Brahmin refused, the antelope added that the sacrifice is beneficial to the animal sacrificed as well as to the sacrificer: "Verily, do thou slay me. Truly do I say, slain by thee I am sure to attain to a righteous end." When the Brahmin weakened, the antelope assumed the Dharma form and preached to the Brahmin, "This slaughter of living creatures is not conformable to the ordinance about sacrifices. . . . The injuring of living creatures forms no part of sacrifices." Thus was removed a lingering doubt which had been in the mind of the Brahmin all the time, for although he had refrained from animal sacrifice, he had wondered if perhaps the sacrifice of animals might not be more efficacious. Section 272 closes with these lines: "Abstention from injury is that religion which is complete in respect of its rewards. The religion, however, of cruelty is only thus far beneficial that it leads to heaven (which has a termination). I have

[61] 3. 17. 4. Hume translation.

[62] *Ibid.*, 8. 15. 1. Hume translation. Nikhilananda translates this as: "who has not given pain to any creature except as approved by scripture."

spoken to thee of that religion of Truth which, indeed, is the religion of those that are utterers of Brahma." [63]

An important further development of *ahiṃsā* is noted in the *Bhagavad Gītā:*

> For seeing in all the same
> Lord established,
> He harms not himself (in others) by himself;
> Then he goes to the highest goal.[64]

This is a deduction of ethical significance drawn from the Upaniṣadic doctrine that the Self of man is identical with the universe; for if each self is identical with the universe, then each self is identical with every other self, and hence he who harms another is in fact harming himself. The *Gītā* also states that by the same token each self delights in the welfare of all beings.[65] The negative principle of non-injury thus seems to become the positive principle of promotion of the good of other living creatures. Caution needs to be exercised in attempting to draw a fully positive doctrine out of the *Bhagavad Gītā* since in a list of moral virtues *ahiṃsā* (harmlessness, non-violence) and *dayā* (sympathy or compassion, from the root *day* meaning "to take part in" or "to have tender feeling for") are listed as separate virtues.[66]

The term "*ahiṃsā,*" coming from the root *han,* "to kill" or "to damage," means literally "not wishing to kill." Hindus have applied *ahiṃsā* in five different ways: one application is vegetarianism, the refraining from the eating of animal flesh. Vegetarianism has a wide variety of interpretations: for some it means refraining from eating beef only; for others no red meat is eaten; for others no meat and no fowl; for others no meat, no fowl, and no fish; for still others no meat, no fowl, no fish, and no animal products such as milk and eggs. A second application of *ahiṃsā* is harmlessness: no violence is to be done to any living creature. This is a negative concept, a letting alone rather than the rendering of positive help. Gandhi gave a Jainist interpretation to *ahiṃsā,* an interpretation repudiated by a passage such as the following from the *Mahābhārata:* "I do not behold the creature in this world that supports life without doing any act of injury to others. Animals live upon animals, the stronger upon the weaker. The mongoose devours mice; the cat devours the mongoose; the dog devours the cat;

[63] The term translated "complete in respect of its rewards" is *sakala dharma* (virtue entire).

[64] 12. 28. Edgerton translation.

[65] 5. 25.

[66] 16. 1–4.

the dog again is devoured by the spotted leopard. Behold all things again are devoured by the Destroyer when he comes."[67] A third application is passive resistance. Gandhi popularized this conception of *ahiṃsā* to such an extent that in the minds of many the whole of the principle is the use of non-violent non-cooperation as a technique to coerce a superior to recognize the rights and desires of an oppressed group. Passive resistance is not the abjuration of force; it is the non-violent rather than the violent use of force. The fourth application of *ahiṃsā*—pacifism—is closely related to passive resistance; it is the refusal to participate in or to support the war effort of one's nation on the ground that killing is wrong. It has a variety of forms ranging from the willingness to do everything for the war effort except pull the trigger of the gun that kills the enemy to the refusal to pay taxes which are used to support the military. The fifth application of *ahiṃsā* is compassion shown to all living creatures based on the conception of the fellowship of life. Three Sanskrit terms suggest the possible forms of compassion: (1) *karuṇa,* intellectual charity, an understanding of the needs and wants of other beings; (2) *dayā,* tender sympathy, an empathetic feeling for others; (3) *maitrī,* active good-doing, promoting the welfare of others by concrete measures. The possibilities of emphases among the five meanings of *ahiṃsā* are almost unlimited.

To the conscientious, dedicated, service-minded Westerner the doctrine of *ahiṃsā* may seem too negative—a hands-off policy rather than helpfulness growing out of a deep sense of concern for others; but the doctrine is based on the assumption that in the last analysis no person can solve another's problems, for each must work out his own salvation. Hence the greater helpfulness is in allowing another to *be,* to function without invisible fetters fastened upon him in the name of concern or love. Letting alone does not mean ignoring; it means recognizing the commonality of hopes and fears in the absolute community of living beings and in the special community of man. *Ahiṃsā* does not summarize the totality of ideal relationships among men, but it does stress the importance of respect for the dignity of the other person. This is fundamental to all human relations, and often is sufficient.

6. *Tapas* AND *Rasa*

Indians often quote Schopenhauer's evaluation: "In the whole world there is no study except that of the originals, so beneficial and so

[67] 12. 15.

elevating as that of the Oupanikhat. It has been the solace of my life, it will be the solace of my death."[68] Yet any Hindu who treasures this encomium has sold his culture short. If Hinduism is only a solace, a comfort in grief, then the Hindu view of life is indeed pessimistic and otherworldly. But Hinduism is far more than a solace to assuage the pangs of living and dying; it is a *sādhana,* a way to fulfillment, perfection, and supreme joy. Hinduism, staying close to the human condition, recognizes that the life of man is both sunshine and shadow, pleasure and pain, and therefore it is not surprising that the "spirit" of Hinduism is pluralistic—there is *tapas* (austerity, withdrawal, mortification, torment) and *rasa* (delight, emotion, pleasure). Sorrow, suffering, agony, and death are unavoidable facts of man's life, and any religion or philosophy which attempts to evade these facts cannot claim to be a complete reflection of, or guide to, man's existence. Conflict between the old and the new, between conservatism and creativity, between restraint and reform, has been a marked feature of life in the subcontinent of Asia for hundreds of years, and never more so than today as India stands poised between the Stone Age and the Atomic Age. Caterpillar tractors and camels pull plows in adjacent fields; at airports fuel for jet planes may be hauled by oxen; Indian scientists sometimes consult astrologers in selecting spouses for their children. A great unfinished battle in India is the struggle between sanctification of the *status quo* in the name of spirituality and rapid change in order to participate in the ongoing life of men and nations.

The tragedy is that full participation in the life of the world is often discouraged in the name of spirituality. Gandhi was censored by his caste council for having crossed the ocean in violation of an old rule of their caste, yet Gandhi held steadfastly to the hallowed caste ideal of following the vocation of one's father: "If my father is a trader and I exhibit the qualities of a soldier, I may without reward serve my country as a soldier, but I must be content to earn my bread by trading."[69] Those families who oppose the desire of their young people to study in European or American universities suspect—correctly in many cases—that the young people, having lived in the West, will not be able to fit into the grooves of Hindu society upon their return; but these families underestimate the power of Hinduism to survive change, and they are not sufficiently aware of the changes that have taken place in Hinduism during the long years of its existence. The climate of Hinduism, which should be *tapas* and *rasa,* often becomes *tapas* versus *rasa.* While there

[68] E.g., Surendranath Dasgupta, *A History of Indian Philosophy,* Vol. 1, p. 40.
[69] *Hindu Dharma,* p. 369.

is little cause for alarm that Hinduism will not survive, there is cause for alarm as to what the conflict may do to it.

Hindu conservatism is most dramatically illustrated in the concept of *tapas*. The term *tapas* is derived from *tapa* meaning heat, torment, pain, or burning. While it usually has the connotation of asceticism, the notion is not that of an effort to curtail appetites, and it is certainly not a punishing of the flesh for the sin of existence, although it may be regarded as an appearance of the dark background of Vedic lore—a persistent awareness of the need for deliverance, a reminder of the pathos of a finite being with infinite aspirations. The heat denoted is chiefly the heat of sexual desire, e.g., in a cosmogonic *mantra* the monistic cosmic principle (*Tat Ekam*, That One) is said to come into being out of its own sexual heat: "What generative principle was enveloped by emptiness—by the might of its own fervour (*tapas*) That One was born." [70] *Tapas* is the life force within, which most easily shows itself in the sex drive, but when retained can build up power that can accomplish almost anything. It was by *tapas* that Umā finally forced her divine husband, Śiva, to pay her the attention she desired. It is by *tapas* that man, the one in whom gods are seated,[71] the "impregnable citadel of the gods," [72] can accomplish the fulfillment of divine aspirations. *Tapas* is conservation for the sake of action; but unfortunately, in Hinduism as in other cultures, a means may become confused with the ends which the means is supposed to achieve. Vegetarianism, harmlessness, celibacy, fasting, vigilance, immobilization, immolation, and many other forms of self-denial have been used in the long history of Hinduism as means for the liberation of the human spirit and have also become ends in themselves.

The conservatism of Hinduism has sometimes entered where one might least expect it. Even the nineteenth-century radicals did not escape the heavy hand of conservatism. Rammohun Roy criticized Hinduism as being chiefly "a peculiar mode of diet," yet when he went to England, he took his Hindu cook with him. Keshub Chunder Sen, the leader who fought for and finally achieved the liberal Brahmo Marriage Act, yielded to the traditional pattern in his daughter's marriage, and thereby lost his effectiveness as a Brahmo Samaj leader. Mahadev G. Ranade, although an advocate of widow marriage, married an eleven-year-old girl to alleviate his father's fears that he might marry a widow. Roland W. Scott concludes his *Social Ethics in Modern Hinduism* with the observation that "the historical function of Hindu spirituality, as

[70] *Ṛg Veda* 10. 129. 3. Edgerton translation.
[71] *Atharva Veda* 11. 8. 32.
[72] *Ibid.*, 10. 2. 31. Edgerton translation.

affirmed in modern times, was largely to sanction social conditions as they developed, trying meanwhile to impose on them its aims and to infuse in them its aspirations." [73]

According to the *tapas* view, life is a suffering from which one ought to escape either by actual withdrawal or by the imaginary glorification of the impoverished life of the people. The first widespread development of this spirit in India was in the sixth century B.C., especially in Bihar and Uttar Pradesh owing to the breakup of tribal societies. Buddhism and Jainism arose and grew in this climate. The Buddha deserted family and possessions to become a homeless wanderer, and established an order of celibate monks to carry on his mission. Jainism glorified the ascetic life, and held that the proper death for the Jain was self-determined starvation. Hinduism stressed non-acquisition and renunciation after the decline of the Guptas and later in the fifteenth and sixteenth centuries when Hindus experienced great suffering as the Mughal empire was being established. Gandhi's praise for the simple life of the Indian village, and his fear and distrust of urban and industrial life are well known. Aurobindo has categorically stated that "there never was a national ideal of poverty in India as some would have us believe." [74]

Gandhi and Nehru exemplify the contrast between Hinduism-as-*tapas* and Hinduism-as-*rasa*. They shared the same hopes for the independence of India, but they were poles apart in the spirit of their lives and in their hopes for India after independence. Gandhi believed in subsistence economy; he wanted to keep India a nation of villages. His loincloth symbolized his conception of the amount of possessions he thought ideal for the Indian, and the spinning wheel symbolized his industrial ideals. On the other hand, Nehru's omnipresent non-utilitarian red rose in his buttonhole symbolized his hopes for a nation with an economy of abundance; and his fascination with airplanes indicated his desire to push India quickly into an industrial age.

The term *rasa* is the key term in Sanskrit poetics. It denotes the emotion proper to aesthetic experience. An ordinary emotion may be painful or pleasurable, but an aesthetic emotion rises above pain and pleasure to pure joy. The emotion is not a response to natural creations such as sunsets, stars, rivers, or trees; it is a response to the creation of a human artist. It is not a pure unity of the real Self in the Brahman, but a unity

[73] P. 230.

[74] *The Renaissance in India*, p. 73. "Would you rather be dead than poor?" asks Maitreya in *The Toy Cart* by King Shudraka. Charuddatta replies, "I'd rather be dead, my friend. Death is only an instant of suffering; but being poor drags on and on. . . . Are the deadly sins five in number? No, let us add a sixth: that is, to be poor." Lal, *Great Sanskrit Plays*, pp. 82, 87.

joyously found in plurality. It is a mental attitude of binding many things together into an organic whole. It is an active emoting, not a passive receiving of stimuli. The eight principal *rasas*—the erotic, the ludicrous, the tragic, the terrible, the heroic, the fearsome, the vulgar, and the miraculous—are believed to be the dominant moods of the human psyche, and as such they are to be worked into literature, drama, music, painting, and sculpture. The artist, says the *Gītā* [75] is one who has yoked his intelligence with the divine, and therefore works a *mārga* in and through his art. Buddhism and Jainism have consistently warned against the enjoyment of drama, dance, and music, but Hinduism has often encouraged both the performance and the enjoyment of such arts, and despite the crises which have overtaken India in conquests and foreign dominations, the enjoyment of art and life has never been entirely crushed. *Artha* (pleasure) as one of the four goals of human life was established early in Hinduism and has remained. The pessimistic view of life as a weary succession of incarnations has always been mitigated by the belief in liberation or deliverance. The *Chāndogya Upaniṣad* specifies that one obligation of the *guru* is to show the pupil "the other side of darkness." [76] The reality of *Satcitānanda* is an insight which even the Hindu has difficulty in holding. It is almost too good to be true! Joy (*ānanda*) is not something to be superimposed on a harsh and cruel world; it is an inherent fact of Reality. Earthly life is neither temporal punishment nor temporal vanity. The world may be *māyā* from one point of view, but it is a *māyā* manifestation of Reality. This is the arena of the quest for the Perfection of Man. Spirituality means the taking of all aims and activities in the framework of growth into the full possibilities of man. This is "the other side of darkness." Rabindranath Tagore understood the *tapas-rasa* polarity of human life and described it in these words: "Man's freedom is never in being saved troubles, but it is the freedom to take trouble for his own good, to make the trouble an element in his joy. It can be made so only when we realise that our individual self is not the highest meaning of our being, that in us we have the world-man who is immortal, who is not afraid of death or sufferings, and who looks upon pain as only the other side of joy. . . . this the keynote of the teachings of the Upanishads: Life is immense!" [77]

According to the *rasa* conception of spirituality, the life of the mind, the life of the body, the life of the individual in familial, vocational, social, and political relationships, and even life as a divine creation, are never ends in themselves but always means toward the full development

[75] 2. 50.
[76] 7. 26. 2. Nikhilananda translation.
[77] *Sādhanā*, pp. 64, 22.

of the real Self. Man is to enter fully into the cosmic evolution which is bringing forth the New Man, the Whole Man, the Superman, the Universal Man. In other words, spirituality is direction to the evolving of the true Self. This is not a submerging or a denying of self, but an affirming of Self. It proceeds from a knowing of which self is the real Self and moves to the realization of that Self. True spirituality is to prize self-development so highly that no light, no new approach, no new idea which promises aid, is rejected. Spirituality is openness to the new, acceptance of the old, welcoming the foreign, and clinging to the familiar, not as new, old, foreign, or familiar, but as promising avenues to the realization of the Ideal Self.

Tapas connotes withdrawal; *rasa* connotes active participation. In the ideal pattern of human life according to Hinduism withdrawal has a part: the fourth stage of life is the time for uninterrupted meditation, for quiet self-examination, for a turning away from the feverish pursuit of earthly rewards. But this period comes only after the active life of formal education, marriage, family responsibilities, vocational pursuits, and all the obligations that fall upon man in society. The true leader in Indian society is sufficiently *tapas*-oriented that he is detached from success and failure—he is indifferent to the happenings of the moment; and because of his detachment he is able to give a better evaluation of changing social and political events. This melody of detached-attachment has been played in various keys by leaders as diverse as Ramakrishna and Nehru, yet its theme has been to be involved, but not overwhelmed, by the task before one. In India religion is more a matter of spiritual culture than of scholastic learning; it is more a matter of doing something which will enhance one's growth intellectually, morally, emotionally, aesthetically, and socially than something to be believed, defended, and propagated. Hinduism does not seek to save the soul, as though the soul were a thing to be preserved in a pure state, as though it had come from the gods and were to be returned at the close of life to the gods. Hinduism seeks to discover and to develop the self through stimulation, guidance, and edification. Hinduism continues to hold before its followers the tantalizing recognition of aspirations and anticipations that are still largely unfulfilled and unsatisfied. Anne Marshall in the Foreword to her charming book, *Hunting the Guru in India,* recounts her skeptical, cautious, and at first halfhearted journey through India to see what sort of nonsense the "holy-men" were up to, and her surprising conclusion that "of all the nations of the world, only India knows how to nourish the soul." Hinduism is *rasa;* it is an emotional challenge to act; man is to seek his true being in his becoming. Hinduism is also *tapas;* it is an invitation to escape from the pressure of the demands of the human condition. Hinduism at its best is a spirit of alternation between inaction and action, between being and doing. In Hinduism the spirit of the ascetic and the spirit of the libertine melt into an Olympian-Dionysian who enjoys life without selling himself to life. The rapture of beauty breaks down austerity; discipline controls and channels passion. Unity is found in diversity; and the diversity of Unity is not ignored. The Infinite is discovered within the bounds of form; the finite reflects the Infinite. The eternal belongs in time; spirit is in matter; God is in Man.

CHAPTER IV
The Quest for Integration

1. HINDUISM AS AN INTEGRATING CULTURE

Social groups are united by many different integrators: blood, language, religion, vocation, devotion to a royal family, etc. But Hindus are united by a common questing for oneness. Although the Indian nation must cope with many divisive factors, such as 179 languages and 544 dialects,[1] scores of religions and sects, and more than 3000 caste groupings, and although the concept of a nation does not harmonize with the Hindu emphasis on primary human relationships, there is one factor within Hinduism upon which she can build, and that is the integrating quest itself. Inclusiveness, not exclusiveness, is the principle of Hinduism. This principle is expressed by Kṛṣṇa in the *Bhagavad Gītā* when he reminds Arjuna, "Whatever form any devotee with faith wishes to worship, I make that faith of his steady."[2] The integrating principle

[1] V. K. Narasimhan *et al.* (editors), *The Languages of India.* Madras: Our India Directories and Publications, 1938, p. vii. The counting of the languages of India is not a clear and simple matter, e.g., "The problem of languages in India is in practice a problem of 12 or 13 languages of which the nine North Indian languages are extremely closely allied, so that even the Census Report of 1921 had to admit: 'There is no doubt that there is a common element in the main languages of Northern and Central India which renders their speakers without any great conscious change in their speech mutually intelligible to one another, and this common basis already forms an approach to a *lingua franca* over a large part of India.'" (R. Palme Dutt, *India, Today and Tomorrow.* Revised and Abridged Edition of "India Today." London: Lawrence and Wishart Ltd., 1955, p. 106.)

[2] 7. 21. Radhakrishnan translation.

of Hindu culture is so strong that it appears in unexpected places, e.g., Kewal Motwami, an Indian sociologist trained in American universities, writes with admirable objectivity, ". . . the core of Indian culture is in the course of disintegration . . . India has all the characteristics of an amorphous, anonymous, unruly mob,"[3] yet later in this same book, Motwami's Western scientific training slips, and he says in strangely teleological language, "India was intended to be one unity, and nature obeyed the plan."[4] Hinduism is *sādhana,* the questing for the Perfection of Man. It is a perfecting which draws no distinction among the disciplines. If Western man is to understand *sādhana* in its integrative aspects he must think of religion, science, philosophy, art, education, politics, marriage, vocation, recreation, economics, literature, drama, and dance not as separate activities with varying aims and methods but as the manifold ways in which the function of being human expresses itself. Perhaps these might be described as "sub-*mārgas.*" A Western educator, accustomed as he is to the division of knowledge and research into colleges, divisions, departments, and courses, is especially ill-conditioned for an understanding of the integrative nature of *sādhana.* The Indologist Louis Renou criticizes Western Sanskritists, Indologists, theosophists, anthroposophists, and teachers of *yoga* for their piecemeal approaches to Hinduism, and concludes, "If Hinduism ever has a future as an integral part of a broad, generally acceptable spiritual movement beyond the borders of the country that gave it birth, this future will be created only by direct reflection from genuinely Indian forms of thought and spirit conceived and expressed by Indians."[5]

The Hindu looks for a common element among apparently different things, for the reality below the appearances, for relationships among the "unrelated." According to the Hindu there are 8,400,000 forms of flora and fauna; yet his emphasis is not on the multiplicity of living forms but on the fact that the same class of being, the *jīva,* occupies these 8,400,000 species. Gandhi suggested that the chief value of Hinduism lies in holding that all life is one.[6] This seemingly noble concept has been carried to the extreme by the Jains who carefully avoid crushing insects as they walk, and who finally die by self-inflicted starvation (a *samādhi* death) as atonement for the necessary destruction of *jīvas* in their diet of fruit and vegetables! This assumption of underlying sameness produces a feeling of appropriateness of elements which to Western eyes seem to be bulging with contradictions. Correspondences are found

[3] *India: A Synthesis of Cultures,* pp. 14–15.
[4] *Ibid.,* p. 41.
[5] *The Nature of Hinduism,* p. 144.
[6] *Hindu Dharma,* p. 39.

which seem fantastic to the non-Hindu. In *Bṛhad-Āraṇyaka Upaniṣad* 1.3.22 the sameness of white ant, mosquito, elephant, "three worlds," and the universe is presented. In the Upaniṣads all these correspondences are reduced to the comprehensive equation that *Ātman* is Brahman.

A Westerner often has difficulty in understanding the integrative aspects of Hindu culture because, whereas in the West the national state and politics are the chief agents of integration, in India the people tend to be united by myth, metaphysics, and art. Modern India may have greater problems in inducing Hindus to rally to the concept of a nation than in getting Hindus and Muslims to live together peacefully. The tales of the *Rāmāyaṇa* and the *Mahābhārata,* the songs of Āḷvārs and the Baūls, the classical dances of India, and the *ragas* of her traditional music are some of the uniting factors. Whether the concept of nation can be superimposed upon these integrators of the people remains to be seen. Radhakamal Mukerjee contends that these aspects of Hinduism gave a unity to the civilization of India as Christianity did to that of Europe,[7] but the parallelism is far from perfect. There has been nothing in Hinduism like Augustine's "City of God" to balance the "City of Man." The Christian Church was able to take over the administration of law and order after the collapse of the Roman Empire; and later, when the state again rose to power, it was the Church that anointed rulers, and that deposed them when they were in conflict with the Church. The leaders in Hinduism were men who retreated to forest *āśramas,* or meditated in temples, or went into silent *samādhis* in caves; the leaders in Christianity were men who opposed the civil authorities until they were at last martyred, or who seized the power of the civil authorities, beheaded kings, and ruled in their stead.

The great strength of Hinduism as integrator of the life of man is its deep sense of the relatedness of things, rooted metaphysically in the concept of the *jīva* which vitalizes all living forms. Man's relationship to animals, to plants, to gods, and to his fellow men does not need to be proved—it is assumed. The natural world is not to be conquered; it is to be appreciated aesthetically and mystically. The orthodox Brahmin still begins his day with a prayer to the sun. During his lifetime the Hindu is expected to repay three debts: (1) his existence as a physical man he owes to his ancestors, and this debt he repays by procreating good progeny and thereby ensuring the continuity of the human race; (2) his existence as an enlightened man he owes to the seers who taught and wrote down the divine truths, and this debt he repays by studying and preserving his cultural heritage and by handing it down to the next

[7] *The Culture and Art of India,* p. 28.

generation; (3) his existence as a divine man he owes to the Supreme Reality, and this debt he repays by worshiping and serving his chosen deity through observation of the sacraments and through fulfillment of the duties assigned to him by his station in life. Even more specifically are the obligations laid down for the householder; each day he and his wife are expected to express the relatedness of things in five acts: Vedic study, offering of water to the forefathers, burning of incense to the gods, giving of food to an animal, and sharing a possession with a fellow man.

The Indian joint family is an admirable device for nurturing the feeling of belonging. From birth to the grave the individuals within a joint family are both supported by and support the other members. Disability by illness or accident holds fewer terrors when one knows that ministering hands and the family purse are available; hunger is more endurable when it is a shared hunger, and joys are increased in the closeness of the familiar grouping. The feeling of being useless or unwanted can hardly arise when one is surrounded by relatives of blood and marriage who depend upon each other for the necessities and the pleasures of living.

Even the much-maligned caste system has an integrative function, for although it may appear to be a way of keeping people in compartments from which they cannot escape, it looks quite different when it is considered as a device to recognize achievement in self-realization. If one accepts the notion of reincarnation and its concomitant, the theory of strict causality in the realm of moral and spiritual growth, then the Brahmin is the person far advanced, and the *Śūdra* the person little advanced on the scale of the Perfecting of Man. There are, of course, many other facets of this complicated social organization, but it ought not to be condemned by either Hindu or non-Hindu without fully recognizing the value of a system that asserts the importance of the development of all men in full dimensions of the human life. An egalitarian society which assumes that no one is better than anyone else might be much worse than a hierarchical society which assumes people differ in their attainments of the full human status and that the full human status is possible for everyone.

The integrating nature of Hindu culture is manifested also in philosophy, where each philosophy is a *darśana*, a point of view, which admits the limits of its own perspective and the possibility and validity of other points of view, rather than where each is a system in mortal combat with other systems, and where philosophers like cannibals feed upon each other's mental productions. Christianity has often functioned as a great divider in Western culture, setting son against father, daughter against mother, until a man's foes are those of his own household. In

India religion is sometimes called a *samaya* (agreement, compact, contract, union). Hinduism seeks the ultimate integration in the great Upaniṣadic affirmations "That thou art" and "*Ātman* is Brahman." Any "that" in its essence is a "thou"; and all are one in Brahman. "Why should I treat my neighbor as myself?" man asks. Hinduism's answer is a most conclusive one, "Because your neighbor is yourself—your Real Self." Here may be a clue for the solution of the most important social problem of our day: how to achieve the unity of man within the diversity of nations.

2. HINDU THOUGHT AS INTEGRATIVE

A charge often made by Western students is that Hinduism lacks system, for example, Lyall said it is characterized by "the entire absence of system" and that it is "a conglomerate of rude worship and high liturgies; of superstitions and philosophies, belonging to very different phases of society and mental culture."[8] Swami Dayananda Saraswati early in the nineteenth century, noting that contradictory doctrines and worship patterns prevented effective propaganda, imposed uniformity by attempting to discover all scientific truths in the Vedas. By going back to the Vedas as the fountainhead of all knowledge, he believed, Hinduism would be able to present a unified front to the world, a front consistent with the scientific knowledge of the West. The Arya Samaj was the institution founded on his integrative assumptions. Students of Hinduism, both Indian and European, have noted the integrative nature of Hinduism, e.g., Radhakrishnan describes Hinduism as "a subtly unified mass of spiritual thought and realisation";[9] and Macnicol believes it is "an encyclopaedia of religions . . . a vast conglomerate, comprehensive in the widest sense, an amalgam of often contradictory beliefs and practices, held together in one by certain powerful ideas and by a system of social regulations."[10] Despite baffling contradictions and differences that puzzle both the foreigner and the Hindu there are many patterns of unity in Hinduism. Sometimes it is a superficial dramatic unity, as in the *Mahābhārata*, an epic only in the sense that there is a dramatic plot upon which seers over a five-hundred-year period hung their ideas; but in reality the lengthy moralizing poem is no more intellectually unified than is the Jewish Talmud—in fact, the description

[8] *Asiatic Studies*. Second Series, pp. 291, 292.
[9] *The Hindu View of Life*, p. 11.
[10] Nicol Macnicol, *The Living Religions of the Indian People*, p. 25.

of the *Mahābhārata* as a Hindu Talmud would not be inaccurate! The Upaniṣads are integrated by common movements of thought, from plurality to unity, from objectivity to subjectivity, and from materialism to spiritualism.[11] Still the first impression of an objective reading of a work like the *Bhagavad Gītā* or *Bhāgavata Purāṇa*, or of a study of a philosophical system like Advaita Vedānta, is that unrelated pluralism rather than related integration is the characteristic thought pattern. Particularly if the student be Western will he be bothered by what he finds, since he looks in vain for the typically Western integration created by system-builders who seek logical harmony. Non-contradiction is the essence of Western integrations. New ideas, not consistent with ideas already entertained as true, must be rejected or altered until their inconsistency is removed. This makes for a continual reordering: Ptolemy is rejected when Copernicus is accepted; Copernicus is modified by Newton; and Newton is partially displaced by Einstein. In India an opposing idea is somehow accommodated, e.g., although Śaṅkara believed the individual soul is not real, he did not exclude the holders of the view from his community, for in commenting on *Vedānta Sūtra* 1.3.19 he says, "Others again, and among them some of ours, are of opinion that the individual soul as such is real."[12] Intellectual integration in India is chronological rather than logical; it is not an historical integration in which every event and every idea is placed in a temporal ordering, but a traditional integration in which a place is found for every concept established as a part of Hindu tradition. Nothing, having entered this culture, ever completely vanishes. Such conservatism may be described positively as the effort to preserve what might be of value to the culture, or negatively as complete indifference to logical contradictions. This may be explained as Hindu tolerance, the unwillingness to reject whatever can possibly be allowed in a great elastic system of ideas and practices; or as Hindu comprehensiveness, the belief that nothing is isolated, everything has significance in a wider sphere than its immediate context; or as Hindu lethargy, the apathy of people living in tropical and semitropical climates who would rather endure an unpleasant situation than make the effort to remedy it.

One technique for conserving ideas and practices has been to allegorize that which can no longer be taken as fact. For example, in the early literature may be found detailed instructions for the performance of elaborate sacrifices, the most elaborate being the Horse Sacrifice which

[11] See Troy Organ, *The Self in Indian Philosophy*, pp. 35–42.

[12] *The Vedānta Sūtras with the Commentary of Śaṅkarācārya*. Translation by George Thibaut. *The Sacred Books of the East*, Vol. 34, pp. 189–190.

required up to ten years for its performance and which only a maharaja could afford. The ritual with its slaughter of thousands of animals was performed until the sacrifice was interpreted allegorically in the Āraṇyakas. According to the new interpretation there was to be no actual sacrifice of animals, but each element of the sacrifice was an allegory of meditation upon nature: he who meditated upon the dawn was as it were meditating upon the head of a horse; the sun-worshiper was as it were adoring the eye of the horse; the air was the life of the horse, etc. Thus the older sacrificial prescriptions were preserved and related to a time when animal sacrifices were no longer in vogue.

By a second procedure, functions, processes, and powers are reified into substances. The power within a magical spell which made the magic happen was originally called *brahman.* This abstract concept was saved by locating the power in a group of magic workers called the Brahmins, and also in the Brahmā, the divine agent who was involved in the process. *Kṣatra,* the power that rules over things, became the Kṣatriyas, the class of people possessing ruling power. It is also interesting to note that the abstract number seven was sometimes expressed by the word *ṛṣi* (sage) since everyone knew there were seven sages, and the number three was similarly called *agni* (fire) since there were three fires in Vedic ceremonies.

A third technique of integrating into Hindu culture that which might be otherwise lost is the use of the negative. We have already noted the emphasis on non-violence or harmlessness (*ahiṃsā*) rather than positive virtues like compassion, helpfulness, and charity, thus indicating a repudiation of violence rather than a commitment to rendering service to another, on the sensible assumption that the most helpful attitude and action in some situations is the avoidance of interference. Again in human relations the negative leaves open a wider range of possibilities, and this is consistent with the Hindu belief that tolerance must be a hallmark of man-to-man relationships. "I do not hate you" leaves open a wide range of possibilities; "I love you" narrows the field considerably! When dealing with problems of ultimate realities *advaita* (non-twoness) is preferred to monism, and *aneka* (non-oneness) to dualism or pluralism. Śaṅkara's conception of the Brahman, for example, is "non-two" since the positive "one" carries with it the connotation of a unit of a species or series—a notion most certainly not applicable to Brahman. In India, as in the West, the Ultimate may be best described by negating the qualities of earthbound beings; the Ultimate is *in*finite, time*less*, space*less*, *un*changeable, etc. A passage in the *Bṛhad-Āraṇyaka Upaniṣad* seems particularly designed to express the *in*expressibility of the Brahman, rather than to give any notion of the Brahman's nature:

> That, O Gārgi, the knowers of Brahman, call the Imperishable. It is neither gross nor fine, neither short nor long, neither glowing red (like fire) nor adhesive (like water). (It is) neither shadow nor darkness, neither air nor space, unattached, without taste, without smell, without eyes, without ears, without voice, without mind, without radiance, without breath, without a mouth, without measure, having no within and no without.[13]

There is no clearer example of the *via negativa,* the *Neti-Neti* way, in the literature of Hinduism. *Neti-Neti* reminds man that his mind is finite, that the problem he poses for himself in knowing Reality is unlimited. *Neti-Neti* calls to mind the caution of Goethe: "Man is not born to solve the problems of the universe, but to find out where the problem begins, and then to restrain himself within the limits of the comprehensible."[14]

Another way the Hindus integrate the intellectual aspects of their culture has been by keeping alive myths and myth-making. They have been, and are today, capable of thinking precisely and clearly—their developments in mathematics are evidence of this—but they have remained somewhat skeptical of words, of precise definitions, and of exact thinking in the realm of theology and metaphysics. Hindus have been so impressed by the unbounded nature of reality that they have preferred contradictions to non-contradictions lest something be left out that ought to be included. No wonder "Indian philosophy" was often regarded by Western scholars in the early part of this century as a self-contradictory expression.[15] But the West has gradually learned to appreciate Indian thought as it has understood the dimensions of the task the Indians have set for themselves in the Hindu tradition. A remarkable instance of this gradual awakening can be traced in three editions of a popular American textbook, A *History of Philosophy* by Frank Thilly and Ledger Wood. In the first edition (1914) the Introduction offers the following apology for omitting Oriental thought:

> A universal history of philosophy would include the philosophy of all peoples. Not all peoples, however, have produced real systems of thought. . . . Many do not rise beyond the mythological state. Even the theories

[13] 3. 8. 8. Radhakrishnan translation.

[14] *Conversations with Eckermann,* Vol. 1, p. 272.

[15] "When I was a student, the term 'Indian Philosophy' was usually regarded as self-contradictory, a *contradictio in adjecto,* comparable to such an absurdity as 'wooden steel.' 'Indian Philosophy' was something that simply did not exist, like a 'mare's nest,' or, as Hindu logicians say, like the 'horns of a hare' or the 'son of a barren woman.'" Heinrich Zimmer, *Philosophies of India,* p. 27.

of Oriental people . . . consist, in the main, of mythological and ethical doctrines, and are not thoroughgoing systems of thought.

In the second edition (1951) the final clause is modified to "are not complete systems of thought"; and in the third edition (1957) it is modified still further to "are rarely complete systems of thought." [16] Part of the reason for the new attitude toward Oriental thought has been the change of attitude toward mythology among Western scholars. When W. Robertson Smith published his scholarly study, *Religion of the Semites*, in 1894 he wrote, ". . . strictly speaking, mythology was no essential part of ancient religion";[17] but the attitude changed so radically in the first half of the twentieth century that in 1953 S. H. Hooke wrote of "the central importance of myth" in religion, and conjectured that Robertson Smith would have been the first to acknowledge this were he alive today.[18] A myth is a story expressing intuitive insights; it conveys untranslatable truths. A myth symbolizes a dimension of richness that cannot be expressed in ordinary language, or may be much better suggested in the language of unbridled imagination than in the sharp outlines of scientific discourses. Although myths are usually associated with primitive peoples and a prepositive level of human thought, it is a great mistake to assume that myths are only historical phenomena. A demythologizing movement such as that of Rudolph Bultmann designed to clear away the stumbling blocks in the interpretation of Christian scriptures created by the scientific world-view is a Western contribution. The Hindu senses that strength is received from scriptures when they are read not in a spirit of literalism but by participating poetically in the inner meaning. Whether there was or was not a fight between the Pāṇḍavas and the Kauravas on the Kurukṣetra battleground is of no consequence when one reads the *Bhagavad Gītā* as an archetype of the eternal conflict between good and evil, or more particularly the conflict between duty and happiness within the human breast. No doubt the Hindu living in the modern world needs to be more careful in distinguishing empirical reality from the never-never land of his imagination, and he needs to examine critically the human ideals supported by his myths, e.g., Rāma's blind fidelity to his father's pledge needs to be weighed against the human pain such fidelity fostered. Also the modern Hindu, reflecting upon the vast storehouse of his culture, must exercise much selectivity. While he may not be willing to shift consciously from "How much of our tradition can we save?" to

[16] Frank Thilly and Ledger Wood, *A History of Philosophy*. Third edition. New York: Henry Holt and Co., 1957, p. 7.

[17] P. 19.

[18] *Babylonian and Assyrian Religion*, pp. x–xi.

"How much of our tradition can we eliminate?", the shift will be made by the pressure of international and intercultural contacts.[19] Yet myth, which has been exploited so effectively in India as a means of preserving insights and of integrating these insights into the lives of generations of men, will surely continue to enrich the art, religion, morality, and thought of the Hindu.

A fifth method of intellectual integration within Hinduism grows out of the tolerant attitude which has already been discussed. An oft-repeated pattern of integration in world history is unifying through the elimination of the opposition by killing those who disagree with the ruling powers, or by confining the dissenters where their views cannot be efficacious, or by destroying their books and forbidding them to speak or write. Any departure from the official point of view is termed heterodoxy, and, if social pressure is not sufficient to enforce the orthodox ideology, the rulers devise rewards for correct believers and punishments for those who deviate from the norm. Joint families and castes have been very effective agents for forcing commonality of practices and beliefs, yet at the same time Hinduism has developed many techniques for allowing diversity within the basic unity. Most of these methods of comprehensive integration have been dualistic in nature, that is, they have provided for two types of mental outlook, or two orders of reality. The ancient *ṛṣis* distinguished between exoteric knowledge taught to the pupil at the early stages of instruction and esoteric or secret knowledge (*upaniṣad*) revealed only after he was sufficiently prepared to receive it. Much stress was placed on spiritual competence (*adhikāra*) by the ancient teachers of Vedic lore. But the esoteric knowledge was not contradictory to the exoteric. Corresponding to the notion of pupil fitness is the notion of a chosen deity (*iṣṭa-devatā*), the view that any deity accepted as one's own is the right deity, for the Lord is in all: "Whatsoever divine form any devotee with faith seeks to worship . . . I ordain that same to be," says Lord Kṛṣṇa to Arjuna.[20] Śaṅkara not only tolerated theism among the followers of his absolutism, but also wrote hymns of praise to the worshiped God. He held two theories of the Absolute: an Absolute without qualities and an Absolute with qualities; one was pure Being (*Sat*), the other Being under the necessary limitations of pluralism within the realm of space and time. Yet it was One Reality—one in the order of Being, the other in the order of becoming. Absolute Being, even when qualified, remains Being. Hence, the uneducated man is not wrong in worshiping his village god; it is his approach to Being. However limited his view of

[19] See Troy Organ, "The Burden of Tradition," *The Mother,* Vol. 2, No. 4, December 1959, pp. 180–182.

[20] *Bhagavad Gītā* 7. 21. Edgerton translation.

god, his view is of the Absolute within the categories of his understanding. Those in the West who have been trained in precise scientific thinking, in Western forms of jurisprudence, and in a creedal religion like Christianity have formed the habit of thinking in dichotomies such as orthodox-heterodox, right-wrong, moral-immoral, and true-false. For them the Hindu efforts to preserve diverse points of view and manifold types of reality in the name of cultural unity may seem to put too much emphasis on unity and not enough on empirical facts and logical consistency. The Hindu reply might be that accommodation of differences in our world is of prime importance today, and until such an attitude pervades peoples and nations the concept of United Nations remains a hope far from being realized.

3. ONENESS IN THE *Ṛg Veda*

"Truth is one, the wise call it by different names." [21] The *Ṛg Veda* not only sets forth the basic unity of all Hindu thought, but also affirms that wisdom consists in recognizing the pluralities into which the one is manifested. The oneness of reality is also stated in the concept of *Ekam Sat* (That One Thing), an objective reality of which all things partake. It is this oneness, the greatest discovery of the Vedic hymns, to which the forest philosophers added the conception of spirituality. *Sat* was a neuter principle, although *ṛṣis* acknowledged that it might be called "Agni, Yama and Mātariśvan." [22] *Ṛg Veda* 10.121 is a hymn to *Kā* (Who), which Max Müller called "A Hymn to the Unknown God." In this hymn *Kā* is described as "present at the beginning," [23] "the sole Lord of created beings," [24] the one who "upheld this earth and heaven," [25] "the giver of soul," [26] "the giver of strength," [27] one "whose commands all beings, even the gods, obey," [28] "the sole king of the breathing and seeing world," [29] the one "who rules over this aggregate of two-footed and four-footed beings," [30] "by whom heaven and the solar sphere were fixed," [31] "by whom

[21] *Ṛg Veda* 1. 164. 46.
[22] *Ibid.* Edgerton translation.
[23] Verse 1.
[24] *Ibid.*
[25] *Ibid.*
[26] Verse 2.
[27] Verse 2.
[28] *Ibid.*
[29] Verse 3.
[30] *Ibid.*
[31] Verse 5.

the sky was made profound and the earth solid," [32] and "among the gods was the supreme god." [33] But such a list of the functions of the Unknown God is matched by the healthy skepticism which lightens and enlivens the *Ṛg Veda.* For example, a *ṛṣi* sang of the proximity and harmony of himself and the natural world: "The heaven is my parent and progenitor: the navel (of the earth) is my kinsman: the spacious earth is my mother";[34] yet on second thought, after listing still more of the wonders of nature, he adds, "I distinguish not if I am this all; for I go perplexed, and bound in mind." [35] Agnosticism, which is more than skepticism, is affirmed also in the *Ṛg Veda:* "You shall not find him, who created these (worlds); something else has come between you (and him)." [36]

Although the *Ṛg Veda* is the oldest literature of man, the hymns are not as primitive as some of the writings to be found in later literature. The oldest gods are the personified and semipersonified powers of nature. Father Sky and Mother Earth were largely ancestral memories by the time of the composition of the earliest hymns, and in their places ruled their offspring: celestial deities, chiefly the sun in its various functions as pathfinder, invigorator, stimulator, and scorcher; atmospheric deities, usually those associated with monsoon storms; and earthy deities, such as rivers, fire, and strong drink. Within the *Ṛg Veda* there seems to be a progression from early nature gods to moral gods like Varuṇa, to gods associated with the Aryan conquest of the Indus Valley, to gods that reflect a feeling for monotheism such as Prajāpati, the father of all. However, due to our inability to establish a chronology of the hymns, a temporal progression is difficult to ascertain. How to relate anthropomorphic deities like Indra, Agni, and Rudra to abstract neuter principles like *Sat, Tat,* and *Kā* remains a puzzle. Vedic literature does indicate a gradual sloughing off of the gods. This is noted in the three stages of development of attitudes toward the sacrifices; first the sacrifices are means of gratification and propitiation of the gods; then they become an end in themselves; and finally the gods become supernumeraries, owing their existence to the sacrifices which they themselves perform.[37]

[32] *Ibid.*

[33] Verse 8.

[34] *Ibid.*, 1. 164. 33

[35] *Ibid.*, 1. 164. 37.

[36] 10. 82. 7. Edgerton translation.

[37] Dorothea Jane Stephen in *Studies in Early Indian Thought* offers eight conceptions of the divine nature in the *Ṛg Veda,* but the ordering is not to be understood as a fixed chronological one.

1. As source of moral law. 7. 86. 6; 7. 88. 5, 6.
2. As source of physical law. 4. 239; 7. 66. 13.
3. As source of physical life. 10. 45. 6; 1. 115. 1.
4. As source of material prosperity. 10. 46. 1.

The sacrificial system may have been the agency through which the important notion of oneness dawned upon the minds of the Vedic Indians. Sacrifices were believed to be magically efficacious without fail; the sun would rise if the priest performed the morning sacrifice, and the sun would not rise if the priest failed to perform the sacrifice. Such belief included a false confidence in the power of the sacrifice, but a true conception of the orderliness of the world. Magic does not need to be dignified as primitive science nor condemned as bastard science, but magic does assume the principle of ordered cause in the world in which it operates. This principle of order (*ṛta*) was the high point of the integration of things in the *Ṛg Veda*. *Ṛta*, the course of things, is the early Hindu conception of natural law. While it was not a principle of morality or jurisprudence, it did include the notion of inner justice, that is, of an inner harmony similar to that of Anaximander and Heraclitus in which the extremeness of opposites was worn off, the wet became dry, and the dry became wet, the hot cold, and the cold hot. Perhaps the regularity of the seasons, the predictability of the monsoons, the rotation of the heavenly bodies, the passing of day into night and of night into day, and other ordered movements in nature, as well as the efficacy of sacrifices, contributed to the Vedic concept of *ṛta*. "The dawn follows the path of *Ṛta*, the right path; as if she knew them before. She never oversteps the regions. The sun follows the path of *Ṛta*" sang a Vedic *ṛṣi*.[38] *Ṛta* was called the father (or overseer) of all. The gods were subject to *ṛta*, but not in the sense of a fixed fate as were the Homeric deities. The parallel concept of *ṛta* among the Greeks was the *Logos*, or pattern of things, not *Moira*, or Destiny. The necessity of *ṛta* was an inner necessity, never an external guidance, nor requirement, nor ordering. *Ṛta* was the nature of things. Rivers flow by *ṛta*; not that they must flow, but that they do. It is the *ṛta* of water to seek a lower level without purpose. When the concept became fixed in the minds of the Vedics, their conception of the world underwent profound change. The world was no longer, as it must have been in pre-Vedic times, a chaos of chance elements, and the world was not an instrument under the direction and control of supernatural agencies; the world was now a predictable, orderly world within which men could organize their lives with confidence that the functioning of things was dependable, neither benevolent nor malevolent, yet so certain that man himself could not escape the causes

5. As priest. 1. 1. 1–5.
6. As sacrifice. 1. 162–163; 10. 13. 4; 10. 90.
7. As abstraction. 10. 121.
8. As the one behind the many. 1. 164. 37, 46; 4. 47. 18; 10. 54. 2; 7. 58. 2.

[38] *Ṛg Veda* 1. 24. 8. Radhakrishnan, *Indian Philosophy*, Vol. 1, p. 79.

he had set in operation. Thus from the conception of *ṛta* grew one of the distinctive aspects of the Hindu view of life: the law of the deed (*karma*). Cause and effect were as operative in the realm of morality as in the realm of natural phenomena. Such was the confidence of the Hindu in the *ṛta* principle in human behavior, that rebirth in a chain of lives was postulated and accepted as necessary to support the doctrine of *karma*.

4. THE GODS AS INTEGRATORS

The Sanskrit word for deity is *deva*. The similarity of *deva* to *deus*, deity, and divine is sufficient to tempt the scholar to attribute to *deva* the denotations and connotations of the Latin and English counterparts. But such parallelism is misleading. One Indologist, Mrs. Rhys-Davids,[39] came to the conclusion that the most satisfactory treatment was to leave "*deva*" untranslated, whereas Mr. Rhys-Davids attempted to use "angel" and "archangel." A *deva* is one who gives something of value to man; sages give knowledge, *gurus* and parents give guidance, guests give happiness, the sun gives light—and all of these are *devas*. The Aryans must have first used *deva* for the lights in the sky, for the term came to mean "the bright and shining ones." As the term became applied to celestial bodies, and then to a wide variety of natural powers, it came to designate that which is fixed and complete. A *deva* was a non-human power at work in the world, which, although anthropomorphized by man's imagination, was transcendent to man. *Devas* were the efficient agents of storm, wind, thunder, lightning, light, and darkness. The three elements of fire, water, and earth were called *devatās*. *Sat* (Being) was called the *parā devatā* (highest divinity). The *Chāndogya Upaniṣad* reports that the varied manifestations of the world were produced by the union of *Sat* with these elements: "That divinity thought 'Well, let me enter into these three divinities by means of this living self and let me then develop names and forms. Let me make each one of the three threefold.' "[40] The Aryan, emphasizing the *deva's* power to bring about change, concluded that nothing had greater potentiality for change than man. If the term *deva* meant a being rich with potentialities, who was more *deva*-like than man? Who had more charisma? So the term came to denote both the powers of the natural world and the powers of man. The Brāhmaṇas contend that there are two classes of *devas:* the god-*devas* and the human-*devas:* "Verily, there are two kinds of gods; for, indeed, the gods are the gods, and the Brah-

[39] See her *Indian Religion and Survival*, p. 31.
[40] 6. 3. 2–3. Radhakrishnan translation.

mins who have studied and teach sacred lore are the human gods."[41] The priestly authors of these works could not yet bring themselves to the notion of a *deva*-nature in all men. The god-*devas* controlled natural phenomena; the human-*devas* controlled the sacrifices which made things happen. Man was the special repository of *deva* energy and strength. Through controlled conservation (*tapas*) man could store power and release it for the accomplishment of desired ends. "Therefore one who knows Man (*puruṣa*, or the spirit) thinks, 'This is *brahman*.' For all 'deities' (potencies, *devatā*) are seated in him, as cattle in a cattle-stall" says a *ṛṣi* in the *Atharva Veda*.[42] The transcendent deities of the early Vedics did not vanish; they became immanent in man.

The Upaniṣads record the breaking away from the *mahā-devas* (the great gods) of the early Vedic hymns. The loss of contact with, and faith in, the divine-*devas* is indicated still more in the Buddhist Suttas where the compound *deva-manuṣā* (divine-human) is used. Yet the concept of *deva* does not entirely vanish in Hinduism, and it is a bit surprising to be informed by a modern Indologist that "the gods are really superfluous in Indian religion."[43] Perhaps god as understood in the West is superfluous, but deity in the second meaning as high potentialities of man in his interpersonal relationships is a viable concept and has remained so to the present day. The essential, but sometimes overlooked, fact is that Hinduism and a theistic religion like Judaic-Christianity have contrary conceptions of divinity. Judaism and Christianity agree that god and man are separate; god's holiness is uniquely non-human. The Judaic-Christian god may not be the "Wholly Other" as Karl Barth used to contend, but on the other hand is most certainly not a "well-developed man"! The Hebrew and the Christian find in the Hindu conception a blurring of the divine-human distinction; they want their god to be God, and their man to be man. No sane Hebrew, not even the most ecstatic prophet, claimed to be God; and the greatest Hebrew of all, Moses, never claimed to be a divinity. Furthermore, no Hebrew attempted to deify him and none worshiped him, either during his life or after his death. Similarly, in Christianity, despite the doctrine of the incarnation, man is not said to be God. Yet in India gods and men, if not of the same order of being, are so closely related that any man who claims to be god will get a sympathetic hearing, and may win a following—at least so it seems to Western eyes and ears.

Perhaps a better way to understand the difference between the Western conception of God and the Hindu conception is to note that in the

[41] *Śatapatha Brāhmaṇa* 2. 2. 6. Radhakrishnan, *Indian Philosophy*, Vol. 1, p. 126.
[42] 11. 8. 32. Edgerton translation.
[43] Louis Renou, *Religion of Ancient India*, p. 68.

West "god" denotes a being whose essence is to be, while in India "god" denotes certain attributes of beings. Although Hinduism does have the notion of "being whose essence it is to be," this, as we have already noted, is Brahman, not God. The attributes which constitute a god can be possessed by animals, by men, and by super-human beings—and they can possess divinity in varying degrees. It is even quite common to refer to some beings as having "semi-divine dignity." [44] In Judaism and Christianity a being either is or is not a god. Plato, for example, argued in a typical Western manner when he reasoned that no god is a philosopher, because a god is wise, and therefore not a *lover* or *seeker* of wisdom.[45] A Western god *is* what he is, he has not *become* what he is, and he will not *become* something other than what he is. A changing god is no god. But in India a god may grow or diminish in divinity. The god-*devas* are beings that have acquired more god-ness than has man. As further evidence for the conception of degrees of the god-state the three types of *avatāras* (incarnations) of Viṣṇu within Vaiṣṇava literature may be cited: there are complete incarnations (*pūrṇāvatāras*), e.g., Rāma-Dasaratha and Kṛṣṇa are often regarded as the two complete *avatāras*; there are also incarnations of a portion of the power of a divine being (*aṃśakṛtāvatāras*), e.g., sometimes Kṛṣṇa of the *Bhāgavata Purāṇa* is so regarded by Vaiṣṇavites who are embarrassed by the stories of Kṛṣṇa's youth found in this *smṛti* writing; and some of the later Vaiṣṇavites allowed a third type of *avatāra*—the partial incarnations of a more or less temporary character (*āveśāvatāras*).

The gradation aspect of the *deva* concept gives to Hinduism a pattern for integrating all living forms. The separation of animals, men, and gods, so essential to Western religions, is rejected. In the Hebrew myth of creation the Creator asks the first man to name the animals as they are brought before him, i.e., to gain control over them, since the name is the power. This seems to the Hindu to separate and to oppose diametrically beings who by nature and by right belong in the same line of evolutionary development. Perhaps the *deva* concept fits the theory of organic evolution better than the typical view of Western religions! The integrative implications of the concept have never been fully worked out. Jainism and Buddhism may be understood to be in part alternative attempts to spell out the practical implications of the theory, the former concluding that all living beings are to be valued and protected, the latter integrating still more by eliminating the concept of beings altogether in a process theory of life.

[44] E.g., see K. M. Panikkar, *A Survey of Indian History*, p. 103.
[45] *Symposium* 204 A.

The refusal to separate men and gods did not spring full-blown from the Aryan mind. Although men and gods were still separated at the time of the formation of the Vedic hymns, the chief concern of the worshipers was achieving earthly blessings for man: food, shelter, children, health, longevity, etc., all on the assumption that the gods were not to be feared, that they were benevolent, and that they would be interested in conferring still more of the blessings already showered down upon the earth. Although men respected the gods, they did not stand in awe of them, and they did not hesitate to give specific orders to the gods, e.g., in a hymn to the rain-god Parjanya, the priest tells the god that enough is enough, "You have rained down rain; now kindly check it!" [46] Gradually the notion of a god in the sky or even in the atmosphere was altered to a god within. The song of India became a song of the soul's quest for God in the heart of man.

5. BRAHMAN AS UNITY

One of the gems of Vedic teaching on the Brahman is found in the third chapter of *Taittirīya Upaniṣad.* A young man named Bhrigu asks his father Varuṇa to instruct him on the nature of Brahman. The father begins with the concise statement that Brahman is that from whence beings are born, by which they live, and into which they enter upon their death.[47] This trilogy—origin, preservation, and dissolution—is the framework for the detailed teaching as the father beginning with the simplest substantial notion, the notion of matter, moves up the evolutionary scale in order to teach Bhrigu that Brahman is the source of all beings, the sustainer of everything, and that into which all beings enter upon departing from this world of name and form: Brahman is matter (*anna*), for material beings are born from matter, live by matter, and departing enter matter; Brahman is life (*prāṇa*), for living material beings are born from life, live by life, and when departing enter into life; Brahman is mind (*manas*), for conscious living material beings are born from mind, live by mind, and upon departing enter into mind; Brahman is intelligence (*vijñāna*), for understanding conscious living material beings are born from intelligence, live by intelligence, and departing enter intelligence; and Brahman is bliss (*ānanda*), because spiritual understanding conscious living material beings are born from bliss, live by bliss, and departing enter bliss. In this teaching Varuṇa conveys the supreme teaching

[46] *Ṛg Veda* 5. 83. 10. Edgerton translation.

[47] Cf. "Of creations I am the beginning, the end and also the middle, O Arjuna." *Bhagavad Gītā* 10. 32. Radhakrishnan translation.

that man, the being in whom the material, the vital, the mental, the intellectual, and the spiritual are harmonized is one with the Absolute, not only in the highest element of his being, but also in each element of his being, and hence there is no element without its peculiar honor and there is no conflict among the elements. Man must not despise the material basis which he shares with the inorganic world, for Brahman is in everything. The teaching session closes with the son chanting a rapture of his newly discovered cosmic unity:

> Oh, wonderful! Oh, wonderful! Oh, wonderful!
> I am food! I am food! I am food!
> I am a food-eater! I am a food-eater! I am a food-eater!
> I am the combining agent! I am the combining agent! I am the combining agent!
> I am the first-born of the world-order!
> Earlier than the gods, in the navel of immortality!
> Who gives me away, he indeed has saved me!
> I, who am food, eat the eater of food!
> I have overcome the whole world! [48]

"Food" is a poetic term for matter. Man is both a material being and a being transcendent to matter, both food and the eater of food, a combiner of matter and spirit. Man is the key to the universe. He is the orderer of pluralities, the center of immortality, the conquerer of the world. The order of the universe resides in him. Therefore he can live out his earthly days with joyous confidence: "I have overcome the world."

As was noted in Chapter II the ontological quest in Hinduism is a search for that which will have no antithesis, and hence will result in no new synthesis. The quest is for an Ultimate behind which, below which, beneath which, and beyond which there is nothing. The Ultimate must be that from which everything else is derived; it is derived from nothing. It must be free from all limitations of space and time, all knowing and being known, all being and becoming. This is the Brahman. The word is derived from a root signifying greatness. Brahman designates that whose greatness is not limited by another, nor by potentialities as yet unfulfilled, nor by change in any form. Brahman includes all opposites, hence has no antithesis. No qualifying characteristics can be assigned to Brahman. Brahman does not exist as things exist, for Brahman also nonexists. Brahman is and is not, but not in the sense that Brahman *is* and *is not*, rather in the sense that Brahman is *and* is not. "No" is the proper response to *every* quality assigned to the Brahman. Brahman is. No!

[48] 3. 10. 6. Hume translation.

Brahman is not! No! So to denote the "existence" of Brahman one must say, "It is not true that Brahman does exist." But even this is inadequate! The full statement would be: "It is not true that Brahman does not exist, and it is not true that Brahman exists, and it is not true that Brahman both exists and does not exist, and it is not true that Brahman neither exists nor does not exist." Brahman is the ground of beings. Without Brahman beings would not exist.

The *Neti! Neti!* doctrine has been offered as the only way to express a non-controvertible statement about Brahman; no matter what one affirms about Brahman, the truth is that one is wrong! However, it might be more appropriate, if less arresting, to suggest that "*Neti! Neti!*" is rather a way of expressing the fact that all statements about Brahman are analogous. There is no one-to-one correspondence between word and referent when speaking about the Brahman as there is in ordinary conversation, e.g., the word "tree" stands for the large plant growing in the yard, whereas the word "Brahman" can represent no thing. So all the words used to define or to describe Brahman—"Being," "Non-Being," "Immanence," "Transcendence," "Consciousness," "Bliss," etc.—are analogies. These words image an image; they do not represent the Brahman. Thinking and verbalizing function in a realm of beings, and Brahman is not a being. Brahman has no attribute such that it can be represented by a word. Brahman negates all our affirmations.

Brahman is One, but not a numerical one, nor a unity of a collection, nor the collection as a whole. Brahman is One as oneness, unification, the principle of integration. Brahman is One only in the sense that there is no other; there is nothing that is not Brahman. Brahman is the non-divisible All from which all things come in a non-divisible way and exist in a non-divisible manner. Brahman cannot even be said to be One as ontologically prior to the existence of things, for this cannot be stated without implying that Brahman and things share in some mode of existence, but Brahman does not exist as things exist, and things do not enjoy the status of Brahman except insofar as they are the manifestations of Brahman under the limiting conditions of name and form, time and space.[49] All things are rooted in Brahman, come from Brahman, return to Brahman, yet there is no diminution or division of Brahman. Brahman does not disperse itself into many "brahmans" or particles of Brahman. The absolute unity of Brahman excludes Brahman from existence, since existing requires actual or potential non-existing. If x exists, then

[49] Brahman and space are equated in some passages of the Upaniṣads. E.g., "Verily, that is called Brahman, that is what the space outside of a person is. . . . Now with reference to the divinities one should meditate on space as Brahman." *Chāndogya Upaniṣad* 3. 12. 7; 3. 18. 1. Radhakrishnan translation.

x could also not exist; or again, if *x* exists, then there must be the possibility of a non-*x* which either does or could exist. But Brahman, being Brahman, cannot be non-Brahman, that is, cannot possess an existential antithesis; and Brahman, being Brahman, cannot be limited by a possible non-Brahman. Brahman's "existence" is not like the existence of *x*.

Not only does the Oneness of Brahman make it impossible to assign existence or non-existence to Brahman, but also the Oneness means that Brahman cannot be known, for to be known is to be the object of the awareness of another; also Brahman cannot know, for to know necessitates a subject being aware of an object. Brahman can only be known by a "knowing" which transcends subject and object, which is not knowing at all. So Brahman can be "known" only by "not knowing": "It is conceived of by him by whom It is not conceived of. He by whom It is conceived of, knows It not. It is not understood by those who [say they] understand It. It is understood by those who [say they] understand It not." [50] The unknowability of Brahman is open to wide misunderstanding. It is not rooted in the transcendence of Brahman, nor in the incompetence of the human mind. It is not that Brahman is so remote, but that Brahman is so immediate. Aristotle in a curious passage [51] conjectures that men, like bats whose eyes are blinded by the daylight, may be unable to grasp the nature of reality because it is too self-evident. Or to change the metaphor, a man seeking Brahman may be like a fish seeking to know water. Brahman is that in which we live and move and have our being; Brahman is without, Brahman is within, Brahman is All. Brahman is unknowable by man because man, being Brahman, cannot achieve the necessary metaphysical distance in order to make Brahman an epistemological object. This is what is meant by the Upaniṣadic statement "*Aham Brahma asmi*" (I am Brahman). These words are an ejaculation of a soteriological insight rather than a metaphysical statement: "I perceive that my essence and the essence of the Brahman are inseparable. I am not an infinitesimal fleck drifting aimlessly on the surface of a minor planet of a second-rate star within one of a million star clouds on the rim of the universe of space. I am Brahman. I have overcome the world." The real Self of man (the *Ātman*) *is* Brahman. But what is the nature of the "is" in this statement? Is it predication, e.g., "This apple is green"? Is it class inclusion, e.g., "Fido is a dog"? Is it class membership, e.g., "Sitting Bull is a member of a vanishing race"? Is it equality, e.g., "2 + 2 are equal to 4"? Is it equivalence, e.g., "IV is equivalent to 4"? Or is it none of these? Rudolf Otto has said, "The

[50] *Kena Upaniṣad* 2. 3. Hume translation.
[51] *Metaphysics* 993 b 10.

word 'is' in the mystical formula of identification has a significance which it does not contain in logic." [52] He suggests that the "mystic copula" of "I am Brahman" might be indicated by forcing the language: "Making the word 'be' into a medium of a higher unity of intransitive and transitive." [53] Such formulations as "I am existed by Brahman," or "Brahman exists me," or "I am essenced by Brahman," or "Brahman essences me" have the additional advantage of suggesting that Brahman, although not acting, is acting from the point of view of the phenomenal world.[54]

The Upaniṣads distinguish two forms of Brahman: (1) the Brahman that is formless, without qualities, and (2) the Brahman that is formed, with qualities.[55] These are not two Brahmans; they are Brahman considered as absolute, that is, abstracted from all points of view, and Brahman considered as relative to a point of view. *Saguṇa* Brahman (Brahman with qualities) is *Nirguṇa* Brahman (Brahman without qualities) considered as though it were (*iva*) an object of human understanding. *Saguṇa* is phenomenalistic Brahman, the Brahman as *Īśvara* (the Lord) who shows himself in the origination, sustenance, and dissolution of the world. *Nirguṇa's* essence is the not-acting foundational source of all beings; *Saguṇa's* essence is the active bringing forth, preserving and destroying of the phenomenal universe. A similar distinction was made in the Christian conception of God by Eckhart, e.g., "God acts. The Godhead does not. It has nothing to do and there is nothing going on in it. It is never on the outlook for something to do. The difference between God and the Godhead is the difference between action and nonaction." [56] This should not induce the sophisticated to turn away from *Saguṇa,* for it is as real as any *thing* in the world is real: trees, animals, buildings, man, art, science, and even the gods. Phenomena are very real to us; it is the world of name and form, of space and time. In the language of Josiah Royce's sea captain, the lights we see in the night sky may not be "damned real" but they are real enough to guide the sailor. *Māyā* is *māyā* only for the enlightened man; for the unenlightened man, the *māyā* objects are very real indeed. Man as Brahman may not need to get out of the path of an elephant as Brahman, but phenomenal man better watch out for phenomenal elephant! Brahman is the one sufficient explanation of the world. It is the material cause and the moving cause of the universe. All that is is Brahman, but Brahman is more than all that

[52] *Mysticism East and West,* p. 84.
[53] *Ibid.,* p. 85.
[54] Cf. "Ātman neither acts nor is affected by acts." *Bhagavad Gītā* 13.31. Lal translation.
[55] E.g., *Matirī Upaniṣad* 6.3.
[56] Raymond Bernard Blakney, *Meister Eckhart: A Modern Translation.* New York: Harper and Brothers Publishers, Torchbook Edition, 1957, p. 226.

is. Existence does not exhaust Brahman. In the poetic language of the *Ṛg Veda,* "He, encompassing the world on all sides, stood out ten fingers' lengths beyond." [57]

Beings are Brahman under the limiting conditions of spatiality and temporality. Beings begin in matter, and end in *ānanda.* The gods, the world, and all that is within the world exist; Brahman is the ground of Existence (*Sat*), the ground of Knowledge (*Cit*), and the ground of Value (*Ānanda*). In Brahman, Existence-Knowledge-Value is a single reality. What a non-subject-object union of Existence, Knowledge, and Value may be lies beyond the capacity of man to know, but this is not because of the transcendence of the One. Brahman is *Ātman;* the fundamental nature of Brahman and the fundamental nature of the Real Self are identified. Only by "self-knowing," which is no *knowing* at all, can man "know" Brahman. The recurring Greek and Hebrew legends of entertaining gods and angels unaware is given a different dimension in Hinduism: man is to awaken to the realization that this is eternal life, that he is the Real, that, in the words of the Zen masters, rivers *are* rivers, trees *are* trees, and mountains *are* mountains.

An interesting fact about the development of Hindu thought is that after the fashioning of the speculative insights found in the Vedas, the first philosophizing, that is, the first efforts to make the insights reasonable, were those of the Sāṅkhya philosophers, who proposed an ontological dualism quite repugnant to the Upaniṣadic monistic idealism. If the Real is one, they argued, then it cannot be known, and if the Real is known, then it cannot be one; therefore each philosopher must decide whether he is committed to knowability or to oneness. The choice must be made between a knowable ontological duality or an irrational ontological unity. The Sāṅkhya philosophers chose the former. Reality, they said, is both *prakṛti* and *puruṣa,* matter and spirit, passivity and activity. Their choice was made on grounds ontological as well as epistemological, for they held that if Reality is one it cannot change, and if Reality changes it cannot be one. The Sāṅkhya philosophers were unwilling to pay the price which the Eleatic philosophers paid. Like Heraclitus, they found the experience of change too real to be denied. So, although the fundamental principle of Indian Vedic speculation was that of an Absolute ontological Unity, the Sāṅkhya philosophers played a dualistic variation on the theme, although they finally returned to the original Unity by arguing that *prakṛti,* upon fulfilling its function as material cause, vanishes. The later schools of Indian philosophy can be interpreted as alternative ways to handle the dilemma of ontological monism and episte-

[57] 10. 90. 1. Edgerton translation.

mological duality. Some tried pluralism, some ritualism, some illusionism. Some shifted the grounds from intellectual knowing to what might be called existential knowing, and one turned upon philosophizing itself and engaged in what might be called metaphilosophizing, a questioning of the whole intellectual enterprise. The reaction of these, the Mādhyamika Buddhists, reminds Westerners of the two reactions of Kant and Boswell to Hume's unrelated world. Hume's philosophy aroused Kant from dogmatic slumbers to develop a philosophy that found room for faith, but Boswell's reaction was to seek consolation in women and alcohol!

One possibility which has not been explored sufficiently is that the unity of Brahman may be a functional unity rather than a structural unity. Only the Mahāyāna Buddhists seem to have thought in these terms. "*Neti! Neti!*" is the response to all substantial overtures to the intellectual grasping of Brahman, but what if "Brahman" be the name we give to the integrating aspects of our experience? Why not regard Brahman as a gentle cosmic force congealing phenomena in a widening unification of being, knowledge, and value? This force need not be completely external to man, for man is uniquely placed as creature and creator in the universe. He is privileged to become the being in which the cosmic *nisus* rises to consciousness and creativity. To this consideration we shall turn after first examining why Absolute Unity pluralizes.

6. THE PLURALIZATION OF BRAHMAN

According to Edith Hamilton the Greek temple is "the creation, *par excellence*, of mind and spirit in equilibrium," the Egyptian temple "reduces to nothingness all that belongs to man" and the Hindu temple is "a conglomeration of adornment." She says of the Hindu temple,

> The lines of the building are completely hidden by the decorations. Sculptured figures and ornaments crowd its surface, stand out from it in thick masses, break it up into a bewildering series of irregular tiers. It is not a unity but a collection, rich, confused. It looks like something not planned but built this way and that as the ornament required. . . . It is decoration, not architecture.[58]

Perhaps if Miss Hamilton had studied Indian culture as fully as she studied the Greek she might have been more sympathetic toward the temples of India. The Indian does not value empty space. "The Indian

[58] *The Greek Way to Western Civilization.* New York: W. W. Norton, 1948, p. 45.

idea is that only things covered with ornaments are beautiful." [59] The harmony and unity of rows of identical columns of a Greek temple would seem monotonous and pointless to the Indian. There are one thousand pillars in the temple at Conjeevaram, and no two are alike. There is unity in Indian art, but it is not the unity of repetition of identical forms; it is unity in diversity. The significant manifestation of a fundamental unity is to be found in the manifoldness of phenomena. The opulence of detail of the roof of a Dravidian temple or *gopuram* (gateway) reveals the Real as the totality of all forms. Tagore says in his novel *Gora*, "The limitless One manifests itself in the limitless Many." [60] In architecture, in poetry, in music, in sculpture, and in every conceivable dimension of Hindu life the theme is repeated. Finitude, rather than being contradictory to infinity, is its necessary explication.

"The gods have a thousand names (*sahasra nāma*)," a statement one sometimes hears in India, means that the gods are part of the shifting, changing forms Reality has taken; it does not mean that the richness of the gods is unnamable. Man is encouraged to look behind the gods for the Absolute One, the Unnamable Integration. Some passages in the Upaniṣads warn against seeing plurality (*nānā*) in Brahman, e.g., "By the mind alone is It to be perceived. There is on earth no diversity. He gets death after death, who perceives here seeming diversity." [61] This, however, is a warning against the subject-object point of view of the world rather than a denial of the power of Brahman to appear pluralistically. The receiver of "death after death" (literally, redeath) is the one who experiences the world as apart from Brahman. He errs existentially by taking phenomena for noumena. It is an error of omission, the failure of becoming what he is; and it is an error of commission, the objectifying of the world and Brahman.

The relation between the Absolute One and the entire pluralistic world of change is not clearly stated in the Upaniṣads. Radhakrishnan puts this even stronger since he believes the relation is not expressed at all: "The inexplicability of the relation between the two is assumed by the Upaniṣads, and the later Vedānta gives it the name of *māyā*." [62] To lend further support to this absence of a conclusion, Radhakrishnan quotes similar observations from two English idealists. "The immanence

[59] Heinrich Zimmer, *The Art of Indian Asia*. New York: Pantheon Books, 1955, Vol. 1, p. 236.

[60] Chapter 20. Goethe once wrote, "Of the Absolute in the theoretical sense I do not venture to speak; but this I maintain, that if a man recognises it in its manifestations, and always keeps his eye fixed upon it, he will reap a very great reward." Quoted by William Ralph Inge, *Christian Mysticism*. London: Methuen and Co., 1899, p. 248.

[61] *Bṛhad-Āraṇyaka Upaniṣad* 4. 4. 19. Hume translation.

[62] *Indian Philosophy*, Vol. 1, p. 186.

of the Absolute in finite centres and of finite centres in the Absolute, I have always set down as inexplicable."[63] "The old question, why God made the world, has never been answered, nor will be. We know not why the world should be: we only know that there it is."[64] Radhakrishnan puzzles further over the pluralization of the Brahman:

> Why should the Absolute Brahman perfect, infinite, needing nothing, desiring nothing, move out into the world? It is not compelled to do so. It may have this potentiality but it is not bound or compelled by it. It is free to move or not to move, to grow itself into forms or remain formless. If it still indulges its power of creativity, it is because of its free choice.[65]

But Radhakrishnan is wrong in this second consideration of the problem. In the first place, is it not obvious that the notion of freedom makes no sense when applied to Brahman? Free choice is a capacity of limited beings; what can it possibly mean to affirm that the Absolute is free? Again, if Brahman were potentiality unrealized, then Brahman would not be the Absolute Brahman. So Brahman is compelled, by Its own nature as the Absolute, to actualize all the actualizable. The fullness of Brahman necessitates that every possible form of being come into existence. Production is a requisite of perfection. Missing links in the great chain of being would be imperfection. Perfection is found in plenitude of beings, and this implies both multiplicity and degrees of perfection. From the principle of perfection we move to the principle of plenitude, and from this to the principle of continuity. There can be no "lower" or "higher" levels of Brahman-manifestation from this point of view. The world and its creatures are necessary for Brahman, for as fullness of Being, Brahman must be in every possible form of being. Individuals are the spectra of Brahman. Individuals are the actualized possibilities of Brahman. A possibility that is never actualized is existentially undistinguishable from an impossibility. An event that may happen, but never does happen, is from the finite point of view the same as an event that never can happen. What makes a possibility what it is, is the fact that it may happen sooner or later; it will happen, but *when* it will happen is uncertain. But in the timeless Brahman "when" has no meaning. All is eternal. It does not happen, It has not happened, nor will It happen. Brahman has not created, does not create, and will not create the gods, the world, and man, although from the finite point of view Brahman

[63] F. H. Bradley, "On Appearance, Error, and Contradiction." *Mind*, Vol. 19, 1910, p. 154.

[64] Thomas Hill Green, *Prolegomena to Ethics*. Oxford: Clarendon Press, 1884, pp. 103–104.

[65] *The Principal Upaniṣads*, p. 63.

has created, does create, and will continue to create the gods, the world, and man. The notion of happening is a finite notion; in the Being of Brahman nothing happens, everything is. If the Absolute is the absolute, then It must realize all potentialities, all possible existences must be brought into being, all possible relationships must subsist. An unrealized possibility within the Absolute would make the Absolute less than absolute; manyness is a possibility which must be actualized in order for the Absolute to be absolute. Necessities are inherent in absoluteness. This is what is involved in such silly questions as: Can God make a rock so big that God cannot raise it? Can God tell a lie? Is God subject to his own laws? Can God make two plus two equal anything other than four? Necessity is of the Absolute. The pluralistic world being a potentiality, and the Absolute not being the Absolute with potentialities, the world by necessity came into being not out of the world's necessity, but out of the Absolute's "necessity." Paul Tillich in his last lecture, culminating a two-year seminar on the history of religions in which he brought his profound understanding of the Western Christian tradition into creative relationships with Mircea Eliade's grasp of Asian religions, said, "Nothing finite can cross the frontier from finitude to infinity. But something else is possible: the Eternal can, from its side, cross over the border to the finite. It would not be the Eternal if the finite were its limit."[66] In other words, for Brahman to be Brahman It must cross over the border into the finite; It must be finitized, pluralized, individualized. Tillich put it in a slightly different fashion, a Judeo-Christian fashion: "The universal bias is the expansion of the Holy within the finite."[67] The Absolute must become the morally good, the socially right, the scientifically true, the empirically real, and the aesthetically beautiful. The finite is the necessary exemplification of the Infinite, not Its limitation. The world is the affirmation of Brahman. All that can be, must be, if Brahman is the All. But the beings of time and space do not exhaust Being. "All beings form his foot," says the *Taittirīya Āraṇyaka*,[68] implying that there are also limbs, torso, arms, legs, and head! Space and time, name and form, do not limit nor exhaust the Brahman. Each individual is the One manyed, and each is essential to the One. "I am Brahman," not only in my *homo*-nature, but also in my *vir*-nature. The problem of the One and the Many is solved in Hinduism in the many-requiredness of the Totally One. Hinduism becomes like Indian music, variations on a theme: variety within structure, freedom within law, liberation within discipline, plurality within unity,

[66] Paul Tillich, *The Future of Religions*. New York: Harper and Row, 1966, p. 63.
[67] *Ibid.*, p. 86.
[68] 3. 12.

manyness within one, diversity within simplicity, manifoldness within the single, finite within the Infinite, relative within the Absolute, the informal within the formal, particularity within universality, unpredictability within predictability, pluralism within monism, variegation within evenness, creativity within staticity, difference within sameness, change within the unchanging, flux within stability, novelty within the established, movement within the unmoved, alternation within the unalterable, indefinite within the definite, design within elements, fluctuation within steadiness, heterogeneity within homogeneity, complexity within the elemental, waywardness within the fixed, *māyā* within Brahman, *jīva* within *Ātman!!!* In Indian music creativity demands the deliberate variegation of the effects of beauty within *rāga* and *tāla*, and the absoluteness of Brahman demands the pluralization of the Brahman. An unsolved problem arises particularly out of this musical analogy: in classical Indian music both well-designed and wayward patterns are part of the total performance. Is the same true in the ontology of Brahman? Are there no moral, nor aesthetic, nor truth distinctions in Brahman? Do both acts of murder and acts of charity exemplify Brahman? Are both required? In all monisms the problems of evil, error, and ugliness are persistent. Hinduism does not appear to have been more successful than other cultures in dealing with this Achilles' heel of philosophies and religions.

7. MAN, THE AGENT OF RETURN

Man, says Aurobindo, "is the greatest of living beings because he is the most discontented, because he feels most the pressure of limitations. . . . [He] is the Divine in the individual ascending back out of limited Nature to its own proper divinity." [69] Man is the point at which the cosmos ceases to pluralize and starts the return to Oneness. The Absolute individuates in order to be absolute; the individual human being, in order to be itself, strives to unity. Man is the key in the cosmic process. In him reality is most fully manifest, for he is the self-aware being. In man the downward manifestation comes to a halt, and turning back, starts the climb to oneness. The hopes of all creation are pinned on him. Only in and through him can all beings come to their full reality.

Brahman is Being; man is Being in the state of becoming. "All things pray except the Supreme" said Proclus, meaning that all things, other than the Supreme, have the potentiality of becoming. Only manifested beings can become. In his temporal condition man has the opportunity

[69] *The Life Divine*, pp. 46, 140.

of entering into the eternal. In the perfection of his Self he realizes the Brahman: "I am Brahman. I have overcome the world." Man-as-he-is *is* Brahman, yet man-as-he-is is Brahman in the *māyā* state, the state of necessary manifestation, a state of pluralization. He becomes Brahman as the perfected individual becomes the cosmic individual; he takes the universe unto himself and transcends it, and thus becomes the Self. In man, and only in man, can Brahman as Being-in-becoming complete the cycle of manifestation and integration. Man is both an essential link in the great chain of beings and also the agent of return. Oneness hangs in the balance in the Perfecting of Man.

The Hindus have tried to state this role of man, but the statements easily become sentimental and even foolish. For the most part it has been an assumption rather than a statement. It is expressed in the love of parents for children, in the tolerance toward manifold ways of behaving in religious matters, in readiness to entertain a variety of opinions in philosophical speculation and argument. One of the best statements comes from Aurobindo:

> Earth-life is not a lapse into the mire of something undivine, vain and miserable, offered by some Power to itself as a spectacle or to the embodied soul as a thing to be suffered and then cast away from it: it is the scene of the evolutionary unfolding of the being which moves toward the revelation of a supreme spiritual life and power and joy and oneness, but includes in it also the manifold diversity of the self-achieving spirit. There is an all-seeing purpose in the terrestrial creation; a divine plan is working itself out through its contradictions and perplexities which are a sign of the manysided achievement towards which are being led the soul's growth and the endeavor of Nature.[70]

[70] *Ibid.*, p. 606.

CHAPTER V
The Quest for Liberation

1. DEVELOPMENT OF THE IDEA OF DELIVERANCE IN THE VEDAS

Indra, the god of the monsoon, impetuous, vigorous, conquering, dominating, the consumer of vast quantities of soma and the slayer of dragons, was the prototype of the Vedic Indian. "Both heaven and earth (are) not equal to one half of me, for I have often drunk of the Soma. I excel the sky in greatness, (I excel) this great earth; for I have often drunk of the Soma," [1] boasted Indra, and his worshipers vicariously shared in his conquests. They emulated the god in their battles, praying to him for victory: "Make me, Indra, (renowned like) a bull amongst my equals, victor over my rivals, the slayer of mine enemies, a sovereign, a lord of cattle. I am the destroyer of mine enemies, like Indra, unharmed and unwounded; may all these my foes be cast down under my feet. . . . I have become triumphant with power, equal to any exploit; I seize upon your minds, your pious observances, your prowess in war. Seizing upon your goods and chattels, may I be victorious; I walk upon your heads; cry aloud from beneath my feet, like frogs from (below) the water, like frogs from (below) the water." [2] The life of these early inhabitants of India may not have been luxurious by modern standards, but they had abundant food, fine robes, and gold ornaments. They developed music, poetry, dance, and other arts. Life was good, and earth—"mother-earth,

[1] *Ṛg Veda* 10. 119. 7, 8.
[2] *Ibid.*, 10. 166. 1, 2, 4, 5.

the widespread delightful earth, this virgin (earth is) as soft as wool"[3]—was enthusiastically enjoyed. So thoroughly did they savor life on earth that they prayed for a full span, i.e., a hundred years.[4] The immortality they wanted was to bear sons who might also enjoy the good earth: "May I obtain immortality through my posterity."[5] A very special reward—too glorious to be more than a dream for most—was to be reborn and to relish again the life of earthly pleasures.[6] Sometimes they dreamed of a heaven (*svarga*), a place of the departed forefathers (*pitṛ-loka*) where the sensuous delights would be forever enjoyed, "where light is perpetual," "where wishes and desires are," "where food and delight are found," and "where there is happiness, pleasures, joy and enjoyment."[7] There they would enjoy the music of the heavenly pipes.[8] *Svarga* was the reward of those who practiced *tapas*, who died in battle, or who made large offerings.[9] Hell, on the other hand, was referred to as a deep pit,[10] a place of darkness[11] where the wicked fall down headlong into caverns to be crushed in *soma* presses.[12] One *ṛṣi* confesses that when he first became aware of death, he feared it, but later he longed for death: "(At first) I beheld him [Yama, the god of death] with anguish inviting me to join the men of olden time, and walking with that fell design; but afterwards I longed for him."[13] But this must not be interpreted to imply a disgust with life, because he adds that he now knows a way of returning from death has been provided.[14]

This would seem to imply that while the joys of *svarga* might match those of earth, some doubt lingered as to the certainty of these joys compared to those of earth. The possibility of a return to earth is suggested in other parts of the *Ṛg Veda*, e.g., a funeral hymn petitions that the vital principle of the deceased go to the heaven, or to the earth, or to the waters, or "abide with thy members in the plants."[15] The notion of transferring the vitalizing force to a plant seems strange, but it does represent a theory of rebirth. The fifth verse of this chapter contains a petition to Agni that the spirit of the deceased be again associated with

[3] *Ibid.*, 10. 18. 10.
[4] *Ibid.*, 10. 18. 4; 10. 161. 4.
[5] *Ibid.*, 5. 4. 10.
[6] *Śatapatha Brāhmaṇa* 1. 5. 3. 14.
[7] *Ṛg Veda* 9. 113. 7–11.
[8] *Ibid.*, 10. 135. 7.
[9] *Ibid.*, 10. 154. 2, 3.
[10] *Ibid.*, 4. 5. 5.
[11] *Ibid.*, 7. 104. 3.
[12] *Ibid.*, 7. 104. 17.
[13] *Ibid.*, 10. 135. 2.
[14] *Ibid.*, 10. 135. 6.
[15] *Ibid.*, 10. 16. 3.

a body. In *Ṛg Veda* 10. 14. 8, another funeral hymn, the soul of the departed is asked to return home again. Of far greater significance for the typical attitude toward the doctrine of rebirth was the concept of "redeath" (*punarmṛtyu*) which begins to appear in the Brāhmaṇas.[16] Although the heavenly life was not spelled out in detail, enough references are made to indicate that it was a desirable existence, at least much to be preferred to existence in hell. The fear arose that as death terminated the pleasures of the earthly life, so a second death (*punarmṛtyu*) might end the pleasures of the heavenly life. One life was as mortal as the other. Furthermore, as the death of earthly life led to the birth of heavenly life, so the death of heavenly life might be supposed to lead to the birth of another earthly life. This return to earth was so undesired that magical methods were introduced in the Brāhmaṇas to avoid the end of the heavenly existence.

The Hindu did not seem to be able to convince himself that the heavenly life was to be preferred to the earthly, and therefore he sometimes referred to an interesting choice that confronts the liberated soul after death. For example, in the *Bhagavad Gītā*[17] reference is made to two paths which the liberated may take, the path of the gods (*devayāna*) and the path of the fathers (*pitṛyāna*). The soul choosing the former does not return to the earth; the soul choosing the latter does return. *Devayāna* is also called *uttarayāna* (the northern way) since it is associated with the northward progress of the sun from winter solstice to summer solstice; these months (January to June) are the auspicious time of the year. *Pitṛyāna* is called *dakṣiṇāyana*, the other six months when the sun is moving toward the equator. They are months in which events such as weddings ought to be avoided. While the assignments of *devayāna* to the auspicious and *pitṛyāna* to the unauspicious does show that one is preferred to the other, it also may be interpreted as an indication of the necessary opposition of the directions and the seasons. While the northern course of the sun is good, it would not be good if the sun continued moving northward after the summer solstice, and finally vanished over the northern horizon. This choice of two ways for the liberated soul to go is strikingly similar to the Buddhist view that a Buddha may become either a Buddha-for-his-own-sake and go into *Parinirvāṇa* or a Buddha-for-the-sake-of-others and return to this life.

The next stage in the development of thought about the life and death of individuals was a questioning of the nature of the heavenly life which

[16] See Keith, *The Sāṁkhya System*, pp. 19–20, and Edgerton, *The Beginnings of Indian Philosophy*, pp. 49, 164. Also *Bṛhad-Āraṇyaka Upaniṣad* 3. 3. 2.

[17] 8. 23–26. Also *Bṛhad-Āraṇyaka Upaniṣad* 6. 2. 15–16, *Praśna Upaniṣad* 1. 9, *Maitrī Upaniṣad* 6. 8.

followed the death of an earthly life and also of the nature of the next earthly life which followed redeath. Because of his acceptance of the concept of cosmic order (*ṛta*), the Hindu could not believe that these lives would be determined by chance. *Ṛta* at work in the succession of mortal lives was called *karma*. This word, which means action or deed in Sanskrit, may be described as the concept of natural causality in the moral sphere. In the moral realm one must sow in order to reap, and one reaps nothing except what has been sown. The doctrine of *karma* was developed in the Upaniṣads and has remained, with modifications, as we shall see when we discuss *bhakti mārga*, an important element in Hinduism to this day. "According as one acts, according as one behaves, so does he become [in the next life]," said an Upaniṣadic seer.[18] Then he spelled out his meaning in more detail: "The doer of good becomes good, the doer of evil becomes evil. One becomes virtuous by virtuous action, bad by bad action. Others, however, say that a person consists of desires." [19] "As is his desire so is his will; as is his will, so is the deed he does, whatever deed he does, that he attains." [20] In the next verse the *ṛṣi* quotes a poem which seems to indicate that at this time the notion of alternation of earthly life and heavenly life was still held:

> Obtaining the end of his action,
> Whatever he does in this world,
> He comes again from that world
> To this world of action.[21]

Other references to *karma* in the Upaniṣads stress the determining factor of action, and do not indicate a two-world theory. "One becomes good by good action, bad by bad action." [22] "The individual soul roams about [in reincarnation] according to its deeds." [23] "[The soul] being overcome by the bright or dark fruits of action, enters a good or an evil womb." [24] The caste system and the conception of the unity of all life was also utilized in the explication of *karma:* "Those whose conduct here has been good will quickly attain a good birth, the birth of a Brahmin, the birth of a Kṣatriya or the birth of a Vaiśya. But those whose conduct has been evil, will quickly attain an evil birth, the birth of a dog, the birth of a hog or the birth of a Caṇḍāla." [25]

[18] *Bṛhad-Āraṇyaka Upaniṣad* 4. 4. 5. Radhakrishnan translation.
[19] A reference to Buddhism?
[20] *Bṛhad-Āraṇyaka Upaniṣad* 4. 4. 5. Radhakrishnan translation.
[21] *Ibid.*, 4. 4. 6. Hume translation.
[22] *Ibid.*, 3. 2. 14. Hume translation.
[23] *Śvetāśvatara Upaniṣad* 5. 7. Hume translation.
[24] *Maitrī Upaniṣad* 3. 2. Hume translation.
[25] *Chāndogya Upaniṣad* 4. 10. 7. Radhakrishnan translation.

The Sanskrit term *saṁsāra* (course, migration) was used to designate a chain of rebirths. The first use of the term in the Upaniṣads links it with the notion of missing the mark of a good life:

> He, however, who has not understanding,
> Who is unmindful and ever impure,
> Reaches not the goal,
> But goes on to reincarnation (*saṁsāra*).[26]

Hence by the time of the formation of the Upaniṣads the early Vedic enthusiasm for life which included the expectation of everlasting *earthly* joys in a heavenly state had been corroded as the notion of redeath made life in heaven as mortal as life on earth, and in addition the concept of heaven itself had been challenged. Man was left with a weary cycle of earthly lives, an indefinite series of revolutions on the crushing wheel of life and death.[27] His last hope was to get off the wheel, to end the life-death cycle altogether. The concept of deliverance had moved from deliverance from death to deliverance from redeath, and from deliverance from redeath to deliverance from rebirth. The negative connotations of human life now outweighed the positive ones. Deliverance was the complete termination of the life-death sequence. What had originated as a desire to escape death, became in the Upaniṣads a desire to transcend both life and death. Liberation had become the *summum bonum* of human life.

2. *Artha, Kāma,* AND *Dharma* AS SECONDARY GOALS; *Moṣka* AS PRIMARY GOAL

Hinduism as a doctrine is complete; it is *theory,* lest practice be blind, and it is *practice,* lest theory be empty. This is one of the significant contributions of Hinduism to human culture: the constant application of theory to practical life and the constant examination of practical life in the light of theory. Neither philosophy alone nor religion alone is *sādhana,* although both religion and philosophy are inherent in and essential to *sādhana.*

Hinduism in its completeness sets before man four areas or goals of life essential to his perfecting. They are also known as *puruṣārthas,* the aims that govern the actions of men. These four are not alternative ways

[26] *Kaṭha Upaniṣad* 3. 7. Hume translation.

[27] Some expositors of Hinduism have worked out fantastically lengthy programs of incarnations, e.g., according to some a *jīva* is granted a human body only after going through 8,400,000 previous incarnations—2,000,000 as a plant, 900,000 as an aquatic creature, 1,100,000 as an insect, 1,000,000 as a bird, 3,000,000 as a cow, and 400,000 as a monkey! Renou, *The Nature of Hinduism*, p. 67.

to live, as are Aristotle's life of pleasure, life of honor, and life of contemplation. The enumeration itself is typically Hindu. "Can any Hindu systematic treatise on any subject be imagined that does not abound in numerical categories?" asks Edgerton.[28] The proclivity to numbering suggests separateness and, possibly, equality in rank, but the four are not completely separate, and they are not equal. They are better identified as four component parts of the whole *sādhana* than as four distinct aims of life. They are the material component (*artha*), the hedonic component (*kāma*), the moral component (*dharma*), and the specifically religious component (*mokṣa*). These four are usually more sharply identified by the virtue associated with each: success, pleasure, duty, and liberation.

The first three are different in context from that of the fourth, although to identify them as philosophies of time and the fourth as a philosophy of eternity does not seem quite apposite[29] because liberation in at least some of its aspects is realized within time. Radhakrishnan states categorically, "Mokṣa or liberation is to be achieved here and now, on earth, through human relations."[30] The distinction is that whereas the first three possess both intrinsic and extrinsic values, the fourth has intrinsic value only, that is, the values of success, of pleasure, and of duty are found both in themselves and in the liberation to which they contribute. In the words of a Tagore song, "*Mukti tore paytaye habe*" (You have to be free). Hinduism is not a way of life which stresses success for its own sake, pleasure for its own sake, and duty for its own sake, even though these three are acknowledged to have intrinsic values; Hinduism insists that in addition these three possess further value in being propaedeutic to liberation. They are not to be despised, yet in themselves they do not constitute the fully human life, nor are they to be regarded as secondary aims only. *Artha, kāma,* and *dharma,* known collectively as the *trivarga* (group of three) were integral to the full life of every man in the Vedic period, but since the sixth century B.C. some Hindus have emulated the Buddha in giving up possessions, in practicing celibacy, and in cutting themselves off from normal social obligations. The tradition of asceticism from Gautama to Ramakrishna has been a viable one.

The term *artha* means literally thing or object. As used in Indian literature *artha* means all the things that a man can amass, possess, share, enjoy, lose, and destroy. The materials required for maintaining a home, for rearing a family, for performing the duties of religion, caste, and citizenship are *artha. Artha* denotes the objects which bring pleasure to

[28] "The Meaning of Sāṅkhya and Yoga," *American Journal of Philosophy,* Vol. 45, 1924, p. 35.
[29] See Zimmer, *Philosophies of India,* Parts II and III.
[30] *Religion and Society,* p. 104.

palate, ear, eye, and total physical well-being. Both material necessities and material luxuries are *artha. Artha* means also the wealth which can be exchanged for the physical goods. The term is even extended to include social and political stability. *Artha,* then, is a very broad term which designates the instruments for success in the worldly life. The man who realizes the *artha* ideal must concern himself with *vārtā,* the means of livelihood through agriculture, husbandry, manufacture, trade, moneylending, etc., and also with *daṇḍanīti,* the indirect means by which he acquires his wealth, namely, politics and jurisprudence. He is a man of *nīti* (worldly wisdom, prudence, practical morality); he is one whose life combines security, prosperity, friendship, knowledge, and action in such a manner that joy and contentment result. The satisfactions of the *nīti* man are not the eternal joys associated with the full Hindu life, but nonetheless they are genuine joys.

Shortly after the formation of the Upaniṣads a number of works were written on the polity aspect of the philosophy of worldly success, of which only the *Arthaśāstra* of Kauṭilya remains. The subject matter of this treatise is *daṇḍanīti* rather than *vārtā* since the author defines his topic as "the science which treats of the means of acquiring and ruling the earth." [31] It is primarily a handbook for monarchs. The program for the education of the king and for techniques of ruling is thoroughly Machiavellian. His education is chiefly training in control of lust, anger, greed, vanity, arrogance, and jealousy, as these will prevent him from absolute rule of his people. Statecraft is largely an efficient system of espionage. Officers must be changed frequently, lest any become entrenched in power and position. In judicial matters the king maintains final authority. General insurrection is avoided by secret measures against sedition. In war total destruction of an enemy is advisable. Internal disturbances should be fomented in the ranks of enemies of superior strength; personal enemies are to be overcome by causing in them blindness, bodily diseases, and deformities.

Similar advice on *daṇḍanīti* is given by the seer Bhīṣma in the *Śanti Parva* of the *Mahābhārata.* The primitive state of man, Bhīṣma tells *Yudhiṣṭhira,* is anarchy. The law of the primitive condition of man is the Law of the Fishes (*mātsya-nyāya*), the big ones devour the small ones. It is "the worst possible of states . . . there is no evil greater than anarchy." [32] The best way to eliminate this unhappy social condition is to become subject to a king: "If a powerful king approaches kingdoms weakened by anarchy, from desire of annexing them to his dominions,

[31] *Arthaśāstra* 15. 1.
[32] *Mahābhārata* 12. 67.

the people should go forward and receive the invader with respect." [33] The divine right of kings was never more clearly stated: "The man that bends his head to a powerful person really bends his head to Indra. . . . A person who is desirous of prosperity should worship the king as he should worship Indra himself." [34] "That man who even thinks of doing an injury to the king, without doubt meets with grief here and goes to hell hereafter." [35] The state is welcomed by those who wish prosperity and property. Private property is a creation of the state. Through fear of the king the property of the weak is secured: "If the king did not exercise the duty of protection, the strong would forcibly appropriate the possessions of the weak, and if the latter refused to surrender them with ease, their very lives would be taken. Nobody then, with reference to any article in his possession, would be able to say 'This is mine.'" [36] But the *Mahābhārata* is no more sanguine about the purposes of the monarch than is the *Arthaśāstra;* the king's benevolence is the velvet which conceals the mailed fist: "The king should (in the matter of taxes) act like the leech drawing blood mildly. . . . A little by little should be taken from a growing subject and by this means should he be shorn. . . . Acting with care and mildness, he should at last put the reins on them." [37] One of the approved methods to induce subservience is covertly to produce disunion among the people, and then step forward to conciliate the people and bask in the role of peacemaker.[38] By displaying the qualities of truthfulness, sincerity, harmlessness, and love the king will be able to consolidate his empire, fill the treasury, and win supporting friends and allies.

In the fifth century in South India the Tamil author Tiruvaḷḷuvar wrote the *Kural,* a collection of maxims obviously indebted to Kauṭilya's *Arthaśāstra,* although it is more concerned with *vārtā* than with *daṇḍanīti.* Wealth is assumed to be universally desired by men, poverty universally shunned:

> Industry will produce wealth;
> Idleness will drive to poverty.[39]
> Many other sufferings will come in the train,
> Of the painful sufferings of poverty.[40]

[33] *Ibid.*
[34] *Ibid.*
[35] *Ibid.,* 12. 68. As we shall note in Chapter VIII there are modifications of this view in the *Mahābhārata* and under certain conditions revolt is sanctioned.
[36] *Ibid.*
[37] *Ibid.,* 12. 88.
[38] *Ibid.*
[39] *Kural* 62. 6. All quotations from the *Kural* are from the H. A. Popley translation.
[40] *Ibid.,* 105. 5.

Men therefore should leave the non-state condition of primitive anarchy, and, becoming members of the state, share in the five jewels: freedom from disease, wealth, good harvests, happiness, and security from external attack.[41]

The impoverished state of both the public and the private sectors of the economy of India today should not be interpreted to mean that Hinduism has blessed poverty, in spite of the words and actions of no less honored leaders than Mahatma Gandhi and Vinoba Bhave. The *Mahābhārata* teaches no anti-materialistic spirituality; on the contrary it states, "Poverty is a state of sinfulness." [42] The *Panchatantra*, the well-known collection of folk stories of India, which has been accurately described as a *nīti-śāstra*, a textbook of the prudent conduct of life, is even more condemnatory of the life of poverty:

A beggar to the graveyard hied
And there "Friend corpse, arise," he cried;
"One moment lift my heavy weight
Of poverty; for I of late
Grow weary, and desire instead
Your comfort: you are good and dead."
The corpse was silent. He was sure
'Twas better to be dead than poor.[43]

Wealth is praised with equal enthusiasm:

A fangless snake; an elephant
Without an ichor-store;
A man who lacks a cash account—
Are names and nothing more.[44]
The wealthy, though of meanest birth,
Are much respected on the earth:
The poor whose lineage is prized
Like clearest moonlight, are despised.[45]

Some passages may seem to be a bit too enthusiastic:

Money gets you anything,
Gets it in a flash:

41 *Ibid.*, 74. 8.
42 *Mahābhārata* 12. 8.
43 *The Panchatantra*, p. 374. Arthur W. Ryder translation.
44 *Ibid.*, p. 207–208.
45 *Ibid.*, p. 219.

Therefore let the prudent get
Cash, cash, cash.[46]

Kāma, the hedonic component of life, is not neglected. The emotional tone of the *Ṛg Veda,* as we have indicated, is that of hopeful expectancy of benefactions from the gods. This optimistic note is especially prevalent in *mantras* celebrating the joys of the stimulating drink soma: "May I, the wise and devout, enjoy the delicious abundantly honored Soma food, which all gods and mortals, pronouncing sweet, seek to obtain. . . . We drink the Soma, may we become immortal. . . . O Soma, drunk by us, be bliss to our hearts. . . . I praise thee now for exhiliration . . . thou art the bestower of heaven." [47] There are one hundred and twenty hymns in the *Ṛg Veda* which celebrate soma, the divine drink reified as a god. The soma drink was enjoyed by men and gods. Unlike the Greeks, the Hindus did not restrain their hedonic pursuits for fear of divine jealousy of human happiness.

A second evidence of the continuous and pervasive lust for life in Indian culture is found in Indian sculpture. While much of it was destroyed by Muslim invaders who, holding that art must be non-representative, were shocked at the Hindu portrayals of the human body in stone, and especially by the erotic positions depicted in the statues. The sculptural remains indicate without question the enthusiasm with which the early Indians sang, ate, drank, danced, and sported.[48] Nothing in any culture can compare with the wild profusion of living forms cut in stone on the high pointed roofs of South Indian temples and gates to sacred enclosures. The artist in his activity shared in the delight (*līlā*) of cosmic creation, and the spectator was caught up in the same joyous emotions. Even a modern Western tourist in India often feels strangely moved by the vigor of classical works of Indian sculpture and painting, and, although classical Indian music and dance are too foreign for the average Westerner to appreciate, he cannot avoid sensing the great emotion depicted in these art forms.

One of the literary sources which conspicuously depicts the path of pleasure (*puṣti mārga*) is the *Kāma Sūtra* of Vātsyāyana (fourth century A.D.). The life of the gentleman of taste, culture, and ease is out-

[46] *Ibid.* p. 374.

[47] *Ṛg Veda* 8.48.1, 3, 4, 6, 15.

[48] As an example of the attitude Western peoples, even artists, held toward Indian art a hundred years ago, consider these observations made in 1864 by Westmacott, a British archaeologist: "There is no temptation to dwell at length on the sculpture of Hindustan. It affords no assistance in tracing the history of art, and its debased quality deprives it of all interest as a phase of fine art. It must be admitted, however, that the works existing offer very curious subjects of inquiry to the scholar and archaeologist." Quoted by Benjamin Rowland, *The Art and Architecture of India.* London: Penguin Books, 1953, p. 1.

lined in detail. After his morning bath, he perfumes his body with paste and incense, rubs his lips with red juice, sweetens his breath with betel leaves, puts on clean clothes, and adds a flower to his coat. After breakfast, he relaxes in a garden swing. Talking parrots, myna birds, and fighting cocks entertain him. Non-professional artistic activities and visiting with friends and companions fill the morning hours. A nap and social calls are enjoyed in the afternoon. In the evening musicians and dancers entertain him until he is ready to retire to his room where all is prepared for love play with his mistress. Picnics, excursions, drinking parties, group games, and worship in temples add variety to his genteel life. Poetry and drama titilate him according to the eight aesthetic emotions (*rasas*): love, humor, pathos, violence, heroism, fear, loathesomeness, and wonder. The *Kāma Sūtra* is a classic textbook for lovers. This book is easily misunderstood by Westerners. It is not a Rabelaisian guide. It may have been an attempt to deal with the problems and frustrations of marriages of arrangement. The treatise gives concrete directions for the wooing of the young bride after the ceremony. The groom is not to rape his bride, but must win her confidence and affection through playful conversation, gestures, and embraces. The bride is to be enticed into the first kiss by playing a game in which a betel leaf is passed back and forth by use of the lips alone. If all other efforts fail to arouse her desire, the husband is advised to threaten to commit suicide and thus to leave the bride a widow! The *Kāma Sūtra* shows the Indian love of classification; it lists sixty-four arts auxiliary to the joys of love, six classes of signs for lovers, fifteen excellent go-betweens, eight signs which reveal the dawn of love, twelve non-coital forms of embrace, ten kinds of kisses, eight kinds of scratchings, eight types of bitings, eighty-four coital positions,[49] twenty-six kinds of men who are successful with women, thirty-four types of women who are easy prey to men, and seventeen signs that a woman has lost interest in her husband. The *Kāma Sūtra* is an effective repudiation of the claim that the ancient Hindu lived a dreamy existence, pursuing only spiritual, other-worldly goals.

The pleasure most highly praised by the Hindu was heterosexual love. Bhartrihari in praising the joys of embracing a lovely woman says, "The *svarga* (heaven) sung by the scriptures is merely secondary." [50] The *Kural* notes

> Love is more delicate than a flower;
> So few attain its perfect bliss.[51]

[49] Masodhra, a commentator, claims there are 729!
[50] *Śṛngāra Sataka*, Section 23.
[51] *Kural* 129.9.

and adds among other suggestions that playfulness is an essential ingredient of successful love-making:

> Bouderie in love is just like salt;
> Too much of it is like too much salt.[52]

The eroticism evident in Hindu sculptures of the female figure is also present in the following description of feminine beauty from the *Vāsavadattā*, the first romantic novel of India: "She was adorned with a waist which seemed full of sorrow through failure to see her moon-like face that was hidden by the burden of her swelling breasts; which appeared to be filled with weariness from the oppression of the urns of her bosom and the circles of her heavy lips; which had apparently conceived a deep resentment for her massy buttocks; which seemed filled with exhaustion from the restraining hand of the Creator who had compressed it exceedingly; and which had become extremely slender, as if on account of its anxious thought: 'Suppose mine own breasts should fall on me like projections from a height?' "[53] To criticize this description and Indian sculptures of the female shape for not being based on natural anatomy is to miss entirely the motive of the artist. The Indian artist does not depict what he sees; he attempts to show an intuitive grasp of the aesthetic object. His art is based on what the object means to him within his cultural assumptions. The artist does not wish to copy nature, nor does he wish to manifest only personal evaluations. Seldom has art been more integrated with its cultural context than in India. Consider the pride of the citizen of modern India who sees in the national flag the green stripe of *artha*, the growing material upon which all reality and value is based, the white stripe of *dharma*, the purity of devotion to the truth, the saffron stripe of *kāma*, the vigor of joyous participation in life, and superimposed on the three stripes the Wheel of the Law symbolizing the disciplined liberty of man at his best.

When the Hindu today speculates as to the ideal life for man on earth, he is likely to appeal to Vālmīki's description of the halcyon days of the reign of Rāma:

> During his reign no woman became a widow. There was no fear of ferocious animals, and diseases were unheard of. The whole kingdom was free from robbers and thieves. Nobody suffered in any way during his

[52] *Ibid.*, 131. 2.

[53] Louis H. Gray, translator, *Vāsavadattā: A Sanskrit Romance by Subandhu*. Delhi: Motilal Banarsadass, 1962, p. 59. Subandhu lived in the seventh century A.D. A similar description of feminine beauty is found in the *Mahābhārata* 3. 46.

rule and the aged had not to perform funeral rites of the young. At that time everybody was happy and virtuous. Nobody attempted to do any violence to anybody out of their respect and love of Rāma. People lived up to one thousand years and had numerous children. Everyone was healthy and free from disease, and the trees always brought forth fruits and flowers. The god Parjanya rained sufficient rains and the wind blew sweetly. Everyone was pleased with his own trade and followed his own vocation. None spoke falsehood and everybody had an auspicious look.[54]

The third component of the *trivarga* is the moral. *Dharma* is the principle of social restraint brought upon the pursuit of possessions and pleasures. Unbridled seeking of wealth and sensual pleasures would be evil indeed. *Dharma,* which is usually translated duty or obligation, expresses the truth that man is man only in society, that the pursuits of wealth and sensual joys become values only when sought in the framework of the duties inherent in one's station in life. The active life of man must be restrained by his participation in the primary groups.

Rāma, the hero of the *Rāmāyaṇa,* is the paradigm of *dharma.* He is called "Justice incarnate," [55] "Vishnu incarnate," [56] "peerless like Indra," [57] and "the most truthful man on earth, and indeed the best of men." [58] Yet, although Rāma is so correct and so righteous, in my opinion he is not an attractive figure. His faultlessness is marred by his all too obvious awareness of his faultlessness. Even his adoring father advises him to be more humble.[59] He is an obnoxious paragon, who cannot cease reminding others of his sterling moral qualities, and, by comparison, of the lesser virtue of others. A brief résumé of the plot of the *Rāmāyaṇa* may support this unfavorable evaluation of a Hindu cultural hero.

Darsarath, king of Kosala, having no issue, pined for a son to perpetuate his line. At last he performed the Horse Sacrifice (*Aśvamedha*) in order to have a son. Four sons were born to his queens: Rāma to Kausalya, Bharata to Kaikeyi, and the twins, Lakshmana and Satrughna, to Sumitra. In due course of time, King Darsarath named his firstborn as his successor. Kaikeyi, however, played upon her husband's emotions reminding him of his long-standing promise to fulfill any two wishes of hers in gratitude for her nursing him after he had been wounded in battle. Darsarath promised to fulfill what she wanted. Whereupon

[54] *Rāmāyaṇa,* Yuddha Kandam, Chapter 86. All selections from Vālmīki's *Rāmāyaṇa* are taken from the translation of Makhan Lal Sen.
[55] *Rāmāyaṇa,* Bala Kandam, Chapter 21.
[56] *Rāmāyaṇa,* Ayodhya Kandam, Chapter 1.
[57] *Ibid.,* Chapter 2.
[58] *Ibid.*
[59] *Ibid.,* Chapter 3.

Kaikeyi asked, "Instead of installing Rāma on the throne, install Bharata in his place, and let gentle Rāma wearing deer-skin and in matted locks pass his life as a mendicant for fourteen years in the Dandaka forest." [60] King Darsarath, reduced to utter despair, could not bring himself to inform Rāma of this tragic change in plans. When Rāma is informed by Kaikeyi of the exile, he is "not a bit pained at these cruel words." [61] He agrees to bestow the kingdom on Bharata; he will even give away his wife, Sītā. In other words, Rāma, "the best of men," thinks first of the precise observance of law, the keeping of promises, the doing of duties, rather than of the human consequences of his actions. When Lakshmana argues that the king has grown mentally weak, that he has come under the influence of a woman and therefore ought not to be obeyed in this regrettable order, Rāma can only reply that it is always the duty of the son to obey his father. Lakshmana—a much more lovable character—replies, "I hate that religion that has fascinated you so much," [62] and vows that he will fight to win back the kingdom which rightfully belongs to Rāma. To this display of allegiance Rāma can only reply, "I think the best course for me is to obey my father's orders." [63] When his mother, seeing his adamant mental state, vows to follow him wherever he goes, Rāma reveals an even more unlovely aspect of his character: not only does he know with certainty what is his own duty, but also he knows what is the duty of others; therefore he advises his mother, "There is nothing more cruel for a woman than to desert her husband. Don't entertain this odious thought. You should serve father so long as he lives. This is your duty." [64] And so proceeds the "White Knight" of Hinduism throughout the epic, ever faithful to his duties of caste and position, ever committed to the importance of truth-keeping, and ever deficient in sensitivity to the nuances of interpersonal relationships. He even allows the joy of the return of Sītā to be corrupted by listening to gossip rather than believing the words of Sītā. This, again, was due to a basic flaw in the flawless one: his inability to establish empathetic relations with others because of his obsession with the concept of complete obedience to law.

The *dharma*-faithfulness of Rāma is probably both cause and effect of an ancient belief that the man who has carried out his obligations faithfully builds up power by which he is able to accomplish magical

[60] *Ibid.*, Chapter 8.
[61] *Ibid.*, Chapter 11.
[62] *Ibid.*, Chapter 13.
[63] *Ibid.*
[64] *Ibid.*

acts. This, which is called "The Act of Truth" (*satyākriyā*), is probably an extension of the belief in the Vedic gods of natural powers.[65] It was further extended in the "truth force" (*satyāgraha*) of Mahatma Gandhi, which Gandhi thought manifested itself in such diverse forms as harmlessness, vegetarianism, devotion to Indian independence, and celibacy.

The more one examines the extension of the *dharma* component of life, the greater is the difficulty to define it. In the words of one Indologist, *dharma* "refers not only to the whole context of law and custom (religion, usage, ethics, good works, virtue, religious or moral merit, justice, piety, impartiality), but also to the essential nature, character, or quality of the individual, as a result of which his duty, social function, vocation, or moral standard is what it is."[66] *Dharma* is the principle by which *artha* and *kāma* are kept within bounds. It prevents the person from setting up either *artha* or *kāma*, or any combination of *artha* and *kāma*, as the sole end of life. It is the valuational check which brings restraint upon the pursuits of wealth and pleasure, reminding the pursuer that while these do belong in the life of man, they are not ends-in-themselves. But neither is *dharma* an end-in-itself, although the *Rāmāyaṇa* comes dangerously close to presenting *dharma* as the sole value of the ideal life. Rāma is a barren and unattractive character because the principle of "duty for duty's sake" overrules the virtues of charity, compassion, forgiveness, and sympathy in Rāmā's relation to father, mother, brother, and wife. The fundamental teaching of Hindu *sādhana* is that *mokṣa*, not duty, nor pleasure, nor possessions, is the end most worth seeking, and this because freedom is the very essence of man. A man may prosper in his business, he may enjoy a variety of the sensed goods of life, and he may channel these pursuits within the total social responsibilities and obligations that are his, but unless these are subservient and ancillary to the realization of his true nature, he is a betrayer of humanity, an unworthy manifestation of the divine spirit, and a contributor to the total suffering of the universe. The Hindus have expressed the same idea in a different fashion. The Vedics divided the life of man into four periods (*āśramas*), each with a span of approximately twenty-five years. The first is the period of the student, the Brahmacarya. This is the period of learning and making second nature the obligations of temperance, sobriety, chastity, and social service. The second is the householder stage, the Gṛhastha. The householder is the provider for the *artha* of

[65] See Eugene Watson Burlingame, "The Act of Truth (*Saccakiriya*): A Hindu Spell and Its Employment as a Psychic Motif in Hindu Fiction," *Journal of the Royal Asiatic Society of Great Britain and Ireland*, 1917, pp. 439–441.

[66] Zimmer, *The Philosophies of India*, p. 163.

the other three *āśramas*. This pursuit is sometimes said to be the most valuable *āśrama*.[67] Even the gods depend for their sustenance upon the householder.[68] During this period the Hindu is expected to marry and bring forth children to insure the continuation of family and caste. The next stage, the Vānaprastha, is sometimes called the hermit stage, although the connotations of "hermit" do not fit the activities of this period. This is the time to relinquish the cleaving to life and its goods; it is the beginning of an attitude of detachment from worldly possessions. The husband and wife turn over property and business to their children and devote more and more time to the study of and meditation upon the scriptures of Hinduism. The last period of life is the Sannyāsa stage; it is a time to forsake the world as far as the individual self is concerned, but it is not a forsaking of the beings in the world. Rather it is a time of identification with others in the unity of sympathy and love. It may take the form of disinterested service to humanity, or of worship of the chosen deity, or of rigorous study of the central intellectual concepts of Hinduism, or of meditative practices which discipline the emotions and will. It is a freeing of self in order to be Self.

3. THE TWO MEANINGS OF *Moṣka*

Man's chief end is *mokṣa*, spiritual freedom. It is the quest for *mokṣa* which has kept philosophy and religion together in India; philosophy cannot be merely an antisepsis of concepts, and religion cannot be blind devotion to inherited values. *Artha, kāma,* and *dharma* culminate and reach fulfillment in *mokṣa*. *Mokṣa* is the transcendence of the limits which bind mortal human life. Any conceptualization of *mokṣa* is a limitation, and hence a falsification. The term is translated as freedom, liberation, or release, but the word *mokṣa*, like freedom, must do double duty: it combines a negative and a positive connotation. A quotation from the *Muṇḍaka Upaniṣad* illustrates the dual function of *mokṣa*: "Taking as the bow the great weapon of the Upaniṣads, one should place in it the arrow sharpened by meditation. Drawing it with a mind engaged in the contemplation of that (Brahman), O beloved, know that Imperishable Brahman as the target." [69] The arrow is freed from the bow by the archer in order to hit the target. Freedom is freedom *from* and freedom *for*, release and opportunity. This duality is nowhere

[67] *Mahābhārata* 12. 12.
[68] *Ibid.*, 12. 23.
[69] 2. 2. 3. Radhakrishnan translation.

more explicit than in the Vedic prayer, "*From* the unreal . . . *to* the real. *From* darkness . . . *to* light. *From* death . . . *to* immortality."

Those who stress the freedom-from component argue that *mokṣa* is the removal of restraints, keeping hands off, leaving alone, relaxing of controls. Any evaluation of the wise or responsible use of freedom is irrelevant to freedom *per se*. To debate how effectively or efficiently a freed man uses his freedom is to discuss matters which may be of great importance in a study of the psychology of the person, but such considerations have nothing to do with the nature of freedom or the reasons for granting freedom. For example, although a man cannot run a mile in three minutes, or create a fugue, or achieve divinity, it makes perfectly good sense to say that he is free to do so. To limit the term freedom to what a man can do is merely to use the word freedom as a designation for what a man can do. Physical freedom is the removal of physical barriers; moral freedom takes away the restraint of laws and mores; spiritual freedom eliminates the blocks that individuals and groups may place in the path of self-realization. What one does with the physical, moral, or spiritual freedom granted is important to the life of the individual and the groups concerned, but these acts are not inherent in the nature of freedom, and anticipations of what one may do when the restraints are removed ought not to be weighed in the determination of whether or not freedom should be granted.

Those who stress the freedom-for component argue that *mokṣa* is the opportunity and ability to actualize inherent potentialities. To tell a man whose broken arm has been in splints for four weeks that the removal of the splints will free his arm is to mock him—for what can he *do* with his liberated arm? In its emaciated condition he finds that the arm is so weak that it cannot even support itself, to say nothing about using it for lifting or carrying objects. To release a $10,000 automobile on the open market does not give meaningful economic freedom to possess this desirable object to the man who has no money. Allowing a madman to possess lethal weapons is not freedom. Meaningful freedom of speech depends on having something to say, freedom of worship on having an object to worship, freedom of action on being able to act. The use which follows the removal of barriers is an inherent aspect of freedom. Freedom that is not meaningful and responsible is not freedom. A nation that grants freedom of action and movement to its citizens cannot allow them to use that freedom to destroy the nation that granted them the freedom. The use of freedom is an inherent element in freedom.

Freedom-from or negative freedom is possibly easier to understand than is freedom-for or positive freedom; at least freedom-from comes to mind first when one is confronted with the idea of freedom. The removal of all limits—that is freedom! But upon second thought, one realizes that the removal of *all* limits would be to lose rather than to gain freedom. Astronauts who have lived for a few days beyond the normal restraining gravitational forces associated with life on the surface of the earth, experience a marked loss of freedom of movement because they are attempting to move in a free environment. To appeal to the *guṇa* theory of the Sāṅkhya philosophers, movement requires the elements of order (*sattva*), activity (*rajas*), and passivity (*tamas*), whether one moves on the surface of the earth, through water, through air, or even through the stratosphere. Some interpret *mokṣa* only negatively: "*Mokṣa* means release from time and space and causality, it does not mean union or communion with God." [70]

The defenders of negative freedom believe that the defenders of positive freedom destroy freedom by placing extraneous limitations on the expression of freedom; the defenders of positive freedom believe that the defenders of negative freedom, confusing license with freedom, destroy freedom by allowing the free man to destroy the very conditions that made freedom possible. The Hindu has attempted to balance the two positions: the arrow is freed *from* the bow *for* the purpose of hitting the target.

The concept of freedom in Hinduism is sometimes interpreted negatively as the absence of restraint, but it is also thought to be positive, the ability to determine one's own actions, e.g., in *Chāndogya Upaniṣad* 7 the learned Nārada comes to Sanatkumāra, the eternal untutored child, for instruction on the nature of Brahman. The argument of the dialogue is that the childlike virtues of love and purity are of more worth than knowledge of the scriptures in the attaining of self-realization. To Nārada's request for instruction, Sanatkumāra asks that Nārada indicate what he knows in order that he may receive further instruction. Nārada states that he knows the four Vedas, the Purāṇas, grammar, methods of appeasing spirits, mathematics, divination, history, logic, polity, divine science, theology, demonology, politics, astrology, snake-charming, and the fine arts, and that he also knows that what he does know has not enabled him to cross "to the other side of sorrow." To this Sanatkumāra says that this is not surprising, since what he has learned is mere "name," that is, he has mastered only the terms needed to talk about things. Knowledge merely represents objects. He who is limited by words is limited indeed; he cannot know reality. "Is there more than name?" asks Nārada. "Assuredly there is more than name," replies Sanatkumāra, and proceeds to instruct Nārada step by step in the full realization of the

[70] R. C. Zaehner, *Hindu and Muslim Mysticism*, p. 7.

Self as the Brahman: "The Soul (*Ātman*), indeed, is below. The Soul is above. The Soul is to the west. The Soul is to the east. The Soul is to the south. The Soul is to the north. The Soul, indeed, is this whole world."[71] The one who understands this thoroughly is self-ruled (*sva-rāj*); the one who does not understand this is ruled by others (*anya-rājan*). The former has freedom; the latter has no freedom.

Mokṣa as release is inherent in the common Indian term *kliṣṭa*, meaning distressed, wearied, faded, worn out, disordered. In India both the six orthodox philosophies which stem from the Vedas and also the non-Vedic philosophies, Jainism and Buddhism, are primarily motivated by the effort to overcome the impediments to the full life for man. The movement of all Indian philosophy cannot be better indicated in outline than to call attention to the Four Noble Truths of Buddhism: to live is to suffer; suffering has a cause; suffering can be stopped; there is a way to end suffering. Patañjali in his *Yoga Sūtras* says that the aim of his philosophical discipline is "to wear away hindrances (*kleśas*),"[72] and in the following sections lists the five hindrances. The chief hindrance to man's liberation, and the one of which the other four partake, is ignorance (*avidyā*). Ignorance is manifested in four ways: (1) in confusing the temporal and the eternal; (2) in identifying the impure as the pure; (3) in supposing there is joy in evil; (4) in believing that the non-soul (i.e., the body) is the self. The second hindrance is egotism or self-assertion (*asmitā*) which is the failure to distinguish between the psychical power of sensing and the spiritual power or consciousness of sensing. The Hindu, for example, would remind Descartes of the "I" behind the *Cogito;* not "I think, therefore I am," but "I am the being who is aware that I argue 'I think, therefore I am.'" The "I" is not the "I" established by the *Cogito* argument. The third hindrance is desire or lust (*rāga*), the attachment to pleasurable experiences which stand in the way of liberation. The fourth is aversion, hatred, or dislike (*dveṣa*), chiefly those discords arising between persons which set man against man hindering the harmony and peace of society. Finally, there is the attachment or cleaving to life (*abhiniveśa*). This is the blindness which makes man unable to see any life other than this earthly physical and psychical life. It is an unwillingness or inability to envisage a life other than the life of sensation, and hence it is a block to the realization of the fullness which can and should be man's.

Patañjali's five hindrances are suggestive, but they do not give the

[71] *Chāndogya Upaniṣad,* 7. 25. 2. Hume translation.

[72] *Yoga Sūtras* 2. 2. See Chapter 10, Section 3, for a fuller discussion of Patañjali and the *kleśas.* All quotations from the *Yoga Sūtras,* unless otherwise stated, are from the Charles Johnston translation.

whole of the doctrine of release. It is this aspect of *mokṣa* which has prompted many students of Hinduism to conclude that the Hindu takes a negative pessimistic attitude toward human life. Of course, it is true that the concept of the Wheel of Life and Death is a stern view of the human condition. The Wheel is not a squirrel cage which man observes from an external detached position; the correct view of the Wheel is from the surface of the rim to which each is chained so he cannot escape the experience of being crushed at the nadir point of the revolution. But whether man looks at his existence cyclically or in some other fashion, the fact remains that he is mortal—he will die. Sometime after the middle of life there comes to the average person the realization that death is not merely something that happens to others. All men die! I, too, shall die! Is this negative and pessimistic? Or is it an existential awareness of the meaning of being human? There is the possibility that instead of regarding freedom-as-release as a pessimistic view of life, it can be interpreted optimistically: the life of man is such that in order to realize its full flowering all that is needed is that the barriers to realization be removed. Take away the evil, and the good will come into its own. Such an interpretation is as defensible as the pessimistic one.

4. *Mokṣa* AS RELEASE

Rousseau declared that man is born free, but society puts him in chains; Hinduism teaches that man is born in bondage and must seek his freedom.[73] His *summum bonum* is his freedom. All other values are fulfilled in *mokṣa*. Hindu intellectuals are sometimes uncritically rhapsodical in their praise of *mokṣa*, e.g., T. M. P. Mahadevan writes, "It is not that every Indian all the time was a philosopher or a man of the spirit; nor that wealth (*artha*) and pleasure (*kāma*) were not pursued by people in India. But there seems to be something in her very soil and air which makes a man at some stage or other in his life realize the futility of finite ends and seek for righteousness (*dharma*) and therethrough release (*mokṣa*) from finitude." [74] The tendency to derive cultural patterns and social habits from "soil and air" has a long and tragic history. Surely we have a right to expect sounder thinking from modern Indian intellec-

[73] This statement must be modified to allow for the view held by some schools of Hindu philosophy that an enlightened one may choose to return. Such an individual is not born in bondage.

[74] "The Religio-philosophic Culture of India," *The Cultural History of India*, Vol. 1, p. 163.

tuals, since one can scarcely imagine a line of thought more conducive to communal disturbances in the subcontinent than for Hindus to argue that the very soil and air of India determine men to become Hindus! Historical factors, rather than geographical and meteorological, have conditioned the Hindu so he seeks release as a supreme value. But the tracing of these factors is not as important as in an analysis of the nature of *mokṣa* itself. From what does the Hindu seek to be free? The answer is to be found in the Upaniṣads; or, more exactly, the *answers* are found in the Upaniṣads, for no consistent philosophy permeates these works. They are a collection of illuminating writings revealing the Hindu quests for reality, spirituality, integration, and liberation within which are the quests for freedom from death, sorrow, *karma*, desire, fear, change, ignorance, finitude, and evil.

The priestly poets of the *Ṛg Veda* understood the longings of the early Indians for life, and expressed this longing in the prayers for a life of a hundred years—a much shorter period by the way than the idyllic life of heroes in Babylonian and Hebrew cultures. The Upaniṣadic sages shared in these hopes. To each of the four stages of life belonged the satisfactions, puzzles, and sorrows so consuming to those within the stage, so insignificant to those in the other stages. Beyond this earthly life was another life, not different from this one. Death could not possess man; the fear of death should not diminish his joy. He was to be free from death; death did not count; he did not need to "see" it:

> The seer sees not death,
> Nor sickness, nor any distress.
> The seer sees only the All,
> Obtains the All entirely.[75]

But, if the post-mortal life is like this life, does it also end in death? Is that life-beyond-life as mortal as this life? The notion of repeated death or redeath (*punarmṛtyu*) disturbed the Hindu.[76] And so the fear of death remained; indeed, the fear of redeath may have been greater than the fear of death, since it was clouded in more mystery than the terminus of the life now lived. The conception of rebirth arose as a logical consequence of the conception of redeath. If this earthly life terminates in a death which leads to another life, then that life also terminates in a death which leads to still another life. In paths now impossible to re-

[75] *Chāndogya Upaniṣad* 7. 26. 2. Hume translation.
[76] The notion of repeated death may be found in *Bṛhad-Āraṇyaka Upaniṣad* 1. 2. 7; 1. 5. 2; 3. 2. 10; 3. 3. 2.

trace, the doctrine of *saṁsāra* arose, and with *saṁsāra* came the weariness of revolutions on the wheel of birth and death.[77] The later Upaniṣads record the search for a release from the whole cycle of birth and death rather than release from death alone: "Brahman knowers become . . . liberated from the womb," that is, from rebirth itself, affirmed a *ṛṣi*.[78] "By knowing God (*deva*) there is a falling off of all fetters; with distresses destroyed, there is cessation of birth and death." [79] The knower of Brahman "cuts the cords of death";[80] he is "liberated beyond death." [81] The state of no-return, of liberation from the whole cycle of birth and death, is the happy note upon which the *Chāndogya Upaniṣad* ends: "He who according to rule has learned the Veda from the family of a teacher, in time left over from doing work for the teacher; he who, after having come back again, in a home of his own continues Veda-study in a clean place and produces [sons and pupils]; he who has concentrated all his senses upon the Soul (*Ātman*); he who is harmless (*ahiṁsant*) toward all things elsewhere than at holy places—he, indeed, who lives thus throughout his length of life, reaches the Brahman-world and does not return hither again—yea, he does not return hither again." [82] By the time of the formation of the *Bhagavad Gītā* the term *nirvāṇa* was used to designate the state of transcendence of both birth and death. While the term itself does not appear in the Upaniṣads, the idea is there. The term

[77] The following poem by the Bengali poet Ramprasad expresses the weariness of rebirth and redeath. The "six oil men" are the passions: anger, coveteousness, sexual appetite, infatuation, pride, and envy.

> Mother, how often round the Wheel of Being
> Me, like a blindfold ox that grinds the oil,
> Are you to drive? Bound to the log of the world,
> You urge me onward—an incessant toil.
> Six oil men rule me—guilty? Through rebirths
> As bird, even eighty lakhs, and beast that's dumb;
> But, sorely hurt, again, again I come.
> The mother takes the child into her lap,
> When the child, weeping, utters the Mother's name,
> I see this everywhere—excepted I;
> Else sinners pardon, crying "Durga," gain.
> Oh, take this binding from my eyes that I
> May see those Feet which ever banish fear.
> Boundless the evil, the evil children are;
> But who did ever of evil mother hear?
> My hope is Ramprasad, O Mother kind,
> May at your Feet in the end station find.

John Alexander Chapman, *Religious Lyrics of Bengal*, p. 13.

[78] *Śvetāśvatara Upaniṣad* 1. 7. Hume translation.

[79] *Ibid.*, 1. 11. Hume translation.

[80] *Ibid.*, 4. 15. Hume translation.

[81] *Muṇḍaka Upaniṣad* 3. 2. 6. Hume translation.

[82] 8. 15. Hume translation.

Brahman may have held some connotations of this transcendent state; *dharma paramaṃ* (supreme station) is certainly designative of the state.

Although the line of development of *mokṣa* as freedom from death was as we have indicated, freedom from fear of death, to freedom from fear of redeath, to freedom from fear of rebirth, and the great hope was that man could be liberated by reaching a state which transcends both birth and death, still there are passages in the Upaniṣads with a quite different approach. One of these is found in *Kaṭha Upaniṣad* in which death is described as a condiment.[83] Death is the sauce which flavors life! Such a passage supports the claim that the Upaniṣads teach conflicting doctrines.

Slightly different approaches to the problem of death are given in the *Mahābhārata.* In the *Bhagavad Gītā* section of the great epic, Kṛṣṇa assures Arjuna not to hesitate to slay his foes, because the killing of the body does not affect the vital principle which inhabits the body. In the *Udyoga Parva* King Dhṛtarāṣṭra is reported to have asked Sanat-sujata, "I hear that thou art of the opinion that there is no death. Again it is said that the gods and the *asuras* practice ascetic austerities in order to avoid death. Of these two opinions, then, which is true?" [84] Sanat-sujata replies that both are true; there is and there is not death. The notion of death, he says, is the result of ignorance. Therefore the *asuras* within their ignorance fear death; whereas the gods, having attained the knowledge of Brahman, see no death at all. The *ṛṣi* concludes, "Knowing that death arises in this way, he that relies on Knowledge, entertaineth no fear of death. Indeed, as the body is destroyed when brought under the influence of death, so death itself is destroyed when it comes under the influence of Knowledge." [85]

A second element in the negative freedoms of *mokṣa* is freedom from sorrow, suffering, misery, frustration, and the loss of the feeling of significance. An expressive word already noted for the attitudes commonly referred to as sorrow is the word *kleśa* meaning distressed, faded, or worn out. In Buddhism this melancholy of life (*dukkha*) is contrasted to *dukkha-dukkha,* the physical and mental pains for which there are rather obvious cures, e.g., a headache which can be cured by an aspirin is *dukkha-dukkha,* whereas an insight into the fleeting character of the satisfactions of human existence is *dukkha.* The Buddha's existential discovery of the sorrows of sickness, old age, death, and asceticism was strictly within Hinduism. Each of the six orthodox philosophies is initially motivated by the desire to cope with the problem of suffering. The

[83] 2. 25.
[84] *Mahābhārata* 5. 42.
[85] *Ibid.*

Upaniṣads speak often of the desire to be freed from sorrow.[86] Sometimes the desire is expressed to pass through sorrow rather than to be liberated from sorrow, as if the desire is to deal with the inevitable rather than to escape the accidental: "Do you, sir, cause me who am such a one, to cross over to the other side of sorrow" is Nārada's request of Sanatkumāra.[87] Sometimes the sorrows of life are described poetically as "the knots of the heart": ". . . release from all knots [of the heart]." [88] "When all desires that dwell within the human heart are cast away, then a mortal becomes immortal and even here he attains to Brahman. When all the knots that fetter the heart are cut asunder then a mortal becomes immortal." [89] "He verily, who knows Supreme Brahman . . . he crosses over sorrow. He crosses over sin. Liberated from the knots of the heart, he becomes immortal." [90]

Mokṣa also means freedom from all causal factors whether they be thought of as *karma,* retribution, law, fate, or even the gods themselves. The doctrine of *karma* may at first have been appreciated as a form of self-determinism, and hence of freedom, but *karma* also was considered to be a prime cause of the miserable state of the person:

> Like the waves in great rivers, there is no turning back of that which has previously been done. Like the ocean tide, hard to keep back is the approach of one's death. Like a lame man—bound with the fetters made of fruit of good and evil (*sad-asad*); like the condition of one in prison—lacking independence; the condition of one in the realm of death—in a condition of great fear; like one intoxicated with liquor—intoxicated with delusion (*moha*); like one seized by an evil being—rushing hither and thither; like one bitten by a great snake—bitten by objects of sense; like gross darkness—the darkness of passion; like jugglery (*indrajāla*)—consisting in illusion (*māyā-maya*); like a dream—falsely apparent; like the pith of a banana tree—unsubstantial; like an actor—in temporary dress; like a painted scene—falsely delighting the mind.[91]

The ways of knowledge and of devotion became in time methods by which *karma* could be neutralized. *Karma* ceases "when He is seen" affirms the *Muṇḍaka Upaniṣad* [92] in an explicit anticipation of the doctrine of divine grace. The concept of fate appears frequently in the *Mahābhā-*

[86] *Muṇḍaka Upaniṣad* 3. 1. 2; *Bṛhad-Āraṇyaka Upaniṣad* 4. 3. 21; *Śvetāśvatara Upaniṣad* 4. 7.
[87] *Chāndogya Upaniṣad* 7. 1. 3. Hume translation.
[88] *Ibid.,* 7. 26. 2. Hume translation.
[89] *Kaṭha Upaniṣad* 2. 3. 14–15. Radhakrishnan translation.
[90] *Muṇḍaka Upaniṣad* 3. 2. 9. Radhakrishnan translation. See also *Muṇḍaka Upaniṣad* 2. 2. 8.
[91] *Maitrī Upaniṣad* 4. 2. Hume translation.
[92] 2. 2. 8. Hume translation.

rata, but it is usually used by the weak-willed to explain away their own failures. Yudhiṣṭhira explains his inability to refrain from gambling on fate: "It would seem then that some of the most desperate and terrible gamblers always depending upon deceit are there. This whole universe, however, is at the will of its Maker, under the control of Fate. It is not free, O learned one. I do not desire, at the command of king Dhṛtarāṣṭra to engage in gambling." [93] Later when challenged to gamble again, he says, "Summoned, I do not withdraw. This is my established vow. And, O king, Fate is all powerful. We all are under the control of Destiny." [94] Dhṛtarāṣṭra, the foster-father of Yudhiṣṭhira, is even more lavish in appeals to fate as an excuse for inability to control his sons and nephews. After the gambling tragedy, he says, "I did not like this business of gambling, but I think I was made to consent to it drawn by Fate." [95] The whole universe is under the controlling influence of fate, he declares on another occasion;[96] and again, "No creature is able to avert Fate. Indeed, destiny, I think is certain to take its course; individual exertion is futile." [97] The argument that these appeals to fate are made by weak-willed men, thus showing only the weak believe in fate, loses some of its force when we note that even Drupada appeals to fate: "The knot destiny cannot be untied. Nothing in this world is the result of our own acts." [98] Sanjaya [99] and Duryodhana also appeal to fate: "I regard fate as supreme and exertions fruitless." [100] Yet fate was never an overruling concept among the Hindus as it was among the Greeks and the Muslims. A *ṛṣi* in the *Maitrī Upaniṣad* contends that although men rightly worship the gods, they ought to progress beyond the gods as causal agents, and quit themselves of all belief in the gods. The highest and truest theism is atheism. "Agni, Vayu, and Aditya; time—whatever it is—breath and food; Brahmā, Rudra, and Vishnu—some meditate upon one, some upon another. Tell us which one is the best?" [101] asks the inquirer. And the *ṛṣi* replies, "These are, assuredly, the foremost forms of the supreme, the immortal, the bodiless Brahma. . . . Verily, these, which are its foremost forms, one should meditate upon, and praise, but then deny." [102] Only after the individual has liberated himself from causality in all its forms,

[93] *Mahābhārata* 2. 58.
[94] *Ibid.*
[95] *Ibid.*, 3. 9.
[96] *Ibid.*, 3. 57.
[97] *Ibid.*, 4. 40.
[98] *Ibid.*, 1. 200.
[99] *Ibid.*
[100] *Ibid.*, 2. 47.
[101] 4. 5. Hume translation.
[102] *Ibid.*, 4. 6. Hume translation.

including belief in divine determination, can he take his proper place in the world of time and place, of name and form. He must attain an intuition of past-present-future as a whole; otherwise he is swept along by momentary causes and events. The dying Bhīṣma declares, "All that is past, all that is future, and all that is present, I behold as clearly as a fruit placed in my hands." [103] To be free from *karma*, fate, time, and gods is to be a liberated person. In the losing of the determining factors is the gaining of the One Reality, or, in the words of the *Maitrī Upaniṣad*, "But in the universal dissolution he attains the unity of the Person—yea, of the Person." [104]

A fourth liberation-from is liberation from desire. Desire or passion (*rāga*) means any emotion which stands in the way of one's fulfillment of duties. Sometimes the term designates those concerns for the body which consume time and attention which could be more profitably spent on service to others, or on mental pursuits, or in meditative exercises. To be "liberated from the body" means to be the master of the body, rather than its servant:

> By ruling over the eleven-gated citadel
> Of the Unborn, the Un-crooked-minded one,
> One sorrows not.
> But when liberated [from the body], he is liberated indeed.[105]

The perfected person is described again as "shaking off the body (*śarīra*) as the moon releases itself from the mouth of Rāhu." [106] He shifts his anxieties from body to the self: "If a person knows the self as 'I am this,' then wishing what, and for desire of what should he suffer in the body?" [107] He ceases to be filled with self-conceit: "Verily, freedom from desire is like the choicest extract from the choicest treasure. For, a person who is made up of all desires, who has the marks of determination, conception, and self-conceit is bound. Hence, in being the opposite of that, he is liberated." [108] Again, "When are liberated all the desires that lodge in one's heart, then a mortal becomes immortal. Therein he reaches Brahma!" [109]

[103] *Mahābhārata* 12. 39.
[104] 4. 6.
[105] *Kaṭha Upaniṣad* 5. 1. Hume translation. The "eleven-gated citadel" is the human body.
[106] *Chāndogya Upaniṣad* 4. 13. Hume translation. In Indian mythology Rāhu is the dragon who causes an eclipse in trying to swallow the moon.
[107] *Bṛhad-Āraṇyaka Upaniṣad* 4. 4. 12. Radhakrishnan translation. Also *Bṛhad-Āraṇyaka Upaniṣad* 4. 4. 6.
[108] *Maitrī Upaniṣad* 6. 30. Hume translation.
[109] *Bṛhad-Āraṇyaka Upaniṣad* 4. 4. 7. Hume translation. *Kaṭha Upaniṣad* 6. 14.

The *Bhagavad Gītā* stresses the elimination of desire for the accomplishment of results. There are three ways of acting according to Kṛṣṇa: (1) to act with concern for results; (2) to act without concern for results, (3) to refrain from action. Arjuna is advised to act without interest in the fruits of action, i.e., he is to be concerned about the doing of his *dharma*. The liberated man should not evaluate his acts in terms of accomplishment nor in terms of the social recognition he may derive from his action. The value of action is in doing what the situation and one's station requires; the results or non-results and the honor or dishonor that may accompany the act should be regarded as completely inconsequential. This message is offered in many places in the *Gītā*, e.g.:

> On action alone be thy interest,
> Never on its fruits;
> Let not the fruits of action be they motive,
> Nor be thy attachment to inaction.[110]

Freedom from the emotion of fear is stressed in many places in the Upaniṣads: "He who knows that bliss of Brahman fears not at any time;" [111] "beyond desires, free from evil, without fear;" [112] "freed from fear in regard to others as full as in regard to himself;" [113] "The bliss of Brahman he who knows fears not from anything at all." [114] And in Vājñavalkya's teachings to King Janaka on the relations of the self to the body and to the universe, freedom from fear is said to be the culmination of the entire teaching: " 'Verily, Janaka, you have reached fearlessness.' Thus spake Vājñavalkya. Janaka [king] of Videha said, 'May fearlessness come unto you, noble Sir, you who make us to know fearlessness.' " [115]

The Hindu seeks also to be free from change; he seeks liberation from the passing away of things. He knows, of course, that things of time and space are subject to generation and destruction, but he believes that he whose vision is limited to things that come to be and pass away has not yet found Reality. On the other hand, he who sees only stability and fixity fails to recognize the world of change as the manifestation of the eternal Brahman. So those who worship non-becoming and see no reality or value in becoming enter into blind darkness, and those who delight in becoming and do not know that the things that become are rooted and

[110] 2. 47. Edgerton translation.
[111] *Taittirīya Upaniṣad* 2. 4. Radhakrishnan translation.
[112] *Bṛhad-Āraṇyaka Upaniṣad* 4. 3. 21. Hume translation.
[113] *Maitrī Upaniṣad* 6. 30. Radhakrishnan translation.
[114] *Taittrīya Upaniṣad* 2. 9. Hume translation.
[115] *Bṛhad-Āraṇyaka Upaniṣad* 4. 2. 4. Hume translation.

grounded in Brahman enter into an even greater darkness.[116] The Hindu seeks to transcend the becoming in his knowledge of Being, and he seeks to avoid the sterility of Being by full participation in the realm of becoming. Generation and destruction belong in the proper view of the world and man's place in it. The liberated man, the man who knows the Absolute as the substratum of the world of myriad things, comprehends and transcends change in both its creative and destructive forms:

> Becoming (*sambhūti*) and destruction (*vināśa*)—
> He who this pair conjointly knows,
> With destruction passing over death,
> With becoming wins the immortal.[117]

The Upaniṣads record that the liberated man is free from ignorance, doubt, intellectual blindness: "All doubts are cut off." [118] He has reached "the shore beyond ignorance." [119] This, however, should not lead to the assumption that the liberated man is the sage, the man of wisdom, for *mokṣa* is the state of freedom from both ignorance and knowledge. Knowledge here means the discursive knowledge which, limited to the categories of name and form, understands everything within these categories. Such knowledge does not liberate:

> Into blind darkness enter they
> That worship ignorance;
> Into darkness greater than that, as it were, they
> That delight in knowledge.[120]

The path of learning is the path of self-conceit (*an-abhimana*).[121] "Therefore one should stand free from determination, free from conception, free from self-conceit. This is the mark of liberation." [122] The Self cannot be realized by being taught by a teacher, nor by self-instruction: "The Soul is not to be obtained by instruction, nor by intellect, nor by much learning." [123] "Therefore," advises the *Bṛhad-Āraṇyyaka Upaniṣad* "let a Brahman become disgusted with learning and desire to live as a child. When he has become disgusted both with the state of childhood and with learning, then he becomes an ascetic (*muni*). When he

[116] *Īśā Upaniṣad* 12.
[117] *Ibid.*, 14. Hume translation.
[118] *Muṇḍaka Upaniṣad* 2. 2. 8. Hume translation.
[119] *Praśna Upaniṣad* 6. 8. Hume translation.
[120] *Īśā Upaniṣad* 9. Hume translation.
[121] *Maitrī Upaniṣad* 6. 28.
[122] *Ibid.*, 6. 30. Hume translation.
[123] *Muṇḍaka Upaniṣad* 3. 2. 3. Hume translation.

has become disgusted with the non-ascetic state and with the ascetic state, then he becomes a Brahman."[124] The world-rejection of Hinduism has been badly misunderstood by some Western scholars. They should note that the state of world-rejection is attained only *after* experiencing the world in all its flavors. *Mokṣa* follows *artha, kāma,* and *dharma.* The practical heresy of the Buddha was his entrance into the final stage of life before going through the earlier stages. Human life is a precious gift to be lived fully and well; the man who turns from it in disgust before savoring all of it reveals an ignorance of saving knowledge. The liberated man transcends both ignorance and discursive knowledge because he knows them. His world-rejection is not the rejection of an innocent. His knowledge is the outcome of doubts conquered, pleasures tasted, sorrows experienced, love shared, and conceptualization surpassed.

The Hindu seeks to be free from finitude. The removal of finite limits has been variously interpreted within the tradition. For Advaita Vedāntists it is the loss of individuality, of the egoism of the finite self; and for others it may mean the end of isolation and loneliness. *Nāma-rūpa* (name and form) is the term often used to signify the limits of the self conceived bodily or separately:

> As the flowing rivers in the ocean
> Disappear, quitting name and form,
> So the knower, being liberated from name and form,
> Goes into the Heavenly Person, higher than the high.[125]

In the instruction of Śvetaketu by his father, Uddālaka, the son is advised to consider the rivers which flow from the ocean and to the ocean again: "As there they know not 'I am this one,' 'I am that one,' even so, indeed, my dear, all creatures here, though they have come forth from Being, know not, 'We have come forth from Being.'"[126] The enlightened man knows that he has come from Being, and that he is Being. Therefore, he does not claim to be a real individual, save in his relation to Being. His reality is the *Ātman,* the universal Self, not the limited finite self commonly associated with the ego. The self as separate and distinct from Reality is a false conception of the real Self—at least according to the interpretation many give to this crucial passage, although, as we have stated and as we shall present later more fully, the finite self regarded as *māyā* by Advaitins is by other Vedāntists not *māyā* when it is properly related to its Lord.

[124] 3. 5. Hume translation.
[125] *Muṇḍaka Upaniṣad* 3. 2. 8. Hume translation. Also found in *Praśna Upaniṣad* 6. 5.
[126] *Chāndogya Upaniṣad* 6. 10. 1–2. Hume translation.

One comparative observation may be appropriate here: whereas in Greece limitlessness was an untidy concept, productive only of ugliness, unhappiness, and general disvalue, in India the notion of limitlessness is associated with value. *Ananta* (endlessness) is *ānanda* (highest bliss). When all limitations are past and when all attributes are inapplicable, then the Brahman is attained—and the Brahman is *Sat* (being), *Cit* (consciousness), and *Ānanda* (bliss). The high value placed upon the absence of limit is witnessed in many facets of Hindu culture: the detailed sculpturing of temples, the music that seems to go on interminably, the cyclical theory of time, the lack of interest in originations and eschatologies, the open canon of scriptures, the unwillingness to draw sharp lines between animals, men, and gods, and the effort to see conflicting philosophies as compatible *darśanas.*

The last freedom-from of *mokṣa* to be mentioned is release from evil (*pāpa*) or sin (*pāpman*). Again and again the Upaniṣads affirm that the man who realizes Brahman, the man who attains *mokṣa,* is free from evil: "All evils turn back therefrom, for that Brahma-world is freed from evil." [127] "If one knows Brahma as understanding and if he is not heedless thereto, he leaves his sins (*pāpman,* in the body and attains all desires." [128] "He, verily, who knows that supreme Brahma, becomes very Brahma. . . . He crosses over sin." [129] "Shaking off evil, as a horse his hairs . . ." [130] "He, verily, who knows it (i.e., the mystic doctrine) thus, striking off evil, becomes established in the most excellent, endless, heavenly world—yea, he becomes established!" [131] "Brahma is lightning, they say, because of unloosing. Lightning unlooses him from evil who knows this, that Brahma is lightning." [132] The Upaniṣads are not definite as to the means by which the individual is freed from evil, but the many references to fire suggest the concept of sacrifice involving fire as the instrument of cleansing and purgation. "He who knows and reverences this fire thus, repels evil-doing from himself." [133] "So, as the top of a reed laid on a fire would be burned up, even so are burned up all the evils of him who offers the Agnihotra sacrifice knowing it thus." [134] "Evil does not overcome him; he overcomes all evil. Evil does not burn him; he burns all evil. Free from evil, free from impurity, free from doubt, he becomes a Brahman." [135] Sometimes the sun is portrayed as the heavenly fire which

[127] *Ibid.,* 8. 4. 2. Hume translation.
[128] *Taittirīya Upaniṣad* 2. 5. Hume translation.
[129] *Muṇḍaka Upaniṣad* 3. 2. 9. Hume translation.
[130] *Chāndogya Upaniṣad* 8. 13. Hume translation.
[131] *Kena Upaniṣad* 4. 9. Hume translation.
[132] *Bṛhad-Āraṇyaka Upaniṣad* 5. 7. Hume translation.
[133] *Chāndogya Upaniṣad* 4. 13. 2. Hume translation.
[134] *Ibid.,* 5. 24. 3. Hume translation. Perhaps this is an instance of sympathetic magic.
[135] *Bṛhad-Āraṇyaka Upaniṣad* 4. 4. 23. Hume translation.

removes sin; thus in *Kaushītaki Upaniṣad* the worshiper is advised to say in refrain to the sun, "Thou art a snatcher! Snatch my sin!", and the priest pronounces absolution, "Whatever evil one commits by day or night, it snatches away." [136] In one of the late Upaniṣads the "fire" that destroys sin is no longer the fire of the sacrifice nor the fire in the heavens, but the fire of self-denial and discipline (*tapas*); " 'This is the door to Brahma!' says he who becomes free of evil by austerity." [137] The Sanskrit word for person (*puruṣa*) has a most interesting composition in this connection; it is made up of *pūrva* (before) and *uṣ* (burn up). A person is one before whom all that is evil is (or ought to be?) burned up. For example, in the *Bṛhad-Āraṇyaka Upaniṣad* this argument is given for classifying the *Ātman* as a person: "Since before (*pūrva*) all this world he burned up (*uṣ*) all evils, therefore he is a person (*puruṣa*)." [138] This same Upaniṣad also states that the burning process is perfected in the liberated man so that in his own being he burns up evil and becomes purified: "Even so one who knows this, although he commits very much evil, consumes it all and becomes clean and pure, ageless and immortal." [139] This shift from an earlier period in which the evil-consuming agent is external, i.e., the sacrificial fire or the sun, to a later period of development in which the person himself is the consumer of evil, is typical of the movement in Hinduism from the early nature gods to the god within.

A different version of freedom from evil is the view that the liberated man is freed from evil, not in the sense that he is able to avoid the doing of evil or the consequences of evil, but in the sense that for him the distinction between good and evil no longer holds. He transcends all moral distinctions, therefore he does no "evil"—and he does no "good." "He is not followed by good, he is not followed by evil, for then he has passed beyond all sorrows of the heart." [140] "Him [who knows this] these two do not overcome—neither the thought, 'Hence I did wrong,' nor the thought 'Hence I did right.' Verily, he overcomes them both." [141] "There he shakes off his good deeds and his evil deeds . . . This one, devoid of good deeds, devoid of evil deeds, a knower of Brahma, unto very Brahma goes on." [142]

> When a seer sees the brilliant
> Maker, Lord, Person, the Brahma source,

[136] 2. 7. Hume translation.
[137] *Maitrī Upaniṣad* 4. 4. Hume translation.
[138] 1. 4. 1. Hume translation.
[139] *Bṛhad-Āraṇyaka Upaniṣad* 5. 14. 8. Hume translation.
[140] *Ibid.*, 4. 3. 22. Hume translation.
[141] *Ibid.*, 4. 4. 22. Hume translation.
[142] *Kaushītaki Upaniṣad* 1. 4. Hume translation.

Then, being a knower, shaking off good and evil,
He reduces everything to unity in the supreme Imperishable.[143]

But this does not necessarily mean that the liberated man can do no evil, or can do no good, although it has been so interpreted by some Hindus; rather it seems to imply that the values appropriate to the life of the unliberated man do not apply to the liberated man. He makes no distinctions between good and evil; he transcends the moral, not by violation, but by keeping the moral without the effort necessary for the unliberated man. The state of the realization of Brahman is founded upon morality although morality itself is not sufficient!

Not he who has ceased from bad conduct,
Not he who is not tranquil, not he who is not composed,
Not he who is not of peaceful mind
Can obtain Him by intelligence.[144]

What are the evils from which man is to be liberated? The Upaniṣads are not very explicit. In one section the five most evil sorts of people are named: those who steal gold, those who drink intoxicating liquors, those who defile the wife of their *guru*, those who kill a Brahmin, and those who consort with anyone guilty of these evils.[145] The *Dharma-Śāstras* later spelled out the moral aspects of Hinduism in full detail.

The aim of *sādhana* is to liberate man from the imperfections of his own nature physically, intellectually, morally, and spiritually. It seeks both a comprehensive *darśana*, that is, a seeing from the point of view of the whole rather than the part, and a comprehensive *mārga*, that is, a way to fulfill all the possibilities of man. The truth will set men free: free from death, sorrow, *karma*, desire, fear, change, ignorance, finitude, and evil, and free for life, love, joy, wholeness, power, service, realization, knowledge, peace, and immortality.

5. *Moṣka* AS OPPORTUNITY

Man seeks liberation in order to become what he is. The full realization of his nature is the goal of positive freedom. *Mokṣa* is the opportunity to become the Perfected Man, to realize the *Ātman*. A man does not become a superman, or an angel, or a god. He becomes himself. He

[143] *Maitrī Upaniṣad* 4. 18. Hume translation.
[144] *Kaṭha Upaniṣad* 2. 24. Hume translation.
[145] *Chāndogya Upaniṣad* 5. 10. 9–10.

cannot become anything else. No being can live the life of another. He lives his own life, but now it is his. There need be no celestial visitant, no opening skies, no illumination from external realms. There is only an awakening. The dimness of sight and intellect is removed. He "sees" and "knows" the Real, the True, and the Good.

Mokṣa is opportunity as well as release, and to fail to attain positive freedom is to commit suicide (*Ātmahanana*), to be a slayer of the Self.[146] The Self, of course, cannot be slain. To slay the Self means to stifle, to smother, and to suppress the Self by carelessness, inattention, and distraction. The Hindu seeks freedom to seek the Freedom which is his end. *Artha, kāma,* and *dharma* contribute to this goal. *Dharma* especially frees man; it does not bind him. To be free is to be so situated that energies may be exerted in the proper channels. For example, one vast difference between the life of the typical Westerner and the life of the typical Hindu is that whereas the Westerner spends years in finding his lifework, the Hindu follows the pattern of his father; thus the energies and time that might have been wasted in seeking his vocation and social position are channeled by caste and *jāti.*

One of the most beautiful and sensitive descriptions of the pilgrimage of the self to the Self is found in *Bṛhad-Āraṇyaka Upaniṣad* 4. 3–4, a portion described by Deussen, ". . . for richness and warmth [it] is unique in the literature of India, and perhaps in the literature of the world."[147] The dramatic setting is an occasion in which Janaka, king of Vedeha, secures an audience with sage Vājñavalkya, and asks, "What light does a person have to guide him through his earthly journey?" Vājñavalkya replies, "He has the light of the sun." (Such naturalistic replies are typical in Hindu scriptures, perhaps to test the profundity and persistence of the questioner.) But Janaka is not to be appeased with this obvious naturalistic answer. "And what does he have to guide him when the sun is set?" he asks. "The moon," replies the *ṛṣi,* still testing his pupil. Fire and speech are next offered as answers. Then Janaka asks, "But when the sun has set, and the moon has set, and the fire has gone out, and speech is hushed, what light does a person here have?" "The soul is his light, for with the soul as his light one sits, moves around, does his work and returns," says Vājñavalkya, and then he instructs Janaka about the various states of the soul. First, there is the state of dream, when godlike he makes pleasant forms for himself. "I'll give you a thousand cows for that," interrupts the king. The *ṛṣi* continues, describing next the state of deep dreamless sleep when the soul is beyond

[146] See *Īśā Upaniṣad* 3.
[147] Paul Deussen, *The System of the Vedānta,* p. 188.

desires, free from evil and without fear. "I'll give a thousand cows," again Janaka offers, and again the offer is ignored. Next there is the soul at death: "This person frees himself from these limbs just as a mango, or a fig, or a berry releases itself from its bond; and he hastens again, according to the entrance and place of origin, back to life." [148] "A thousand cows," sounds the refrain. Finally, the released soul is described: "when are liberated all the desires that lodge in one's heart, then a mortal becomes immortal." [149] "I will give you, noble sir, a thousand cows," again adds the king. Following this last offer of the king, the *ṛṣi* continues to describe the liberated soul, and adds, "The *Ātman* is unseizable, for it cannot be seized. It is indestructible, for it cannot be destroyed. It is unattached, for it does not attach itself. It is unbound. It does not tremble. It is not injured. . . . One sees the Soul just in the soul. One sees everything as the Soul." [150] At last the king comprehends, and makes his final, and his only acceptable, offer: "I will give myself."

Mokṣa is self-determinism. Man's final growth and his final estate rests on himself. His future is in his hands. His positive liberation is God-realization. "He, verily, who knows that supreme Brahma, becomes very Brahma," sings the *ṛṣi* [151]—a passage which so impressed Anquetil Duperron that he made it the title of his Latin translation of the Upaniṣads: *Quisquis Deum intelligit, Deus fit.* But God-realization is Self-realization. Man is the Self, the Self to be created, the Self to be discovered. Man *is* the Self, yet he must *become* the Self. Until he *knows* who he is, he is less than he is. Nothing less than the fullest realization of his being is required. "We have found a strange footprint on the shores of the unknown. And Lo! it is our own." [152]

The Upaniṣads, like scriptures in other cultures, have much more to say about the losing of earthly pains and sorrows than the gaining of heavenly joys. Nonetheless the state of liberation is depicted as the fulfillment of all goals: "He obtains all worlds and all desires who has found out and who understands that Self." [153] It is a state of joy: "He becomes one who goes beyond [the lower] Brahma, even to the state of supreme divinity above the gods; he obtains a happiness undecaying, unmeasured." [154] "Delight eternal one enjoys." [155] It is a state of peace:

[148] 4. 3. 36. Hume translation.
[149] 4. 4. 7. Hume translation.
[150] 4. 4. 22, 23. Hume translation.
[151] *Muṇḍaka Upaniṣad* 3. 2. 9. Hume translation.
[152] A. S. Eddington, *Space, Time and Gravitation*. Cambridge: The University Press, 1920, p. 201.
[153] *Chāndogya Upaniṣad* 8. 7. 1. Hume translation.
[154] *Maitrī Upaniṣad* 4. 4. Hume translation.
[155] *Ibid.*, 6. 20. Hume translation. Also 6. 34.

"The One who rules over every single source, in whom this whole world comes together and dissolves, The Lord, the blessing-giver, God adorable —by revering Him one goes forever to this peace."[156] It is an immortal state: "Those who know this become immortal."[157] Above all it is a freedom to be free: "By knowing God one is released from all fetters."[158]

"To become Brahman" does not mean to become transformed into a Being different from what we are now; it means to enter fully into an eternal form of freedom. The *Bhagavad Gītā* correctly refers to it as Brahman-*nirvāṇa* (*nirvāṇamayaṃ brahma*).[159] This state of freedom is to be experienced here and now; it is not located in a post-death time, for it is not subject to time. Freedom as goal is no far-off event anticipated after leaving this mortal flesh; it is to be enjoyed in every moment. The term "goal" does not appropriately represent its nature; it is *mārga* as well as goal. *Mokṣa* is present possession as well as future attainment. Realization connotes a quality of living consistent with the desired achieving. A few Hindus have caught the vision of this view of *sādhana* and applied it to education. For example, Ananda Acharya has said, "I am persuaded . . . that the most efficient way of helping the student of soul-philosophy is not to give him any so-called academic philosophy at all, but to confer upon him the privilege of a free hand, and allow him, as it were in his own right, to bring out to his own introspection, and shape and mould, all the hidden forces of logic and light that lie dormant in his own higher nature, needing no interference or compulsion from without, but only a favorable spiritual and ethical stimulus, in the shape of affinity or real friendship with the impersonal individuality of a living, historical, and national culture."[160] Rabindranath Tagore carried into practice the *mārga* of freedom. Remembering his own unhappy experience thirty years earlier in a schoolroom where the world vanished, "giving place to wooden benches and straight walls staring at me with the blank stare of the blind,"[161] he established in 1901 a boys' school near Bolpur in West Bengal where his pupils might learn that the life of man is in harmony with all existence. He named the school Śantiniketan, the abode of peace. Tagore held that "where the eagerness to teach others is too strong, especially in the matter of spiritual life, the result becomes meagre and mixed with untruth."[162] The object of

[156] *Śvetāśvatara Upaniṣad* 4. 11. Hume translation.

[157] *Bṛhad-Āraṇyaka Upaniṣad* 4. 4. 14. Hume translation. Also *Chāndogya Upaniṣad* 8. 6. 6.; *Śvetāśvatara Upaniṣad* 3. 3. 7; *Kaṭha Upaniṣad* 6. 8.

[158] *Śvetāśvatara Upaniṣad* 1. 8. Hume translation. Also 1. 11; 2. 15; 4. 16.

[159] 2. 72; 5. 24, 25, 26.

[160] *Brahmadarsanam*, pp. vii–viii.

[161] *Santiniketan, 1901–1951*. Santiniketan: Visva-Bharati Press, 1951, p. 1.

[162] *Ibid.*, p. 8.

education, he said, is "the freedom of mind which can only be achieved through the path of freedom." [163] To illustrate his theory of education, Tagore enjoyed recounting the following incident:

> I well remember the surprise and annoyance of an experienced headmaster, reputed to be a successful disciplinarian, when he saw one of the boys of my school climbing a tree and choosing a fork of the branches for settling down to his studies. I had to say to him in explanation that "childhood is the only period of life when a civilized man can exercise his choice between the branches of a tree and his drawing-room chair, and should I deprive this boy of that privilege because I, as a grown up man, am barred from it?" What is surprising is to notice the same headmaster's approbation of the boys' studying botany. He believes in an impersonal knowledge of the tree because that is science, but not in a personal experience of it.[164]

Mokṣa is the capstone and summary of the Hindu quest. It is freedom to be and to become, freedom from all that ensnares and entangles man in the confusions and conflicts of life, and freedom to love and enjoy life in all dimensions, here and hereafter. It is the freedom to be free. No limits can be set to this liberation. "In all worlds they possess unlimited freedom." [165] The man of *mokṣa,* the man who has entered Brahman-*nirvāṇa,* is the human paradigm, the ideal of the Perfection of Man.

[163] *Ibid.,* p. 11.
[164] *Ibid.,* pp. 2–3.
[165] *Chāndogya Upaniṣad* 8. 4. 3. Hume translation.

CHAPTER VI

The Ideal of the Perfected Man

1. MAN AND THE WORLD

"The first assertion of soul comes to man with too violent an emphasis upon the separateness from nature, against which it seems ready to carry out a war of extermination," wrote Rabindranath Tagore.[1] While the context of his remark gives no clue, one can assume that the poet had in mind the oldest of the systematic philosophies of India, the Sāṅkhya, with its conception of the spiritual principle (*puruṣa*) and the material principle (*prakṛti*). According to these early philosophers *puruṣa* is so separate from *prakṛti* that it is never aware of the other's existence, and the grand finale of the cosmic evolution is the extermination of *prakṛti*. This dualistic metaphysical system is in striking contrast to the *Ātman*-Brahman doctrine of the Upaniṣads, yet as an orthodox system it is designed to give rational support and explanation to the speculative insights of the *śruti* literature. Its "too violent an emphasis upon the separateness from nature" was corrected in the later Vedāntic philosophies. Tagore also sought to restore man and the world to proper perspective. His life's work was the fulfillment of his petition: "Oh, grant me my prayer that I may never lose the bliss of the touch of the one in the play of the many." [2] But Tagore did not become lost in an immanentism; he sought the one both within and without, both far and near,

[1] *Personality*, p. 94.
[2] *Gitanjali* 63.

both in activity and in passivity. He was fond of quoting the *Īśā Upaniṣad* to support his view:

> It moves. It moves not.
> It is far, and It is near.
> It is within all this,
> And It is outside of all this.[3]

Tagore's seeking for the spiritual in the material is strikingly opposed to that of Hiriyanna, who held that "The final end of the Vedānta, in common with all higher religions, is to transform man into a spiritual being by killing the animal in him." [4]

Man and the physical world are opposed only in the minds of those who do not know who they are and what the world is. The greater the realization of the true nature of man, the less the separation of man and the world, and at the level of the Perfection of Man the essence of man and the essence of totality admit of no fundamental distinction—*Ātman* is Brahman. The hominization of the universe is the goal of both man and the world. In the words of Aurobindo, "Man is there to affirm himself in the universe, that is his first business, but also to evolve and finally to exceed himself: he has to enlarge his partial being into a complete being, his partial consciousness into an integral consciousness; he has to achieve mastery of his environment but also world-union and world-harmony; he has to realise his individuality but also to enlarge it into a cosmic self and a universal and spiritual delight of existence." [5] Hinduism has stated this goal in many ways—theistically, pantheistically, atheistically, naturalistically, monistically, dualistically, personally, and impersonally, by means of knowledge, of works, of psychic discipline, and of grace—but the notion of the infinitude of expansion is the keystone of Hinduism. Without expansion there is no *sādhana*, and without *sādhana* Hinduism becomes merely religious and philosophical talk. Philosophy and science within Hindu culture must always take man into account. The real cannot exclude man. The Hindu scientist does not

[3] *Īśā Upaniṣad* 5. Hume translation. See *Personality*, p. 44, and *The Religion of Man*, p. 118. Tagore wrote in his essay "The Philosophy of Our People" as follows: "The Ishopanishad has strongly asserted that man must wish to live a hundred years and so go on doing his work; for, according to it, the complete truth is in the harmony of the infinite and the finite, the passive ideal of perfection and the active process of its revealment; according to it, he who pursues the knowledge of the infinite as an absolute truth sinks even into a deeper darkness than he who pursues the cult of the finite as complete in itself." *Tagore For You*. Edited by Sisirkumar Ghose. Calcutta: Visva-Bharati, 1966, pp. 19–20.

[4] Mysore Hiriyanna, *Popular Essays in Indian Philosophy*, p. 3.

[5] *The Life Divine*, p. 610.

keep himself out of his subject matter as the Western scientist believes he does, because for him man and the real world are inseparable. Facts and values are not as distinct as the Western scientist believes.[6] *Sat,* as we have already noted, means both being and good. Truth is existential truth, a truth which concerns man's total being. Ontology includes axiology. Any theory of reality which does not cope effectively with the basic problem of human suffering will be ultimately rejected. All science, education, social planning, economics, and politics must come before the bar of human good. Gandhi opposed industrialization because he believed the life of man in his primary relationships would be impoverished by crowding families into slums around factories. The problems of the cities in Europe and America may yet make Western peoples rethink what is ultimately for the good of man in the area of economic growth. Man is not the crown of creation in Hinduism as he is in Judaism (in Hinduism, e.g., he is not admonished to press animals into his servitude); yet man is superior to other beings since he is the being in whom pluralization can be held in check and integration can have its genesis. In his *being* he is a *jīva,* a living being like any animal or plant; but in his *becoming* he is the Perfected One, a status impossible for a mere animal, plant, or god. The goal of self-realization is not a turning inward that cuts off the outward perspective. Inward vision does not necessitate outward ignorance, and exterior knowledge does not require inner blindness. Not only is it "not wisdom to be only wise, and on the inner vision close the eyes," but also it is impossible to separate the two, claim the Upaniṣads. To know the Self is to know the All, and to know the All is to know the Self.

The Hindu is aware of the deceptive appearances of the world. The "snake" in the rope, the "flower" in the sky, the "moon" in the still pool of water are well known to him, and are frequently discussed in his philosophical writings. He is prepared to recognize the difference between the objects of the dream world and the objects of the waking world, and he is willing to admit that the latter are not necessarily the real objects. Indeed, he acknowledges that both the waking world and the dreaming world are *māyā.* But to recognize the *māyā* character of the world does not mean to die to the world; rather it means to see that the world is

[6] Michael Polyani, *Personal Knowledge.* New York and Evanston: Harper and Row, 1958. This book is a well-formulated challenge to this point of view. The author says, "The purpose of this book is to show that complete objectivity as usually attributed to the exact sciences is a delusion and is in fact a false ideal. . . . For as human beings, we must inevitably see the universe from a centre lying within ourselves and speak about it in terms of a human language shaped by the exigencies of human intercourse. Any attempt rigorously to eliminate our human perspective from our picture of the world must lead to absurdity." Pp. 18, 3.

the *māyā* of Brahman. The world is *māyā,* but to describe it as illusory or false is not to tell the whole story. The world is an appearance, but it is a *false* appearance only when man forgets that it is an appearance and takes it for reality. Then its "reality" is false. When the world is seen as an appearance of Brahman, when it is understood as rooted and grounded in Brahman, when it is known as one of the infinite manifestations of Brahman, then it is an appearance *of Reality.* As long as the world is seen as an appearance and that of which it is an appearance is known, it is not a false appearance; it is the Real under the categories of finite human sensation and knowledge. When so seen, it is valued as a help and not as a hindrance to man in his pilgrimage to the Self. The world is the *līlā* of Brahman, the joyous proliferation of the plenitude of Being, the necessary manifestation of the All, the non-telic activity of the Absolute. From the point of view of man the pluralization of Brahman in a space-time world cannot be said to be non-purposive, for only under such conditions can man exist, i.e., man, the being whose essence is to become, can become only in such a world. There is no conception of Manushi Buddhas in Hinduism, no beings who attain the *nirvāṇa* state while in a form other than a human form. Only man can be perfected. Hence, there is "no status superior to that of humanity." [7]

When we consider the importance of the world for the realization of the fullness of man's being and destiny, we are surprised that the natural world is so ill-appreciated in India. There is a strange lack of awareness of the beauty of nature. India has no rich tradition of landscape painting as does China. The mountains are loved, not for their beauty and majesty, but for being the homes of the gods. The Ganges River is not groomed to enhance its beauty; rather its banks are defaced with burning ghats and *dobhi* washings, and its water is polluted with garbage and corpses. Hindu temples are not landscaped with trees, shrubs, lawns, and flowers as are the Buddhist and Shinto temples of Japan. Art in India is theocentric and anthropocentric. How could Indian artists have forgotten that man can become Man only in a world? For all that is great and praiseworthy in the art of India, there are curious lacunae. One is the failure to appreciate the natural world. Another is the peculiar fact that in none of his work in stone did the Indian artist discover stone. He treated stone as wood! At Sanchi the fences of stone are cut to look like wooden rails.

Man is unique among all living beings, for in him the questing which is part of life itself rises to consciousness. Man takes on his own spiritual evolution. In man the thirst to live becomes a thirst for quality of life.

[7] *Mahābhārata* 12. 300.

While Hinduism is a culture in which this quest is in some respects seen at its best, it is also a culture in which sometimes one sees sad evidences of a non-hierarchical evaluation. Gandhi's companions report that they once saw him refuse to remove an ant that was biting his toe because he said the insect deserved his daily food. There is a hierarchy of life in Hinduism and man is the apex of the hierarchy, yet there is not a hierarchy in the sense that all lives are thought worthy to be lived. Fortunately, in modern India few Hindus oppose mosquito control, but unfortunately for the economy of the country, monkeys, rats, and unproductive cows are allowed to take their toll of food which is needed by the human population.

Hinduism does not teach that the life of man in the world can ever be one of uninterrupted bliss. There is no romantic "and they lived happily ever after" to the story of man in India. A myth about Śiva, retold in the *Kumarasambhava* of Kālidāsa, expresses the life of man in the world. Śiva has lost his beloved Sati, and has retired as an ascetic into the Himalayas. Sati, now reborn as Parvati, seeks to win Śiva's affection and love. Kāma, the god of love, attempts to arouse erotic passion in Śiva, but this only angers Śiva, and he kills Kāma. Parvati then engages in *tapas*. Śiva finally notices Parvati, and asks her why she is practicing such dreadful austerities. When he learns that it is Sati reincarnated as Parvati, he joins her in wedlock; but now the basis of their relationship is love plus penance. In other words, love to be all that love should be must be rooted in sorrow and restraint. Joy and pain belong in the self-realized man.

2. MAN AND SOCIETY

Hinduism is sensitive to change and movement in the macrocosmos and in man as a manifestation of Reality, but it is insensitive to the meaning of human history. Indian history was not written by Indians until recent years when the desire arose to write a history counteracting the British interpretation of the life and culture of India. This omission was due in part to the cyclical theory of time. Events that take place in *kalpas* have little chronological significance; they cannot be ordered in a line of progress. The Hindu does not ignore the social aspects of man's life. He always thinks of himself as belonging to a family, a *jāti*, a *varṇa*, a *gotra*, a village. The *dharma* view of human life is the view of social relationships and obligations. But he does not emphasize the obligation to improve the social groups to which he belongs; he must do his duties, pay his debts to benefactors, transmit the ancestral line and lore to the next generation, but he does not expect to improve the pattern or the quality of social life. Conformity rather than melioration has been the social imperative. Gunnar Myrdal has summarized the contemporary situation in India in this forceful manner:

> People's attitudes to work and life, hardened by stagnation, isolation, ignorance and poverty, and underpinned by tradition and often by religion, are frequently found to be inimical to change of any kind. As this book illustrates, the situation varies in regions and communities in the vast realm that is India. But people, even, and not least, the poorest people, often set their sights, not upon individual progress, but upon mere survival, and then they can still less be expected to have the inclination, and the daring, to aim at an intentional, concerted, co-operative effort to remake society. Until this whole system of traditional attitudes has been changed there is a frail basis for democratic planning in the Indian sense.[8]

The Hindu is not unaware of man's sociality. To this day many Indians working in cities send their paychecks to the joint family of their home village. The author recalls conversing with a successful man in Calcutta who had lived in that city for thirty-five years during which time he had married and reared a family, yet home for him was not Calcutta, but the Bengal village where he was born and reared and where the members of his joint family still resided. This man felt no responsibility to improve the economic and social life of Calcutta, because, as he insisted, his real home was his village. Social progress is often a foreign concept for the Hindu. Society is only the environment for the Perfecting of Man. Prime Minister Nehru saw clearly the problem India faced in becoming a modern nation. In many respects he was a tragic figure; he had received a excellent Western education and had caught the enthusiasm of Western economic, social, and political progress, and yet he inherited the mantle of Gandhi, a man who was mainly repelled by Western values. Nehru's public life constantly demanded compromises between his ideals and the realities of Indian life. A man who was fascinated by airplanes was called to lead a nation where the bullock cart is the most extensive means of travel! The symbol of the Congress Party remains to this day a pair of yoked oxen. Nehru in *The Discovery of India* speaks of "the intense individualism of the Indo-Aryans," which, while it led to the production of superior human types giving an idealistic and ethical background to the whole culture and producing an astonishing flowering of civilization and culture chiefly among the upper classes, also led the Indians "to attach little importance to the social

[8] Introduction to Kusum Nair, *Blossoms in the Dust*, p. xiv.

aspect of man, of man's duty to society. For each personal life was divided and fixed up, a bundle of duties and responsibilities within his narrow sphere in the graded hierarchy. He had no duty to, or concept of, society as a whole, and no attempt was made to make him feel his solidarity with it." [9] This individualism or exclusiveness, continues Nehru, "was to grow into a very prison for the mind of our people—not only for the lower castes, who suffered most from it, but for the higher ones also. Throughout our history it was a weakening factor, and one might perhaps say that along with the growth of rigidity in the caste system grew rigidity of mind, and the creative energy of the race faded away." [10] Nehru held that it was India's flaunted tolerance which stood in the path of social progress. The people endured rather than eliminated the traditional burdens which prevented growth and improvement. Thus "only the shell of what used to be so full of life and meaning remained." [11]

Mrs. Kusum Nair, an Indian journalist, traveled extensively in 1958–59 throughout the villages of India to determine the extent to which the peasant communities desire change and a higher standard of living. Her discoveries are not encouraging. "The basic problem, therefore, of how to bring about rapid change in a people's social and economic values within the framework of democratic planning, remains," she concludes.[12] Since independence the villagers have depended on resources and pressures from external agencies for what progress has been achieved and at every new level of induced prosperity there is the danger of stabilization. Her visit to Sevagram, the *āśrama* of Mahatma Gandhi which he designed as a showplace of what could be achieved through his methods, is a dramatic illustration of the current situation in India. She found the cottage of Gandhi, Bapu Kuti, preserved as a silent museum. According to Mrs. Nair a daily prayer meeting is conducted in the compound under the tree Gandhi had planted. A vacant white cushion at the prayer meeting reminds the audience of the absent Bapu. Immediately after the *āśrama* prayers, reports Mrs. Nair, over one hundred outcaste families gather to hold their prayers. They are led in prayer by a Japanese Buddhist priest. These are the outcastes who had followed Dr. Ambedkar into the Buddhist fold, only to find themselves not "ex-untouchables" but "neo-Buddhistic outcastes." Thus, Sevagram, which was to be a model village, "is riven into two hostile blocs, one of caste-Hindus and the other of Buddhists who were previously Harijans. There is complete segregation and social boycott between them. There has been no im-

[9] *The Discovery of India*, p. 61.
[10] *Ibid.*
[11] *Ibid.*, p. 62.
[12] *Blossoms in the Dust*, p. 197.

provement in the status of the Harijans since they embraced a new religion. They continue to be treated as untouchables."[13] The Harijans even refuse to send their children to the *āśrama* school based on Gandhi's famous "basic education," for it condemns the Harijans to remain tillers of the soil. Instead, their children walk four miles away from the village to study in a conventional school. Although Sevagram was nurtured by Gandhi and is now covered by the Community Development program, Mrs. Nair agrees with the villager who told her, "We have made no progress in development work or anything. Our economic condition is very poor; worse than what it used to be."[14] Her own conclusion is: "Obviously, though the 'revolution' came to Sevagram under the personal direction of Gandhi himself, it has proved to be of a wholly transient character. Almost everything that was achieved in the village in Gandhi's time in the social and economic fields is lost already, in less than a decade after his death."[15]

The basic reason for the unprogressive conception of human society in Hinduism is rooted in the fact that *sādhana* is often conceived as perfection of the individual self. Western scholars have not ignored this aspect in their criticism of Hinduism. Schweitzer speaks of "the inactive ethic of perfecting the self alone"; he misses in Hinduism an "active, enthusiastic love of one's neighbour."[16] Renou notes, "Generally speaking, deliverance according to Indian doctrines is always individual, never collective."[17] Hindu leaders have also noticed this deficiency and have attempted to remedy it. Śaṅkara in a puzzling passage suggests a correlation of altruism and psychological egoism, ". . . an agent even when acting for some extrinsic purpose is impelled by an intrinsic motive."[18] Vivekananda turned the Ramakrishna movement from mystical self-contemplation to active social service; Tagore established Śriniketan, the Institute of Rural Reconstruction, as an integral part of his collection of schools at Śantiniketan, and in the last years of his life expressed his opinion that this institution was nearer to his ideals than any other of the complex; and Radhakrishnan, who wrote in 1928, "Self-perception is the aim of religion, but until this aim takes hold of society as a whole, the world is not safe for civilisation and humanity,"[19] although one of the greatest Indian scholars of this century, gave himself unsparingly

[13] *Ibid.*, p. 187.
[14] *Ibid.*
[15] *Ibid.*, pp. 187–188.
[16] *Indian Thought and Its Development*, p. 5.
[17] *The Nature of Hinduism*, p. 75.
[18] *The Vedānta-Sūtras with the Commentary by Śaṅkarāchārya*, 2. 2. 3. 7. Translated by George Thibaut. *The Sacred Books of the East*. Vol. 34, p. 435.
[19] *The Religion We Need*, p. 30.

to the life of his country not only as teacher and educational administrator but also Vice-President and later as President of the nation. But even the thought and activities of these leaders leaves something to be desired. Perhaps it can be indicated by noting a line from Tagore who once wrote, "We have our greatest delight when we realize ourselves in others." [20] But the issue is not the presence or the absence of delight. The question is: Is self-realization *possible* at all except as we realize ourselves in others?

William Theodore de Bary writes, "It will be seen that the system of the four stages of life seeks to resolve the conflict between two ideals, namely, consolidation and progress of society on the one hand and the spiritual emancipation of the individual on the other." [21] But this seems to be a Western sympathetic interpretation. There is no conflict between "two ideals" for there is only one ideal: the ideal of the spiritual emancipation of the individual. Social progress is an ideal for Western man, but not for the Hindu. This, as we have noted previously, is the stumbling block of modern India: her Hindu population has not had the concept of a nation, to say nothing of a community of nations. The redemption of society has not been a viable goal. Society has been only the backdrop for the great cosmic-human event, the Perfection of Man. Those courageous prophetic leaders who have envisaged a beloved community have thought in terms of the *āśrama* ideal—a small utopian retreat—rather than in terms of a frontal attack on the whole of society. Nehru was the great exception, and he throughout his life engaged in an ill-concealed battle against Hinduism. In religious matters he called himself an agnostic, and upon dedicating an atomic research center announced that this center should be the temple of the future. He regarded Śantiniketan as "one of the focal points of Indian culture," [22] and praised Tagore in these words: "More than any other Indian, he has helped to bring into harmony the ideals of the East and the West, and broadened the bases of Indian nationalism." [23] His highest praise of Tagore was that he was a humanist: "Tagore was the great humanist of India." [24] But, unfortunately, these social ideals have not been dominant in Hinduism or in India. Most Hindus have either been woefully deficient in social vision or they have thought in terms of a closely knit community. Keshub Chunder Sen, the "morning star of the Indian renaissance," illustrates this point. His words and acts were often, if not radical, at least far in

[20] *The Religion of Man*, p. 49.
[21] *Sources of Indian Tradition*, p. 220.
[22] *The Discovery of India*, p. 257.
[23] *Ibid.*
[24] *Ibid.*, p. 258.

advance of the times. Yet when he thought of the ideal man in the ideal society, he did not dream of a nationwide social revolution. Instead he thought of a small communistic community. In 1872 he established such a community near Calcutta. This short-lived experiment was like Western counterparts such as Brook Farm, Fruitlands, Amana, and Koinonia, chiefly a haven of safety from an evil society rather than a direct solution of social problems. To this day India is dotted with *āśrama* communities when her real need is to develop a sense of national identity and solidarity.

3. MAN AND GOD

The gods of the Indo-Aryans were the reified powers of natural phenomena: the crashing thunder of the monsoon storms, the heat and light of the sun, the wetness of gentle rains, the darkness of the night, the coolness of the wind from Himalayan peaks. A *deva* was a giver, hence there were *devas* for everything that man believed he received rather than accomplished by his own efforts. There were *devas* of prosperity, health, illness, and death. The *devas* were anthropomorphized, even superanthropomorphized, since they were often equipped with extra legs, arms, heads, and eyes to signify their superhuman capacities. Power was their distinguishing characteristic. They were not essentially moral nor were they markedly good, at least by human standards, although none was fully demonic. Even an angry, ferocious god like Rudra might use his destructive powers to eliminate that which brought harm to man. Because the Vedic deities were not moral agents, the *Ṛg Veda* sometimes encourages human morality without divine sanctions, e.g., benevolence is enjoined in these terms: "The inhospitable man acquires food in vain. I speak the truth—it verily is his death. He cherishes not Aryaman nor a friend; he who eats alone is nothing but a sinner." [25] The gods were not fully personalized; hence the Vedics did not establish close relationships with their gods as did the Semitic tribes with Yahweh or Marduk.

By the time of the formation of the Brāhmaṇas and the Upaniṣads the denotation of *deva* had been enlarged such that anything having power was a *deva*. The charisma itself was the divine essence, and it might be found in a man, an animal, a plant, a river, or even a stone. Brahman the Real could be revered only in the forms of Its manifestation. The gods in the Upaniṣads, and still more in the epics, become the mythopoetic creations symbolic of the foundation of beings. The gods become cultural archetypes. Neither gods nor men denote absolute reality. They

[25] 10. 117. 6.

are both phenomenal. They are experienced reality, not Reality itself. *Ātman*-Brahman is the Real; men and gods are the apparent. "A god is to Brahman as a *jīva* is to *Ātman*" is a proportion which, although not sharp and clear, does suggest the man-god relationship. As a god is revelatory of transcendent Reality, so the essence of a man is revelatory of the immanent Reality. But immanent Reality and transcendent Reality are equivalent—*Ātman* is Brahman. Man and god are two means by which the One Reality is manifested. Man is *Ātman*-Brahman manifested in the realm of space and time; god is *Ātman*-Brahman manifested in the ideal realm of the imagination. But to say that a man is real and a god is ideal is not to say that one *is* and the other *is not*. The order of their being is different. Man is a real being; a god is an ideal being. Man and god are identical in essence, but different in form. Man is real potentiality; a god is ideal fulfillment. Man is to be fulfilled as god is fulfilled, but not like god's fulfillment, for god's fulfillment is a static fulfillment—there are no possibilities in gods. A god is like a perfect circle—perfect in its ideation and in its ideality, but not perfect in its reality. Man is to be perfected beyond god, for he is to be perfected in dynamic reality. The attainment of god-realization is not the ideal goal of human life. Divinization began to be depreciated by the Indo-European tribes even before they reached India, for while still in Iran some of the tribes concluded the *devas* were to regarded no longer as gods, but only as demons. Those who immigrated into the valley of the Indus River were the more conservative *deva*-worshipers, but they also ceased to revere the *devas*. The Upaniṣads are the best evidence of the twilight of the gods. The Self, the *Ātman*, not god, is to be realized, claim the Upaniṣads. The *Ātman* can be realized only by man. According to Śaṅkara, "Deities like Brahmā and Indra taste only a particle of the unlimited Bliss of Brahman and enjoy, in proportion, their shares of that particle." [26]

Are the gods necessary at all? They are not needed for creation, for salvation, for moral ideals, nor for moral sanctions, but they do enrich man's understanding of the world. They dramatize the environment in which the human lot is cast. They inspire man to aspire for ideality. If they are not metaphysical necessities, at least they are axiological assets. Hinduism would be possible without its gods, but it would be much impoverished. The Hindu gods demythologized are symbols of the full realization of man's potentialities. A god may be a symbol of self-realized man. The word "god" is adjectival, not nounal. But there is a subtle and important distinction to be made: man extended and fulfilled is not god but man still. When the essence of man is realized in its fullness, man

[26] *Ātmabodha* 58. Nikhilananda translation.

is god-*like*, divine, deified. Yet in this state he is greater than god; his becoming-being is rich with real possibilities, whereas god's fixed-being is complete in its ideality. Man is to be deified; and the Universe is to be hominized.[27] Man's deification is his fulfillment *as Man*, not his transformation into god, nor his absorption into the great ocean of reality. Tagore saw this clearly and proclaimed it courageously:

> In India, there are those whose endeavour is to merge completely their personal self in an impersonal entity which is without any quality or definition; to reach a condition wherein mind becomes perfectly blank, losing all its activities. . . . Such realization of transcendental consciousness accompanied by a perfect sense of bliss is a time-honored tradition in our country, carrying in it the positive evidence which cannot be denied by any negative argument of refutation. Without disputing its truth I maintain that it may be valuable as a great psychological experience but all the same it is not religion. . . . man is more perfect as a man than where he vanishes in an original indefiniteness.[28]

In Hinduism all theologies, all metaphysics, all cosmologies, must come before the bar of human good. This is the basic humanism of India. This humanism must not be correlated with Western brands, for it is not the claim that man is the only reality; rather it is the claim that human value is an ultimate value. Human value means Brahman most fully represented and presented in the realm of time and space. Brahman remains the ultimate *ānanda*, but under the limitations of time and space Brahman-as-man is the apex of value. This is the realm in which no status is superior to that of humanity.

Man is the possible. That is why the Puraṇas say that the life of man is desired even by the gods of heaven, since it is only through a human incarnation that final liberation can be achieved. The human body is the house of endeavors, a gateway of salvation, says Tulasīdāsa.[29] Tulasīdāsa also says the devotee of Rāma is greater than Rāma.[30] Man is on the mainline to the Self; the gods are on a sidetrack! It is the Self that is to be attained. God-realization is but a poetic metaphor for Self-realization.

> Man is a spirit veiled in the works of energy and moving to self-discovery. He is a soul growing in Nature to self, a divinity and eternal existence, a

[27] "Today human life is not in the hands of nature; world-nature is being subjected to the hand of man." Johannes B. Metz, "Future of Faith in a Hominized World." *Philosophy Today*, Vol. 10, 4/4, Winter, 1966, p. 291.

[28] *The Religion of Man*, pp. 117–118.

[29] Raymond Allchin, *Kavitāvalī*, p. 51.

[30] *Dohāvalī*, verse 3.

> wave of the God-ocean, an inextinguishable spark of the supreme Fire, identical even in reality with the ineffable Transcendence from which he came, greater even than the godheads he worships. . . . To find his real and divine Self, to exceed his outward, apparent, natural self, is the greatness of which he alone of beings is capable. He has the spiritual capacity to pass to a supreme and extraordinary pitch of manhood, and that is the first aim which Indian culture proposed to him, to live no more in the first crude type of an undeveloped humanity . . . but to become a perfected semi-divine man.[31]

The theology of Hinduism has been badly understood by literal-minded Westerners. What can be made of a religion that admits there are no gods, or one god, or thirty-three, or three hundred thirty-three million? How seriously can one regard such numbering when informed that there may be one and a half gods? [32] How can one revere a god that is portrayed with a necklace of human skulls, a belt of human hands, feeding upon a corpse? Such questions reveal a fundamental failure to understand the nature of mythopoetic thinking. The great canon of Hindu religious literature—if an indefinite, ever-growing collection of writings can be called a canon—contains myths, legends, fairy tales, epics, hymns, proverbs, stories, discourses, and teachings of the widest possible variety. There have been no councils, no boards of directors, no censors, no committees, to select or edit these writings. Furthermore in this culture there has been no series of intellectual revolutions such as the ancient Ionian, the Copernican, the Darwinian, the Marxian, and the Freudian to challenge the fundamental assumptions upon which the traditional lore was built. In India is a rich human cultural tradition which until very recent years has been largely untouched by the philosophical, scientific, religious, biological, social, and psychological revolutions which have convulsed the West since the sixth century B.C. India has needed no Descartes or Kant to create one world safe for scientific investigation and another world safe for morality and religion, for she has not experienced the bifurcation of science and religion which marked and marred Western intellectual development. Western man has preserved a rich tradition of poetry, drama, literature, art, and religion and a second rich tradition of science, technology, engineering, and mechanics, and until the middle of the twentieth century he has been able to live a full and abundant life without facing up to the meaning and significance of the value-fact hiatus of his existence. In Hinduism the Westerner can look in upon

[31] Aurobindo, "The Indian Conception of Life," *The Indian Philosophical Congress Silver Jubilee Commemoration Volume*, 1950, p. 174–175.

[32] *Bṛhad-Āraṇyaka Upaniṣad* 3.9.1.

a culture which places higher value on myth than on utility. Here is a people who have not yet lost the ability to listen to the poetic spirit and to find in it more than entertainment, comment, or protest. Poetic truth has not been lost. The symbolic use of language still comes naturally for these people. They are embarrassed by the literal-minded assumptions of Western visitors. The author recalls being shown through a temple by a Hindu friend who carefully explained that Lakṣmī had appeared at this very spot centuries ago. But when a skeptical "Really?" was tossed to the guide, the response was "Well, so we believe." What will happen in India as the factually oriented, critically analytic minds of modern individuals set out to solve the enormous problems of this large nation? One emancipated Hindu in conversation offered the hypothesis that Hinduism in a couple of generations will be kept alive by old women and nostalgic-minded philosophers!

A great mistake in the approach to Indian life and thought made by both native and Western scholars is the assumption that Indian culture is spiritual, ergo religious, and ergo God-intoxicated. But India has far more to teach about man than about God. Humanism, not theism or pantheism, is the message of Hinduism. As Western peoples become more confused about the condition of man and less confident of the good life for man and society, a consideration of the insight of this living five-thousand-year-old culture may be of great value. Max Müller, the Indologist whose enthusiasm sometimes strayed from the accustomed paths of scholarly restraint, spoke more insightfully than perhaps he realized when he expressed his feeling that Western peoples might derive from India "that correction which is wanted in order to make our inner life more perfect, more comprehensive, more universal, in fact, *more truly human.*" [33] Western humanisms—there are many philosophies that assume that approbative title—are usually correlated with naturalism. Humanism in the West might be called an *external* humanism; it has been largely concerned with the outer paraphernalia that make man's life healthy, serene, variegated, exciting, and happy. Humanism in India may be said to be an *internal* humanism; it has been largely concerned with the ideas, emotions, attitudes, and disciplines of man.

4. THE PERFECTED MAN

The ideal of the Perfected Man permeates Hinduism, yet the ideal is nowhere realized in its literature. In the epics, if any place, one would

[33] *India, What Can It Teach Us?*, p. 6. Italics are mine.

expect to find a paradigm of humanity, yet the objective scholar finds moral flaws in the characters of the *Rāmāyaṇa* and the *Mahābhārata:* Rāma is too easily moved by gossip, is stubborn beyond all reason, pontificates on the duty of others, and causes great suffering in order to keep the letter of the foolish words of his father; Sītā is a model of humble obedience to her husband, but she lacks Draupadī's spirited confidence in action; Draupadī, on the other hand, is far too swayed by the emotion of revenge; Yudhiṣṭhira tells a complete lie to bring about the death of his *guru;* Bhīma kills Duryodhana by a foul blow which violates the basic rules of fair fighting; Arjuna kills Bhīṣma, the grandsire of the Kauravas, by shooting him while hiding behind an effeminate warrior with whom Bhīṣma will not fight. Strangely enough, Bhīṣma, chief of the "villainous" Kauravas, comes as close as anyone in either epic to being the Perfected Man. It is he through whom the lengthy moralizing of the *Mahābhārata* is given, yet he renounces marriage and the throne to gratify a whim of his aged father. The curious anti-heroic character of the heroic Pāṇḍavas and the heroic character of some of the Kauravas prompted one Indologist (Adolph Holtzmann) to contend that the original *Mahābhārata* had glorified the Kauravas but was altered, as the figure of Kṛṣṇa became magnified in later centuries.[34]

The non-realization of the ideal is an extremely important fact in Hindu thought. The ideal of Perfection remains an ideal; it is beyond being, but not beyond imagination. Man's potentiality exceeds his actuality. He is never all that he can be; or to state this in a different form, were man to become what he potentially is, he would cease to be man. His being *as man* is his eternal becoming. Man is the being that includes the potentiality of becoming more than his status as man. Man Perfected is more than man. As Kṛṣṇa says,

> Rid of passion, fear, and wrath,
> Made of Me, taking refuge in Me,
> Many by the austerity of knowledge
> Purified, have come to My estate.[35]

If there were a concept of *hybris* in Hinduism, it would not be the overweening pride of man, but the jealousy of gods directed toward man, the being who can attain the divine estate. A god is a god, but a man is more than a man!

The ideal of a superior man (*Uttamapuruṣa,* literally "an excellent spirit") has ethical, metaphysical, and religious aspects which have been

[34] See V. S. Sukthankar, *On the Meaning of the Mahābhārata,* pp. 13–15.
[35] *Bhagavad Gītā* 4. 10. Edgerton translation.

variously emphasized in different periods. In the Vedic period the Perfected Man was the one engaged in prayers and actions pleasing to the gods. Before the time when the ceremonies became so complicated that a professional class was needed to perform them, the head of the family conducted all Vedic rites. With the entrance of professionalism came the notion of absolute correctness of every aspect of the elaborate sacrifices. The Perfected Man was the sacerdotal man. The priest who could perform without error was a "human god." In the Upaniṣadic period the notion of esoteric doctrine was added to the criteria for perfection. The *Uttamapuruṣa* was the wise man who could instruct others in secret learning which would make all that was knowable known and all that was realizable realized. Later in the Puraṇic and epic periods the ideal man was the man mature enough to assume the duties of the tribal assembly (*sabhā*), the man who had undergone the training and received the instruction requisite for leadership in the community, and the man devoted to a god (the *bhakti* man), the man of meditative practices (the *dhyāna* man), and the man whose body and spirit were well disciplined (the *yoga* man). In the *Bhagavad Gītā* the Perfected Man is described as the man of stabilized wisdom (*sthitiprajña*).[36] He is presented by Kṛṣṇa as a man who has overcome the desires of the flesh, who is at peace with himself, who is stoically indifferent to pleasure or pain, good or evil, who has no selfish aims or personal hopes, and who makes no demands of others. This is the man, says Kṛṣṇa, who attains peace.[37] The Perfected Man has been viewed in many different ways by Hindu leaders: for Ramakrishna he is the mystic lost in his adoration of his deity, for Aurobindo the *yogi* proficient in meditation, for Gandhi the Satyāgraha steadfastly loyal to Truth and expressing this loyalty in active participation in social improvement, for Tagore the Supreme Man, "infinite in his essence . . . finite in his manifestation," [38] and for Radhakrishnan the free spirit.[39] In all Indian thinking on Man Perfected says Gokhale, certain postulates are common: "these are that perfection is a moral phenomenon. It is also emotion, intellectual and spiritual. But perfection, though it begins with man turning inward, can find fulfillment only when he turns outward towards the world, and, like a benevolent spirit, uses his moral and spiritual force as an instrument for bringing about desired changes in the world." [40]

There have been attempts to spell out in concrete and simple outline

[36] *Ibid.*, 2. 54.
[37] *Ibid.*, 2. 72.
[38] *The Religion of Man*, p. 118.
[39] Paul Schilpp, *The Philosophy of Radhakrishnan*, pp. 64–65.
[40] *Indian Thought Through the Ages: A Study of Dominant Concepts*, p. 213.

the exact qualities of the Ideal Man. For example, Viśiṣṭādvaita Vedāntism has listed seven qualities: (1) *viveka,* purification of mind resulting from the taking of only pure food; (2) *vimoka,* the leaving of all desires; (3) *abhyāsa,* the ability to contemplate an object without interruption; (4) *kriyā,* the habit of doing one's own duties; (5) *kalyāna,* truth speaking; (6) *anavasāda,* not being disturbed by physical miseries; and (7) *anuddharśa,* satisfaction with one's own condition.[41] But the dry bones of a list fail to convey the image of an attractive figure. Better a Rāma or a Bhīṣma than a catalog of virtues. The Ideal Man concept has been misinterpreted as either legalism or Gnosticism, but it is neither a form of obedience to ceremonial or moral law nor a God-intoxication, a turning from life, a killing of the body, or an other-worldly dreaming. It is an exalted humanism—or better, hominization—which holds before man an ideal for approximation.

The Perfected Man is described both as *videhamukta* and *jīvanmukta.* The former denotes the being who has attained the state of elimination of all *karma* so that there are no causes of another incarnation; the latter denotes the being who is liberated in life. The *jīvanmukta* is free while living. His *mokṣa* is not postponed until death. For him death does not count. This state is adumbrated in Islam as "Dying before you die" and in Christianity as "O death, where is thy victory? O death, where is thy sting?" There are no definite rules for the life of the *jīvanmukta.* Some forsake the active life; some lead a life of useful activity; some are indifferent to the world; some are motivated by sympathy for all creation. In other words, part of the freedom of the free man is the freedom to be himself. He is free because there is no longer a self to bind him. He is conscious only of the *Ātman.* There is no loss of self, only an enlargement. The "I" and the "Thou" are taken up in a comprehensive reality in which nothing is lost. The *jīvanmukta* no longer makes distinctions between himself and the other self. His value distinctions are timeless; his liberation is now, the eternal now. *Mokṣa* is now, for it cannot be at any other time. It is always *now* when *mokṣa* is. Time does not limit nor contain *mokṣa.* It *is* whenever man is ready for it. His liberation is fundamentally a new perspective. Nothing happens, nothing needs to happen, and yet there is a new orientation. He now *sees* what before he merely was. He awakens to who he is. *Ātman* is Brahman.

The belief that the *jīvanmukta* has passed beyond good and evil has been both prized and despised by Hindus. Radhakrishnan praises the concept: "The pure and perfect are laws unto themselves. The imperfect

[41] Rangacharlu Garu, "Visishtadvaitism: What it teaches us." *The Vaishnavite,* Vol. 1, 1898, pp. 69–73.

have to accept laws made by others and recognised by society."[42] Sircar, recognizing the condition and offering no criticism, states that the *jīvanmukta* "has no virtues nor vices, no good nor evil; rights, duties and values are categories that have no meaning for him. He is an onlooker of life and its claims. . . . But no definite law can be laid down how a *jīvanmukta* should behave himself. Theoretically he is open to no influences."[43] Rāmānuja rejects the notion of *jīvanmukti*. Liberation, for him, is the final attainment of an unbroken fellowship with Brahman. The liberated are modes of Brahman, and stand in the relation of fellowship and equality to it.[44] *Mukti* for Rāmānuja is always *videha*. The liberated pass into a state of actual communion with Īśvara, a condition which is not possible before the forsaking of the vital and bodily sheaths of the soul. R. C. Bose severely criticizes the conception of *jīvanmukti*: "The system has proved a refuge of lies to many a hardened sinner. The perplexed minds which have found shelter in its solution of the problem of existence are few indeed, but the number of wicked hearts which have been composed to sleep by the opiate of its false hope, is incalculable."[45] Identification of the hypocrites would be most difficult. In any case Bose's criticism is wide of the mark, because abuse of a system is not necessarily an indictment of the system. What seems to be implicit in the doctrine of *jīvanmukti* is that the person in this state is impervious to the requirements and restrictions of common morality not because he is a violator of this morality but because he keeps it without notice of the sanctions such as fear of punishment, desire for social approval, and pursuit of material gains which control the lives of ordinary men.

A discussion of the Perfected Man is open to serious misunderstandings. One is the problem of putting the state in time, and yet not making it a time-bound state. It is an eternal condition which may be or may not be in time. This is what is meant by the distinction between *jīvanmukti* and *videhamukti*, but this distinction must not be overemphasized. It is rather a way of proclaiming that the Perfected One is indifferent to the presence or absence of the physical conditions of earthly life. The quality of a complete value experience does not depend upon its temporal extension. The limiting conditions of space and time neither aid nor detract from the highest values.

Another misunderstanding is in making a sharp distinction between the Perfected Man as *jīva* and the Perfected Man as *Ātman*. Much of

[42] *Indian Philosophy*, Vol. 1, p. 507.
[43] Mahendranath Sircar, *Comparative Studies in Vedāntism*, p. 271.
[44] See his commentary on *Vedānta Sūtra* 4. 4. 4.
[45] Quoted by W. S. Urquhart, *The Vedānta and Modern Thought*, pp. 174–175.

the language about the Perfected Man necessarily implies that it is the individual man who is perfected, but the Hindu ideal is not the ideal of the Renaissance Man, that is, he is not a monadic individual cut off from social and cosmic contexts. Radhakrishnan, in what can only be explained as a moment of unguarded enthusiasm, once wrote that the aim of Hinduism is to make all men prophets.[46] But a prophet is a man against the group; the prophet sets himself as it were outside his social environment and from this detached point of view levels his criticism upon it. On the other hand, there is also the monistic absorptionist tradition in Hinduism which would identify all Hinduism with Advaita Vedāntism. For example, Miss Heimann writes, "In fully developed Hinduism, no personal survival of liberated man is ever hoped for, nor does Hinduism rely on the constant support of any God-person."[47] Miss Heimann's statement is consistent with her assumption, evident in many essays, that Śaṅkara's Vedānta is "fully developed Hinduism." Her writings would lead to the conclusion that believers in personal survival or in a supporting deity are cases of arrested development! However, the doctrine of the Perfected Man is the view that nothing of value is lost. The true individuality remains; the false distinctions which separate men from each other are seen for what they are. The Universal Man (*Viśvātman*), or the Gnostic Being in the terminology of Aurobindo, does not slough off the matter or the spirit. The Perfected Man finds himself, knows himself, and fulfills himself. He becomes humanized; he learns to empathize with others so that he respects, tolerates, aids, and loves others. He becomes hominized; he becomes the generic man, unable to set himself apart from other men. He becomes divinized; he sees the Godhead in all and embraces God-in-man. He becomes Brahmanized; the gods fade away as he intuits the unity of being and value in Reality.

5. THE PERFECTING MAN

Although a distinction is often made between *jīvanmukti*, salvation within life, and *videhamukti*, salvation after discarding the bonds of bodily existence, a better term for the human ideal, a term which avoids the implications of time, is *Ātmansiddhi*, the perfection of the full potentialities of man. If man's potentialities are finite and temporal, then their perfection must be within the limits of time and space; but

[46] *The Heart of Hindusthan*, p. 22.
[47] *Facets of Indian Thought*, p. 61.

if man's potentialities are infinite and eternal, then perfection cannot be defined within any limits. The latter may be a way of saying that perfection is an ideal never attained, but ever calling forth effort. Perfecting Man, not Perfected Man, is the *telos*. Hinduism is not a Donatism, demanding that man must be perfect in order to be a Hindu; it is concerned with the melioristic direction of man's life, individually and generically. "The individual's aim of perfection is the same as the group's aim of culture, complete, balanced and practical—the realisation of the Universal Self and the Universal Community."[48] That is to say, perfection is to the individual as culture is to the group: a process of becoming rather than a state of being. The individual seeks perfecting as society seeks "culturing." Miss Heimann correctly states the perfectionism of Hinduism:

> This ideal of the final goal of Perfection is a Western postulate, not an Indian one. The West thinks on results, believes in facts which ultimately can be reached and fulfilled. . . . The Western ideal rests in perfection, the fulfillment of a distinct aim which can be accomplished by limitation and selection only. The end, the ideal, is static and changeless in its perfected individuality. By contrast, the Indian is never satisfied with any static end. . . . For him there cannot be a resting-place in a personal perfection, in a distinct single survival. The end of development is for all phenomena a final re-flow into the general receptacle of the "Ocean," the Brahman, the universal reservoir out of which all forms sprang forth and into which all of them, in the end, are reabsorbed.[49]

Mokṣa or *mukti* is a process. Part of the difficulty Westerners have in understanding Hinduism is rooted in the fact that static categories of Western essentialism miss the dynamic character of Indian thought. Hindu soteriology is progressive. Christianity, having rooted its atonement in an historical event, is constantly puzzling as to whether salvation is a reality already accomplished or an invitation to assist in the soteriological process. Hinduism, having no such historical event, has less difficulty in making salvation a process. The life of each man is an evolution, a *pravṛtti mārga*, a path of progress. Schweitzer conceived of ethics as the "maintenance of one's own life at the highest level of becoming more and more perfect in spirit,"[50] yet because of his conviction that Indian thought is "world and life negation," he was unable to perceive the degree to which Hinduism approximated his own definition.

[48] Mukerjee, *The Culture and Art of India*, p. 18.
[49] *Facets of Indian Thought*, pp. 142–143.
[50] *Indian Thought and Its Development*, p. 260.

Hinduism is a pursuit, an endeavor, a striving. According to the *Mahābhārata* it is the "pursuit of Brahman or self-knowledge" that is immortality.[51] This continuous endeavor toward fulfillment is a promise, and, like all ideals, a forever falling short of the goal. This is cause for despair only for those who have been unaccustomed to think of proximate ideals; for those who have held communion with the gods, the ordinary life has been raised to a new dignity, or in the words of a Zen master, the fragrance remains in the robes. Hiriyanna expresses his own conviction thus:

> Some Indian thinkers admit *jīvanmukti,* which means that the goal of life can be reached here on this earth; others do not recognize it and so make it realisable hereafter—in a future existence. If I may conclude by expressing a personal opinion, the question whether the highest value is attainable is not of much consequence. We may grant that it is not finally attained and that man's reach will always exceed his grasp. What really matters is the deliberate choosing of it as the ideal to be pursued, and thereafter making a persistent and continued advance toward it.[52]

The Perfecting Man is a man of forward-looking enthusiasm. The stereotype of the Indian is that of a sleepy lazy individual, e.g., "In the somewhat enervating climate of India . . . human life tended to become recessive physically." [53] In the areas of art, literature, philosophy, and religion the Indians have been very vigorous. Whereas the ancient Greeks advised moderation in all things, "Nothing in excess" being one of the two mottoes sufficiently prized to be placed at the entrance to the temple at Delphi, the Hindus have sought to derive full worth of each idea, each value, each way, by pushing it to what Aurobindo has called "a fine excess." He speaks of "a tendency of the Indian mind which is common in all its activities, the impulse to follow each motive, each specialization of motive even, spiritual, intellectual, ethical, vital, to its extreme point and to sound its utmost possibility." [54] Self-assertion is pushed to dissatisfied regality, self-denial to satisfied nudity. Yet this is not the end, for in the extremes the Hindu seeks for a rule which will result in a measure of harmony and balance. The Buddha is a classical example of this existential dialectic. As a young prince he lived in three palaces, one for each season of the year. A retinue of servants, mistresses, and a doting father were ready to satisfy his desires. When he turned from

[51] 5. 42.
[52] *The Quest for Perfection,* p. 35.
[53] John Noss, *Man's Religions.* Third edition. New York: The Macmillan Company, 1956, p. 464.
[54] *The Renaissance in India,* p. 19.

this way of life, he wrenched the hair from his head, changed his royal robes with the first beggar he met, and finally, according to legends, reduced his diet to a few grains of rice a day. After his enlightenment he established the Middle Way, the way that avoided the extremes of pleasure and asceticism. The Indian makes distinctions only to turn upon them and to deny all distinctions. Again from Aurobindo: "Balance and rhythm, which the Greeks arrived at by self-limitation, India arrived at by its sense of intellectual, ethical and aesthetic order and the synthetic impulse of its mind and life." [55] The life of Keshub Chunder Sen is a good example of "fine excess." Two years before his death he said, "I am partial to the doctrine of enthusiasm. To me a state of being on fire is the state of salvation. . . . Coldness and hell have always been the same to my mind. Around my own life, around the society in which I lived, I always kept burning the flame of enthusiasm." [56] Mozoomder commenting on this says, "The entire society of the Brahmo Samaj was exceedingly fervid in his time. His disciples were distinguished not so much by intellect, as by a certain emotion, by an intense enthusiasm, the best impulses of his nature kept always aglow. He developed ever new occupations for them, he never suffered them to take repose." [57] Swami Vivekananda stimulated his audiences at the Parliament of Religions in Chicago in 1893. Unhappily, the enthusiastic idealism of Tagore, Aurobindo, Vivekananda, and Nehru has touched far too few citizens of the modern state of India. The warning of the *Talmud*, "He that does not increase shall cease. . . . One who is not always striving to improve will come to an end," [58] needs to be sounded throughout the Indian nation.

To end on a somber note about contemporary India does not fairly present the nobility of the ideal of the Perfecting Man. The world is the sport (*līlā*) of Brahman the Blissful (*ānanda*). Man at his best is existentially aware of his Brahman nature. In the *Taittirīya Upaniṣad* the *ṛṣi* in an inspiring passage attempts to state the happiness of the knower of Brahman, but he finds no words adequate to the task:

> Wherefrom words turn back,
> Together with the mind, not having attained—
> The bliss of Brahma he who knows,
> Fears not from anything at all.[59]

[55] *Ibid.*, p. 23.
[56] P. C. Mozoomder, *Keshub Chunder Sen and His Times*, pp. 14–15.
[57] *Ibid.*, p. 16.
[58] Judah Goldin, *The Living Talmud*. New York: The New American Library, p. 67.
[59] 2. 9. Hume translation.

The Perfecting Man is the reality to be attained; the Perfected Man is the ideal to be approximated. The mark of both is the note of joy.[60]

[60] Some scholars have interpreted Hinduism in quite a different fashion from the one presented in this volume. For example, Mrs. Sinclair Stevenson in *The Heart of Jainism*, London: Oxford University Press, 1915, p. 1, writes, "If, therefore we would try reverently and sympathetically to grasp the inner meaning of an Indian faith, we must put aside all thought of the perfectly developed personality which is our ideal, and of the joy and zest that come from progress made and powers exercised, and, turning our thoughts backwards, face for a while another goal, in which death, not life, is the prize, cessation not development the ideal." The explanation that Mrs. Stevenson's view is due to her preoccupation with Jainism is contravened by noting that the excellent Hindu scholar Mysore Hiriyanna says, "the primary aim of Jainism is the perfection of the soul." *Outlines of Indian Philosophy*, p. 173. Some scholars have interpreted Christianity in almost the same fashion in which Hinduism is presented in this volume. For example, F. H. Cleobury in *Christian Rationalism and Philosophical Analysis*, London: James Clarke and Co., 1959, p. 140, writes, "We must postulate, then, that the awareness of God is one which actually realizes the ideal which animates all our intellectual instincts. The rational instinct to seek consistency and unity, and to include ever more data—more facts—within the systematic unity, is, fundamentally, an instinct to expand our awareness to greater similarity with that of God. But we have postulated that exact similarity as between consciousnesses is complete identity. It follows that *if* a rational being *could* bring to completion the task which he sets himself of expanding his knowledge and systematizing it, he would *become* reality—become God. The task of increasing our 'grasp' of truth and reality is not a process of copying something wholly external—it is a process of increasing unity *with* reality. We need not be in the least shocked by this thought. It is not pantheistic; it is quite compatible with orthodox Christianity."

CHAPTER VII

The Way of Thought

1. THE IMPORTANCE OF KNOWLEDGE IN EARLY HINDUISM

"Not without knowledge . . . does anyone find perfection," asserts the *Mahābhārata*.[1] Knowledge of reality is the key to self-realization in Hindu culture. This is what makes Hinduism unique among the cultures of man. No other people, not even the Greeks, placed a higher value on knowledge, or gave it a more central position. Originally the knowledge sought was a name which would give the knower magical power. If the one name, the True Name, of the All could be found, the knower would have power over all that is, both in this life and the next, in this world and all other worlds. Knowledge was power. This was believed long after the earlier magical view ceased to be operative. Even the knowledge sought by the six classical systems of philosophy was more than an intellectual knowing; it was a *mārga* to the realization of man's highest good. Abstract speculation was not incomprehensible to these philosophers. They were aware of the satisfactions of the pure love of knowledge. *Jijñāsa* is the Sanskrit term for this intellectual motivation. However, the philosophers were so man-centered that their quest for knowledge was subordinated to *mumukṣā*, the desire for liberation. Soteriological motivations overrode the purely cognitive motivations. Knowledge was a means to the cessation of suffering, a way to end fear of death, rebirth,

[1] 12. 231.

and redeath, a technique for stepping out of the finite into the infinite, out of time into eternity, a method of moving from darkness into light, from death into immortality, from unreality into reality. The Greeks took an aseptic attitude toward knowledge; knowledge must be clear and precise; there must be no fuzziness, no error, no confusion. For the Hindus, the adequacy of representation of reality was given prior value to exactness of statement and purity of argument. Entertaining a suspicion that reality could not be pigeonholed, they were prepared to accept knowledge that was vague. Since Brahman could not be precisely identified as Being or as Non-Being, they accepted statements about It which were not entirely consistent with each other. A people who placed deep dreamless sleep above the waking experience as the psychological state most likely to convey the nature of reality may not have prized vagueness above clarity, but they acknowledged that clarity might be insufficient. Though willing to admit that reality might be beyond the categories of all thought, they still sought to know what could be known. To describe them as "too human to be logical" [2] may overstate the situation, but it does correctly identify the tendency of Hindu philosophy. Sometimes they expressed the inadequacy of ordinary knowing and ordinary intellectual categories in a paradoxical riddle:

> The blind one found the jewel;
> The one without fingers picked it up;
> The one with no neck put it on;
> And the one with no voice gave it praise.[3]

Even the philosophy of Śaṅkara was not a fully rational metaphysical system. His philosophy was not a "Science of Reality" as Mahadevan has called it,[4] but a "Philosophy of Value" as it has been called by Ram Pratap Singh:

> The one great truth which has escaped the attention of the interpreters of Śaṅkara who have consequently found in his works a system of pure and diluted relationalism is that it is primarily and pre-eminently a Philosophy of Value. . . . Śaṅkara's philosophy concerns itself with the problem of "appearance and reality" only in so far as this is necessary to bring out in bolder relief the value-side of the universe. For Śaṅkara the truth of the universe is constituted by the value it possesses.[5]

[2] William Archer, *India and the Future,* p. 23.
[3] *Taittirīya Āraṇyaka* 1. 11. 5. Quoted by Zimmer, *Philosophies of India,* p. 409.
[4] T. M. P. Mahadevan, *The Philosophy of Advaita,* p. 9.
[5] *The Vedānta of Śaṅkara,* p. 11.

For Śaṅkara truth was truth only if and when it set men free; this is another way of saying, as has been said throughout this study, that Hindu philosophy can only be understood as *sādhana.*

Philosophical speculation in the *Ṛg Veda* is for the most part of a very limited and restrained form. Many of the hymns are good poetry; most are poor philosophy. For centuries these hymns have had no vital part in Hinduism. A few of the hymns can be adapted for use much as the Christian uses the ancient Hebrew psalms: liturgical instruments whose ideas are not to be examined closely. Their meaning is the medium, i.e., the sounds, not the ideas, mold the hearer. This is not surprising, since they are the work of priests rather than seers. The authors were concerned about the human existential response to the semipersonalized powers of nature, not about clear and precise formulation of ideas. In the early Vedas the goal was the securing of the material goods of life. These hymns are not the outpouring of a primitive people; they are the designed product of sophisticated priests to be used in the rites performed for wealthy patrons. Their priestly authors had no intention of cluttering their petitionary ritualistic poetry with profound thought forms. Only in the late Upaniṣads do we find the specific philosophizing mood at work. Most clearly this mood is found in the Hymn of Creation,[6] in its quest for the Reality that was before realities came into being, in its hypothesis that desire was the first seed of being, and in its confession that no one knows for certain—perhaps even the "overseer in the highest heaven" does not know. The bulk of the hymns must have been carefully guarded by the priests as tools of their trade. Presumably all that was required of the patrons for whose benefit the rites were performed was that they bear the expense of the sacrifices.

The *Atharva Veda* is the product of a different strain of Vedic religion. It is the result of sacerdotal tendencies in which the stress was placed on the efficacy of the rite itself rather than upon the charisma of the priests. This movement was a "Protestant" emphasis on the priesthood of all believers. The hymns became magical charms to effect the realization of the plethora of wants of the average man: the healing of a broken bone, the blessing of a first tooth, the growing of hair on a bald pate. Yet this movement does not indicate an irrational trend in Vedic thought, e.g., in *Atharva Veda* 8. 10 almost every stanza ends with the phrase "Who knows thus," meaning that only the person who knows the meaning of the ritual will receive benefits from its observance. The esoteric power of the rite can be released only by knowing the secret word.

The movement from priest to ritual to knowledge culminated in the

[6] *Ṛg Veda* 10. 129.

earliest Upaniṣads. The secret knowledge alone is sufficient to attain the ultimate goals of human striving: "He who knows the Supreme Brahman verily becomes Brahman." [7] "This one, devoid of good deeds, devoid of evil deeds, a knower of Brahma, unto very Brahma goes on." [8] This knowledge does not fit the structure of ordinary knowing, since the Brahman to be "known" is "immediately present and directly perceived." [9] The reality sought is the Self within all things, including the knower. To suggest the immediacy of the Brahman the Upaniṣad identifies it as that which breathes in (*prāṇa*), out (*apāna*), about (*vyāna*), and up (*udāna*); it is the seer of seeing, the hearer of hearing, the thinker of thinking, the understander of understanding.[10] The practical technique recommended is that the seeker of reality pursue *pāṇḍitya* (scholarship, learning, erudition) until the luster wears off and he returns to fundamentals and desires to live as a child. But this is not yet the end of the line. The child is one who has reduced life to its fundamentals, but the child is also one who is caught up in these fundamentals; he does not possess the detachment needed by the true knower. Hence the seeker must turn from the childlike life and take on the life of the *muni*. *Muni*, which is commonly translated ascetic, does not—or need not—designate a holy man who specializes in abuse of the body; a *muni* is an inspired man, a man who has an ecstatic vision. He may become a teaching seer, a hermit who has taken a vow of silence, a laborer for the good of man, or a mystic who enjoys his own vision of Truth. Finally *paṇḍita*, child, and *muni* must all be transcended in order to become a *Brāhmaṇa* (a knower of Brahman). To literalize these as three stages of the process of knowing Brahman would be misleading. They are images to affirm that the knowledge *mārga* lies beyond scholarship, beneath direct experience, and behind ecstasy. Both effort and the giving up of effort must be transcended. Learning and the giving up of learning, immediacy and the rejecting of immediacy, and illumination and the turning from illumination must be experienced and transcended. This is the secret knowledge, the *upaniṣad*. The *jñāna mārga* of the Upaniṣads was a rare jewel which the Hindus once possessed and lost. Later other *mārgas* forced their way into *sādhana* and sometimes crowded out altogether the amazing discovery of the *ṛṣis* that liberation was to be liberated from the liberating techniques themselves.

The *Bhagavad Gītā*, popularly referred to as the layman's Upaniṣad, offers a compromising *sādhana*, although it functions beautifully in its

[7] *Muṇḍaka Upaniṣad* 3. 2. 9. Nikhilananda translation.
[8] *Kaushītaki Upaniṣad* 1. 4. Hume translation.
[9] *Bṛhad-Āraṇyaka Upaniṣad* 3. 4. 1. Hume translation.
[10] *Ibid.*, 3. 4. 1, 2.

scriptural role of offering to each pilgrim that which he wishes to hear and that which will be for his good. In keeping with the lay character of the *Gītā*, liberating and perfecting knowledge is described either as knowledge of God's nature, e.g.,

> My wondrous birth and actions
> Whoso knows thus as they truly are,
> On leaving the body, to rebirth
> He goes not: to me he goes, Arjuna.[11]
>
> At the end of many births
> The man of knowledge resorts to Me.[12]
> Who Me the unborn and beginningless
> Knows, the great lord of the world,
> Undeluded, he among mortals
> Is freed from all evils.[13]

or as knowledge of the separateness of the self and the body, e.g., "Such a man is said to have transcended the gunas." [14] "Brahman does not cause anyone's reward or punishment. Wisdom is prevented by ignorance, and delusion is the result. But, like the sun, knowledge reveals Brahman to those whose ignorance is removed by self-realization." [15]

Jñāna mārga is praised in many passages in the *Śanti Parva*, i.e., Book 12 of the *Mahābhārata*, by the venerable Bhīṣma in his final teachings to the Pāṇḍavas: "No man ever attains to success by means other than the acquisition of knowledge, the practice of penances, the subjugation of the senses, and renunciation of everything." [16]

> I shall expound to thee the two paths. . . . Listen with concentrated attention, O child, to me, as I tell thee the place that is reached by one with the aid of knowledge, and that other place which is reached with the aid of acts. The difference between these two places is as great as the limitless sky. . . . By acts, a living creature is destroyed. By knowledge, however, he becomes emancipated. For this reason, Yogins who behold the other side of the ocean of life never betake themselves to acts. Through acts one is forced to take rebirth, after death, with a body composed of the six and ten ingredients. Through knowledge, however, one becomes transformed into that which is Eternal, Unmanifest, and Immutable.[17]

[11] 4. 9. Edgerton translation.
[12] *Ibid.*, 7. 19. Edgerton translation.
[13] *Ibid.*, 10. 3. Edgerton translation.
[14] *Ibid.*, 14. 25. Lal translation.
[15] *Ibid.*, 5. 16, 17. Lal translation.
[16] 12. 239.
[17] 12. 241.

Bhīṣma in elaborating the advantages of *jñāna mārga* over *karma mārga* says that the path of knowledge leads to the ending of grief and decrepitude, that the state of fulfillment resulting therefrom is one which transcends the states of conscious existence, of pain, and of destruction, and that it is a state in which "they cast equal eyes on everything, become universal friends and devoted to the good of all creatures." The "man of knowledge, without undergoing destruction, remains existent forever." [18]

2. ŚAṄKARA, THE EXPONENT OF *Jñāna Mārga*

The Upaniṣads are the fountainheads of Hindu *sādhana*. They have many common points of view, and they also have many conflicts. This is not surprising, since they were composed by seers over many generations. Inconsistencies made it necessary for an investigation (*mīmāṁsā*) in order that a harmonious view of the teachings might be developed. By selection and isolation two systems were devised, one concerned chiefly with ritual, the other with metaphysics. These are known as Pūrva Mīmāṁsā, the *karma mārga* aspects of *sādhana*, and Uttara Mīmāṁsā, the *jñāna mārga* aspects of *sādhana*. According to Hindu legend, Jaimini was the author of the first, Bādarāyaṇa the author of the second. A second reason for the appearance of these interpretations was the nature of the Upaniṣads as speculations. They are insightful and doctrinaire rather than logical and discursive. They are largely conclusions for application to life, rather than hypotheses supported by evidence and reason. They are not irrational but transrational, in the sense that their propositions often lie beyond that which is dialectically defensible. They are *śruti*, revelatory, rather than argumentative. In India, as elsewhere, men have not been willing to leave untouched the irrational, the non-rational, or even the transrational. Bādarāyaṇa, known as The Arranger (*vyāsa*), lived in either the third or fourth century A.D. He was one of the best of the systematizers, and in time his *Brahma Sūtras* (or *Vedānta Sūtras*) replaced all others as the accepted rational interpretation of the Upaniṣads. His work, which was in fact the culmination of Vedic thought, became the basis for much of the philosophical development of Hindu *sādhana*. These *sūtras* were to thought as the Brāhmaṇas were to ritual. All contributions to *jñāna mārga* had to take Bādarāyaṇa into account.

Bādarāyaṇa placed premium value on conciseness. He is said to have

[18] *Ibid.*

rejoiced more in the elimination of a word than in the birth of a son! The *sūtras* of Bādarāyaṇa are intellectual shorthand *par excellence*. Confucius's *Analects* are verbose by comparison. These aphorisms are so skeletal that they can be made intelligible only with commentaries. Perhaps they were designed as mnemonic devices for students who memorized the teaching rather than as actual outlines of the teaching, that is, as reminders for those who knew, not as instructional tools for the uninformed. Philosophy as reasoned argument had at last entered Hindu culture. The four Vedas (*Ṛg, Yajūr, Sāma,* and *Atharva*), each with its four sections (Saṁhitas, Brāhmaṇas, Āraṇyakas, and Upaniṣads), had attained scriptural authority. Next the *Brahma Sūtras* challenged scholars in ancient India to supply argumentative content to the bare bones of the *jñāna mārga* rooted in the Upaniṣads. The commentators took a scholastic attitude toward the Vedas as a whole, particularly toward the *Brahma Sūtras* as the summary of Vedic thought. Yet this approach did not stifle originality of thought. For one thousand years, from Śaṅkara (ninth century) to Baladeva (eighteenth century) commentaries on the Upaniṣads, the *Bhagavad Gītā,* and the *Brahma Sūtras* constituted the bulk of the work in philosophy. Śaṅkara, the first commentator, was also the greatest. His presentation of *jñāna mārga* remains to this day the classic presentation, and he continues to have more followers than any other. Some scholars have estimated that at least seventy-five percent of the Hindu philosophers in India today are Advaita Vedāntins, i.e., followers of Śaṅkara.[19] The system of Śaṅkara is unquestionably one of the grandest, if not *the* grandest, of all Hindu intellectual creations, yet it is a serious mistake, frequently committed, to consider all Hindu philosophy as Advaita Vedāntism. This propensity must have originated among the followers of Śaṅkara a few generations after his life, if we can judge from the emotional outbursts of Rāmānuja against Śaṅkara and his disciples. To this day it is not unusual for scholars to refer to Advaitism as "the Summum of all Hindu thought." [20]

Although Indologists agree in assigning precise dates for the life of Śaṅkara (788–820) his life remains "mostly a bundle of historically unverifiable legends." [21] He was the founder of a Neo-Vedāntic movement directed chiefly at Buddhism, a movement which continued with vigor in India for at least two centuries after his death. Śaṅkara set for himself the task of defeating Buddhism on its own chosen grounds in a concen-

[19] Richard Garbe, "Vedānta," *Encyclopedia of Religion and Ethics,* edited by Hastings, Vol. 12, p. 597.

[20] E.g., Heimann, *Facets of Indian Thought,* pp. 69 (footnote 1), 141, 142, 143.

[21] Sukumar Datta, "Monasticism in India," *The Cultural History of India,* Vol. 2, p. 592.

trated back-to-Brahmanism movement. During his short life he attempted to stem Buddhism on two fronts, the practical and the theoretical.

Śaṅkara's battle with Buddhism on the practical front took the form of establishing four monasteries (*maṭhas*) in the four corners of India: Joṣī Maṭha in the Himalayas, Sṛṅgerī Maṭha in Mysore, Sārada Maṭha in Gujarat, and Govardhana Maṭha in Orissa. These were surely established to overcome the influence of the highly successful Buddhistic monasteries. This innovation must be understood within an ancient Hindu tradition of the spiritual aspirant passing from the state of living in a joint family into a state of homelessness (*āgārasmā anāgārīyam*). It was a relaxation of ties with the primary group, although not necessarily a break with broader human ties. For some Hindus the joint family had been interpreted as the training ground for the wider relationships which finally culminated in the existential condition of seeing all living forms as one, as *Ātman-Brahman,* although for others it was "a flight of the alone to the Alone." The tradition of the homeless wanderer (*parivrājakas*) was at first shared by Hinduism and its prodigal offspring, Buddhism. The wanderer was known as the *sannyāsin* (one who casts off home and worldly life), or as the *śramana* (one who toils for spiritual life), or as the *bhikṣu* (one who lives on alms). The founder of Buddhism lived the wandering life after breaking from his family. But within Buddhism there also developed another practice: the coming together of the wanderers at fixed places at the time of the monsoons when travel was difficult. From this annual congregating developed the practice of coenobium, a settled life together throughout the year. Some of these monasteries became famous for the high quality of the lives of the monks, and under the patronage of the Gupta emperors (320–500) they developed into centers of instruction in Buddhist doctrines. A university system thus came into being. The largest and best of these was at Nālandā in northeast India. Students came to Nālandā from all parts of India as well as from China and other neighboring countries. Buddhism was established in Tibet in the seventh century by Tibetans who had studied at Nālandā. In its heyday the university had ten thousand students studying under a well organized program of both group and independent studies. Śaṅkara established his four *maṭhas* in an effort to head off the tide of Buddhism by means of a Neo-Vedāntic revival. The establishment of additional Buddhist universities in northeast India, such as those at Odantapura and Vikramaśīla, may have been an effort on the part of the Buddhists to counter reviving Hinduism. The Hindu-Buddhist conflict ended with the Muslim invasions in the tenth and eleventh centuries. Hindus and Buddhists were unable to unite against the common enemy, and Buddhism ceased to be a major influence in India.

Śaṅkara's battle with Buddhism on the theoretical front was an effort to defend *jñāna mārga* as a complete *mārga,* one far more effective than the path of enlightenment outlined in Buddhism. To designate the disputes as battles is not to overstate the case, for the followers of the schools often met in actual debates in which all the techniques and tricks of public persuasion were used to silence opponents and to build prestige for one's self and one's school.

> If a Buddhist for example could defeat a great Nyāya or Mīmāṁsā thinker in a great public debate attended by many learned scholars from different parts of the country, his fame at once spread all over the country and he could probably secure a large number of followers on the spot. Extensive tours of disputation were often undertaken by great masters all over the country for the purpose of defeating the teachers of the opposite schools and of securing adherents of one's own.[22]

Thus it is not surprising to find emotionally toned words in the writings of Śaṅkara and his opponents.

A second reason for the bellicose nature of Śaṅkara's writings is that he was caught between the realism of the Hindu philosophers who affirmed the reality of the individual self and the external world and the idealism of the Buddhists who denied a real self and a real world. Śaṅkara was disturbed to find himself criticized by orthodox Hindus as too sympathetic to Buddhism, if not in fact a Buddhist. Śaṅkara, therefore, had to explain carefully that he did not share with Buddhism the concept of the world as a phenomenal structure of "point-instants," that the self and the world were real because they are rooted in the Brahman, the Reality behind all mental and material phenomena, and that they were ideal in the sense that as phenomena *per se* they are *māyā.*

A third area of conflict between Śaṅkara and the Buddhists, an area both practical and theoretical, had to do with the *mārga* which would lead to *mokṣa.* The *mārga* of Buddhism was primarily a transformation of the will. Enlightenment (*bodhi*) followed a realistic handling of desire (*tṛṣṇā*) and cleaving (*upādāna*). According to Buddhism by getting rid of the cleaving or clinging to the objects of desire one could enjoy the pleasures of life and finally attain *nirvāṇa,* a state in which desires have been extinguished; but according to Śaṅkara *mokṣa* could be attained only through *jñāna mārga,* the knowledge of one's perfect identity with Brahman. When this knowledge is acquired, the individual becomes a *jīvanmukta,* one liberated through living in the world, and at physical death is completely merged into the Brahman. But once again

[22] Surendra Nath Dasgupta, *A History of Indian Philosophy,* Vol. 1, p. 406.

the conflict was particularly fierce because of the similarity of the points of view. The Buddhists approached *mārga* from the volitional aspect, and Śaṅkara from the cognitive aspect, yet the *mārga* of the Buddhists was a volition which includes knowing, and the *mārga* of *Śaṅkara* was a knowing that is self-awareness rather than a subject-object form of knowing. In religion and philosophy the worst battles are fought between supporters of similar theories!

The theories of Śaṅkara have, as we have already indicated, won the approval of a majority of the philosophers of India, and they have also aroused sharp opposition. Rāmānuja, who lived two centuries after Śaṅkara, consistently refers to Śaṅkara as "our opponent." His commentary on the *Brahma Sūtras* offers as an opening evaluation of Śaṅkara's philosophy:

> The entire theory rests on a fictitious foundation of altogether hollow and vicious arguments, incapable of being stated in definite logical alternatives. . . . The theory therefore must needs be rejected by all those who, through texts, perception, and the other means of knowledge—assisted by sound reasoning—have an insight into the true nature of things.[23]

Even in the twentieth century emotional opposition continues; for example, a leader of the *Śaiva Siddhanta* school in South India is reported to have said, "I would rather see all India become Christian than that it should fall a prey to the Vedānta of Śaṅkara.[24]

The times in which he lived forced Śaṅkara to be combative. Not only did he wage a battle against the Buddhists, but also he had to defend his views against those who wanted to develop joint *mārgas*, a *jñāna-karma mārga* or a *jñāna-bhakti mārga. Sūtras* 3. 4. 25 and 26 of the *Brahma Sūtras* forced Śaṅkara to clarify his position on knowledge and works as ways of liberation, for they seem to take different stands on the importance of works: "For this very reason there is no need of the lighting of fires and so on." [25] "And there is need of all (works), on account of the scriptural statement of sacrifices and the like: as in the case of the horse." [26] In commenting on the first *sūtra* Śaṅkara writes ". . . the lighting of the sacrificial fire and similar works which are enjoined on the different āśramas are not to be observed, since man's purpose is effected

[23] *The Vedānta-Sūtras with the Commentary of Rāmānuga. The Sacred Books of the East*, Vol. 48, p. 39.

[24] "*Ich sähe lieber, Indien würde christlich, als dass es dem Vedānta des Çamkara zur Beute fiele.*" H. W. Schomerus, *Der Çaiva-Siddhanta eine Mystik Indiens*, p. 20.

[25] *The Brahma Sūtras* 3. 4. 25. Radhakrishnan translation.

[26] *Ibid.*, 3. 4. 26. Radhakrishnan translation.

through knowledge."[27] And in commenting on the second *sūtra* he writes, "Under the preceding Sūtra we have arrived at the conclusion that as knowledge effects its own end the works enjoined on the āśramas are absolutely not required. With reference to this point the present Sūtra now remarks that knowledge has regard for all works enjoined on the āśramas, and that there is not absolute non-regard."[28] Yet he does not find a contradiction between the two *sūtras*. Works are useful as means to knowledge; they do not produce liberation. Liberation comes only from knowledge, but works may be needed to produce the knowledge which in turn will produce the liberation. So, indirectly, works are productive of liberation. In the words of Śaṅkara: "Knowledge having once sprung up requires no help toward the accomplishment of its fruit, but it does stand in need of something else with a view to its own origination."[29] Works may serve as a purifying agent: "Works are the cleansing away of uncleanliness, but knowledge is the highest way. When the impurity has been removed by works, then knowledge begins to act."[30] *Mokṣa* is not something that can be *attained*. Ignorance disappears, and *mokṣa* is. But Śaṅkara is not adverse to admitting that through effort one may put himself into the condition in which *mokṣa* may be. Moral acts and religious rites may lead to many good things, e.g., earthly prosperity and heavenly bliss, but they do not lead to liberation. Śaṅkara will not accept a combination of *karma mārga* and *jñāna mārga*, nor will he allow that a previous study of Pūrva Mīmāṁsā is necessary or valuable as preliminary to Uttara Mīmāṁsa. Saving knowledge is not a matter of faith; it is the result of inquiry. Why must an effort be made to know Brahman? Is not Brahman known without effort, since Brahman is one's self? The answer is that Brahman must be known through a *mārga*, i.e., through a discipline or effort, because each thinks he knows the self. Each in his ignorance thinks the body, or the mind, or the sense organs is the self. This "knowledge," which is in fact ignorance, must be removed. The self as knower attempts to know the self as an object, and this is impossible, for the self is essentially subject. As long as the self insists on imposing objective attributes upon the subject it remains ignorant of the self. But the effort needed is not a trying harder to know; it is the making of a clear distinction between the self and the non-self. Non-discrimination between the self and the non-self is *avidyā* which masquerades as *vidyā*. Śaṅkara rejects *karma mārga* because he rejects the notion of a

[27] *The Vedānta-Sūtras with the Commentary by Śaṅkarācārya. The Sacred Books of the East*, Vol. 38, p. 306.
[28] *Ibid.*, pp. 306–307.
[29] *Ibid.*, p. 307.
[30] *Ibid.*

gradual liberation (*krama-mukti*), as if one might be one-third or one-half liberated. Yet implicit in *karma mārga* is the notion of step-by-step movement toward the goal of *mokṣa* or away from self-deception. Śaṅkara is committed to the notion of instantaneous liberation (*sadya-mukti*), although he does grant that there are gradations of steps toward the condition in which liberation is. The notion of an evolutionary process of liberating is a Sāṅkhya view, not shared by Śaṅkara. To bring the aspirant to the level where self-knowing is possible Śaṅkara grants that ceremonial and domestic duties, worship and prayer, may be helpful, but when the highest knowledge has arisen all such *dharmas* and *karmas* are unnecessary.[31]

As illustrative of the manner in which Śaṅkara worked the magic of his interpretation to disclose *jñāna mārga* where it might not be expected to be found, let us follow his treatment of *jñāna mārga* in the *Bhagavad Gītā*. Secondarily, this will also illustrate why the *Gītā* has been so well received in India as a scripture, for having a nose of wax it can be turned in the direction one wishes to go. Whether one is a proponent of *bhakti* or *jñāna*, or *karma*, one can find support for one's position in the *Gītā*. Śaṅkara fully exploits the *Gītā* to support his own view. Thus in his commentary on 2. 10 he writes, "Then, it is the opinion of some that *Kaivalya, Mukti*, or *Nirvāṇa* is not attained *alone* by the knowledge of *ātman* derived from the total abandonment of all work but that the decision prevailing throughout the entire *Bhagavad Gītā* is that *jñāna* accompanied by the performance of those actions prescribed in the *Srutis* and the *Smṛtis* such as the *Agani-hotrya-yagna*, is the means of obtaining that goal." [32] Śaṅkara cites the passages which the defenders of *karma mārga* use to support their case: "If you desist from this most righteous war, then you shall be failing in the performance of your duty and consequently incur sin. . . . To act is thy proper path . . . Therefore be thou always doing actions." [33] Having done justice to his opponent's argument, Śaṅkara begins his refutation with the sweeping statement, "This argument, however, does not hold good." [34] His argument is that the *Gītā* clearly distinguishes the path of *jñāna* and the path of *karma*, and also that it marks out two entirely distinct principles of action. The *jñāna*

[31] Vamdeo Sastri, a modern Vedāntist, states the Advaita position on *jñāna mārga* as follows: "In short, for us Salvation comes, not by righteousness but by knowledge, not by casting out of sin, though we long to be delivered from it, but by emerging out of ignorance." Quoted by Lyall, *Asiatic Studies*, Second Series, p. 86.

[32] S. C. Mukhopadhyaya, *The Bhagabat Gita with the Commentary by Shri Shankaracharya*, pp. 22–23. Transliteration of Sanskrit terms has been changed to agree with the form used throughout, which is that of L. Renou, *Grammaire Sanscrite*, Paris, 1930.

[33] *Ibid.*, p. 23.

[34] *Ibid.*

mārga outlined in 2. 11–31 is entirely free from any reference to *karma mārga.* It is called the Sāṅkhya way. Śaṅkara then, points out that in 2. 39 Kṛṣṇa makes a transition in his conversation with Arjuna: "This what I have described to you is the path of Sāṅkhya, now hear this of Yoga." [35] He also cites 3.3: "In former times I had spoken of two courses, of which the Sāṅkhyas follow the path of *Jñāna.*" [36] In this same verse Kṛṣṇa defines *karma mārga* as the path of the Yogis as distinguished from the path followed by Sāṅkhyas. Śaṅkara adds, "Thus the two courses of Sāṁkhya-*budhi* and Yoga-*budhi* being distinguished from each other by the Supreme Being in the *Gītā* itself, the two things *Jñāna* and *Karma* cannot be the resort of one and the same individual, for *Jñāna* implies want of duality as well as freedom from every relation such as the doer or perceiver in the *ātman,* whereas *karma* or action presupposes that there are as many *ātmans* as there are individuals and *ātman* is a *Karta* or a doer." [37] What would be the meaning, Śaṅkara asks, of Arjuna's question in 3. 1 as to the superiority of *jñāna* or *karma* if the two could be combined in the same individual? If Kṛṣṇa had been teaching the simultaneous institution of *jñāna* and *karma* by the same individual the question would be meaningless. Obviously the union of the two paths had never been intended nor spoken of. Having separated the two *mārgas,* Śaṅkara then demonstrates that the *jñāna mārga* does not in any way require the performance of Vedic rites nor of moral action: "Just as the actions of the Supreme Being . . . cannot be said to be intermingled with his divine wisdom, so it is with the wise, for in both cases there is an equal want of any desired end as well as the notion of personal instrumentality. The knower of truth never imagines himself the doer of any acts nor does he intend their consequences." [38] Persons who possess the knowledge of the highest truth engage in actions solely to induce others to lead a virtuous life. They are on a higher plane where it is no longer necessary to act, but still they act knowing that their action and non-action are both the same. Liberation results from *jñāna mārga; karma mārga* seems required only to make possible the life of man at the lower level of *māyā* reality. Śaṅkara concludes, "Thus it is clearly proved that in the *Gītā* the condition of Self-knowledge without any admixture of *Karma* is marked as the only path of *mokṣa.*" [39]

Later in his commentary on the *Bhagavad Gītā* 2. 39 Śaṅkara grants that *karma mārga* is a path that may be followed by beginners. *Karma*

[35] *Ibid.,* p. 24.
[36] *Ibid.*
[37] *Ibid.*
[38] *Ibid.,* p. 27.
[39] *Ibid.,* p. 28.

mārga is for those at the earliest stages of the pilgrimage of the soul who are as yet ignorant and impure in heart (*avidvat*); *jñāna mārga* is the proper path for the more advanced who are pure-hearted (*vidvat*).[40] *Karma mārga,* he advises, will "lop off the overgrowths of ignorance in your minds,"[41] that is, it will get at the effects of ignorance but not at the causal factors.

Śaṅkara's position on the soteriological efficacy of only *jñāna mārga* makes it necessary for him to comment fully on *Bhagavad Gītā* 3. 1, "If you regard *jñāna mārga* as more excellent than *karma,* why urge me into battle?" Some interpret this passage, says Śaṅkara, to mean that the *Gītā* teaches the combination of *jñāna* and *karma* in the same individual, and that mere *jñāna* in the absence of *karma* is opposed to Vedic doctrine. But Śaṅkara believes this is a false view of *śruti* doctrine: "It is the conjoining opinion of all the Upaniṣads, Itihāsas, Purāṇas and Yogas that for the *Mumukshu* . . . the renunciation of work is the only direct cause of *mokṣa.*"[42] Later in his commentary on 3. 1 Śaṅkara indicates why he regards *jñāna* and *karma* as contraries: the former has no duality while the latter is always dual, i.e., in the *jñāna* form of knowing there is no dichotomy between knower and known, whereas in *karma* there is always a distinction between the actor and the deed. He concludes, "It is invariably held that *mokṣa* ensues from *Jñāna* and *Jñāna* only."[43] The reader is surprised to note that Śaṅkara, having come to such a definite conclusion in his comments on 3. 1, weakens this position in his comments on 3. 3 with an acknowledgment of a proper role for *karma mārga:* "The *Jñāna mārga* was meant for the Sāṅkhyas, i.e., for men who after attaining the stage of intellectual discrimination between *ātman* and non-*ātman* through the study of the Vedānta, renounced all *Karma* and left the world and all its concerns, and the *Karma mārga* which was meant for the *yogis* who lived in the world."[44] Śaṅkara, here as elsewhere, assumes the *māyā* nature of the material universe, and hence gives no liberating power to the *mārga* inherently part of this world. *Jñāna mārga,* he says, "without any admixture of *Karma* is marked as the only path of *mokṣa.*"[45] On the other hand, Śaṅkara says that verse 55 of the eleventh book is the essence of the whole *Gītā-śāstrā.* This verse adumbrates the entire spectrum of *mārgas:* "O Pandava, one who is engaged in my service (*karma mārga*), who considers Me as the Highest (*jñāna mārga*), who has given himself

[40] *Ibid.,* p. 61.
[41] *Ibid.,* p. 62.
[42] *Ibid.,* p. 92.
[43] *Ibid.,* p. 93.
[44] *Ibid.,* p. 94.
[45] *Ibid.,* p. 28.

entire to Me (*bhakti mārga*), who is void of attraction and who has no hatred against my being (*yoga mārga*) attains me." [46] Śaṅkara, however, persists in his opinion that there is but one *mārga:* "Possessed of wisdom, his doubt caused by ignorance is cut asunder by the conviction that to live in the true nature of the self is the only means of attaining to the Highest Bliss." [47]

Śaṅkara was more restrained in his rejection of a *bhakti-jñāna mārga* than he was in his rejection of a *karma-jñāna mārga.* This may have been due to the fact that his opponents here were Hindus rather than Buddhists, although this supposition should not be pressed. He does say in the *Vivekachundamani,* "Of all things which help the attainment of liberation, *bhakti* is the greatest." [48] But it is clear that for him *bhakti* is only a "help." On the other hand in his commentary on *Bhagavad Gītā* 18:55, "By devotion he verily knows me," Śaṅkara without question takes *bhakti* as identical with *jñāna:* "By pure devotion he knows Me as the essence of all *Upādhis,* the Supreme *Purusha* resembling *Ākāsha,* i.e., secondless pure consciousness, undecaying, and deathless." [49] Also in his commentaries on the *Brahma Sūtras* he notes that knowing and meditating are used interchangeably: ". . . in the Vedānta texts the terms 'knowing' and 'meditating' are seen to be used one in the place of the other." [50] He observes that in the *Chāndogya Upaniṣad* 4.1.4 the *ṛṣi* states, "He who knows that he knows what he knows is thus spoken of by me" and later in 4.2.2 says, "Teach me, sir, the deity which you meditate on," and also in the same Upaniṣad is found "Let a man meditate on mind and Brahman" and "He who knows this shines and warms through his celebrity, fame and glory of countenance." [51] Śaṅkara also says that meditation in itself is of the nature of work, and thus is incapable of producing liberation. *Karma* cannot produce *mokṣa,* even when it is disguised in the form of *bhakti.*[52] Nevertheless a man ought to meditate "at whatever time, in whatever place and facing whatever region, he may with ease manage to concentrate his mind," [53] and he ought to repeat these meditations up to his death, since, like works,

[46] Mukhopadhyaya, *op. cit.,* p. 273.
[47] *Ibid.,* p. 374. Commentary on 18. 10.
[48] Satanath Tattvabushan, "The Philosophy of Śaṅkaracharya," *Three Great Acharyas: Śaṅkara, Rāmānuja, Madhwa,* p. 107.
[49] Mukhopadhaya, *op. cit.,* p. 394.
[50] *The Vedānta-Sūtras with the Commentary by Śaṅkarācārya,* 4. 1. 1. *The Sacred Books of the East,* Vol. 38, p. 332.
[51] *Ibid.*
[52] *Ibid.,* pp. 345–349.
[53] *Ibid.,* p. 351.

they may not bring forth liberation, but they are a help to the knowledge which will bring liberation.[54]

His favorable attitude toward religious worship has been something of a problem for his followers for three reasons: (1) it violates his principle that only through knowledge can the self be liberated; (2) he taught that Īśvara (the Lord) is *māyā;* (3) he held that worship has no part in the life of the *jīvanmukta.* A prayer attributed to Śaṅkara seems to express a guilt of "worshipping" the Absolute, which cannot in fact be an object of space, or of thought, or of words: "Forgive me, O Śiva, my three great sins. I came on a pilgrimage to Kāśi forgetting that you are omnipresent; in thinking about you, I forget that you are beyond thought; in praying to you I forget that you are beyond words." [55] Worship is founded on the duality of man and God, whereas the Perfected Man will realize that there is no duality between his real self and Brahman. Religious worship is a phenomenon of the lower stage of the development of man; the *jīvanmukta* does not worship: "One who is beyond all gods does not salute a god." [56]

Śaṅkara not only accepted *bhakti* as an allowable step leading to *jñāna mārga* which alone could result in *mokṣa,* but also he provided hymns to be used by the man in the lower stages of *sādhana.* For the rank beginner he composed a hymn to the Divine Mother:

> No father have I, no mother, no comrade,
> No son, no daughter, no wife, and no grandchild,
> No servant or master, no wisdom, no calling:
> In Thee is my only haven of refuge,
> In Thee, my help and my strength, O Bhavāni!
>
> . . . .
>
> I know neither Brahmā nor Vishnu nor Śiva,
> No Indra, sun, moon, or similar beings—
> Not one of the numberless gods, O Redeemer!
> In Thee is my only haven of refuge,
> In Thee, my help and my strength, O Bhavāni! [57]

In typically tolerant Hindu fashion he composed hymns both to Śiva and to Viṣṇu:

> Him do I cherish, the Lord of living creatures, the Almighty One, the Slayer of sin,

[54] *Ibid.,* p. 352.
[55] Radhakrishnan, *The Brahma Sūtras,* pp. 37–38.
[56] Venkataramanan, *Select Works of Śrī Śaṅkarāchārya,* p. 265.
[57] Nikhilananda, *Self-Knowledge (Ātmabodha), An English Translation of Śaṅkarachārya's Ātmabodha,* pp. 242, 244.

Who is adored by all,
Within whose matted locks the Ganges wanders murmuring:
Him do I cherish—Śiva, the Great God, the One without a second, the Destroyer of lust.[58]
Save me from pride, O Vishnu! Curb my restless mind.
Still my thirst for the waters of this world's mirage.
Be gracious, Lord! to this Thy humble creature,
And rescue him from the ocean of the world.[59]

He composed hymns petitioning forgiveness:

Even before I saw the light of this world, my sins from previous births,
Through which I passed because of desire for the fruit of my deeds,
Punished me as I lay in my mother's womb.
There I was boiled in the midst of unclean things:
Who can describe the pain that afflicts the child in its mother's womb,
Therefore, O Śiva! O Mahādeva! O Śambhu! forgive me, I pray, for my transgressions.[60]

Even though Śaṅkara himself knew the *siddhi* which transcended time and its ravages, he wrote of the sorrows of finitude common to the man caught in the meshes of time and space:

Sunrise and sunset, daylight and darkness,
Winter and springtime, come and go;
Even the course of time is playful;
Life itself soon ebbs away;
But man's vain hope, alas! goes onward,
Tireless onward evermore.[61]

Perhaps the most remarkable of all his *bhakti* poems are his verses which celebrate liberation itself:

Om. I am neither the mind, intelligence,
ego, nor chitta,
Neither the ears nor the tongue,
nor the senses of smell and sight;
Neither ether nor air,
nor fire nor water nor earth:
I am Eternal Bliss and Awareness

[58] *Ibid.*, p. 266.
[59] *Ibid.*, p. 253.
[60] *Ibid.*, p. 276.
[61] *Ibid.*, p. 287.

—I am Śiva! I am Śiva!

. . . .

I have no form or fancy:
  the All-pervading am I;
Everywhere I exist,
  and yet am beyond the senses;
Neither salvation am I,
  nor anything to be known:
I am Eternal Bliss and Awareness
  —I am Śiva! I am Śiva! [62]

A comparison of this hymn with the ones quoted previously reveals the amazing spread of sophistication of the hymns of Śaṅkara. In the first hymn the worshiper stands removed from Brahmā, Viṣṇu, and Śiva, and worships only Bhavāni, the Divine Mother, Mother Earth herself. In the second and third hymns the worshiper identifies as the object of his worship the gods Śiva and Viṣṇu. Here they are distinguished from each other, and from the worshiper himself. But in the last hymn the hiatus between worshiper and worshiped has been closed: "I am Śiva! I am Śiva!" Yet, because the aspirant has not yet attained the *jīvanmukti* state, Śaṅkara graciously allows an act of worship, a *bhakti mārga*, even in the life of the man who recognizes "I am Eternal Bliss and Awareness." Such a person is almost ready for the Supreme Bliss, *Ātman* is Brahman, *Tat tvam asi.*

3. *Jñāna Mārga* IN THE *Yogavāsiṣṭha*

The *Yogavāsiṣṭha* is a huge book of 64,000 lines. It is recognized within Hinduism as authoritative on *jñāna*. The legendary author is Vālmīki, the reputed author of the Sanskrit *Rāmāyaṇa*. The *Rāmāyaṇa* delineates the outer life of the culture hero Rāma, telling how he fought and slew the evil king Rāvana. The *Yogavāsiṣṭha*, which is also called the *Jñāna-vāsiṣṭha*, the *Vāsiṣṭha-Rāmāyaṇa*, and the *Mahā-Rāmāyaṇa*, describes the inner life of Rāma, telling how he triumphed over the foes within himself. Some Indologists have claimed that it is a religious rather than a philosophical treatise; Winternitz, for example, said it was "*mehr eine religioses Werk*." [63] Farquhar and Radhakrishnan think it is primarily religious, but S. N. Dasgupta and B. L. Atreya regard it as a philosophical work. Of course, the distinction between religion and phi-

[62] *Ibid.*, pp. 302, 304.
[63] *Geschichte der Indischen Litteratur*, Vol. 3, p. 443.

losophy in Hindu *sādhana* is, as we have already noted, more a reflection of the prejudices of the scholar than an objective character of a literary work. Perhaps the popular style in which it is written is one reason why an intellectual may be inclined to classify it as religious rather than as philosophical. Scholars have estimated the date of its composition as early as the fifth century A.D. and as late as the thirteenth. The dramatic situation is very simple. Rāma is about to depart with the *ṛṣi* Viśvāmitra to protect him from the demons who have been disturbing his religious rites, but he is possessed with doubts about the meaning of life: "Is there any place where there is no suffering? Is there any creature which is not ephemeral? Is there any dealing which is free from deception?" [64] Vāsiṣṭha, the family priest, is brought to dispel Rāma's doubts and fears. The *yoga* of Vāsiṣṭha is the result.[65]

Although the *Yogavāsiṣṭha* and Śaṅkara express many similar views, neither refers to the other. One point of difference has to do with their treatment of the *śruti* tradition. The *Yogavāsiṣṭha,* unlike Śaṅkara, rejects authority as a source of knowledge: "There is only one ultimate source of knowledge, namely, one's own direct experience, which is the ground and source of all other *pramāṇas*." [66] Authorities are to be accepted as a source of information, subject, however, to the evaluations of reason: "A reasonable statement, even of a child, should be accepted, while the unreasonable ones should be discarded like a piece of straw, even though they are made by the Creator Himself." [67] The "reason" which the *Yogavāsiṣṭha* lauds is direct knowing or intuition, not public logicality. "Mere knowledge of the inexistence of the world, without subduing the passions, is known as knowledge without practice, and is of no good to its possessor." [68] The admonitions are sometimes extremely pragmatic, bordering on intellectual relativism: "The method by which a man makes progress is best for him. He should not change it for another, which is neither proper for him, nor pleases him, nor is fruitful of good to him." [69] What is intended in such passages is an emphasis on the importance and necessity of each person's perfection through his own efforts. *Siddhi* is the result of self-nurture, not a grace of the gods: "Vishnu is unable to give

[64] *Yogavāsiṣṭha* 1. 27. 31. All quotations are taken from the B. L. Atreya translation.
[65] The ancient Indian authors appear to have loved a situation in which an important activity is arrested in order that the meaning of the event may be examined and the perplexities may be cleared away. Cf. the *Bhagavad Gītā* in which the battle is delayed in order for Arjuna to understand why it is his *dharma* to fight. Again there is the long section at the close of the *Mahābhārata* in which Bhīṣma postpones his death to enlighten Yudhiṣṭhira on a variety of questions.
[66] 2. 19. 16.
[67] *Ibid.*, 2. 18. 3.
[68] *Ibid.*, 3. 22. 2. 31.
[69] *Ibid.*, 6b. 130. 2.

knowledge to one who does not think for himself, even if He is worshipped for long and is very much pleased." [70] "The self is the only friend of the self, and the self is the only enemy of the self. If one does not save oneself, there is no other way left." [71]

The *Yogavāsiṣṭha*, like Śaṅkara, holds that liberation can be attained only through *jñāna mārga*. It itemizes at length the methods by which men try unsuccessfully to attain liberation: penances, renunciations, pilgrimages, distribution of alms, baths in sacred rivers, concentrations, *yoga*, sacrifices, performances of duties, fasts, worship listening to a *guru*, etc.[72] These may open the doors of heaven, but they do not lead to the ending of *saṁsāra*, to enlightenment, to perfection. It should be noted that the *Yogavāsiṣṭha* appears to be excessively concerned with liberation as escape from the pangs of man's pilgrimage through earthly lives. The problem of the work is set at the opening when Rāma requests, "Great Sire, I wish to learn from thee how I may escape the miseries which arise from one's connection with this world." [73] Śaṅkara could not have stated more strongly and positively the sole sufficiency of *jñāna mārga*: "There is in fact no other course for crossing over the ocean of *saṁsāra* for a bound man than knowledge." [74] He also would agree with the observation that a distinction must be made between the *jñānin*, the one who has an intuition of the object of knowledge, and the *jñāna-bhandu*, the one who has a discursive awareness of the object of knowledge, and that only the *jñānin* has the knowledge which liberates. Liberating knowledge requires much practice; it is a *mārga*, a way along which one must move—hence the title of the book "The *Yoga* (or *mārga*) of Vāsiṣṭha."

Although the *Yogavāsiṣṭha* and Śaṅkara agree in emphasizing *jñāna mārga*, there is an important difference: for Śaṅkara the way of knowledge is both necessary and sufficient, whereas for the *Yogavāsiṣṭha* the way of knowledge is necessary but not sufficient. Hence Śaṅkara stresses renouncing the life of the householder and living the life of the recluse, while the *Yogavāsiṣṭha* places value on the household life as assistance to the perfecting way of *jñāna*. According to Śaṅkara, *jñāna* and *karma* are separate paths suitable for different kinds of people or of people at different stages of self-realization; according to the *Yogavāsiṣṭha*, *jñāna* and *karma* constitute a joint method. When a Brahmin asks *ṛṣi* Agasti, "Oh great sage! that art informed in all the ways and truths of virtue, and knowest with certainty all the Śāstras, I am in a doubt which I

[70] *Ibid.*, 5. 43. 10.
[71] *Ibid.*, 6b. 162. 18.
[72] *Ibid.*, 6b. 199. 31; 6b. 174. 24; 5. 3. 8; 3. 6. 4; 6b. 197. 18. See also Atreya, *The Philosophy of the Yogavāsiṣṭha*, p. 413.
[73] *Yogavāsiṣṭha* 1. 1. 5. 51.
[74] *Ibid.*, 5. 67. 2.

pray you will kindly remove. Tell me whether a man's acts or his knowledge or both of these, is in your opinion, the cause of his emancipation." Agasti replies, "As the flight of birds in the air is effected by means of both their wings, so the highest state of emancipation is attained through the instrumentality of both knowledge and acts." [75] In the Mitra translation Chapters 88 and 89 of Book 5 are entitled "A Discourse on Yoga Meditation" and "A Lecture on Rationalistic Meditation"; Chapter 13 of Book 6 is entitled "The Two Yogas of Knowledge and Reasoning." Throughout there is a firm conviction of the unity of the world: "That man that relies on his firm faith in the unity is said to be truly liberated and perfect in his knowledge." [76] Knowledge remains for the *Yogavāsiṣṭha* the sole means for the liberation of man, but the author is so convinced of knowledge as a living experience that he does not hesitate to value works as equal to knowledge. Knowledge without works is dead; unless knowledge is active, it cannot lead to human perfection. Knowledge without action is mere belief. Hence there must be a *yoga*, a practice in which the individual empathizes his identity with Brahman, merges his mental life into the Absolute Reality, and channels the vital powers of his body into the paths that lead to the ending of *saṁsāra*. More specifically, the *Yogavāsiṣṭha* advises meditating on one's identity with Brahman on the theory that one becomes what one consistently and persistently affirms himself to be; it details the process of inhalation and exhalation of the breath in order that the state between inhalation and exhalation may be prolonged; and it suggests techniques for restraining the tendency of the mind toward objectification, since by this tendency one constantly holds before one's self the false assumption that the world is other than one's own nature, or the equally false assumption that one's finite self is the center of thinking, feeling, and willing. The *jñānin* saves himself through direct knowledge, an intuition applied in the usual pattern of *karma* and *dharma*. Hence, the *jñāna-karma mārga* is the *mārga* of the *Yogavāsiṣṭha,* although salvation is through *jñāna* alone.

The strength of the *Yogavāsiṣṭha* presentation of *sādhana* is its emphasis on the process nature of self-realization. The process is presented as a seven-stage (*bhūmikā*) movement from the dawning of the desire for liberation to final and complete attainment.[77] The first stage is the awareness of one's ignorance, one's narrow self-centeredness. The second stage is the reflection on the nature of the worldly life and the genesis of distaste for transitory pleasures. The next stage is the acquiring of a feeling of non-attachment to the objects of sense. The fourth stage is the posi-

[75] *Ibid.*, 1. 1. 2. 4–7.
[76] *Ibid.*, 5. 79. 20.
[77] *Ibid.*, 3. 118. 3–16; 6a. 120. 1–8; 6a. 126. 4–73.

tive feeling of the reality within. The fifth stage is the giving up of attachments to the objective world. The sixth stage is a state of pure bliss; the objects given up in the previous stage are now seen to be no objects at all. In the last stage all distinctions are negated. The last stage is a transcendental state (*tūryātīta*), although it need not be interpreted as a state beyond the earth-bound state. Perhaps a clearer statement would be that it is a state in which being earth-bound or not being earth-bound makes no difference. The individual in the seventh stage is in the world but not of the world. The sufferings of life and the enjoyments of life are alike to him. Nothing can subtract or distract him from his bliss. His is an absolute delight.

The one who has attained, the *jīvanmukta*, is described thus: "He who is not delighted with his delights, nor dejected in his distress; who looks only within himself for his peace and solace, is verily called the liberated man in his lifetime. . . . This is the liberated soul, which reclines in its intellectuality, and has its mind ever fixed in it; which delights in intellectual culture and his repose therein." [78] His "desire" is not properly a desire, "since it is pure desire relating to universal weal and happiness." [79] "The sage whose mind is freed in his life-time, conducts himself unconcerned in this world; he smiles secure at its occurrences, and is regardless of the first, last and middle stages of his life: namely, the pains of his birth and death, and the whole course of his life." [80] "He is attentive to his present business, and unmindful of every other object about him: he is devoid of cares and desires, and his thought is of his internal cognitions only." [81] "He is free from anxiety in all places; he tolerates whatever he happens to meet with; he sees the light of reason in his soul, and walks in the romantic groves of his musings." [82] "He neither rejoices nor laments at his lot, nor envies nor hankers after the fortune of another; but pursues his own business in quiet silence." [83] "He speaks agreeably to every one, and utters gently what he is required to say: he is never put out of countenance, who understands the intentions of others." [84] The *Yogavāsiṣṭha* teaches that the *tūryātīta* state may last for one moment or it may last for years, but it always puts the life of man into a new perspective. He ceases to be attached to or repelled by the objects of experience. He does not disregard what he has got, nor does he regard what he has not. He appears to be an ordinary man save

[78] *Ibid.*, 6 supplement 159. 1. 3.
[79] *Ibid.*, 3. 22. 1. 5.
[80] *Ibid.*, 5. 18. 2.
[81] *Ibid.*, 5. 18. 3.
[82] *Ibid.*, 5. 18. 4.
[83] *Ibid.*, 5. 18. 7.
[84] *Ibid.*, 5. 18. 9.

for the fact that "his face is never without the lustre of cheerfulness." [85] His rapport with others is complete: "He deals as a boy with boys, and as a veteran with old people; he is youthful in the society of young men, and is grave in the company of the aged and wise." [86] One striking difference between the Perfected Man as depicted in the *Bhagavad Gītā* and in the *Yogavāsiṣṭha* is that in the former he is said to act in a disinterested or unattached manner, while in the latter he is depicted as one who enters fully in the life of man, mingling with his fellow men in joys and sorrows, yet is not overcome by these experiences. Although deriving neither gain nor loss from observance or neglect of the acts of life, he is enjoined by Vāsiṣṭha to act in conformity with the prescribed rules of conduct of his society: "The wise man derives no positive nor permanent good by his doing of any act prescribed by custom or usage; nor does he lose anything by his neglect of them; wherefore it is best for him to stand in the middle course, and according to the common rules of society and his country." [87] The metaphors of the *Yogavāsiṣṭha* show the serious effort to convey the attractiveness of the *jīvanmukta:* he is "as a sea of delight," [88] "as refreshing as the full moonbeam," [89] "as firm as mountain rocks," and his passage is as "the flight of birds." [90]

At the close of the book the author inserted an epilogue, a *bon voyage* to the pilgrim who seeks to follow the admonitions of the *Yogavāsiṣṭha,* which reveals once again the remarkable qualities of this work on Hindu *sādhana:* "May your hearing of these serve to lead you to your utter indifference of this world, and to the desire of your liberation in it, while you are alive herein. May this lead to your continued prosperity in order to engage your attentions toward the perfection of your knowledge and devotion, and to the discharge of the duties of your station without falling." [91]

4. *Jñāna Mārga* AS KNOWING

The way of thought of the Vedānta philosophers is not the acquiring of knowledge; it is not a positive attaining of potential information, nor a conclusion of a line of argument, nor an inference from experience and experiment. *Jñāna mārga* is not founded on the Enlightenment assump-

[85] *Ibid.*, 6a. 116. 3.
[86] *Ibid.*, 5. 77. 14.
[87] *Ibid.*, 6 supplement 199. 4.
[88] *Ibid.*, 5. 77. 19.
[89] *Ibid.*, 5. 7. 19.
[90] *Ibid.*, 1. 1. 2. 4–7.
[91] *Ibid.*, 6 supplement 215. 17.

tion that the world is rational and that the human mind is competent to know the world. This would be the case if *jñāna* were discursive knowing, but *jñāna* does not contain a hiatus between the subject and the object. The Vedāntists do not object to scientific knowing, the knowing that preserves a subject-object epistemological dichotomy; they simply declare that this is not a *mārga* leading to the liberation of man. There is a vast difference between the assumptions of the *jñāna* and the scientific forms of knowledge; the former does not agree with the latter in the final intelligibility of the world. The *cit*-ness of reality does not mean that the world is basically rational in any human sense; it means that the rationality of man is an emergent from a fundamental feature of the real. The appearance of reason reveals a potentiality of reality.

While Western minds tend to think of reality as an unknown waiting to be captured in the categories of human thought, the Hindu thinks of reality as self-revealing. All that is needed is the removal of obstructions. There is no capture. The hindrances to knowledge are removed, and behold!—reality is manifest. Reality was there all the time, but because of human *ajñāna* it was not known. Gauḍapāda distinguished five sorts of false identifications which prevent man from knowing the Absolute Reality, the True Self. These aspects of *māyā* he also called *koṣas* (sheaths) of the Self. Only as a man understands the illusory or hiding nature of the *koṣas* does he penetrate to the *Ātman*. These *koṣas* are the identification of himself (1) with his physical body (*annamaya*), (2) with the vital breath in his physical body (*prāṇamaya*), (3) with his mind as active agent in desiring and reasoning (*manomaya*), (4) with his consciousness of being an ego (*vijñānamaya*), and (5) with the elemental pleasure of existence (*ānandamaya*). In *jñāna mārga* all of these forms of self-identification must be seen for what they are: false identifications. Śaṅkara tended to use *māyā* and *avidyā* (or *ajñāna*) indiscriminately, but among later Vedāntic authors there was a growing differentiation: *māyā* is the principle of individuation, *avidyā* is the principle of obscuration. The former is ontological; the latter is epistemological. Śaṅkara's identification of the two may have been a designed effort to demonstrate that the phenomenal self and the phenomenal world are strictly correlative; the distinctions between psychological and ontological, between knower and known, between subjective and objective, and between *Ātman* and Brahman are merely verbal distinctions. Later Vedāntists distinguished three strands or veils of *ajñāna* which were capable of being interpreted either subjectively or objectively: (1) those which cause a thing to appear as non-existent, (2) those which cover its revealing aspect and make it non-revealing, and (3) those which cover the bliss aspect.

Jñāna mārga of Advaita Vedāntism is a *via negativa.* By the elimination of the false the true is revealed. Man does not discover reality. He does not reach it by effort, either mental or physical. Rather he removes the obstructions so that reality reveals itself. Take away ignorance and truth is uncovered. Brahman is revealed when the *upādhis,* the individualizing determinations, are recognized by the intellect. "As a lighted lamp does not need another lamp to manifest its light, so Ātman, being Consciousness itself, does not need another instrument of consciousness to illumine Itelf." [92] The seeker has found the object of his quest. Now he knows, and yet his knowing is a non-knowing. He does not stand off from Brahman and recognize the reality of Brahman. He understands that he *is* Brahman, and that he has always been Brahman. Only his ignorance prevented him from realizing his own true Being.

In the total process of self-realization nothing happens, no change takes place, no attainment is achieved, no new level is reached, no metaphysical structures are changed, no new processes are innovated. This is obviously a difficult point to convey, although whether it is due to the novelty of the idea or the errors of scholarly interpreters is impossible to say. Max Müller blamed it on the interpreters:

> The fatal mistake which interpreters of the Vedānta-Philosophy both in India and Europe have made is to represent this absorption or recovery . . . as an approach of the individual soul towards God. There can be no such approach where there is identity; there can be only recovery or restitution, a return, a becoming of the soul of what it always has been, a revival of its true nature.[93]

Jñāna mārga differs from the other *mārgas* in its central aspect: the other *mārgas* involve a duality—a god to be loved, an act to be done, a body to be disciplined—but in *jñāna mārga* there is no duality. *Jñāna* is not ordinary knowledge, the form of knowing which differentiates knower and known; *jñāna* is the intuitive grasp of Self by self. The ideal aspired after by the Vedāntists is the elimination of even the smallest interval between the subject and the object. There is no consciousness of something by something. There is no attainment of something that was not; there is only the unfolding of the latent infinitude of the apparently finite.

The seemingly paradoxical nature of *jñāna* is presented in the *Kena Upaniṣad,* one of the briefest of the Upaniṣads. Brief as it is, it is still a composition of two somewhat unrelated parts. The first part, consisting

[92] Śaṅkara, *Ātmabodha* 28. Nikhilananda translation.
[93] *Six Systems of Indian Philosophy,* p. 222.

of thirteen verses, is a poetic section probably added later to a simple prose section. The problem to be considered is raised in the opening passage: what is the reality upon which the phenomenal world of human experience depends? The answer is that the reality must be found within; it is the subject of apprehending, not an object of mind; it is the essence of the apprehending agencies: "the ear of the ear, the mind of the mind, the speech of the speech, the breath of the breath, the eye of the eye." [94] To call this a form of subjective idealism would err in two ways: it would in the first place imply a duality of things-as-seen and things-as-they-are, which is completely foreign to the absolutism of the Upaniṣads, and in the second place it would err in making Reality an active subject in a subject-object context, but Brahman is not an object of knowing nor an active subject which knows an objective phenomenon. As a continuation of the answer to the question, the teacher adds that eye, speech, and mind do not take one to the reality of phenomena: "Other, indeed, it is than the known; and also it is above the unknown." [95] Hence "We know not, we understand not how one would teach It." [96] The pupil admits that he does not think that he knows It, and yet he does not think that he does not know It. The pupil senses that Reality is apprehended both in the knowing and in the not-knowing, for It is the subject of both knowing and not-knowing, and the teacher illuminates the student's insight further by adding, "It is conceived of by him by whom It is not conceived of." [97] That is, he who knows that Reality is not an object to be conceived of, knows Reality. "He by whom It is conceived of, knows It not." [98] He who conceives of Reality fails to understand that Reality is not a reality toward which one can take a subject-object, knower-known relationship. "It is not understood by those who [say they] understand It." [99] He who says he understands errs in thinking Brahman is an object. "It is understood by those who [say they] understand it not." [100] Those who know that Reality cannot be understood in the objective manner in which things are understood know that Reality is not a thing to be known, and this constitutes in itself a "knowing" of Reality.

The knowledge needed, according to Śaṅkara, is the recognition that the *Ātman* and the Brahman are identical. The discovery brings the peace that ends all anxiety. The knowing is not so much the acquiring of a philosophical truth as the acquiring of a truth philosophically. It is a

[94] *Kena Upaniṣad* 1. 2. Radhakrishnan translation.
[95] *Ibid.*, 1. 4. Radhakrishnan translation.
[96] *Ibid.*, 1. 3. Hume translation.
[97] *Ibid.*, 2. 3a. Hume translation.
[98] *Ibid.*, 2. 3b. Hume translation.
[99] *Ibid.*, 2. 3c. Hume translation.
[100] *Ibid.*, 2. 3d. Hume translation.

knowing that brings peace and freedom to the human spirit by the opening of the mind to a fact that is rather than to a fact that is to be, by a present possession and not a future attainment. Although the phenomenal *jīva* is actually *Ātman*, and although *Ātman* and Brahman are the same from different points of view, the fact of these realities must be realized by human endeavor. Fact must become *realized* fact. Śaṅkara compared the search and the discovery to one who lost a jewel, and who found that it was never lost at all, for it was on his person all the time: "Though *Ātman* is an ever present reality, yet because of ignorance *Ātman* is realized. It is like the case of the ornament on one's neck." [101] An even better metaphor would be to compare the quest for the *Ātman* to that of a person searching for lost spectacles, only to discover that the very spectacles for which he was seeking were the spectacles he was using in the search. It is through *Ātman* that *Ātman* is found. Nothing is changed in the discovery other than the recognition that one's so-called "knowledge" is ignorance. Self-realization is the realization of what is one's innate character. This theme is found in many parables in Hindu and Buddhist lore, e.g., a prince brought up as a peasant discovers that he is of royal blood; a tiger cub reared among a flock of sheep discovers that he is a tiger; a prodigal son is slowly and kindly led to the state where he can endure the wondrous revelation that his wealthy master is his own father.

But the process does not end here. The end is not an eternal state of static bliss. The process is never over. As long as man is incarnate he needs to continue establishing himself in the Brahman. The *jīvanmukta*, the ideally liberated man, is, as we have said previously, the Perfecting Man. His true being is his becoming. A "leaping spark," a "blinding light," an "ephemeral vision," or an "angel chorus" may be adequate designations for what a Western mystic calls his vision, but for the Hindu there must be a process of constantly renewing insight. "What is *jñāna*?" asked Ramakrishna, the great Bengali mystic. "It is to know one's own Self and to keep the mind in It." *Jñāna* is a *mārga*.

5. *Jñāna* AS *Mārga*

Jñāna mārga is more than a momentary illumination. Śaṅkara taught that the pupil (*śiṣya*) must practice four disciplines of spiritual knowledge (*sādhanacatuṣṭaya*). The first instrument of this *mārga* is the practice of discriminating between the real and the unreal. He must be constantly aware of the fact of this difference, and must be always attempt-

[101] *Ātmabodha* 44. Nikhilananda translation.

ing to distinguish appearance from reality. This discipline should lead to the second: the renunciation of any hedonic satisfactions that might handicap the pursuit of the real. This is not to be interpreted as a Stoic refusal to acknowledge pain or pleasure, nor as Epicurean non-involvement; it is not the rejection of pleasure as such, but the rejection of any pleasure which disrupts the quest for reality. The third discipline according to Śaṅkara is the ethical foundation of the *mārga.* Śaṅkara mentions six subdisciplines under this heading: (1) calmness (*sama*), a steady and undisturbed pursuit of the knowledge which will make all knowable known; (2) self-control (*dama*), the keeping of the organs of sense and of all actions under control of the overriding desire to realize the real; (3) settledness (*uparati*), the restraining of the mind from drifting back to the contemplation of the objects of sense experience; (4) forbearance (*titikṣa*), the ability to be so attached to the main goal of one's life that physical suffering, anxiety, and grief in no way disturb the *mārga;* (5) complete concentration (*samādhāna*), the placing of all mental powers on the goal of liberation; (6) faith (*śraddhā*), the affirming frame of mind toward a *guru* as guide to Vedāntic wisdom. The last discipline is the longing for liberation (*mumukṣā*) without which the pupil would never remain steadfast in the long journey to his spiritual goal. It is a confidence in knowledge expressed in action. *Śraddhā* is close to the will to believe as analyzed by William James in his well-known essay. The *Chāndogya Upaniṣad* expresses the idea in this fashion: "When one has faith, then he thinks. One who has not faith does not think. Only he who has faith thinks. But one must desire to understand faith." [102] In other words, in order for *jñāna* to be a way of *sādhana* there must be a feeling of reality about the quest; one who does not think of human life as a long quest for *Satcitānanda* would certainly not engage in this or in any *mārga.* Secondly, there must be confidence that the way of thought is an effective and sufficient method for the attainment of the ideal goal. Śaṅkara makes a similar observation in his commentary on the *Bhagavad Gītā* when he notes that devotion to action is a *mārga,* not because action will lead directly to liberation, but because devotion to action may lead to the attitude of devotion to liberating knowledge. By being purely and exclusively intellectual one tends to lose faith in the intellect. The importance of knowing in the life of man must not blind him to the fact that he experiences the world in many ways.

Śaṅkara's four disciplines can be subsumed under one: an intense one-pointedness of mind (*ekāgratā*), a self-control which empties the mind of all activities, thoughts, emotions, concerns, and volitions save that of

[102] 7. 19. 1. Radhakrishnan translation.

the perfecting of man. The *Kaṭha Upaniṣad* compares the life of man to that of a journey made in a chariot.[103] The body is the chariot, the intellect (*buddhi*) is the chariot-driver, the senses are the horses, and the self (*Ātman*) is the passenger. Safely reaching the end of the journey depends chiefly upon the control of the horses by the chariot-driver. Thus "he who has the understanding of a chariot-driver, a man who reins in his mind—he reaches the end of his journey." [104] Only the man with controlled mind will realize the *Ātman*.

Further evidence that *jñāna* is acknowledged by Śaṅkara as a *mārga*, that is, as a process, is the fact that he refers to four stages of the evolution of the emancipating development: (1) *sālokya*—the overcoming of *rajas* and *tamas*, and through *sāttva* living in the presence of Īśvara, the qualified Brahman; (2) *sāmipya*—the constant associating with Īśvara in acts of worship; (3) *sārūpya*—the consciousness of identity with the form and power of Īśvara; (4) *sāyujya*—the state of absolution of all difference from Īśvara, yet lacking still an identification with the unqualified Brahman. "Through repeated practice," Śaṅkara assures us, "knowledge purifies the embodied soul stained by ignorance, and then itself disappears." [105] Knowledge vanishes when Reality is. But since Reality always "is," "knowledge" never is. Knowledge is an achievement which is no achievement. It attains nothing. Realization is a negative affair, a refusing to give assent to the unreal, a turning away from the illusion of unrealizedness. The knowing that liberates is a negating of the "knowledge" that is ignorance. The happening that happens is a non-event; the achievement is a non-achievement. Man becomes what he is, although in fact he does not *become* at all; he is what he is, and his is-ness is his becoming. His ignorance, his finitude, his limits, are not sloughed off; they are seen as *māyā*. Man's identity with Reality is a fact, although to state it in this form suggests none of its dynamic character. *Ātman* is *Brahman* is a fact*ing*, a real*ing*, a becom*ing*, and a be*ing*. Man, even the *jīvanmukta*, because of the space and time limitations within which he operates, must continue to follow *jñāna* as a *mārga*. Only the truth that is a *way* of truth liberates.

According to the Vedānta the created world is a Self-forgetfulness, and salvation is Self-awareness. The primal ignorance can become identified, and hence overcome, only in the creature for whom Self-consciousness is a possibility. Man is that creature. Only he can know that he knows. Only in him can objectification and plurification turn back upon Itself. *Jñāna mārga* is man redeeming the world.

[103] 1. 3. 3–9.
[104] 1. 3. 9. Hume translation.
[105] *Ātmabodha* 5. Nikhilananda translation.

CHAPTER VIII
The Way of Action

1. THE IMPORTANCE OF ACTION

The *Mahābhārata* records a legend that the gods once placed the four Vedas on one side of a balance scale and the *Bhārata* on the other, and, upon noting that the latter outweighed the former, decided to call it the *Mahābhārata,* the great battle, "being esteemed superior both in substance and gravity of importance" to "the four Vedas with their mysteries." [1] The meaning of the legend is that the way of action, the way defined and praised in the great epic, is better than the ways of thought, devotion, and discipline combined. *Karma mārga* is to be preferred to any combination of the other *mārgas.* The *Mahābhārata* is particularly insistent on the superiority of *karma mārga* to *jñāna mārga.* In the *Udyoga Parva* of the *Mahābhārata,* Kṛṣṇa reports a difference of opinion among the Brahmins as to whether liberation from the earthly life and attainment of final peace depends upon works or knowledge:

[1] *Mahābhārata* 1. 1. A number of references to and quotations from the *Mahābhārata* will occur in this chapter. Therefore, a caveat should be mentioned about using the *Mahābhārata* as a source of information about Hinduism. The epic has gone through many emendations and accretions until the basic plot has become largely a carrier for anachronous moralizing and theologizing. Donald A. Mackenzie once suggested that for a Westerner to understand what has happened to the *Mahābhārata,* he should imagine that "the *Iliad* survived to us only in Pope's translation, and our theologians had scattered through it, say, metrical renderings of Bunyan's *Pilgrim's Progress,* the *Thirty-nine Articles of the Church of England,* the *Westminster Confession of Faith,* Fox's *Book of Martyrs,* and a few representative theological works of rival sects." *Indian Myth and Legend,* p. 139.

"Some say that success in the world to come depends upon work. Some declare that action should be shunned and that salvation is attainable by knowledge."[2] He settles the argument by affirming that knowledge has value only insofar as it leads to action. Knowledge is the theory; action is the practice. Or in a typical Indian metaphor, action is the eating: "Though one may have a knowledge of eatable things, yet his hunger will not be appeased unless he actually eats. Those branches of knowledge that help the doing of work, bear fruit, but not other kinds, for the fruit of work is of ocular demonstration. A thirsty person drinks water, and by that act his thirst is allayed. This result proceeds, no doubt, from work. Therein lies the efficacy of work. If anyone thinks that something else is better than work, I deem his work, and his words are meaningless."[3] Kṛṣṇa continues by arguing that it is by work that the gods flourish, the wind blows, the sun rises, fire burns, rivers flow, rain descends; it was by work that Indra attained the highest position among the gods; and it is by combining a life of study, austerity, and work that men attain the status of saints.[4] In the *Bhagavad Gītā* Kṛṣṇa argues that man's material nature is a composite of three strands (*guṇas*) resulting in a never-ending stimulus to activity: "For no one even for a moment remains at all without performing actions: for he is made to perform action willy-nilly."[5]

In another passage of the *Mahābhārata* the relative worth of activity is asserted in a second weighing illustration. This time it is the four *āśramas* or periods of human life that are compared: the student or preparatory period, the householder period, and the two periods of retirement—the hermit and the Sannyāsa periods. "The four different modes of life were at one time weighed in the balance. The wise have said, O King, that when domesticity was placed on one scale, it required the three others to be placed on the other for balancing it."[6] The householder period is the period of active pursuit of *dharma* (religion), *kāma* (pleasure), and *artha* (profit). Activity is in this case described as of equal importance to *mokṣa* (liberation).

Again the importance of works is emphasized when the Hindu considers the rebirth of the individual in a series of incarnations. The quality of the action in the incarnate state is both the result of the actions of previous states and the cause of actions in the future states. In the causal law of moral nature it is only through good works that one becomes

[2] 5. 29.
[3] *Ibid.*
[4] *Ibid.*
[5] 3. 5. Edgerton translation.
[6] 12. 12.

good, and only through bad works that one becomes bad. But when the Hindu considers the *tat tvam asi* doctrines of the Upaniṣads, his thoughts take a different turn. The great unborn Self, the *Ātman*, is not born nor does it die; it is in no wise affected by action: "In the space within the heart lies the ruler of all, the lord of all, the king of all. He does not become greater by good action nor inferior by bad action."[7] Śaṅkara, as we noted in the previous chapter, having identified the real self as the *Ātman*, consistently denied the value of works. The conclusion of the *Bhagavad Gītā*, he argued, is that salvation is attained by knowledge alone, not by knowledge conjoined with works.[8] Therefore, the enlightened man who has seen the immutable Self and the man who is eager for emancipation have only to renounce all works.[9] In a discussion of the relative merits of knowledge and works as soteriological methods, Śaṅkara in one passage curiously identifies the path of knowledge as the path of the gods, the path of works as the path of the fathers, and a third path, which he says is neither knowledge nor works, as the "path on which they repeatedly return to the existence of small animals."[10] In commenting on *sūtra* 3. 3. 31 he identifies this explicitly as the path of "worms, birds, and creeping things," and says that faith and works cannot by themselves lead to liberation: "Not by faith and austerities alone, we reply, unaided by knowledge, can that path be attained."[11] Conversely, although salvation is attained only through knowledge, works are needed as an indirect means to the goal, since through works knowledge comes to be. According to *sūtra* 3. 4. 26, "there is need of all works, on account of the scriptural statement of sacrifices and the life; as in the case of the horse." Śaṅkara's commentary on this *sūtra* is so well-put that we shall quote it at length:

> We now consider whether knowledge has absolutely no need of the works enjoined on the different āśramas, or whether it has some need of them. Under the preceding Sūtra we have arrived at the conclusion that as knowledge affects its own end the works enjoined on the āśramas are absolutely not required. With reference to this point the present Sūtra now remarks that knowledge has regard for all works enjoined on the āśramas, and that there is not absolute non-regard. But do not the two Sūtras thus contradict each other? By no means, we reply. Knowledge having once sprung up requires no help towards the accomplishment of its fruit, but it

[7] *Bṛhad-Āraṇyaka Upaniṣad* 4. 4. 22. Hume translation.
[8] *Commentary on Bhagavad Gītā* 2. 10.
[9] *Ibid.*, 2. 21.
[10] *The Vedānta-Sūtras with the Commentary by Śaṅkarācārya*, 3. 1. 17. *The Sacred Books of the East*, Vol. 38, p. 124.
[11] *Ibid.*, p. 234.

does stand in need of something else with a view to its own origination. . . . Again the passage "That word which all the Vedas record, which all penances proclaim, desiring which men live as religious students, that word I tell thee briefly, it is Om" (*Kaṭha Upaniṣad* 1.2.15), likewise intimates that the works enjoined on the āśramas are means of knowledge. Similarly Smṛti says, "Works are the washing away of uncleanliness, but knowledge is the highest way. When the impurity has been removed, then knowledge begins to act." The phrase, "as in the case of the horse," supplies an illustration on the ground of suitability. As the horse, owing to its specific suitability, is not employed for dragging ploughs but is harnessed to chariots; so the works enjoined on the āśramas are not required by knowledge for bringing about its results, but with a view to its own origination.[12]

Some of the followers of Śaṅkara have carried the recognition of the role of works far beyond anything envisaged by Śaṅkara, e.g., an Advaitist acknowledging, "we must rise to Jñāna Yoga, not by leaps and bounds, but on the stepping stone of Karma Yoga to the next higher stage," warns, "those who attempt at a cross-grained ascent against the course of nature, and, before being qualified for Jñāna Yoga, betake themselves to the worship of Nirguna Brahman, the ultimatum of the Vedānta, far from attaining liberation, are punished with hell for rejecting the Karma Kānda." [13]

Just as the proponents of *jñāna mārga* came to recognize the place of works within their *mārga*, so the defenders of *bhakti mārga* and *yoga mārga* saw that *karma mārga* was inherent in their *mārgas*. The *Mahābhārata* prescribes two ways of life, the way of activity and the way of renunciation. In one passage Bhīṣma advises a life of action: "The man reft of action can never obtain success." [14] He notes that for a person who is capable of action, not to act is to fail in duty; for a life of renunciation is a hypocritical life. In curious exaggeration he states that if the goals of life were to be obtained by renunciation then mountains and trees, animals of the forests, and creatures of the seas could obtain it! Although this argument is a flagrant violation of the distinction between a necessary cause and a sufficient cause, it does indicate the importance of action. However, in the same *parva* the way of renunciation is proclaimed with equal fervor by Bhīṣma, the grand old man of the epic. A person, beholding the origin of creatures, their growth, decay, and death taking place according to natural law, neither delights nor grieves

[12] *Ibid.*, pp. 306–307.
[13] Mahamahopadhyaya Kamakhya Nath Tarkabagisa, *Lectures on Hindu Philosophy*, Part I, p. 5.
[14] 12.10.

in the lot of his life. He does not expect mortal things to be immortal, nor limited experiences to be unlimited. Good fortune or ill fortune are equally regarded:

> If I get without trouble a copious repast, I do not scruple to enjoy it. On the other hand, I pass many days together without eating anything. Sometimes people feed me with costly viands in profusion, sometimes with a small quantity, sometimes with even less, and sometimes I get no food whatever. . . . Sometimes I sleep on an elevated bedstead of the best kind. Sometimes I sleep on the bare ground. I am sometimes clad in rags, sometimes in sackcloth, sometimes in raiments of fine texture, sometimes in deerskins, sometimes in robes of the costliest kind. I never reject such enjoyments as are consistent with virtue and as are obtained by me without effort. I do not, at the same time, strive for attaining such objects as are difficult of acquisition.[15]

To point out that the earlier section deals with the life of the Kṣatriya and the latter with the life of the Brahmin is to miss the fact that both are given by Bhīṣma in reply to Yudhiṣṭhira's request of how he ought to pattern his own life. At one time in Indian culture the two ways, the path of action (*pravṛtti mārga*) and the path of renunciation (*nivṛtti mārga*), were regarded as exclusive, but with the coming of the notion of acting without self-interest, a notion most clearly presented in the *Bhagavad Gītā*, the two paths became harmoniously blended.

Efforts to determine the relative importance of the four *mārgas* by appeal to the age of each have not proved to be of great value, partly because chronology is always a problem in Indological studies, and partly because all the *mārgas* can be rooted in the earliest Vedas. N. K. Brahma claims that the *jñāna mārga* has its source in the *Ṛg Veda*, the *bhakti mārga* in the *Atharva Veda*, and the *yoga mārga* in the *Sāma Veda*,[16] but from what is known of all primitive cultures we may justifiably postulate that *karma mārga*, which includes both the ceremonially right and the morally right, antedates the ways of thought, emotion, and discipline. Man acts and then finds reasons for his action.

Hinduism, by reason of its long tradition of intellectual tolerance, has escaped the pitfalls of orthodoxy; it has not fared so well in the area of right acting. Orthopraxy with its rigid ceremonies and casuistic morality has often been the pattern of Hindu life. The *Ṛg Veda* distinguishes between the morally straight (*ṛju*) and the morally crooked (*vṛjina*).[17] The gods were the upholders of moral and natural righteousness (*ṛta*).

[15] *Ibid.*, 12.179.
[16] *Philosophy of Hindu Sādhanā*, p. 76.
[17] 4.1.17.

Ceremonial purity and moral worth were often confused. The term *karma* was used in a narrow sense in the Vedas to designate the sacrifices to the deities and in a broad sense to designate moral behavior and physical acts as well as the rites and ceremonies of adoration of and petition to the gods. *Karma mārga* as used in this chapter should be understood to include action in general (*karma*), dutiful action (*dharma*), ritualistic action (*saṁskāra*), and social service (*yajña*). Śaṅkara and his school, making a distinction between the status of *jñāna* as an end and *karma* as a means or support of *jñāna*, limited the denotation of *karma* to meditation (*dhyāna*) and reflection (*vicāra*). The truth of the charge of orthopraxy against Hinduism will become obvious in this chapter. Orthopraxy is a temptation whenever a people seek to spell out in detail the minutiae of correct behavior. When emphasis is placed on the rightness of external acts, formality displaces humanitarian concerns. A group of Hindus who believed that their low position in society was due to the legalism and ceremonialism of their culture once burned a copy of Manu's *Dharma Śāstra* as a public protest.[18] A similar occurrence took place at Mahad near Bombay on December 24, 1927, at the instigation of Dr. Ambedkar, the outstanding Untouchable who later was chairman of the committee that wrote the Constitution of India.[19] Unfortunately, Hindus have sometimes overstressed legalities and have neglected the wise observation of the *Mahābhārata* that exactness in these areas remains a dark and uncertain quality: "The truth about religion and duty is hid in caves." [20]

2. *Dharma*

Dharma is the primary virtue in the active life of the Hindu. No other term so adequately connotes concern for the preservation of traditional values. The word *dharma* appears at least fifty-six times in the *Ṛg Veda* [21] and is found among both pre-Indian Aryans and pre-Aryan Indians. The *Sanātana Dharma* (eternal *dharma*) may offer to modern India, both Hindu and non-Hindu, a foundation for a culturally united nation, i.e., it may *if* the Hindus are willing to give up post-Vedic accretions and the non-Hindus are willing to accept as foundation of law and morality that which developed in India before Hinduism or Brahmanism came into being.

[18] *The Hindu Literary Supplement*, Madras, September 2, 1934.
[19] Dhananjay Keer, *Dr. Ambedkar, Life and Mission*, p. 96.
[20] 3.311.
[21] *The Cultural History of India*, Vol. 2, p. 424. The observation of P. V. Kane.

The term *dharma* is almost impossible to translate. In some contexts words such as duty, morality, righteousness, justice, and benevolence seem appropriate; in other contexts words such as law, religion, essence, order, rule, nature, and truth seem to catch the meaning. The term is derived from the root *dhṛ*, meaning to uphold, support, or nourish. *Dharma* connotes the conserving of a thing. It is manifested in acts that preserve realities and values. *Dharma* is not the act. The act *per se* is *karma*. Hence, the most precise statement would be to identify *karma* as the action by which *dharma* is outwardly manifested. No act is a full expression of *dharma*, and none fails to express some *dharma*. In the words of the *Mahābhārata*, "There is no act that is wholly meritorious, nor any that is wholly wicked." [22] *Dharma* acts may be ordinances, rites, or ceremonies associated with magic, sacrifices, sacraments, or worship to which evaluative terms such as proper, effective, required, and correct are applied. *Dharma* acts may be ways of behaving considered to be ethical or moral to which approval or disapproval words like good, bad, right, wrong, moral, and immoral are applied. The concept of *dharma* underlies all ceremonial, ethical, social, religious, and political ideas of the Hindus. *Dharma* is both reality and ideality. The *dharma* act may be chiefly prescriptive, i.e., a chosen act intended to preserve a value, or it may be chiefly descriptive, i.e., an act flowing from the nature of a thing. In either case it is related to *ṛta*, the ancient conception of the orderliness of the world. One of the most comprehensive definitions of *dharma*—a definition which has the merit of including both descriptive and prescriptive aspects—is that formulated by Bhagavan Das:

> That which holds a thing together, makes it what it is, prevents it from breaking up and changing into something else, its characteristic function, its peculiar property, its fundamental attribute, its essential nature,—is its dharma, the law of its being primarily. That which makes the world-process what it is and holds all its parts together as One Whole, in a breakless all-binding chain of causes-and-effects, is the Law (or totality of laws) of Nature or Nature's God, dharma in the largest sense, the world order. . . . That scheme or code of laws, which binds together human beings in the bonds of mutual rights-and-duties, of causes-and-consequences of actions arising out of their temperamental characters, in relation to each other and thus maintains society, is human law, *mānava dharma*. Yet again, the code of life based on Veda (all-science of the laws of nature in all her departments), the due observance of which leads to happiness here and hereafter is Dharma. Briefly, Dharma is characteristic property, scientifically; duty, morally and legally; religion with all its proper implications, psycho-

[22] 12.15.

logically and spiritually; and righteousness and law generally; but Duty above all.[23]

The human *dharma*, i.e., *dharma* in the affairs of men, denotes an ordered life in an ordered world. It is the cohesive ideal in society. Without *dharma* there might be human individuals in various relations to each other, but there could be no human society. *Dharma* is both the essence of society and the virtue that makes the good society. The *dharma*-centered society is so foreign to Western human-rights–and–liberty–centered society that there is small hope for "one world" until this important difference between India and the West is reconciled. The basic notion of *dharma* is constraint. To show *dharma* is to order one's thoughts, passions, and affections in accordance with a rule of a place for everything and everything in its place.

According to the *Ṛg Veda*, *dharma* was established in the world when Viṣṇu made his three strides covering the entire universe.[24] Scholars differ as to what is symbolized by the three steps, but the myth implies an ordering of the universe. A second interesting account of the origin of *dharma* is found in the Upaniṣads. According to this account, in the beginning the world was only *Ātman*. The *Ātman* had no delight, hence it split itself into two, the male and the female, and from the consequent sex union the world of living forms came into being. At this point the *ṛṣi* comments, "He was not developed. He created further a better form, Law (*dharma*). . . . Therefore there is nothing higher than Law. So a weak man controls a strong man by Law, just as if by a king." [25]

The classic symbol of *dharma* is the bull, whose four feet are truth (*satya*), purity (*śauca*), compassion (*dayā*), and charity (*dāna*). The *dharma* man is the man who stands firmly in a full and happy life which culminates in self-realization and liberation. But to stand firm as a bull does not mean to be bullish! In the concept of *dharma* there is no simple rule for distinguishing right from wrong, the correct from the incorrect. Much is left to the lights of the individual. The *Mahābhārata* advises, "What should be done and what should not, cannot be ascertained easily." [26] To illustrate this point Kṛṣṇa in this section of the epic tells the story of Kausika, an ascetic, who was so faithful in telling the truth that he was known as The Truthteller. Robbers who were pursuing a group of wealthy travelers, knowing of the reputation of Kausika, approached him and asked him where the travelers had gone. Kausika

[23] *The Science of Social Organization*, Second edition, Vol. 1, pp. 49–50.
[24] 1. 22. 18.
[25] *Bṛhad-Āraṇyaka Upaniṣad* 1. 4. 14. Hume translation.
[26] 8. 69.

truthfully told the exact route they had taken. Whereupon the robbers overtook the travelers, and slew them all. Kṛṣṇa adds, "In consequence of that great sin consisting in the words spoken, Kausika, ignorant of the subtleties of morality, fell into a grievous hell." Kṛṣṇa then notes that sometimes the knowledge distinguishing virtue and sin can be determined by reason, and sometimes by appeal to scripture, but that there is no infallible way. There is a fundamental telic principle, as we have been saying again and again, namely, the Perfection of Man, but the application of that principle depends upon the practical wisdom of individuals, not upon the blind following of rules.

There are five sources of *dharma.* The first is the Vedic literature itself. This *śruti* (divine revelation) material according to tradition was "seen," not composed, by the *ṛṣis.* It is its own authority, and is often treated in a manner quite similar to the scholastic use of the Bible and Aristotle. A second source is found in a body of literature known as the Vedāṅgas. These books were composed to guide the transferral of the Saṁhitās and other oral materials into written form. The Vedāṅgas specifically dealing with secular and religious duties are known as the *Dharma Sūtras,* which, as the title indicates, were composed in the aphoristic style. There are many collections of these *sūtras.* The dates of composition are thought to be between 600 and 100 B.C. A third source of *dharma* is the collection known as the *Dharma Śāstras,* works which came into being at about the same time as the *Dharma Sūtras.* Some of these works are metrical, some prosaic. They represent the response to demands of Hindu society for interpretations of the vast *dharma* literature. These works are *smṛti,* not *śruti,* and are often denoted by the term *smṛti* itself. The word *smṛti* means memory, tradition, or recollection of what was previously established as knowledge. The relation of *smṛti* to *śruti* is quite similar to the relation of Talmud to Torah within Judaism. There is no claim that the *smṛtis* are revealed; they are clearly man-made. Their claim to authority is that they are the works of men whose minds were thoroughly saturated in the Vedas. When some observation in a *smṛti* work cannot be directly traced to *śruti,* the assumption is that the original *śruti* has been lost. A fourth source of *dharma* is custom, or "the practice of the good" (*ācāra*). To insure that custom is not the personal whim of an individual, the Hindu community has at various periods provided for a council of elders (*pariṣad*) which can be called to decide a special issue. Custom and *smṛti* are about equal in authority. A fifth way to determine *dharma* is to appeal to the view of an author, especially a *śiṣṭa,* i.e., a person who has studied the Vedas and who in addition has the appropriate moral character to speak on these matters. Vāsiṣṭha defines a *śiṣṭa* as one whose heart is free from all personal desires.[27] He is also known as an *ekavākyatā,* a man who has an opinion. Expressions like "Some say this, but my opinion is . . ." and "Manu has said, but I believe . . ." are allowable and appreciated, if the scholarly and moral credentials of the author are creditable. The sixth source of *dharma* is known as *ātmatuṣṭi,* the satisfaction of one's own heart or conscience. This is the final court of appeal, for if one is a *śiṣṭa,* he cannot be obligated to accept as his *dharma* any act that is not fully consistent with his own conscience. Hindu *dharma* is not external compulsion placed upon a man's behavior; it is fundamentally what appeals to the mind and heart of the person who is qualified to judge in these matters. Of course, people differ widely in their *dharma* proficiency depending directly upon the degree of their self-realization. Kālidāsa argued that a highly cultured person can be trusted to follow his own conscience. The poet Tagore wrote, "The inner voice of the people has begun to tell them that neither the scriptures nor tradition nor the force of personality could set a wrong right—the moral standpoint alone counted." [28] The ethic of Universal Man—to use Tagore's phrase—is still in the formulative stage. Gandhi also made moral decisions on the basis of conscience, and did not hesitate to condemn the literal use of the *Dharma Śāstras:* "The shastras would be death-traps if we were to regulate our conduct according to every detail given in them or according to that of the characters therein described." [29] Gandhi's efforts to identify the sanctions for his moral decisions are interesting but mystifying. Some of the *Dharma Śāstra* of Manu he rejected as "interpolations." "I hope they are later interpolations," he said.[30] Some sections he rejected as "contrary to known and accepted morality," [31] and about still other parts he said, "we must reject them in the light of positive experience and scientific knowledge." [32]

The *Sanātana Dharma* includes all the *mārgas.* It appeals to the three dimensions of the human being, the affective (*icchā*), the cognitive (*jñāna*), and the conative (*kriyā*). In its restrictive, disciplinary aspect it is a *yoga mārga,* but as a duty or requirement it is necessarily limited to the observable, external behavior of the human being. The internal life of the affections cannot be legislated. For example, one can be coerced to bow the head, to say "I am sorry," and to promise to avoid a repetition of an offending act, but one cannot be forced to *feel* penitent. Every

[27] *Vāsiṣṭha Dharma Sūtra* 1. 6.
[28] *Towards Universal Man,* p. 344.
[29] *Hindu Dharma,* p. 23.
[30] *Ibid.,* p. 370.
[31] *Ibid.,* p. 219.
[32] *Ibid.,* p. 402.

detail of the life of the individual is legislated in *dharma* literature except the life of the mind and the heart! What appears to be a formal, rigid legalism turns out to be a provision for the liberation of the imaginative, artistic, and creative endeavors of man. When the social and ceremonial activities of man are comfortably channeled in ways that have acquired the status of custom, the individual is free to concentrate on what Spinoza has called the sharable goods of life. By regulating the external life of man, Hindu *dharma* releases the internal life. The fewer decisions that the individual has to make in the area of overt behavior, the greater is the liberty to grow in the inner life of art, science, literature, music, philosophy, and religion. To observe that this does not always happen is merely to note that in every dimension of life practice does not fulfill the promises of theory.

Karma mārga, the path of action, is the application of *dharma* leading to the Perfection of Man. Indian and Western scholars have classified the *mānava dharmas* in many different ways; some of the *dharmas* relate to the ordinary life of man, some to man as a seeker of emancipation, some to sex activities, and some to the tragic situations of life. Pandurang Vaman Kane, in his excellent *History of Dharmashastra,* recommends classifying the dharmas into five groups: (1) *varṇa dharmas,* those having to do with the duties of the classes in Hindu society: (2) *āśrama dharmas,* those associated with the four stages of the ideal life of a Hindu; (3) *varṇāśrama dharmas,* the rules and requirements for the life of a man of a particular class and in a particular stage of his life; (4) *naimittika dharmas,* the techniques for expiating the *karma* resulting from the doing of that which is forbidden; (5) *sādharaṇa dharmas,* the duties common to all humanity. For our purpose in examining the *mārgas* we shall first consider the *sādharaṇa dharmas,* next the *varṇa dharmas,* and then the *āśrama dharmas.* Following this we shall consider the religious ceremonial rites and indicate upon whom each of them is obligatory.

The important fact about the *dharmas,* not to be lost in an examination of their intricacies, is that although some of them are the outgrowth of superstition and primitive magic, they are rooted in the fundamental view of man as a social being living in an ordered universe.

3. *Sādharaṇa Dharma*

Hinduism does not affirm that all men are created equal. The doctrine of the inequality of men is fundamental to Hindu society; it is inherent in the doctrines of *karma* and *saṁsāra.* Birth and death are transition points in the causal chain of lives of an individual. "Every man is born in the world fashioned by himself" says the *Śatapatha Brāhmaṇa*.[33] The child at birth is the product of karmatic influences of its previous incarnations; its psychological make-up, physical differentia, and even its class membership are determined by causes now coming to fruition. Hinduism openly and frankly recognizes the differences among men by holding that the greater responsibility falls upon the well-endowed persons in society, and the greater punishment must be inflicted when these fail in their obligations. In practice, however, the rights and the privileges of Brahmins often overshadow their obligations. Tagore was one who saw that civil justice requires equality: "Among the doctrines of the new age that have come to us is the one that makes all men equal before the Law. Whether a Brahman kills a low-caste Sudra or a Sudra kills a Brahman, it is murder all the same, and calls for the same punishment. No ancient injunction in this regard can sway the scales of justice."[34] Panikkar argued, "Democracy and caste are totally opposed. . . . the one is based on equality, and the other on inequality of birth."[35] Nehru left no doubt where he stood. In the social organization of today, he wrote, caste "has no place left. . . . It was an aristocratic approach based on traditionalism. This outlook has to change completely, for it is wholly opposed to modern conditions and the democratic ideal."[36] Even Radhakrishnan refers to "the undemocratic character of the institutions associated with Hindu religion."[37] The argument of caste-minded men for inequalities of rights, duties, and hence of punishment, is based on the conception of the development of the individual over many incarnations. If caste may be described as a merit system, at least the merits are earned, not awarded by a capricious fate or a whimsical society. Between the tenth and the eighteenth centuries two egalitarian movements ran their courses within Hinduism—the Bhakti and the Tantric movements—but neither made a major alteration in the basic Hindu conception of the inequalities of men. A poem of the Śaiva mystic Pattakiriar expresses the poignant longing of those who labored for equality:

> When shall our race be one great brotherhood,
> Unbroken by the tyranny of caste,
> Which Kapila in early days withstood,
> And taught that men once were in times once past.[38]

[33] 6. 2. 2. 27.
[34] *Towards Universal Man*, p. 344. See also *Nationalism*, p. 135.
[35] K. M. Panikkar, *Caste and Democracy*, p. 37.
[36] *The Discovery of India*, p. 394.
[37] *Modern India and the West*, p. 350.
[38] Quoted by Mukerjee, *The Culture and Art of India*, p. 318.

Gandhi believed in both the equality of men and *varṇa dharma.* He accomplished this feat by claiming that all occupations were of equal value, therefore all classes are of equal worth. He sometimes did the work of a scavenger to give empirical evidence to his claim. But in spite of precept and example, he did not convince many Indians of the basic equality of men or occupations. Today the democratic nation of India is making an effort to establish the theory and practice of human equality in a land of many tongues, races, religions, and castes.

Although Hinduism divides men into four classes on the basis of their development in the process of perfection, it does insist that all men belong to one great human race. This has not been a universal view among the cultures of man. The ancient Egyptians believed that only Egyptians were men; Asians and Africans were not people! The *Merikarē,* an early Egyptian writing, after speaking of the miserable life of the Asian, adds, "Trouble thyself not about him; he is only an Asiatic." [39] Aristotle represented well the Greek attitude when he advised Alexander to treat Asian peoples as "plants and vegetables," and when he described slaves as living tools.[40] Hinduism, on the other hand, has made a distinction between the duties of all men and the duties of men within castes, thus recognizing that the society of men is more than homogenous grouping in joint families, clans, and occupational classes. There are everyman *dharmas,* duties that properly belong to man because he is man. These are fundamental to the maintenance of society and the state. The British were able to take advantage of this lawfulness in their rule of India. The *sādharaṇa dharmas* are often presented in the *smṛtis* as lists of virtues such as truthfulness, mercy, patience, non-injury, self-control, and benevolence. Bhīṣma identifies nine duties belonging to all the four orders equally: (1) suppression of wrath, (2) truthfulness of speech, (3) justice, (4) forgiveness, (5) begetting children upon one's wedded wives, (6) purity of conduct, (7) avoidance of quarrels, (8) simplicity, and (9) maintenance of dependents.[41] The Edicts of Aśoka may be cited as an example of "the *dharma* of everyone." Sometimes the essence of *sādharaṇa dharma* is stated as not doing to others what one would not like done to one's self.

To illustrate the universal duties of men we shall turn to the *Kural,* an ethical poetic writing assigned to Tiruvaḷḷuvar, a priest of the Tamil outcaste group who flourished in the third century A.D. He lived in Mayilāpur, now Mylapore a suburb of Madras, where he earned his

[39] *Merikarē* 98. Quoted by John A. Wilson in H. Frankfort, H. A. Frankfort, John A. Wilson, and Thorkild Jacobsen, *Before Philosophy.* London: Pelican Books, 1949, p. 47.

[40] *Politica* 1253 b 30.

[41] *Mahābhārata* 12.60.

livelihood by weaving. Hinduism, Buddhism, Jainism, and Christianity have all claimed him, and according to legend his remains lie beneath the cathedral of St. Thomas in Mylapore. The *Kural* has often been called the Tamil Veda. It has been well received by many peoples. Albert Schweitzer said of it, "There hardly exists in the literature of the world a collection of maxims in which we find such lofty wisdom." [42] The *Kural* has been selected by UNESCO as one of the works to be translated into all modern languages. It is divided into three parts: *dharma, artha,* and *kāma,* or, in Tamil, *aram, porul,* and *inbam.* The absence of *mokṣa* indicates the predominately ethical interests of the author. After four opening poems in which the author praises God, the natural world, the seers, and abstract virtue, he takes up the themes that to him matter most—the virtues of home, wife, and children. The highest human virtues are those of the home: "True home life is true virtue." [43] "He who lives home life worthily is chief among all who strive." [44] He will have a place among the gods in heaven.[45] His wife is his most precious possession:

> What is more precious than a wife,
> If strength of purity is hers?
> . . . .
> The worth of a wife is a man's good fortune.[46]

The love of man and wife is like "the bond of soul and body." [47] True love, however, is not easy to attain; it "is more delicate than a flower." [48] Tiruvaḷḷuvar offers many hints as to how the perfect bliss of married love might be attained, perhaps the most penetrating: "In lover's quarrels the loser always wins." [49] Children are a man's jewels, he says.[50] His descriptions of little incidents of the home reveal his own childlike heart:

> The gruel that children's little hands have stirred
> Is sweeter far than nectar.
> The touch of children's hands is a joy to the body,
> To listen to their prattle is joy to the ear.[51]

[42] Thirumalaimuthuswami, *A Bibliography on Thirukkural*, p. 3.
[43] *Kural* 5. 9.
[44] *Ibid.*, 5. 7.
[45] *Ibid.*, 5. 10.
[46] *Ibid.*, 6. 4, 10.
[47] *Ibid.*, 113. 2.
[48] *Ibid.*, 129. 9.
[49] *Ibid.*, 113. 7.
[50] *Ibid.*, 6. 10.
[51] *Ibid.*, 7. 5–6.

The love of wife and children spreads into wider human relations:

> Love gives rise to affection for all . . .
>
> . . . .
>
> The living soul subsists by love;
> The loveless are but skin and bone.[52]

One of the most immediate ways of sharing love is to entertain a guest:

> The wealth and joy of home life have one end,
> To cherish guests and show them kindnesses.
>
> . . . .
>
> He'll be a welcome guest to gods above,
> Who, having cherished the parting guest awaits the coming guest.[53]

The virtues of primary personal relations which the poet praises include: kindly speech, "Humility and kindly speech are jewels rare";[54] gratitude, "Never forsake the friendship of those who've helped you in trouble";[55] self-control, "Self-control will lead one to the immortals";[56] forbearance, "Though others do you ill, 'tis better, knowing their suffering, to do no ill";[57] unselfishness, "For one to enjoy alone his hoarded wealth is far worse than begging";[58] truthfulness, "Let no one tell a lie knowingly";[59] kindness, "It is the creed of the pure never to give pain to others, even if they could by it gain supreme wealth";[60] non-injury, "What is the sum of all virtues? It is not taking life";[61] and desirelessness, "There is in this world no greater good than desirelessness." [62] The poet blesses learning:

> The learned are said to have seeing eyes;
> The unlearned have only two sores on their faces.
>
> . . . .
>
> Learning is excellent imperishable wealth;
> All else is not real wealth.[63]

[52] *Ibid.*, 8. 4, 11.
[53] *Ibid.*, 9. 1, 6.
[54] *Ibid.*, 10. 5.
[55] *Ibid.*, 11. 6.
[56] *Ibid.*, 13. 1.
[57] *Ibid.*, 16. 7.
[58] *Ibid.*, 23. 9.
[59] *Ibid.*, 30. 3.
[60] *Ibid.*, 32. 1.
[61] *Ibid.*, 33. 1.
[62] *Ibid.*, 37. 3.
[63] *Ibid.*, 43. 3, 10.

Sometimes the *Kural* sounds like *Poor Richard's Almanac:*

> Industry will produce wealth;
> Idleness will drive to poverty.[64]

Sometimes it resembles the *Tao Te Ching:*

> It is easy for anyone to talk;
> It is hard to act according to one's speech.[65]

And sometimes it reminds the reader of the *Book of Proverbs:*

> Wisdom is a tool for guarding against ruin;
> It is an inner fortress which even foes cannot destroy.[66]

Tiruvaḷḷuvar advises men to engage in the simple occupations of life:

> Roam where one will, the world follows the plough;
> Farming, though toilsome, is the best labour.[67]
> . . . .
> Even though it be but gruel and pure water,
> There is nothing sweeter than the good of toil.[68]

But he does not identify the simple life with the life of poverty:

> Many other sufferings will come in the train
> Of the painful suffering of poverty.[69]

As we read the *Kural* we forget that it is the work of a simple Indian weaver of the third century, and think of it as a work of a great practical humanitarian of any culture or time. The *Kural* may be Hindu, but it is also human and humane. It reminds us that the basic primary virtues are the common denominator of all human morality. The *Kural* is an example of *sādharaṇa dharma.* The Hindus were not slow to develop the principles of harmonious human relationships. One Western scholar states in the preface to his volume on Hindu ethics that he has written his book "feeling confident that it will be a pleasure to many and a grief to none to know that truthfulness, generosity, kindness of heart,

[64] *Ibid.*, 63. 6.
[65] *Ibid.*, 67. 4.
[66] *Ibid.*, 43. 3.
[67] *Ibid.*, 104. 1.
[68] *Ibid.*, 107. 5.
[69] *Ibid.*, 105. 5.

purity of soul, forgiveness, and compassion were taught in India as everyday precepts long before the Christian era." [70] This is the moral duty of all men to all men. This is *sādharaṇa dharma.*

4. *Varṇa Dharma*

Varṇa dharma is the *dharma* of social planning. The principle of planning as conceived within Hinduism makes movement from vocation to vocation, from profession to profession, impossible. It is the obligations and rules necessary for a well-organized society. As a *dharma* it deals with duties, not rights, with social utility and self-realization rather than class identity and individual privileges. Although *varṇa dharma* may not have been designed to distinguish the high and the low, the good and the bad, the fact is it has acquired value distinctions. The Brahmin is the one who has moved further along in development toward the Perfection of Man than has a member of other classes; hence he is better, although, since Hinduism has no theory of the inevitable progress of the individual, he may slip from the status he has attained.

The origins of the caste system cannot be established. Majumdar says there are about as many theories of caste origins as there are writers on the subject.[71] Caste appears to have originated in northwestern India among the invading Aryans as a technique to avoid assimilation with the darker-skinned aboriginals. Before coming into India the Aryans distinguished between the nobility (*kṣatra*) and the common people (*viś*) of their own tribes. Perhaps they had also participated in an ancient Iranian division into priests, warriors, agriculturalists, and artisans. After settling in the Indus valley they were confronted with the problem of maintaining their own identity. They began to distinguish themselves as Aryans (nobles) from the conquered peoples, whom they called Dāsas (black ones) or Asuras (non-shining ones). The former term came to mean slaves; the latter term came to mean demons. In the *Ṛg Veda* these peoples are described as black in color, speechless (probably meaning that they did not speak the Aryan tongue), without rites, without any purpose in life, and without the gods (*adevas*). Those Aryans who married Dāsas fell in the social scale of the conquerors. As religious rites became more complicated, those who were in charge of the sacrificial lore were shown special deference, and they rose in the social ranks. By the close of the Vedic period a fourfold division of society had been accepted and had been given religious sanction.

[70] Edward Washburn Hopkins, *Ethics of India*, p. xii.
[71] D. N. Majumdar, *Races and Cultures of India*, p. 289.

One of the religious sanctions for the caste system can be found in the *Ṛg Veda* in the myth of Puruṣa, the primeval man who existed before the foundation of the universe. Puruṣa is the primordial sacrifice, slain before the foundations of the world were laid. The gods immolated him, making the firmament from his navel, heaven from his head, earth from his feet, space from his ear, etc. Man also came from him: "His mouth became the Brahmin, his arms the Kṣatriya, his thighs became the Vaiśya, and the Śūdra was born from his feet." [72] These classes of men are not called *varṇas* in the *Ṛg Veda,* but later the term *varṇa* was used to signify the priestly scholars, the warriors and rulers, the merchants, and the serfs or laborers. The fact that *varṇa* means color has caused some to make the facile assumption that the classification was a color distinction. However, *varṇa* also means species, kind, character, nature, and form. When the Portuguese came to India in the sixteenth century, they used their word *casta* for *varṇa.* This word, which means an unmixed race, a tribe, or a clan, is a poor translation, for it connotes groups that rise and fall in a social scale, but the four *varṇas* are fixed. Meanwhile another Sanskrit term began to be used—the term *jāti. Jāti* means origin or birth, and it came to be used especially for the subclasses within the four *varṇas,* of which there are today about three thousand. Sometimes the word "caste" is used only for *jāti,* e.g., this was Gandhi's meaning when he said, "I hold there is nothing in common between caste and *varṇa.* Whilst *varṇa* gives life, caste kills it, and untouchability is the hatefulest expression of caste." [73] The practical difference is that *varṇa* emphasizes duties, whereas *jāti* emphasizes privileges. But since *varṇa* and *jāti* were both translated as "caste," confusion resulted. We shall avoid adding to the confusion by using *varṇa* to denote the four fixed classes, by using *jāti* for the subclasses, which are usually occupational groups, and by using "caste" only for the entire *varṇa-jāti* system.

The term *jāti* offers an interesting contribution to the study of man. The *jāti* of a man is the result of *nāmika* (that which refers to the name [*nāma*], the sum of qualities properly belonging to the individual) and *gotrika* (that which belongs to the family [*gotra*], the sum of qualities which the individual derives from his heredity). *Jāti* is the result of individual differences plus inherited characteristics. An individual is a combination of heredity, environment, and a uniqueness which is truly his own. Speculations on *jāti* differ according to whether the emphasis is

[72] *Ṛg Veda* 10. 10. 12. In the Brāhmaṇas the *varṇa* system is found among the gods, e.g., Agni and Bṛhaśpati are Brahmins; Indra, Varuṇa, Soma, and Yama are Kṣatriyas; Vasus, Rudra, and the Maruts are Vaiśyas; and Pūṣan is a Śūdra. See *Maitrāyaṇi Sāmskāra* 1. 10. 13. Also *Satápatha Brāhmaṇa* 14. 4. 2. 23–25.

[73] *Hindu Dharma,* p. 34.

placed on the inherited aspects or on the individual aspects. Gandhi usually stressed the heredity aspects, e.g.,

> I believe that just as everyone inherits a particular form so does he inherit the particular characteristics and qualities of his progenitors, and to make this admission is to conserve one's energy. That frank admission if he will act upon it would put a legitimate curb upon our ambitions and thereby our energy is set free for extending the field of spiritual research and spiritual evolution." [74]

Gandhi reflected a late point of view. The class distinction may have been originally based on the *guṇas: rajas* (active individuals), *sattva* (intellectual types), and *tamas* (sluggish people). *Bhagavad Gītā* 4. 13 can be used as a proof-text for such a claim: "The fourfold order was created by Me according to the divisions of quality (*guṇa*) and work (*karma*)." [75] *Śruti* support is found in *Chāndogya Upaniṣad,* where the son of an unmarried serving girl is accepted as a Brahmin by a *guru* because he truthfully acknowledges his illegitimate birth. The *guru* says, "A non-Brahmin would not be able to explain thus. Bring the fuel, my dear. I will receive you as a pupil. You have not deviated from the truth." [76] Yet during the centuries emphasis came to be applied to a man's birth rather than to his character. When Muslims came to India in the eleventh century, bringing with them the practice of proselytism, Hindus reacted by ossifying their customs and traditions. The *jāti* system became more rigid. The differences that mattered were localized in problems of intermarriage, inter-dining, and occupation. The number of *jātis* increased on extremely flimsy bases, e.g., the oil pressers of Bengal belonged to a single *jāti* until a new technique was introduced: a hole was made at the bottom of the mortar in which the oil seeds were pressed. Those who adopted the innovation became a separate *jāti,* and the two, those who used a mortar with a hole in the bottom and those who used the old method of mopping up the oil with a cloth, set up restrictions against each other.[77] Thus the concept of individual and class differentiation in the words of Radhakrishnan "degenerated into an instrument of oppression and intolerance" and tended "to perpetuate inequality and develop the spirit of exclusiveness." [78] Aurobindo, likewise, said, "It has become a name, a shell, a sham and must either be dissolved in the crucible of an individualist period of society or else fatally affect with weakness and falsehood the

[74] *Young India,* Sept. 20, 1927.
[75] Radhakrishnan translation.
[76] 4. 4. 5. Hume translation.
[77] G. Slater, *The Dravidian Element in Indian Culture,* p. 51.
[78] *The Hindu View of Life,* p. 93.

system of life that clings to it."[79] Gandhi, a curious combination of innovator and reactionary, was in this respect very conservative. He seemed to want to hold on to many fixed ways of thinking and acting as he led his people on new paths of passive resistance to political independence. Nehru minced no words:

> It is sometimes said that the basic idea of caste might remain but its subsequent harmful development and ramifications should go; that it should not depend on birth but on merit. This approach is irrelevant and merely confuses the issue. In a historical context a study of the growth of caste has some value, but obviously we cannot go back to the period when caste began; in the social organization of today it has no place left. If merit is the only criterion and opportunity is thrown open to everybody, then caste loses all its present-day distinguishing features and, in fact, ends.[80]

The *varṇa-jāti* structure of society in India has been of paramount interest to travelers since the days of Alexander, and the evaluations of the system have been multiform. Flavius Arrian, the Greek historian who lived in the first century A.D., reported there were seven classes of Indians: (1) tillers of the soil, (2) nomadic herdsmen, (3) handcraftsmen and retail dealers, (4) warriors, (5) superintendents who spied on the people for the benefit of the rulers, (6) rulers of state, and (7) "Sophists," the least numerous, but the ones in supreme place of dignity and honor. Arrian added that the customs of the country prohibited intermarriage among the classes and movement among trades or classes.[81] The French missionary Dubois, who lived in India from 1792 to 1823, said,

> After much careful thought I can discover no other reason except caste which accounts for the Hindus not having fallen into the same state of barbarism as their neighbors and as almost all nations inhabiting the torrid zone. Caste assigns to each individual his own profession or calling; and the handing down of the system from father to son, from generation to generation, makes it impossible for any person or his descendents to change from the condition of life which the law assigned to him for any other. Such an institution was probably the only means that the most clear sighted prudence could devise for maintaining a state of civilization amongst a people endowed with the peculiar characteristics of the Hindus.[82]

[79] *The Human Cycle*, p. 11.
[80] *The Discovery of India*, p. 394.
[81] *Indika* XI, XII. See R. C. Majumdar, *The Classical Accounts of India*, pp. 224–226.
[82] *Hindu Manners, Customs and Ceremonies by the Abbé J. A. Dubois*, p. 160. Translated by Henry K. Beauchamp.

Many Westerners who have known and loved India have condemned the caste system, e.g., Mountstuart Elphinstone, John Stuart Mill, and Henry Maine, but few have rivaled the Indians themselves in vilification, e.g., Swami Vivekananda once said, "But in spite of all the ravings of the priests, caste is simply a crystallized social institution, which doing its service is now filling the atmosphere of India with stink." [83] Radhakamal Mukerjee writes, "Today she [India] finds that caste men are not good men, and caste society an unjust and evil society." [84] Govindā-Dāsa condemns it wholesale:

> The utter rout, the hopeless breakdown of the whole system of caste is exemplified in every nook and corner of India—from the days of Cyrus, Darius and Alexander, downwards through the bitter agony of the Moslem occupation of the country; the widespread ruins of architecture testifying for all those who have eyes to see or ears to hear that the Hindu polity of those 2500 years has failed to be the bulwark of Hindu faith and the channel for conveying uncontaminated its culture. The Kshatriya has proved a rotten reed in the defence of the country; the Vaishya has not brought wealth to the land, nor the Brahman, learning—unless the useless knowledge of the sacrificial art can be called "learning." Judged by the present-day condition of India, it must be said that the caste-system as now working has to be abolished altogether, if the Indian people are to have a new lease of life.[85]

The deterioration of the caste system can be described as a shifting of emphasis from *varṇa* to *jāti*, from the broad duties inherent in one's culture, character, and profession or occupation to the narrow rights and privileges of one's birth. For example, all Brahmins are believed to have descended from seventy-two *ṛṣis*, and all descendants from one *ṛṣi* are said to be a *gotra*. Intermarriage within a *gotra* is forbidden, and as the *varṇa*-system becomes weaker a Brahmin father may be more anxious that his daughter not marry a Brahmin of his *gotra* than that she not marry outside the Brahmin *varṇa*. He is more concerned about the *gotra* label or name than about the duties associated with Brahmin stature. The rigidity of the caste system is largely a matter of restrictions regarding intercaste marriages. This is a distinct problem which we shall examine later in this chapter.

The *Dharma Śāstra* of Manu, the most important of the forty-seven *Dharma Śāstras*, lists the duties of the four *varṇas* as follows: the Brahmins are to study and teach Vedic lore, to conduct sacrifices, to give and

[83] Quoted by K. M. Panikkar, *Hindu Society at Cross Roads*, p. 77.
[84] *The Indian Scheme of Life*, p. vi.
[85] *Hinduism*, p. 443.

receive gifts;[86] the Kṣatriyas are to protect the people, to give gifts, to study the Vedas, and to abstain from sensual pleasures;[87] the Vaiśyas are to tend cattle, to give alms, to sacrifice, to study the Vedas, to lend money, to cultivate the land;[88] the Śūdras are to serve meekly the other castes.[89] In this list, as in most lists, the line of distinction is between the three upper *varṇas* and the Śūdras, not between Brahmins and non-Brahmins. Note, for example, that Brahmins, Kṣatriyas, and Vaiśyas are to study the Vedas, but this is not mentioned as a Śūdra duty. As a matter of fact, the Śūdras were forbidden to study the Vedas. Śaṅkara accepted this view. In his commentary to *Vedānta Sūtra* 1. 3. 38 he quotes with approval the following passages from the Vedas: "The ears of him [i.e., a Śūdra] who hears the Veda are to be filled with molten lead and lac. . . . For a Śūdra is like a cemetery, therefore the Veda is not to be read in the vicinity of a Śūdra." [90] He also agrees that the tongue of a Śūdra is to be slit "if he pronounces" the Vedas, and his body to be cut through "if he preserves it." [91] Only the members of the three upper *varṅas* are to study the Vedas, to participate in Vedic sacrifices, and to bestow gifts in Vedic fashion. Śaṅkara recognizes that this general rule may at times be altered, e.g., if a Śūdra, despite the rule, somehow acquires Vedic knowledge, he will be liberated, "since knowledge in all cases brings about its fruit." [92] Śaṅkara acknowledges that the Ithihāsas and the Purāṇas may be taught to Śūdras. He quotes the *Mahābhārata* to support this view: "He is to teach the four castes." [93] But to make sure that his principal point is not lost, Śaṅkara adds as a concluding remark: "It remains, however, a settled point that they (the Śūdras) do not possess any such qualification with regard to the Veda." [94]

Brahmins, Kṣatriyas, and Vaiśyas are twice-born, i.e., the male members of these *varṇas* undergo at puberty a sacrament marking their spiritual birth, whereas the Śūdras are once-born, i.e., they do not have a spiritual birth. The supreme *varṇa dharma* for the twice-born is to engage in self-perfecting; the chief obligation for the once-born is to serve the twice-born, knowing that their status as Śūdras is the result of karmatic forces and that the twice-born state is a possibility for them in later in-

[86] 1. 88.

[87] 1. 89.

[88] 1. 90.

[89] 1. 91. A similar listing of the duties of each of the four *varṇas* is given in the *Mahābhārata* 12. 60.

[90] *The Vedānta Sūtras with the Commentary by Śaṅkarācārya. The Sacred Books of the East*, Vol. 34, p. 228.

[91] *Ibid.*

[92] *Ibid.*, p. 229.

[93] *Ibid.*

[94] *Ibid.*

carnations. Again it should be noted that the four *varṇas* are hierarchical; yet there is no necessity that each individual go through the four *varṇas*, i.e., Vaiśyas and Kṣatriyas do not need to anticipate becoming Brahmins as part of their *sādhana*. Even the necessity of twice-bornness is denied by the supporters of *bhakti mārga*. Radhakrishnan once wrote, "The ideal of the Hindu dharma is to make all men Brahmins." [95] This is a loose and misleading statement, for certainly the caste system is not a spiritual ladder to be ascended rung by rung. *Mokṣa* for Kṣatriyas and Vaiśyas does not depend upon their attaining the status of Brahmins. Perhaps Radhakrishnan meant that the ideal is to make all men *like* Brahmins, although even this interpretation is subject to serious emendation. The ideal is to attain the Perfection of Man, a perfection which transcends the caste system.

The Brahmins are given extremely high status in the Hindu lawbooks: "The gods are invisible deities, but Brahmins are visible deities." [96] "A Brahmin, whether learned or not, is a great deity." [97] Their duties are chiefly concerned with the conservation of Vedic lore. Their privileges are numerous. Kane, stating, "It is desirable that a comprehensive list of all the privileges claimed by brahmanas (though not always conceded as the sequel will show) should be set out once for all," [98] itemizes the privileges listed in the *Dharma Śāstra*: [99]

1. They must serve as *guru* to all the *varṇas*.
2. They must expound the proper duties and conduct for all classes.
3. They may eat sacrificial food.
4. They cannot be given corporal punishment.
5. They are free from taxation.
6. They may keep all found treasure.
7. They do no sin by dying without leaving an heir.
8. They are favored on the roadways.
9. Killing a Brahmin is the greatest sin.
10. Threatening or striking a Brahmin is severely condemned.
11. They receive lighter punishments for certain offences.[100]
12. They cannot be called as litigant by a member of a lower *varṇa*.

[95] *The Heart of Hindusthan*, p. 22.
[96] *Viśnu Dharma Sūtra* 19. 20.
[97] *Manu Dharma Śāstra* 9. 317.
[98] *History of Dharmashastra*, Vol. 2, Part I, p. 138.
[99] *Ibid.*, pp. 138–154.
[100] E.g., there is lighter punishment for adultery committed by a Brahmin than for adultery committed by a Śūdra. On the other hand, a Śūdra who steals is to be fined eight times the worth of the stolen goods; a Vaiśya sixteen times the worth of the goods; a Kṣatriya thirty-two times the worth of the goods; and a Brahmin sixty-four or one hundred twenty-eight times the worth of the goods. *Manu Dharma Śāstra* 8. 336–338.

13. They may be guests at *śrāddhas* (oblations to the dead).
14. They are the only ones who can perform certain sacrifices.
15. They are required fewer days of mourning than other *varṇas*.[101]

The limitations on the Śūdras are many: they cannot study the Vedas, nor perform Vedic rites, nor engage in most of the sacraments; they cannot attain merit by giving gifts to Brahmins; they cannot cook for Brahmins, nor eat with them, nor touch them; they are to spend their whole life in the householder stage. Yet the Śūdras have certain advantages: they may follow any vocation, except those specially reserved for Brahmins and Kṣatriyas; they may engage in moneymaking occupations; they are freed from the round of daily rites; they may eat any food and drink any drink they desire; they are much less restricted as to whom they may marry.

Rammohun Roy once stated the practical meaning of Hinduism in daily life as "a peculiar mode of diet." [102] "What and with whom may I eat?" sometimes seems to be the fundamental problem in *varṇa dharma.* G. S. Ghurye in *Caste and Class in India,* taking dining as the differentium, claims that the caste system divides men into five groups: (1) the twice-born; (2) those at whose hands the twice-born can take food cooked with ghee; (3) those at whose hands the twice-born can take water, but not food; (4) those at whose hands the twice-born cannot take food or drink, but whose touch is not defiling; (5) those at whose hands the twice-born cannot take food or drink, and whose touch is defiling.

Despite the obvious defects, problems, and injustices of the caste system, the system pervades the lives of many in India who are not Hindus. The caste structure has entered Islam with divisions into Sayed, Mughal, Sheikh, and Pathan. Zoroastrianism in India has developed similar divisions: Atharvas, Rathaesthas, Vastryafshuyans, and Huiti. Jews and Christians in India have also formed groups analogous to castes.[103] The Syrian Christians of Kerala have their own castes. L. K. A. Iyer claims, "There are a large number of Christians in the Southern Districts of the Madras Presidency who even boast of their being firmer and truer adherents of the caste system than the Hindus." [104] Over four hundred *jātis* have been formed among the Outcastes or Untouchables in India, the people whom Gandhi called the Harijans (Children of God), and

[101] Ten days for a Brahmin; one month for a Śūdra.

[102] Roland W. Scott, *Social Ethics in Modern Hinduism,* p. 40.

[103] J. H. Hutton, *Caste in India.* Fourth edition, p. 2.

[104] *Anthropology of the Syrian Christians.* Ernakulam, 1926, p. 218. T. S. Wilkinson in "Urban Community and the Church," *The United Church Review,* August 1964, pp. 171–174, states that Indian Christians tend to treat converts from Scheduled castes as "second class Christians."

who constitute about fifteen percent of the total population of India. One Indologist has speculated, "Modern India, having created a caste of chauffeurs from the menials who tend motor-cars, is almost ripe for a Rolls Royce caste rejecting food or marriage with the Fords." [105]

The most serious charges against *varṇa dharma* are that it directs the attention of people to ceremonies and magical practices rather than to moral issues, deadens human sympathies toward the less fortunate people of society, fragments and narrows the compass of humanitarian concerns, and places a higher value on birth than on character and attainment. Ambedkar, an Untouchable who earned a doctorate at Columbia University, suffered all his life at the hands of people inferior to him in education yet "superior" to him by reason of being *varṇa* men. Office helpers in the government buildings at New Delhi used to slam interoffice communications on his desk as an expression of their attitude toward his untouchability. In conversation with Gandhi on August 14, 1931, Dr. Ambedkar said, "Gandhiji, I have no homeland. . . . How can I call this land my own homeland; and this religion my own wherein we are treated worse than cats and dogs, wherein we cannot get water to drink? No self-respecting Untouchable worth the name will be proud of this land." [106] Ambedkar also concluded that the Untouchable could not claim Hinduism. "To the Untouchables," he said, "Hinduism is a veritable chamber of horrors." [107] In desperation shortly before his death he and thousands of other Untouchables embraced Buddhism in hopes of improving their lot.

The government of India has tried many ways to eliminate the scourge of untouchability. The providing of government scholarships for "Ex-Untouchables" in universities and colleges is one way. By 1963 the number of such scholarships had risen to fifty-five thousand. In 1961 an inquiry was sent out from the office of the Commissioner for Scheduled Castes and Tribes to all the state governments to determine how many of the assisted students had earned degrees, what type of degrees they had earned, etc. But by mid-1963 the Commissioner had not received a single reply from the state governments.[108] If this is a fair sample of the absence of human concern among caste-minded men, then caste stands condemned as a crime against humanity. Is this also a condemnation of *varṇa?* Gandhi was convinced that untouchability was the result of a

[105] R. E. Enthoven in a review of N. K. Dutt's *Origin and Growth of Caste in India* in *The Journal of the Royal Asiatic Society*, January 1932. Quoted by Hutton, *Caste in India*, p. 117.

[106] Keer, *Dr. Ambedkar, Life and Mission*, p. 162.

[107] *What Congress and Gandhi Have Done to the Untouchables*, p. 307.

[108] Harold Isaacs, *India's Ex-Untouchables*, p. 18.

false valuational hierarchy which had entered Hindu social thinking. He once wrote in a letter to Dr. Ambedkar, "Untouchability is the product . . . not of the caste system, but of the distinction between high and low that has crept into Hinduism and is corroding it. . . . The moment untouchability goes, the caste system itself will be purified, that is to say, according to my dream, it will resolve itself in the true Varna Dharma, the four divisions of society, each complementary of the other and none inferior or superior to any other, each as necessary for the whole of Hinduism as any other." [109] Gandhi's dream remains, as yet, unfulfilled.

5. *Āśrama Dharma*

The *āśramas* are the four stages of the ideal life of the Hindu. The *āśrama dharmas* are the duties and obligations appropriate to the individual as he progresses toward the supreme goal. They are designed to insure that each person in the Hindu community will have the necessary opportunity to advance toward the state of liberation. The word *āśrama* comes from *śram* meaning to exert energy. The implication is that each of the life stages embodies an expenditure of effort toward specific ends and that the whole scheme is directed toward *mokṣa*. If the *varṇas* can be said to emphasize nature, the *āśramas* stress nurture.

The *āśramas* are not mentioned in the *Ṛg Veda* as *āśramas*, although references are made to students, householders, and ascetics. There are also references in the *Upaniṣads* to students of sacred learning who lived in the house of their teacher.[110] We know that by the time of the Buddha the four *āśramas* had been established, since the Buddha left the life of the householder to assume the role of a wandering ascetic. The Hindu community did not favor the Buddhist tendency to omit or shorten the householder stage, nor did it approve opening the ascetic stage to women.

The *āśrama* scheme of man's life is a functional division. The four functions in chronological order are preparation, production, service, and retirement. They constitute a rhythm of inner-direction and outer-direc-

[109] *Hindu Dharma*, pp. 358–359. Another side of Gandhi's work is revealed by Taya Zinkin: "I visited Gandhi's eldest sister, Ralihat Behen, shortly before she died at over ninety. When I tried to make her talk about her brother she exploded into toothless anger and tears: Gandhi's insistence on mixing with unclean people, on being his own sweeper, and his trips over the sea, had led to the excommunication of the whole family. For Ralihat Behen this had meant a lifetime of ostracism and humiliation by the people about whom she minded: the orthodox of her own sub-caste and neighbourhood. Far from feeling proud of her brother, she stood there, doubled up by rheumatism, calling him a man so selfish that he had not cared what harm he had done to his family." *Caste Today*, pp. 49–50.

[110] *Chāndogya Upaniṣad* 2. 23. 1.

tion. The first is an inner-directed stage of training for the second and third, which are both outer-directed. In the second stage the person maintains the entire society, and in the third he shares his experiences for the good of all. The final stage is again inner-directed; the individual, having contributed at least as much as he has received, now prepares himself for release from life itself. Efforts to link the four *āśramas* with the four ideal ends of man's life—*artha, kāma, dharma,* and *mokṣa*—are not very helpful and ought not to be attempted, since all four *āśramas* may be said to be the *dharma* of man. Manu condemned a man who sought *mokṣa* without going through the first three stages,[111] but there are many deviations from this norm. A *sādhu* may skip the second or third *āśrama,* or he may skip both. Many modern Hindus in practice recognize only one *āśrama,* the householder stage, the first being regarded as preparation for the householder stage, and the last two as largely of historical interest. The four stages are outlined in the classical writings of Hinduism with the Brahmins chiefly in mind, although since *mokṣa* is a possibility for any of the twice-born, Kṣatriyas and Vaiśyas theoretically may also move through the four *āśramas.* In practice few other than Brahmins participate in the third and fourth *āśramas.* Stylistically, it has been said that the Brahmins move through all four, the Kṣatriyas reach the third, the Vaiśyas attain only to the second, and the Śūdras live a life of preparation for participation in the *āśrama dharma* in another incarnation. Although the *āśramas* are well delineated in the *Dharma Śāstras* and in the other *smṛti* writings, they may best be understood as a paradigm of the ideal life rather than a program of careful and minute observation for Hindus. The fact that perhaps not one Hindu in a thousand today patterns his life in careful obedience to the *āśramas* as described in the literature does not invalidate the scheme as a model of how life ought to be lived.

The four *āśramas* are known as Brahmacarya, Gṛhastha, Vānaprastha, and Sannyāsa. The first stage is the life of the student in which he receives instruction in the Vedas, learns meditative disciplines, develops self-control, and prepares himself for his life responsibilities. In the Gṛhastha *āśrama* the young man marries, rears a family, continues his studies without formal guidance by a *guru,* engages in his occupation, and supports those of his family in the other *āśramas.* Vānaprastha is a time for checking attachment to worldly possessions, of turning over the family occupation to sons, of guiding others on the basis of one's own experiences, and of paying more attention to the perfecting and liberating processes of life. In the Sannyāsa *āśrama* the ties with family, occupation,

[111] *Manu Dharma Śāstra* 6. 35.

and all worldly matters are cut and full attention is given to the goal of *mokṣa*. This, in briefest outline, is the *āśrama* pattern for human life. We shall now examine each *āśrama* in more detail.

The formal education of the Brahmin boy, according to Manu, normally begins not later than his eighth year. Prior to this he should have seven free years to experience without restraint the world of color, form, sound, taste, and odor. However, if the boy displays promise of great intellectual attainments, the formal education may begin as early as the fifth year. It begins when the boy goes to the home of his prospective *guru* with fuel in hand requesting permission to be a pupil in the home of the teacher. If he is accepted, he is invested with a three-strand thread, standing for control of thoughts, actions, and desires, to be worn during his entire life; he is also given a staff, symbolic of the authority of the *guru* over him during the Brahmacarya years. His *guru* serves *in loco parentis* for the five months of each year during which time he lives in the *guru's* home.

The education outlined for the Brahmacarin in ancient Hinduism was a forest education, not a town education. Its purpose was to prepare the boy for participation in the great heritage of the Indo-Aryan. It was a vocational education, but not an occupational one, i.e., it was a training for the vocation of being a man, a being who has the unique opportunity of self-perfection.[112] It was first of all an education in discipline of the body. The pupil served his *guru* in complete loyalty. He collected fuel for the fires in the home, tended the house and the cattle, made a daily round of begging for his food, went to bed after the *guru's* retirement, arose before the *guru* wakened, and served the *guru* in the spirit of obedience and reverence. His body was hardened and conditioned by eating simple food, wearing the minimum of clothing, walking without an umbrella, and observing complete chastity. It was an existential education, an education of living close to a great man who embodied the ideal toward which the pupil should strive. It was an education through work—truly a *karma mārga*—rather than a bookish education. It was a training

[112] Hinduism does not think of a man chiefly in terms of what he does to make a living, as is usually the case in the West. In the *āśrama* plan for life, earning a living occupies only the second period; during the first a Hindu is supported by those of his family who are in the second period, and during the third and fourth periods he is supported both by his previous earnings and by those of his family who are in the second period. The difference between the Western and the Hindu views of man can be illustrated by what is expected in answer to the question "Who is he?" The answer expected in the West is an identification of his occupation, e.g., "He is a carpenter . . . . a farmer . . . a lawyer, etc." In India the proper Hindu reply would name his *jāti* and *gotra*, and perhaps his sect and language, e.g., "He is a Bharadwaja Vadama Brahmin." In other words, "Who is he?" in Hinduism elicits a response about status in self-perfecting.

in *dharma;* the pupil was to learn his duties and how to do them. He was to learn to do what was expected of him without inner struggle; he was to acquire an identification of himself and his *dharma.* He was to listen to the expounding of the Vedas from the lips of his *guru,* to recite this wisdom until it was a part of his very being, and to meditate upon the meaning of what was spoken.

The Brahmacarya *āśrama* guaranteed the conservation and transmission of Vedic wisdom. When the boy left his *guru* at the age of sixteen, he was expected to carry with him habits of study and meditation that would remain with him throughout his life, to be picked up again as a full-time occupation in the last *āśrama.* At the end of the training period the Brahmacarin took a ceremonial bath, made a formal offering to his *guru* in gratitude for his instruction, and returned home, where he was honored by his family with gifts of fine clothes and an umbrella. Shortly thereafter he was to marry and to enter the second *āśrama.*

The education of Kṣatriyas and Vaiśyas was slightly modified. Formal instruction for them began in the eleventh or twelfth year and ended in the twenty-second or twenty-fourth.[113] The reason for the early education of the Brahmins was based on the principle that those with the richer endowments had greater obligations to the community and were to assume these community responsibilities as soon as possible. Girls of the twice-born *varṇas* were to receive instruction in their homes in the duties and responsibilities pertaining to the life of wife, mother, and homemaker. Through the centuries the forest retreats of *gurus* have been modified and supplemented by hermitages, institutions for advanced studies, and schools in kings' courts.

Just how the ancient pattern of *guru* education can fit into modern life with its need for skills in science, business, and industry is a problem the Hindu has not solved. How much time can be taken out of necessary technological and professional training in order to insure a spiritual integrity? Unfortunately, the answer given by many Hindus seems to be "None." Coomaraswamy, the perceptive and imaginative Indian whose long residence in America gave him the detachment necessary for significant evaluations of his native land, once said, "Of all Indian problems the educational is the most difficult and most tragic." [114] "The beauty and logic of Indian life," he added, "belong to a dying past." [115] Many hope that "the wonder that was India" [116] can continue to enrich a world of jet travel, television, automation, and atomic energy.

[113] *Manu Dharma Śāstra* 2. 38–40.
[114] *The Dance of Shiva,* p. 137.
[115] *Ibid.,* p. 131.
[116] A. L. Basham, *The Wonder That Was India.*

The second *āśrama* is the Gṛhastha. This is the householder stage of human life. In ancient India marriage was expected, and to this day one rarely finds a mature man or woman in Hindu India who is not, or has not been, married. It was and is a social duty and a sacramental necessity. The elaborate techniques for preventing failure in marriage, including details of sexual intercourse as in the *Kāma Kalpa,* are further indications of the high value placed upon marriage. Marriage is woman's sacrament. While happiness in marriage was not forgotten—the *Dharma Śāstras* state that one of the purposes of marriage is for pleasures both sexual and non-sexual—the main purposes of marriage were to beget offspring, to fulfill specific *dharmas,* and to perform proper sacrifices to the gods. To quote again from Coomaraswamy, marriage in Hindu culture is "an impersonal contract, undertaken as a social debt, by men and women alike, not for happiness, but for the fulfillment of social and religious duties." [117] The education of the boy in the home of his *guru* and that of the girl in the home of her parents were both designed to prepare for Gṛhastha. "The man is not man alone, but his wife and children also," said Manu.[118] According to Vālmīki "the wife is the better half of man. . . . A woman can never be happy even with a hundred sons, without the husband. Her life is then like a lyre without the strings, or a chariot without its wheels. The gifts of the father, mother, and the son are limited. It is only the husband's gifts that are unlimited. . . . Husband is the highest God to a woman." [119] Also from the *Rāmāyaṇa:* "A woman cannot live without her husband." [120] It was this high regard for the husband which among other factors accounted for the appearance of the cruel practice of *satī.*[121]

The Gṛhastha is the most valuable of all the *āśramas,* says the *Mahābhārata.*[122] The reason for this is that the householder is the supporter of all: "The gods, *pitris,* guests, and servants all depend (for their sustenance) upon the person leading a life of domesticity." [123] More obligations fall upon the householder than upon those in the other stages of life. He must discharge each day five *dharmas.* (1) His debt to Brahmā the creator he discharges by studying and teaching the Vedas. (2) His debt to his ancestors is discharged by offering food and water to their

[117] *The Dance of Shiva,* p. 126.

[118] *Manu Dharma Śāstra* 9. 45.

[119] *Rāmāyaṇa, Ayodhya Kandam,* Chapter 18, pp. 196, 199. Makhan Lal Sen translation.

[120] *Ibid.,* Chapter 15.

[121] See C. E. Buckland, *Bengal Under the Lieutenant-Governors,* Vol. 1, pp. 160 ff., for an account of the last legal *satīs.* See Basanta Kumar Chattopadhayaya, "Sahamaran or Sati," *The Mother,* Vol. 8, No. 8, April, 1966, pp. 317–320, for a recent defense of the practice. See also *Mahābhārata* 1. 160.

[122] 12. 12.

[123] *Ibid.,* 12. 23.

memory. (3) His debt to the *devas* is discharged by a fire oblation. (4) His debt to the lower animals is expressed by a gift of food to an animal, perhaps nothing more than a few crumbs for ants. (5) His debt to his fellow humans is to be expressed by some gesture of hospitality. Throughout the day from the time of awakening before rising to that of going to sleep, the householder's life has been prescribed in the *Dharma Śāstras.* For example, while dining he is advised to face the east for long life, the south for fame, the west for prosperity, and the north for truth.[124] Finally, there were the complicated Vedic sacrifices which the householder was expected to perform. These we shall consider later. Small wonder that Vyāsa, the supposed author of the *Mahābhārata,* says, "A life of domesticity is the most difficult of all the four modes of life." [125] Yet when Yudhiṣṭhira, disgusted with life, expressed a desire to renounce the householder state and become a Sannyāsin, Vyāsa dissuaded him with the argument that the highest duty of man lies in living the full life of the householder.[126]

The *smṛti* writings contain many observations about women, their strengths and weaknesses, their virtues and vices, and how men ought to cope with them. Diametrically opposed views can be found in the scriptures of Hinduism. Bhīṣma says that women are never impure [127] and also that they are as frightful as Atharvan rites which can bring destruction upon even unseen foes.[128] Yet the ideal wife is described in most attractive terms:

> She who speaks sweetly to her husband and is a clever manager of household affairs, is a true wife. She who is one in spirit with her lord, and devotes her whole self to his happiness, is a true wife. He whose wife decorates her person with sandal paste, and perfumes her body after her daily ablution, talks little and agreeably, partakes of small quantities of food, is ever fond of him, and is constantly engaged in acts of piety and virtue with a view to bringing happiness and prosperity to the home, and is ever ready to yield to procreative desires of her lord, is not a man, but the lord of heaven.[129]

Again a different evaluation can be found in the *Rāmāyaṇa.* When Rāma goes in pursuit of the golden deer, he orders his brother Lakshmana to guard Sītā. Sītā upon hearing a cry, thinks Rāma is in danger and asks

124 *Manu Dharma Śāstra* 2. 51, 57.
125 *Mahābhārata* 12. 23.
126 *Ibid.*
127 *Ibid.,* 12. 165.
128 *Ibid.,* 12. 213.
129 *Garuda Purāṇa* 108.

Lakshmana to go in search of Rāma. But Lakshmana refuses to disobey the order given to him by Rāma. When Sītā turns upon her brother-in-law, calling him a defiler of his life, a hypocrite, and a villain, Lakshmana replies, "Worshipful lady, you are a goddess to me. I dare not reply to your words. It is not at all strange for a woman to use unjust and improper words; it is rather the nature of a woman, and it is everywhere to be found. They are fickle, irreligious and crooked, and they bring about family dissensions. . . . I was simply obeying the mandate of the eldest brother, but you have accused me on account of your womanly nature."[130] Yet Sītā has been chosen as the model of wifely virtues, and she is usually portrayed in proper wifely submission to her husband. One can speculate how the role of woman in India would have been different had Draupadī, the powerful and scheming wife of the five Pāṇḍavas, been selected as the model!

The *Dharma Śāstras* contain detailed prescriptions for the selection of spouses. Husband and wife should be of the same *varṇa* but of different *gotras*. The bride should be younger than the groom. Manu recommends the age of twenty-four for the man and eight for the girl.[131] Pre-puberty marriages were encouraged, probably because of the great importance attached to the virginity of brides. Such early marriages did not occur in Vedic times. Manu taught that the bride should have no bodily defects, a pleasant name, a graceful walk, moderate hair, small teeth, and a soft body.[132] He advised against marrying women with red hair, women who talk much, women who have red eyes, and women with inauspicious names.[133]

After marriage the wife must constantly revere her husband as a god, even though he is unfaithful to her.[134] The woman must never be independent,[135] and never unguarded.[136] Nothing should be done by the wife according to her own will.[137] If she becomes a widow she can never remarry.[138] A widow cannot even mention the name of another man.[139] However, the husband-wife relationship was not merely one of domination and submission; wives and husbands also knew the harmony so beautifully expressed in the *Mahābhārata*: "Thou are mine and I am thine, while all that is mine is thine also! He that hateth thee hateth me as

[130] *Rāmāyaṇa, Aranya Kandam,* Chapter 17.
[131] *Manu Dharma Śāstra* 9. 94.
[132] *Ibid.,* 2. 10.
[133] *Ibid.,* 2. 8. 9.
[134] *Ibid.,* 5. 154.
[135] *Ibid.,* 5. 141; 9. 3. See also *Mahābhārata* 1. 174.
[136] *Ibid.,* 9. 12.
[137] *Ibid.,* 5. 147.
[138] *Ibid.,* 5. 163.
[139] *Ibid.,* 5. 157. Divorce has been possible in Hindu society only since 1869.

well, and he that followeth thee followeth me." [140] Marriage was so desirable that provision was made for a girl to secure her own husband if her father failed to find a husband for her by three years after the beginning of her menstruation.[141] The *Mahābhārata* records, "The son is one's own self; the wife is one's friend; the daughter, however, is the source of trouble." [142] In Kālidāsa's play *Shakuntala*, Kashyapa, the father of Shakuntala, expresses relief when his daughter leaves home: "A daughter never really belongs to her father. I'm glad she has gone to her husband." [143]

The householder stage of life is terminated when the grandchildren arrive, gray hairs appear, and the wife ceases to be capable of bearing children. The husband and wife, having been together through many joys and sorrows, now enter together into the third *āśrama*, the period of gradual giving up of desires for possession of worldly goods. The Vānaprastha *āśrama* is based on the sensible recognition that life in a family and in an occupation is not always conducive to the psychological and mental conditions needed for the attainment of *mokṣa*. Although Vedic study is continued during the Gṛhastha *āśrama*, the cares of the family often crowd out concerns for the fundamental goal of life. Hence the third period was established as a period in which the individual begins a semiretirement from the daily responsibilities of home and work in order to spend more time in contemplation and meditation. He does not yet become a wandering ascetic; he remains in the home and observes more faithfully the rites of the Gṛhastha *āśrama*. The rather indefinite nature of this stage has resulted in many different opinions of what it means in modern society. One is not far wrong to think of it as a halfway stage between the busy, anxious householder life and the quiet life of the ascetic. The one in the third *āśrama* continues to enjoy the social life of family and community, but with a detachment not possible for the householder. No longer is he the financial supporter of persons in the other *āśramas*, nor is he yet a single-minded seeker of enlightenment; he is rather a selfless worker for the good of all. With the immediate pressures of home and family partially removed, he is able to serve the community in active administrative positions or in advisory capacities to those in positions of authority. He can serve as counselor, peacemaker, judge, teacher, and friend to the young and the middle-aged. His years

[140] 3. 12.

[141] *Manu Dharma Śāstra* 9. 90.

[142] *Mahābhārata* 1. 161. The reference to the son as the self of the father is a notion that goes as far back as *Ṛg Veda* 5. 4. 10. It is clearly affirmed in the *Mahābhārata*: "For their own good fathers yearn after sons who bring them salvation from out of this world in that beyond." 7. 173. See also 1. 159 and 3. 12.

[143] Lal translation. P. Lal, *Great Sanskrit Plays*, p. 46.

of experience are available to the community as a source of wisdom and direction for policy-making and adjudication of the inevitable conflicts of men in society. The third stage of life is a time for objective concern for the welfare of men in civic and social affairs and also for subjective concern for thought, meditation, and prayer. Men and women in this *āśrama* have enough detachment to see problems of home, community, state, and nation in perspective. Individuals within this *āśrama* may differ in the direction in which they wish to expend their energies; the *rajas* type of person may choose to be active in a public capacity, whereas the *tamas* or *sattva* person may only give advice when he is asked to express an opinion, but otherwise he spends his days in quiet study and reflection.

This *āśrama* has had particular significance for India following independence, because in trying to establish herself as a member of the community of national states India is attempting to be strong in an area of Hindu weakness. The great philosopher-president of India has written, "Indian culture has failed to give political expression to its ideals. The importance of wealth and power to give expression to spirit, though theoretically recognized, was not practically realized." [144] To state this in a different fashion: the hiatus between theory and practice has been spanned in theory but not in practice! One of the positive features of Hinduism is that there is no status for the unattached individual within the social structure, but on the other hand "the compartmental division of Hindu society is beset with grave defects." [145] Kumuran continues, "In the first place we failed to develop a corporate national life, and with us caste has taken the place of the nation. Even more serious, however, was the continued degradation of the communities described as 'untouchable.' " [146] Caste has been modified by the Indian Constitution, although this legal modification may not be enough. Even the broad-minded Rabindranath Tagore feared nationalism. He defined a nation as the "organized self-interest of a whole people, where it is the least human and the least spiritual." [147] He felt that nationalism is the displacement of the moral man by the political man. Nationalism, he believed, leads to greed for power. Tagore, a child of wealth and privilege, longed for the simple life of the village Indian, the only man who knows true freedom, a freedom "from the isolation of self, from isolation of things." [148]

[144] Radhakrishnan, *Eastern Religions and Western Thought*, p. 55.

[145] M. R. Sampat Kumaran, "Hindu Social Ideals," *Triveni*, Vol. 10, May 1938, p. 24.

[146] *Ibid.* This seemingly obvious point of view has been completely denied by some Indians, e.g., "India has always felt herself to be a nation, though the obstacles to her realisation of her nationhood have been many and tremendous and though internal dissensions and external invasions have been ever and anon hindering such self-realisation." K. S. Ramaswami Sastri, *Hindu Culture and the Modern Age*, p. 49.

[147] *Nationalism*, p. 26.

[148] *Ibid.*, p. 153.

Yet Tagore, despite his words, did much to place Indian nationalism on a broader base by bringing together into his great mind and heart the ideas and ideals of both East and West. Gandhi's outstanding service to his native land was to awaken the people to independence; Tagore's contribution was to awaken Indians to a feeling of interdependence with men everywhere. Tagore's university, Visva-Bharati, is a concrete example of his blending of nationalism and internationalism. Thanks to leaders like Tagore and Nehru the world is watching the coming into existence of a new sort of nationalism, a nationalism that is more humanistic than nationalistic, more committed to the creation of an environment for the fullest development of man than for the amassing of wealth and power. Only the most romantic idealist would assert that this model has appeared in the subcontinent of Asia, but only the most ignorant and prejudiced would deny that some of the ingredients are operative in India today.

The man in the third stage of life has the opportunity and the incentive to give himself in service to his fellow men. It is somewhat misleading to emphasize that Hindu *dharma* is concerned with duties rather than with rights, although this is the usual line of argument. The concept of the rights of man has not been well formulated in India; indeed, these rights were so foreign that when Indians originated the independence movement they had to appeal to European history for the concept. The authorities to whom they appealed were Milton, Burke, Garibaldi, Mazzini, and Mill. Paradoxically it was from an English education foisted upon the Indians that they got the ideas which led to the independence movement. In order to sell the idea of independence to Hindus, Gandhi appealed to *dharma* as the motivation for freedom: "What we want to do should be done not because we object to the English or that we want to retaliate, but because it is our duty to do so." [149] He believed that no declaration of human rights was necessary in the Indian Constitution because they are implicit in a non-violent society.[150] He wrote, "The true source of rights is duty. If we discharge our duties, rights will not be far to seek." [151] The authors of the Constitution of India did not follow his directive; they listed many rights of the citizen: equality, freedom of speech, freedom of assembly, freedom of association, freedom of movement, freedom of residence, the right to own property, and the right to engage in a chosen occupation.[152]

Hinduism is most certainly not unaware of the need for social justice (*sāmya*), but it recognizes that social justice should be a concern of an

[149] *Hind Swaraj, or Indian Home Rule,* p. 95.
[150] *Constructive Programme, Its Meaning and Value,* p. 14.
[151] *Young India,* January 8, 1925.
[152] *The Constitution of India,* Part III, Sections 14–35.

individual during only a portion of his development. Higher wages, shorter hours of labor, improved working conditions, and job security are for Hinduism not ends in themselves but necessary conditions for the enrichment of the character of individuals, and if they are not utilized for this end, their value is considerably diminished. If this approach seems too individualistic for Western minds, perhaps Westerners ought to ask themselves if they are not guilty of thinking in Hobbesian terms that the governmental unit has values transcending those of the individual. When the Hindu thinks of man and society, he does not forget that society's reason for existence is the promotion of man's final and ultimate good.

Law in the *Dharma Śāstras* is rooted in the concept of *dharma*, and is therefore both a positive law to be discovered in the nature of things and a created law growing out of custom and conscience. Hindu law is therefore neither Roman nor English but partakes of the nature of both. The *Mahābhārata* teaches that "anarchy is the worst possible of states," and that the man "that bends his head to a powerful person really bends his head in Indra." [153] But the right to rule does not give the king license to rule cruelly or unjustly. Kings are elected and crowned by the people,[154] and the king who fails to protect his subjects is to be destroyed by popular revolt: "That king who tells his people that he is their protector but who does not or is unable to protect them, should be slain by his combined subjects, like a dog that is affected with the rabies and has become mad." [155]

A political state is originated to create private property, thus ending the condition of nature in which the strong at their will seize the possessions of the weak. In the state of nature there is no property: "Nobody then, with reference to any article in his possession, would be able to say 'This is mine.' Wives, sons, food, and other kinds of property, would not then exist." [156] In such a situation unrighteousness would be the practice of everyone: "In the absence of royal protection men would disregard or even injure their very mothers and fathers if aged, their very preceptors and guests and seniors. If the king did not protect, all persons possessed of wealth would have to encounter death, confinement, and persecution, and the very idea of property would disappear." [157] Thus, the Hindu thought of the state as coming into being in order to create private property.

[153] 12. 68.
[154] *Ibid.*, 13. 61.
[155] *Ibid.*
[156] *Ibid.*, 12. 68.
[157] *Ibid.*

The Hindu conception of justice is founded, as we have already noted, on the principle of the inequality of men, e.g., the ancient wergeld payable for murder of a Kṣatriya was one thousand cows, of a Vaiśya one hundred cows, and of a Śūdra ten cows. Even interest rates were different for men of different *varṇas:* 2 percent for Brahmins, 3 percent for Kṣatriyas, 4 percent for Vaiśyas, and 5 percent for Śūdras.[158]

The advice for collecting taxes was offered without the guile we moderns might be tempted to read into it:

> A king should milk his kingdom like a bee gathering honey from plants. He should act like the keeper of a cow who draws milk from her without boring into her udders and without starving the calf. He should in the matter of taxes act like the leech drawing blood mildly. He should conduct himself towards his subjects like a tigress in the matter of carrying her cubs, touching them with her teeth but never piercing them therewith. He should behave like a mouse which though possessed of sharp and pointed teeth still cuts the feet of sleeping animals in such a manner that they do not at all become conscious of it. A little by little should be taken from a growing subject and by this means should he be shorn.[159]

Manu allowed for war between sovereign states only after conciliation had failed.[160] He also provided rules for the fair conduct of war: only open battles were allowed, no concealing of weapons, no use of poison, no firebrands, respect for non-combatants, and no attack on sleeping people or on the wounded. The conception of a universal kingdom in which peace is perpetual was envisioned in the *Mahābhārata.* Yudhiṣṭhira early in the epic notes that although there are kings who in every province are benefiting themselves and their subjects, no king has achieved the status of "the imperial dignity" (*samrāj*). He means that a universal monarch who would bring all peoples together in peace and prosperity has not yet appeared.[161] Yudhiṣṭhira finally becomes the *samrāj,* the embodiment of eternal law (*sanātana dharma*). At the close of the *Mahābhārata* Yudhiṣṭhira refuses to enter the heavenly realm without his faithful dog. Whereupon the dog, assuming its true status as Dharma, the god of righteousness, says,

> Thou art well born, O king of kings, and possessed of the intelligence and the good conduct of Pandu. Thou hast compassion for all creatures, O

158 P. S. Sivaswamy Aiyar, *Evolution of Hindu Moral Ideals,* p. 92.
159 *Mahābhārata* 12. 88.
160 *Manu Dharma Śāstra* 7. 198.
161 2. 15.

> Bharata, of which this is a bright example. . . . Hence, O king, there is no one in Heaven that is equal to thee. Hence, O Bharata, regions of inexhaustible felicity are thine. Thou hast won them, O chief of the Bharatas, and thine is a celestial and high goal.[162]

All of these matters of polity belong to the man in the third *āśrama.* He has freed himself from the pressing obligations of his family and home and he does not yet give full attention to the goal of *mokṣa,* therefore he can benefit his fellow men with guidance based on the riches of his experiences. Hence the Vānaprastha *āśrama* is often called the *dharma āśrama.* But in time these matters must also be given up, and the quester for perfection enters the last period when all attention is given to the ultimate goal of life.

To refer to the Sannyāsa *āśrama* as a retirement is misleading, for it is not a retirement from labor. It involves extremely exacting demands on the individual. *Smṛtis* hold that this *āśrama* is only for men of the first *varṇa,* and, we might add, it is only for exceptional males within this group. At last the candidate for liberation takes up completely the task of devoting all his time and energy to meditation and contemplation. He renounces family, economic pursuits, human fellowship, and political activities. He engages in solitary meditation under natural surroundings. He begs for his food, accepts no money, owns no property, collects no disciples, and does no teaching. He makes no reference to his past life. When spoken to, he responds by repeating the name of God. He restrains his passions and senses. He aims for nothing other than *mokṣa.* For one man it may mean extreme *tapas,* for another adoration of his god, and for another identification with Reality. This stage is not a stunt of self-denial or physical torture. It is a return to the life of the student lived years ago in the home of the *guru;* although now it is different, since the Sannyāsin returns to his studies and his meditations with the rich resources derived from full participation in the life of man. Brahmacarya is the time of planning; Gṛhastha is the time of nurturing; Vānaprastha is the time of sharing the products of planting and nurturing; and Sannyāsa is the time of reaping the harvest. To individuals in the other *āśramas,* the fourth *āśrama* may seem to be a most undesirable existence, a wandering ascetic enjoying none of the pleasures and satisfactions of human life; but to the *Sannyāsin* his lifelong petition takes on unspeakable meaning and significance: "Lead me from the unreal to the real. . . . from darkness to light . . . from death to immortality." The ancient prayer ceases to be mere petition; it becomes an existential experience.

[162] 17. 3.

6. THE *Saṁskāras*

Karma mārga includes both moral action and ceremonial action. In the Vedic age ritual (*dravya*) and knowledge (*jñāna*) were sometimes in conflict, although they were not mutually contradictory. The way of knowledge was expressed in the Upaniṣads, the way of ceremony and sacrifice in the Brāhmaṇas. A translator of the Brāhmaṇas once described them as follows: "For wearisome prolixity of exposition, characterized by dogmatic assertion and flimsy symbolism rather than by serious reasoning, these works are perhap not equalled anywhere." [163] The Pūrva Mīmāṁsā or Karma Mīmāṁsā school of thought, which is rooted in the *Mīmāṁsā Sūtra* of Jaimini (c. fourth century B.C.), originates in, supports, delineates, and expounds the ritualistic aspects of the Vedas as the Vedānta or Uttara Mīmāṁsā identifies itself with the intellectualistic aspects. The Karma Mīmāṁsā includes the act of knowing as part of the total ritualistic action leading to *mokṣa*, but its central concern is the examination of *dharma* as expressed overtly in the rituals. The principle of reality is the self-as-actor (*ahaṁ-kāra*).

These rituals have come to be known as *saṁskāras*, a word usually translated as sacraments. Sacraments in the Christian tradition are acts regarded as visible signs of an invisible spiritual work, but in Hinduism a *saṁskāra* is not merely a ceremonial act representative of a covert operating force, rather it is itself operative. *Saṁskāras* are thought to operate in two ways: negatively they remove evil, positively they generate fresh desirable qualities. From an objective point of view one can assert that Hindu *saṁskāras* and Christian sacraments serve the same psychological and cultural function, i.e., they celebrate important steps in the life of an individual.

Gautama in his *Dharma Śāstra* lists forty *saṁskāras*. Other digests give twenty-five. In the *Gṛhya-Sūtras*, the first systematic description of the *saṁskāras*, the following sixteen are described.

1. *Garbhādhāna*, a ritual to insure conception.
2. *Puṁsavana*, the nourishment of the child in the womb.

[163] J. Eggeling, *The Sacred Books of the East*, Vol. 12, p. ix. The Brāhmaṇas and the sacrifices which they describe are prime instances of what Macdonell calls the Indian "tendency to exaggeration." *A History of Sanskrit Literature*, p. 278. Macdonell amplifies, "The almost incredible development of detail in ritual observance; the extraordinary excesses of asceticism; the grotesque representations of mythology in art; the frequent employment of vast numbers in description; the immense bulk of the epics; unparalleled conciseness of one of the forms of prose; the huge compounds habitually employed in the later style, are among the many striking manifestations of this defect of the Indian mind." *Ibid.*, p. 10.

3. *Sīmantonnayana,* the insuring of proper mental formation of the child in the last month of pregnancy.
4. *Jātakarman,* the birth ceremony.
5. *Nāmakaraṇa,* the giving of a name to the child.
6. *Niṣkramaṇa,* the taking of the child out of the house for the first time.
7. *Annaprāśana,* the first feeding of solid food.
8. *Cūḍākaraṇa,* the first cutting of the hair.
9. *Karṇavedha,* the boring of the ear lobe for ornaments.
10. *Vidyārambha,* the beginning of study by the learning of the alphabet.
11. *Upanayana,* the initiation of study under a *guru.*
12. *Vedārambha,* the beginning of Vedic studies.
13. *Keśānta,* the first shaving of the beard.
14. *Samāvartana,* the homecoming after completion of studies under a *guru.*
15. *Vivāha,* the marriage ceremony.
16. *Antyeṣṭi,* the funeral rites.

Most of these have fallen into oblivion in modern times. We shall consider briefly only three of the *saṁskāras: Upanayana, Vivāha,* and *Antyeṣṭi.*

Upanayana is extremely important for it marks the induction of the boy into the clan. *Vedārambha* indicates the beginning of elementary education; *Upanayana* is the beginning of secondary education. It is the second birth, the spiritual birth, of the twice-born. In a very real sense it is the beginning of the Brahmacarya *āśrama,* since the education which precedes this was for the most part haphazard and unplanned. The passage of the initiate from childhood to student years is marked by a last meal with his mother, a gift of loincloth and girdle, and, perhaps most important of all, the investure with the sacred thread (*yajñopavīta*) to remind him throughout his life that a twice-born man always lives under *dharma.*

The *saṁskāra* of marriage (*Vivāha*) is designed to impress upon the couple that in entering the married state they assume special *dharmas.* The dedication of emotional harmony is beautifully expressed in the words recited by the bridegroom to the bride: "Thy heart shall dwell in mine; my mind thou shalt follow with thine; in my words shalt thou find joy; to me shalt thou adhere; in me shall thy thoughts dwell; to me shalt thy veneration be bent." The actual completion of the marriage ceremony is the seven steps taken together by bride and groom. A very significant feature in Hindu marriage is the requirement of continence during the first three nights of married life. This is a reminder that marriage is not license for sexual pleasures but a relationship sanctioned and controlled by the community.

The funeral rite (*Antyeṣṭi*) makes much use of fire. Cremation of the corpse is the central act. The disposal of the corpse by fire may be a continuation of the ancient Vedic belief that Agni was the messenger between men and gods.

In addition to the *saṁskāras* the Hindu during his householder years may engage in rituals and ceremonies which do not have the status of *saṁskāras,* but which may in the ordinary passing of the days assume great importance in the life of the individual. These include regulations for rising in the morning, brushing the teeth, lighting of fires, entertaining of guests, dining, giving of gifts, and going to bed at night. The danger of ceremony taking over the humanitarian and moral aspects of religion is ever present. Some Hindus today are calling attention to this danger: "One great hardship under which Hinduism labours is its load of ritualism and ceremonial observances. The sooner its followers can lighten this load and devote themselves to the essentials of religion, the greater will be its chances of survival." [164] The restrictions that have grown around the caste system need careful and courageous revamping. For example, four of the yearly festivals are sometimes interpreted as reminders that the *varṇa* distinction is a temporary one: Rakṣābandhana symbolizes that all are Brahmins working for universal good, Vijayadaśami that all are Kṣatriyas protecting righteousness, Deepāvalī that all are Vaiśyas creating works of art and illumination, and Holī that all are Śūdras engaging in physical merrymaking. As India moves into the modern world changes in sacraments and holy days are inevitable. But those who would hastily and completely eliminate these aspects of life must remember how much of the life of man is enriched by ceremonies.

7. *Karma* AS *Mārga*

Karma mārga has behind it the sanctity and authority of the Vedic moral and sacrificial tradition. Modern psychologists support the assumption of *karma mārga* that man is an active being, a creature who is always planning, practicing, completing, failing, and starting over again. He is a being who is restless, anxious, and fretful. In moments of repose he gains strength and direction for more activity. Those who favor the path of works believe that through the performance of moral and ceremonial acts man will reach a state of desireless action and finally will

[164] P. S. Sivaswamy Aiyar, *Evolution of Hindu Moral Ideals,* p. 207.

attain a liberation which transcends all *karmas* and *dharmas*. Life is to be lived and outlived. Man should do his work in the world, but he should not allow the work to possess him. He must work without desire for the fruit of action. Rabindranath Tagore once translated *Īśa Upaniṣad* 2 in these words: "Doing work in this world thou shouldst wish to live a hundred years. Thus it is with thee and not otherwise. Let not the work of man cling to him." [165] He then offered the following comment:

> Only by living fully can you outgrow it. When the fruit has served its full term, drawing its juice from the branch it dances with the wind and matures in the sun, then it feels in its core the call of the beyond and becomes ready for its career of a wider life. But the wisdom of living is in that which gives you the power to give it up. For death is the gate of immortality. Therefore it is said, Do your work, but let not your work cling to you. For the work expresses your life so long as it flows with it, but when it clings, then it impedes, and shows, not the life, but itself.[166]

One of the serious dangers of *karma mārga* is that its supporters may attempt to reduce the good life to the observance of rules and regulations. There is an inelasticity and unimaginativeness inherent in the doctrine of *dharma* so conceived which is incompatible with an open-ended society. The future of man is more than that which can be predicted upon the basis of the present condition of man. Yet consider this typical statement of a traditional-minded Hindu: "Not only everything that we believe today, everything that we practice today, can be and is assigned to some pigeon-hole of *dharma*, but all that we shall think tomorrow and act tomorrow has pigeon-holes ready for them." [167] In the first place, this is simply not true; no human culture has "pigeon-holes" ready for a world of interplanetary and interstellar travel, of complete genetic controls, of thoughts and emotions electromagnetically determined, of life forms created by artificial means, and of social organizations undreamed of as yet. In the second place, if it were true that everything man will think and do tomorrow has categories and classifications ready within Hinduism, there are no epistemological methods for determining a weight for this so-called truth. The value of *karma mārga* does not depend upon making irresponsible claims for it. *Karma mārga* has been, and will surely continue to be, a valuable ingredient in man's *sādhana* without tying it to a scholastic interpretation of *dharma*.

The goal of Hinduism is not that all men become Brahmins, nor that

[165] *Personality*, p. 64.
[166] *Ibid.*, pp. 64–65.
[167] Govindā-Dāsa, *Hinduism*, p. 80.

all men be liberated from the wheel of *saṁsāra;* it is that the promises inherent in man be actualized, that this universe be hominized, that all human faculties be unfolded and liberated in an active, creative life of the spirit. The goal of *karma mārga* is to transcend *karma mārga.* The notion of agency must be given up. The act is to become disinterested. The actor must lose himself in the act. The act, not the actor or the *telos* of the act, must become the all. The self must forswear selfishness, and then forswear the self by which selfishness is forsworn. Duty is to be replaced by spontaneity. The actor must be able to say, "It is not I that acts, but Reality-Spirit-Love (*Satcitānanda*) that acts through me." Man-perfecting ceases to be a *dharma*-constrained man. He fulfills all *dharmas* without awareness of *dharma.* He accomplishes through non-accomplishment. He does not *do dharma;* he *is dharma.*

CHAPTER IX
The Way of Devotion

1. THEISM IN EARLY HINDUISM

Hinduism, as we noted in the opening chapter, is best understood as *sādhana,* the quest for the perfection of potentialities in all dimensions of man's being. *Bhakti mārga,* the way of devotion, is religion *per se,* for it is primarily the directing of the emotions toward the being who epitomizes man's highest values. Theism may be described as an unstable compromise between a transcendent theology, the belief in a god whose existence is outside the natural world, and an immanent theology, the belief in a god whose existence is within the natural world. Total transcendence is deism; total immanence is pantheism. The great religions of the Western world—Judaism, Christianity, and Islam—tend towards deism by reason of their emphasis on the separation between God and the created world, while Hinduism tends toward pantheism in its emphasis on the inseparability of God, man, and the world. But to accept Barth's conclusion, "India is radically pantheistic and that from its cradle onward," [1] as the complete and final truth regarding Hindu speculation about God would be as hasty and superficial as to declare that the West is radically deistic. Theism may be defined as the belief in the existence of a personal being distinct from man, a being who is both transcendent to and immanent in the world as creator, preserver, and redeemer, a being with whom man can establish communicative relations. God is

[1] A. Barth, *Religions of India,* p. 8.

a being that exists, not being that subsists. God is personal in the sense that God and man can address each other. God is within the world, but God is not exhausted by the world. God fashioned the world, is the source and sustenance of the highest values of goodness, beauty, and truth, and offers to man a way of salvation.

The *devas* of the Aryan Indians meet this criterion of theistic beings, although at an early date the Aryans began moving toward radical immanentism. This is evident in *Ṛg Veda* 10. 129. In this hymn the ancient *ṛṣi* sought to identify that which was before either existence or non-existence. His setting of the scene is masterful. It was a time before immortals and mortals, before day and night, before light and darkness. Desire (*kāma*) entered as "the first seed of thought" making distinctions between male and female, energy and receptivity, force and that upon which force needs to operate in order to be force. At this point in the poem the *ṛṣi*, apparently feeling that he may have gone too far in his speculations, retreats and asks himself the fundamental epistemological question, "What are the grounds of knowing such things?" He radically shifts the direction of his speculations from the quest of an impersonal cosmic principle to a personal "overseer in the highest heavens" who knows these matters, and then with a final flashback to his previous courageous speculations, adds that perhaps even the overseer does not know the ultimate cosmogony. The shift from the unknown first principle, later called Kā (Who), to the personal surveyor of the heavens indicates the instability of theism in the period of the *Ṛg*. The *devas* were the natural powers incompletely personified and anthropomorphized.[2] Varuṇa is the most interesting of the *devas* from the theistic point of view. He is the creator who "has spread the firmament as a bed for the sun."[3] He is the "supreme monarch over all worlds."[4] He is the god of cosmic order; he prepares a path for the sun,[5] controls the flow of rivers,[6] divides day from night,[7] waters "earth, mid-air, and heaven,"[8] uses the sun to measure the earth,[9] and supports both heaven and earth.[10] In other words, Varuṇa is the god of cosmic order. He is

[2] Maurice Bloomfield refers to the Vedic gods as cases of "arrested personification." *The Religion of the Veda*, p. 85. Nicol Macnicol says, "In no case is the process of anthropomorphization anything like complete." *Indian Theism from the Vedic to the Mohammedan Period*, p. 17.

[3] *Ṛg Veda* 5. 85. 1.

[4] *Ibid.*, 8. 42. 1; 5. 85. 3.

[5] *Ibid.*, 7. 87. 1; 1. 24. 8.

[6] *Ibid.*, 2. 28. 4; 1. 24. 8; 7. 87. 1, 5.

[7] *Ibid.*, 7. 87. 1.

[8] *Ibid.*, 5. 85. 4.

[9] *Ibid.*, 5. 85. 5; 8. 41. 4; 8. 42. 1.

[10] *Ibid.*, 8. 41. 10.

also the sustainer and benefactor of man. He "has given strength to horses, milk to cows, determination to the heart";[11] he is the "chief guide of men";[12] he is the one about whom men say, "no one rules for the twinkling of an eye apart from thee";[13] he destroys the Asuras, the enemies of men and *devas*.[14] He is "considerate to created beings,"[15] "observant of holy vows,"[16] "possessed of understanding,"[17] and wise and intelligent.[18] He is the one "who protects men by his acts, as the herdsman guards the cattle."[19] Therefore, men approach Varuṇa boldly and petition him for general protection, "Keep off all danger from me, Varuṇa,"[20] for riches, "May I never be devoid of well regulated riches,"[21] and for happiness, "make me this day happy."[22] Varuṇa is the very center of religious devotion, the one "in whom all pious acts are concentrated."[23] Men may also seek moral guidance from Varuṇa: "Keep us all our days in the right path."[24] But beyond this, and far more important from the theistic point of view, Varuṇa is the god to whom men appeal for forgiveness of sins. He, the god of cosmic and moral order, is also the god who is willing and able to restore men to moral purity when they stray from the path of moral rectitude. Therefore, almost every petition to Varuṇa contains a request for forgiveness: "If, Varuṇa, we have ever committed an offence against a benefactor, a friend, a companion, a brother, a neighbour, or, Varuṇa, a dumb man, remove it from us."[25] "Cast off from me sin, Varuṇa, as if it were a rope."[26] "May we be free from sin against that Varuṇa, who has compassion upon him who commits offence."[27] "Varuṇa, loosen for me the upper, the middle, the lower band; so, son of Aditi, shall we, through faultlessness in thy worship, become freed from sin."[28] Thus Varuṇa stands out distinctly from the other Vedic nature deities as the god of theistic promise.

[11] *Ibid.*, 5. 85. 2.
[12] *Ibid.*, 2. 28. 3.
[13] *Ibid.*, 2. 28. 11.
[14] *Ibid.*, 5. 85. 5.
[15] *Ibid.*, 10. 85. 17.
[16] *Ibid.*, 12. 1. 4.
[17] *Ibid.*, 7. 87. 4.
[18] *Ibid.*
[19] *Ibid.*, 8. 41. 1.
[20] *Ibid.*, 2. 28. 6.
[21] *Ibid.*, 2. 28. 11.
[22] *Ibid.*, 1. 25. 19.
[23] *Ibid.*, 8. 41. 6.
[24] *Ibid.*, 1. 25. 12.
[25] *Ibid.*, 5. 85. 6.
[26] *Ibid.*, 2. 28. 5.
[27] *Ibid.*, 7. 87. 7.
[28] *Ibid.*, 1. 24. 15.

He is a personal deity who creates and sustains the world; he transcends the world in his creative role, yet he is immanent in the world as its ordering agent; he is a god deeply involved in the quest for righteousness; he is constantly sympathetic to the needs of men, he desires to communicate with mortals; and he is a god who stands ready to forgive the sins of men who turn in penitence to him. Macdonell says, "Varuṇa's character resembles that of the divine ruler in a monotheistic belief of an exalted type." [29] Radhakrishnan observes that the theism of the Vaiṣṇavas with its emphasis on *bhakti* "is to be traced to the Vedic worship of Varuṇa, with its consciousness of sin and trust in divine forgiveness." [30]

As the sacrificial rites of the Aryans became more complex the emphasis shifted from the *devas* to both the rites themselves and the priests who performed the rites. A sacerdotal attitude to the sacrifices replaced the gods as agents through which benefactions might be attained. Even the gods were believed to perform sacrifices. A sacrifice performed without error was believed to accomplish unfailingly the result for which it was intended. The Horse Sacrifice (*aśvamedha*) would effectuate any result desired. But there could be no deviation in the ritual. An improperly conducted sacrifice would have no result or perhaps harmful results. As the ritual became more significant in the life of the Vedic Indians the position of the priests became more important and more dangerous. The priests risked their personal welfare in the act of sacrificing. The elaborate ceremonies finally required a division of responsibilities: the *Hotṛ* tended the fire, the *Adhvaryu* used the sacrificial instruments, the *Udgātar* sang the chants, and the *Brahmin* supervised the entire operation to ensure that everything was done according to custom. The *Brahmins*, upon whom fell the major responsibility for the effectiveness of the sacrifice, came to be known as the "human gods." [31] When errors were committed —an ill-timed lighting of the fire, an incorrect use of an instrument, or the mispronunciation of a word—additional rites and petitions were necessary to purge the guilt of the priests and to avoid consequent evil. The god invoked in such circumstances was Viṣṇu. He was a minor god in Vedic times. Although he is celebrated in few of the hymns of the *Ṛg Veda*, two later myths assigned to him the position of the beloved of men, a position which earlier had been assigned to Varuṇa. According to one myth he and Indra had slain Vṛtra, the demon who almost destroyed the world. In the myth of the three steps Viṣṇu alone among the gods traverses the three cosmic regions. Two of these regions men know, earth and sky; but the third, the highest heaven, cannot be known by

[29] A. A. Macdonell, *Vedic Mythology*, p. 3.
[30] *Indian Philosophy*, Vol. 1, p. 78.
[31] *Śatapatha Brāhmaṇa* 2. 2. 2. 6.

men, "nor can soaring birds pursue it." [32] Viṣṇu became the messenger of men and gods, a sun-god like Prometheus, who could plead for men before the thrones of the gods. The third step signified the heavenly goal to which the worshiper hoped to pass from cursed death and re-death, "that highest place of Viṣṇu." [33] Varuṇa was a god of majesty, but Viṣṇu was a god of the domestic circle, a god who lived with men and who conveyed the prayers of men to the highest gods. As "friend of the pious," [34] "giver of happiness," [35] "granter of protection," [36] and "best of the doers of good deeds," [37] he satisfied man's longing for a theistic god, and he has remained to this day in India the most loved of the gods. It is he who, out of compassion for men, comes back as an *avatāra* (earthly manifestation) in each age to protect the good, to destroy the wicked, and to reestablish *dharma* on the earth.[38] It is he who will come again as Kalkī the tenth *avātara.*

The religion of the ancient Vedics appears to have forked in two directions after the early stages of the relatively simple rites of praise and petition and the later complicated sacerdotalism. One direction was the popular way of magic-mongering. This religion is seen in the charms and incantations of the *Atharva Veda:* charms to destroy hostile priests, to insure success in love-making, to grow hair, to bless a first tooth, to banish sterility, to eliminate fear objects, etc. The other direction was the sophisticated way of speculation, which resulted in the Upaniṣads with their movements from plurality to unity, from objectivity to subjectivity, and from materialism to spiritualism. Both of these ways led away from theism, one back to magic and animism, the other on to philosophy. If we ignore the former, we can trace the development of the ancient Hindu religion in three periods: (1) the Vedic period, in which the gods were satisfied by punctilious performance of rituals; (2) the Brāhmaṇic period, in which the rituals were at first the means for controlling the gods, and then acts which did not require theistic dynamics; (3) the Upaniṣadic period, in which the developing monistic speculations removed altogether the necessity for the Vedic gods. In the Upaniṣads the names of Vedic gods such as Indra, Varuṇa, and Agni are found, but the attitude toward them changed radically. The second half of the *Kena Upaniṣad* is an early myth which clearly points to the new attitude. Brahman at this time was thought to be a being in the class of beings. The myth begins when Brahman had won a victory, and

[32] *Ṛg Veda* 1. 155. 5.
[33] *Kaṭha Upaniṣad* 3. 9.
[34] *Ṛg Veda* 1. 154. 5.
[35] *Ibid.,* 1. 156. 1.
[36] *Ibid.*
[37] *Ibid.,* 1. 156. 5.
[38] *Bhagavad Gītā* 4. 8.

the gods, thinking that Brahman was a god like themselves, rejoiced in this as a triumph for all the gods, "Ours indeed is this victory! Ours indeed is this greatness."[39] But when Brahman appeared before them, they did not understand what It was. Agni, the fire-god, being selected to discover who Brahman was, approached Brahman. But before he could speak Brahman asked, "Who are you?" "I am Fire," replied Agni. "I have power to burn everything." Whereupon Brahman placed a straw before Agni and challenged him to burn it. But Agni was unable, and returning to the gods reported his failure: "I have not been able to find out this—what this wonderful being is."[40] Vāyu, the wind-god, tried next, but he was unable to move the straw. Lastly, Indra sought to understand Brahman, and with the help of Umā, the daughter of the Himalayas, he knew Brahman.[41] The *ṛṣi* says, "Therefore, verily, these gods, namely Agni, Vāyu, and Indra, are above the other gods, as it were; for these touched It nearest, for these and [especially] he [i.e., Indra] first knew It was Brahma."[42] The gods thus discovered that their power was not their own but the power of Brahman. The impotence of the gods before Brahman is noted elsewhere in the Upaniṣads, e.g., the *Bṛhad-Āraṇyaka Upaniṣad* states that anyone, god or man, who attains the mystic knowledge (*upaniṣad*) that he is Brahman, becomes "this All" and that "even the gods have not power to prevent him becoming thus."[43] The *ṛṣi* adds that the discovery that man can become Brahman, and hence be greater than the gods, is not pleasing to the gods. How ridiculous, therefore, says the *ṛṣi*, for people to say "Worship this god! Worship that god!"[44] when all the time they are themselves all the gods, and greater than the gods. Hence, all works of those who know not the truth about Brahman merely perish.[45] The *Muṇḍaka Upaniṣad* adds that the doers of deeds do not understand the folly of what they do: "Thinking sacrifice and merit is the chiefest thing . . . they re-enter this world, or a lower."[46] The Vedic rites themselves are "unsafe boats."[47]

Yet the fact remains that there are many references to the Vedic gods

[39] *Kena Upaniṣad* 3. 1. Hume translation.

[40] *Ibid.*, 3. 6. Hume translation.

[41] The use of Umā may be a way of saying that knowledge of Brahman comes through meditation, since the Himalayas have always been the retreat for mystics and mendicants.

[42] *Kena Upaniṣad* 4. 2. Hume translation. The expression "as it were" is the translation of *iva*, a word connoting phenomenalism. When it appears, it suggests that the objects under discussion are to be understood as real or valuable only from the relative point of view of a finite perspective. The term *māyā* appears only twice among the dozen oldest Upaniṣads, *Śvetāśvatara* 4. 10 and *Bṛhad-Āraṇyaka* 2. 5. 19, but the term *iva* is used frequently.

[43] 1. 4. 10. Hume translation.

[44] *Ibid.*, 1. 4. 6. Hume translation.

[45] *Ibid.*, 1. 4. 15. See also *Chāndogya Upaniṣad* 5. 24. 1.

[46] 1. 2. 10. Hume translation.

[47] *Ibid.*, 1. 2. 7. Hume translation.

in the Upaniṣads. Śaṅkara solved the problem arising from both theism and absolutism in the same literature by distinguishing two levels of knowledge, the lower or phenomenal (*aparā vidyā*) and the higher or noumenal (*parā vidyā*). God-talk belongs to the lower level. God-talk is justified pragmatically but not metaphysically. Śaṅkara, in what was in some respects an anticipation of William James's "will to believe," allowed a place for theistic religion as well as for rituals as propaedeutic to the true view of things. According to Śaṅkara, the gods exist only on the phenomenal level. When the individual existentially realizes *Ātman* is Brahman, the phenomenal level will be seen for what it is and will accordingly be given up as part of the *māyā* world. A note of criticism may be interjected here: if belief in gods and the observance of ceremonies are to be allowed, what are the criteria for selecting which gods and which ceremonies are accepted? Surely not all gods, rites, and practices, are permitted. Does Śaṅkara open the floodgates to superstition, idolatries, and orgies? Śaṅkara did not ridicule theism, but instead composed many lovely prayers and hymns, of which the following are samples: "O Lord, even after realizing that there is no real difference between the individual soul and Brahman I beg to state that I am yours and not that you are mine. The wave belongs to the ocean and not the ocean to the wave."[48] "Nowhere exists in all the world another sinner to equal me; nowhere a Power like Thyself for overcoming sinfulness. O Goddess, keeping this in mind, do Thou as it pleases Thee."[49] Yet the movement of Advaita Vedāntism has been, and is, toward immanentism and away from the transcendency inherent in the middle position we have identified as theism. A hymn composed by an Advaita Vedāntist expresses the inadequacy of ritualistic worship:

How can one ever invoke the All-pervading Absolute?
How give a seat to That which is the one Support of all?
How can one bring offerings to That whose nature is Pure Awareness,
Or purify That which is ever pure?

Why should one bathe with water That which is ever free from stain,
Or offer clothes to That which folds the universe in Itself?

Why should one place a sacred thread on Him who needs no support?
What is the use of flowers for One insensitive to smell?

How can perfume be pleasing to Him who is totally unattached,
Or jewels set off the beauty of Him who is all beauty's Source,
Futile are offerings of food to One who is ever satisfied!

[48] Quoted by Radhakrishnan, *The Brahma Sūtras*, p. 38.
[49] Quoted by Mukerjee, *The Culture and Art of India*, p. 261.

How can one circumambulate Him who is boundless in all directions?
How contrive to salute Him who is One without a second?
How can hymns be pleasing to That which the Vedas cannot reveal?

How can one wave lights before the Self-luminous Lord, the All-pervading Reality,
And how, as an image, can He be installed who stands complete within and without?

Therefore it is that perfect knowers of Brahman, always and under all conditions,
Commune with the Lord through contemplating their total identity with Him.[50]

The Ramakrishna-Vivekananda movement is an interesting illustration of the religious problem inherent in Advaitism. This movement is regarded by its propagandists as a modern presentation of the teachings of Śaṅkara, yet room is found for worship and other theistic practices. Ramakrishna had not the slightest doubt of the reality of his special deity, Kālī. A. C. Das of Calcutta University reveals an experience which shows that theism remains a problem for the Advaita Vedāntist:

> Some years ago I submitted an essay to *Vedanta and the West*, the organ of the Ramakrishna Mission at Los Angeles in the U.S.A. In this paper I wrote: "If one wants to get to the core of Hinduism as a religion, one must understand the theistic movement which has its roots in the Veda and Upaniṣads, and has had its periodic fruitions, chief among the latest being Sri Ramakrishna, Swami Vivekananda, Mahatma Gandhi, Sri Aurobindo, and Rabindranath." This apparently annoyed the editor, and the paper was returned with the apology that it was not in line with the principles of the journal. He said that Ramakrishna was an Advaitist, an exponent of Absolutist Vedānta and therefore no theist. With this I still disagree.[51]

By the end of the fourth century B.C. most of the Upaniṣads had been composed. Even if the Upaniṣads are correctly characterized as non-

[50] Quoted by Nikhilananda, *Self-Knowledge*, pp. 52–53. Nikhilananda identifies the author only as "an advanced Non-dualist."

[51] *A Modern Incarnation of God*, p. vii. The disciples of Śaṅkara have often been impatient with any who challenged their philosophy. When the followers of Madhva referred to Advaita Vedāntism as a disguised Buddhism, the Śaṅkarites were furious. George A. Grierson reports, "As may be expected, the rupture with Brahmaism brought upon them vigorous attacks from the followers of Śaṅkara and in one work, entitled *Pāṣandachapeṭikā*, or 'Slap in the Face of the Heretics,' they were all, as a body, genially consigned to the utmost torment of hell." *Encyclopaedia of Religion and Ethics*, edited by Hastings, Vol. 2, p. 545.

theistic, it would be a mistake to conclude that theism by this time had become intellectually unrespectable and that only in the popular religions of illiterate tribes was theistic religion kept alive. The chief reason for this caveat is that by this time the earliest form of the *Bhagavad Gītā*, one of the greatest theistic works in all Hindu literature, had been composed, a treatise which remains to this day the best-loved and most-read religious work in India. To examine theism in India after the Upaniṣads requires that distinctions be made among three great theistic traditions: Vaiṣṇavism, the religion directed toward the god Viṣṇu; Śaivism, the worship of Śiva; and Śāktaism and Tantrism, religions founded on the principle of female energy, which we shall examine in the next chapter. But first we must examine the psychological state called *bhakti*, the distinctively theistic attitude toward a god.

2. *Bhakti*

Bhakti is a vague and elastic term coming from the root *bhaj* meaning to be attached to, to be devoted to, or to resort to. The term is not ancient, but the feelings it denotes are very ancient in Hindu culture. The basic *bhakti* emotion is a complex mixture of fear, awe, fascination, love, and dependence. *Bhakti*, more than any other term, expresses the Hindu attitude toward a deity—an attitude midway between the Hebrew fear of the unapproachable Yahweh, the god who would not show his face, and the Greek fascination for the anthropomorphic Olympians, who delighted in appearing unannounced among men. The taking of an attitude of deference toward the source of vital energy is as old as the *Ṛg Veda*. In India anything which is honored may become a god. Confusion enters when a Western mind, attempting to understand Indian thought, assumes that the term denotes a supernatural, omniscient, omnipotent, omnipresent, First Cause of the cosmos. This confusion would not appear if due account were taken of both the Greek and the Hebrew strains in Western thought. According to the Hebrews the word "god" denotes the Holy One, the being before whom man and the whole creation stand in awe and submission; but according to the Hellenes the word "god" denotes any object, image, or idea toward which man takes an attitude of extreme worth. For example, the Greeks said "Love is a god," by which they did not reify or deify love, but rather they signified that love was of such a nature that it should be honored with the noblest description they knew. "Love is a god" means that love is divine-like, worthy of highest regard, and ought to be treated with utmost respect. God is adjectival for the Greek mind. Christianity in its theology, as well as its anthropology, cosmology, and morality, is an unstable compound of Hebrew and Greek elements. A greater awareness of Christianity's hybrid origins should make Western man better able to understand and appreciate the Hindu conception of deity.

The best translation of *bhakti* is "devotional faith." *Bhakti* is an excluding emotional attitude; it is taken toward one object, not toward many. It tends to displace other attitudes. Because of its excluding nature, some have thought that *bhakti* is essentially monotheistic. Rūpa Goswāmin's definition of *bhakti* encompasses both of these exclusions: "the loving worship and service of Lord Kṛṣṇa, uninterrupted by the desire for anything else, and unenveloped by *jñāna, karma,* and such other things." [52] The province of *bhakti* as an intense and existentially important attitude is religion. One could not properly be said to take a *bhakti* attitude toward music, food, art, or people. When it is said in Hinduism that one may take a *bhakti* attitude toward almost anything, what is meant is either that one may confer divinity or "semidivinity" upon an object, and then take a *bhakti* attitude toward it, or that one may express *bhakti* toward a revered object by means of the traditional artefacta of worship: flowers, fruit, incense, fire, water, etc. *Bhakti* is more than an attitude of deference; it also implies the taking of refuge in a god for protection, for assistance, or for special benefits, with confidence that the god is approachable and that he reciprocates with the same love that the devotee has for the god. *Bhakti* appears to have developed as a *mārga* in India after the ways of work and thought had been formulated and practiced, although there are a few hints of *bhakti* in the Upaniṣads. The earliest use of the term is in the *Śvetāśvatara Upaniṣad:* "These subjects which have been declared shine forth to the high-souled one who has the highest devotion (*bhakti*) for God and for his spiritual teacher as for God." [53] The promise of Kṛṣṇa to Arjuna at the close of the *Bhagavad Gītā* is one of the finest expressions of *bhakti* in all Hindu literature:

> Think only of me,
> Have faith in me,
> Worship me.
> You cannot fail to find me.
> I love you, Arjuna, so promise you this.

[52] Quoted by Brahma, *Philosophy of Hindu Sādhanā,* p. 255, from Rūpa Goswāmin's *Bhaktirasāmṛtasindhu.*

[53] 6. 23. Radhakrishnan translation. See also *Bṛhad-Āraṇyaka Upaniṣad* 3. 7.

Throw away your dharmas—
Have faith in me.
That is enough, I promise you.[54]

Another excellent expression of *bhakti* is the hymn with which the *Kural* opens:

As letters all have "A" as first,
So the world has the adorable God as First.
What use is lore, if the learned will not bow
Before the feet of Him, the all wise One?
. . . .
The head that bows not at the feet of the Lord, of eightfold worth,
Is useless as a senseless sense.
Who then can swim this wide earthly sea?
Not they who cling not to our Lord's feet.[55]

By the twelfth century *bhakti* had developed in both North and South India and had been given its fullest analysis and defense in the works of the Viśiṣṭādvaita teachers, especially in the writings of Rāmānuja. Rāmānuja gave it a strong moral flavor, demanding an elaborate preparation which included such items as diet, living for God, thinking about God, service to others, truthfulness, compassion, non-violence, cheerfulness, and hopefulness. By the sixteenth century, under the influence of the Bengali Vaiṣṇavite Caitanya, *bhakti* had become a *rasa* (emotional mood), "a curious mixture of the aesthetic, the erotic, and the religious." [56] In this extreme form *bhakti* was prized above *mokṣa*. Emancipated individuals engaged in *bhakti* experiences because they believed that the state of emancipation alone was not enough.[57] Rāmānuja had made similar statements, e.g., he said that while *mokṣa* is an excellent thing, compared to the love of God it is as a mustard seed set beside Mount Meru.[58]

Two ancient works on *bhakti*, the *Bhakti Sūtras* of Śāṇḍilya and of Nārada, illuminate the nature of the way of devotion. These *sūtras*, unlike the *Vedānta Sūtras*, do not require a commentary to make sense of them. No definite dates have been assigned for their composition, although the Śāṇḍilya *sūtras* are the older. Śāṇḍilya treats *bhakti* from the Advaita point of view in his contention that *bhakti* is necessary

[54] 18. 65–66. Lal translation.
[55] 1. 1–2, 9–10.
[56] Sushil Kumar De, *Bengal's Contribution to Sanskrit Literature and Studies in Bengal Vaiṣṇavism*, p. 123.
[57] *Ibid.*, p. 118.
[58] In his commentary on *Bhagavad Gītā* 6. 47.

only in the unenlightened state; whereas Nārada, treating *bhakti* from the Dvaita point of view, holds that devout worship of a personal god is an aspect of the enlightened state. Nārada defines *bhakti* as "the highest form of devotion to God." [59] Śāṇḍilya defines *bhakti* as "extreme attachment towards God." [60] Note that for both the attitude is toward a single god, and also that both emphasize the unique nature of the emotion, i.e., it is an extreme or superior attachment (*parā anurakti*). *Parā* calls attention to the fact that *bhakti* emotion is not to be confused with *prema, kāma, prīti,* or other terms denoting a sensual or physical love. "A love without it is simply a passion of paramours," says Nārada.[61] That is, a love without the *bhakti* element is only passion. According to Śāṇḍilya, "*Devabhakti* or devotion towards God is not love on account of its association with others." [62] The meaning is that the true *bhakti* attitude can be taken only toward a deity. The difference between the love which is *bhakti* and other forms of love is the presence of *prapatti* (absolute surrender) only in the former. In *bhakti* the devotee seeks exclusively the welfare of the object of his devotion, while in *prema, kāma,* and *prīti* the lover is also concerned with his own pleasure. This distinction must not be taken to mean that the *bhakta* derives no enjoyment from the experience; the difference is a difference of direction of attitude. The *bhakta* sets all affections on the object of his devotion; the lover seeks personal pleasure as well as pleasure for his beloved. Śāṇḍilya seems more sympathetic to the pleasant psychological states of the devotee than does Nārada, since he lists as marks of the *bhakti* relationship "veneration, delight in objects resembling Him, joy in His presence, pain in His absence, indifference towards other objects, feeling of glory in Him, living for His sake, feeling that everything is His, feeling that all is one, absence of hostility towards Him." [63] But Nārada offers as psychological benefits only "feeling extreme restlessness in forgetting Him." [64] The object-oriented Nārada says, "God alone is to be worshipped always with calmness of mind and fulness of heart," [65] but the subject-oriented Śāṇḍilya contends the devotee should direct the mind to "self and Self," [66] that is, both to finite self (*jīva*) and to Īśvara (the personal Brahman).

[59] *Sūtra* 2. All quotations from Nārada are from the translation by Lala Kannoo Mal entitled *The Aphorisms of Nārada.*

[60] *Sūtra* 2. All quotations from Śāṇḍilya are from the translation by Jadunath Mozoomdar entitled *Religion of Love, or Hundred Aphorisms of Śāṇḍilya.*

[61] *Sūtra* 23.

[62] *Sūtra* 18.

[63] *Sūtra* 44.

[64] *Sūtra* 19.

[65] *Sūtra* 79.

[66] *Sūtras* 29–31.

This slight difference of emphasis in the interpretation of *bhakti* in Nārada and Śāṇḍilya must not hide the fact that for both the emotion is an extreme one. *Bhakti* is not a warm feeling of joy derived from idly basking in the presence of one's god. As Shashibhusan Dasgupta has said, "the view that it may be possible to attain some religious experience through an intense emotion or even through some strong sensation is not very uncommon in the field of Indian religious thought." [67] Not sufficient notice has been taken among students of Indian thought that the Middle Way of the Buddha, the path of moderation, was a reaction against another path, the path of extremes. The tendency to push to excess is Indian; witness the size of the great Indian epics, the length of an Indian classical music concert or dance program, the tendency of each scripture to describe itself as superior to others, the lavish use of the *deus ex machina* in Indian fiction, the profusion of carved objects on the roofs of Dravidian temples, and even the riot of colors in the saris of Indian women. Buddhism thrived much better among the pragmatic and phlegmatic Chinese than among the idealistic and emotional Indians.

The defenders of *bhakti mārga* differ as to whether devotion includes knowledge. Rāmānuja says it does. *Bhakti,* he says, is knowledge which has assumed the form of devotion.[68] This is the view of the four great schools of Vaiṣṇavism, schools founded by Rāmānuja, Vallabha, Nimbārka, and Madhva. But this is not the opinion of Caitanya. The Bengali school holds that the best form of devotion (*uttamā bhakti*) stands by itself; it has no knowledge component, nor does it involve *karma.* Nārada and Śāṇḍilya, as might be expected, differ at this point. Nārada says, "Love is its own reward." [69] Śāṇḍilya, admitting that love is not knowledge [70] and that love does not depend upon exertions for its growth as does knowledge,[71] grants that knowledge may assist in bringing about love,[72] although he denies that love is a means toward knowledge.[73] According to the *Bhāgavata Purāṇa, karma* yields *bhakti,* and *bhakti* in turn yields *jñāna:* "Actions done for the satisfaction of the Lord, produce devotion towards Him, and that devotion produces knowledge." [74] The problem inherent in comparisons of the use of the term *bhakti* among the various authorities and scriptures is, as we have already indicated, the

[67] *Obscure Religious Cults,* p. 154.
[68] *Śrī Bhaṣya* 1. 2. 23.
[69] *Sūtra* 30.
[70] *Sūtra* 4.
[71] *Sūtra* 5.
[72] *Sūtra* 9.
[73] *Sūtra* 15.
[74] 1. 5. 35. J. M. Sanyal translation.

loose and comprehensive manner in which the term is used. At the lowest level *bhakti* is blind faith in the object of devotion; at the highest level it is direct realization. The term is used both for the process in which *bhakti* serves as a means for liberation and for the realized goal itself. The former, which is known as *gauṇī bhakti* is a steppingstone to goals transcending itself. Its values are all extrinsic. There is always the danger that an individual may savor this emotion so much that it degenerates into an exclusive love valued for its own sake. These introvertive, solipsistic emotions can result in pathological conditions of a schizophrenic nature. The second form of *bhakti* is called *parā bhakti* or *sādhyā bhakti*. This refers to the *bhakti* state as inherent in *mokṣa* itself. The *jīvanmukta* in this state forgets self and sees nothing but an all-encompassing love which embraces the universe in joy. *Bhakti* is the goal (*sādhyā*), not merely the means (*mārga*). Nārada thinks of *bhakti* as both the means and the goal, but Śāṇḍilya thinks *bhakti* is only a means to enlightenment. According to the supporters of *gauṇī bhakti*, the offering of water, of *tulasī* leaves, of lotus and other flowers, and of fruit, the recitation of the names of god, the listening to stories of the lives of Kṛṣṇa and Rāma, and the serving of the devotees of God are works of merit whose values are in the acts themselves, not in the remote goal which they may realize. Supporters of *sādhyā bhakti* insist that the blessed state of the *bhakta* transcends any other experience within time and space. The benefactions of the gracious Lord may be symbolized in the *bhakti* acts which the *gauṇī bhakta* assumes to be the totality of *bhakti*, but these are only adumbrations of *mokṣa*. *Gauṇī bhakti* is formal (*vaidhī*) *bhakti*; it is the lower phase, the phase of prayers, meditations, ceremonies, pilgrimages, and image worship. *Sādhyā bhakti* is supreme (*mukhyā*) *bhakti*. The first step in *bhakti*, continues the *sādhyā bhakta*, is a respectful dependence upon God, a positive expectant attitude of waiting. There can be no *bhakti* without this; but to settle for this, to conclude that this is the *summum bonum* of *bhakti*, is to prize *bhakti* far too cheaply. Ear cannot hear and eye cannot see what lies in store for the devotee of the Lord. Thus it was that Arjuna begged forgiveness from Kṛṣṇa after the theophany for having assumed that his previous experience of deity was adequate, "And I have presumed, from love and casual regard, called you Krishna, Yadava, and friend, thinking you a friend, unmindful of your glory. I have lowered you in laughter, in resting, eating and walking, alone and in company. Forgive me, Krishna." [75] A *sādhyā bhakta* does not deny or belittle the value of an active devotional life (*śuddha śrāddha*); he does, however, want to keep it in perspective as a means for the realiza-

[75] *Bhagavad Gītā* 11.41–42. Lal translation.

tion of supreme ends. Temporal *rasa* is not to be compared to eternal *rasa.*

Bhakti is the heart of theistic religion. It is an emotion which individuates and separates the subject and the object, man and his god. Both are persons; one is the finite *bhakta,* the other is the infinite Bhagavan. Rāmānuja and the other Viśiṣṭādvaitins hold that even in the state of liberation the separateness of the individual and Īśvara remains. Śāṇḍilya, following the Advaita tradition, maintains that the *bhakti* state ends upon liberation.[76] Śaṅkara allows both *bhakti* and *karma* as supports for *jñāna mārga,* although he denies that either is a feature of the liberated state, the state transcending all dualities.

Bhaktas differ as to whether effort is a feature of the *bhakti mārga,* although in general they, unlike those who stress *yoga,* hold that complete surrender to God (*prapatti*) is sufficient to elicit divine grace (*prasāda*). Two kinds of *prapatti* are distinguished: one-pointed *prapatti* addresses itself to God for the granting of worthy boons, the most desirable being salvation itself; one-only-pointed *prapatti* craves only the knowledge and love of God. The doctrine of grace is rooted in the early Vedic literature. In a hymn to Vāc (personified speech) the *deva* displays a gracious attitude to men: "He who eats food (eats) through me; he who sees, who breathes, who hears what is spoken, does so through me. . . . whomsoever I will, I render formidable, I made him a Brahman, a Rishi, or a sage." [77] In the *Kaṭha Upaniṣad* it is declared that one becomes freed from sorrow "when through the grace (*prasāda*) of the Creator he beholds the greatness of the Soul (*Ātman*)." [78] Again in the *Śvetāśvatara Upaniṣad* the *ṛṣi* states that man's vision of God is itself granted by divine grace: "Through the grace (*prasāda*) of the Creator he sees the Lord and his greatness." [79] The doctrine of election is stated even more clearly in the *Muṇḍaka Upaniṣad:*

> This Soul (*Ātman*) is not to be obtained by instruction,
> Nor by intellect, nor by much learning.
> He is to be obtained only by the one whom He chooses;
> To such a one that Soul (*Ātman*) reveals His own person.[80]

The *bhakti* schools have differed as to whether the grace of God is a divine response to human effort or a divine initiative that tantalizes man into action. Rāmānuja, for example, says that without *prasāda* man

[76] *Sūtra* 31.
[77] *Ṛg Veda* 10. 125. 4, 5.
[78] 2. 20. Hume translation.
[79] 3. 20. Hume translation.
[80] 3. 2. 3. Hume translation.

could not make the effort required to liberate the Self from the lower self, and without God a *yogi* is in danger of mental breakdown.[81] In this connection Zaehner has offered an interesting translation of *Bhagavad Gītā* 6. 47: "But of all Yogins I consider that one the most integrated who worships me with faith, his inmost soul lost in me."[82] Because of the excesses to which many of the *bhakta* have gone in their efforts to experience the love of God, supporters have often been obliged to defend *bhakti* as a "religion of healthy-mindedness" rather than a manifestation of the "sick soul," to use William James's well-known classification. One of the most interesting defenses of *bhakti* as an ingredient in the fully human life is found in the *Bhāgavata Purāṇa*. We shall quote it at length, and then turn to two types of *bhaktism:* Vaiṣṇavism and Śaivism.

> A person who has never heard the discourses of Sri Hari, his ears may be regarded as holes. O Suta, the tongue of the person who has never sung on the glories of Sri Hari may be regarded as contemptible as that of the tongue of a frog. A head even though furnished with a crown or a silk turban, but never bending down to the lotus-like feet of *Mukunda* (the Lord Vishnu) may be regarded as nothing but an useless burden to the body. The hands although adorned with golden bracelets but which have never been used to offer flowers devotedly to the lotus feet of Sri Hari may be regarded as useless as the hands of a dead person. The eyes which have never seen the beauty of Sri Hari may be regarded as vain beautiful marks of eyes on the plumes of a peacock. The feet that have not walked to the places hallowed by the association of the Lord Sri Hari may be regarded as trunks of trees. The persons who have never taken the dust of the feet of devotees of the Lord, though physically living, are to be regarded as useless as corpses. And that [one] who has not enjoyed the smell of the *Tulasi* leaves placed on Sri Hari's feet, although breathing, should be regarded as dead. The heart of the person may be regarded as hard as stone, who does not feel pricked with conscience and overwhelmed with *bhakti* on hearing Sri Hari's name sung, and even though moved in heart if his eyes do not shed tears and the hairs of his body do not stand erect with feeling of reverence and awe.[83]

3. VAIṢṆAVISM

The religion known as Vaiṣṇavism or Bhāgavata first appeared in India in the fifth century B.C. as part of a general Kṣatriya protest move-

[81] His commentary on *Bhagavad Gītā* 2. 63.
[82] R. C. Zaehner, *Hindu and Muslim Mysticism*, p. 195.
[83] 2. 3. 20–24. Sanyal translation.

ment against the Brahmins, a protest which also manifested itself in the rise of Buddhism and Jainism. It was a monotheistic religion, as another name for it indicates—Ekāntika. The term Bhāgavata relates the religion to a very ancient *deva* named Bhaga probably of Indo-European origin who is mentioned in the Vedas, although his function and personality are indistinct.[84] In one passage Agni is praised by being called Bhaga, the one who "rules over wealth," [85] and in another Bhaga is mentioned in the context of riches.[86] The term came to mean the power of goodness, and still later it was changed to Bhagavat, the god who possesses beneficences which he will give to his devotees. Vaiṣṇavism, of course, is the religion of Viṣṇu, the all-pervading solar deity of the Vedas whose peculiar place was the sun at its zenith, i.e., a position higher than that of any other deity. As the god of the three steps, he was able to move into all the cosmic regions. In the Brāhmaṇas he is described as the supreme god.[87] Viṣṇu and Bhagavat were in time united into a single god, thus creating the very heart of Vaiṣṇavism, *viz.*, belief in the existence of but one god, a god both benevolent and omnipotent.

Another fountainhead of Vaiṣṇavism is the Vāsudeva-Kṛṣṇa cult, a sectarian movement built around a culture hero of the Vṛṣṇi or Sātvata clan of the Kṣatriya *varṇa* in northwest India.[88] This cult was a revolt against the elaborate and mechanical forms of worship into which the ancient Vedic sacrifices had deteriorated, and also against the Brahmins who had seized control of the rituals. The myth of this cult is centered on the hero Vāsudeva-Kṛṣṇa, but how much is legend and how much is history cannot be confidently determined. Indologists have divided opinions on this matter; e.g., Vāsudeva-Kṛṣṇa has been identified as a popular deity foisted upon Viṣṇu (Hopkins), as a solar deity (Barth), as a vegetation deity (Keith), and as a king, probably of royal descent, who was elevated to divinity in the stories built around him (Bhandarkar, Seal, Grierson, Raychoudhuri). The myth locates him in Mathurā, and narrates how he became head of a confederation of tribes which foiled the attempt of his evil uncle Kaṇsa to become tyrant of Mathurā. By the second century B.C. Vāsudeva-Kṛṣṇa was worshiped as "the god of gods" (*devadeva*) according to an inscription discovered at Besnagar which records the erection of a Garuḍa column to him.[89] The one who erected the column, a man named Heliodora, called himself a Bhāgavata;

[84] John Dowson, *A Classical Dictionary of Hindu Mythology and Religion, Geography, History, and Literature*, p. 43.

[85] *Ṛg Veda* 2. 1. 7.

[86] *Ibid.*, 10. 125. 2.

[87] *Aitareya Brāhmaṇa* 1. 1; *Śatapatha Brāhmaṇa* 14. 1. 1.

[88] *Bhagavad Gītā* 10. 37.

[89] *Epigraphia Indica*, Vol. 10, Inscription No. 669.

he was in fact an ambassador of the Macedonian king Antialkidas. Another item of evidence for the hypothesis that the worship of Vāsudeva may have come from the Greeks is the reference of Megasthenes to the worship of "Herakles" at the city "Methora" near the river "Jobares." [90]

A third element contributing to the development of Vaiṣṇavism was the worship of Nārāyaṇa. Nārāyaṇa was a sage who according to tradition wrote a hymn in praise of Puruṣa the Cosmic Soul.[91] In later Brahmanic times Nārāyaṇa was worshiped as the Soul he had praised in his hymn: "all this visible world, all that is, and all that is to be." [92] According to another tradition the close relationship of Nārāyaṇa and Nara (the original eternal man) was expressed in the association of Kṛṣṇa and Arjuna in the *Bhagavad Gītā* and also in the Upaniṣadic story of the two birds in a single tree.[93] In the *Mahābhārata* Nārāyaṇa is identified with Hari or Kṛṣṇa.[94]

During the years in which Vāsudeva-Kṛṣṇa legends were coalescing with the Viṣṇu and Nārāyaṇa legends—a process which was completed by the third century B.C.[95]—a new element was developing which was to change radically the character of the religion. Bhandarkar speculates that as Vaiṣṇavism spread it came into contact with this new element about the first century A.D. A nomadic tribe living near Mathurā worshiped a cowherd deity called Vāsudeva-Kṛṣṇa. These people, whom Bhandarkar identifies as Abhiras, had many tales about their divine hero, his humble birth, the massacre of innocents, his boyhood mischievousness and pranks, the threats on his life, etc. When these stories were integrated with the Viṣṇu-Bhaga-Vāsudeva-Kṛṣṇa-Nārāyaṇa god and cult, the result was an intensely emotional religion, a viable alternative to decadent ritualism and entrenched priesthood. This religion is found in the *Bhagavad Gītā*, a work put together between 100 B.C. and A.D. 100. The *Gītā* remains to this day one of the finest expressions of *bhakti mārga* and also a source of devotional strength for all Hindus who are sympathetic to religious worship. Edgerton has described it as "India's favorite Bible." [96] Gandhi said it was "an infallible guide to conduct." [97] Schweitzer, while denying that the *Gītā* presents a mysticism corresponding to Christian

[90] Radhakrishnan, *Indian Philosophy*, Vol. 2, p. 493.

[91] *Ṛg Veda* 10. 90.

[92] *Ibid.*, 10. 90. 2.

[93] *Muṇḍaka Upaniṣad* 3. 1. 1. *Śvetāśvatara Upaniṣad* 4. 6. A quotation from *Ṛg Veda* 1. 164. 20.

[94] 10. 344.

[95] Bharatan Kumarappa, *The Hindu Conception of Deity as Culminating in Rāmānuja*, p. 91.

[96] *The Bhagavad Gītā*, p. vii.

[97] *The Story of My Experiments with Truth*, p. 323.

mysticism, characterized it as "an attempt undertaken by magnificent, unimpassioned thought to gain recognition for the idea of self-devotion to God by action within the world-view of world and life negation." [98] Hopkins found it "an ill-assorted cabinet of primitive philosophical opinions." [99] The *Gītā*, like all genuine scriptures of mankind, has sufficient ambiguity to allow its readers to find support for almost any doctrine or practice they wish to believe and to follow. If this were not the case, the work would be neglected and thus cease to be a living scripture. *Bhakti mārga* is in the *Bhagavad Gītā* for those who seek *bhakti*—but so is *karma, jñāna,* and *yoga.* The *Gītā* offers both the Upaniṣadic doctrine of an impersonal Absolute and the Vaiṣṇava doctrine of a loving, redeeming Kṛṣṇa; it offers monistic Vedānta metaphysics and also dualistic Sāṅkhya. Kṛṣṇa is the god of the *Gītā,* yet worshipers of Śiva also use the *Gītā* in their worship. The unfinished nature of the *Gītā* is part of its charm. Even though it has been supplemented by commentaries, by the *Pāñcaratra Saṁhitas,* and by the Purāṇas, it has been supplanted by none. It remained the best exposition of devotional religion within Hinduism until the systematic philosophical exposition by Rāmānuja in the eleventh century, a treatment consisting mainly of commentaries on the *Bhagavad Gītā* and the *Vedānta Sūtras.* The development of Bhaktism in India in the one thousand years from the compiling of the *Gītā* to Rāmānuja had as its center four events: (1) the writing of the two great epics of India, (2) the lives and works of the Āḷvārs, (3) the philosophical activities of Śaṅkara, and (4) the writing of the *Bhāgavata Purāṇa.*

The epics of India, the *Mahābhārata* and the *Rāmāyaṇa,* grew out of stories which were part of the folklore of the Indian people in pre-Buddhistic times. The period of the formation of the epics was the eight centuries from 400 B.C. to A.D. 400. The *Rāmāyaṇa* is much the more integrated of the two, and is of far less significance in the development of *bhakti.* The chief value of the *Rāmāyaṇa* for *bhakti mārga* is that in this epic Rāma, the *avatāra* of Viṣṇu, is the hero who stresses the life of *dharma.* The *Mahābhārata* contains a considerable amount of didactic material, especially Book 12, the *Śanti Parva,* in which the dying Bhīṣma relieves himself of the amassed wisdom of his years for the benefit of the Pāṇḍavas. The *Bhagavad Gītā,* which is Book 6 sections 25 to 42 of the *Mahābhārata,* is the high point of the *bhakti* teaching of the epic. Although the *Mokṣadharma Parva* (Book 12, sections 174–367) and the *Anugītā Parva* (Book 14, sections 16–51) are also rich in *bhakti* material, they contain little that is not found in the *Bhagavad Gītā.* The religion

[98] *Indian Thought and Its Development,* p. 191.
[99] Edward Washburn Hopkins, *Religions of India,* p. 399.

of devotion and submission to the grace of the Lord is presented as equal to or surpassing any other religion:

> The religion followed by a person that is devoted with his whole soul to Nārāyaṇa is regarded as similar or equal in merit to the system of the Sāṅkhyas. By adopting that religion one attains to the highest end and attains to emancipation which has Nārāyaṇa for its soul. That person upon whom Nārāyaṇa looks with compassion succeeds in becoming awakened. No one, O king, can become awakened through his own wishes.[100]

The life and work of the Āḷvārs constitute one of the most fascinating chapters in the history of the religions of Hinduism. The Āḷvārs were twelve wandering troubadors living in south India in the seventh and eighth centuries A.D. who composed and sang songs of devotion to Viṣṇu in the Tamil language. Some of these poets were of low birth, one was an outcaste, and one was a woman. Their contribution to the philosophical understanding of Hinduism is almost nil, but their songs are rich contributions to the *bhakti* movement. These songs were compiled in a single volume called *Nālāyira Prabandam* (Book of Four Thousand Hymns) about A.D. 900. Among Tamil-speaking Vaiṣṇavites this collection remains to this day as cherished as the Sanskrit Vedas. Many of the Āḷvārs have been canonized and worshiped in south India. The word *āḷvār,* meaning one deep in wisdom, is not quite appropriate, since *bhakti,* not *jñāna,* is the forte of these minstrels. A poem by Āḷvār Toṇḍaraḍipoḍi shows the typical *bhakti* attitude toward knowledge:

> Truth have I forsworn! Caught in the snares
> Of wily dames of flowing locks, come I
> An erring soul. Refuge for all the sins
> That teem the world, O gracious Lord Ranga!
> 'Tis but my certain hope Thy grace will save
> Which makes me bold to come to Thee and wait.[101]

The effort of the individual to restrain his loving devotion in order to labor in the path of action is expressed in this song from Nammāḷvār:

> Alas! my heart, wouldst thou now start ahead
> Of me to reach His feet and praise His grace
> So fired by zeal, so goaded by thy love?
> But tarry now, I prithee, let us work
> Together up to Him of hue of *pūvai* flower;

[100] *Mahābhārata* 12. 349.
[101] Quoted by R. W. Frazer, *Indian Thought Past and Present,* p. 221.

And weave into wreaths of honied song
Which wellest forth from tongue, unhelped by mind.[102]

Another song from Nammāḷvār is on a common theme of the Āḷvārs, the desire to depart this life in order to be forever with the Lord:

When shall I join my lord, who poison is
For evil deeds, and nectar for the good?
Husband of her who haunts the lotus-bloom,
Cowherd who thought no scorn to graze the cows
Who overpaced the world in his two strides![103]

The Āḷvārs provided the ground and the inspiration out of which Rāmānuja's teachings grew, and in addition they set a pattern of music and poetry which has remained a part of the religion of the common people of India, particularly in south India, as is evidenced by this Canarese folksong:

I worshipped a stone I could see and could feel
And therefore have now neither strength nor ally.
I visited oft with the fool and the rogue.
And, like a mad elephant, wounded my friends.
Was wise but for folly; in sinning was brave.
Oh, Vishnu, Lord, speedily save!
    Chorus—I see how foolish I have been
        And cry against the dread Vishnu—
        "Oh, wilt thou never mark the scene
        Of strife and sorrow so undue."

I made many vows and am weary of sin,
For nothing delights or can profit me now.
Each temple I've circled and circled again
Till, weary and worn, I am worse than before,
And nothing is left but thy love or the grave.
Oh, Hari, Lord, speedily save!

The quack and the fool were as gurus to me,
So simple was I, so defiled and unclean,
Purandala's grace I now strive to obtain
So pure and so good, ever worthy of praise.
Thou canst not refuse the protection I crave.
Oh, Hari, Lord, speedily save![104]

[102] Alkondavalli Govindāchārya, *The Holy Lives of the Āzhvārs or Drāvida Saints*, pp. 221–222.

[103] J. S. M. Hooper, *Hymns of the Āḷvārs*, pp. 85–86.

[104] Charles E. Gover, *The Folk-Songs of South India*, pp. 47–48.

At the very time the last Āḷvārs were composing and singing their hymns of adoration to Viṣṇu, Śaṅkara was promulgating metaphysical monism and world illusionism as the true doctrine of the Upaniṣads. Śaṅkara, as we have already noted, taught that *jñāna* is the only *mārga* which can bring men to *mokṣa* and that *bhakti* is useful only at the early preparatory stages of *sādhana*. Although according to Śaṅkara's position any god is as good as another, since for him all are of the phenomenal rather than the real world, his own preference was for Śiva. His attack on Vaiṣṇavism was direct and harsh: "We have, in what precedes, refuted the opinion of those who think that the Lord is not the material cause but only the ruler, the operative cause of the world." [105] That is, he had refuted the dualistic doctrine that God created the world out of stuff independent of his own nature. Next he refuted the opposite opinion that God is the material cause of the world, a view held by Vaiṣṇavites: "The so-called Bhāgavatas are of the opinion that the one holy (*bhagavat*) Vāsudeva, whose nature is pure knowledge, is what really exists." [106] He does this by arguing from Advaita Vedāntic principles that creation, world, and gods are all *māyā* rather than reality. Vaiṣṇavism, according to Śaṅkara, is incomplete, dealing as it does with only the world of appearance and not with the world of Reality, the "world" of Brahman. Again Śaṅkara says he does not object to the Vaiṣṇava emphasis on inculcating concentration of mind on the Highest Being under the forms of reverential approach, but to do this on the grounds that the individual self (*jīva*) has sprung from the highest Self (*Ātman*) is once again to confuse badly the orders of phenomena and noumena. If Vāsudeva be the highest Self as the Vaiṣṇavites claim, then from this Self the finite selves could not originate, for if that were the case the nonpermanency of the finite self would also belong to the Self from which it originated. Having demonstrated that the Bhāgavata hypothesis has no rational basis, he then in the next *sūtra* points out that there is no scriptural passage that can be cited in favor of the Vaiṣṇava position.[107] Śaṅkara also calls attention to passages that are contradictory to the Vaiṣṇava position.[108] The spirited attack of Śaṅkara and his followers on Vaiṣṇavism revealed the need for intellectual defenses of *bhakti* and *prapatti* other than the unsystematic treatment offered in the *Bhagavad Gītā* and the emotional support of the saintly Āḷvārs. Before the end of the ninth century there arose in Tamil land the teachers, theologians,

105 *The Vedānta-Sūtras with the Commentary by Śaṅkarācarya*, 2. 2. 42. *The Sacred Books of the East*, Vol. 34, p. 439.
106 *Ibid.*, p. 440.
107 *Ibid.*, 2. 2. 43.
108 *Ibid.*, 2. 2. 45.

and philosophers who were to do for the intellectual side of Vaiṣṇavism what the Āḷvārs did for the emotional side. These men were known as *ācāryas*. The greatest of them was Rāmānuja.

The fourth significant event in *bhakti* development between the compilation of the *Bhagavad Gītā* and the work of Rāmānuja was the writing of the *Bhāgavata Purāṇa*, the second most important work in Vaiṣṇavism.[109] The *Bhāgavata Purāṇa* or *Śrimad Bhāgavatam* was probably composed in the tenth century at Kānchi, a famous south Indian seat of learning. This work is one of eighteen Purāṇas (ancient narratives), books written as their name suggests to record legends and stories which had theretofore been passed down orally from generation to generation. The Purāṇas are so important that they have been called the Fifth Veda, an honorific title which has also been applied to the *Mahābhārata* and to the Tantric scriptures. A purāṇa was expected to cover five topics: (1) creation of the world, (2) eschatology of the world, (3) genealogies of gods, demons, sages, and kings, (4) cosmic cycles, and (5) accounts of royal dynasties. The *Bhāgavata Purāṇa* fits the model, but its importance in Vaiṣṇava tradition is largely centered on Book 10, which contains accounts of the birth of Kṛṣṇa, his mischievous boyhood, his amorous delights with the milkmaids (*gopīs*), his destruction of the tyrant Kaṇsa, his marriages, his miracles, and his many heroic exploits. This portion of the *Bhāgavata Purāṇa* was later expanded and exploited into an erotic Vaiṣṇavism especially by the Bengali followers who regarded the love of Kṛṣṇa and the *gopīs* as the epitome of the divine-human encounter. According to the *Bhāgavata Purāṇa* all the *gopīs* were madly in love with Kṛṣṇa the cowherd. They would slip away at night from their husbands' beds to meet Kṛṣṇa on the banks of the Yamunā River to dance a circle dance (*rāsa-pañcādhyāya*). Kṛṣṇa multiplied himself so each *gopī* enjoyed him and was enjoyed by him in the fullness of coital love. While for some Indians the stories of Kṛṣṇa and the *gopīs* represent "man's profoundest communion with God" and the "ecstasy of universal salvation," [110] others "entirely disbelieve the truth of these stories" holding that "no more mischievous though well-intentioned misrepresentations have ever sullied the fair name of a great man." [111] Renou, refusing to commit himself on the religious values of the erotic passages, finds other values: "I cannot say whether religious feelings profited greatly by this

[109] Some students of Indian religions would not place the *Bhāgavata Purāṇa* in a secondary position. E.g., Radhakamal Mukerjee writes, "The Bhāgavata is the greatest scripture in India. Its influence on the life of her millions has been greater than even that of the Bhagavadgītā." *The Lord of the Autumn Moons*, p. 47.

[110] Mukerjee, *The Lord of the Autumn Moons*, pp. 5, 19.

[111] Chintaman V. Vaidya, *Epic India*, p. 422.

development, but it was an undoubted gain for literature." [112] Radhakrishnan dismisses these passages from the Hindu conscience by saying they "clearly indicate the non-Aryan origin of Kṛṣṇa." [113] These matters will be discussed after considering the work of Rāmānuja.

Śarma likens the progress of Vaiṣṇavism to a river system: ". . . the fountain of Vaiṣṇava bhakti rises in the *Gītā*, passes through the songs of the Āḷvārs, gathers its waters in the system of Rāmānuja and flows out later . . . in varied streams all over India." [114] The position of Rāmānuja in Vaiṣṇavism is always recognized as that of a great systematizer. He is said to have gotten the direction of his life from a priest who taught him at an early age that devotion is the only unfailing cause of salvation. Most of his long life was spent at Śrīraṅgam where he was in charge of the shrine. He was deeply impressed by the Āḷvārs, so much so that he requested commentaries be written on the hymns. But it was Śaṅkara who, with his disciples, more than anyone else shaped the course of Rāmānuja's teachings by presenting an interpretation of Hindu tradition which Rāmānuja believed to be false and pernicious. Śaṅkara, by reestablishing Hinduism on its ancient Vedic foundations, effectively opposed the threat of Buddhism and won back many pious and thoughtful people who had strayed from the Vedic tradition; but in doing so he created a Vedāntic religion far too erudite for the common man who felt a need for divine love and sustenance which he could not find in the impersonal Brahman nor in the *jñāna mārga* which Śaṅkara claimed to be the only path to liberation. Rāmānuja sought to modify the monism of Śaṅkara in order to allow room for the claims of the heart, not merely because he knew this was what the common man wanted and needed, but also because he believed this was the true interpretation of the Upaniṣads, the *Vedānta Sūtras*, and the *Bhagavad Gītā*. The emotional tone of Rāmānuja's argument is startling. His first evaluation of Śaṅkara's conception of the Brahman sets the pattern: "The entire theory rests on a fictitious foundation of altogether hollow and vicious arguments, incapable of being stated in definite logical alternatives." [115] Ill-will between Advaitins and Viśiṣṭādvaitins has continued through the centuries. For example, Thibaut in the introduction to his translation of Śaṅkara's commentary on the *Vedānta Sūtras* expressed his scholarly opinion after much argument and evidence that "in some important points their

[112] *Religions of Ancient India*, pp. 72–73.

[113] *Indian Philosophy*, Vol. 1, p. 496.

[114] D. S. Śarma, *Studies in the Renaissance of Hinduism in the Nineteenth and Twentieth Centuries*, p. 40.

[115] *The Vedānta-Sūtras with the Commentary of Rāmānuga. The Sacred Books of the East*, Vol. 48, p. 39.

[*Vedānta Sūtras*] teaching is more closely related to the system of Rāmānuga that to that of Śaṅkara." [116] Thibaut reports that certain followers of Śaṅkara attacked him for having made this evaluation, charging him with "philosophical incompetency" and contending he was "hopelessly theistic due to early training." [117] Otto reports that a follower of Rāmānuja once said to him, "I would sooner become a Christian than acknowledge the teachings of Śaṅkara." [118] Name-calling continues to this day: Sures Chandra Chakravarti, an Advaitist, says Rāmānuja was a "middle-class intellect" who "pandered to the cry of the populace," [119] and P. N. Srinivasachari, a Viśiṣṭādvaitist, accuses the Advaitists of having a "superiority complex." [120]

Rāmānuja stayed within the Vedāntic tradition, rooting his teachings in the Upaniṣads, but he rejected the monism of Śaṅkara for a modified monism (*viśiṣṭādvaita,* literally "modified non-dualism"). *Tat tvam asi* did not mean for him the absolute identity of *Ātman* and Brahman but an expression of the truth that in Brahman everything has its Self. The Absolute for him is an embodied whole consisting of the Brahman, individual souls, and the physical world. Brahman is the Soul of which the selves and the world are the body. All three are different, distinct, eternal, and inseparable. The oneness of the Absolute is a unity of differences which together form a living organism. The cause of the world and individual selves is the omniscient and omnipotent God Himself who for "nothing else than sport" [121] (*līlā*), creates, sustains, and redeems the world. The term "Brahman" denotes "the highest Person (*purushottama*), who is essentially free from all imperfections and possesses numberless classes of auspicious qualities of unsurpassable excellence." [122] Rāmānuja emphasized the gracious love of God which he found in the *Gītā* and the religious experience of the Āḷvārs. His emphasis on the grace of God is seen in one of his favorite quotations from the Upaniṣads:

> This Soul (*Ātman*) is not to be attained by instruction,
> Nor by intellect, nor by much learning.

[116] *The Vedānta-Sūtras with the Commentary by Śaṅkarācārya. The Sacred Books of the East,* Vol. 34, p. cxxvi.

[117] *The Vedānta-Sūtras with the Commentary of Rāmānuga. The Sacred Books of the East,* Vol. 48, p. ix.

[118] Rudolf Otto, *India's Religion of Grace and Christianity Compared and Contrasted,* p. 22.

[119] *The Philosophy of the Upaniṣads,* p. 154.

[120] *The Philosophy of Viśiṣṭādvaita,* p. xliii.

[121] *The Vedānta-Sūtras with the Commentary of Rāmānuga,* 2.1.33. *The Sacred Books of the East,* Vol. 48, p. 477.

[122] *Ibid.,* 1.1.1, p. 4.

He is to be obtained only by the one whom he chooses;
To such a one that Soul (*Ātman*) reveals his own person.[123]

He points out that according to the *Bhagavad Gītā* God is "the friend of all beings,"[124] a companion,[125] and one who loves men.[126] In his commentary on the *Gītā* Rāmānuja refers to God as "the sole Reservoir of all illustrious attributes, the antithesis to all evil,"[127] "the ocean of infinite mercy, compassion, beauty, sweetness, dignity, bounty, affection,"[128] and "the natural boundless ocean of all the exalted countless glorious attributes, such as beauty, compassion and condescension, love and clemency, sweetness and dignity and bounty, courage, valour and daring, wisdom, lordship."[129] God's grace does not violate the law of *karma;* it always acts in accordance with the principle of moral causality, since *karma* is an expression of God's own mode of action, not something external to him. Man's response to that loving grace is *bhakti.* Rāmānuja says at the opening of his commentary on *Bhagavad Gītā* 2, "The purpose of this work . . . is to make an exposition of that one-pointed and perfect Loving Faith or Devotion," and he adds, "In order to achieve this Bhakti, the realizing of the nature of one's own *ātma,* is a necessary preliminary step."[130] In other words Rāmānuja holds that *jñāna mārga* is a means to *bhakti.* Also in his proem to his commentary on *Bhagavad Gītā* 13 he says, "In the First Division comprising the First Six Lectures, it was shown that there were two Paths, *viz.,* Karma-Yoga and Jñāna-Yoga, by which an aspirant can achieve actual soul-realization. It also shows that such soul-realization or soul-cognition is ancillary (or steppingstone) to God-Love known as Bhakti, or the Means by which to reach the Supreme Goal, *viz.,* the Blessed Lord Vāsudeva, Who is Parabrahm."[131] The highest goal of human life, then, is not Self-realization, the *Ātman-bodhi* of Śaṅkara, but loving devotion to the Lord. Rāmānuja did not make perfectly clear whether *bhakti* is merely man's response to God's gracious love, or whether man's devotion is an active agent in *sādhana.* As a result two schools appeared among his followers: the "monkey school" (*Markaṭa Nyāya*) which supports the view that man aids his salvation as a

[123] *Kaṭha Upaniṣad* 2. 23. Hume translation.
[124] *Bhagavad Gītā* 5. 29. Edward J. Thomas translation.
[125] *Ibid.,* 11. 41.
[126] *Ibid.,* 18. 64.
[127] *Bhagavad Gītā with Srī Rāmānujāchārya's Viśiṣṭādvaita Commentary,* p. 6. A. Govindacharya translation.
[128] *Ibid.,* p. 315.
[129] *Ibid.,* p. 385.
[130] *Ibid.,* p. 87.
[131] *Ibid.,* p. 397.

young monkey helps by clinging to its mother, and the "cat school" (*Mārjāra Nyāya*) which contends that man does not aid his salvation as a kitten does not help in its being carried.

Rāmānuja taught that individuality of selves remains in the liberated state. This is assumed in his conception of oneness as relatedness, but in addition he argues pragmatically that no one would seek liberation if it meant individual annihilation. A man suffering pain sets out to find a release from the pain, he says, but "If, on the other hand he were to realize that the effect of such activity would be the loss of personal existence, he surely would turn away as soon as somebody began to tell him about release. . . . No sensible person exerts himself under the influence of the idea that after he himself has perished there will remain some entity termed 'pure light!' "[132] However, liberation for Rāmānuja does not include a bodily individuality, for he says that liberation in the full sense is not possible as long as a man lives in the embodied state.

In the work of Rāmānuja the Vaiṣṇava religion received intellectual footing for the *bhakti* practices it had developed over many centuries. The principles of *Bhagavad Gītā* were now systematized, the *Vedānta Sūtras* could now be used to support Vaiṣṇavism, the emotionalism of the Āḷvārs would no longer stand without philosophical foundation, and above all the Hindus were offered an alternative to Advaita Vedāntism with its reduction of individual men, the physical world, and the gods to the status of *māyā*. New hope and new courage entered Vaiṣṇavism. Rāmānuja interpreted the words of Kṛṣṇa to Arjuna, "Grieve not,"[133] as advice to give up efforts to expiate sins, to adopt Kṛṣṇa in lieu of such efforts. Man is encouraged to make a start, to commence *bhakti mārga*. To begin is to insure success, for the fruition is in the hands of the Lord. Rāmānuja's message encouraged men to launch out with joy on their *sādhana*. The four centuries following Rāmānuja witnessed one of the great religious reformations in India, a renewal of equality and brotherhood. Vedāntists like Madhva, Nimbārka, and Vallabha offered modifications of Śaṅkara's extreme non-dualism, but they introduced little that is strikingly different in the area of *mārga*.

The next development in Vaiṣṇavism appeared in the north. Kṛṣṇa of the *Bhāgavata Purāṇa* began to be presented as the cowherd lover of the *gopīs* rather than the destroyer of tyrants and demons. *Bhakti* shifted from man's response of gratitude for the freely offered grace of God to an erotic love enjoyed as archetypal of the man-god relationship. Although Kṛṣṇa was said to have had eight principal wives and 16,100

[132] *The Vedānta-Sūtras with the Commentary of Rāmānuga. The Sacred Books of the East*, Vol. 48, p. 70.

[133] *Bhagavad Gītā* 18. 66.

secondary wives, and although he had ten sons and one daughter by each wife, the cult leaders at Vṛndāvana, the forest home of Kṛṣṇa, began in the tenth century to dwell on the pre-marital and extra-marital exploits of Kṛṣṇa with the cowgirls. The *Bhāgavata Purāṇa* says that Kṛṣṇa had an unnamed favorite among the *gopīs*. She is later identified as Rādhā. A cult celebrating the love dalliances of Rādhā and Kṛṣṇa began at Vṛndāvana near Mathurā and spread particularly into northeast India, especially into Bengal where the ground had been laid by many erotic practices. Rādhā's willingness—nay, her longing—to engage in adulterous love (*parakīyā rati*) with her paramour was interpreted as symbolic of the longing of the human soul for union with god. Secret, illicit sex love rather than love within marriage was selected because the elements of risking discovery, of planning for trysts, and of uniting for pleasure rather than the fulfillment of marriage vows made this form of love emotionally like the unfathomable communion of man and god. In *parakīyā rati* Rādhā demonstrated her complete selflessness in giving herself to her lover with everything to lose. In similar dedication each man should give himself to the Lord. As might be expected, students of religion have puzzled over this variation on the *bhakti* theme. Archer speculates that the change of emphasis at this time was due to changes in marriage forced upon the Hindus by the Muslim invasions. Hindus, he argues, were forced to regulate marriages rigidly in order to avoid intermarriage with Muslims. This resulted in the loss of romantic marriages in favor of utilitarian arrangements. The loves of Kṛṣṇa were then "an exact sublimation of intense romantic needs" and the emphasis on Rādhā was "a substitute for wishes repressed in actual life." [134] Archer's hypothesis smells of the scholar's study! Poetry is no substitution for sex! It certainly was not in India; for soon the devotees of Lord Kṛṣṇa began emulating the exploits of Rādhā and Kṛṣṇa by staging their own enactments of the Vṛndāvana experiences. Sex and religion are always closely related, and seldom have they been more closely related than in the Rādhā-Kṛṣṇa cult of the Vaiṣṇavites in the twelfth to the fifteenth centuries. One of the earliest of the love poets of Vaiṣṇavism was Jayadeva, the court poet of King Lakṣmaṇasena, who reigned in the last half of the twelfth century. His *Gītā Govinda* (*Cowherd in Song*) is a lyrical drama based on the love of Kṛṣṇa for Rādhā, their estrangement and final reconciliation. Vidyāpati, a fourteenth-century poet of Mithili in that part of India now known as the state of Bihar, composed songs of the idyllic love of Rādhā and Kṛṣṇa. The songs portray both the joy of union and the agony of separation. Many are framed as the words of Rādhā.

[134] W. G. Archer. *The Loves of Krishna*, pp. 74, 73.

O friend, there is no end to my joy!
Mādhava is home for ever.
The pain I suffered for the heartless moon
Ended in bliss.
My eyes live on his face.
Lift up my dress, fill it with gold,
Yet never will I let him go again,
He is my shelter in the rains,
Ferry boat on the river.
He is my warmth when the winter is hard,
Cool breeze in the summer months.
Nothing else I need.[135]

The poems of Vidyāpati are beautiful love poems—there is no doubt about that. But are they religious poems? One critic compares them to the Hebrew *Song of Songs*, and argues that the allegorical interpretation of Vidyāpati's poetry ought to be given up as Christians have given up the allegorical interpretation of the *Song of Songs:* "The result is a clear gain to literature in the acknowledgement of this lyricism for what it is, masterpieces of sex-love, the glorification of the sex interest as supreme. To persist in treating such songs as teaching the divine truth of religion is as poor criticism as it is bad religion." [136] A Vaiṣṇavite might reply by pointing out that it is difficult for a man in one cultural tradition to determine what is good or bad in the religion and literature of another culture.

In the same century in which Vidyāpati was singing of the love of Rādhā and Kṛṣṇa, Rāmānanda was preaching *bhakti* in Banaras as the means of attaining salvation. His work was so successful that within half a century Bhāgavata was the leading religion of north India. The greatest of his disciples was a fifteenth-century poet Kabīr, who though born of Muslim parents became a disciple of Rāmānanda and worshiped Rāma as his god. He lived during the time of some of the worst persecutions by the Mughal rulers. The Emperor Sikandar Lodi finally banished Kabīr from Banaras, yet Kabīr's influence resulted in a synthesis of Islam and Hinduism known as Sikhism. A sect honoring Kabīr survives to this day, the Kabīrpanthī. Many of his songs have been preserved in the Sikh *Ādi Granth*. He was a radical in many ways: he rejected caste completely, placed no confidence in any scriptures, set no store by the four divisions of life, and dismissed all philosophies. For him religion is *bhakti*, and *bhakti* is religion. Although he sometimes uses the wife-husband relationship to illustrate what should be the relationship be-

[135] W. G. Archer, *Love Songs of Vidyāpati*, p. 52. Translated by Deben Bhattacharya.
[136] Melville T. Kennedy, *The Chaitanya Movement*, p. 255.

tween man and God, he is free from sexual implications. "All are wives of Rāma: unmovable Purusha is the Husband." [137] Kabīr is indiscriminate in the use of names for his god—Rāma, Hari, Śiva, Śakti, Govinda, Nārāyana, Brahmā, Allah, and Kundā. "Kabīr is a child of Rāma and Allah, and accepteth all gurus and pirs." [138] "Rāma, Khudā, Śakti, Śiva are one: tell me how you distinguish them?" [139] His god is to be found within: "Search in thy heart, search in thy heart of hearts; there is his place and abode." [140] His denunciation of the externalities of religion is often very harsh:

Why perform so many ceremonies? . . .
You (wear) tilaks on your forehead, (carry) rosaries in your hands, and (put on sectarian) dresses.
People think that God is a plaything.[141]

Devotion, sacrifice and rosary, piety, pilgrimage, fasting and alms.
Nine bhaktas, Vedas, the Book, all these are cloaks of falsehood.[142]

If union with God be obtained by going about naked
All the beasts of the forest shall be saved.[143]

Some shave men's locks and hang the black cord on their necks,
And pride themselves on the practice of Yoga.
What credit is there in causing your seat to fly?
Crow and kite also circle in the air.[144]

The greatest hindrance to *bhakti* is sin, said Kabīr, and the greatest sin is pride in learning or in ceremonies. He is reported to have addressed a Brahmin, "Thou art a Brahmin, I am a weaver of Banaras; how can I be a match for thee? By repeating the name of God I have been saved, while thou, O Pandit, shalt be lost by trusting to the Vedas." [145] *Bhakti* itself, he said, would not suffice unless it be a true *bhakti* of the heart.

[137] *Bījak, Ramainī* 27. The *Bījak* is the chief scripture of the Kabīrpanthī. There are two English translations, the Prem Chand translation (Calcutta, 1890) and the Ahmad Shah translation (Cawnpore, 1911). The most accessible sources of Kabīr poetry are F. E. Keay, *Kabir and His Followers*, G. H. Westcott, *Kabir and Kabir Panth*, and Max Arthur Macauliffe, *The Sikh Religion*, Vol. 6. Rabindranath Tagore published *One Hundred Poems of Kabir*, but according to Ahmad Shah these poems are based on an inaccurate Bengali translation, and the collection as a whole is not the work of Kabīr. All quotations from the *Bījak* are from the Ahmad Shah translation, and all quotations from the *Ādi Granth* are from the Macauliffe translation.

[138] *Ādi Granth, Prabhati* 2. A *pir* is a Muslim saint.

[139] *Bījak, Śabda* 48.

[140] *Ādi Granth, Prabhāti* 2.

[141] *Ādi Granth, Bhairau* 6.

[142] *Bījak, Śabda* 113.

[143] *Ādi Granth, Rag Gauṛī* 4.

[144] *Bījak, Ramaini* 71.

[145] Macauliffe, *The Sikh Religion*, Vol. 6, p. 242.

What availeth devotion, what penance, what fasting and worship,
To him in whose heart there is worldly love?
O man, apply thy heart to God;
Thou shall not obtain Him by artifice.[146]

The goal of *bhakti mārga* is reabsorption in God, but Kabīr does not elaborate on what that reabsorption means other than that it is a most desirable state:

When the body dieth, to what abode shall the pious man's soul go?
It shall unite with Him who is beyond expression and indestructible.[147]

Another who spoke against the intellectualization of religion stemming from Śaṅkara was Tulsīdāsa, the author of the Hindi *Rāmāyaṇa* or *Rāmacharitmānasa* (*The Lake of the Deeds of Rāma*) as Tulsīdāsa preferred to call it. In the Tulsīdāsa version Rāma becomes the embodiment of the divine. Book seven, for example, ends with the poet's own confession of devotional faith:

Rāma alone is all beautiful, all wise, full of compassion, and of loving-kindness for the destitute, disinterested in his benevolence, and the bestower of final deliverance; whom else can I desire? There is no other Lord like Rāma, by whose favour, however slight, even I the dull-witted Tulsīdāsa has found perfect peace.

Again in the *Kavitāvalī*, a collection of verses, Tulsīdāsa says,

I have but one faith, O Rām, that I am called yours:
—Yours, O friend of the wretched is the compassion, and mine the wretchedness.[148]

Bhakti is the only *mārga*; *jñāna* is the path of fools:

Those who knowingly ways of devotion forsake,
And for learning alone long laborious ways take,
Are like fools who in search of the milk-weed will roam
To get milk—leaving all their rich milch-cows at home.
Those, Garur, who for bliss have all other means tried,
From true worship of God blindly turned aside,
Are like blockheads who try at the ignorant notion,
Of crossing without any boat the great ocean.[149]

[146] *Ādi Granth, Gaurī* 6.
[147] *Ibid., Gaurī* 18.
[148] F. R. Allchin (translator), *Kavitāvalī*, p. 154.
[149] *Rāmāyaṇa, Chaupai* 110. A. G. Atkins translation.

The fullest description of *bhakti* is found in the third book of the *Rāmāyaṇa* when Lakshmana inquires from Rāma the difference between God and the soul. Rāma begins by confirming that knowledge according to the Vedas is the means to salvation, but he says there is a more excellent way, the way of *bhakti*. *Bhakti* is independent of knowledge. It involves using the senses for the enrichment of attitudes toward the deity. *Bhakti* has nine elements: (1) devotion to all manifestations of Rāma, (2) devotion for saints, (3) devotion for *gurus*, (4) singing hymns of praise to Rāma, (5) repeating the name of Rāma, (6) self-restraint, (7) seeing the whole world as full of Rāma, (8) contentment, and (9) guilelessness.[150] There is nothing very distinctive or original in this list nor in any of the discussions of *bhakti* in the *Rāmāyaṇa* of Tulsīdāsa. The chief impact of the *Rāmāyaṇa* in Hinduism has been in offering to the devout the characters of Rāma and Sītā as models of the dutiful life. The narration of their devotion is greater than any oral insights they give on the ideal life for man. The Hindi version of the epic remains one of the most influential works in India. H. H. Wilson has opined that it has "more influence upon the whole body of Hindu population than the whole voluminous series of Sanskrit composition." [151]

Between the thirteenth and the seventeenth centuries the *bhakti* renaissance made its appearance in Marāṭhā in the form of poets who composed short lyrics (*abhaṅgas*) filled with religious longing. The greatest of these Vaiṣṇavites were Jñāneśvar, Miktā Bāī, Nāmadeva, Janābāī, Edanāth, and Tukārāma. We shall confine our examination to Tukārāma, a Śūdra tradesman, who has been called "the Robert Burns of India." [152] A group in south India known as the Wārkarī keep the message of Tukārāma alive by reciting his poems in worship services. Some claim to know by heart as many as four thousand of his poems. The Prārthana Samaj of Bombay uses the poems of Tukārāma regularly in worship. Although no consistent philosophy can be constructed from his poems, two features do loom large in his writings: a sense of sin and a rather consistent opposition to Absolutism. His deep sense of sin is expressed in over three hundred of the poems, e.g., "Now save me from shame, I am a heap of transgressions. I am encased in the net, head and toes. Protect, oh protect me. Look on me graciously." [153] "I call myself his servant, but I do not act as tho' I were; my inward and outward parts are at variance. I show myself singing and dancing to the people, but the love of Nārāyaṇa dwells not within me." [154] His opposition to Absolutism

[150] III. *Doha* 38.
[151] *Encyclopaedia Britannica*, Vol. 13, p. 509.
[152] *Indian Interpreter*, January 1913, p. 173.
[153] J. N. Fraser and K. B. Marathe (translators), *The Poems of Tukārām*, Vol. 1, p. 163.
[154] *Ibid.*, p. 125.

is best illustrated by an event in his life. A learned Brahmin came to Tukārāma one day with a book expounding Advaita Vedāntism and asked permission to read it to him. Tukārāma, not wishing to dishonor a Brahmin, agreed, but insisted on placing a blanket over his head during the reading because he did not want the sight of the world to disturb him while listening—at least, so he said. After reading for an hour, the Brahmin lifted the blanket and discovered Tukārāma with fingers in his ears! Tukārāma explained, "I cannot listen to the doctrine that God and His worshipper are one. . . . Between Himself and His worshipper God has drawn a line; that line we must recognize. A man may have perfect insight into God's nature, but he does not acquire God's power to create, preserve, and destroy; these attributes belong to God alone. So long as God in His three forms exercises these powers Himself let us mortals be humble and claim no identity with Him." [155] God was to him "mother, father, brother, and bosom friend." [156] Philosophical knowledge is in vain: "We may enter on dry discussion, but you remain beyond them; we are only thrusting imaginary torments on our selves." [157] "Weary not thyself; search not the forest of philosophy." [158] "Men may dispute over arguments they have learned; and yet know nothing of the secret truth. Learned men may preach, and yet never attain their desire, the happiness of the self." [159] "Let the burden of knowledge rest on God's head; it is well for us to be ignorant as we are." [160] Men are to live joyfully in the presence of God: "It is well that I am born and came to possess a human body. This was a great acquisition; it has made me fit for happiness. I received organs, hand, foot, ear, eyes, and mouth to speak; these have gained for me, thee, O Nārāyaṇa." [161] "The body which we possess in this world, lo! the gods covet it. We are blessed in our births, we have become the slaves of Viṭhobā. In attaining this mortal life we have found being, mind and happiness." [162] "After many a re-birth, you have secured at last this gain: you have entered a human body, so grasp the feet of Vitthala." [163] Therefore, says Tukārāma, all men should sing in complete confidence:

> God is ours, yea, ours is he,
> Soul of all the souls that be.

[155] J. N. Fraser and J. F. Edwards, *The Life and Teachings of Tukārām*, pp. 102–103.
[156] Fraser and Marathe, *The Poems of Tukārām*, Vol. 1, p. 77.
[157] *Ibid.*, p. 81.
[158] *Ibid.*, p. 168.
[159] *Ibid.*, p. 187.
[160] *Ibid.*, p. 216.
[161] *Ibid.*, p. 121.
[162] *Ibid.*, p. 231.
[163] *Ibid.*, p. 309.

God is nigh without a doubt,
Nigh to all, within, without.

God is gracious, gracious still;
Every longing he'll fulfill.

God protects, protects his own;
Strife and death he casteth down.

Kind is God, ah, kind indeed:
Tuka he will guard and lead.[164]

Vaiṣṇavism in Bengal had meanwhile developed a different type of *bhakti*. Religions in Bengal by the fifteenth century were in need of reform. Hinduism had become largely the observation of minute restrictions. Corrupt and degrading forms of Buddhism lingered on. Ancient superstitions and magic associated with local gods such as Manasā, the serpent goddess, and Maṅgala-Caṇḍi, a goddess of wealth, claimed the attention of the untutored. Muslim rule was a constant source of irritation. The times were ripe for a revival of devotional attitudes. Caitanya, the man who brought about the revival, was born in 1486 at Navadvīpa on the Ganges. He was converted to Vaiṣṇava *bhaktism* as a young man while at Gayā where he had gone to perform his father's funeral rites. Upon his return he was dismissed as a madman by the people of Navadvīpa who witnessed him shouting Kṛṣṇa's name, laughing, weeping, and falling into trances. But a few joined him in daily *kīrtanas* (congregational singing in praise of a god). The sole source for his *bhakti* came from the *Bhāgavata Purāṇa*. Caitanya thought of Kṛṣṇa as an *avatārin* rather than as an *avātara*, i.e., as the source of all incarnations, as God himself. He believed Kṛṣṇa to be superior to Vāsudeva. *Bhakti* for him was not a means to *mokṣa*, but an end in itself, a *rasa* with no ethical component, the highest stage in the order of realization. *Bhakti* was *mokṣa*, a direct vision, an experience. *Bhakti* was *prema*-love, a love that was more than a sexual love, although the joyous submission of sexual intercourse between devoted lovers was held by Caitanya to be the paradigm and symbol of the love between man and God. According to Bengali Vaiṣṇavism Caitanya once had a meeting with Rāmānanda in which Caitanya asked what was the best way to realize God.[165] Rāmānanda replied that it was to adhere to one's worship practices, in other words, to follow the *dharmas* of one's *varṇa* and *āśrama*. Caitanya's response was "You are still on the surface; go deeper into truth." A long

[164] Nicol Macnicol, *Psalms of Marāṭhā Saints*, p. 73.
[165] *Sri Sri Chaitanya Charitamrita, Madhya-Līlā*, Chapter 8. All quotations are from the Nagendra Kumar Ray translation.

discussion followed in which Rāmānanda offered a variety of new answers, each one moving closer to the final answer, and to each Caitanya admonished him to penetrate deeper, "to work well and to offer the result of all good actions to the Lord Krishna . . . to renounce one's own religion and to take Krishna as guide . . . to have faith in God based on reason . . . to have faith in God apart from reason . . . to have a loving faith in God, a faith rooted in devotion . . . to give loving obedience to God . . . to have a loving friendship with God . . . to have loving affection for God." At last Rāmānanda confessed, "The best way to realise God, Oh Lord, is conjugal Love, and this is to love him as the lover loves a beloved one! . . . And all the sweetness of the first four species of love dwells in the last. And these four are loving faith, loving obedience, loving friendliness, and loving affection. And the last is loving conjugal associations with the Lord which at a higher stage of realisation is entirely possible and is millions of times sweeter than ordinary sex-association. . . . It is the be-all and the end-all of realisation." The conversation concluded with the agreement that the love of Rādhā for Kṛṣṇa is the most sublime of all loves, the very model for man in his self-realization. A similar progression is indicated in the view of Caitanya Vaiṣṇavism that liberation moves through five stages: (1) *sālokya,* being in the same place with God; (2) *sāmipya,* nearness to God; (3) *sārupya,* likeness to God; (4) *sārśti,* equaling the glory of God; (5) *sāyujya,* absorption in God.[166] The last stage should not be interpreted monistically, for this would destroy the possibility of the enjoyment of God which is the essence of *mokṣa* for Vaiṣṇavas. The early followers of Caitanya disagreed in their interpretations of the Rādhā-Kṛṣṇa theme; some held that Rādhā was his wife, others that she was his mistress. Kṛṣṇadāsa Kavirāja, the author of the *Sri Sri Chaitanya Charitamrita,* the authoritative biography of Caitanya, settled the matter by putting the second view in the mouth of Caitanya, and this has remained the teaching of the sect, i.e., the love of the human soul for God is like *parakīya* love.[167]

Caitanya's own *bhakti* experiences began with imagining that he was Rādhā longing for her beloved Kṛṣṇa. Although his ecstatic states were like the feminine role in erotic passion, Caitanya was himself a man of moral purity. However, his emphasis on the feminine in his *bhakti-rasa* and *bhakti-līlā* inaugurated a dangerous element which has occasionally led to homosexuality, transvestitism, and other forms of sexual behavior

[166] *Chaitanya Charitamrita* 2. 6.

[167] "The stories of Rādhā-Kṛṣṇa stand alone in Hindu literature in this respect. In Sanskrit drama a married woman is nowhere represented as faithless or as the object of other men's love." Nisikanta Chattopadhyaya, *The Yatras, or The Popular Dramas of Bengal,* pp. 11–12.

often regarded as deviations from the normal.[168] Some of Caitanya's followers regarded him as in incarnation of Rādhā. The emphasis on femininity remains a dominant element in Bengali Vaiṣṇavism, e.g., Sadhu Nityagopal, a twentieth-century leader of the sect, has written, "When a man endowed with supreme, love-tinged devotion, obtains the competency for that union, he becomes conscious of himself as Rādhā, the Supreme Goddess. As cool water can obtain warmth through heat, so a man can, through the supreme union of love, obtain the feelings and sentiments of a woman. When a man obtains them, his nature also resembles that of a woman. His movements also resemble those of a woman. A man who attains femininity through the supreme union of love is not a common man. Therefore, when he obtains the nature of a woman, when he gains the emotions of a woman, he does not win those of an ordinary woman. He wins those of the Supreme Prakriti and Supreme Śakti through the supreme union of love. She who is the Supreme Prakriti, is, indeed, Rādhā. She who is the Supreme Śakti, is indeed, Rādhā." [169] Caitanya is sometimes regarded as the one in whom the Rādhā element and the Kṛṣṇa element combined: "Rādhā is the ultimate development of love to Lord Krishna. She is the energy Divine, called Hladini, and hence Rādhā-Krishna are one and the same. But for the sake of Divine play they separated into two bodies. And now they have been united and made manifest as Lord Chaitanya." [170]

Caitanya made a pilgrimage to Vṛndāvana and was responsible for establishing a center of learning there. His last years were spent at Purī in almost continual worship interspersed with ecstatic trances of great intensity. Kṛṣṇadāsa Kavirāja reports that he raved like a lunatic, blood oozed from his skin, his body swelled and shrank, he threw himself on the ground, and sometimes did physical violence to himself. Caitanya once described his seizures as epileptic fits.[171] Accounts of his life at Purī suggest advanced insanity: "And the Lord passed his days in dancing as the various feelings moved him. For now it was remorse, now sorrow, now humility and now impatience, now pleasure and now patience and now again anger, that moved the Lord thus. And in all these he passed

[168] See Shashibhusan Dasgupta, *Obscure Religious Cults,* Part 1, for a discussion of the Sabjiyā cult.

[169] Quoted by Nityapadanda Abadhut, *Philosophy of Union by Devotion,* pp. 31–32.

[170] *Chaitanya Charitamrita, Adi-Līlā,* Chapter 1. The psychologist C. G. Jung holds that in every man there is the "*anima*" (a compensating feminine element) and in every woman there is the "*animus*" (a compensating masculine element). He says there is a tendency to treat *animus* and *anima* as *enkekalymmenoi* (veiled ones). See "Aion" in *The Collected Works of C. G. Jung,* Vol. 9, Part. 2.

[171] Sushil Kuman De, *Early History of the Vaiṣṇava Faith and Movement in Bengal,* p. 102, footnote 1.

his days." [172] The work of organizing the cult and of transforming Caitanya into a god was largely accomplished by the six teachers known as the Gosvāmins (literally cow-lords) of Vṛndāvana, especially Kṛṣṇadāsa Kavirāja who wrote, "What the Upanishads call One Brahman without a second is the halo of the body of Lord Chaitanya. What is named as Paramatma or Indwelling Guiding Spirit is but a partial manifestation of Him. And what is called Bhagavan possessed of six attributes is He Himself. There is no higher principle (Truth) than Lord Chaitanya-Krishna." [173] The school of thought growing out of the Caitanya renaissance is known as Acintya-Bhedābheda or Gauḍīya, but it is the life rather than the thought of Caitanya which is important both for his followers and for the development of *bhakti* in India. The stories of the birth and childhood of Caitanya seem to be lifted from the *Bhāgavata Purāṇa,* so similar are they to those of Kṛṣṇa. Although Caitanya was once a schoolteacher, he gave up his position, refused to read books, and wrote only a few lines. Once a Brahmin came to Caitanya reporting that he was being ridiculed for erring in pronunciation while reading aloud the *Bhagavad Gītā.* He said to Caitanya, "I do not care whether I am correct in my pronunciation. Whenever I read, I visualize the beautiful Sri Kṛṣṇa sitting on Arjuna's chariot and giving his instructions to him. This produces ecstasy in my heart, and I cannot stop my study." Caitanya replied, "It is you who has acquired the full eligibility to read the *Gītā.*" [174]

Bhakti mārga in Bengali Vaiṣṇavism differs from the other forms we have noted this far in its extreme emotionalism. Man's highest good is self-realization in the form of intense emotional joy; there is no appeal to intellectual satisfactions, no regard for the social life of man, and no moral admonitions. All is personal emotional exaltation. De offers this criticism of the Caitanya movement, "Its feelings and ecstasies are all inward; they live in and for themselves. But being unrelated and isolated, they lose virility, and become liable to delirious abandon and consuming excess of passionate sentimentality. Emotion in itself is not to be deprecated; it should take its proper place in every religious system; but, to save it from morbidity, it must be related to will and intellect, to life and reality." [175]

Whatever may be the deficiencies of Caitanya Vaiṣṇavism as a religion, it has produced some of the finest lyrics in the library of love poetry. The tender charm of Rādhā's blushing pride as she recounts Kṛṣṇa's playful

[172] *Chaitanya Charitamrita, Madhya-Līlā,* Chapter 2.

[173] *Ibid., Adi-Līlā,* Chapter 1.

[174] *Chaitanya Charitamrita* 2. 9. Narendra Nath Law, "Śrī Kṛṣṇa and Śrī Caitanya," *Indian Historical Quarterly,* Vol. 23, 1947, pp. 267–268.

[175] *Early History of the Vaiṣṇava Faith and Movement in Bengal,* p. 547.

love antics comes through even in English translation. What better analogue could be found for God's search for the human soul than the flute call of Kṛṣṇa? Three seventeenth-century poems illustrate the high quality of this literature:

> He knows that at noon day when I go to bathe, the sandy pathway on the Jumna side is hot. He steals thither and waters the path for me; and as I behold him doing this, my heart feels the silent pang of love. When alone I go to the bathing ghat he sees my footprints and kisses them. My heart again feels the pangs of silent love. But abashed I stand aside, thinking what will the people say.[176]
>
> Though always near me he cannot repose a moment, fearing lest he lose sight of me. He regrets that I am not the sandal whose perfumed content he can always feel. Like one in possession of sudden wealth after a whole life's labour, he knows not what to do with me. He decorates my hair with the wreath of Mālati flowers. With a candle in his hand he wakes the whole night and beholds my face times without number, each time weeping for joy. He softly touches my feet and adorns them with scarlet Alṭā dye.[177]
>
> You do not choose right hours and times to play on your flute, my love. Out of season you play, and my heart goes forth to you without any control. When I sit in the company of my elders your flute calls me by my name. Can you not imagine, my love, to what shame I am put? From the other bank of the river you sound your flute and I hear its sound across the stream from this bank. Do you not know, my love, that it is my luckless fate that I know not how to swim across the river? [178]

Bhakti is also found today in Bengal in the activities of the Bāuls, the troubadours who move from village to village giving spontaneous expression in music and song to their simple religious faith. The term Bāul may come from a Sanskrit word meaning crazy—a derivation which disturbs the Bāuls not in the least. Their unconventional songs express no subtle philosophy or theology, only their love of God. Vaiṣṇavism and Sūfism are the backgrounds out of which they have grown, but the Bāuls have no interest in orthodoxy either Hindu or Muslim. Their deity is often addressed as "The Man of the Heart" or as an unknown bird which mysteriously flies in and out of its cage, the human body. They seem to have borrowed the notion of the human body as the microcosm of the universe from tantric and yogic sources. The following two songs are typical of the songs they sing in the villages:

176 Dinesh Chandra Sen, *The Vaiṣṇava Literature of Mediaeval Bengal*, p. 203.
177 *Ibid.*, pp. 215–216.
178 *Ibid.*, p. 217.

The Simple Man was in the Vṛindāvan of my heart,
Alas how and when did I lose Him,
That now no peace I know, at home or abroad?
By meditation and telling of beads, in worship and travail,
The quest goes on forever;
But unless the Simple Man comes of Himself,
Fruitless is it all;
For He yields not to forcefulness of striving.[179]

> Methinks, by this time I have become mad; otherwise, why should I feel so troubled inside every now and then? When I remain quiet with the undisturbed mind, I see that Some One speaks loudly from within,—"I am here, here I am!" In the dimness of the sky of my heart, methinks, I see Some One come to my side; He moves, He speaks, He plays,—He smiles, —He indulges in hundred other sports! . . . If I try to leave Him off and live alone, I cannot; it seems, He has settled His dwelling in the core of my heart.[180]

Rabindranath Tagore loved the songs of the Bāuls and did much to bring them to the attention of Indian intellectuals; but to describe Tagore as "the greatest of the Bāuls of Bengal" [181] does justice to only one side of the many talents of that genius. There is certainly a Bāul-like quality in some of the poems of Tagore, e.g.;

> My song has put off her adornments. She has no pride of dress and decoration. Ornaments would mar our union: they would come between thee and me; their jingling would drown thy whispers. My poet's vanity dies in shame before thy sight. O master poet, I have sat down at thy feet. Only let me make my life simple and straight, like a flute of reed for thee to fill with music.[182]

Vaiṣṇavism remains one of the most lyrical forms that Hinduism has taken. It is the poetic religion of India.

4. ŚAIVISM

The second major form that *bhakti* has taken in India involves the worship of Śiva. Śiva was not one of the gods of the *Ṛg Veda,* at least no god was known by that name, although Śiva appears to be a development

[179] Quoted by Kshitimohan Sen, *Mediaeval Mysticism of India,* p. 232.
[180] Quoted by Dasgupta, *Obscure Religious Cults,* p. 181.
[181] *Ibid.*, p. 187.
[182] *Gitanjali* 7.

from Rudra the Howler, the Vedic god of the destructive aspects of nature. Rudra may have been the god formed by merging of native gods such as Sarva, the lord of thunderbolts, Bhava, the god of land and air, and Urga, the ruler of the lower world. He was a malevolent deity, feared by gods and men. The fact that Rudra did not share in the *soma* sacrifice suggests that he was not an Indo-Aryan god. He was father of the Rudras or Maruts, the storm gods whose steeds were the whirlwinds. Rudra was not always destructive; he could be appeased, and when appeased he was said to be "auspicious."[183] "showerer of benefits,"[184] "bestower of food,"[185] and "guardian against disease."[186] "Harm us not"[187] appears as a frequent petition in the hymns to Rudra. "*Śiva*" (auspicious) as applied to Rudra may have been an expression of hope, a hope that he might become kindly, just as the ancient Athenians called the Erinys, the avenging spirits, by the euphemistic title "Eumenides," the gracious ones. When Rudra ceased to be one of the gods of India, Śiva became his historical successor and remains to this day a god of destruction; but, since destruction and reproduction are associated in Indian thought, Śiva is also the god who perpetually restores the world and the creatures within the world. In his reproductive capacities he is worshiped with phallic symbols both male and female, the *liṅga* and the *yoni*. Brahmā, Viṣṇu, and Śiva constitute the Trimūrti, the three great gods of Hinduism. While Viṣṇu is often portrayed sleeping on his couch and Brahmā has almost vanished, Śiva remains the god of activity. He is Naṭarāja, the dancer with his right foot on the demon of evil and his left foot in the air poised for additional destruction if needed. One of Śiva's hands is raised in the position of blessing; another hand points to the free foot to symbolize his liberating powers; still another hand holds a drum symbolizing sound, the beginning of creation; the fourth hand holds fire to signify that Śiva is the god of destruction, the god of the ending as well as the beginning. His body is adorned with the trophies of his exploits: a tiger-skin tunic, an elephant-hide cloak, and a snake neckpiece represent evil beasts he has destroyed; the skulls forming his necklace are those of successive Brahmās whom he has destroyed; his blue neck is the result of poison he swallowed to prevent it from reaching mankind; and the River Ganges in his matted locks reminds his worshipers he once saved mankind from a flood. The third eye in the middle of his forehead is the weapon with which he reduced Kāma the god of love to ashes, and with

[183] *Ṛg Veda* 1. 114. 9.
[184] *Ibid.*, 1. 114. 3.
[185] *Ibid.*, 7. 46. 1.
[186] *Ibid.*, 7. 46. 2.
[187] *Ibid.*, 1. 114. 8; 7. 46. 4.

which on another occasion he destroyed one of the heads of Brahmā. Further evidence of his strength is his bull Nāndī and his *śakti* consort Pārvatī, who has the ability to change herself into different personalities ranging from Umā the ascetic to Kālī the horrible black mother of death. The *bhakti* cults of devotion to this god have an undercurrent of fear. Rudra-Śiva is a god of strength, vigor, and destruction. These traits are reflected in the art forms of the Śiva cults. One of the most curious artistic representations of Śiva is the *ardhanarīśvara*, Śiva as half-man and half-woman. There probably could be no more fitting representation of the oxymoronic character of this destructive-auspicious deity. According to a Tamil legend, in the beginning Śiva said there should be no separation between himself and his Śakti; therefore he declared that the right side of himself be Śiva and the left Pārvatī in an eternal union.

There are numerous stories of rivalries between Viṣṇu and Śiva. The followers of the two gods have sometimes contributed to the strained relations, e.g., Śaṅkara has been said to be an *avatāra* of Śiva, and Bhāgavata teachers have even joined in the claim, only they have added that Viṣṇu directed Śiva to become incarnate in Śaṅkara in order to win followers to his false teachings and thus give Viṣṇu an opportunity to glory in their destruction![188] Today one is more likely to find harmony, e.g., at Chidambaram both Śiva and Viṣṇu images are placed in the center of the temple of Naṭarāja.

The Śaiva cults are not as well organized as the Vaiṣṇava. They are more modified by local legends and customs. They also tend to run to extremes, sometimes taking on repulsive practices such as eating nauseating foods, using human skulls as begging bowls, and smearing the body with ashes from funeral pyres. Yet the cults are united in the worship of Śiva, or of one of his Śaktis, or of an animal associated with him such as Nāndī or Ganeśā. Deity is concretely conceived, and the relationship between God and man is very personal. The *Āgamas* or *Tantras*, a vast collection of esoteric scriptures, is assigned a place equal or even superior to the Vedas. These will be considered in the next chapter. The chief *bhakti* legacy of Śaivism is the work of sixty-three poet-saints (Aḍiyars or Nāyanmars), the Śaiva counterparts to the Āḻvārs. These poets lived between the second and the ninth centuries A.D. Two collections of their poems are highly regarded: the *Dēvārām*, the works of Sambandar, Apparsvāmi, and Sundararmūrti, who lived in the seventh and eighth centuries, and the *Tiruvāchakam*, the work of Māṇikya Vāchaka, who lived in the ninth century.

[188] Grierson, "Bhakti-mārga" in *Encyclopaedia of Religion and Ethics*, edited by Hastings, Vol. 2, p. 551.

The principal sects of Śaivism are the Liṅgāyata or Vīraśaivism and Kashmir Śaivism. The members of the former live in south India, and are identified by the *liṅga* which they wear at all times on a cord around the neck. They observe five rules of conduct (*pañcācāra*): (1) *liṅgācāra,* daily worship of the *liṅga* as the representation of Śiva; (2) *sadācāra,* following a profession and leading a strictly moral life, including the feeding of wandering teachers of the sect; (3) *śivācāra,* the recognition of complete equality of all members of the sect; (4) *bhṛtyācāra,* complete humility before Śiva and his devotees; (5) *gaṇācāra,* willingness to vindicate any adverse remarks about Śiva or the practices of Śaivism. The Kashmir form of Śaivism has through the centuries been more idealistic and monistic than the Liṅgāyata and has avoided extremes in sexuality and austerity. Both sects agree that only by surrender to the grace of Śiva can the fetters that bind the individual to *saṁsāra* be broken. In the words of Māṇikya Vāchaka,

> To me, mean as I was, with no good thing, Thou didst grant grace,
> That I, with mind erewhile embruted—pure one!—should
> Become commingled love, in soul-subduing rapture melt!
> Thou cam'st in grace on this same earth, didst show Thy mighty feet
> To me who lay mere slave,—meaner than any dog,—
> Essential grace more precious than a mother's love.[189]

The medical aspects of the ancient Rudra remain in the Śaiva notion that Śiva removes the four fetters (*pāśas*) that have attached themselves to the soul: (1) *mala,* that which conceals the power of the soul; (2) *karma,* the impression of deeds; (3) *māyā,* the material causes of all things, and (4) *rodhaśakti,* the power that regulates the other three fetters. Śiva, the physician of the soul, is to be sought within, as a poem of Tirunāvukkarasu states:

> I sought Him and I found.
> Brahm sought in vain on high.
> Vishnu delved vainly underground.
> Here in my soul found I.[190]

The Śaivas love to dwell on the theme that Śiva comes to man uninvited. "He is the thief that stole my heart away," sings Sambandar.[191] Māṇikya Vāchaka says the same in this song:

[189] The *Tiruvasagam,* or *Sacred Utterances of the Tamil Poet, Saint and Sage Māṇikka-Yāçacar,* p. 5. Translation by G. U. Pope.

[190] *Hymns of the Tamil Śaivite Saints,* p. 55. Translations by F. Kingsbury and G. E. Phillips.

[191] *Ibid.,* pp. 13, 27.

Came down in grace and made e'en me to be His very own.
Henceforth before no man I bow; I fear but Him alone.
Now of His servants' servants I have joined the sacred
throng,
And ever more and more I'll bathe in bliss, with dance
and song.[192]

Śaivism is strictly monotheistic, as a song from Śiva Vākyar declares:

There is but one God in all the world, none else.
That One is God, the Lord of all that is,
He never had beginning, never hath an end.
O God! I once knew naught of what thou art,
And wandered far astray. But when Thy light
Pierced through the dark, I woke to know my God.
O Lord! I long for thee alone. I long
For none but Thee to dwell within my Soul.[193]

Mokṣa in Śaivism is chiefly a release. A heaviness permeates the life of the Śaivite. His love for God is not fed by the joy of the emotion as in Vaiṣṇavism; he loves God for having liberated him from the burdens of life. "Release is theirs, and theirs alone, who call at every time upon the Lord of all," [194] says Tirunāvukkarasu. As is the case for all *bhaktas*, the Śaivites believe that the only way of release is through *bhakti*:

Even if you read the Veda
The Sāma and the Rik
And know the Śāstras six
You still may never know
The great Divine Śivam.[195]

The wonder of wonders to which the Śaivite returns again and again is that the grace of God cannot be won—it is freely bestowed.

Fool's friend was I, none such may know
The way of freedom; yet to me
He shew'd the path of love, that so
Fruit of past deeds might ended be.
Cleansing my mind so foul, He made me like a god.
Ah who could win that which the Father hath bestowed? [196]

[192] *Ibid.*, p. 95.
[193] Quoted by Frazer, *Indian Thought Past and Present*, p. 269.
[194] Kingsbury and Phillips, *op. cit.*, p. 57.
[195] A song of Śiva Vākyar. Frazer, *op. cit.*, p. 269.
[196] A song of Māṇikya Vāchaka. Kingsbury and Phillips, *op. cit.*, p. 127.

5. *Bhakti* AS *Mārga*

Bhakti becomes a *mārga* in Hinduism from both negative and positive motivations. Negatively *bhakti* becomes a *mārga* because of the inability of man to realize the Self by means of works and knowledge. To be aware of one's duty is not necessarily to do one's duty: "Lord, I know what *dharma* is, but I cannot practise it; I know what *adharma* is, but I have no power to resist it." [197] *Karma mārga* as moral behavior deteriorated through the impossibility of observing all the rules of *varṇa, jāti, gotra,* and *āśrama; karma mārga* as *saṁskāras* collapsed through the multiplication of details of the ceremonies and rituals until it was almost impossible to perform a rite without some violation of the prescriptions. Positively *bhakti mārga* reflects the fact that man is a conative as well as a cognitive being. To curb the rich emotions of man is to cripple his individual development and generic evolution as much as would stifling the intellectual dimensions of his life. Part of the greatness of Śaṅkara as a human being was his willingness to enjoy *bhakti,* even though he knew the deficiency of the way of religious devotion. If his petitions to gods seem paradoxical in view of his theory of Brahman, they also honestly reflect the paradoxical nature of human life; the intellectual is still emotional, and the emotional is intellectual, yet they are not identical. To personalize the universe is as dishonest as to universalize the personal, yet both are needed, and neither alone is true to the whole. Śaṅkara knew that the world is rooted and grounded in the impersonal Brahman, yet he practiced devotion to the gods of his faith: "O Lord, even after realising that there is no real difference between the individual soul and Brahman, I beg to state that I am yours and not that you are mine. The wave belongs to the ocean, and not the ocean to the wave." [198]

Bhakti as a *mārga* is somewhat confusing in Hinduism because conflicting statements are made about it. It is praised as the easiest of all the *mārgas:* "The way of love is easier than other methods." [199] No exertions are required: "Love does not depend upon exertions for its growth like knowledge." [200] It follows the objective path, and deals with concrete things. The goal set before the pilgrim is the attractive goal of love and devotion to a responsive god who redeems those who put their trust in him. The devotee is wooed along the path, becoming more and more

[197] Quoted by Radhakamal Mukerjee, *The Indian Scheme of Life,* p. 32, from the *Prapanna Gītā.*

[198] Quoted by Radhakrishnan, *The Brahma Sūtras,* p. 38.

[199] Nārada *Sūtra* 58.

[200] Śāṇḍilya *Sūtra* 7.

aware of his god in personal terms. The sum and substance of *bhakti mārga* is "Follow the object, concentrate your attention on the object, love it with all your heart, seek nothing else, think of nothing else, make it your own, dedicate your self to it and you will realise it." [201] But the way of *bhakti* is also described as a difficult way, one fraught with the dangers of sentimentality, eroticism, and erraticalness. If the way that liberates is an emotional way, then some defenders may conclude that any intensely emotional way will liberate; and if intensity is characteristic of the liberating emotion, some may think that the quality of the liberation depends on the degree of the intensity of the emotion. The Middle Way (*mādhyama mārga*) was finally pushed out of India. The line that separates the sane and the insane in any intense emotion is thin indeed. Only the most tolerant of families and communities welcome the prophets of a faith. Jesus was at one time considered insane by his friends.[202] A Ramakrishna or a Caitanya in a modern scientifically oriented society would probably be incarcerated in an asylum for the mentally deranged. *Bhakti* is also confusing because it is said to be both sudden and gradual. This confusion is related to the cat grace and monkey grace controversy among the followers of Rāmānuja; both schools agreed that salvation is chiefly from the Lord, but whereas the former held that the experience of enlightenment comes almost unexpected, the latter held that only by an effort of the devotee does enlightenment at last come. Śāṇḍilya supports the theory of effort: "There is provision for gradual progress leading towards Final Emancipation." [203] *Bhakti mārga* as process is constructed of many ingredients: listening to scriptures and stories about God, praising God for creating, preserving, and saving the world, worshiping God in images, offering flowers and *tulasī* leaves, serving God and his devotees, longing for God as for a child, a friend, and a spouse, being absorbed in God in a trance-like identity with Him, and finally, closing of the separation between God and man.

How can the same path be easy and hard, spontaneous and effortful? The answer is that the way of *bhakti* is dual; it is a way capable of two distinct variations. One is the way of *bhakti per se*, a way of loving God with all one's energy. Its effectiveness depends upon the psychological nature of the individual. An intellectualistic or an activistic person may find it a very difficult way; some people are constitutionally unqualified for mystical experiences or for deep overwhelming emotions. They are mesomorphs and ectomorphs according to Sheldon's classification. Others generate without effort the rich emotional outlets of art and worship.

[201] Brahma, *Philosophy of Hindu Sādhanā*, p. 243.
[202] The *Bible*, Mark 3. 21.
[203] *Sūtra* 80.

For them *bhakti* is self-justifying and self-sustaining; it is active but not effortful. Hinduism constantly stresses man's life as both active (*pravṛtti*) and passive (*nivṛtti*), e.g., the *Mahābhārata* advises both action, "He that is reft of action can never have success. . . . Therefore, one should betake himself to action" [204] and inaction, "All acquisitions are certain to end in destruction. Hence I never set my heart upon the acquisition of any objects." [205] The fact is, as the *Bhagavad Gītā* clearly states, man should act, yet he must not act for the fruits of action; he should be active in his acting, yet he should be passive in his desire to accomplish through his acting. The way of *bhakti* is also the way of *prapatti*, the way of loving God with all the force derived from God. Not my will, but thine, is the theme of *prapatti*. The aspirant relies on the grace of the Lord to bestow upon him the ability to do what the way demands. Self-surrender is man's response to God's offer. Inherent in the *bhakti mārga*, so conceived, is the notion that the individual is elected to liberation: "This Ātman cannot be attained by the study of the Vedas, or by intelligence, or by much hearing of sacred books. It is attained by him alone whom It chooses. To such a one Ātman reveals Its own form." [206] But if the Lord makes the initial offer, does he offer his benefactions to all, or does he elect some to receive and others to be denied benefits? And if the Lord does select individuals, what is the ground for the selection? How is selection reconciled with the doctrine of *karma*? Buddhism, the great do-it-yourself religion, holds that liberation is within the grasp of anyone who makes the effort; but Rāmānuja contended that without divine grace the effort to liberate would never be effectual, and he warned that anyone who omits God in the *mārga* is heading for mental breakdown.[207] These problems wait for solution. However, the *bhakta* feels little compulsion to work out the intellectual grounds of his faith and his experience. He has tasted, and therefore knows existentially that the Lord is good. What more does he need? His life is an eternal play of emotion. "A mortal *jīva* once raised to the plane of *suddha-bhakti* or pure life-to-life devotion to Him calmly views even mortal phases of *rasa* as essentially immortal. The veil of death is then immediately withdrawn from all life. All life is then in full *rasa* and in eternal *rasa*. . . . All phases of mortal pleasures and pains are transformed into amusements of self-concealment (*līlā*) of the will-to-enjoy. . . . Life, all life, is then really merged in True life and His eternal *līlā* of *rasa*." [208]

[204] 12. 10.

[205] 12. 179.

[206] *Kaṭha Upaniṣad* 1. 2. 23; *Muṇḍaka Upaniṣad* 3. 2. 3. Nikhilananda translation. See also Rāmānuja, *Śribhāṣya* 1. 1. 1.

[207] See his commentary on *Bhagavad Gītā* 2. 61–63.

[208] Bhagabat Kumar Goswami, *The Bhakti Cult in Ancient India*, pp. 410–411.

One of the distinctive features of *bhakti mārga* is its attitude toward caste. It is usually denied that caste restrictions affect the *mārga*, but this does not mean that the social restrictions of caste are repudiated. Both Kṛṣṇa Bhāgavatism and Śiva Bhāgavatism were more favorably received by foreigners (*mlecchas*) and Śūdras than by the twice-born. The *varṇāśrama dharma*, which limited worship to the upper classes, is repudiated. For example, in the *Mahābhārata* the venerable Bhīṣma says of Kṛṣṇa, "He is the Eternal God, pervading all beings, and ever blessed. He, of whom thou hadst asked me, is known by the name of Vasudeva. He it is whom Brahmanas and Kshatriyas and Vaiśyas and Śūdras, having distinctive features of their own, humbly serve and worship with restrained hearts and performing their own duties." [209] According to the *Bhāgavata Purāṇa* "the merit of this *Bhāgavata Purāṇa* is capable of granting the desired end to all alike." [210] Śāṇḍilya says, "Even the lowest classes have a right to follow the path of love." [211] And Nārada agrees that *bhakti mārga* is for all: "*Bhakti* is the only method to be resorted to by all desirous of emancipation." [212] Rāmānuja advised that men ought to fulfill their caste duties even though all men are equal in worship: "Hence a man of special distinction or character ought always to show the example to the world, by first playing himself the part in all duties assigned to his caste (*varṇa*) and order of life (*āśrama*). If he should fail to do so, he commits sin—the sin of not having benefitted the world by example." [213] In other words, soteriological egalitarianism ought not to entail sociological egalitarianism. In the thirteenth, fourteenth, and fifteenth centuries the *bhakti* movement proclaimed the removal of all caste distinctions, and many Vaiṣṇava leaders emerged from the Śūdras and Untouchables. Among these were Kabīr, Dādu, Raīdas, Dhannā, Nāmadeva, Nanda, Ravidās, and Chokamela. The reaction of some Brahmins to this leveling is neatly illustrated in the sarcastic words of a sage named Atri: "Those Brahmins who are devoid of Vedic lore study the Śāstras; those devoid of Śāstric lore study the Purāṇas, and earn their livelihood by reciting them; those who are devoid of Purāṇic reading become agriculturalists; and those who are even devoid of that become Bhāgavatas." [214] Caitanya is reported to have said, "A man of low caste is not for his low caste unfit to serve the Lord, nor is a Brahmin of high caste fit for it merely by virtue of his being of a higher caste. For the

[209] 6. 66.
[210] 2. 1. 12.
[211] *Sūtra* 78.
[212] *Sūtra* 33.
[213] *Bhagavad Gītā with Śrī Rāmānujāchārya's Viśishṭādvaita Commentary*, 3. 21. Govindāchārya translation.
[214] Quoted by Mukerjee, *The Culture and Art of India*, pp. 121–122.

truly low is he who does not serve the Lord." [215] But Caitanya was concerned only with the elimination of caste in religious matters; he did not teach the elimination of caste as a social institution. Still the tendency of *bhakti mārga* in India has been to discourage caste as a dominant feature of Hindu religious life. A Bengali *sadhu* named Nityagopal who died in 1910 has stated the position very explicitly: "Even persons of very low descent, unlettered women, the Vaishyas who are intent on cultivation, trade, etc., and the Shudras, if they obtain His shelter, reach the supreme goal like the virtuous Brahmins and the great-souled, royal sages who have been refuged in the Lord." [216]

Bhakti mārga is religion *per se*. If the philosophical, the social, and the religious components of Hindu *sādhana* can be separated, the religious component is *bhakti mārga*. It refrains from subjectifying the ground of reality and value; the object of worship remains an object, and the worshiper remains a subject. Transcendent reality is not collapsed into immanent reality. Thus the essence of religion, the confrontation with an Other believed to exist as a reality external to man yet enough like man to insure communication, is preserved. Man is not alone in the universe. The Other is not man writ large. It is a theistic God, and *bhakti mārga* is religious devotion directed to this God. Religious emotion is elevating, inspiring, and uplifting, but it is God, not the emotion, that saves man. *Bhakti* is not a psychological bath to be indulged in when one wants an emotional plunge or purgation; it is a devotion of love directed to the God who redeems. To love this God with all one's being is to give one's life a focal point outside the finite self and beyond finite space and time. This is the great asset in dignifying the human condition.

But what happens to the divine condition? When God is worshiped as the personal God, He easily degenerates into a limited being of finite form and qualities. The relationship between man and God tends to become a relation between equals. When God becomes a limited divinity, all hope of liberation by means of *bhakti mārga* is gone. As Radhakrishnan has stated so well, "The moment we reduce the Absolute to an object of worship, it becomes something less than the Absolute. To have a practical relationship with finite will, God must be less than the Absolute, but if He is less than the Absolute, then He cannot be the object of worship in any effective religion. If God is perfect, religion is impossible; if God is imperfect, religion is ineffective." [217] A limited di-

[215] *Chaitanya Charitamrita, Antya-Līlā*, Chapter 4.

[216] Abadhut, *Philosophy of Union by Devotion*, p. 188. This volume is a translation of Nityagopal's *Bhaktiyoga-Darsan*.

[217] *Indian Philosophy*, Vol. 1, p. 97.

vinity cannot be entrusted with full soteriological responsibilities any more than can a limited humanity. Yet *bhakti mārga* requires that God be a person. Arjuna was horrified when, after the theophany had been granted to him, he realized in his personification of God he had made God less than God. A limited divinity is no real divinity, yet an unlimited divinity is one with which man can establish no relations. *Bhakti* must be transcended. Religion must become non-religion. Effective Hinduism must be a religionless Hinduism. This is the end to which this line of argument points. *Bhakti mārga* pursued in isolation from other *mārgas* terminates in limiting paradoxes. *Jñāna mārga* and *karma mārga,* however, fare no better when pursued alone; *jñāna* leads to cold intellectualism, and *karma* to legalism or sacerdotalism. Thus, we reach more evidence of the wisdom of the Hindus in their remarkable practice of tolerance and accommodation. Room is found in the life of man for devotion, for knowledge, and for action in an existential harmony which seeks the Perfection of Man in all the dimensions of his potentiality.

Bhakti mārga's focus on God also raises a serious question about the relation of man to his fellow men. Ritschl once said that the difference between Hindu *bhakti* and Christian *bhakti* is the difference between a circle with its one focus and an ellipse with its two foci. Hindu *bhakti,* he thought, focuses on God alone, Christian *bhakti* on God and also on service to men. This observation does not do full justice to Hinduism. Man does not exist detached from his fellow men in Hinduism, and certainly he is not saved in isolation. The Perfecting Man, the *jīvanmukta,* is the *Ātman*-Man, the Universal Man, not the *jīva*-man, the monadic man. Man must learn to shift the center of his life from *jīva*-consciousness to God-consciousness, but this does not imply the cutting of ties of interest and concern for one's fellow men. *Mukti* is freedom from the individualistic inlook, and the attainment of the divine outlook, a view which sees others as part of the Self. Enlightenment is a passage from the narrow view to the broad view. Man is man only as he seeks the perfection of that which sets him apart from both animals and gods—the potentiality to become Man.

Śaṅkara allocated *karma mārga* and *bhakti mārga* to the lower spheres of illusion and ignorance, and therefore gave them secondary and supporting roles. But Rāmānuja sought to establish *bhakti's* claim to the world of reality. This view was shared by Nārada and Śāṇḍilya: "Bhakti is indeed greater than action, knowledge and yoga. . . . Love is its own reward." [218] "Love is superior to others, as they are in need of it. . . . Love, as had been declared in the Scripture [i.e., the *Gītā*] is superior to action, wisdom and yoga." [219]

[218] Nārada *Sūtras* 25, 30.
[219] Śāṇḍilya *Sūtras* 10, 22.

The best indication of the high evaluation placed upon *bhakti mārga* is the conviction of many *bhaktas* that *mokṣa* itself is but a stage on the way to union with God. *Jñāna mārga* seeks the elimination of ignorance and the acquisition of true knowledge about the world; *karma mārga* seeks the perfect fulfillment of all duties moral and ceremonial; *bhakti mārga* seeks the unsharable and ineffable experience of the grace of God. The three *mārgas* constitute a whole. Without a *bhakti*, *jñāna* and *karma* would be incomplete. An episode in the lives of three of the earliest Āḷvārs illustrates the integral path. Poygai, Bhutattar, and Pey once took refuge in the tiny corridor of a house during a heavy rain. There was room enough for one man to lie down, or for two to sit, or for three to stand. The three therefore stood closely pressed together that each might be sheltered from the rain. But as they stood they became aware of the presence of a Fourth, one invisible but present. According to the *bhakti* interpretation of this story, it is a parable of the three *mārgas*. One Āḷvār perceived the Divine through *jñāna*, one through *karma*, and one through *bhakti*, but only when all three met was each aware of the presence of the Fourth.

CHAPTER X
The Way of Discipline

1. THE MYTH OF *Yoga*

The fourth *mārga* suffers from its popularity. Probably no other aspect of Indian culture is more widely known and discussed than *yoga*. It is cheapened by misunderstandings about its nature and purpose. In India thousands of self-styled *yogis* amaze the crowds both native and tourist with their "yogic" tricks, and in the West *yoga* is offered as a panacea guaranteed to improve health, skin color, sexual potency, memory, human relations, business, marriage, religion, etc.[1] *Yoga* is a favorite topic for Sunday newspaper supplements, paperback books, YMCA programs, and popular lectures. Classes in *yoga* are given by *yoga* clubs formed for the mutual encouragement of faddists. The yogic cult attracts the idle rich, the unsuccessful, and the lonely, as well as those who seek the novel for its own sake. While *yoga* has developed largely within India and within Hinduism, it is neither Indian nor Hindu exclusively. Yogic discipline is an inherent and necessary part of the full hominization of the universe. Recently *yoga* has been adapted for and recommended to Christians.[2] Before we can examine *yoga* in Hindu *sādhana* we must identify the myth of *yoga*, the falsities and half-truths which have accrued around

[1] The bibliography contains a number of titles of books of this character.

[2] E.g., J. M. Deċhanet, *Christian Yoga*. London: Burnes and Oates, 1960. Shyam Sundar Goswami, *Jesus Christ and Yoga*. London: L. N. Fowler, n.d. Aelred Graham, *Zen Catholicism*. New York: Harcourt, Brace and World, Inc., 1963.

the concept and practice of this *mārga*. These misrepresentations will be classified under four headings: (1) *yoga* as physical culture, (2) *yoga* as mental training, (3) *yoga* as shamanism, and (4) *yoga* as status symbol.

Yoga as physical culture consists of breathing techniques, bodily postures, and isomorphic exercises supposed to improve health and physical well-being. Changes in diet, sleeping habits, working conditions, and attitudes toward people may be recommended. Smoking and the drinking of alcoholic beverages will probably be eliminated. Exercise in fresh air, regular bowel movements, the drinking of more water, and other health-promoting measures are generally advised. A person in normal health will profit from such sensible good health measures. *Yoga*, so conceived and so practiced, can be a great asset to an individual. This desirable form of *yoga*, known as *haṭha yoga*, is not the full meaning of *yoga*.

Yoga is again sometimes presented as a form of mental training. This is known as *rāja yoga*. Psychologists differ as to what percentage of his mental ability the average person uses, but they agree that few work to their full intellectual capacity. Within limits improvement can be made in certain clearly identifiable abilities, such as memory, by conscious dedication and practice of simple techniques; but improvement in thinking in general is questionable, partly because of the inability to make reliable empirical studies of such behavior.[3] Melioration of physical health brought about by *haṭha yoga* may also be expected to nurture improvements of a psychological nature. Constipation, headache, nervousness, irritability, and ill health of any sort are obvious hindrances to clear and critical thinking. *Yoga* has even been regarded as a form of psychotherapy similar to Couéism which brings about a wide variety of psychological benefits. Again—within limits—changes of attitudes, e.g., from pessimism to optimism, or from lethargy to dynamism, will inaugurate changes in behavior, if these attitudes are amenable to volitional controls. But few, if any, psychiatrists maintain that man's behavior is fully subject to his volition. Despite benefits to be derived from *rāja yoga*, *yoga* as a *mārga* is given short shrift in being classified as a therapy for mental and psychological improvement.

The third misrepresentation of *yoga* is far more serious. We have called it shamanism. The shaman in primitive societies is the wonder-working medicine man who controls the spirits. *Yoga* is often praised in India for the miracles (*siddhis*) the *yogi* is said to perform. Early Euro-

[3] See Paul L. Dressel and Lewis B. Mayhew, *General Education: Explorations in Evaluation*. Washington, D.C.: American Council on Education, 1954, pp. 202–206. Also see Troy Organ, *The Art of Critical Thinking*. Boston: Houghton Mifflin Co., 1965, pp. xi–xiii.

pean travelers to India brought back stories of legerdemain, the most astonishing being the famed rope trick. Through the years some Indians have found it profitable to keep alive the legends of India as a land of mystery, and to this day modern tourists sometimes seek out the occult, and some natives are happy to satisfy the tourists' desire! The uneducated villager tends to accept uncritically the general primitive attitude toward esoteric powers at work in the natural world, but the educated Indian takes a different attitude, e.g., "But all those wonder-working Yogic powers, which are amply described in Hindu, Jain, and Buddhistic writings, are things about which the best attitude now is one of suspended judgment." [4] Śriśa Chandra Vasu says of the "true yogis," "*Siddhis* (psychic powers) are no ambition of their souls; they do not court them; nor are they elated if they produce some phenomena now and then. Their eyes are bent upon *mokhsha;* these students of Yoga do not tarry in their course to pick up these baubles of *Siddhis*." [5] Vachaspati Miśra concurs: "But a yogin whose mind-stuff is concentrated must avoid these [*siddhis*] even when brought near to him. One who longs for the final end of life, the absolute assuagement of the three-fold anguish, how could he have any affection for these perfections which go counter to the attainment of that goal?" [6] Likewise Jajineswar Ghosh refers to "the unenlightened zeal of those who believe and assert that the *yogi's* career is always rendered glorious by a dazzling chain of miracles." He adds, "It is unfortunate that a mere side-issue has been so often stressed in discussing the merit of Yoga as a system of philosophy and a code of morals." [7] According to Swami Sivananda, "There is no such thing as miracle or Siddhi." [8] The *siddhis* play no part in the *Bhagavad Gītā*. Unfortunately, some Westerners seem intent upon fastening the *siddhi* label on Hinduism. A recent delightful travelogue is a case in point. Dom Denys Rutledge in his *In Search of a Yogi* recounts his pilgrimage from Banaras to Rishikesh seeking a *yogi* who could perform or who had witnessed the performance of miracles. In Rutledge's own words, "This is an account of a journey in India from Banaras up towards the source of the Ganges, undertaken at the turn of the year 1959–60 at the conclusion of a task in the Poona district. Fundamentally, it was an enquiry into the

[4] C. N. Krishnaswami Aiyar, *Three Great Acharyas: Śaṅkara, Rāmānuja, and Madhwa,* p. 44.

[5] *An Introduction to Yoga Philosophy. The Sacred Books of the Hindus,* Vol. 15, Part 4, pp. 4–5.

[6] Quoted by James Naughton Woods, *The Yoga-Sūtras of Patañjali,* or *The Ancient Hindu Doctrine of Concentration of Mind,* p. 266.

[7] *A Study of Yoga,* pp. 13–14.

[8] *Practical Lessons in Yoga,* p. 243.

claim of the Indian Yogi to control matter by mind, to control the world of phenomena by the spirit even to the extent of calling it into existence and dissolving it." [9] He concluded at the end of his journey, "I had not found any evidence for the existence of such powers among yogis." [10] However, the author did not therefore conclude that the *yogis* are frauds, since he would not exclude such possibilities: "I would not like it to be thought that I consider powers such as the siddhis non-existent in this life." [11] The author, who by the way is a Benedictine monk, holds that belief in *siddhis* is shared by Hinduism and Christianity: "Both Hindu and Christian believe this can be done, and that this is in fact, or should be, the normal state of things, in which the material and visible world is completely subject to the spiritual and unseen." [12] The difference, he says, is that whereas the "Christian believes he will be able to do this fully only after death . . . the Hindu Yogi believes that he can do it here and now by his own natural powers." [13] While ignoring Rutledge's interpretation of Christianity, one cannot but observe that his attitude toward Hinduism is clouded by an all too obvious desire to accept it from the lips and practices of its less qualified representatives. Surely Rutledge knows that not all who call themselves *yogis* are worthy of the name. As one Hindu scholar has written,

> In India many understand by the word Yogi, those hideous specimens of humanity who parade our streets bedaubed with dirt and ash—frightening the children, and exhorting money from timid and good-natured folk by threats, abuse and pertinacity of demand. Of course, all true Yogis renounce any fraternity with these. If these painted caricatures by any stretch of language can be called Yogis, surely their yoga (communion) is with ash and dirt, with mud and money. . . . Looking on the disgusting spectacle of ash-besmeared and lazy beggar, the horrible self-inflictions of the Haṭha Yogi, and inhumane apathy of the recluse, no wonder that many should think that Yoga is after all a great humbug, not worth the consideration of any sane man.[14]

Rutledge's search for a *yogi* specializing in *siddhis* displays a woeful lack of understanding of Hinduism. His book cries for a parallel volume written by a Hindu who tours the various sites in Europe where Christian

[9] *In Search of a Yogi*, p. xi.
[10] *Ibid.*, p. 232.
[11] *Ibid.*
[12] *Ibid.*, p. xi.
[13] *Ibid.*
[14] Śriśa Chandra Vasu, *An Introduction to Yoga Philosophy. The Sacred Books of the Hindus*, Vol. 15, Part 4, pp. 2–3.

miracles are reputed to have taken place in quest of a cleric who can do similar miracles.[15]

The fourth misrepresentation of *yoga* is the treatment of *yoga* as a status symbol. Among some groups the *yogi* is thought to be a unique person whose abilities set him apart from the ordinary run of humanity. *Yoga* has a strange fascination for many Westerners, possibly because it includes the patient inward look so contrasting to the Western external view of things. Self-styled *yogis* may be found in Europe and America enjoying the envy of their more conventional fellows, and many Westerners delight in referring to these individuals as their *gurus*. Some of these followers by turning their backs on the one safe foundation of Western civilization, its scientific attitude and accomplishments, in order to adopt Eastern *yoga*, become pitiable imitators, ridiculous in the eyes of both Eastern and Western peoples. Books that offer to teach *yoga* in ten easy lessons cheapen and misrepresent an important Indian tradition, and Westerners who adopt yogic practices as a form of spiritual calisthenics form a rootless fringe belonging to neither Western nor Indian society. C. G. Jung writes, "I wish particularly to warn against the oft-attempted imitation of Indian practices and sentiments. As a rule nothing comes of it except an artificial stultification of our Western intelligence."[16] And in another essay Jung writes in similar vein,

> If I remain so critically adverse to yoga, it does not mean that I do not regard this spiritual achievement of the East as one of the greatest things the human mind has ever created . . . my criticism is directed solely against the application of yoga to the peoples of the West. The spiritual development of the West has been along entirely different lines from that of the East and has therefore produced conditions which are the most unfavourable soil one can think of for the application of yoga. . . . In the

[15] In fairness to Rutledge, it should be noted that some well-educated Hindus have acknowledged miracles of the most astonishing type. For example, Śriśa Chandra Vasu, who has been quoted above in criticism of the *siddhis*, also holds that without a shadow of doubt *yogis*, rather than waiting for future incarnations in order to settle karmatic debts, create all the bodies their *karma* requires, each with an artificial mind in its artificial body: "These artificial bodies with artificial minds in them walk through the earth in hundreds—they are distinguished from ordinary men by the fact that they are perfectly methodical in all their acts, and automatic in their lives. All these artificials are controlled by the consciousness of the Yogi. One consciousness controlling hundreds of automatons. Every one of these automatons has a particular destiny, a particular portion of the *sanchati karma* to exhaust. As soon as that destiny is fulfilled, the Yogi withdraws his ray from it, and the 'man' dies a sudden death—a heart failure generally." Introduction to *Patañjali's Yoga Sūtras with the Commentary of Vyāsu and the Gloss of Vachaspati Miśra*. Translated by Rāma Prasāda. *The Sacred Books of the Hindus*, Vol. 4, p. xi.

[16] "The Psychology of Eastern Mysticism," *The Collected Works of C. G. Jung*, Vol. 2, p. 568.

course of the centuries the West will produce its own yoga, and it will be on the basis laid down by Christianity.[17]

Renou is far less restrained in his condemnation of Western imitators of Indian *yoga;* he says of them:

All that these people succeed for the most part in getting out of Hinduism is an artificial vocabulary and arbitrary interpretations chosen haphazardly from the total field. . . . Let us always remember that India is an Eldorado for charlatans. If Hinduism ever has a future as an integral part of a broad, generally acceptable spiritual movement beyond the borders of the country that gave it birth, this future will be created only by direct reflection from genuinely Indian forms of thought and spirit conceived and expressed by Indians.[18]

2. THE SĀṄKHYA METAPHYSICS

The terms *yoga* and *yogi* are not found in the early Upaniṣads, but in the later Upaniṣads both the terms and the basic ideas of yogic discipline are found. The word *yogi* first appears in *Maitrī Upaniṣad* 6. 10 in the teachings of *ṛṣi* Śākāyanya to a king named Bṛhadratha.[19] The *yogi* is said to be the individual who attains a unified state with the Brahman by means of restraint of breath (*prāṇāyāma*), withdrawal of senses (*pratyāhāra*), meditation (*dhyāna*), concentration (*dhāraṇa*), contemplation (*tarka*), and absorption (*samādhi*).[20] This experience of unity is described as a "joining"[21] of the breath, the senses, and the mind in a state which transcends selfhood until there is no longer any distinction between pain and pleasure.[22] A second treatment of yogic ideas is found in *Śvetāśvatara Upaniṣad* 2. Here *yoga* is presented as a *mārga*. The *yogi* is to sit on a clean level spot with a pleasant view near the sound of running water protected from the wind.[23] He is to hold his head, chest, and neck erect.[24] His breathing is to be diminished, and his mind must become undistracted.[25] The results he can expect from such practices

[17] "Yoga and the West," *The Collected Works of C. G. Jung*, Vol. 2, p. 537.

[18] *The Nature of Hinduism*, p. 144.

[19] 2. 1–6. 28.

[20] *Ibid.*, 6. 18.

[21] *Yoga* is from the root *yuj* meaning to join, to unite, or to yoke, and it carries the connotation of exertion, diligence, zeal, and enthusiasm.

[22] *Maitrī Upaniṣad* 6. 21.

[23] *Ibid.*, 2. 10.

[24] *Ibid.*, 2. 8.

[25] *Ibid.*, 2. 9.

include a clearer understanding of the five cosmic elements—earth, water, fire, air, and space,[26] improved health and physical well-being,[27] and finally a vision of God and release from all fetters.[28] Scattered throughout the Upaniṣads is what may be regarded as a third contribution to *yoga mārga;* this is the listing of four types of experience which became associated with yogic practices: (1) Light, e.g., "Therefore, verily, on crossing that bridge, if one is blind he becomes no longer blind." [29] (2) Color, e.g., "The form of this Person is like a saffron-coloured robe, like white wool, like the [red] Indragopa insect, like a flame of fire, like a [white] lotus-flower, like a sudden lightning flash." [30] (3) Sound, e.g., "It is the sound thereof that one hears by covering the ears thus. When one is about to depart (from this life one does not hear this sound." [31] (4) Forms, e.g., "Fog, smoke, sun, wind, fire, fireflies, lightning, crystal moon, these are the preliminary forms which produce the manifestation of Brahman in Yoga." [32] *Yogis* can be divided according to sense preferences into photists, chromatists, audiles, and morphists.

The greater contribution of the Upaniṣads to the development of *yoga mārga,* however, is not found in insights into the nature of the psychological state of the *yogi* but in insights into the metaphysical view of the cosmos which underlies *yoga.* This is a dualism quite distinct from the predominant monism of the Upaniṣads. For example, Brahman is not always presented as the unitary Ground of Being. It is also sometimes said to be dual: "Verily, there are two forms of Brahman, the formed and the formless, the mortal and the immortal, the unmoving and the moving, the actual (existent) and the true (being)." [33] The next two verses attempt to clarify the two forms of Brahman by distinguishing between the sun which gives warmth and the "person in the region of the sun." Verses 4 and 5 attempt to cast further light by distinguishing between the eye and the "person in the eye." Radhakrishnan thinks that this is the same distinction Plato makes between the Form of the Good in *The Republic* and the Demiurgos in the *Timaeus,* but perhaps Eckhart's distinction between God and Godhead (*Gott* and *Gottheit*) is closer to the Upaniṣads. Śaṅkara utilizes his distinction between lower and higher forms of knowing to distinguish between the phenomenal and

[26] *Ibid.,* 2. 10–11.
[27] *Ibid.,* 2. 12–13.
[28] *Ibid.,* 2. 14–15.
[29] *Chāndogya Upaniṣad* 8. 4. 2. Hume translation. See also *Muṇḍaka Upaniṣad* 2. 2. 9. and *Śvetāśvatara Upaniṣad* 4. 18.
[30] *Bṛhad-Āraṇyaka Upaniṣad* 2. 3. 6. Hume translation.
[31] *Ibid.,* 5. 9. 1. Radhakrishnan translation. See also *Maitrī Upaniṣad* 2. 6.
[32] *Śvetāśvatara Upaniṣad* 2. 11. Radhakrishnan translation.
[33] *Bṛhad-Āraṇyaka Upaniṣad* 2. 3. 1. Radhakrishnan translation.

the noumenal Brahmans. The dual nature of Reality appears most clearly in the *Maitrī Upaniṣad:* "There are, assuredly, two forms of Brahman: the formed and the formless. Now that which is formed is unreal; that which is the formless is the real." [34] "There are, verily, two forms of Brahman, time and the timeless." [35] "There are, verily, two Brahmans, to be meditated upon, sound and non-sound. By sound alone is the non-sound revealed." [36] The concept of Nature (*prakṛti*) consisting of the three *guṇas* is also introduced in the *Maitrī Upaniṣad.*[37] Matter is here described dualistically as that which the *yogi* enjoys: "He is an enjoyer, for he enjoys the food of Nature." [38] These dualistic passages are either the basis for or the expression of Hinduism's foundational system of philosophy, the Sāṅkhya. The equivocal expression "the basis for or the expression of" is required because of the mystery surrounding the Sāṅkhya. Some scholars deny that the Sāṅkhya is derived from or related to the Upaniṣads, maintaining that it is an independent doctrine.[39] If there is truth in the legend that a scholar named Kapila lived in the seventh century B.C. and composed the fundamental principles of the Sāṅkhya system, then his ideas may well have been appropriated by late Upaniṣads such as the *Maitrī*, the *Śvetāśvatara*, and the *Kaṭha*. The same district of India which produced this dualistic challenge to idealistic monism also produced Buddhism; indeed, there is a persistent tradition in India that the Sāṅkhya philosophy was used by the Buddha as the basis for his own thought and practice. The Sāṅkhya had become so well-established by the time of the composition of the *Bhagavad Gītā* that the author (or authors) of that work attempted to blend the monism of the Upaniṣads with the by-then unassailable dualism of the Sāṅkhya. The Sāṅkhya may be described as "Hinduism's foundational system of philosophy" for this, the oldest of the intellectual systems or viewpoints (*darśanas*), is a genuine philosophy, not commentary or exposition upon Vedic speculations but reasoned argument for an intellectual position. Reasoning, rather than appeals to Vedic authority, constitutes the dominant methodology of the Sāṅkhya. It is built upon Upaniṣadic insights, but, unlike philosophies such as the Vedāntic, it goes radically beyond the teachings of the Upaniṣads. It delineates the problems with which all systems of Indian philosophy deal, and it presents a metaphysic contrary to the dominant monism of the Upaniṣads. All other *darśanas*, in the words of Thadani,

[34] 6. 3. Radhakrishnan translation.
[35] *Ibid.*, 6. 15. Radhakrishnan translation.
[36] *Ibid.*, 6. 22. Radhakrishnan translation.
[37] *Ibid.*, 6. 10.
[38] *Ibid.*
[39] M. Hiriyanna, *Essentials of Indian Philosophy*, p. 106.

are but amplifications, commentaries, and criticisms of Sāṅkhya ideas and conclusions.[40] While it may be an overstatement, it is not an untruth, to observe that Hindu philosophy is predominantly an effort to square the Sāṅkhya with the Upaniṣads. This observation, together with the view that the Upaniṣads are speculations rather than philosophy, is the justification for the extreme statement of Davies: "The system of Kapila, called the Sāṅkhya or Rationalistic, in its original form, and its theistic development by Patañjali, contains nearly all that India has produced in the department of pure philosophy."[41] Since *yoga mārga* presupposes the Sāṅkhya metaphysics, it is necessary to present this theory of reality before discussing Patañjali's systematization of *yoga*.

Although Sāṅkhya stems from the time of the Buddha, the sixth century B.C., the earliest extant Sāṅkhya text is the *Sāṅkhya Kārika* of Īśvara Kṛṣṇa, a work of the third century A.D. The term *sāṅkhya* (discriminative wisdom) is highly appropriate for the philosophy whose outstanding characteristic is the distinction it draws between spirit and matter. The *Sāṅkhya Kārika* begins in the typical pattern of Indian philosophy by stating the end to be achieved by means of the philosophy: relief from the triad of misery, i.e., misery brought upon us by ourselves, misery brought about by others, and misery inflicted by non-human agencies. This misery cannot be removed by empirical means, i.e., by any means knowable by perception.[42] There is no certainty about earthly good fortune, nor about the common means for the alleviation of the pains that afflict man. The religious practices for dealing with human misery are no more successful than the empirical methods, for they often involve the very misery they claim to remove, e.g., the Vedic rites inflict pain and death upon the sacrificial animals. But Sāṅkhya offers a better way, a way that distinguishes the evolved (or manifested), the unevolved (or unmanifested), and the knower (or subject).[43] Sāṅkhya, as distinguished from the joint philosophy Sāṅkhya-Yoga, is a *jñāna mārga*. The theory of evolution is unique and important in Sāṅkhya. Of the two basic ways of explaining the origin of the world—origination, i.e., from many ultimate simple atomic reals to the physical universe, and evolution, i.e., from a single complex all-pervasve substance to the physical universe—Sāṅkhya selects the second. Evolution is utilized by the author of the *Sāṅkhya Kārikā* to distinguish two primary principles, that which is not evolved but does evolve and that which is not evolved and does not evolve, and also two

[40] N. V. Thadani, *The Secret of the Sacred Books of the Hindus*, p. xliv.
[41] John Davies, *The Sāṅkhya Kārikā of Īśwara Krishna*, p. v.
[42] *Sāṅkhya Kārikā* 1.
[43] *Ibid.*, 2.

derived and secondary principles, that which is evolved and does evolve and that which is evolved and does not evolve.

The primary principles are known as *prakṛti* and *puruṣa*. *Prakṛti* is translated as nature, matter, root-matter, or primordial matter, but it cannot be accurately translated since there is no idea quite like it in Western philosophy. Perhaps the Latin *procreatrix* (cosmic energy) is the best translation into a Western language. *Prakṛti* is undeveloped matter containing within itself the possibilities of all physical things. It is universal potency. It is that which can become anything. Aristotle's notion of prime matter is the closest Western counterpart: "a matter out of which the so-called elements come-to-be . . . an originative source . . . the matter which underlies, though it is inseparable from, the contrary qualities";[44] "a first thing, which is no longer, in reference to something else, called a 'thaten,' this is prime matter."[45] *Prakṛti* is the material cause which requires only an efficient cause to determine the direction in which it moves by removing obstacles in that direction. A difference between the Aristotelian prime matter and the Sāṅkhya *prakṛti* is that whereas for Aristotle the form must be imposed upon the material potentiality, in Sāṅkhya the potentialities both material and formal—to use Aristotelian terms—are in *prakṛti*. *Prakṛti* has the potentiality of becoming anything and everything, but without the presence of *puruṣa* no potentiality will be actualized. *Prakṛti* is composed of three constituents or component factors (*guṇas*) each bearing a distinctive aspect of the physical. The *guṇas* are not independently existing units which unitedly produce or constitute *prakṛti*, since they depend for their reality on *prakṛti* as much as *prakṛti* depends for its reality upon the *guṇas*. The *guṇas* are interdependent, and the *guṇas* and *prakṛti* are also interdependent. The three *guṇas* are *rajas* (the attribute of activity), *tamas* (the attribute of passivity), and *sattva* (the attribute of direction). For anything to be or to act there must be both motion and pattern. Motion involves also a correlated inertia. The similarity to Aristotle's efficient cause, formal cause, and material cause is striking. In the primordial state the three *guṇas* are in equilibrium—and nothing happens.

The other primary principle, *puruṣa*, is often called spirit, but "the subjective" might be a better designation, and *prakṛti* would then be "the objective." The role that *puruṣa* plays in the system is that of final cause, as is stated in one of the five arguments given for its existence:

[44] *De Generatione et Corruptione* 329 a 25, 30, 31.

[45] *Metaphysics* 1049 a 25. By use of the coined word "thaten" (ἐκεῖνον) Aristotle means that unlike a chair which is wooden and a ring which is golden, there is nothing which is related to prime matter such that it can be said to be "thaten."

"because all composite objects are for another's use."[46] This is a case of unconscious teleology, for *puruṣa* is unaware of *prakṛti*. The creation of the concept of *puruṣa* by the *Sāṅkhya* philosophers must have been the result of their awareness of the purposiveness of the world. A world in which there is design is a world in which there must be reference to an end not inherent in the world processes themselves. *Puruṣa* is the principle for the sake of which *prakṛti* evolves. *Puruṣa* does not evolve; but by being what it is, it causes *prakṛti* to evolve. The mechanism of the relating of *prakṛti* and *puruṣa* is a weak link in the Sāṅkhya philosophy. How unconscious inactive *puruṣa* can stimulate *prakṛti* to an awareness of *puruṣa* and to the realization of *puruṣa* as its own end, remains unexplained. Unlike *prakṛti*, which is single, *puruṣa* is manifold. Each *puruṣa* is static, passive; it is an enjoyer, a witness (*sākṣin*),[47] although how it can be a witness and still be passive is puzzling.

Perhaps the difficulty experienced in understanding the Sāṅkhya metaphysics is the result of thinking of *puruṣa* and *prakṛti* as separate independent principles, forgetting that "without the 'subjective,' there would be no 'objective,' and without the 'objective' there would be no 'subjective.' "[48] Again the author of the *Sāṅkhya Kārika* writes, "For the perception of Nature by the spirit and for the isolation of the spirit, there is union of both,—like that of the halt and the blind; and from this union proceeds evolution."[49] The image of a sure-footed blind man carrying a cripple with good sight on his shoulders is a striking analogue of the *prakṛti-puruṣa* relationship, although it suffers from the possibility of false interpretations, e.g., the relationship of *prakṛti* and *puruṣa* is not one of mutual choice as would be that of a blind man and a cripple, and again, *prakṛti* and *puruṣa* cannot act alone as could the two men. In other words, the *prakṛti-puruṣa* relationship is not engaged in in order to act *well*, but to act *at all*. Further, in the present cosmic age a *prakṛti-puruṣa* relationship is the only way in which anything can be.

Besides the two primary principles there are the two derived and secondary principles. These are resultants of the disturbance of the equilibrium of the *guṇas* in the presence of *puruṣa*. That which is evolved and from which others evolve consists of three subprinciples: (1) the principle of intellect, both cosmic (*mahat*) and individual (*buddhi*); (2) the principle of individuation or egoism (*ahaṁ-kāra*); and (3) the principle of the five subtle elements (*tanmātras*)—sound, color, touch, taste, and

[46] *Sāṅkhya Kārikā* 17. Quotations are from the translation by S. S. Suryanarayana Sastri unless otherwise indicated.
[47] *Ibid.*, 19.
[48] *Ibid.*, 52. Ganganatha Jha translation.
[49] *Ibid.*, 21. Jha translation.

odor. That which is itself evolved and from which others do not evolve consists of four subprinciples: (1) the principle of arrangement of sensations into percepts and concepts, i.e., the mind (*manas*); (2) the principle of the five sensory organs—sight, hearing, touch, taste, and odor; (3) the principle of the five motor organs—speech, grasping, walking, evacuation, and reproduction; and (4) the principle of the five gross elements—space, air, fire, water, and earth. *Sattva* predominates in *manas; tamas* predominates in the subtle and gross elements; *rajas* predominates in none, but is involved in the activity of everything. The evolutionary process begins when the balance of *sattva-rajas-tamas* is disturbed by the presence of *puruṣa.*

The entire cosmic evolution is for the sake of the emancipation of the *puruṣas.*[50] A *puruṣa* is kept in bondage by *prakṛti*—association with *prakṛti* is its bondage—yet the bondage is also the means of its liberation. Spirit is liberated in and through—and from—matter. The "higher" is redeemed by means of the action of the "lower." The Sāṅkhya philosophy makes a unique contribution; for *mokṣa* is not interpreted as a union of the individual with Reality, but as a disunion. *Puruṣas* are cut off from *prakṛti* by means of the evolutes. *Prakṛti* ceases to act, having fulfilled its function: "As a dancer desists from dancing, having exhibited herself to the audience, so does Primal Matter desist, having exhibited herself to the spirit." [51] *Puruṣa* at last views *prakṛti,* and sees it for what it is—the instrumentality of *puruṣa's* liberation; and *prakṛti* never again comes into view of *puruṣa.*[52] The final end is "eternal and absolute isolation" of *puruṣa* from *prakṛti.*[53]

This, in brief, is the argument of the *Sāṅkhya Kārikā.* It obviously challenges the *tat tvam asi* doctrine of the nature of the self and the self's realization. Its *mārga,* as we have already noted, is a *jñāna mārga,* a becoming aware of the separateness of *puruṣa* and *prakṛti.* At the hands of Patañjali the *mārga* shifted from *jñāna* to a form worthy of a new name—a *yoga mārga.*

3. THE *Yoga* OF PATAÑJALI

The *Yoga Sūtras* is a collection of *sūtras* (threads of an argument) which, while assuming for the most part the Sāṅkhya metaphysical system, shifts the perspective from the problem of cosmic evolution to the

[50] *Ibid.,* 56.
[51] *Ibid.,* 59.
[52] *Ibid.,* 62.
[53] *Ibid.,* 68. Jha translation.

problem of man's salvation. It undertakes far more seriously than does the *Sāṅkhya Kārikā* a therapy for relieving man from his threefold misery. The *Yoga Sūtras* is traditionally assumed to be the work of a man named Patañjali who lived in the second century B.C. It is organized into four chapters, each dealing with a definable aspect of the discipline: the first chapter deals with the general theory of *yoga;* the second presents the technique recommended for self-realization; the third discusses the *siddhis* or psychic powers attainable by yogic discipline; and the fourth describes the final emanipation. Charles Johnston has suggested the following titles for the four chapters: "Spiritual Consciousness," "Means of Soul Growth," "Spiritual Powers," and "Mechanism of Salvation."

One difference between the Sāṅkhya and the Yoga system of Patañjali is that God is a factor in Yoga and not in Sāṅkhya. Although Sāṅkhya has often been described as atheistic, the true state of affairs is that the concept of deity is not utilized as an explanatory device in its metaphysics; there is no categorical denial of the existence of deity. In Patañjali, on the other hand, the existence of God is affirmed and used as a metaphysical principle. God for Patañjali is the *Puruṣa* of *puruṣas.* God stands somehow outside the *puruṣas* and *prakṛti,* since he is the mediator between the two. He is the adjustor of *karma,* the efficient and formal cause of *karma.* He also directs *prakṛti* to the liberation of the *puruṣas.* He is the guide of the entire cosmic evolution. Devotion to God is one of the means for progress in yogic discipline. God is not a creator, and does not in fact seem to be required by the system. Moreover, the concept of God contradicts the causal nature of *karma* and turns it into a program of rewards and punishments under the control of a personal agent. The relation between *puruṣas* and God is not clear. Perhaps God was introduced by Patañjali as a means to explain how inactive *puruṣas* and unconscious *prakṛti* can be related, although just how a deity can bridge this hiatus is not made clear. Radhakrishnan and Garbe suggest Patañjali introduced a personal God as a concession to popular feelings.[54]

Patañjali emphasizes the pluralistic nature of *puruṣa* more than does the author of the *Sāṅkhya Kārikā.* The *puruṣas* are individual and separate, and in the liberated state they preserve their separate identities. The empirical self is a complex of nature and spirit, *prakṛti* and *puruṣa. Mokṣa* is the liberation of an individual *puruṣa* from the *prakṛti* component. More specifically, Patañjali, having introduced a new term in his Yoga system,

[54] Radhakrishnan, *Indian Philosophy,* Vol. 2, p. 371. Garbe, "Yoga," *Encyclopaedia of Religion and Ethics,* edited by Hastings, Vol. 12, p. 831, and *The Philosophy of Ancient India,* p. 15. See also A. Berriedale Keith, *The Sāṁkhya System,* p. 68, and P. Tuxen, *Yoga,* p. 56.

the term *citta* which combines the Sāṅkhya *buddhi, aham-kāra,* and *manas* as the highest manifestation of the *prakṛti* principle, contends that liberation is the isolation of a *puruṣa* from *citta. Puruṣa,* as transcendent Self, cannot come into its own until it has left behind the particularizing discursive rational mind and its activities. In Patañjali's conception of *mokṣa* there is the underlying notion of a fall from a halcyon state of purity through involvement with *citta.* The aim of *yoga mārga,* therefore, is to return the *puruṣas* to their original state by suppressing the *rajas* and *tamas* aspects of *prakṛti,* especially the tantalizing activity of *citta. Citta* is the tempter, offering the delights of mentation; but *citta* is also the mediator through which *puruṣa* regains its lost status, a status of omniscience in which *prakṛti,* having been seen as *prakṛti* and not as *prakṛti-puruṣa,* is rendered impotent to bind *puruṣa* to *saṁsāra* and consequent misery. Although the liberation of *puruṣa* is a liberation both from body and mind, Patañjali emphasizes the supression of the mental activities, possibly because suppression of the physical is less difficult.

Vedavyāsa in his commentary on the first *sūtra* of the *Yoga Sūtras* identifies five states of the mind (*citta*) according to their fitness for *yoga.* The least fit is the *kṣipta citta,* the wandering mind in which there is an excess of *rajas.* It moves restlessly from one object to another and is a slave to passions. The *mūḍha citta* is the mind with an excess of *tamas.* It is easily absorbed and led astray by overpowering emotions such as anger. It is sluggish and inclines toward sleep. The third type of mind is *vikṣipta citta,* the generally abstracted, but occasionally steady, mind. It is obsessed with *sattva* insofar as *sattva* is light, pleasant, and enjoyable. It seeks the pleasurable and avoids the painful. While it tends toward the good, it easily slips back into evil. It resists discipline that requires tenacious adherence to a line of action. The fourth type of mind, the *ekāgra citta,* is entirely filled with *sattva.* As the name indicates, it is the one-pointed mind. It can devote itself unwaveringly to a single object of meditation. Such a mind is ready for the last stage, since these four types can also be regarded as preparatory stages leading to the final and proper stage. The fifth stage is the *niruddha citta,* the restrained or restricted mind, the mind in which all mental activities are arrested. The *citta* in the *niruddha* stage is a fit instrument for leading the *puruṣa* to its liberation. The ordering of these five stages points up most clearly the main emphasis in the *sādhana* techniques of the *yoga mārga* of Patañjali: the suppression of mental activities.

Patañjali gives two lists of obstacles to mind control. The first list is found in *sūtra* 30 of the first chapter. This is a rather comprehensive enumeration of obstructions to overcoming the first three states of the mind, chiefly the mind as dominated by *rajas* and *tamas,* in order to enter upon the single-pointed state which will lead to *niruddha citta.* Nine obstacles are named: (1) disease of body and/or mind, (2) inertia, (3) doubt and indecision, (4) frivolity, (5) laziness, (6) intemperance, (7) erroneous knowledge, (8) inability to attain a state of concentrated contemplation, and (9) unsteadiness of the mind in the state of contemplation. The next *sūtra* lists other physiological and psychological problems faced by the individual who sets himself on the *yoga* path: "Grieving, despondency, bodily restlessness, the drawing in and sending forth of the life-breath, also contribute to drive the psychic nature to and fro." [55] The second list [56] is directed specifically to the practice of yogic discipline. Chapter 2 opens with the practical suggestion of the use of austerities (*tapas*), spiritual study (*svādhyāyā*), and complete resignation to the will of God (*praṇidhāna*) as techniques of concentration. The aims of these techniques according to Patañjali are two, one positive and one negative. The positive aim is to bring about a vision of the *puruṣa* in its pure state of non-relatedness to *prakṛti;* the negative aim is to overcome the emotional and intellectual weaknesses to which human beings are prone. These afflictions and hindrances to concentration are known as the *kleśas.* There are five *kleśas:* (1) *avidyā,* ignorance or false opinion about the objective world; (2) *asmitā,* identification of the *puruṣa* and the *citta;* (3) *raga,* emotional weakness of man which prompts him to seek and to attach himself to things merely for the pleasure they are able to give; (4) *dveṣa,* man's tendency to avoid and to hate those things which give him pain; and (5) *abhiniveśa,* attachment to life and fear of death. These two lists of obstacles to yogic practices suggest the serious pursuit of a rigorous program of self-discipline which characterizes *yoga mārga.* Patañjali makes no effort to hide the severe physical and psychical demands of his plan for the Perfection of Man. The *kleśas* must be "worn away." [57] He does not promise that the grace of God will step in and preternaturally wipe away all that clouds the perfect vision. His way is for activists, not for wishful dreamers. Human life is a vale of tears: "To him who possesses discernment, all personal life is misery." [58] A serious malady requires a serious therapy.

Patañjali spells out his *yoga mārga* in eight *aṅgas* (parts, limbs, means, aids).[59] The first five are aids to psychical purification; the remaining three are the degrees of concentration which the *yogi* experiences. The first *aṅga* is *yama.* This is a list of five moral practices stated negatively

[55] *Yoga Sutras* 1. 31.
[56] *Ibid.,* 2. 3–11.
[57] *Ibid.,* 2. 2.
[58] *Ibid.,* 2. 15.
[59] *Ibid.,* 2. 29–3. 12.

which should control the behavior of the *yogi*. The five are almost the same as the *Pañca Sīla* of Buddhism: non-injury, non-telling of falsehoods, non-stealing, non-engagement in acts of sexual impurity, and non-covetousness. No one can expect to progress on the path leading to liberation from *prakṛti* apart from a sound moral foundation. The second *aṅga* is five positive moral and spiritual requirements (*niyamas*) which should be practiced after the development of the habit of avoiding the sins of the previous list. These include purity in mind and body, an attitude of contentment, the ability to engage in austerities, the study of sacred books and application of the study to one's self, and devotion to God. The last two *niyamas* include elements of *jñāna* and *bhakti*. Patañjali includes both knowledge and devotion as parts of *yoga*. His psychological insight is often excellent, e.g., he writes, "When transgressions hinder, the weight of the imagination should be thrown on the opposite side." [60] That is, when one begins to experience difficulties and temptations while practicing the restraints and the observances, the best form of attack is an indirect one, e.g., if tempted to hate another person, instead of trying to put down hatred directly, one should begin to think of the good qualities of the person. The third *aṅga* deals with the problem of the posture (*āsana*) of the *yogi*. Patañjali recommends no specific meditative position, but merely recommends that the one chosen be steady and easy. Other teachers of *yoga* have developed eighty-four postures, some elaborate and complicated. *Prāṇāyāma* (breathing), the fourth limb of *yoga*, is given slight treatment; it ought to be regular, and it will vary according to time and place. The fifth *aṅga* (*pratyāhāra*) is the state of abstraction or withdrawal of the senses from their objects. It is recommended as a means of encouraging the inward look and discouraging being caught up in externalities. The last three *aṅgas* are the stages of inner progress of the *yogi* toward *mokṣa: dhāraṇā* (attentive concentration on a single object), *dhyāna* (prolonged holding of the mind on an idea), and *samādhi* (trance contemplation in which the sense of separateness of the subject and the object has vanished). But these three are external to the final goal, warns Patañjali.[61] Even *samādhi* is an *aṅga*, an aid, not the goal. The goal is being, not knowing—a state of the *puruṣa*, not a state of the *citta*. The body becomes quiescent in *samādhi*, but the *citta* is still active. *Samādhi* is the highest activity, but *mokṣa* is not an activity.

In Chapter 3 of the *Yoga Sūtras* Patañjali lists the psychic powers [62]

[60] *Ibid.*, 2. 33.

[61] *Ibid.*, 3. 8.

[62] In later *yoga* literature the psychic powers were commonly listed under eight heads: (1) *animā*, the power to diminish in size at will; (2) *mahimā*, the power to increase

resulting from *saṁyana* (the group name for *dhāraṇa, dhyāna,* and *samādhi*), including such items as "knowledge of past and future,"[63] "an understanding of the sounds uttered by all beings,"[64] "knowledge of previous births,"[65] "power to make the body invisible,"[66] "knowledge of the lunar mansions,"[67] "cessation of hunger and thirst,"[68] "power of ascension,"[69] "power to traverse the ether,"[70] etc. These are the lesser goals of *yoga;* they are not to be despised, nor are they to be sought. Patañjali breaks into the middle of their recitation to caution, "These powers stand in contradistinction to the highest spiritual vision. In manifestation they are called magical powers."[71] One wonders why, if these powers are contrary to the end sought, he devotes so much of Chapter 3 to their enumeration. His list has titillated the imagination of his readers, and has caused much harm by misleading people to seek the "magical powers" rather than the "spiritual vision."

Chapter 4 is devoted to *kaivalya* (absolute independence, absolute freedom, absolute isolation). The term *kaivalya* is used by Patañjali rather than *mokṣa* to indicate the special conception of liberation as independence from cares, troubles, works, and the claims of other people upon the life and attention of the *yogi. Kaivalya* connotes the individual nature of this liberation. An individual saves only himself; he cannot save others, and others cannot save him. *Yoga* is a *svādhyāyā,* a study of one's own being and one's own welfare. Each must realize his own *kaivalya.* In the *kaivalya* state man realizes a trans–*puruṣa-prakṛti* condition; he is neither body nor mind, but something beyond both. Since *kaivalya* lies beyond knowing, there is little Patañjali can say about it, therefore he is very restrained in his remarks: "When all veils are rent, all stains washed away, his knowledge becomes infinite; little remains for him to know."[72] When one fully is, knowledge loses its savor. The objective, the *prakṛti,* having vanished, there is no thing to be known. *Citta* is no more. A trans-subjective *puruṣa* is all. Patañjali's book concludes with a magnificent

in size at will; (3) *laghimā,* the power to overcome gravity at will; (4) *prāpti,* the power to obtain anything or reach any place at will; (5) *prākāmya,* the power to fulfill any wish at will; (6) *īśatvā,* the power to control energies of nature at will; (7) *vaśitvā,* the power of self-command and freedom from being influenced; and (8) *kāmavasāyita,* the power of stopping all desires at will.

63 *Yoga Sūtras* 3. 16.
64 *Ibid.,* 3. 17.
65 *Ibid.,* 3. 18.
66 *Ibid.,* 3. 21.
67 *Ibid.,* 3. 27.
68 *Ibid.,* 3. 30.
69 *Ibid.,* 3. 39.
70 *Ibid.,* 3. 42.
71 *Ibid.,* 3. 37.
72 *Ibid.,* 4. 31.

summary: "Absolute freedom comes when the qualities, becoming devoid of the object of the *puruṣa,* become latent; or the power of consciousness becomes established in its own nature." [73]

4. THE MEANING OF *Yoga*

Patañjali was an editor of *yoga,* not an innovator. His *Yoga Sūtras* is a selection from a large collection of ideas and practices which were current in India long before the second century B.C. As editor he emphasized and neglected according to his personal evaluations. His work is the definitive one in this field, yet Hindus have not accorded to it a *śruti* status, and therefore have not hesitated to modify *yoga* through the centuries. Patañjali's *yoga* is a conservative form of psychological discipline. He was fully aware of the dangers inherent in man's discovery of the powers latent in his own being, and cautioned against preoccupation with these powers. Other adepts in *yoga* have been less cautious.

Yoga requires introspective attitudes seldom found outside India. Western psychiatrists are much interested in "the Indian mind" and in its possible contributions to Western cultures. C. G. Jung has written, "An Indian, inasmuch as he is really Indian, does not think, at least not what we call 'think.' He rather perceives the thought." [74] Jung argues that thinking for the Indian is increasing one's vision, entering more fully into the truth one already has; thinking for a Western man is solving problems, conquering the unknown, bringing more of nature under man's power. The Indian thinks to appreciate; the Westerner thinks to possess. The Indian civilizes the world by accommodating himself to it; the Western man civilizes the world by controlling it. "We in the West," writes Jung "have become split into a conscious and an unconscious personality. We are highly disciplined, organized, and rational on one side; but the other side remains a suppressed primitive, cut off from education and civilization. This explains our relapses into barbarity." [75] In India, on the other hand, there is a civilization "which has brought every essential trace of primitivity with it, embracing the whole man from top to bottom. . . . That is presumably the reason why India seems so dreamlike: one gets pushed back into the unconscious, into that

[73] *Ibid.,* 4. 34. Rāma Prasada translation.

[74] "What India Can Teach Us," *The Collected Works of C. G. Jung,* Vol. 10, p. 527. Nirad C. Chaudhuri has written, "There is no such thing as thinking properly so called among the Hindus, for it is a faculty of the mind developed only in Greece, and exercised only by the heirs of the Greeks. A very large part of what is called Hindu thinking is wooly speculation or just mush." *The Continent of Circe,* p. 151.

[75] *Ibid.,* p. 528.

unredeemed, uncivilized, aboriginal world, of which we only dream, since our consciousness denies it. India represents the other way of civilizing man, the way without suppression, without violence, without rationalism."[76] The factor that makes the difference is *yoga. Yoga,* says Jung, is the Indian's most important exercise. "Yoga is the most eloquent expression of the Indian mind and at the same time the instrument continually used to produce this peculiar attitude of mind."[77]

Yoga shares with all varieties of Hindu *sādhana* the conviction that man is a unique and marvelous entity whose nature is to perfect his being, to transcend the limitations of his mortal existence by the realization of a freedom which is absolute and unconditioned. *Yoga* also differs from the other *mārgas* in certain emphases. We shall consider five of its distinguishing characteristics.

In the first place, according to *yoga* man is the epitome of the universe. He is a microcosm of the macrocosm. The universe is man writ large. In man are all the potencies (*devatā*) of the All. "Therefore one who knows Man thinks, 'This is *Brahman.*' For all deities are seated in him, as cattle in a cow-stall."[78] Since man reveals the universe, by looking within himself a man can discover what is without—or, perhaps more accurately, he can discover there is in fact no "without" or "within," that outer and inner are two expressions of the same Reality. Therefore, he does not need to conquer the external world; instead of possessing the world, he has the ineffable experience of being the world. *Haṭha,* the term used for the *yoga* that is exclusively physical, is composed of the words sun (*ha*) and moon (*ṭha*). The *yogi* realizes his nature as "sun," "moon," and everything else of the "external" world. The human consciousness is capable of infinite expansion. Man can function at many levels in addition to his "normal" awareness. Inherent in this fact is a great danger of *yoga;* the *yogi* may prefer to trifle with the occult rather than strive for the Perfection of Man. His horizons may contract rather than expand. The early stages of postures, breathing exercises, and pinpoint concentration are preparatory, not terminal. Although Gandhi swore that he had nothing to do with *yoga,* his view of man's nature was essentially *yogic:* "Unless we have the realization that the body is the house of God, we are less than men."[79]

The second characteristic of *yoga* is its assumption that the spiritual can be controlled by the material. Bodily conditioning is for the purposes

[76] *Ibid.*

[77] "The Psychology of Eastern Mysticism," *The Collected Works of C. G. Jung,* Vol. 2, p. 560.

[78] *Atharva Veda* 11. 8. 32. Edgerton translation.

[79] Quoted by Pyarelal, *Mahatma Gandhi: The Last Phase,* Vol 1. Ahmedabad: Navajivan Publishing House, 1956, p. 62.

of mental development and spiritual attainment. The term *yoga,* which originally meant a yoke of draft animals, came to mean the yoking or controlling of the senses. In the Upaniṣads the senses are sometimes described as horses.[80] *Yoga* dignifies the body of man and gives it a valuable purpose. "Sādhanā has to be done in the body, it cannot be done by the soul without the body." [81] There is no Docetism or Gnosticism in *yoga,* no despising the body in its physical role. Long before the James-Lange theory of the emotions was formulated, before modern psychoanalysis and psychosomatic medicine, the Indians discovered the non-physical impact of the physical. What man eats and how he walks, talks, senses, breathes, and sleeps affect his thinking, hoping, and aspiring. Man is what he does. The *tapas* or austerities of *yoga* need not be unpleasant, nor need they injure the body. The *Haṭhayoga Prakīpika* lists the *tapas* as six forms of behavior to be avoided: overeating, strenuous exercise, idle chatter, hard vows, needing to be with people, and restlessness.[82] The distinction between the "lower" functions and the "higher" functions of man's life loses significance when the so-called lower are understood as contributory to the realization of man's noblest aspirations.

A third distinguishing feature of *yoga* is the effort to "reverse" human behavior. There must be a shift from concern for the preservation of the empirical self to the restoration of the *puruṣa* to its original state. One must cease looking for one's essence in externals; the external and the internal must be found within. This reversal includes immobility of the body, arresting the breath, restraining the thoughts, and even the returning of semen. The senses must be withdrawn from their objects like a tortoise that withdraws its legs into its shell.[83] The reversal is based on the view of opposition between the phenomenal and the noumenal. "Death" is really a new birth into life; "time" is the eternal sliced into meaningless moments; "space" is an erroneous measurement; "right" and "wrong" are limited and spurious evaluations of reality; "pain" and "pleasure" are distinctions having no support in the nature of things. Aurobindo contends that the reversal is part of the evolution which is the entire meaning of life: "A change into a higher consciousness or state of being is not only the whole aim and process of religion, of all higher askesis, of Yoga, but it is also the very trend of our life itself, the secret purpose found in the sum of its labour." [84]

[80] *Kaṭha Upaniṣad* 3. 4. *Maitrī Upaniṣad* 2. 6.
[81] Aurobindo, *Bases of Yoga,* p. 134.
[82] 1. 15.
[83] *Bhagavad Gītā* 2. 58.
[84] *The Life Divine,* p. 648.

Yoga's fourth mark is its emphasis on conation. *Yoga* is disciplined action, earnest striving. Activity, not rationalism or emotionalism, is the keynote. Śaṅkara can be said to have assigned will a prior evaluational status to love, and thought a still higher status; Caitanya placed the order as love-thought-will in descending order; but Patañjali established the priority as will-thought-love. *Yoga* is a voluntarism which assumes that physical and psychical controls will bring about changes in mental attitudes and spiritual values. Self-analysis and self-effort are regarded as means of curing psychological disorders. *Yoga* is something to do. A yogic way of life is vigorous; it demands that senses, appetites, emotions, and thoughts be kept in strict control. Selected habits are to be encouraged and developed. Drifting must be avoided. By nurturing the desired activities the *yogi* takes on his own salvation. He relies on no organization or community for his own modifications. When the term union is used in connection with *yoga*, it does not mean union in an Advaita Vedānta sense of absorption into Reality, nor a Viśiṣṭādvaita Vedānta sense of loving adoration of God; rather it means a state in which distracting forces are ended and all conflicts resolved. "Union" describes an inner harmony of interests, rather than an identity with the Absolute or a devotion to a deity.

Finally, the way of the *yogi* is a progressive way. His movement along the path can be measured. Liberation comes by degrees, not by sudden illumination. The eight *aṅgas* may be regarded as steps toward the goal. *Yoga* is a planned program for disciplining man toward his perfection. Vyāsa in his *Bhāsya* divides the progress into seven stages: (1) conviction that all external goods are productive of suffering; (2) assurance that passions which prompted the *yogi* to see the external goods have suffered attenuation so it is no longer necessary to keep a strict watch over these passions; (3) vision of freedom and repose which ends all questioning and doubts; (4) faith in the knowledge of the difference between mind (*citta*) and the source as the means of attaining the goal; (5) recognition that mind has completed its task by leading the individual through enjoyment and suffering to renunciation of everything that is foreign to its inmost nature; (6) recognition that constituents of mind must organize themselves for a fresh set of experiences; and (7) discovery that the highest and the inmost are identical.[85]

Yoga as a system of philosophy and *yoga* as discipline must be carefully distinguished. Yoga philosophy has been characterized as theistic Sāṅkhya, and was opposed by the other classical systems of Indian philosophy. But *yoga* as discipline is not opposed by the *darśanas*. It is

[85] 2. 27.

accepted as an essential human discipline by all Hindu philosophies and religions. Something of the genius of the Hindu went into *yoga*, and *yoga* remains an ingenious effort to put the entire human being into action toward the Perfection of Man.

5. TANTRIC *Yoga*

The most radical development in *yoga* after Patañjali was a synthesis of *yoga* and *bhakti* known as Tantra. The differences between the *yoga* of Patañjali and some forms of Tantra are so great that it is almost misleading to use the term *yoga* for both.[86] The most striking innovation was the introduction of a sexual element in Tantric *yoga*. Today Indian journalists sometimes use the expression "woman tantric" as equivalent to prostitute.[87] At the same time the Tantra system of worship is said to have occupied "a position of supreme importance in the religious life of Hindus all over India for at least the last four or five hundred years." [88] It has been estimated that two-thirds of Hindu religion as practiced today and one-third of Hindu medicine is Tantric.[89] A Hindu scholar thinks the penetration of Tantric ideas is even more thorough: "Hinduism in its present form involves, no doubt, 'a double framework,' Vaidika and Tantrika, but Tantrika wings have not simply been added from time to time to the ancient Vaidika mansion. The process has been in the nature of a remodelling of the old structure in which its ground-plan has subsisted, but the edifice has been permitted to wear a new form and expression suited to new times and conditions. . . . The general body of Hindu ideas, beliefs, and practices will, on examination, be found to be permeated through and through by the cult of the Tantra, indeed so much so that the whole now bears a definitely Tantrika character." [90] The Tantric scriptures have been called the Fifth Veda.

Tantrism has received much condemnation from both Indians and foreigners. Elliot said that it preserves and emphasizes what is "super-

[86] See Rajendra Lal Mitra, *The Yoga Aphorisms of Patañjali*, p. lxi.

[87] A news item in *The Statesman* (Calcutta) for December 28, 1965, reads as follows: "Mr. P. C. Sen, West Bengal Chief Minister, asked the Inspector-General of Police, Mr. U. Mukerjee, on Monday to make a special inquiry into the conduct of a young woman tantric, who is said to have chosen the Jadavpur area as her field of operation. The Chief Minister's inquiry order follows an S O S from a married woman who had appealed to Mr. Sen to save her husband from the clutches of the tantric."

[88] Chintaharan Chakravarti, *Tantras, Studies on their Religion and Literature*, p. 49.

[89] A. S. Geden, "Tantras," *Encyclopaedia of Religion and Ethics*, edited by Hastings, Vol. 12, p. 192.

[90] Swami Pratyagatmānanda, "Tantra as a Way of Realization," *The Cultural Heritage of India*, Vol. 4, pp. 227, 229.

ficial, trivial and even bad in Indian religion, omitting and neglecting the higher sides."[91] Murdock characterized Tantrism as "the latest and most corrupt form of Hinduism. The religious system of some of them is perhaps the most degraded on the face of the earth."[92] Tantrism has been condemned as black magic, obscenity, and vulgarity; it has been dismissed as "lust, mummery, and superstition."[93] Some scholars have claimed that the Tantras were compiled in order to spread licentiousness among the people, and have recommended the total annihilation of the literature for the good of the unsuspecting.[94] These evaluations are based partly on the questionable moral behavior of some self-styled tantrics and partly on ignorance of the Tantric writings. No translation of any Tantra text was published in India until about 1900, and none in the West before 1913 when Sir John Woodroffe published his translation of the *Mahānirvāṇa Tantra.* Scholarly studies of the Tantra are largely limited to the twentieth century.

The word *tantra* comes from the root *tan* meaning a discipline, a system, literally a web or pattern. It is an organizing of the life of man, especially his physical life, for the realization of ideal ends appropriate for him in view of his unique place in the universe. Although the earliest scriptures do not antedate the fifth century A.D., Tantric ideas and practices are very ancient in India. A *Ṛg Vedic ṛṣi* refers to his praises of Indra as embracing the *deva* sexually: "My praises, all-acquiring, concentrated and eager, glorify Indra: they embrace Maghavat as wives embrace a husband; as women embrace a man free from defect for the sake of protection."[95] Furthermore, each Vedic *deva* has a *śakti,* a spouse, who is his energy. The *śakti* is an emanation of the god who brings the divine power to man and who makes the god approachable for man. Śiva, the deity especially associated with Tantrism, has 1008 names, and for each of his names he has a *śakti.* This means there are 1008 approaches to the god! *Śaktis* of Śiva most often appealed to are Kālī, Durgā, Bhairavī, Chaṇḍī, Pārvatī, Umā, Kamārī, and Gaurī. The feminine nature of a *śakti* is not necessarily a sexual attribute; to refer to a *śakti* as female is to note that it is a source of energy, productivity, and growth. *Śakti* is the inherent power of things so that they do what is their nature to do. The *śakti* of fire is to burn, of water to moisten, of the hand to grasp. *Śakti* as a cosmic person is the Divine Mother, the productive

[91] Charles Norton Edgecumbe Elliot, *Hinduism and Buddhism: An Historical Sketch,* Vol. 2, p. 283.

[92] John Murdock, *The Religious History of India,* p. 138.

[93] See Swami Pratyagatmānanda, *op. cit.,* p. 227.

[94] See Chintaharan Chakravarti, "Ideals of Tantra Rites," *The Indian Historical Quarterly,* Vol. 10, p. 486.

[95] 10.43.1.

dynamism of all creation. The *Ṛg Veda* refers to the power of the gods as a single *Śakti*.[96] In Tantrism the concept of *śakti* is not that of an abstract kinetic energy, but a vital, personal entity which is called *Caitanya* (Pure Consciousness) or *Pārā Śakti* (Supreme Being of Power). The notion of life has been expressed in two forms of *śakta*, the right-handed, which insists on animal sacrifices, and the left-handed which emphasizes coitus as the origination of life. Animal sacrifices survive in a few Kālī temples; the sexual practices are not publicly displayed except in images. While the conception of *śakti* as power is Hindu, the worship of *śaktis* appears to be borrowed from the early primitive peoples of India. Some scholars think that *śakti* worship arose first among the Dravidians; others locate the original home in Bengal. An interesting empirical evidence for a Bengal origin is the fact that the *Mahānirvāṇa Tantra* recommends three species of fish for Tantrics, and these three are especially found in Bengal—Śāla, Boāl, and Ruhi.[97]

In the Śiva-Śakti syndrome Śiva is wisdom and Śakti is energy. Tantrism, stressing power, comes into prominence in times calling for action. The first century of great development of Tantrism was the ninth century A.D., when a protest was needed against the fatalistic lethargy which was the practical result of Śaṅkara's philosophy of the unreality of the space-time world. Again in the late nineteenth and early twentieth centuries there was a burst of enthusiastic growth in Tantrism when Bengalis actively resisted the partition of their state. At that time they made the song *Bande Mātaram* (Bow to the Mother) their patriotic hymn. The British Government in 1906 declared the singing of the hymn illegal. Today all over India there occurs at the time of the ending of the monsoon and the beginning of the growing season a joyous autumnal celebration of the power of growth in nature. This is known as Durgā-pūgā in the east, as Rāmalīlā in the north, and as Dusserah in the south, but in each case it is a worship of *śakti*.

Indian philosophers do not agree as to the source of the Tantras. Radhakrishnan insists, "Śakti worship, there is no doubt, prevailed among the non-Aryans, and was gradually adopted by the Aryans." [98] Others argue for a Chinese origin; still others root it in Mahāyāna Buddhism. But D. N. Bose contends, "The Tantras are, in fact, the elaboration of the religious principle and philosophy of the Vedas and the Upanishads." [99] There are many evidences for an indigenous growth of Tantrism within Hinduism. The rites and rituals of the *Atharva Veda* are similar

[96] 3. 55.
[97] 6. 7–8.
[98] *Indian Philosophy*, Vol. 1, p. 487.
[99] *Tantras: Their Philosophy and Occult Secrets*, p. 38.

to those in Tantrism. There are passages in the Upaniṣads which have the unmistakable flavor of the Tantras, e.g., "As a man, when in the embrace of a beloved wife, knows nothing within or without, so this person, when in the embrace of the intelligent Soul, knows nothing within or without. Verily that is his [true] form in which his desire is satisfied, in which the Soul is his desire, in which he is without desire and without sorrow." [100] A Śāṇḍilya aphorism indicates that divine love is of the same order as human love: "Perfection of Love towards the Lord is to be inferred by the same marks by which human love is judged." [101] Again the *śakti* element is found throughout the Vedas. In the famous creation hymn sexual desire is named as the first cause of the formation of the world,[102] and in the *Śvetāśvatara Upaniṣad* the womb (*yoni*) is suggested as one of the possible First Causes,[103] yet actual *śakti* worship does not appear in Hindu literature before the *Mahābhārata*.[104] The use of *soma* in Vedic worship is well known, and charm words like AUM, Khaṭ, Kaṭ, and Phaṭ appear also in the Upaniṣads and Āraṇyakas.[105] The sacrifices of goats, sheep, bulls, horses, and even humans are described or referred to in the Vedas.[106]

The philosophical background of the Tantras is largely Sāṅkhya; Śiva is the guiding *puruṣa*, and Śakti is the dynamic *prakṛti*. The evolution and diversity of the world are explained by the interaction of the *guṇas*, and human differences are accounted for by the dominant *guṇa:* if *tamas* predominates, the person is akin to animals; if *rajas*, he is heroic; and if *sattva*, he is like a god. One of the greatest helps for Tantrism came from Vaiṣṇavism. According to Vaiṣṇavism *śakti* is an essential attribute of the Supreme Being. Rādhā, the embodiment of *śakti*, the supreme power of the Lord, has no separate existence from Kṛṣṇa. Rādhā is the Lord Himself in the fullness of joy and energy. She is the primordial element which manifests itself in loving companionship with the Lord. In the *Bhāgavata Purāṇa* energy and joy (*śakti* and *ānanda*) are blended in the person of God. Kṛṣṇa eternally delights in playing with his own *śaktis*, the powers inseparable from himself. The Rādhā-Kṛṣṇa love relationship had three distinct patterns in Bengali Vaiṣṇavism. Caitanya

[100] *Bṛhad-Āraṇyaka Upaniṣad* 4. 3. 21. Hume translation.
[101] *Sūtra* 43.
[102] *Ṛg Veda* 10. 129. 4.
[103] 1. 2.
[104] 4. 6; 6. 23.
[105] *Taittiriyā Āraṇyaka* 4. 27; *Atharva Veda* 13. 1. 15; 13. 3. 6; *Kaṭha Upaniṣad* 2. 15–17.
[106] A Brahmin named Bānabhaṭṭa who lived in the courts of King Harsha in the seventh century A.D. reports in his *Harsa-carita* the sale of human flesh! Cowell and Thomas translation, pp. 92, 136, 263.

placed himself in the role of Rādhā longing for Kṛṣṇa. For him the desire of the human soul for God is like that of a devoted woman for close companionship with her beloved. Caitanya did not think of his experience of God as sexual, but in describing the relationship of man and God as the relation of a woman and a man, he opened the floodgates for eroticism. The Vaiṣṇava poets, such as Jayadeva, Caṇḍīdāsa, and Vidyāpati, thought of themselves in the role of the cowherd female companions of Rādhā and Kṛṣṇa longing for chances to witness the love-making of Rādhā and Kṛṣṇa. The observer attitude—a Peeping Tom attitude!— is midway between that of Caitanya and the Vaiṣṇava Sahajiyā cultists. The latter contended that the barriers between God and man should be broken down, and that as divine *līlā* (play) was expressed in the erotic pleasures enjoyed by Rādhā and Kṛṣṇa so man should enter into this divine enjoyment in acts of sexual intercourse, especially of a *parakīyā* nature, i.e., outside the bonds of marriage. Illegal coitus was regarded as man's most exciting experience, and hence as a fitting approximation of the overpowering joy of immediate relations between man and God. In the intimacy of sexual love the devotee is Rādhā submitting herself to her divine lover. How much of Bengali Vaiṣṇavism was the result of Tantrism and how much of Tantrism was due to the impact of Bengali Vaiṣṇavism is difficult to determine, but in any case some of the post-Caitanya cults are accurately described as Tantric.

The supporters of Tantra place a very high value on their scriptures. According to Tantrism the basic scriptures of Hinduism are the *Āgamas* and the *Nigamas*. These Tantric terms are equivalent to the traditional *śruti* and *smṛti* distinction, except that for Tantrism the Tantras are the *Āgamas* and the Vedas are the *Nigamas*. The demotion of the Vedas to the status of tradition rather than revelation is based on a Tantric interpretation of the four cosmic ages. According to this ancient Hindu belief, the world moves through four ages (*yugas*): *Krita, Treta, Dvapara,* and *Kālī*. *Krita* is the Golden Age, the age in which men were fully devoted to *dharma*: "By the study of the Vedas, by Dhyana and Tapas, and the conquest of the senses, by acts of mercy and charity men were of exceeding power and courage, industry and prowess, adherents of the true Dharma, good and truthful, and, mortals though they were, they were yet like Devas and went to the abode of the Devas." [107] In this age men had the Vedas to guide them in the path of devotion and duty. In the *Treta Yuga, dharma* and the Vedic rites were neglected: "For men, through their anxiety and perplexity, were unable to perform these rites

[107] *Mahānirvāṇa Tantra* 1. 21–22. All selections are from the translation of Sir John Woodroffe, whose pseudonym is Arthur Avalon.

in which much trouble had to be overcome, and for which preparation had to be made. In constant distress of mind they were neither able to perform nor yet were willing to abandon the rites."[108] The *smṛtis* were their source of guidance. The *Dvapara Yuga* was a time when men were blinded by passion and afflicted by ills of mind and body. The Purāṇas were their source of instruction and help. Finally, the *Kālī Yuga* arrived. This, the present age, is by far the worst: "Dharma is destroyed, an Age full of evil customs and deceit. Men pursue evil ways. The Vedas have lost their power, the *Smṛtis* are forgotten, and many of the Purāṇas, which contain stories of the past, and show the many ways (which lead to Liberation, will, O Lord! be destroyed."[109] In this age through the grace of the Lord the *Āgamas* have been given to men. They are the announcers of Vedic knowledge to men living under the tragic conditions of the *Kālī Yuga*. The *Āgamas* are sometimes called *Śrutiśakhā-viseṣah*, a specific branch of the Vedas. They contain the rites and ceremonies which are to continue throughout the *Kālī* Age, a period of time which began in 3102 B.C. and is to continue for 432,000 years. There is no authoritative canon of *Āgamas*. In addition to eighteen so-called *Śiva Tantras* there are many others in India, Nepal, Tibet, China, and Mongolia. Because of the secretive nature of Tantric cults, there are probably hundreds of manuscripts yet unknown to scholars. Few have been translated into Western languages. They are usually cast in the form of dialogues between Śiva and his *śakti* Pārvatī. According to Woodroffe an *Āgama* is structured to cover seven topics: (1) creation of the universe, (2) destruction of the universe, (3) modes for worship of *devas*, (4) spiritual exercises, (5) instruction in a preparatory rite (*puraśca-raṇa*), (6) magical powers, and (7) forms of *yoga*. The esoteric character of the *Āgamas*, with their use of mystical symbols, secret letters, diagrams, circles, charms, spells, and other forms of mystical meaning make very dull reading for non-devotees.

The Tantric view of man is more special and important than its view of God and the world. A man is a rare and priceless being. According to the *Viśvasāra Tantra* "There is no birth like unto the human birth. Both Devas and Pitṛs desire it. For the Jīva the human body is of all bodies the most difficult to come by. For this it is said that human birth is attained with extreme difficulty. . . . It is said in all the Śāstras that of the Jīva's eighty-four lakhs[110] of births the human birth is the most fruitful. In no other birth can Jīva acquire knowledge of the truth. Human birth is the stepping-stone to the path of liberation. But rare are

[108] *Ibid.*, 1. 30–32.
[109] *Ibid.*, 1. 38–39.
[110] I.e., 8,400,000.

the meritorious who come by it." [111] Tantric *sādhana* is the recovery of a lost identity, the union of Śiva and Śakti, Divine Wisdom and Divine Power; and the human body, which is the microcosm of the macrocosm, is the agency of *sādhana*. The outwardly directed behavior must be reversed; there must be an inner-directed behavior so energy will be redirected from the dissipating of the inner life to the strengthening of the inner life. Tantra *yoga* may seem to be identical with the *yoga* of Patañjali, but the emphasis on the human body as the medium through which *sādhana* is accomplished is uniquely Tantric. Each person must become aware of the subtle body within the physical body, and, being aware, must assist the activity of the elements of this body.

The student who accepts uncritically the priority of objective knowledge has difficulty in taking seriously the Tantric analysis of the mystical body of man, but the student who recognizes that all knowing is an appraising, that objectivity "is not a counsel of self-effacement, but the very reverse—a call to the Pygmalion in the mind of man," [112] may be able to appreciate the esoteric physiology of Tantrism. A few examples may help. The question, "How long is a minute?" is not univocally answered, "Sixty seconds." Sixty seconds spent holding one's breath under water and sixty seconds spent saying farewell to a dear friend *seem* very different in length. How long an experience *feels* may be very different from how long an experience *is*. Psychological time is as real as clock time. In India there is an interesting belief that the higher up the ladder of perfection a being moves, the quicker time passes for him until, at liberation, time is no magnitude at all.[113] In all cultures there are pictorial and figurative expressions of the feeling of things and events which violate scientific terminology. Western people are well acquainted with a "frog" in the throat, "butterflies" in the stomach, "lead" in the feet, "stars" in the eyes, "springs" in the toes, "jelly" in the legs, a "lion" in the heart, and "rocks" in the head. The soul is located in the blood by the Hebrews and in the breath by the Greeks. A Western man when puzzled scratches his head, but a Chinese scratches his knee. Perhaps such considerations make the student more receptive to the conception of a snake coiled at the base of the spine!

The *Āgamas* contend that the universe consists of several layers of existence, from the lowest plane of the physical to the highest plane of perfect bliss. This cosmic organization is repeated in the "feeling body" of man. In each human being there are *chakras* (centers) connected

[111] Quoted by Woodroffe, *Principles of Tantra*, p. 95.
[112] Michael Polanyi, *Personal Knowledge*, p. 5.
[113] F. O. Schrader, *Introduction to the Pāñcarātra and the Ahirbudhnya Saṁhitā*, p. 27.

with the cosmic planes, so that by introspection a man is able to understand the nature of the universe and by certain esoteric techniques may control externalities. The Upaniṣadic *tat tvam asi* (That thou art) becomes *ham sah* (I am That). When these *chakras* are properly utilized, they make the powers of the macrocosm available in the microcosm. These six centers—they are also called wheels, disks, and lotuses (*padmas*)—are imagined to be located in the spinal cord. To each *chakra* is assigned a fundamental sound, an animal symbol, an element, a specific number of lotus petals, a symbolic form, and a deity; but the important feature of each *chakra* is the physical and psychical functions it governs. The *chakras,* their location, and their functions are as follows: (1) *Mūlādhāra.* This *chakra* is located at the base of the spinal column midway between the anus and the genitals. It presides over matter in its grossest state, governs the subconscious movements of the body, and controls the sense of smell. It encloses the mysterious psychic energy known as the *Kundalinī,* the coiled-serpent power. As the most elemental of all forces it is the creative energy which must be awakened in order to move up the *nadis,* or invisible conduits connecting the *chakras* to all parts of the body, charging man's entire being with energy, and thus enabling him to establish dynamic harmonies with the entire universe. (2) *Svādhisthāna.* The second *chakra* is at the level of the genitals. It governs the lower vital being, and presides over the water-state (*apas*) of matter. The sense of taste is assigned to this *chakra.* (3) *Manipura.* This *chakra* is imagined to exist at the level of the navel, and governs the sense of sight. It is associated with the fire-state (*agni*) of matter. The bodily movements are under its jurisdiction. (4) *Anāhata.* The *chakra* at the level of the heart presides over the air-state (*vāya*) of matter. The sense of touch is thought to be its province, and, like the Western view which puts emotions in the heart, it governs the emotional life of man. (5) *Viśuddha.* At the level of the throat is placed the *Viśuddha chakra,* the center of the expressive and externalizing mind. The sense of hearing is controlled here, and in addition it controls the mind in its functions of communication and objectification of feelings and sensations. (6) *Ājñā.* The sixth center is between the eyebrows at the spot where Śiva's third eye is located. This is the center of command for all acts of willing. It may be thought of as the *chakra* of mind proper (*manas*). According to the Tantric mystic view of the body there is a seventh point which is thought to be at the level of the crown of the head, but it is not a *chakra.* This is the *Sahasrāra,* the "Lotus of One Thousand Petals," which governs the highest reaches of the mind, the state that leads to intuition. It is the microcosmic correlative to the macrocosmic Śiva-Śakti union.

The aim of Tantric *yoga* is to open and cleanse the principal *nadis* which connect the *chakras* in order that the coiled-serpent power in the *Mūlādhāra* can be released. Thus each individual human being can become a point of radiation of the cosmic energy. The joyous union of Śiva and Śakti is to be repeated in millions of forms in the world, especially in the human form which is strikingly designed for this purpose. Man is uniquely qualified to mirror the cosmic *līlā*. Each man is privileged to offer his own variation of joy in the universal polyphonic concert.

Tantrism has developed other methods besides the *yoga* techniques of Patañjali for the realization of integration of man and the cosmos. In the process of its development Tantrism has looked askance, even with ridicule, at many of the common Hindu customs. For example, the *Kulārvaṇa Tantra* states, "If the mere rubbing of the body with mud and ashes gains liberation, then the village dogs who roll in them have attained it." [114] One of the controversial methods introduced by the *Tantras* is the *Pancha Makāras*, often called the 5 M's. The idea behind the 5 M's seems to be the changing of the *telos* of the normal human activities. A man is to do all things in consecration to the Lord rather than for the sake of his own being. He is to awaken himself to becoming a channel of cosmic joy. The five *makāras* are *madya* (wine), *māṁsa* (meat), *mātsya* (fish), *mudrā* (cereal), and *maithuna* (sexual union). The five symbolize respectively: (1) the intoxicating experience of God, (2) the consigning of all things to one's inner growth, (3) the identification of oneself with all the pain and pleasure in the universe, (4) the relinquishing of association with evil, and (5) the union of Śiva and Śakti. The practical problem for the Hindu is whether the 5 M's are to be engaged in literally or symbolically. *Maithuna*, in particular, raises serious difficulties. Those of the left-handed Tantra have followed the 5 M's literally. They argue that the development devotee reaches a state known as *Kaula*, a state which lies beyond all morality. Indians who are not Tantrics have often questioned this defense. The following caricature of the *Kaula* state from a tenth-century drama, the *Karpūramañjari* of Rājaśekhara, is typical:

> As for black-book and spell—they may all go to hell!
> My teachers excused me from practice for trance.
> With drink and with women we fare mighty well,
> As on—to salvation—we merrily dance.
>
> A fiery young wench to the altar I've led.
> Good meat I consume, and I guzzle strong drink;

[114] Quoted by Ernest A. Payne, *The Śaktas*, p. 11.

And it all comes as alms,—with a pelt for my bed.
What better religion could anyone think?

Gods Vishnu and Brahm, and the others may preach
Of salvation by trance, holy rites, and the Vedies.
'Twas Uma's fond lover alone that could teach
Us salvation plus brandy plus fun with the ladies.[115]

Tantra places a high value on women. Every woman is a *śakti.* Some Tantrics have held that a woman is necessary for the salvation of a man. Śiva and Śakti in embrace represent wisdom and power, whereas Śiva alone is knowledge without strength, and Śakti alone is energy without direction. The symbol of *maithuna* also reminds the Tantrist that enlightenment (*mukti*) and enjoyment (*bhukti*) go together, that the ecstasy of sexual intercourse is the nearest physical approximation to the joy of liberation. The Tantrist believes no other symbol can express so well the closeness of God, the love of God, and the thrill of union with God.

Tantrism has provided many aids to worship in addition to the *makāras.* The goal of Tantric worship is to attain a feeling of the identity of worshiper and the object of his worship. Here something of the vigor and enthusiasm which accompanied the ancient Vedic sacrifices survives. All the senses are to be used in worship. *Mantras* are based on the cosmic significance of elemental sound. *Maṇḍalas* and *yantras* are figures with mystical meanings which are used as objects of meditation. Incense, hand gestures, bodily postures, food and drink, baths, flowers, and many other aids are used lavishly. The full dedication of the Tantric to his deity is indicated in a song from Rāmaprasāda:

Of what use, O brother! is this body if it does not melt in love for Dakṣinā?
Oh, fie, fie, to this tongue if it does not utter the name of Kālī.
Those eyes are sinful which see not the form of Kālī.
Oh, how wicked is the mind which does not sink under her feet.
May thunder strike those ears which do not hear Her sweet name, make copious tears flow from the eyes. For what purpose does their existence serve?
Oh, should we desire to have the hands which fill the belly, if they are not joined together to hold sandal paste, Javā flowers, and bael leaves?
Oh, of what use are the feet, and wholly without purpose is the work they do by day and night, if they do not willingly and gladly carry us there where images of Kālī are enshrined? [116]

[115] Quoted by Payne, *The Śaktas*, p. 30. Translation by C. R. Lanman.
[116] Quoted by John Woodroffe, *Principles of Tantra*, p. 679.

Tantrism is probably the least understood and most misrepresented aspect of Hinduism. Much remains to be done in the scholarly study of this interesting *mārga.*

6. *Yoga* as *Mārga*

Yoga, like *karma* and unlike *jñāna* and *bhakti,* is a *kriyā mārga,* a way of action. It is built around the belief that the universe is dynamic and that the salvation of man must correspond in method and goal with that of the universe. In *jñāna* and *bhakti mārgas* man puts himself into position for something to happen; in *yoga* and *karma mārgas* he makes it happen, or at least has a key function in the happening. *Yoga mārga* differs from *karma mārga* in the degree of freedom and joy which marks the *yogi* as contrasted with the restriction which shapes the life of the one who chooses the path of *karma* as his special way of life. *Yoga* puts all of man into action. It is a way of discipline, but the discipline proceeds from within the individual rather than from the society in which he lives.

Yoga mārga is a positive way, a way of reestablishing a lost unity by means of life affirmation. Unlike the negative way—the *Neti! Neti!* way —of the Advaitists, *yoga* affirms human life in all its active dimensions. It uses the physical and the material with complete enthusiasm. But the use to which it puts the physical is a sublimation or substitution transcending the limited. The life of the body is caught up in the life of the spirit. The whole man serves divine ends. The ordinary becomes sacramental. Eating, drinking, breathing, sensing, copulating, and sleeping becomes conducive to the end of the Perfection of Man without ceasing to contribute to the health of the body and the total enrichment of human life. They are elevated to new telic levels without diminution of physical satisfaction. In Tantra *yoga* the sex act is sublimated as the creative union of Śiva and Śakti without ceasing to express the love of man and woman. The carnal is no longer non-spiritual; the spiritual is no longer non-carnal. Together they form a union which destroys the difference between matter and spirit without loss of the values of either. Śiva is Śakti, and Śakti is Śiva. Yājñavalkya offers a number of suggestive analogies of the disciplined life of the *yoga*-adept: he is "like the fixed and upward flame of a lamp that is full of oil and burns in a breezeless spot," "like a rock which is incapable of being moved in the slightest degree by even a heavy downpour from the clouds," "as a man of cool courage and determination, while ascending a flight of steps with a vessel full of oil in his hands, does not spill even a drop of the liquid if frightened and threatened by persons armed with weapons." [117] The *yogi* in his training becomes aware of his involuntary actions, such as breathing and digesting, not in order to develop neurotic attitudes, nor to attempt to keep these activities consantly under his control, but to become fully aware of who and what he is, of what he can and cannot do, and through this self-knowledge to direct his whole being to the ends selected as most worthy of being sought.

Yoga mārga is an individualistic way of liberation. The social dimension is absent. Patañjali presents the psychological requirements and techniques, but he makes no reference to social prerequisites or results. Perhaps we can assume from absence of reference to caste that he intended his *yoga* for all men regardless of caste. Tantra *yoga* is more explicit. According to the *Mahānirvāṇa Tantra* there are five castes in the *Kālī Yuga*, the fifth caste being the *Sāmānya*, the common or lowborn.[118] This is a way of stating that no one is outside the caste system. Each caste has but two *āśramas*, the householder and the mendicant. The first and the third stages of life, the student and the hermit stages, do not exist in the *Kālī Yuga* because they require a stricter observance of rules and regulations than is possible in the decadent times of this age. This is a leveling process, and the *Mahānirvāṇa Tantra* does not hesitate to draw the conclusion: "When the Kali Age is in full sway, the Vipras [Brahmins] and the other castes have equal right to enter into both these stages of life." [119] Equality of all to enter upon the paths leading to the Perfection of Man does not, however, mean that all social distinctions are eliminated. This, as we have noted in the previous chapter, was also the situation in Vaiṣṇavism and Śaivism. Eliade argues that *yoga* attempts cosmicization," but that its techniques are "antisocial" and even "antihuman." [120] The "cosmicization" process is particularly evident in Tantra. But surely "antisocial" and "antihuman" are too strong characterizations. The social is not emphasized in *Yoga Mārga*, but in Tantra the rites and rituals of worship do require group behavior. "Antihuman" is very misleading. The aim of *yoga* is to realize man's human condition. Man is a being in process; his nature is to be transitory. He is the being who can attain *mokṣa*, a freedom transcending dualities, a return to primordial unity. *Mokṣa* is an integrative consciousness of freedom "which exists nowhere in the cosmos, neither on the levels of life nor on the levels of 'mythological divinity,' " [121] but which exists only in the Supreme Being.

[117] *Mahābhārata* 12. 317.
[118] 8. 5.
[119] 8. 12.
[120] Mircea Eliade, *Yoga: Immortality and Freedom*, p. 97.
[121] *Ibid.*, p. 100.

If *yoga* is "antihuman," it is so in asserting that man should not settle for less than his full potentialities. It is against any human life that does not set for itself the realization of *mokṣa.*

Yoga mārga has ofen been in conflict with the other *mārgas.* The *Mahānirvāṇa Tantra* admits that the Vedic ceremonies of *karma mārga* were once valuable, but claims that they have become useless: "The Vedic rites and Mantras which were efficacious in the First Age have ceased to be so in this. They are now as powerless as snakes, the poison-fangs of which are drawn." [122] The *Mahānirvāṇa Tantra* continues that there is only one *mārga* now, and that anyone who tries another is a sinner: "No other path is there to salvation and happiness in this life or in that to come like unto that shown by the Tantras which give both happiness and Liberation. . . . The fool who would follow other doctrine heedless of Mine is as great a sinner as the slayer of a Brāhmaṇa or of a woman, or a parricide; have no doubt of that." [123] The conflict was symmetrical; for we have evidence from other sides. Thus in *The Laws of Manu* there is the claim that one can ignore the *yoga* techniques if one follows *karma mārga* faithfully: "If he keeps his organs and his consciousness under subjection, he can attain his ends without further tormenting his body by Yoga." [124] Śaṅkara flatly denied that *mokṣa* could be obtained solely by *yoga:* "the highest beatitude (the highest aim of man) is not to be attained by the knowledge of the Sāṅkhya-*smriti* irrespective of the Veda, nor by the road of Yoga-practice." [125] Again Śaṅkara refuted the claims of *yoga mārga* in his *Aparoksānubhutī* by suggesting alternatives: "The best posture is neutrality toward all objects. The best regulation of breath is the contemplation of the delusion of the world. The best withdrawal of the senses from objects is the identification of self with them. The highest contemplation is the realisation of the Whole, the Absolute, or the Brahman without reference. The highest samādhi is the complete cessation of any kind of mental activity." [126] The opposition to *yoga mārga* seems however to have been an opposition only to the claims of *yogis* that *yoga* alone was the path to salvation. *Yoga* became assimilated into the other *mārgas* as disciplinary aspects. Each *mārga* requires some form of control of the life of man, some regulatory preparations for the liberated state. The senses must be subdued, the mind must be emptied, the desires must be redirected. According to the *Kena Upaniṣad* the Self cannot be known by him who has knowledge; it can be known only by

[122] 2. 15.

[123] 2. 20, 13.

[124] 2. 98.

[125] *The Vedānta-Sūtras with the Commentary by Śaṅkarācārya,* 2. 1. 3. *The Sacred Books of the East,* Vol. 34, p. 298.

[126] Quoted by Mukerjee, *The Culture and Art of India,* p. 262.

him who has no knowledge.[127] This has been taken to mean that the preparation for knowing is of quite different character from the knowing. This method of accommodation of all *mārgas* into one's own is common among Hindus. Pratyagatmānanda's generalization on Tantra *mārga* is correct, although definitely in need of further clarification: "For the common aspirant, however, it serves out a mixed prescription of *karma, jñāna, yoga,* and *bhakti,* all 'scientifically' combined, graded and graduated, and regulated, according to varying conditions and needs." [128] The "prescription" according to *yoga mārga* might be this: *karma mārga* alone is too occupied with the externalities of the soteriological process; *bhakti mārga* errs in attempting to make the emotions, which are in fact resultants, the completely effective instruments of liberation; *jñāna mārga* correctly identifies the importance of knowledge as an ingredient, but it does not pay enough attention to the existential nature of self-realizing knowledge, and too easily ignores the physical component of all knowing. But when *yoga* assigns each to its proper place, and when it disciplines the total *rajas-tamas-sattva* organism we call man, then *karma, bhakti,* and *jñāna* become interdependent stages of the process leading to the Perfection of Man.

[127] 11.

[128] "Tantra as a Way of Realization," *The Cultural Heritage of India,* Vol. 4, p. 238.

CHAPTER XI
Human Catholicism

On November 11, 1866, Keshub Chunder Sen led a small group of Indians in the establishment of the Brahmo Samaj of India, taking at that time as the motto of the organization:

> The wide universe is the temple of God.
> Wisdom is the pure land of pilgrimage.
> Truth is the everlasting scripture.
> Faith is the root of all religion.
> Love is the true spiritual culture.
> The destruction of selfishness is the true asceticism.
> So declare the Brahmos.

Five years earlier, before having broken with the organization called simply "Brahmo Samaj," Keshub had described Brahmoism as "Human Catholic Religion." [1] The term is ideally suited to designate the homo-

[1] "Brahmoism is anti-sectarian; catholicity is its distinguishing characteristic; love is its very life. It is not the religion of a particular community, epoch or country; it is universal religion; it is Human Catholic Religion. It is this which clearly distinguishes Brahmoism from all systems of faith. While they are founded upon the peculiarities of time and place, Brahmoism stands upon a basis co-extensive with human nature, upon principles that are catholic and universal. While they seek to divide mankind into distinct and hostile parties, Brahmoism goes forth to bring all mankind to a state of unity and harmony. While they confine their love within their own respective sects, Brahmoism extends the holy current of love to the whole human race. The former is a battle-field in which communities strenuously fight against each other, actuated by inveterate jealousy, or the maddening spirit of fanaticism. The latter is the Kingdom

centricism which has been emphasized in this study of the Perfection of Man. The Perfected Man is the Universal Man.[2] Individuality is not lost but is elevated and dignified as each man mirrors the Ideal Man according to his own talents. Both the Man and all men participate in the goal of the perfecting process; thus catholicity is manifested idealistically and pluralistically. Hinduism so conceived is a *Viśvajanaina,* a catholic religion. The *Bhagavad Gītā,* the one scripture common to all Hindus, is sometimes referred to as "the gospel of humanity." Rabindranath Tagore was characterized by Nehru as "the great humanist of India." [3] A fine Bāul song celebrates the glories of man, and sets the theme for this final chapter:

> Man, man, everyone speaks of man!
> What is man?
> Man is health, man is life, man is the jewel of the Heart;
> Very few on earth know the truth of Man.
> Man knows a love which other creatures know not,
> And man alone knows the depths of such love.
> Man's love helps him to know the Real Man;
> Thus man knows Man;
> The strength of man-in-Man is understood by man alone.[4]

Hinduism is the *sādhana* of man. It is a system of thought and life aiming at the Perfection of Man through knowledge, morality, faith, and love. It glorifies man as the being who is capable of knowing and living in accord with the highest truths of the universe. The difference between the early Vedic hymns and the Brahmāṇas on the one hand and the Upaniṣads on the other is that whereas the emphasis in the hymns and the Brahmāṇas is on cosmo-physical notions and ritualistic matters, the emphasis in the Upaniṣads is increasingly anthropocentric. Even in the earliest hymns the gods are primarily instruments through which man may secure what he desires. The centrality of man is a constant theme throughout the development of Hinduism. Turning to the epics, in the *Mahābhārata* the dying Bhīṣma is finally allowed to disclose the truth of truths, the secret doctrine transcending all others, the *upaniṣad:* "This

---

of peace, in which all mankind are a brotherhood and Love reigns supreme." From the third tract of Keshub Chunder Sen's "Tracts for the Times," in Prosanto Kumar Sen, *Biography of a New Faith,* Vol. 1, p. 250.

[2] Brajendranath Seal delivered a lecture entitled "Rammohun Roy, the Universal Man" at the death anniversary of Rammohun Roy held at Bangalore on September 24, 1924, and another entitled "Rammohun's Universal Humanism" at Calcutta on December 31, 1933.

[3] *The Discovery of India,* p. 258.

[4] Quoted by Mukerjee, *The Culture and Art of India,* p. 357.

is the secret and supreme doctrine I announce to you. There is nothing in the universe higher than man." [5] In the *Rāmāyaṇa* Tulsīdāsa says, "Know the devotee of Rāma to be greater than Rāma." [6] "Listen, O brother man," sang Caṇḍīdāsa, "the truth of man is the highest truth, there is no truth above it." [7] The real atheism in Hindu *sādhana* is not to have faith in man. Not to have faith in one's self and in one's fellows is to be unworthy of the potentialities of the human status. Each individual is a candidate for becoming fully man. He who does not labor for the Perfection of Man in his own being is not fit to be a man. He ought to be a non-knowing animal or a non-becoming god! Aurobindo in his characteristic poetic manner writes, "Man is a spirit veiled in the works of energy and moving to self-discovery. He is a soul growing in Nature to self, a divinity and eternal existence, a wave of the God-ocean, an inextinguishable spark of the supreme Fire, identical even in reality with the ineffable Transcendence from which he came, greater even than the godheads he worships." [8] Radhakrishnan in his typical succinct prose states, "Man is an unfinished experiment." [9] The history of Indian thought, writes A. Chakravarti, "is the history of Humanism with a bias towards spirituality. We may say, in short, that Indian philosophy is a running commentary on the text, 'Thanks that I am a man.'" [10]

Swami Vivekananda in a lecture given on September 19, 1893, at the Parliament of Religions in Chicago offered the electrifying challenge: "Come up, O lions, and shake off the delusion that you are sheep." [11] Hinduism charges man to become what he is, to enter fully into the realities of his own nature. In the words of Martin Heidegger, man is called to desert inauthentic being and to enter into authentic being. Another way to state this would be to ask man, the god who has forgotten himself, to realize his full nature. Hinduism has been defined as "a system of spiritual discipline for the discovery of God within." [12] The "God within" that must be discovered is Man in his complete being. The use

5 *Mahābhārata* 12. 300.

6 *Dohāvalī* 3.

7 Quoted by Tagore, *The Religion of Man*, p. 113.

8 "The Indian Conception of Life," *The Indian Philosophical Congress, Silver Jubilee Commemoration Volume*, 1950, p. 174. Aurobindo has also written, "Man is God hiding himself from Nature so that he may possess her by struggle, insistence, violence and surprise. . . . The animal is Man disguised in a hairy skin and upon four legs; the worm is Man writhing and crawling towards the evolution of his Manhood. Even crude forms of Matter are Man in his inchoate body. All things are Man, the Purusha." *Thoughts and Glimpses*. Calcutta: Arya Publishing House, 1941, p. 15.

9 *The Brahma Sūtras*, p. 153.

10 "Humanism and Indian Thought." Miller Lectures, University of Madras, p. 27.

11 *The Complete Works of Swami Vivekananda*, Vol. 1, p. 9.

12 P. T. Raju, "The Development of Indian Thought," *Journal of the History of Ideas*, Vol. 13, 1952, p. 548.

of the term "God" may be misleading—particularly to Western minds, but the term "discovery" may be even more misleading, for it usually connotes a purely cognitive awareness of hitherto unknown realities. While it is correct to say that for Hinduism man is the being who must come to know his own being, it is incorrect to construe this "knowing" in either a discursive or an intuitive fashion. Self-realization is a process, not a cognitive state. Man's "being" is a becoming. His is-ness is in process such that he never *is* with the finality of God or beast. In process he *creates* his being. Man creatively discovers what he is, and what he "is" is what he can become. Man is a process, not a status. Man is what he *becomes*, not what he is. Blackham says of the philosophy of Heidegger, "A man is possibility, he has the power to be. His existence is in his choice of the possibilities which are open to him, and since this choice is never final, once for all, his existence is indeterminate because not terminated." [13]

The *sādhana* theory of man, the theory of man as striving for Perfection, is the heart of Hinduism. In the words of Ramakrishna, "The contented man is no man; he is no more than a brute." [14] *Sādhana* is the effort of man to achieve what the seers have presented in theory. Knowledge in Hinduism cannot be mere knowledge; worship cannot be mere worship; morality cannot be mere morality; discipline cannot be mere discipline. *Sādhana* in all its forms—knowledge, worship, morality, and discipline—must not, and cannot, be divorced from the goal. And conversely, the goal cannot be considered as viable, or even as a goal, in the absence of the means for achieving the goal. Hinduism is a life-centered philosophical-religious-ethical discipline. When an Indian philosopher attacks Western philosophy for being only philosophical, what he means is that Western philosophy is usually presented and understood in the absence of *sādhana*. At its lowest it is a collection of university courses in ethics, aesthetics, logic, metaphysics, epistemology, and history of ideas, which when successfully completed give the student credits toward an academic degree! Western philosophy in spite of its life-centered Greek origins tends to deteriorate into a science or a metascience. The epistemological dimensions of philosophy are important, but when philosophy becomes merely epistemology, as it has in recent language-analysis movements, it carves out for itself a very small portion of the human enterprise. In so doing it leaves an area of life for religion, but the result is a philosophy which denies life-demands and a religion which denies thought-demands. Hinduism, when rightly understood, is neither philoso-

[13] H. J. Blackham, *Six Existentialist Thinkers*. New York: Harper and Brothers, 1959, p. 88.

[14] "The Path of Perfection," *Works*, Vol. 1, p. 224.

phy nor religion; rather it is a way of life which includes rationally definable goals plus the means for the realization of these goals plus an effort toward the goals. The goals are as meaningless without the means as are the means without the goals. Hinduism may be defined as the attempt of a specific culture to answer two related questions: "What is man, actual and ideal?" and "How can actual man become Ideal Man?"

Mankind is still in the making. Man must continue to be in the making. His ultimate *dharma* lies in the service of ideals he cannot possibly achieve. His salvation is in losing self in quest of a Perfection beyond realization. The Perfection of Man is inherent in his perfect*ing*, not in a flawless state of complete fulfillment. The *nisus* of man, which may once have been automatic or unconscious, has through the evolutionary process become conscious. Man takes on his own future, his own becoming, or, as we can say for man alone, his own being. However, his future is not determined. This is the *karma* principle which is so frequently misunderstood. *Karma* is the law of cause and effect in the totality of human becoming. Man eats the fruits of his *karma*, but he also sows the seeds of his *karma*. His present is causally determined by his past, and the future lies within his hands inasmuch as he is able to initiate now the causes which will have results in the future. To regard Hinduism as fatalism is a serious error, since the cause and effect relationship in human affairs is the presupposition of any theory of meaningful freedom. Man's coming-to-be, which is his self-realization, is not a playing with the self, not an introvertive activity having little or no relation to the world of external phenomena, for man must realize himself in relations to other men, to nature, and to God.

Man alone is less than a man. Man is man only in community. Man does not live alone, and man does not perfect himself alone. Liberation is a project of humanity, not of individual men. Man, therefore, "must disabuse his mind once for all of the notion that he can reach his spiritual goal apart from others." [15] This is one of the distinctions between Hinduism and Buddhism, especially Theravāda Buddhism. The Buddha's forsaking of the householder stage was a violation of a basic Hindu responsibility, for a man's duties to family are never to be forsaken, and the description of an *arhat* (Theravāda monk) as one who walks alone like a rhinoceros seems to the Hindu to be the proper metaphor, for one who walks alone is not acting like a human! Feuerbach's observation that man with man is God [16] is very similar to the Hindu position. In the Hindu tradition there have been many ways of viewing and implementing the sociality of man. The *Ātman* concept of man in Advaita Vedānt-

[15] M. Hiriyanna, *The Quest After Perfection*, p. 77.

[16] *Principles of the Philosophy of the Future*, Section 60.

ism gives an interesting sanction for moral behavior at the phenomenal level: one ought to treat one's neighbor as one's self because one's neighbor is one's Self. Keshub Chunder Sen established in February 1872 a closely knit communal group of his followers based on the theory that only collectively could men attain *mokṣa*. The institution, Bharat Ashram, at Belgharia seven miles north of Calcutta lasted five years. One of the members of the *āśrama*, Bijay Krishna Goswami, wrote, "There is no salvation through individual spiritual culture. All together in quest of salvation and bound by ties of family must advance towards the Kingdom of Heaven. It is selfishness to tread the solitary way to righteousness. We must enter the Kingdom of Heaven taking all with us." [17] P. K. Sen also comments, "Keshub's soul was set on collective *sādhana*—marching Heavenward together—on constructing a communistic Family that would serve as a perfect example of the brotherhood of man." [18] Radhakrishnan has upheld the doctrine of *sarvamuktivāda* (simultaneous salvation), the view that liberation from human individuality will not be effected until the cosmic eschatological moment when Īśvara enters the Absolute.[19] Elsewhere Radhakrishnan has written, "The world is in dreadful need of these heroic spirits who have the courage of their vision of human oneness to assume the new leadership." [20] The mission of man on earth is to hasten the time when all men will see the Godhead in each, and each will seek the Godhead in all. The salvation of man is in the production and discovery of a new center of his existence, a movement from self-centeredness to identification with the Being whose center is everywhere and whose circumference is nowhere.

The Hindu conception of salvation is even wider than humanity, for, although not often stated, behind the doctrines of *dharma* and *mokṣa* is the assumption that liberation and perfection is the birthright of all *jīvas*. Anything that is a life may experience *mokṣa*; man has the direct possibility, the *jīvas* in other bodily forms have the indirect possibility. The refusal of Yudhiṣṭhira to enter the heavenly regions without his dog is one of the few places in Hindu literature where the liberation of subhumans is implied.[21]

[17] Quoted by P. K. Sen, *Keshub Chunder Sen*, p. 112.

[18] *Ibid.*, p. 101.

[19] See P. T. Raju, "The Development of Indian Thought," *Journal of History of Ideas*, Vol. 13, 1952, p. 546.

[20] *The Religion We Need*, p. 32.

[21] *Mahābhārata* 17. 3. According to primitive religions all spirits—animal, plant, human, world, and divine—are assumed to be of equal dignity and worth. A strange custom of plant-marriage practiced in some parts of India illustrates this belief. Betty Heimann reports as follows: "If a widower or a widow wants to get married again, the unmarried partner must first win the same status as his consort in symbolically marrying a tree or shrub. If his extra-human partner fades or dies, then he has attained

Again man is man only in nature. To say that man must live in the universe may sound as foolish as Margaret Fuller's decision to accept the universe, but there is a profound issue at stake. Martin Buber in commenting on Albert Einstein's conception of the universe has noted that "this universe can still be thought, but it can no longer be imaged, the man who thinks it no longer really lives in it." [22] Albert Einstein in a conversation with Rabindranath Tagore on July 14, 1930, contended that the world is a unity independent of the human factor, but Tagore argued that man and the universe are mutually dependent: "The entire universe is linked up with us . . . it is a human universe . . . This world is a human world—the scientific view of it is also that of the scientific man. There is some standard of reason and enjoyment which gives it truth, the standard of the Eternal Man whose experiences are through our experiences." [23] Einstein disagreed, and added with candor, "I cannot prove that my conception is right, but that is my religion." [24] The Hindu, no less candidly, must admit that his faith that man is the fullest expression of the universe and that man's highest values depend upon the mode of existence which we call the "universe" is equally beyond proof. The question is what constitutes the universe? Is it in time and space, or is it beyond time and space? At this point the Einsteinian view and the Hindu view are strikingly alike—the universe transcends space and time. The conceptions of Brahman and of a finite but unbounded universe both portray a cosmos in which the measurements of temporality and spatiality are inadequate. Can man live in such a universe? Perhaps the answer depends as much on what man is as on the nature of the universe; and at this point Hinduism has much to say, since, for the Hindu, man is not as H. L. Mencken once said, a sick fly taking a dizzy ride on a gigantic flywheel, but the being in whom Reality comes to Self-consciousness. Apart from him Being would not be being. He more than mirrors the universe—he is the universe pluralized.

In the third place man stands in an integral relation to God. Hinduism deifies man and humanizes God. God and man tend to blend into god-man or man-god. Hence the worship of *gurus, sadhus,* and *ṛṣis,* and hence the references to semidivine beings, as though divinity were a sliding

---

the equality in status with his widowed associate, and no impediment now stands in the way of their union. The Indian dogma of the essential unity of all beings is here carried to the extreme. . . . If by any chance a younger brother intends to get married before his elder brother has chosen a wife, then this elder brother must first be wedded symbolically. He has to embrace the trunk of a tree; the tree then is assumed to be his wife." *The Facets of Indian Thought,* pp. 66, 165.

[22] *Between Man and Man.* London: Fontana Library, 1961, p. 165.

[23] *The Religion of Man,* p. 222.

[24] *Ibid.,* p. 223.

scale on which a being might be placed as having more or less of the attribute of divinity. In Christianity man and God remain distinct orders of being. One is Creator; the other is created. Although God became man once in the Incarnation, Christians do not claim this estate for themselves, nor do they allow any man to claim divinity. In Christianity anyone asserting himself to be God would be considered either insane or blasphemous. God is the Holy, the Absolutely Other. Man in his redemption does not become God. God became incarnate in history in the person of Jesus the Christ. Only He is *Deus-Homo.* Although this is the official doctrine, the language of devotion offers other views, for example, the prayer of Origen used in the prayers at the Offertory in *Missale Romanum:* "Grant us to be partakers of his divinity, who deigned to become partaker of our humanity." In Hinduism each man is an incarnate deity, and each birth is an incarnation. "True incarnation is not, as popular philosophy defines it, the absolute perfection of the divine nature embodied in mortal form; it is not the God of the universe putting on a human body—the infinite becoming finite in space and time, in intelligence and power. It simply means God manifest in humanity—not God made man, but God in man." [25] Karl Barth, a twentieth-century leader of Protestant theology, who had insisted in his early writings that God is "Wholly Other," later admitted he had gone too far, and wrote a remarkably different essay in which he confessed, "I should indeed have been somewhat embarrassed if one had invited me to speak on the humanity of God—say in the year 1920." [26] His eyes, he said, had been opened "to the fact that God might actually be wholly other than the God confined to the musty shell of the Christian-religious self-consciousness, and that as such He might act and speak." [27] Barth then coming to what he described as a "*Retraktation*" wrote, "It must now quite frankly be granted that we were at that time only partially in the right. . . . What expressions we used—in part taken over and in part newly invented!—above all, the famous 'wholly other.' " [28] After his agonizing preliminary, Barth came to the heart of his retraction: "It is precisely God's *deity* which, rightly understood, includes his *humanity*. . . . No, God requires no exclusion of humanity, no non-humanity, not to speak of inhumanity, in order to be truly God. . . . In this divinely free volition and election, in this sovereign decision (the ancients said, in His decree), God is *human.*" [29]

[25] Keshub Chunder Sen in his lecture "Great Men." Quoted by P. K. Sen, *Keshub Chunder Sen*, p. 59.

[26] *The Humanity of God.* London: Collins, 1961, p. 38.

[27] *Ibid.*, p. 40. Note the use of "wholly other" rather than "Wholly Other."

[28] *Ibid.*, p. 42.

[29] *Ibid.*, pp. 46, 50, 51. Curiously Barth blamed the Bible for his former inadequate conception: "The stone wall we first ran up against was that the theme of the Bible

If Hinduism is a humanism, it is not a humanism which excludes God, as does a typical Western humanism. Western humanism might be described as a limited humanism, but Hinduism is unlimited in its humanism because for it the human contains latent indefinite potentialities. God in man is a possession; but more—God in man is a task calling forth strenuous activity. The quest for God in Hinduism does not drive man away from man. "If I could persuade myself that I could find Him [God] in a Himalayan cave," wrote Gandhi, "I would proceed there immediately. But I know that I cannot find Him apart from humanity." [30]

In the previous four chapters on the *mārgas* we have noted some of their dependent relationships. There are three positions which can be taken relating these paths to the Perfection of Man: (1) they may be kept separate, (2) they may be complementary or preparatory to each other, and (3) they may be synthesized into an integral *mārga*.

Although Hinduism's basic temper is one of tolerance and compromise, there has been genuine conflict among the proponents of the various *mārgas*. The Advaitists and the Viśiṣṭādvaitists have not minimized their differences of opinion about the *mārgas*. An Advaita book such as the *Pāṣandachapeṭikā* (*Slap in the Face of the Heretics*) and the observation of a Śaiva Siddhantist that Śaṅkarites "prey" upon the populace [31] violate the traditional spirit of tolerance. Some Indian philosophers have regarded the *mārgas* as absolute alternatives, e.g., "Jñāna and karma alike reject bhakti, but bhakti is entirely indifferent to these. Jñāna, again, rejects karma, if karma is anything but wholly subservient, and similarly with karma's attitude to jñāna." [32] Others have taken the *sattva, rajas,* and *tamas* classification of the types of men and have added to this the division into introvertic (*daivī*) and extrovertic (*āsurī*) to yield six types of men, and have then argued that each type of man will necessarily select a *mārga* suitable to his personality. For example, an introvertive

---

is the deity of *God*, more exactly God's *deity*—God's independence and particular character, not only in relation to the natural but also to the spiritual cosmos; God's absolutely unique existence, might, initiative, above all, in His relation to man. Only in this manner were we able to understand the voice of the Old and New Testaments." *Ibid.*, p. 41. Barth said in a lecture given in Geneva at the Rencontres Internationales on September 1, 1949, "The Christian message is the message of the humanism of God. . . . the Christian message is not a case of a classical humanism nor of a new humanism which is to be rediscovered today, but rather of the humanism of God." Karl Barth, *Against the Stream*. London and Southampton: Camelot Press, 1954, p. 184. Dietrich Bonhoeffer also called attention to the anti-humanity tendency in Christianity: "There is a very real danger of our drifting into an attitude of contempt for humanity. . . . Even God did not despise humanity, but became Man for Man's sake." *Letters and Papers from Prison*. Translated by Reginald H. Fuller. New York: The Macmillan Company, 1953, pp. 24, 25.

[30] *Harijan*, August 29, 1936.

[31] R. W. Frazer, *Indian Thought Past and Present*, p. 72.

[32] Kalidas Bhattacharyya, *Alternative Standpoints in Philosophy*, p. 321.

sattva person will probably turn to *jñāna mārga*, and an extrovertive *rajas* person will find fulfillment in some form of *karma mārga*. The problem of relating six types of persons to only four *mārgas* is not puzzling when we note that there are conflicts within each of the *mārgas*: in *karma mārga* the emphasis may be on *dharma* (social duties, caste obligations, and moral restrictions) or on *saṁskāra* (ceremonies, rituals, rites, and sacraments); in *jñāna mārga* the emphasis may be on *vidyā* or *prajñā* (discursive knowledge, science, and learning) or on *dhyāna* or *jñāna* (meditation, direct knowledge, and wisdom); in *bhakti mārga* the emphasis may be on *prema* or *kāma* (active love and devotion) or on *prapatti* (surrender to the grace of the Lord); and in *yoga mārga* the emphasis may be on *haṭha* (physical discipline and bodily control) or on *rāja* (psychical discipline and mental control).

Many Hindus have supported the view that the *mārgas* are complementary to each other. For example, Swami Sivananda, speaking of the four ways, said, "These divisions are not hard and fast. There is no demarcation between one another. . . . Every Yoga [*mārga*] is a fulfillment of the preceding one." [33] Mal agrees, "The four methods . . . are not antagonistic to one another, but are, on the contrary, complementary. They all show the different methods of the Hindu religion are in harmony with each other. Each has its own proportion of importance, as it helps to lead the soul forward on its journey to the spiritual beatitude, the aim of all religions." [34] Some passages of the Upaniṣads suggest a harmony of the *mārgas*, e.g., "But those who seek for the Self by austerity, chastity, faith and knowledge, they, by the northern route, gain the sun." [35] While there is little opposition to the view that there is danger in excessive intellectualism, or emotionalism, or moralism, or asceticism, if each of the respective *mārgas* be pursued without due regard to the composite nature of man, the problem of the proper relationship of the four ways is not easily settled. According to an oft-repeated metaphor, the progress of man is like the flight of a bird in which one wing is *bhakti*, the other wing is *jñāna*, and the tail which acts as a rudder keeping balance between the wings is *yoga*. Śaṅkara accepted *karma* and *bhakti* as preparatory to *jñāna*, the only liberating *mārga*. Rāmānuja contended that *karma* and *jñāna* are aids to *bhakti*: "In the First Division comprising the First Six Lectures, it was shown that there are two Paths, viz., *Karma-Yoga* and *Jñāna-Yoga* by which as aspirant can achieve actual soul-realization. It was also shown that such soul-realization or soul-cogni-

[33] *Practical Lessons in Yoga*, pp. 11–12.

[34] Lala Kannoo Mal, *The Aphorisms of Narada*, p. 8.

[35] *Praśna Upaniṣad* 1. 10. Radhakrishnan translation. See also *Muṇḍaka Upaniṣad* 1. 2. 11 and *Śvetāśvatara Upaniṣad* 4. 17.

tion is ancillary (or stepping-stone) to God-Love known as *Bhakti*, or the Means by which to reach the Supreme Goal." [36] The *Bhāgavata Purāṇa*, oddly enough, gives in one passage the ordering of *karma* to *bhakti* to *jñāna*: "Actions done for the satisfaction of the Lord, produce devotion towards Him, and that devotion produces knowledge." [37] Brahma accepts this same ordering, and adds, "Karma, Bhakti and Jñāna may be regarded as disciplines suiting three different stages in the course of the development of the Sādhaka." [38] Govindācārya Swāmin offers the suggestion that *karma* leads to *jñāna*, and that *jñāna* is supportable only insofar as it is productive of *bhakti*.[39] Mouni Sadhu believes that until *rāja* and *haṭha yoga* have been mastered, it is impossible to practice *jñāna*.[40] Radhakrishnan argues that *jñāna, bhakti,* and *karma* are necessary, and names the dangers of pursuing any one in the absence of the restraining influences of the others, but he does not indicate which of the three is prior in temporal or axiological order:

> Each of them makes its own contribution to the whole, and is penetrated by the others. . . . The first reveals to us the truth, the second instills a love for it, and the third moulds life. Mere knowledge unvivified by the warmth of feeling, leads to icy coldness of heart; mere emotion, unlit by knowledge, is hysteria; mere action, unguided by wisdom and uninspired by love, is meaningless ritual or feverish unrest. All the three enter into the integral experience of a perfect life.[41]

It is interesting to note that on the next page Radhakrishnan remembers to add *yoga mārga*: "The Yoga discipline is intended to train the mind to hear the mighty voice of the silence within." [42] The Brahmo Samaj, the leading movement of the nineteenth-century renaissance of Hinduism, made many efforts to provide for the spectrum of *mārgas*. Two of the founders, Devendranath Tagore and Rammohan Roy, were vastly different types of men, the former emotional, the latter rational. Two hymns of the Brahmo Samaj on the same theme reveal this difference. The first is by Rammohan; the second is by one of the Tagore family.

> Remember the last fearful day,
> Others will speak, but thou shalt be silent;

[36] Proem to Rāmānuja's commentary on *Bhagavad Gītā* 13. A. Govindāchārya translation.
[37] 1. 5. 35.
[38] *Philosophy of Hindu Sādhanā*, p. 98.
[39] See Frazer, *Indian Thought Past and Present*, p. 233.
[40] *Concentration*, p. 42.
[41] *The Heart of Hindusthan*, pp. 9–10.
[42] *Ibid.*, p. 11.

Much care can preserve a grass, or a log of wood,
But no care can keep thy body from decay;
Therefore know the truth, leave vanity and worldliness,
Be resigned in spirit, and contemplate on the Great God.[43]

How much (is) Thy mercy,
I will not forget in life,
Day and night I will weave strung around (my) heart,
I will no more lie chained in the love of the world,
I will keep Thee in my soul,
Wealth, life, body, mind, I will give Thee all.[44]

Keshub Chunder Sen made full provision for the four *mārgas* in his movement, dividing his followers in 1876 into four groups depending upon the *mārga* each disciple preferred. He defined the four *mārgas* as union with God by introspection (*yoga*), by love (*bhakti*), by knowledge (*jñāna*), and by service to fellow men (*karma*), but in his own experience he preferred an organic union. He wrote in his autobiography, *Jeevan Veda,*

> When the love of God grew within me into a rapture, I felt that to give my feelings due steadiness, *Yoga* (communion with God by mental concentration) was necessary. This excitement of the devotional sentiment might be merely temporary, I must seek the means to give it permanence. *Bhakti* sweetens *Yoga,* but *Yoga* converts *Bhakti* into pure reverence. Perhaps *Bhakti* might have led me to superstition, perhaps *Yoga* might have led me to pantheism. But by the combination of the two, the gardens of Divine Love grew upon the mountains of communion.[45]

Perhaps the only conclusion that can be reached is that the *mārgas* are complementary and that each is necessary to temper the others, but the one given priority depends upon the preferences of the individual. The great Hindus of this century can be classified according to the *mārgas:* Rabindranath Tagore's *mārga* was *bhakti,* Mahatma Gandhi's *karma,* Aurobindo Ghose's *yoga,* and Sarvapalli Radhakrishnan's *jñāna*—yet none of these men excluded the other *mārgas* completely from his life. A composite or mixed (*miśrā*) *mārga* would be as ridiculous as a composite ideal man unless one of the *mārgas* is dominant, but the possibility of a synthesis into an integral *mārga* is a challenging and stimulating idea.

In *jñāna-karma-bhakti-yoga,* Hinduism offers ingredients of the full

[43] Quoted by P. C. Mozoomdar, *The Faith and Progress of the Brahmo Samaj,* p. 190.
[44] *Ibid.,* p. 194.
[45] Quoted by P. C. Mozoomdar, *Keshub Chunder Sen and His Times,* pp. 177–178.

life for man, but a Plato is lacking to write a *Philebus* prescribing the mixture of the ingredients. Two features of Indian life and thought have made such a mixture difficult. One is the tendency to let the aspect of the subject with which one is dealing at the moment crowd out all other aspects. Max Müller noticed this tendency in his study of early Vedic religion. It was the tendency to recognize the existence of only the god worshiped at the moment and to assign to that god the other gods as its powers. Max Müller called this kathenotheism or henotheism. Others have called it opportunistic monotheism. The second is the tolerance of contrary and conflicting points of view. Contradictions may even be entertained on the ground that they represent alternative viewpoints. This tolerance may grow out of an emphasis on peace, or it may be the result of an inherent sluggishness produced by the hot climate. The Hindu is invited to a life of reason, a life of action, and a life of love and joy which is to be channeled towards the goals most worth seeking. Science, religion, and art are to be mingled and directed to the *summum bonum*. Man is invited to play the theme of the Perfection of Man with four possible variations.

The *Bhagavad Gītā*, the source of much practical wisdom in Hinduism, is often distorted by interpreters who read into it the *mārga* they prefer. As Brajendranath Seal has said, "Each commentator accepts those passages of the *Gītā* which support his own preconceived dogma and distorts the meaning of the conflicting passages to harmonize with his dogma." [46] Seal argues that the *mārgas* are organically connected, and that they are unified in being centered on the Self; but he dodges the issue of the synthesis of the *mārgas* in the life of the individual. He says, "It would suffice for any one individual to follow the course of discipline laid down in any one of these divisions." [47] This, of course, would not be a synthesis of the *mārgas* in the life of the person, and on this issue Seal has nothing to say: "But it is a moot point whether any single individual may choose to go through the three courses successively." [48] Perhaps Seal has shown great wisdom in not trying to force the *Gītā* into even a single unified *mārga*. The life of each man is his to fashion. The synthesis of the

[46] *The Gītā: A Synthetic Interpretation*, p. 1. Cf. R. C. Zaehner's observation on the reforms Debendranath Tagore introduced into the Brahmo Samaj: "Debendranath rejected whatever did not agree with his own views, and compiled a selection of suitable passages from the Upanishads, the Epic, and elsewhere which he entitled Brahma Dharma, and this was to rank as the sacred book of the sect. This method of selecting only those parts of the scripture which fit in with one's own ideas was to be typical of the modern reformers and is particularly noticeable in the case of Gandhi." *Hinduism*, p. 201.

[47] *Ibid.*, p. 17.

[48] *Ibid.*

mārgas must be personalized and individualized. The great merit of the *Gītā* is in stating clearly and unequivocally the ingredients out of which a man must create his own synthesis. The balance (*samatvam*) cannot be prescribed; it must be achieved by each individual.

Rabindranath Tagore in an address in the chapel of Manchester College, Oxford University, on May 25, 1930, said,

> We in India are unfortunate in not having the chance to give expression to the best in us in creating intimate relations with the powerful nations, whose preparations are all leading to an enormous waste of resources in a competition of brow-beating and bluff. Some great voice is waiting to be heard which will usher in the sacred light of truth in the dark hours of the nightmare of politics, the voice which will proclaim that "God is over all," and exhort us never to covet, to be great in renunciation that gives us the wealth of spirit, strength of truth, leads us from the illusion of power to the fullness of perfection, to the *Śāntam,* who is peace eternal, to the *Advaitam,* who is the infinite One in the heart of the manifold. But we in India have not yet had the chance.[49]

Since 1947 India has had her chance, but thus far she has not fulfilled Tagore's hopes. Instead of bringing forth treasures from her five-thousand-year-old culture, the modern nation of India seems intent upon creating in the subcontinent of Asia a Europe of Asia. Thus far she has repeated the errors of Europe and America: conflicts among the states, conflicts between the states and the central government, conflicts between the public sector and the private sector, between Communists and non-Communists, between Muslims and Hindus, between labor and management, between the rural and the urban districts, and among political parties—and to these she has added tensions over language, caste, food and drink restrictions, cow protection, etc. Unhappily, the "wonder that was India." [50] has become the "crisis of India." [51] But it is too early to announce the end! India remains "a world in transition." [52] The big question is whether India can develop into a independent nation that is more humanistic than nationalistic, a nation that makes room for manyness without jeopardizing oneness. Can there arise a political state whose end is the Perfection of Man? Such a nation would inspire the peoples of the world to the realization of a human catholicism, a condition in which each person seeks reality, spirituality, integration, and liberation. The ideals are implicit in Hinduism: "Meet together, talk together, let

[49] *The Religion of Man,* pp. 235–236.
[50] A. L. Basham, *The Wonder That Was India.*
[51] Ronald Segal, *The Crisis of India.*
[52] Beatrice Pitney Lamb, *India, A World in Transition.*

your minds apprehend alike. . . . Common be your intention; common be the wishes of your hearts; common be your thoughts, so that there may be thorough union among you." [53] The realization is future. Man is yet to be led from the unreal to the real, for darkness to light, from death to immortality.

[53] Ṛg *Veda* 10. 191. 2, 4.

*Bibliography**

GENERAL

Abhedananda, Swami, *India and Her People*. New York: Vedanta Society, 1906.
Abid Husain, S., *Indian Culture*. Bombay: Asia Publishing House, 1963.
Abid Husain, S., *The National Culture of India*. Bombay: Asia Publishing House, 1961.
Acharya, Ananda, *Brahmadarsanam, An Introduction to the Study of Hindu Philosophy*. New York: The Macmillan Co., 1917.
Acharya, P. K., *Elements of Hindu Culture and Sanskrit Civilization*. Lahore: Mehar Chand Lachham Das, 1939.
Acharya, P. K., *Glories of India*. Allahabad: Jay Shankar Brothers, 1952.
Agarwalla, V. S., *India as Known to Panini*. Lucknow: University of Lucknow, 1953.
Akhilananda, Swami, *Mental Health and Hindu Psychology*. New York: Harper and Brothers, 1951.
Andrews, C. F., *The Renaissance in India*. London: Young People's Missionary Movement, 1912.
Appasamy, Aiyadurai Jesu Dasan, *Temple Bells*. London: Student Christian Movement Press, 1930.
Arapura, *Radhakrishnan and Integral Experience*. Bombay: Asia Publishing House, 1966.
Archer, William, *India and the Future*. London: Hutchinson and Co., 1917.
Arnold, Edwin, *East and West*. London: Longmans and Co., 1896.
Atmananda, Swami, *The Four Yogas*. Bombay: Bharatiya Vidya Bhavan, 1966.
Aurobindo, *The Foundations of Indian Culture*. New York: The Sri Aurobindo Library, 1953.
Aurobindo, *The Human Cycle*. Pondicherry: Sri Aurobindo Ashram, 1949.

* Works listed in this bibliography include both those used in this study and those recommended in five areas of study in Hinduism: General, *Jñāna Mārga*, *Karma Mārga*, *Bhakti Mārga*, and *Yoga Mārga*.

Aurobindo, *The Ideal of Human Unity*. Pondicherry: Sri Aurobindo Ashram, 1950.
Aurobindo, "Life-Value of Indian Philosophy." *Calcutta Review*, Vol. 63, May 1937.
Aurobindo, *Lights on Life Problems*. Bombay: Sri Aurobindo Circle, 1950.
Aurobindo, *The Renaissance in India*. Calcutta: Arya Publishing House, 1946.
Aurobindo, *The Riddle of This World*. Calcutta: Arya Publishing House, 1943.
Aurobindo, *Savitri—A Legend and a Symbol*. Pondicherry: Sri Aurobindo Ashram, 1950.
Aurobindo, *The Supernatural Manifestation upon Earth*. Pondicherry: Sri Aurobindo Ashram, 1952.

Bagchi, Prabodh Chandra (translator), *Pre-Aryan and Pre-Dravidian in India*. Essays by Sylvain Levi, Jean Przyluski and Jules Bloch. Calcutta: University of Calcutta, 1929.
Baij Nath, Lala, *Hinduism: Ancient and Modern*. Lucknow: Vaishya Hitkari, 1899.
Banerjea, J. N., *Development of Hindu Iconography*. Calcutta: University of Calcutta, 1956.
Banerjee, G. N., *India as Known to the Ancient World*. London: Humphrey Milford, 1921.
Barnett, L. D., *The Antiquities of India*. London: Philip Lee Warner, 1913.
Barnett, L. D., *The Heart of Hinduism*. London: John Murray, 1924.
Barnett, L. D., *The Heart of India*. London: John Murray, 1913.
Barth, A., *Bulletin on the Religions of India*. Calcutta: Firma K. L. Mukhopadhyaya, 1960.
Barth, A., *The Religions of India*. Translated by J. Wood. London: Kegan Paul, Trench, Trubner and Co., 1891.
Barua, Beninadhab, *A History of Pre-Buddhistic Indian Philosophy*. Calcutta: University of Calcutta, 1921.
Basham, A. L., "Hinduism," in *The Concise Encyclopaedia of Living Faiths*. Edited by R. C. Zaehner. New York: Hawthorne Books, 1959, pp. 225–260.
Basham, A. L., *Studies in Indian History and Culture*. Calcutta: Sambodhi Publishers, 1964.
Basham, A. L., *The Wonder That Was India: A Survey of the Culture of the Indian Sub-continent Before the Coming of the Muslims*. London: Sidgwick and Jackson, 1954.
Basu, Srisa Chandra (translator), *The Gheranda Samhita. Sacred Books of the Hindus*, Vol. 15, Part 2. Allahabad: The Panini Office, 1914.
Baynes, Herbert, *The Evolution of Religious Thought in Modern India*. London: S.P.C.K., 1889.
Beck, L. Adams, *The Story of Oriental Philosophy*. New York: Farrar and Rinehart, 1928.
Beidler, William, *The Concept of the Self in the Upanishads and Bhagavad Gītā*. A Ph.D. dissertation written by a Fulbright student at Osmania University.
Belvalkar, S. K. and Ranade, R. D., *History of Indian Philosophy*. Poona: Aryabhushan Press Office, 1927.
Bennet, Allan, *The Wisdom of the Aryans*. London: Kegan Paul, Trench, Trubner and Co., 1923.

Bernard, Theos, *Hindu Philosophy*. New York: Philosophical Library, 1947.
Bernard, Theos, *Penthouse of the Gods*. New York: C. Scribner's Sons, 1939.
Bernard, Theos, *Philosophical Foundations of India*. London: Rider and Co., 1948.
Besant, Annie, *Hindu Ideals*. Benares: Theosophical Publishing Society, 1904.
Bhagavan Das, *Ancient Solutions of Modern Problems*. Adyar: Theosophical Publishing House, 1933.
Bhagavan Das, *The Essential Unity of All Religions*. Madras: Theosophical Publishing House, 1940.
Bhagavan Das, *The Science of Peace*. Benares: Theosophical Publishing Society, 1904.
Bhandarkar, D. R., *Some Aspects of Ancient Indian Culture*. Madras: University of Madras, 1940.
Bhandarkar, R. G., *Collected Works of Sir R. G. Bhandarkar*. Edited by N. B. Utgikar and V. G. Paranjpe. Poona: Bhandarkar Oriental Research Institute, Vol. 1, 1933; Vol. 2, 1928; Vol. 3, 1927; Vol. 4, 1929.
Bhargava, P. L., *India in the Vedic Age*. Lucknow: Upper India Publishing House, 1956.
Bhattacharya, B. C., *Indian Images*. London: Thacker and Co., 1922.
Bhattacharyya, Benoytosh (translator), *Sādhanamālā*. Gaekwad's Oriental Series, Vols. 26, 41. Baroda: Oriental Institute, 1925, 1928.
Bhattacharyya, Hari Mohan, *Studies in Philosophy*. Adyar, Madras: Theosophical Publishing House, 1915.
Bhattacharyya, Kalidas, *Alternative Standpoints in Philosophy*. Calcutta: Das Gupta and Co., 1953.
Bhattacharyya, Kalidas (editor), *Recent Indian Philosophy*. Vol. 1. Calcutta: Progressive Publishers, 1963.
Bhattacharya, K. K. (translator), *Institutes of Parāśara*. Calcutta: Asiatic Society, 1887.
Bibliotheca Indica. Calcutta: Asiatic Society, 1848–
Bion, Walter Arnold, *Catalog of the Library of the Asiatic Society of Bengal*. Calcutta, 1884.
Bissoondoyal, Basdeo, *Hindu Scriptures*. London: P. R. Macmillan, 1960.
Blair, Chauncey J., *Heat in the Rig Veda and Atharva Veda*. New Haven: American Oriental Society, 1961.
Bloomfield, Maurice, *A Vedic Concordance*. Cambridge, Mass.: Harvard University Press, 1906.
Bose, Abinash Chandra, *Hymns from the Vedas*. Bombay: Asia Publishing House, 1966.
Bose, Ram Chandra, *Hindu Philosophy Popularly Explained*. New York: Funk and Wagnalls, 1884.
Bose, Sudhindra, "The Oriental Point of View—An Approach." *Prabuddha Bharata* (Calcutta), February 1936.
Boss, Medard, *A Psychiatrist Discovers India*. Translated by Henry A. Frey. Calcutta: Rupa and Co., 1966.
Bouquet, A. C., *Hinduism*. London: Hutchinson's University Library, 1948.
Brahma, Nalini Kanta, *Philosophy of Hindu Sādhanā*. London: Kegan Paul, Trench, Trubner and Co., 1932.
Brahmachari, Gangananada, "Hinduism: What It Means." *The Mother*, Vol. 8, No. 9, May 1966, pp. 379–383.

Brahmananda, Swami, *The Eternal Companion*. Hollywood: Vedanta Press, 1947.
Brown, George William, *The Human Body in the Upanishads*. Jubbulpore: Christian Mission Press, 1921.
Brown, George William, "The Sources of Indian Philosophical Ideas," in *Studies in Honor of Maurice Bloomfield*. New Haven: Yale University Press, 1920, pp. 75–88.
Brown, W. Norman, "The Basis for the Hindu Act of Truth." *The Review of Religion*, Vol. 5, 1940.
Brunton, Paul, *Indian Philosophy and Modern Culture*. New York: E. P. Dutton and Co., 1921.
Brunton, Paul, *The Spiritual Crisis of Man*. London: Rider and Co., 1952.
Burch, George Bosworth, "The Hindu Concept of Existence." *The Monist*, Vol. 50, No. 1, January 1966, pp. 44–54.
Butterworth, A., *The Substance of Indian Faith*. Camberley: the author, 1926.

Chaitanya, Krishna, *A New History of Sanskrit Literature*. New York: Asia Publishing Co., 1962.
Chakravarti, A., *Humanism and Indian Thought*. Madras: University of Madras, 1935.
Chakravarti, K. C., *Ancient Indian Culture and Civilization*. London: Luzac and Co., 1952.
Chakravarti, Sures Chandra, *Human Life and Beyond*. Calcutta: University of Calcutta Press, 1947.
Chang, Kun, *A Comparative Study of the Kaṭhinavastu*. Gravenhage: Mouton and Co., 1957.
Chatterjee, Satischandra, *The Fundamentals of Hinduism: A Philosophical Study*. Calcutta: Das Gupta and Co., 1950.
Chatterjee, Satis Chandra, "Hinduism," in *Silver Jubilee Commemoration Volume of The Indian Philosophical Congress*, 1950, pp. 119–130.
Chatterjee, Satis Chandra, and Datta, D. M., *An Introduction to Indian Philosophy*. Calcutta: University of Calcutta, 1939.
Chatterji, Suniti Kumar, *The Indian Synthesis, and Racial and Cultural Intermixture in India*. Ahmedabad: Gujarat Viday Sabha, 1953.
Chattopadhyaya, Debriprasad, *Lokāyata: A Study in Ancient Indian Materialism*. New Delhi: People's Publishing House, 1959.
Chaudhuri, Nirad Chandra, *The Autobiography of an Unknown Indian*. London: Macmillan and Co., 1951.
Chaudhuri, Nirad Chandra, *The Continent of Circe*. London: Chatto and Windus, 1965.
Childe, V. Gordon, *The Aryans*. London: Kegan Paul and Co., 1926.
Childe, V. Gordon, *New Light on the Most Ancient East*. London: Routledge and Kegan Paul, 1952.
Chirol, Valentine, *India Old and New*. London: Macmillan and Co., 1921.
Clark, Walter E., *Indian Conceptions of Immortality*. Cambridge: Harvard University Press, 1934.
Clayton, A. C., *The Rig-Veda and Vedic Religion*. London: Christian Literature Society for India, 1913.
Coleman, Charles, *The Mythology of the Hindus*. London: Parbury, Allen and Co., 1832.

Coomaraswamy, Ananda K., *The Dance of Shiva*. Bombay: Asia Publishing House, 1948.
Coomaraswamy, Ananda K., *Hinduism and Buddhism*. New York: Philosophical Library, 1943.
Coomaraswamy, Ananda K., *The Message of the East*. Madras: Ganesh and Co., 1909.
Coomaraswamy, Ananda K., *A New Approach to the Vedas*. London: Luzac, 1933.
Coomaraswamy, Ananda K., *Time and Eternity*. Ascona, Switzerland: Artibus Asia, 1947.

Dahlquist, Alan, *Megasthenes and Indian Religion*. Stockholm: Almquist and Wiksell, 1962.
Damodaran, K., *Indian Thought*. Bombay: Asia Publishing House, 1967.
Dandekar, R. N., *Vedic Bibliography*. Bombay: Karnatak Publishing House, 1946.
Darmsteter, James, *The Sacred Books of the East*. New York and London: The Colonial Press, 1900.
Das, Avinasa-Chandra, *Rig Vedic India*. Calcutta: University of Calcutta, 1921.
Das, A. C., *Studies in Philosophy*. Calcutta: Firma K. L. Mukhopadhyay, 1962.
Das, Ras-Vihari, *The Self and the Ideal*. Calcutta: Calcutta University Press, 1935.
Dasgupta, Shashi Bhusan, *Aspects of Indian Religious Thought*. Calcutta: A. Mukherjee and Co., 1957.
Dasgupta, Surendra Nath, *Hindu Mysticism*. Chicago, London: The Open Court Publishing Co., 1927.
Dasgupta, Surendra Nath, *A History of Indian Philosophy*. Cambridge: Cambridge University Press, Vol. 1, 1922; Vol. 2, 1932; Vol. 3, 1940; Vol. 4, 1949; Vol. 5, 1955.
Dasgupta, Surendra Nath, and De, S. K., *History of Sanskrit Literature* (*Classical Period*). Calcutta: University of Calcutta, 1947.
Dasgupta, Surendra Nath, *Indian Idealism*. Cambridge: The University Press, 1933.
Dasgupta, Surendra Nath, *Philosophical Essays*. Calcutta: Calcutta University Press, 1942.
Datta, D. M., *Chief Currents in Contemporary Philosophy*. Calcutta: University of Calcutta, 1961.
Datta, Dhirendra Mohan, "India's Debt to the West in Philosophy." *Philosophy: East and West*, Vol. 6, No. 3, October 1956, pp. 195–212.
Datta, Hirendra-Natha, *Indian Culture, Its Strands and Trends*. Calcutta: Calcutta University Press, 1941.
De, S. K., *Aspects of Sanskrit Literature*. Calcutta: Firma K. L. Mukhopadhyay, 1959.
De, Sushil Kumar, *History of Sanskrit Literature*. Calcutta: University of Calcutta, 1947.
deBary, Wm. Theodore (editor), *Approaches to the Oriental Classics: Asian Literature and Thought in General Education*. New York: Columbia University Press, 1959.
deBary, Wm. Theodore and Embree, Ainslee T., (editors), *A Guide to Oriental Classics*. New York: Columbia University Press, 1964.

deBary, Wm. Theodore, Hay, Stephen H., Weiler, Royal, and Yarrow, Andrew, *Sources of Indian Tradition*. New York: Columbia University Press, 1958.

Delaire, Jean, *The Story of the Soul in East and West*. London: Philosophical Publishing House, 1949.

Desmukh, P. S., *The Origin and Development of Religion in Vedic Literature*. London: Oxford University Press, 1933.

Devanandan, Paul David, *Christian Concern in Hinduism*. Bangalore: Christian Institute for the Study of Religion and Society, 1961.

Devanandan, Paul David, *The Concept of Māyā*. London: Lutterworth Press, 1950.

Devanandan, P. D., *The Dravida Kazhagam: A Revolt against Brahmanism*. Bangalore: Christian Institute for the Study of Religion and Society, 1960.

Devanandan, P. D., *Living Hinduism: A Descriptive Survey*. Bangalore: Christian Institute for the Study of Religion and Society, 1958.

Devanandan, Paul David, "The Renaissance of Hinduism. A survey of Hindu Religious History from 1800 to 1910." *Theology Today*, Vol. 12, pp. 189–205.

Devi, Akshaya-Kumari, *The Evolution of the Rigvedic Pantheon*. Calcutta: Vijaya Krishna Bros., 1938.

Dilger, Wilhelm, *Salvation in Hinduism and Christianity*. Translated by Luise Oehler. Mangalore: Basel Mission Press, 1908.

Diwan-Chmad Obhrai, *Song of the Soul, or the Sacred Science of Self*. Lahore: Civil and Military Gazette, 1939.

Dixit, V. V., *Relation of the Epics to the Brāhmana Literature*. Poona: Oriental Book Agency, 1950.

Dowson, John, *A Classical Dictionary of Hindu Mythology and Religion, Geography, History, and Literature*. Sixth edition. London: Kegan Paul, Trench, Trubner and Co., 1928.

Dutt, P. G., "The Doctrine of Māyā." *The Philosophical Quarterly*, April 1936.

Dutt, R. C., *Ancient India*. London: Longmans, Green and Co., 1893.

Dutt, Romesh Chunder, *A History of Civilization in Ancient India*. 3 vols. Calcutta: Thacker, Spink and Co., 1889–90.

Dvivedi, Manilal N. (translator), *The Jivanmukti-Viveka*, or *The Path to Liberation in this Life by Swami Śri Vidyāraṇyasarswati*. Bombay: Tookaram Tatya, 1897.

Eaton, Gai, *The Richest Vein, Eastern Tradition and Modern Thought*. London: Faber and Faber, 1949.

Edgerton, Franklin, *The Beginnings of Indian Philosophy*. London: Allen and Unwin, 1965.

Edgerton, Franklin, "Dominant Ideas in the Formation of Indian Culture." *Journal of the American Oriental Society*. Vol. 62, September 1942, pp. 151–156.

Edgerton, Franklin, "The Upanishads: What do they seek, and why?" *Journal of the American Oriental Society*, Vol. 49, 1929, pp. 97–121.

Edwardes, Allen, *The Rape of India: A Biography of Robert Clive and a Sexual History of the Conquest of Hindustan*. New York: The Julian Press, 1966.

Elliot, Charles Norton Edgecumbe, *Hinduism and Buddhism: an Historical Sketch*. London: E. Arnold and Co., 1921.

Faddegon, Barend, *The Vaiçeṣika System*. Amsterdam: J. Muller, 1918.

Farquhar, J. N., *The Crown of Hinduism*. London: Oxford University Press, 1915.

Farquhar, J. N., *An Outline of the Religious Literature of India*. London: Oxford University Press, 1920.

Farquhar, J. N., *A Primer of Hinduism*. London: Oxford University Press, 1912.

Fausset, Hugh I'Anson, *The Flame and the Light*. London: Abelard-Schuman, 1958.

Frazer, R. W., *Indian Thought, Past and Present*. London: Unwin, 1915.

Frazer, R. W., *A Literary History of India*. London: Unwin, 1897.

Fryer, John, *A New Account of East India and Persia*. London: Hakluyt Society, 1909–1915.

Garbe, Richard, *The Philosophy of Ancient India*. Chicago: Open Court Publishing Co., 1897.

Garratt, Geoffrey Theodore (editor), *The Legacy of India*. Oxford: The Clarendon Press, 1937.

Geldner, K. F., *Der Rig-Veda. Harvard Oriental Series*, Vols. 33–35. Cambridge, Mass.: Harvard University Press, 1951.

Ghoshal, Upendra Nath, *Studies in Indian History and Culture*. Bombay: Orient Longmans, 1957.

Giri, Mahadevananda, *Vedic Culture*. Calcutta: Calcutta University, 1947.

Glasenapp, Helmuth von, *Der Hinduismus*. München: Kurt Wolff Verlag, 1922.

Glasenapp, Helmuth von, *Immortality and Salvation in Indian Religions*. Translated by E. F. J. Payne. Calcutta: Susil Gupta India, 1963.

Gode, P. K., *Studies in Indian Literary History*. Bombay: Singhi Jain Shastra Shikshapith, 1953.

Goetz, H., *The Crisis of Indian Civilization in the 18th and 19th Centuries*. Calcutta: University of Calcutta, 1938.

Gokhale, B. G., *Ancient India, History and Culture*. Bombay: Asia Publishing House, 1952.

Gokhale, B. G., *Indian Thought Through the Ages: A Study of Some Dominant Concepts*. Bombay: Asia Publishing House, 1961.

Gokhale, B. G., *The Making of the Indian Nation*. Bombay: Asia Publishing House, 1958.

Goldstucker, Theodore, *Inspired Writings of Hinduism*. Calcutta: Susil Gupta, 1952.

Gonda, Jan, *Die Religionen Indiens. I, Veda und älterer Hinduismus*. Stuttgart, 1960.

Gonda, Jan, *Epithets in the Ṛgveda*. Gravenhage: Mouton and Co., 1959.

Gonda, Jan, *Notes on Brahman*. Utrecht: J. L. Beyers, 1950.

Gonda, Jan, *Some Observations on the Relations between "Gods" and "Powers" in the Veda*. The Hague: Mouton and Co., 1957.

Gonda, Jan, *The Vision of the Vedic Poets*. The Hague: Mouton and Co., 1963.

Gongulee, Kumudini Kant, *Self-control and Self-realization*. Dacca: Nagendra Kumar Ray, 1916.

Goshal, Kumar, *The People of India*. New York: Sheridan House Publishers, 1944.

Gough, Archibald Edward, *The Philosophy of the Upanishads and Ancient Indian Metaphysics*. London: Kegan Paul, Trench, Trubner and Co., 1882.
Gough, Archibald Edward (translator), *The Vaiśeṣika Sūtras of Kaṇāda with Comments from the Upaskāra of Śaṅkara-miśra and the Vivṛitti of Jaya-nārāyaṇatarkaparichānana*. Benares: E. J. Lazarus and Co., 1873.
Govindā-Dāsa, *Hinduism*. Madras: G. A. Natesan and Co., 1924.
Gowan, Herbert H., *A History of Indian Literature*. New York: D. Appleton and Co., 1931.
Gray, Louis H. (translator), *Vāsavadattā: A Sanskrit Romance by Subandhu*. Delhi: Motilal Banarsidass, 1962.
Grierson, G. A., *The Modern Vernacular Literature of Hindustan*. Calcutta: Asiatic Society, 1889.
Griffith, Ralph T. H., *The Hymns of the Atharva-Veda*. Benares: E. J. Lazarus and Co., 1895.
Griffith, Ralph T. H., *The Hymns of the Ṛgveda*. Benares: E. J. Lazarus, 1889.
Griffith, Ralph T. H., *The Texts of the White Yajurveda*. Varanasi: M. L. Abhimanyu, 1957.
Griswold, Hervey De Witt, *Brahman: A Study in the History of Indian Philosophy*. New York: The Macmillan Co., 1900.
Griswold, Hervey De Witt, *Insights into Modern Hinduism*. New York: Henry Holt and Co., 1934.
Griswold, Hervey De Witt, *The Religion of the Rigveda*. London, New York: Oxford University Press, Humphrey Milford, 1923.
Grousset, René, *The Civilization of India*. Translated by Catherine A. Phillips. New York: Tudor, 1939.
Growse, F. S., *Mathunā: A District Memoir*. North-Western Provinces and Oudh Government Press, 1880.
Guénon, René, *East and West*. Translated by William Massey. London: Luzac and Co., 1941.
Guénon, René, *Introduction to the Study of the Hindu Doctrines*. Translated by Marco Pallio. London: Luzac and Co., 1945.

Haas, William S., *The Destiny of Mind: East and West*. London: Faber and Faber, 1956.
Haigh, Henry, *Some Leading Ideas of Hinduism*. Madras: Christian Literature Society for India, 1928.
Hammet, Frederick S., "Ideas of the Ancient Hindus Concerning Man," *Isis*, Vol. 28, 1938.
Harcourt, Henry, *Sidelights on the Crisis in India*. London: Longmans and Co., 1924.
Harper, Edward B., *Religion in South Asia*. Seattle: University of Washington Press, 1964.
Harrison, Selig S., *India: The Most Dangerous Decades*. Princeton: Princeton University Press, 1960.
Heimann, Betty, *Facets of Indian Thought*. New York: Schocken Books, 1964.
Heimann, Betty, *Indian and Western Philosophy, A Study in Contrasts*. London: George Allen and Unwin, 1937.
Hein, Norvin J., "Hinduism," in *A Reader's Guide to the Great Religions*. Edited by Charles J. Adams. London: Collier-Macmillan, 1965, pp. 45–82.
Hillebrandt, Alfred, *Lieder des Rigveda*. Leipzig: J. C. Hinrichśsche, 1913.

Hillebrandt, Alfred, *Vedische Mythologie*. Breslau: 1891–1902.

Hiriyanna, Mysore, *The Essentials of Indian Philosophy*. London: George Allen and Unwin, 1932.

Hiriyanna, Mysore, *Indian Philosophical Studies*. Mysore: Kavyalaya Publishers, 1957.

Hiriyanna, Mysore, "The Message of Indian Philosophy." *The Philosophical Quarterly*, Vol. 16, April 1940, pp. 14–28.

Hiriyanna, Mysore, "A Neglected Ideal of Life," in *Indian Philosophical Congress Silver Jubilee Volume*, Calcutta, 1950, pp. 222–227.

Hiriyanna, Mysore, *Outlines of Indian Philosophy*. London: George Allen and Unwin, 1932.

Hiriyanna, Mysore, *Popular Essays in Indian Philosophy*. Mysore: Kavyalaya Publishers, 1952.

Hiriyanna, Mysore, *The Quest After Perfection*. Mysore: Kavyalaya Publishers, 1952.

Holdich, T. H., *India*. London: Henry Frowde, 1905.

Hopkins, Edward Washburn, Epic Mythology. Strassburg: Verlag Von Karl J. Trübner, 1915.

Hopkins, Edward Washburn, *Legends of India*. New Haven: Yale University Press, 1928.

Hopkins, Edward Washburn, *The Religions of India*. Boston: Ginn, 1898.

Howells, G., *The Soul of India*. London: Alexander and Shepherd, 1913.

Humayun Kabir (editor), *Green and Gold*. Calcutta: Asia Publishing House, 1957.

Humayun Kabir, *The Indian Heritage*. Bombay: Asia Publishing House, 1955.

Hume, R. A., *An Interpretation of India's Religious History*. New York: Fleming H. Revell Co., 1911.

Husain, Yusuf, *Glimpses of Medieval Indian Culture*. Bombay: Asia Publishing House, 1957.

Hypes, James Lowell, *Spotlights on the Culture of India*. Washington: Daylion Co., 1937.

Ingalls, Daniel H. M. (translator), *An Anthology of Sanskrit Court Poetry*. Cambridge: Harvard University Press, 1964.

International Bibliography of the History of Religions. Leiden, Netherlands: E. J. Brill, 1954.

Jackson, R. J., *India's Quest for Reality*. London: Buddhist Lodge, 1938.

Jacobs, Hans, *Western Psychotherapy and Hindu Sadhana*. London: International Universities Press, 1961.

Jaini, J. L. (translator), *The Atma-siddhi, or The Self-Realization of Shrimad Rajchandra*. Ahmedabad: Shrimad Raja Chandra Gyan Pracharak Trust, 1960.

Jha, Ganganatha (translator), *Mīmāṁsā Sūtra. Gaekwad's Oriental Series*, Vols. 66, 70, 73. Baroda: Oriental Institute, 1933, 1934, 1936.

Jones, John Peter, *India: Its Life and Thought*. New York: The Macmillan Co., 1908.

Kaegi, Adolph, *The Rig Veda: the Oldest Literature of the Indians*. Boston: Ginn and Co., 1886.

Kama Khya Nath Tarkabagisa, *Lectures on Hindu Philosophy*. Part 1. Translated by Akhil Chandra Chatterji. Calcutta: Gopal Chandra Mookerjee, 1910.

Kamath, M. A., *Hinduism and Modern Science*. Mangalore: Sharada, 1947.

Kanal, S. P., *Dialogues on Indian Culture*. Delhi: Panchal, 1956.

Kane, P. V. and Joshi, C. N., *Uttararamacarita of Bhavabhuti*. Delhi, 1962.

Karmarkar, A. P. and Kalamdani, N. B., *Mystic Teachings of the Haridāsas of Karṇāṭaka*. Dharwar: Karnataka Vidyavardhaka Sangha, 1939.

Karmarkar, A. P., *The Religions of India*. Lonarla: Mira Publishing House, 1950.

Keay, F. E., *A History of Hindi Literature*. Calcutta: Association Press, 1920.

Keith, A. Berriedale, *Classical Sanskrit Literature*. Oxford: The Clarendon Press, 1923.

Keith, A. Berriedale, *A History of Sanskrit Literature*. Oxford: The Clarendon Press, 1928.

Keith, A. Berriedale, *Indian Mythology. The Mythology of All Races*. Edited by Louis Herbert Gray. Vol. 6, pp. 1–250. Boston: Marshall Jones Co., 1917.

Keith, Arthur Berriedale, *Rigveda Brāhmaṇas. Harvard Oriental Series*, Vol. 25. Cambridge, Mass.: Harvard University Press, 1920.

Keith, Arthur Berriedale, "Some Problems of Indian Philosophy." *Indian Historical Quarterly*, Vol. 8, 1932, pp. 426–441.

Keith, A. B. (translator), *The Veda of the Black Yajur School entitled Taittitiya Sanhitā*. Cambridge, Mass.: Harvard University Press, 1914.

Kesavan, B. S. and Kulkarni, V. Y. (editors), *National Bibliography of Indian Literature: 1901–1953*. New Delhi: Sāhitya Akademi, 1962.

Kolanda, Rao P., *East versus West, A Denial of Contrast*. London: George Allen and Unwin, 1939.

Konow, Stan and Tuxen, Paul, *The Religions of India*. Copenhagen: E. C. Gad Publishers, 1949.

Kosambi, D. D., *The Culture and Civilization of Ancient India in Historical Outline*. London: Routledge and Kegan Paul, 1965.

Kosambi, D. D., *An Introduction to the Study of Indian History*. Bombay: Popular Book Depot, 1956.

Kosambi, Damodar Dharmanand, *Myth and Reality*. Bombay: Popular Prakashan, 1962.

Krause, Charlotte, *The Kaleidoscope of Indian Wisdom*. Bhavnagar: Phulchandji Ved, 1929.

Krishnamachariar, K., *History of Classical Sanskrit Literature*. Madras: T. T. Devasthanams Press, 1937.

Krishnaswami Aiyangar, S., *Ancient India*. London: Luzac and Co., 1911.

Krishnaswami Aiyangar, S., *Some Contributions of South India to Indian Culture*. Calcutta: Calcutta University, 1923.

Kulandran, S., *Resurgent Religions*. London: Lutterworth Press, 1957.

Lacombe, Oliver, "Reflections on Indian Philosophy." *Diogenes*. No. 24, 1958, pp. 32–41.

Lahiri, Anadi Kumar, *Comparative Studies in Philosophy*. Calcutta: the author, 1963.

Lal, Chaman (editor), *Spiritual Stories from India*. Tokyo: Charles E. Tuttle Co., 1964.

Lal, P. (translator), *Great Sanskrit Plays in Modern Translation*. New York: New Directions, 1963.

Lal, Shyam, *Retransformation of Self*. Gwalior: G. S. Nivas, 1927.
Lamb, Beatrice Pitney, *India, A World in Transition*. New York: Frederick A. Praeger, 1963.
Lane-Poole, S., *Mediaeval India*. Calcutta: Susil Gupta, 1951.
Law, Narendra Nath, "Age of the Ṛgveda." *The Indian Historical Quarterly*, Vol. 36, Nos. 2–4, 1960, Supplement; Vol. 37, Nos. 1–4, 1961, Supplement.
Law, Narendra Nath, *Studies in Indian History and Culture*. London: Luzac and Co., 1925.
Lemaitre, Solange, *Hinduism*. Translated by J. F. Brown. New York: Hawthorne Books, 1959, 1960.
Luckmidas, Keshavjee R. (compiler), *Modern India Thinks*. Bombay: D. B. Taraporevala Sons and Co., 1932.
Lyall, Alfred C., *Asiatic Studies*. London: John Murray, 1899.

McCrindle, John Watson (translator), *Ancient India as Described in Classical Literature*. London: Archibald Constable and Co., 1901.
McCrindle, John Watson, *Ancient India as described by Megasthenes and Arrian*. Calcutta: Thacker, Spink and Co., 1877.
MacDonald, Kenneth Somerled, *The Vedic Religion*. London: Nisbet and Co., 1881.
Macdonell, Arthur Anthony, *A History of Sanskrit Literature*. London: D. Appleton and Co., 1929.
Macdonell, Arthur Anthony, *Hymns from the Rig-Veda*. London: Oxford University Press, 1923.
Macdonell, Arthur A., *India's Past: A Survey of Her Literature, Religions, Languages and Antiquities*. Oxford: Clarendon Press, 1927.
Macdonell, Arthur A. and Keith, A. B., *Vedic Index of Names and Subjects*. London: John Murray, 1907.
Macdonell, Arthur Anthony, *Vedic Mythology*. Strasbourg: R. J. Trübner, 1897.
Macdonell, Arthur Anthony, *A Vedic Reader for Students*. Oxford: Clarendon Press, 1917.
Macfie, J. M., *Myths and Legends of India*. Edinburgh: T. and T. Clark, 1924.
Mackay, E., *Early Indus Civilizations*. London: Luzac and Co., 1948.
MacKenzie, Donald A., *Indian Myth and Legend: Myth and Legend in Literature and Art*. London: Gresham Publishing Co., 1910.
McLaurin, Hamish, *Eastern Philosophy for Western Minds*. Boston: The Strafford Co., 1933.
Macnicol, Nicol, *Hindu Scriptures*. London: J. M. Dent and Sons, 1938.
Macnicol, Nicol, *India in the Dark Wood*. London: Edinburgh House Press, 1930.
Macnicol, Nicol, *The Making of Modern India*. London: Oxford University Press, 1924.
Madhava, Son of Mayana, *A Handbook of Hindu Pantheism*. Translated by Nandalal Dhole. Calcutta: Dhole's Vedanta Series, 1886.
Mahadevan, R., "The Conception of Personality in Indian Materialism," *The Philosophical Quarterly*, Vol. 14, October, 1938.
Essays in Philosophy Presented to Dr. T. M. P. Mahadevan on his Fiftieth Birthday. Madras: Ganesh and Co., 1962.
Mahadevan, T. M. P., *Outlines of Hinduism*. Bombay: Chetana, 1960.

Mahadevan, T. M. P., "The Re-Discovery of Man," in *Proceedings of 30th Indian Philosophical Congress*, Nagpur, 1955, pp. 3–22.
Mahadevan, T. M. P., *Time and the Timeless*. Madras: Upanishad Vihar, 1953.
Maitra, Harendranath, *Hinduism: The World Ideal*. London: Cecil Palmer and Hayward, 1916.
Maitra, S. K., *The Spirit of Indian Philosophy*. Benares: the author, 1947.
Maitra, Susil Kumar, *Fundamental Questions of Indian Metaphysics and Logic*. Calcutta: Chuckervertty, Chatterjee and Co., 1956.
Maitra, Susil Kumar, *Studies in Philosophy and Religion*. Calcutta: Chuckervertty, Chatterjee and Co., 1941.
Maity, Pradyot Kumar, *Historical Studies in the Cult of the Goddess Manasā*. Calcutta: Punthi Pustak, 1966.
Majumdar, R. C., Raychaudhuri, H. C. and Datta, Kalinkar, *An Advanced History of India*. London: Macmillan and Co., 1958.
Majumdar, R. C., *Ancient India*. Banaras: Motilal Baranasidas, 1952.
Majumdar, R. C., *The Classical Accounts of India*. Calcutta: Firma K. L. Mukhopadhyay, 1960.
Majumdar, R. C. and Pusalkar, A. D., (editors), *The History and Culture of the Indian People*. London: George Allen and Unwin, 1951.
Mal, Bahadur, *A Story of Indian Culture*. Hoshiarpur: Vishveshvaranand Vedic Research Institute, 1956.
Malkani, G. R., *The Meaning and Problem of Philosophy*. Amalner: Indian Institute of Philosophy, 1930.
Malkani, G. R., "Spirituality—Eastern and Western." *The Philosophical Quarterly*, Vol. 37, No. 2, July 1964, pp. 103–110.
Malkani, G. R., *Vedantic Epistemology*. Amalner: The Indian Institute of Philosophy, 1953.
Mankar, G. A., *A Sketch of the Life and Works of the Late Mr. Justice M. G. Ranade*. Bombay: Caxton Printing Works, 1902.
Mankekar, D. R., *Twenty-two Fateful Days*. Bombay: Manaktalas, 1966.
Manshardt, Clifford, *The Hindu-Muslim Problem in India*. London: George Allen and Unwin, 1936.
Marshall, John Hubert and others, *Mohenjo Daro and the Indus Civilization*. London: Arthur Probsthain, 1931.
Masson-Oursel, Paul, *Ancient India and Indian Civilization*. Translated by M. R. Dobie. London: Kegan Paul, Trench, Trubner and Co., 1934.
Masson-Oursel, Paul, *Comparative Philosophy*. London: Kegan Paul, Trench, Trubner and Co., 1926.
Mees, G. H., "*The Psychology of Anima and Animus and Conceptions of Eastern Schools*." Ninth All India Oriental Conference, Trivandrum, 1940.
Mehta, G. L., *Understanding India*. Bombay: Asia Publishing House, 1959.
Mehta, P. D., *Early Indian Religious Thought*. London: Luzac and Co., 1956.
Mishra, Mahamahopadhyaya Umesha, *History of Indian Philosophy*, Vol. 1. Allahabad: Tirabhukti Publications, 1957.
Mishra, Umesha, *Conception of Matter According to Nyāya-Vaiçesika*. Allahabad: the author, 1936.
Mitchell, John Murray, *Hinduism, Past and Present*. London: Religious Tract Society, 1897.
Mitra, Sisirkumar, *The Future of India*. Madras: Sri Aurobindo Library, 1941.
Mitra, Sisirkumar, *The Vision of India*. Bombay: Jaico Book Co., 1949.

Modak, Manorama R., *The Land and the People of India*. New York: J. B. Lippincott Co., 1945.

Mohana Simha, M. A., *The Mysticism of Time in Rig Veda*. Lahore: Atma Ram and Sons, 1939.

Monier-Williams, Sir Monier, *Brahmanism and Hinduism*. New York: Macmillan and Co., 1891.

Monier-Williams, Sir Monier, *Buddhism, in its Connexion with Brahmanism and Hinduism, and its Contrast with Christianity*. London: John Murray, 1889.

Monier-Williams, Sir Monier, *Hinduism*. Calcutta: Susil Gupta, 1877.

Monier-Williams, Sir Monier, *Indian Wisdom*. London: William H. Allen and Co., 1875.

Monier-Williams, Sir Monier, *Religious Thought and Life in India*. London: John Murray, 1883.

Monro, W. D., *Stories of Indian Gods and Heroes*. London: George G. Harrap, 1911.

Mookerji, Radha Kumad, *Hindu Civilization*. London: Longmans, Green and Co., 1936.

Mookerji, Radha Kumad, *Men and Thought in Ancient India*. London: Macmillan and Co., 1924.

Moore, Charles A. (editor), *The Indian Mind*. Honolulu: East-West Center Press, 1967.

Moreland, W. H. and Chatterjee, Atul Chandra, *A Short History of India*. Fourth edition. London: Longmans, Green and Co., 1956.

Morgan, Kenneth W. (editor), *The Religion of the Hindus*. New York: Ronald Press, 1953.

Morrison, John, *New Ideas in India during the Nineteenth Century*. London: Simpkin, Marshall and Co., 1906.

Motwani, Kewal, *India: A Conflict of Cultures*. Nagpur: Nagpur University, 1946.

Motwani, Kewal, *India: A Synthesis of Cultures*. Bombay: Thacker and Co., 1947.

Mudaliyar, S. Sabaratna, *Essentials of Hinduism*. Madras: Maykandan Press, 1915.

Mukerjee, Radhakamal, *The Culture and Art of India*. London: George Allen and Unwin, 1959.

Mukerjee, Radhakamal, *Dimensions of Values*. London: George Allen and Unwin, 1964.

Mukerjee, Radhakamal, *The Flowering of Indian Art: the Growth and Spread of a Civilization*. Bombay: Asia Publishing House, 1964.

Mukerjee, Radhakamal, *The Fundamental Unity of India*. London: Longmans and Co., 1914.

Mukerjee, Radhakamal, *A History of Indian Civilization*. Bombay: Hind Kitabs, 1958.

Mukerjee, Radhakamal, *The Indian Scheme of Life*. Bombay: Hind Kitabs, 1951.

Mukerjee, Radhakamal, *The Philosophy of Personality*. Bombay: Allied Publishers, 1963.

Mukerji, Chuni, *A Modern Hindu View of Life*. London and Calcutta: S.P.C.K., 1930.

Mukerji, Nirod, *Standing at the Crossroads*. New Delhi: Allied Publishers, 1964.
Mukharji, Dhan Gopal, *Disillusioned India*. New York: E. P. Dutton, *c*. 1930.
Mukharji, Dhan Gopal, *The Face of Silence*. New York: E. P. Dutton, 1930.
Mukharji, Dhan Gopal, *My Brother's Face*. London: Thornton Butterworth, 1936.
Mukharji, Dhan Gopal, *A Son of Mother India Answers*. New York: E. P. Dutton and Co., 1928.
Müller, F. Max, *Heritage of India*. Calcutta: Susil Gupta, 1951.
Müller, F. Max, *A History of Ancient Sanskrit Literature*. London: Williams and Norgate, 1860.
Müller, F. Max, *India: What Can It Teach Us?* New York: Funk and Wagnalls, 1883.
Müller, F. Max (editor), *The Sacred Books of the East*. 50 volumes. Oxford: The Clarendon Press, 1879–1925.
Müller, F. Max, *The Six Systems of Indian Philosophy*. London and New York: Longmans, Green and Co., 1928.

Naipaul, V. S., *An Area of Darkness*. London: Andre Deutsch, 1964.
Narahari, H. G., *Ātman in Pre-Upanishadic Vedic Literature*. Madras: Vasanta Press, 1944.
Narahari, H. G., "The Meaning of Brahman and Ātman in the Ṛgveda." *Indian Culture*, Vol. 3, December 1941–March 1942.
Narahari, H. G., " 'Soul' in the Ṛgveda." *Review of Philosophy and Religion*, Vol. 11, April 1942.
Narang, Gokul Chand, *Glorious Hinduism*. New Delhi: New Book Society of India, 1966.
Narang, Gokul Chand, *Real Hinduism*. Lahore: New Book Society, 1947.
Narasimham, P., "The Individual in Progress." Miller Lectures, University of Madras, 1939–1940.
Narasimham, P., "The Quest after Perfection." Miller Lectures, University of Madras, 1939–1940.
Naravane, V. S., *The Elephant and the Lotus—Essays in Philosophy and Culture*. Bombay: Asia Publishing House, 1965.
Naravane, V. S., *Modern Indian Thought*. Bombay: Asia Publishing House, 1964.
Naravane, V. S., *Stories from the Indian Classics*. Bombay: Asia Publishing House, 1962.
Narayanaswami Aiyar, K., *The Thirty-two Vidyas*. Madras: The Adyar Library and Research Center, 1962.
Natarajan, P., *The Word of the Guru*. Bangalore: Gurukula Publishing House, 1952.
Nath, Rai Bahadur Lala Baij, *Ancient and Modern Hinduism*. Meerut: Office of the Vaishya Hitkari, 1899.
Nath, Rai Bahadur Pandit Kashi, *The Ideals of Hinduism*. Bombay: D. B. Taraporevala, 1932.
Nehru, Jawaharlal, *Jawaharlal Nehru's Speeches*. The Publications Division, Ministry of Information and Broadcasting, Government of India. Vol. 1, 1949; Vol. 2, 1954; Vol. 3, 1958.
Nehru, Jawaharlal, *The Unity of India*. London: Lindsay Drummond, 1941.

Nikhilananda, Swami, *The Essence of Hinduism.* New York: Ramakrishna-Vivekananda Center, 1946.

Nikhilananda, Swami, *Hinduism: Its Meaning for the Liberation of the Spirit.* New York: Harper and Brothers, 1958.

Nirvedananda, Swami, *Hinduism at a Glance.* Bengal: Vidyamandira, 1944.

Noble, Margaret Elizabeth and Coomaraswamy, Ananda K., *Myths of Hinduism.* London: Harrap, 1920.

Noble, Margaret Elizabeth, *The Web of Indian Life.* Mayavita, Almora: Advaita Ashrama, 1904.

Northrop, Filmer S. C., *The Meeting of East and West.* New York: The Macmillan Co., 1946.

Oldenberg, Hermann, *Ancient India, Its Language and Religion.* Chicago: Open Court, 1898.

Oldenberg, Hermann, *Die Indische Philosophie.* Leipzig: B. G. Teubner, 1913.

Oldenberg, Hermann, *Die Religion des Veda.* Berlin: W. Hertz, 1894.

O'Malley, Lewis Sydney Steward, *Modern India and the West: A Study of the Interaction of their Civilizations.* London: Oxford University Press, 1941.

O'Malley, Lewis Sydney Steward, *Popular Hinduism.* Cambridge: University Press, 1935.

Organ, Troy, "The Self as Discovery and Creation in Western and Indian Philosophy," in *East-West Studies on The Problem of the Self.* Edited by P. T. Raju and Alburey Castell. The Hague: Martinus Nijhoff, 1968, pp. 163–176.

Organ, Troy, *The Self in Indian Philosophy.* The Hague: Mouton and Co., 1964.

Organ, Troy, "The Philosophy of India." *The Ohio University Review,* Vol. 1, 1959, pp. 59–72.

Pal, Bipin Chandra, *The New Spirit.* Calcutta: Sinha, Sarvadhikari and Co., 1907.

Pal, Bipin Chandra, *The Soul of India.* Calcutta: Choudhury and Choudhury, 1911.

Pal, Bipin Chandra, *Speeches.* Calcutta: Rames Chandra Choudhury, 1908.

Pal, Dhirendra Nath, *Hindu Philosophy.* Calcutta: Oriental Publishing Co., n.d.

Pal, Kumar, "Ambivalence." *Review of Philosophy and Religion,* Vol. 10, April 1944.

Pandit, M. P., *Aditi and Other Deities in the Veda.* Madras: Sri Aurobindo Study Circle, 1958.

Pandya, Manubhai C., *Intelligent Man's Guide to Indian Philosophy.* Bombay: D. B. Taraporevala and Sons, 1935.

Panikkar, K. M., *Common Sense About India.* New York: The Macmillan Co., 1960.

Panikker, R., "Does Indian Philosophy Need Re-orientation?" *The Philosphical Quarterly,* Vol. 30, October 1957, pp. 189–199.

Parab, B. A., *The Miraculous and Mysterious in Vedic Literature.* Bombay: The Popular Book Depot, 1952.

Pearson, E. Norman, *Space, Time and Self.* Adyar: Theosophical Publishing House, 1957.

Petavel, J. W. and Sen, Kiran Chandra (translators), *Behula: The Indian "Pilgrim's Progress."* Calcutta: R. Cambray and Co., 1923.
Peterson, Peter, *Hymns from the Rigveda.* Bombay: Government Central Book Agency, 1888. Poona: Bhandarkar Oriental Research Institute, 1924.
Phillips, Maurice, *The Evolution of Hinduism.* Madras: M. E. Publishing House, 1903.
Phillips, Maurice, *The Teaching of the Vedas.* London: Longmans, Green and Co., 1895.
Piggott, S., *Prehistoric India.* Harmondsworth, Middlesex: Penguin Books, 1950. London: Cassell and Co., 1962.
Pitt, Malcolm, *Introducing Hinduism.* New York: Friendship Press, 1955.
Potter, Karl, "Are the Vaiśeṣika 'Guṇas' Qualities?" *Philosophy East and West,* Vol. 4, October 1954.
Potter, Karl, "More on the Unrepeatability of Guṇas." *Philosophy East and West,* Vol. 7, April-July 1957.
Potter, Karl, *Presuppositions of India's Philosophies.* Englewood Cliffs, New Jersey: Prentice Hall, 1963.
Powell-Price, J. C., *A History of India.* London: Thomas Nelson and Sons, 1955.
Prabhavananda, Swami and Manchester, Frederick, *The Spiritual Heritage of India.* Garden City: Doubleday and Co., 1963.
Prabhavananda, Swami, *Vedic Religion and Philosophy.* Madras: Ramakrishna Math, 1938.
Prajnanananda, Swami, *Philosophy of Progress and Perfection.* Darjeeling: Ramakrishna Vedanta Ashrama, 1958.
Prasad, Beni, *The State in Ancient India.* Allahabad: The Indian Press, 1928.
Prasad, Jwala, *Introduction to Indian Philosophy.* Allahabad: The Indian Press, 1928.
Prasad, Rajendra, *Autobiography.* Bombay: Asia Publishing House, 1957.
Prasad, Rajendra, *At the Feet of Mahatma Gandhi.* New York: Philosophical Library, 1955.
Pratt, James Bissett, *India and Its Faiths.* Boston: Houghton Mifflin Co., 1915.
Purnalingam Pillai, M. S., *A Primer of Tamil Literature.* Madras: Ananda Press, 1904.
Pym, Michael, *The Power of India.* New York: G. P. Putnam's Sons, 1930.

Radhakrishnan, Sarvepalli, "The Ancient Asian View of Man," in *Man's Right to Knowledge.* New York: Columbia University Press, 1954, pp. 9–15.
Radhakrishnan, Sarvepalli, *et al.* (editors), *A. R. Wadia: Essays in Philosophy Presented in His Honour.* Madras: G. S. Press, 1954.
Radhakrishnan, Sarvepalli and Raju, P. T., (editors), *The Concept of Man.* London: Allen and Unwin, 1960.
Radhakrishnan, Sarvepalli and Muirhead, J. H., *Contemporary Indian Philosophy.* London: George Allen and Unwin, 1936.
Radhakrishnan, Sarvepalli, *East and West.* London: George Allen and Unwin, 1955.
Radhakrishnan, Sarvepalli, *East and West in Religion.* London: George Allen and Unwin, 1949.
Radhakrishnan, Sarvepalli, *Eastern Religions and Western Thought.* London: Oxford University Press, 1939.

Radhakrishnan, Sarvepalli, *The Essentials of Psychology*. London: Henry Frowde, Oxford University Press, 1912.

Radhakrishnan, Sarvepalli, *Freedom and Culture*. Madras: G. A. Nateson and Co., 1946.

Radhakrishnan, Sarvepalli, *Gautama the Buddha*. Bombay: Hind Kitabs, 1945.

Radhakrishnan, Sarvepalli, *Great Indians*. Bombay: Hind Kitabs, 1949.

Radhakrishnan, Sarvepalli, *The Heart of Hindusthan*. Madras: G. A. Nateson and Co., 1945.

Radhakrishnan, Sarvepalli, *The Hindu View of Life*. London: George Allen and Unwin, 1927.

Radhakrishnan, Sarvepalli *et al.*, *History of Philosophy, Eastern and Western*. London: George Allen and Unwin, 1952.

Radhakrishnan, Sarvepalli, *Indian Philosophy*. London: George Allen and Unwin, Vol. I, 1923; Vol. II, 1927.

Radhakrishnan, Sarvepalli, *Kalki, or The Future of Civilization*. London: Kegan Paul and Co., 1929.

Radhakrishnan, Sarvepalli, *Occasional Speeches and Writings 1952–1959*. Government of India, Publications Division, 1960.

Radhakrishnan, Sarvepalli, *Radhakrishnan: Comparative Studies in Philosophy Presented in Honour of his Sixtieth Birthday*. London: George Allen and Unwin, 1951.

Dr. S. Radhakrishnan Souvenir Volume. Moradabad: Darshana International, 1964.

Radhakrishnan, Sarvepalli, *Recovery of Faith*. London: George Allen and Unwin, 1956.

Radhakrishnan, Sarvepalli, *The Reign of Religion in Contemporary Philosophy*. London: Macmillan and Co., 1920.

Radhakrishnan, Sarvepalli, *The Religion We Need*. London: Ernest Benn, 1928.

Radhakrishnan, Sarvepalli and Moore, Charles A., (editors), *A Source Book in Indian Philosophy*. Princeton, New Jersey: Princeton University Press, 1957.

Raghavan, V., *The Indian Heritage: An Anthology of Sanskrit Literature*. Bangalore: Indian Institute of Culture, 1956.

Ragozin, Z. A., *Vedic India*. London: T. Fisher Unwin, 1886.

Rai, Lajpat, *Unhappy India*. Calcutta: Banna Publishing Co., 1928.

Raja, Chitenjoor Kunhan and Sastri, Satalur Sundra Suryanarayana, *Manameyodaya*. Madras: The Adyar Library, 1933.

Raja, C. Kunhan, *Poet-Philosophers of the Ṛgveda*. Madras: Ganesh and Co., 1963.

Raja, C. Kunhan, *Some Fundamental Problems in Indian Philosophy*. Delhi: Motilal Banarsidass, 1960.

Rajagopalacharai, C., *Hinduism*. New Delhi: Hindustan Times Press, n.d.

Raju, P. T., *Comparative Philosophy: Idealistic Approaches, Eastern and Western*. Baroda: M. S. University, 1956.

Raju, P. T., "The Development of Indian Thought." *Journal of the History of Ideas*, Vol. 13, 1952, pp. 528–550.

Raju, P. T., *Idealistic Thought of India*. Cambridge: Harvard University Press, 1953.

Raju, P. T., *Indian Idealism and Modern Challenges*. Chandigarh: Panjab University Publication Bureau, 1961.

Raju, P. T., *Indian Philosophy: A Survey* (1917–1942). Edited by R. N. Dandekar. Poona: Bhandarkar Oriental Research Institute, 1942.

Raju, P. T., "Indian Philosophy: Its Attitude to the World." *The Vedānta Kesari* (Madras), November, December 1944.

Raju, P. T., "Metaphysical Theories in Indian Philosophy," in *Essays in East-West Philosophy*. Edited by C. A. Moore. Honolulu: University of Hawaii Press, 1951.

Raju, P. T., *Thought and Reality—Hegelianism and Advaita*. London: George Allen and Unwin, 1937.

Raju, P. T., "The Western and the Indian Philosophical Traditions." *The Philosophical Review*, Vol. 61, No. 2.

Ramachandra Dikshitar, V. R., *Studies in Tamil Literature and History*. London: Luzac and Co., 1930.

Ramakrishna Centenary Memorial, *The Cultural Heritage of India*. First edition, 3 vols. Calcutta: Belur Math, 1937. Second edition, 4 vols. Calcutta: The Ramakrishna Mission, Institute of Culture, 1953–1962.

Ramaswami Aiyar, C. P., *Fundamentals of Hindu Faith and Culture*. Madras: Ganesh and Co., 1959.

Ramaswami, Aiyar, C. P., *Phases of Religion and Culture*. Bombay: Hind Kitabs, 1949.

Ramaswami Sastri, K. S., *Hindu Culture and the Modern Age*. Annamalainagar: Annamalai University, 1956.

Ramatirtha, Swami, *In Woods of God-realisation*. Sixth edition. Lucknow: Rama Tirtha Publication League, 1937.

Ramdas, *In the Vision of God*. Anandashram, Ramnagar, Kahangad: S. I. Rlys, 1935.

Ranade, Mrs. Ramabai, *The Miscellaneous Writings of the Late Honorable Mr. Justice M. G. Ranade*. Bombay: Manroanjan Press, 1915.

Ranade, Ramachandra Dattatraya, *A Constructive Survey of Upanishadic Philosophy*. Poona: Oriental Book Agency, 1926.

Ranade, Ramchandra Dattatraya, *Indian Mysticism: Mysticism in Maharashtra*. Poona: Bilvakunja Publishing House, 1933.

Ranade, R. D., *Pathway to God*. Sangli: Adhyatma Vidya Mandir, 1954.

Ranade, R. D., *Philosophical and Other Essays*. Bombay: Gurudeo Ranade Satkar Samiti, 1956.

Rao, M. V. Krishna, *The Growth of Indian Liberalism in the Nineteenth Century*. Mysore: H. Venkataramiah and Sons, 1951.

Rao, P. Nagaraja, "In Defence of Individuality," in *D. R. Bhandarkar Commenoration Volume*. Calcutta, 1940.

Rao, T. A., Gopinath, *Elements of Hindu Iconography*. London: Probsthain and Co., 1914.

Rapson, E. J., *Ancient India*. Cambridge: Cambridge University Press, 1914.

Rawlinson, Hugh George, *India: A Short Cultural History*. London: Cresset Press, 1937. New York: Praeger, 1952.

Ray, Benoy Gopal, *Contemporary Indian Philosophers*. Allahabad: Kitabistan, 1947.

Redding, Saunders, *An American in India*. Indianapolis: Bobbs-Merrill, 1954.

Reed, Elizabeth A., *Hindu Literature*. Chicago: S. C. Griggs and Co., 1891.

Regnaud, P., *Materiaux pour Servir a L'Histoire de la Philosophie de L'Inde*. Paris: F. Vieweg, Libraire-Editeur, Librairie A. Franck, 1876.

Renou, Louis *et al.*, *Classical India and Vedic India.* Translated by Philip Spratt. Calcutta: Gupta, 1957.

Renou, Louis, *The Destiny of the Veda in India.* Delhi: Motilal Banarsidass, 1915.

Renou, Louis, *Hinduism.* London: Prentice Hall International, 1961.

Renou, Louis, *Indian Literature.* Translated by Patrick Evans. New York: Walker and Co., 1964.

Renou, Louis, *The Nature of Hinduism.* Translated by Patrick Evans. New York: Walker and Co., 1962.

Renou, Louis, *Religions of Ancient India.* London: Athlone Press, 1953.

Reyna, Ruth, *The Concept of Māyā from the Vedas to the Twentieth Century.* London: Asia Publishing House, 1962.

Rhys-Davids, C. A. F., "Man and His Becoming in the Upanishads," in *Indian Linguistics* (Lahore), 1933.

Rhys-Davids, C. A. F., *Indian Religion and Survival.* London: Allen and Unwin, 1934.

Rhys-Davids, T. W., *Buddhist India.* London: T. Fisher Unwin, 1903.

Ricker, Hans-Ulrich, *The Secret of Meditation.* Translated by A. J. Pomerans. London: Rider, 1955.

de Riencourt, Amaury, *The Soul of India.* New York: Harper and Brothers, 1960.

Riepe, Dale, "Emerson and Indian Philosophy." *The Journal of the History of Ideas,* Vol. 28, January–March 1967, pp. 115–122.

Riepe, Dale M., "Indian Naturalism." *The Philosophical Quarterly* (Amalner), Vol. 25, July 1952.

Riepe, Dale, *The Naturalistic Tradition in Indian Thought.* Seattle: University of Washington Press, 1961.

Risley, Herbert, *People of India.* Calcutta: Thacker, Spink and Co., 1908.

Rolland, Romain, *Prophets of the New India.* London: Cassell and Co., 1930.

Ronaldshay, Earl of, *The Heart of Aryavarta.* London: Constable and Co., 1925.

Roof, Simons, *Journeys on the Razor-Edged Path.* New York: Thomas Y. Crowell, 1959.

Ross, Floyd H., *The Meaning of Life in Hinduism and Buddhism.* London: Routledge and Kegan Paul, 1952.

Roy, Dhirendranath, *The Spirit of Indian Civilization.* Calcutta: University of Calcutta, 1938.

Roy, Kaviraj A. P., *The Quest of the Infinite.* Calcutta: the author, 1958.

Roy, M. N., *Science and Superstition.* Dehradun: Indian Renaissance Association, 1940.

Roy, Satis Chandra, *Religion and Modern India.* Calcutta: Asutosh Library, 1923.

Ryder, Arthur W., *Kalidasa: Translations of Shakuntala and Other Works.* London: J. M. Dent and Co., 1912.

Sachau, Carl Edward (translator), *Alberuni's India.* London: W. H. Allen and Co., 1879.

Saiyidain, K. G., *The Humanistic Tradition in Modern Indian Educational Thought.* Madison, Wisconsin: Dembar Educational Research Services, 1967.

Saksena, Krishna, *Nature of Consciousness in Hindu Philosophy*. Benares: Nand Kishore and Bros., 1944.
Saksena, S. K., "Authority in Indian Philosophy." *Philosophy East and West*, Vol. 1, October 1951.
Samartha, S. J., *The Hindu View of History: Classical and Modern*. Bangalore: Christian Institute for the Study of Religion and Society, 1959.
Santinatha, Sadhu, *Critical Examination of the Philosophy of Religion*. Amalner: Institute of Philosophy, 1938.
Santinatha, *Sādhanā, or Spiritual Discipline—Its Various Forms*. Poona: S. Santinatha, 1938.
Sarkar, Benoy Kumar, *The Folk Element in Hindu Culture*. London: Longmans, Green and Co., 1917.
Sarkar, Benoy Kumar, *Hindu Achievements in Exact Science*. New York: Longmans, Green and Co., 1918.
Sarkar, Benoy Kumar, *What is Hinduism?* Madras: The Madras Law Journal Office, 1945.
Sarkar, Kishori Lal, *The Hindu System of Religious Science and Art*. Calcutta: Sarasi Lal Sarkar, 1898.
Sarkar, Mahendranath, *Eastern Lights*. Calcutta: Arya Publishing House, 1935.
Sarkar, M. N., "The Immanent and the Transcendent." *Prabuddha Bharata* (Calcutta), Vol. 35, November 1930.
Sarkar, Mahendranath, *The Mystical Experience and Samadhi*. Calcutta: Bharati Madhavidyalaya, 1946.
Śarma, D. S., *Hinduism Through the Ages*. Bombay: Bharatiya Vidya Bhavan, 1956.
Śarma, D. S., *A Primer of Hinduism*. Madras: Macmillan, 1929.
Śarma, Dittakavi Subrahmanja, *Studies in the Renaissance of Hinduism in the Nineteenth and Twentieth Centuries*. Benares: Benares Hindu University, 1944.
Śarma, D. S., *The Tales and Teachings of Hinduism*. Bombay: Hind Kitabs, 1948.
Śarma, D. S., *What is Hinduism?* Madras: Madras Law Journal Press, 1945.
Sastri, S. Subramanya and Srinivasa Aiyangar, T. R. (translators), *Jīvanmuktiviveka*. Madras: The Adyar Library, 1938.
Sastri, S. S. Suryanarayana, *Collected Papers of Professor S. S. Suryanarayana Sastri*. Madras: University of Madras, 1961.
Sastry, K. S., Ramaswami, *Hindu Culture*. Madras: S. Ganesan, 1922.
Sastry, N. Sivarama and Rao, G. Hanumantha (editors), *Prof. M. Hiriyanna Commemoration Volume*. Mysore: Mysore Printing and Publishing House, 1952.
Savarkar, V. D., *Hindutva*. Poona: V. G. Ketkar, 1942.
Sawal, Maharajadhiraj Shri, *Eastern Light of Sanatan Culture*. Calcutta: Thacker, Spink and Co., 1933.
Schilpp, Paul Arthur (editor), *The Philosophy of Sarvepalli Radhakrishnan*. *The Library of Living Philosophers*. New York: Tudor Publishing Co., 1952.
Schultz, M., *Hindu Philosophy*. Madras: Theosophist, 1910.
Schuyler, Jr., Montgomery, *A Bibliography of the Sanskrit Drama*. New York: A. M. S. Press, 1965.

Schweitzer, Albert, *Indian Thought and its Development*. Translated by Mrs. Charles E. B. Russell. New York: Henry Holt and Co., 1936.
Seal, Brajendranath, *The Gītā: A Synthetic Interpretation*. Calcutta: Sadharan Brahmo Samaj, 1964.
Seal, Brajendranath, *The Positive Sciences of the Ancient Hindus*. London, New York: Longmans, Green and Co., 1915.
Seal, B. N., *Syllabus in Indian Philosophy*. Bangalore: University of Mysore, 1924.
Segal, Ronald, *The Crisis of India*. London: Johnathan Cape, 1965.
Sen, D. N., "The Upanishads in Relation to Practical Life," in *Proceedings of the Fourth Indian Philosophical Congress*. Calcutta: University of Calcutta, 1930, pp. 145–154.
Sen, Gurn Prosad, *An Introduction to the Study of Hinduism*. Calcutta: Thacker, Spink and Co., 1893.
Sen, S. C., "The Conception of the Self in the Upanishads," in *Proceedings of the First Indian Philosophical Congress*. Calcutta: The Calcutta Philosophical Society, 1927, pp. 211–224.
Sen, Saileswar, *A Study on Mathuranatha's Tattvacintamanirahasya*. Wageningen: H. Veenman en Zonen, 1924.
Sen, Sukumar, *History of Brajabuli Literature*. Calcutta: University of Calcutta, 1935.
Sethna, K. D., *The Indian Spirit and the World's Future*. Pondicherry: Sri Aurobindo Ashram, 1953.
Sethi, Narendra K. (editor), *Hindu Proverbs and Wisdom*. Mt. Vernon, N.Y.: Peter Pauper Press, 1962.
Shah, A. B., *Scientific Method*. Bombay: Allied Publishers, 1964.
Shah, K. T., *The Splendour that was India: A Survey of Indian Civilization*. Bombay: D. B. Taraporewala Son and Co., 1930.
Shahani, R. G., *Indian Way*. London: Probsthain, 1951.
Shamasastry, R., "The Concept of Mukti in Indian Philosophy," in *Jha Commemoration Volume*. Poona: Oriental Book Agency, 1937, pp. 349–358.
Shankarananda, Swami, *Anatomical Alphabet and Comparative Study of Literature*. Poona: the author, 1956.
Sharma, Chandrahar, *A Critical Survey of Indian Philosophy*. London: Rider and Co., 1960.
Sharma, Chandrahar, *Indian Philosophy*. Benares: Nand Kishore and Bros., 1952. New York: Barnes and Noble, 1962.
Sharma, Sripad, *Our Heritage and its Significance*. Bombay: Hind Kitabs, 1947.
Sharma, S. N., *The Jewel of Hindi Literature*. Bombay: the author, 1954.
Sharpe, E., *The India that is India*. London: Luzac, 1934.
Sharpe, E., *Shiva, or The Past of India*. London: Luzac, 1930.
Shastri, D. Ranjan, "Çarvaka Philosophy." *The Humanist Way*, Calcutta, Vol. 4, No. 3, 1950.
Shastri, Hari Prasad, *Wisdom from the East*. London: The Shanti-Sadan Publishing Co., 1948.
Shastri, Prabhu Dutt, *The Essentials of Eastern Philosophy*. New York: The Macmillan Co., 1928.
Shekhar, I., *Sanskrit Drama: Its Origin and Decline*. Leiden: E. J. Brill, 1960.
Shende, N. J., *The Religion and Philosophy of the Atharvaveda*. Poona: Bhandarkar Oriental Research Institute, 1952.

Shils, Edward A., *The Intellectual Between Tradition and Modernity: The Indian Situation*. The Hague: Mouton, 1961.
Shrikhande, V. B., "The Nature of the Self," in *Proceedings of the First Indian Philosophical Congress*, 1927, pp. 105–119.
Siddhanta, N. K., *The Heroic Age of India*. London: Kegan Paul, Trench, Trubner and Co., 1929.
Simha, Charv Chandra, *The Problems of Hindu Philosophy*. Calcutta: S. C. Gupta, 1912.
Singer, Milton, "The Cultural Pattern of Indian Civilization." *Far Eastern Quarterly*, Vol. 15, pp. 23–36.
Singer, Milton, *Traditional India: Structure and Change*. Philadelphia: American Folklore Society, 1959.
Singh, Mohan, *Who Am I?* Delhi: Rajkamal Publications, 1948.
Sinha, A. K., *A World-view Through A Reunion of Philosophy and Science*. Calcutta: Library of Philosophy, 1959.
Sinha, Devabrata, "The Concept of Self as Sākṣin." *Calcutta Review*, Vol. 138, pp. 68–76.
Sinha, Jadunath, *The Foundation of Hinduism*. Calcutta: Sinha Publishing House, 1955.
Sinha, Jadunath, *History of Indian Philosophy*, Vol. 2. Calcutta: Central Book Agency, 1952. Vol. 1. Calcutta: Sinha Publishing House, 1956.
Sinha, Jadunath, *Indian Psychology of Perception*. London: Kegan Paul, Trench, Trubner and Co., 1934.
Sinha, Jadunath, *Indian Realism*. London: Kegan Paul, Trench, Trubner and Co., 1938.
Sinha, Jadunath, *Introduction to Indian Philosophy*. Agra: Lakshmi Narain Agarwal, 1949.
Sinha, Nandalal (translator), *The Vaiśeṣika Sūtras of Kanāda. The Sacred Books of the Hindus*, Vol. 6. Allahabad: The Panini Office, 1923.
Sivananda, Swami, *All About Hinduism*. Sivanandanagar: Sivananda Literature Research Institute, 1961.
Sivananda, Swami, *World's Religions*. Rishikesh, India: The Sivananda Publication League, n.d.
Skorpen, Erling, "The Whole Man." *Main Currents in Modern Thought*, Vol. 22, No. 1, September–October 1965, pp. 10–16.
Slater, G., *The Dravidian Element in Indian Culture*. London: Ernest Benn, 1924.
Slater, T. E., *The Higher Hinduism in Relation to Christianity*. London: Eliot Stock, 1902.
Smart, Ninian, *Doctrine and Argument in Indian Philosophy*. London: Allen and Unwin, 1964.
Smith, Donald E., *India as a Secular State*. Princeton: Princeton University Press, 1963.
Smith, Huston, "Accents of the World's Philosophies." *Philosophy East and West*, Vol. 7, Nos. 1 and 2, April-July 1957, pp. 7–19.
Sorokin, Pitirim A., *Forms and Techniques of Altruistic and Spiritual Growth*. Boston: The Beacon Press, 1954.
Spear, Percival, *India, A Modern History*. Ann Arbor, Michigan: University of Michigan Press, 1961.

Spiegelberg, Frederic, *Spiritual Practices of India*. San Francisco: The Greenwood Press, 1952.

Srinivasa Iyengar, P. T., *Outlines of Indian Philosophy*. Benares: Theosophical Publishing Society, 1909.

Stephen, Dorothea Jane, *Studies in Early Indian Thought*. Cambridge: Cambridge University Press, 1918.

Strauss, Otto, *Indische Philosophie*. Münich: Verlag Ernst Reinhart, 1925.

Subba Rao, T., *A Collection of Esoteric Writings*. Bombay: Rajaram Tukaram, 1910.

Sugiura, Sadajiro and Singer, Jr., Edgar Arthur (editors), *Hindu Logic as Preserved in China and Japan*. Philadelphia: University of Pennsylvania, 1900.

Sukthankar, Vishnu Sistam, *Ghate's Lectures on the Rig Veda*. Poona: Oriental Book Agency, 1926.

Syamananda, Brahmachari, *Self-realization*. Benares: Govinda Chandra Mukhopadhyya, 1926.

Tara Chand, *The Influence of Islam on Indian Culture*. Allahabad: The Indian Press, 1936.

Tawney, R. H. (translator), *Stories from Somadeva's Kathasaritsagara*. Bombay: Jaico Publishing House, 1956.

Thadani, N. V., *The Secret of the Sacred Books of the Hindus*. Delhi: Bharati Research Institute, 1953.

Thomas, P., *Epics, Myths and Legends of India*. Bombay: D. B. Taraporevala and Sons, 1940.

Tiele, C. P., *Outlines of the History of Religion to the Spread of the Universal Religions*. Translated by J. Eastlin Carpenter. London: Trubner and Co., 1877.

Tilak, Bala Gangadhara, *The Arctic Home in the Vedas*. Poona: Arya-Bhushana Press, 1903.

Tiwari, Brij Gopal, *Secularism and Materialism in Modern India*. Jabalpur: Jabalpur Co-operative Printing and Publishing Society, n.d.

Ui, Hakuju (translator), *The Vaiśeṣika Philosophy according to the Daśopadārthaśāstra*. London: Royal Asiatic Society, 1917.

Underwood, A. C., *Contemporary Thought in India*. London: Williams and Norgate, 1930.

Upadhyaya, Bhagwat Saran, *India in Kalidasa*. Allahabad: Kitabistan, 1947.

Upadhyaya, B. S., *Women in the Rig Veda*. Banaras: Nand Kishore and Bros., 1941.

Urquhart, Margaret, *Women of Bengal*. Calcutta: Association Press, 1925.

Urquhart, William Spence, *Pantheism and the Value of Life with Special Reference to Indian Philosophy*. London: The Epworth Press, 1919.

Urquhart, William Spence, *The Upanishads and Life*. Calcutta: Association Press, 1916.

Useem, John and Useem, Ruth Hill, *The Western-Educated Man in India*. New York: The Dryden Press, 1955.

Vable, D., *An Introduction to Modern India and Hinduism*. Jaipur: Apollo Publication, 1962.

Vanamali, Vedantatirtha (translator), *Gṛhya-Sūtras of Gobhila*. Calcutta: Metropolitan Printing and Publishing House, 1940.

Vaswani, T. L., *The Aryan Ideal*. Madras: Ganesh and Co., 1922.
Vaswani, Thaverdas Lilaram, *Atmagnan, or Life in the Spirit*. Madras: Ganesh and Co., 1922.
Venkataramanayya, N., *Rudra-Śiva*. Madras: Madras University, 1941.
Venkatasubbiah, A., *Vedic Studies*. Mysore: Surabhi and Co., 1932.
Venkateswara, S. V., *Indian Culture through the Ages*. London: Longmans, Green and Co. Vol. 1, 1928; Vol. 2, 1932.
Vidyarthi, Mohan Lal, *India's Culture through the Ages*. Kanpur: Tapeshwari Sahitya Mandir, 1952.
Voitinsky, V. S., *India: The Awakening Giant*. New York: Harper, 1957.
Vreede, Franz, *A Short Introduction to the Essentials of Living Hindu Philosophy*. London: Oxford University Press, 1953.

Wadiyar, Jaya Chamarajendra (translator), *Dattatreya: The Way and the Goal*. New York: The Macmillan Co., 1957.
Ward, Barbara, *India and the West*. London: Hamish and Hamilton, 1961.
Ward, Barbara, *The Interplay of East and West*. London: George Allen and Unwin, 1957.
Ward, William, *Account of the Writings, Religion and Manners of the Hindoos*. Four volumes. Serampore: Mission Press, 1811.
Ward, William, *A View of the History, Literature and Mythology of the Hindoos*. Two volumes. Serampore: Mission Press, 1818.
Warrier, A. G. Krishna, "Brahman as Value." *The Adyar Library Bulletin*. No. 25, 1961, pp. 477–504.
Watts, Alan W., *The Legacy of Asia and Western Man: A Study of the Middle Way*. London: John Murray, 1937.
Weber, Albrecht, *The History of Indian Literature*. London: Kegan Paul, Trench, Trubner and Co., 1914.
Wheeler, Robert Eric Mortimer, *The Indus Civilization*. Cambridge: Cambridge University Press, 1953.
Wilkins, W. J., *Hindu Mythology: Vedic and Puranic*. Calcutta: Thacker, Spink and Co., 1882.
Wilkins, W. J., *Modern Hinduism*. London: T. Fisher Unwin, 1887.
Wilson, G. E., *The Masnavai*. London: Arthur Probsthain, 1910.
Wilson, Horace Hayman, *Essays and Lectures on the Religions of the Hindus*. London: Trubner and Co., 1961.
Wilson, Horace Hayman, *Religious Sects of the Hindus*. Calcutta: Susil Gupta, 1958.
Wilson, Horace Hayman, *Rig-Veda-Sanhita: A Collection of Ancient Hindu Hymns of the Rig-Veda*. 6 vols. Poona: Ashtekar and Co., 1925–1928.
Wilson, Horace Hayman, *Sketch of the Religious Sects of the Hindus*. Calcutta: Bishop's College Press, 1846.
Wilson, Horace Hayman (translator), *The Vishnu Purana: A System of Hindu Mythology and Tradition*. Calcutta: Punthi Pustak, 1961.
Wilson, Horace Hayman, *Works*. 12 vols. London: Trubner and Co., 1862–1871.
Winslow, J. C., *The Christian Approach to the Hindu*. London: Edinburgh House Press, 1958.
Winternitz, Moriz, *A History of Indian Literature*. Calcutta: Calcutta University Press. Vol. 1, 1927. Translated by S. Ketkar. Vol. 2, 1933. Translated by S. Ketkar and H. Kohn.

Winternitz, Moriz, *Some Problems of Indian Literature*. Calcutta: Calcutta University Press, 1925.

Wiser, Charlotte Viall and Wiser, William H., *Behind Mud Walls in India*. London: George Allen and Unwin, 1932.

Wofford, Clare and Wofford, Harris, *India Afire*. New York: John Day Co., 1951.

Wood, Ernest, *An Englishman Defends Mother India*. Madras: Ganesh and Co., 1929.

Wood, Ernest, *The Glorious Presence*. London: Rider and Co., 1952.

Woodward, Frank Lee, *Manual of a Mystic*. Edited by C. A. F. Rhys-Davids. *Pali Text Society Translation Series*, Vol. 6. London: Oxford University Press, 1916.

Yale, John, *A Yankee and the Swamis*. London: George Allen and Unwin, 1961.

Yusuf Ali, A., *A Cultural History of India during the British Period*. Bombay: D. B. Taraporevala Sons and Co., 1940.

Zacharias, *An Outline of Hinduism*. Alwaye: St. Joseph's Seminary, 1956.

Zimmer, Heinrich, *The King and the Corpse: Tales of the Soul's Conquest of Evil*. New York: Pantheon Books, 1948.

JÑĀNA MĀRGA

Abhedananda, Swami, *Attitude of Vedānta Towards Religion*. Calcutta: Ramakrishna Vedanta Math, 1947.

Abhedananda, Swami, *Our Relation to the Absolute*. Calcutta: Ramakrishna Vedanta Math, 1946.

Abhedananda, Swami, *The Path of Realization*. Calcutta: Ramakrishna Vedanta Math, 1939.

Abhedananda, Swami, *Vedānta Philosophy, Self-Knowledge. Ātma-Jñāna*. New York: Vedanta Society, 1905.

Abhedananda, Swami, "The True Nature of the Ātman," in *Vedānta Kesanī*. Madras: Ramakrishna Math, Vol. 28, 1941–42.

Apte, Raghunath N., *The Doctrine of Māyā: Its Existence in the Vedāntic Sūtra, and Development in the Later Vedānta*. Bombay: publishing house not given, 1896.

Apte, Raghunath N., *The Theosophy of the Upanishads*. London: Theosophical Publishing Society, 1896.

Apte, V. M. (translator), *Brahma-Sūtra Shānkara-Bhāshya*. Bombay: Popular Book Depot, 1960.

Asokananda, Swami, *The Influence of Indian Thought on the Thought of the West*. *Prabuddha Bharata*, XLI, April 1931.

Athalye, D. V., *Neo-Hinduism*. Bombay: D. B. Taraporevala Sons and Co., 1932.

Atreya, Bhikan Lal, *Deification of Man: its Methods and Stages According to the Yogavāsiṣtha*. Moradabad: Darshana Printers, 1963.

Atreya, Bhikan Lal, *The Elements of Indian Logic*. Second edition. Benares: The Indian Bookshop, 1934.

Atreya, Bhikan Lal, *The Philosophy of Yogavāsiṣṭha*. Adyar: Theosophical Publishing House, 1936.

Atreya, Bhikan Lal, *The Yogavāsiṣṭha and its Philosophy*. Benares: The Indian Bookshop, 1932.

Atreya, Bhikan Lal, *Yogavāsiṣṭha and Modern Thought*. Benares: Indian Bookshop, 1954.

Bagghi, Sitansusekhar, *Inductive Reasoning: A Study of Tarka and its Role in Indian Logic*. Calcutta: Orient Press, 1953.

Bahirat, B. P., *The Philosophy of Jñānadeva*. Pandharpur: Pandharpur Research Society, 1956.

Balakrishna, *The Veda and the Systems of Philosophy*. Ajiner: publishing house not given, 1933.

Ballantyne, J. R., *Hindu Philosophy*. Calcutta: J. Ghose and Co., 1879.

Banerjea, K. M., *Dialogues on the Hindu Philosophy, Comprising the Nyaya, The Sankhya, The Vedant*. Madras: Christian Literature Society for India, 1903.

Banerjee, Nikunja Vihari, *Concerning Human Understanding*. London: George Allen and Unwin, 1958.

Banerjee, N. V., "The Problem of Self-Knowledge," in *25th Indian Philosophical Congress Silver Jubilee Commemoration Volume*, 1950, pp. 180–185.

Barnett, Lionel David, *Brahma Knowledge: an Outline of the Philosophy of the Vedānta as set forth by the Upanishads and by Śānkara*. London: John Murray, 1907.

Belvalkar, Shripad Krishna (translator), *The Brahma-Sūtras of Bādarāyaṇa. Poona Oriental Series*, Vol. 13. Poona: Bhandarkar Oriental Research Institute, 1923.

Belvalkar, S. K., *Vedānta Philosophy*. Poona: Bilvakunja Publishing House, 1929.

Besant, Annie, *The Wisdom of the Upanishads*. Benares: Theosophical Publishing Society, 1907.

Bhaduri, Sadananda, *Studies in Nyāya-Vaiśeṣika Metaphysics*. Poona: Bhandarkar Oriental Research Institute, 1947.

Bhagavan Das (translator), *Mystic Experiences. Tales of Yoga and Vedānta from Yogavāsiṣṭha*. Banaras: Indian Bookshop, 1928.

Bhagavan Das, *A Search for the Science of the Self in the Principles of Vedānta-Yoga*. Benares: The Indian Book Shop, 1938.

Bhattacharya, Asutosh Sastri, *Studies in Post-Śaṅkara Dialectics*. Calcutta: University of Calcutta, 1936.

Bhattacharya, Chandrodaya, "On Self-Awareness." *Journal of the Philosophical Association*, Vol. 3, No. 9–10, July–October 1955, pp. 49–70.

Bhattacharya, M. L., *A Lecture on Vedānta Philosophy*. Agra: Mokerji Bros., 1895.

Bhattacharya, V., "The Doctrine of Ātman and Anātman." All India Oriental Conference, Lahore, 1928.

Bhattacharyya, Hari Mohan, "The Conception of the Soul in the Nyāya System." *The Philosophical Quarterly*. Calcutta. Vol. 10, July 1935.

Bhattacharyya, K. C., *Studies in Vedāntism*. Calcutta: University of Calcutta, 1909.

Bhattacharyya, Kokileswar, *An Introduction to Advaita Philosophy*. Calcutta: University of Calcutta, 1924.

Bhattacharyya, Krishnachandra, *Studies in Philosophy*. Edited by Gopinath Bhattacharyya. Calcutta: Progressive Publishers, Vol. 1, 1956; Vol. 2, 1958.
Bhattacharyya, Vidhushekhara, *The Āgamaśaṣtra of Gauḍapāda*. Calcutta: University of Calcutta, 1943.
Bihari, B., *Mysticism in the Upanishads*. Gorakhpur: Gita Press, 1940.
Bloomfield, Maurice, *The Religion of the Veda: The Ancient Religion of India, from the Rig Veda to the Upanishads*. New York and London: Putnam, 1908.
Brahmananda, Swami, *Spiritual Teachings of Swami Brahmananda*. Mylapore, Madras: Sri Ramakrishna Math, 1933.
Brooks, F. T., *Tattva-Darshanan*, or *the Mind-Aspect of Salvation*. Madras: Vyasashrama Book Depot, 1910.
Brough, John, *The Early Brahmanical System of Gotra and Pravara*. A translation of the *Gotra-Pravara-Mañjarī* of Purusottama-Pandita. Cambridge: Cambridge University Press, 1953.
Buch, Maganlal, *The Philosophy of Śaṁkara*. Baroda: A. G. Widgery, 1921.
van Buitenen, J. A. B., *The Maitrāyanīya Upaniṣad*. The Hague: Mouton and Co., 1962.
Burch, George B., "The Hindu Concept of Existence." *The Monist*, Vol. 50, No. 1, January 1966, pp. 44–54.
Burch, George B., "Search for the Absolute in Neo-Vedānta: The Philosophy of K. C. Bhattacharyya." *International Philosophical Quarterly*, Vol. 7, No. 4, December 1967, pp. 611–667.

Chakravarti, Sures Chandra, *The Philosophy of the Upanishads*. Calcutta: University of Calcutta, 1935.
Chakravarti, Sures Chandra, *Theory of Unreality*. Calcutta: University of Calcutta, 1922.
Chari, C. T. K., "The Psychic Quest for the Self." *The Aryan Path*, Vol. 23, No. 7, July 1952, pp. 312–317.
Chari, C. T. K., "The Psychic Veil of the Self." *The Aryan Path*, Vol. 21, No. 10, October 1950, pp. 440–442.
Chatterjee, M., *Our Knowledge of Otherselves*. Bombay: Asia Publishing House, 1945.
Chatterjee, Mohini M. (translator), *Ātmanātma-viveka and Ātmabodha by Shrimat Śaṅkarāchārya*. Bombay: Bombay Theosophical Publishing House, 1932.
Chatterjee, Mohini M. (translator), *Viveka-chūdāmaṇi*, or *Crest-jewel of Wisdom of Sri Śaṅkarāchārya*. Adyar, Madras: Theosophical Publishing House, 1932.
Chatterjee, Satis Chandra, "The Basis of World Philosophy." 28th Indian Philosophical Congress, 1953, pp. 3–21.
Chatterjee, Satis Chandra, "The Hindu Conception of Self," in *Prabuddha Bharata*, 1945.
Chatterjee, Satis Chandra, "Identity of the Self," 26th Indian Philosophical Congress, 1951, pp. 143–150.
Chatterjee, Satis Chandra, *The Nyāya Theory of Knowledge*. Calcutta: University of Calcutta, 1950.
Chatterji, Jagadish Chandra, *Hindu Realism: being an Introduction to the Metaphysics of the Nyāya-Vaiśeshika System of Philosophy*. Allahabad: The Indian Press, 1912.

Chatterji, Jagadish Chandra, *India's Outlook on Life: The Wisdom of the Veda.* New York: Kailoe Press, 1931.
Chaudhuri, Anil Kumar Ray, *The Doctrine of Māyā.* Calcutta: Das Gupta and Co., n.d.
Chaudhuri, Anil Kumar Ray, *A Realistic Interpretation of Śaṅkara Vedānta.* Calcutta: University of Calcutta, n.d.
Chaudhuri, Anil Kumar Ray, *Self and Falsity in Advaita Vedānta.* Calcutta: Progressive Publishers, 1955.
Chennakesavan, Mrs. Sarasvati, "Are Mind and Self Identical?" 30th Indian Philosophical Congress, 1955, pp. 161–164.
Chennakesavan, Mrs. Sarasvati, "Mind and Consciousness: A comparison of Indian and Western Views." 28th Indian Philosophical Congress, 1953, pp. 187–192.
Chennakesavan, Saraswati, *The Concept of Mind in Indian Philosophy.* Bombay: Asia Publishing House, 1960.
Coomaraswamy, Ananda K., *Figures of Speech or Figures of Thought.* London: Luzac and Co., 1946.
Coomaraswamy, Ananda K., "Recollection, Indian and Platonic." *Journal of the American Oriental Society* (New Haven), Suppl. 3, April–June 1944, pp. 1–18.

Dandoy, G., *Essay on the Doctrine of the Unreality of the World in the Advaita.* Calcutta: A. Rome, 1919.
Das, A. C., "Advaita Vedānta and the Liberation in Bodily Existence." *Philosophy East and West,* Vol. 4, No. 2, July 1954. Also Ch. III in A. C. Das, *Studies in Philosophy.* Calcutta: Firma K. L. Mukhopadhyay, 1962.
Das, Adhar Chandra, "Mysticism and Unity in Nature." *Vedānta Kesarī,* 28, March 1941.
Das, Ras-Vihari, *The Essentials of Advaitism: Suresvara's Naiskarmyasiddhi, Explained in English.* Lahore: Motilal Banarsi Das, 1933.
Das, Saraj K., *Systematic Study of the Vedānta.* Calcutta: S. K. Das and Co,. 1931.
Das, Saroj Kumar, *A Study of the Vedānta.* Calcutta: University of Calcutta Press, 1937.
Das, Saroj Kumar, *Towards a Systematic Study of the Vedānta.* Calcutta: University of Calcutta, 1931.
Dasgupta, Shashi Bhusan, *Aspects of Indian Religious Thought.* Calcutta: A. Mukherjee and Co., 1957.
Date, Vinayak Hari, *Vedānta Explained, Śaṅkara's Commentary on the Brahmasūtras.* Vol. 1. Bombay: Bookseller's Publishing Co., 1954.
Datta, D. M., "The Interpretation of Vaiseshika Categories," in *Proceedings of the 13th Indian Philosophical Congress.* Madras: G. S. Press, 1955.
Datta, Dhirendra Mohan, "Inward and Outward Advaita Vedānta." *The Philosophical Quarterly,* Vol. 30, Oct. 1957, pp. 165–172.
Datta, Dhirendra Mohan, *The Six Ways of Knowing: A Critical Study of the Vedānta Theory of Knowledge.* London: George Allen and Unwin, 1932.
Datta, Dvijadas, *Vedāntism,* or *Lectures on the Vedānta.* Comilla: Sarva-Dharma-Samanvaya-Asrama, n.d.
Deussen, Paul, *Outlines of Indian Philosophy: with an Appendix on the Philosophy of the Vedānta in its Relations to Occidental Metaphysics.* Berlin: Karl Curtins, 1907.

Deussen, Paul, *Outline of the Vedānta System of Philosophy According to Shankara.* Translated by J. H. Woods and C. B. Runkel. New York: The Grafton Press, 1906.

Deussen, Paul, *The Religion and Philosophy of India: The Philosophy of the Upanishads.* Edinburgh: T. and T. Clark, 1906.

Deussen, Paul, *The System of the Vedānta, according to Badarayana's Brahma-sūtras and Çankara's Commentary.* Translated by Charles Johnston. Chicago: The Open Court Publishing Co., 1912.

Deutsch, Eliot, *The Bhagavad Gītā.* New York: Holt, Rinehart and Winston, 1968.

Deutsch, Eliot S., "The Justification of Hindu 'Polytheism' in Advaita Vedānta." *East-West Center Review,* Vol. 1, No. 3, February 1965, pp. 55–61.

Deutsch, Eliot, "The Self in Advaita Vedānta." *International Philosophical Quarterly,* Vol. 2, No. 1, March 1966, pp. 5–21.

Devanji, Prahlad Chandrashekha (translator), *Siddhantabindu by Madhusūdanasarasvati: a Commentary on the Daśaśloki of Śaṁkarācārya. Gaekwad's Oriental Series,* Vol. 64. Baroda: Oriental Institute, 1933.

Devaraja, N. K., *An Introduction to Śaṅkara's Theory of Knowledge.* Delhi: Banarsidass, 1962.

Devi, Akshaya Kumari, *Quintessence of the Upanishads.* Calcutta: Vijaya Krishna Bros., n.d.

Dixit, Shriniwas, "A Critical Evaluation of the Vaiśeṣika Categories." *The Philosophical Quarterly* (Amalner), Vol. 31, April 1958.

Dutt, Nripendra Kumar, *The Vedānta: Its Place as a System of Metaphysics.* Calcutta: University of Calcutta Press, 1931.

Dutta, Sitha Natha, *Śaṅkaracharya: His Life and Teachings.* Calcutta: Elysium Press for the Society for the Resuscitation of Indian Literature, 1899.

Field, Claude, *A Little Book of Hindu Wisdom* and *A Little Book of Eastern Wisdom.* London: George G. Harrap and Co., 1907.

Freeman, James Montague, "Myth and Metaphysics in Indian Thought." *The Monist,* Vol. 50, No. 4, October 1966, pp. 517–529.

Ghate, V. S., *The Vedānta: A Study of the Brahma-Sūtras with the Bhasyas of Sankara, Ramanuja, Nimbarka, Madhva, and Vallabha.* Poona: Bhandarkar Oriental Research Institute, 1923.

Gopal, Madan, "India's Problem of Problems: The Fixed Attitude." *The Aryan Path,* Vol. 14, December 1943, pp. 539–543.

Gotama, *The Nyāya Sūtras of Gotama.* Translated by S. C. Vidyabhusana. *The Sacred Books of the Hindus,* Vol. 8. Allahabad: The Panini Office, 1930.

Guénon, René, *Man and His Becoming, According to the Vedānta.* Translated by Charles Whitby. London: Rider and Co., 1945.

Guha, Abhayakumar, *Jivātman in the Brahma-Sūtras.* Calcutta: University of Calcutta, 1921.

Harrison, Max Hunter, *Hindu Monism and Pluralism.* London, Bombay, Calcutta, Madras: Oxford University Press, Humphrey Milford, 1932.

Heimann, Betty, "Plurality, Polarity, and Unity in Hindu Thought: A Doxographical Study." *Bulletin of the School of Oriental Studies.* (University of London), Vol. 9, 1937–1939, pp. 1015–1021.

Hiriyanna, Mysore (translator), *Kenopanishad with the Commentary of Śrī Śaṅkarāchārya*. Srirangam: Sri Vain Vials Press, 1912.
Hiriyanna, Mysore (editor and translator), *Vedānta-sāra: A Work on Vedānta Philosophy*. Poona: Oriental Book Agency, 1929.
Horrwitz, E., *Veda and Vedānta*. Calcutta: Advaita Ashram, 1937.
Hume, Robert Ernest, *The Thirteen Principal Upanishads*. London: Oxford University Press, 1921. Second edition, revised, 1931.

Ingalls, Daniel Henry Holmes, *Materials for the Study of Navya-Nyāya Logic. Harvard Oriental Series*, Vol. 40. Cambridge: Harvard University Press, 1951.
Isherwood, Christopher (editor), *Vedānta for Modern Man*. New York: Harper and Bros., 1945.
Isherwood, Christopher (editor), *Vedānta for the Western World*. Hollywood and New York: The Marcel Rodd Co., 1946.
Iyer, B. R. Rajam, *Rambles in Vedānta*. Calcutta: S. P. League, 1946.
Iyer, K. A. Krishnaswami, *Vedānta*, or *the Science of Reality*. Madras: Ganesh and Co., 1930.
Iyer, M. K. V., *Advaita Vedānta—According to Śaṅkara*. Bombay: Asia Publishing House, 1930.

Jagadananda, Swami, *A Thousand Teachings of Śrī Śaṅkarāchārya*. Madras: Sri Ramakrishna Math, 1949.
Jha, Ganganatha, *The Nyāya Philosophy of Gautama*. Allahabad: Allahabad University, n.d.
Jha, Ganganatha, *The Philosophical Disciplines*. Calcutta: Calcutta University Press, 1928.
Jha, Ganganatha, *Shaṅkara Vedānta*. Allahabad: The Allahabad Law Journal Press, 1939.
Jha, Ganganatha, *The Tarkabhāṣā* (by Keśavmiśra), or *Exposition of Reasoning*. Second revised edition. Poona: Oriental Book Agency, 1924.
Joad, C. E. M., *Counter Attack from the East. The Philosophy of Radhakrishnan*. London: Allen and Unwin, 1933.
Johnston, Charles (translator), *The Awakening to the Self*. New York: privately printed, 1897.
Johnston, Charles, *The Crest Jewel of Wisdom*. London: John M. Watkins, 1964.
Johnston, Charles, *The Great Upanishads*. New York: Quarterly Book Department, 1927.
Josyer, G. R., *Sanskrit Wisdom*. Mysore: International Academy of Sanskrit Research, 1960.

Kaviraj, Gopinath, *Gleanings from the History and Bibliography of the Nyāya-Vaiśeṣika Literature*. Calcutta: Firma K. L. Mukhopadhyaya, 1961.
Keith, A. Berriedale, *Indian Logic and Atomism, an Exposition of the Nyāya and Vaiçesika Systems*. Oxford: The Clarendon Press, 1921.
Keith, Arthur Berriedale, "New Theories as to Brahman," in *Jha Commemoration Volume*. Poona: Oriental Book Agency, 1937, pp. 199–215.
Keith, A. Berriedale, *The Religion and Philosophy of the Veda and Upanishads. Harvard Oriental Series*, Vols. 31, 32. Cambridge: Harvard University Press, 1925.

Kirtikar, Vasudeva Jagannath, *Studies in Vedānta*. Bombay: D. B. Taraporevala Sons, 1924.
Kitch, Ethel May, *The Origin of Subjectivity in Hindu Thought*. Chicago: The University of Chicago Press, 1917.
Krishna Rao, C. R., *Madva and Brahma Tarka*. Udipi, Madras: Majestic Press, 1960.
Krishnananda, Swami, *The Realization of the Absolute*. Ananda Kutir, Rishikesh: The Yoga-Vedanta Forest University, 1952.
Krishnasvami Aiyar, C. N., *Shri Madhva and Madhvism*. Madras: G. A. Natesan and Co., 1907.
Krishnasvami Aiyar, C. N. and Tattvabhushan, Pandit Sitanath, *Śri Śaṅkarāchārya*. Madras: G. A. Natesan and Co., n.d.
Krishnaswami Ayar, R., *The Great Equation; An Exposition of the Doctrine of Advaita Vedānta*. Bombay: Chetana, 1963.

Lacombe, O., *L'Absolu selon le Vedānta*. Paris: Librairie, Orientaliste, Paul Geuthner, 1937.
Langley, G. H., "The Conception of Universal Spirit in the Upanishads and of its Identity with Individual Spirit." *The Indian Philosophical Review*, Vol. 3, 1920, pp. 109–128.
Levy, John, *The Nature of Man According to the Vedānta*. London: Routledge and Kegan Paul, 1956.
Londhe, D. G., "Śaṁkara's Conception of the Absolute," in *Proceedings of the Fourth Indian Philosophical Congress*, (Madras), 1928. Calcutta: University of Calcutta, 1930, pp. 163–170.

Madhavananda, Swami, *Bṛhadāranyaka Upaniṣad*. Calcutta: Advaita Ashrama, 1934.
Mahadevan, T. M. P., *Gauḍapāda: A Study in Early Advaita*. Madras: University of Madras, 1954.
Mahadevan, T. M. P., *The Philosophy of Advaita*. London: Luzac and Co., 1938. Madras: Ganesh and Co., 1957.
Mahadevan, T. M. P., "Soul: One or Many?" *Proceedings of the 19th Indian Philosophical Congress*, December 1944, pp. 1–15.
Mahadevan, T. M. P., *The Upanishads, Selections from the 108 Upanishads with English Translation*. Madras: G. A. Natesan and Co., 1940.
Maitra, Susil Kumar, *Madhva Logic*. Calcutta: University of Calcutta, 1936.
Maitra, Susil Kumar, *The Spirit of Indian Philosophy*. Benares: the author, 1947.
Majumder, Jnanendra Lal, "The Philosophy of Gauḍapada." *Indian Historical Quarterly*, Vol. 23, 1947, pp. 1–16.
Malkani, Ghansamdas Ratanmal, Das, R., and Murti, T. R. V., *Ajñāna*. London: Luzac and Co., 1933.
Malkani, G. R., *Metaphysics of Advaita Vedānta*. Amalner: The Indian Institute of Philosophy, 1961.
Malkani, G. R., *Philosophy of the Self*. Amalner: The Indian Institute of Philosophy, 1939.
Malkani, G. R., "Self-consciousness and Consciousness of Other Minds," in *The 33rd Indian Philosophical Congress*, Selected Papers, 1958, pp. 33–37.
Malkani, G. R., A *Study of Reality*. Bombay: The Modern Book Stall, 1927.

Mazumdar, A. K., "Knowledge and Self-Knowledge," in *The 24th Indian Philosophical Congress*, Madras, 1949, pp. 43–47.

Mehta, Rohit, *The Intuitive Philosophy*. Adyar: The Theosophical Publishing House, 1950.

Mehta, S. S., *A Critical Survey and Summary of the Leading Upanishads*. Bhavnagar: Saraswati Press, 1908.

Mehta, S. S., *A Manual of Vedānta Philosophy as revealed in the Upanishads and Bhagavadgītā*. Bombay: publishing house not given, 1919.

Menon, Y. Keshava and Allen, Richard F., *The Pure Principle*. East Lansing, Michigan: Michigan State University Press, 1960.

Milburn, R. Gordon, *The Religious Mysticism of the Upanishads*. London: Theosophical Publishing House, 1924.

Mishra, Umesha, *Conception of Matter According to Nyāya-Vaiçeṣika*. Allahabad: Allahabad Press, 1936.

Mitra, Vihari-Lala (translator), *The Yoga-Vāsishtha-Mahārāmāyana of Vālmiki*. Calcutta: Bonnerjee and Co., Vol. 1, 1891; Vol. 2, 1893; Vol. 3, 1898; Vol. 4, 1899.

Modi, P. M., "Relation between the Two Aspects of Brahman." *Indian Historical Quarterly*, Vol. 17, June 1941, pp. 160–171.

Mukerji, A. C., *The Nature of Self*. Allahabad: The Indian Press, 1938.

Mukerji, A. C., *Self, Thought and Reality*. Allahabad: Allahabad Indian Press, 1957.

Mukerji, M. N., "Teachings of the Upanishads." *Indian Review*, Vol. 41, December 1940.

Mukharji, Nalinimohan Sastri, *A Study of Śaṅkara*. Calcutta: University of Calcutta, 1942.

Mukhopadhyaya, Govindagopal, *Studies in the Upaniṣads*. Calcutta: Sanskrit College, 1960.

Mukhopadhyaya, Paramathanath, *Introduction to Vedānta Philosophy*. Calcutta: The Book Co., 1928.

Mukhopadhyaya, S. C. (editor), *The Bhagabat Gita with the Commentary by Shri Shankaracharya*. Calcutta: The Proprietor, 1902.

Müller, F. Max, *Three Lectures on the Vedānta Philosophy*. London: Longmans, Green and Co., 1894.

Müller, F. Max (translator), *The Upanishads*. Second impression. *The Sacred Books of the East*, Vols. 1, 15. London: Oxford University Press, 1926.

Murty, K. Satchidananda, *Revelation and Reason in Advaita Vedānta*. London: Asia Publishing House, 1961.

Nagaraja Sarma, R., *Reign of Realism in Indian Philosophy. The Dwaita Vedānta of Madhva*. Madras: National Press, 1937.

Nakamura, Hajime, *Ways of Thinking of Eastern Peoples: India-China-Tibet-Japan*. Honolulu: East-West Center Press, 1964.

Narain, K., *A Critique of Madhva, Refutation of the Śaṅkara School of Vedānta*. Allahabad: Udayana Publications, 1964.

Narain, K., *An Outline of Madhva Philosophy*. Allahabad: Udayana Publications, 1962.

Narasimha, B. V., *Self-realization, Life and Teachings of Sri Ramana Maharshi*. Fifth edition. Tiruvannamalai: T. V. Venkataraman, 1953.

Narayanaswami Aiyar, K. (translator), *Laghu-Yogavāsiṣṭha*. Madras: Thompson and Co., 1896.
Narayanaswami Aiyar, K. (translator), *Thirty Minor Upanishads*. Madras: The Vasanta Press, 1914.
Narayanaswami Aiyar, K. (translator), *Yoga Vasiṣṭha*. Madras: K. N. Aiyar, 1914.
Nikhilananda, Swami (editor), *Self-knowledge* (*Ātmabodha*), *An English Translation of Sankara-charya's Ātmabodha*. New York: Ramakrishna-Vivekananda Center, 1946.
Nikhilananda, Swami, *The Upanishads*. London: Phoenix House, Vol. 1, 1951; Vol. 2, 1954; Vol. 3, 1956; Vol. 4, 1958.
Nikhilananda, Swami (translator), *Vedāntasāra of Sadānanda*. (*The Essence* [*sāra*] *of the Doctrines of Vedānta*.) Mayavati: publishing house not given, 1931.

Pal, Dhirendra Nath, *Śaṅkara the Sublime*. Calcutta: S. C. Gupta, 1912.
Pandeya, R. C., *The Problem of Meaning in Indian Philosophy*. Delhi: Motilal Banarsidass, 1963.
Pessein, J. F., *Vedānta Vindicated*. Trichinopoly: St. Joseph's Industrial School Press, 1925.
Ponniah, V., *The Saiva Siddhanta Theory of Knowledge*. Annamalainagar: Annamalai University, 1952.
Prabhavananda, Swami and Isherwood, Christopher (translators), *The Crest-Jewel of Discrimination by Śaṅkaracharya*. Hollywood, Calif.: Vedanta Press, 1947.
Prabhavananda, Swami and Manchester, Frederick, *The Upanishads*. Hollywood: Vedanta Society of Southern California, 1948. Mentor Book, 1957.
Prasad, Jwala, *History of Indian Epistemology*. Delhi: Munshi Ram Manohar Lal, 1956.
Prasad, Jwala, *Indian Epistemology*. *The Punjab Oriental Series*, No. 25. Lahore: Punjab Sanskrit Book Depot, 1939.

Radhakrishnan, Sarvepalli, *The Brahma Sūtra: The Philosophy of Spiritual Life*. London: George Allen and Unwin, 1960.
Radhakrishnan, Sarvepalli, "The Doctrine of Māyā in the Vedāntic Philosophy." *International Journal of Ethics*, July 1914.
Radhakrishnan, Sarvepalli, *The Ethics of the Vedānta and Its Metaphysical Presuppositions*. Madras: The Guardian Press, 1908.
Radhakrishnan, Sarvepalli, "The Metaphysics of the Upanishads." *The Indian Philosophical Review*, Vol. 3, 1920, pp. 213–236, 346–362.
Radhakrishnan, Sarvepalli, *The Philosophy of the Upanishads*. London: George Allen and Unwin, 1935.
Radhakrishnan, Sarvepalli, *The Principal Upanishads*. London: George Allen and Unwin, 1953.
Radhakrishnan, Sarvepalli, *Vedānta According to Śaṅkara and Rāmānuja*. London: George Allen and Unwin, 1928. (First published as part of *Indian Philosophy*, Vol. 2.)
Raghavendracharya, H. N., *The Dvaita Philosophy and Its Place in the Vedānta*. Mysore: University of Mysore, 1941.

Rai, Dalpat, *The Upanishads: An Introduction to their Study*. Lahore: Arobans Press, 1897.
Raj Chandra, *The Ātma-siddhi*, or *The Self-realization of Shrimad Rajchandra*. Translated by J. L. Jaini. Ahmedabad: Shrimad Raja Chandra Gyan Pracharak Trust, 1960.
Rama Vasu (translator), *Vedānta-parijāta-saurabha of Nimbarka and Vedānta-kaustubha of Srīnivāsa. Commentaries on the Brahma-Sūtras*. Calcutta: Bibliotheca, Indica, No. 259, 1940. Calcutta: Royal Asiatic Society of Bengal, 1940–1943.
Ramana Maharshi, *The Collected Works of Ramana Maharshi*. Edited by Arthur Osborne. London: Rider and Co., 1959.
Ramana Maharshi, *Erase the Ego*. Bombay: Bharatiya Vidya Bhavan, 1963.
Ramana Maharshi, *Maharshi's Gospel*. Tiruvannamalai: Sri Ramanasraman, 1949.
Ramana Maharshi, *The Quintessence of Wisdom*, or *The Thirty Verses of Sri Ramana*. Madras: S. Viswanathan, 1955.
Ramana Maharshi, *Self-Enquiry*. Tiruvannamalai: Sri Ramanasraman, 1952.
Ramana Maharshi, *Spiritual Instruction*. Tiruvannamalai: Sri Ramanasraman, 1948.
Ramana Maharashi, *The Teachings of Bhagavan Sri Ramana Maharshi in His Own Words*. Edited by Arthur Osborne. London: Rider and Co., 1962.
Ramana Maharshi, *Truth Revealed*. Tiruvannamalai: Sri Ramanasraman, 1950.
Ramana Maharshi, *Who Am I?* Eighth edition. Tiruvannamalai: Sri Ramanasraman, 1955.
Ramananda and Starr, Meredith, *Ātma-jnan*, or *The Garden of the Heart*. London: William Rider and Son, 1914.
Ramanujachari, V. K. (translator), *The Vedanta-Sutra*. Kumbakonam: the author, 1930.
Ramasubba, Sastri R., *Hindu Religion, Vedānta Philosophy and Modern Psychology*. Trivandrum: Sridhava Power Press, 1922.
Randle, Herbert Niel, *Indian Logic in the Early Schools*. London: Humphrey Milford, Oxford University Press, 1930.
Rangacarya, Malur Rao Bahadur (translator), *The Sarva-siddhānta-saṅgraha of Śaṅkarācārya*. Madras: Government Press, 1909.
Rangacharya, Malur Rao Bahadur and Varadaraja Aiyangar, M. B. (translators), *The Vedānta-sūtras with the Śrī Bhāshya of Rāmānujāchārya*, Vol. I. Madras: The Brahmavadin Press, 1899.
Rao, B. A. Krishnaswamy, *Outlines of the Philosophy of Sri Madwacharya*. Tumkur: privately published, 1951.
Rao, K. B. Ramakrishna, *Ontology of Advaita with Special Reference to Māyā*. Mulki: Vijaya College, 1964.
Rao, T. Bhujanga, "Dreamless Sleep (Suṣupti) in Vedānta." *Vedānta Kesarī*, Ramakrishna Math, Madras, Vol. 32, September 1945.
Rawson, Joseph Nadin, *The Katha Upaniṣad*. Oxford: Oxford University Press, 1934.
Roy, S. S., *The Heritage of Śaṅkara*. Allahabad: Udayana, 1965.

Samartha, S. J., *Introduction to Radhakrishnan*. New York: Association Press, 1964.

Sandal, Pandit Mohan Lal, *Philosophical Teachings in the Upanisats. The Sacred Books of the Hindus*, Extra V. Allahabad: The Panini Office, 1926.
Sarkar, Mahendranath, *Comparative Studies in the Vedānta*. London: Oxford University Press, 1927.
Sarkar, Mahendranath, *Hindu Mysticism According to the Upanishads*. London: Kegan Paul, Trench, Trubner and Co., 1934.
Sarkar, Mahendranath, *The System of Vedāntic Thought and Culture*. Calcutta: University of Calcutta, 1925.
Sarma, D. S., *Dialectic in Buddhism and Vedānta*. Banaras: Nand Kishore and Bros., 1952.
Sarma, Nagaraja, *The Reign of Realism in Indian Philosophy, Exposition of Ten Works by Madhva*. Madras: The National Press, 1937.
Sastri, Alladi Mahadeva (translator), *The Bhagavad-gītā with the Commentary of Shri Shankarāchārya*. Madras: Minerva Press, 1897.
Sastri, A. Mahadeva, *The Vedānta Doctrine of Śrī Śaṅkarāchārya*. Madras: Minerva Press, 1899.
Sastri, Kokileswar, "Māyā in Śaṅkara-Vedānta: Its Objectivity," in *Jha Commemoration Volume*. Poona: Oriental Book Agency, 1937, pp. 327–342.
Sastri, Kokileswar, *A Realistic Interpretation of Śaṅkara-Vedānta*. Calcutta: University of Calcutta, 1931.
Sastri, S. Kuppuswami, *Compromises in the History of Advaitic Thought*. Madras: The Kuppuswami Sastri Research Institute, 1946.
Sastri, S. Kuppuswami, *A Primer of Indian Logic according to Annambhatta's Tarkasamgraha*. Madras: P. Varadachary and Co., 1932.
Sastri, S. Sitaram and Jha, Ganganatha, *The Upanishads and Śrī Śaṅkara's Commentary*. Madras: V. C. Seshacherri, 1898–1901.
Sastri, Vidyaratna Kokileswar, *An Introduction to Adwaita Philosophy*. Calcutta: University of Calcutta, 1926.
Satprakashananda, Swami, *Methods of Knowing according to Advaita Vedānta*. London: George Allen and Unwin, 1965.
Schomerus, H. W., *Der Caiva-Siddhanta eine Mystik Indiens*. Leipzig: J. C. Hinrichs'sche Buchhandlung, 1912.
Sen, Sris Chandra, *The Mystic Philosophy of the Upanishads*. Lucknow: Upper India Publishing House, 1937.
Sengupta, Bratindra Kumar, *A Critique on the Vivarana School*. Calcutta: Firma K. L. Mukhopadhyaya, 1959.
Seshadri, P., *Sri Sankaracharya*. Trivandrum: The University of Travancore, 1949.
Sharma, B. N. K., *A History of Dvaita School of Vedanta and its Literature*. Bombay: publishing house not given, 1960–1962.
Shastri, Prabhu Dutt, *The Doctrine of Māyā in the Philosophy of the Vedānta*. London: Luzac and Co., 1911.
Singh, Jaideva, "Some Problems in Connexion with the Nyāya Theory of Perception." *The Philosophical Quarterly* (Calcutta), Vol. 10, No. 4, 1935.
Singh, R. P., "The Individual Self in the Vedānta of Śaṅkara," in *25th Indian Philosophical Congress*, Part 1, Calcutta, 1950, pp. 141–147.
Singh, Ram Pratap, *The Vedānta of Śaṅkara—a Metaphysics of Value*, Vol. 1. Jaipur: Bharat Publishing House, 1949.
Sinha, Dababrata, *The Idealist Standpoint, A Study in the Vedāntic Meta-*

physic of Experience. Santiniketan: Centre of Advanced Study in Philosophy, 1965.

Sivananda, Swami, *Ātma Bodha of Śrī Śaṅkarāchārya*. Rishikesh: The Divine Life Trust Society, 1936.

Sivananda, Swami, *Dialogues from Upanishads on Knowledge of the Self*. Amritsar: Em. Airi, 1936.

Slater, T. E., *Studies in the Upanishads*. Madras: Christian Literature Society for India, 1897.

Sreeram, Lala (translator), *Vicārasāgara: Metaphysics of the Upaniṣads*. Calcutta: the author, 1885.

Srinivasa Aiyangar, T. R. (translator), *Sāmānya Vedānta Upanisads*. Madras: The Adyar Library, 1941.

Srinivasachari, P. N., *Studies in Vedānta*. Madras: P. Vavadachari and Co., 1941.

Srinivasachari, P. N., A *Synthetic View of Vedānta*. Mylapore: India Printing Works, 1940.

Srinivasa Chari, S. M., *Advaita and Viśiṣṭadvaita*. Bombay: Asia Publishing House, 1961.

Srisa Chandra Vasu and Bhattacharya Vidyabhusana, Pandit Ramaksyaya (translators), *The Brihdāranyaka Upaniṣad with the Commentary of Śrī Māhhvāchārya Called Ānandatīrtha. Sacred Books of the Hindus*, Vol. 22. Allahabad: The Panini Office, 1933.

Srisa Chandra Vasu (translator), *The Upanishads. Sacred Books of the Hindus*, Vol. 1. Allahabad: The Panini Office, 1909.

Srivastava, S. N. L., "Śaṁkara on God, Religion and Morality." *Philosophy East and West*, Vol. 7, Nos. 3 and 4, October 1957 and January 1958, pp. 91–105.

Subba Rau, S. (translator), *The Vedānta-Sūtras with the Commentary of Madhyacharya*. Madras: Thompson and Co., 1904.

Sundrar-Rama Aiyar, *The Vedānta: Its Doctrine of Divine Personality*. Srirangam: Sri Vanivalas Press, 1923.

Swami, Shree Purohit and Yeats, W. B., *The Ten Principal Upanishads*. London: Faber and Faber, 1937.

Tattvabushan, Sitanath, "The Philosophy of Śaṅkaracharya," in *Three Great Acharyas: Śaṅkara, Rāmānuja, Madhwa*. Madras: G. A. Natesan, 1923, pp. 75–109.

Telivala, Mulachandra Tulasidasa, *How Far Śaṅkarāchārya Truly Represented the View of the Author of the Brahma-sūtras*. Bombay: Nirnaya Sagar Press, 1918.

Thibaut, George (translator), *The Vedānta-Sūtras with the Commentary by Śaṅkarāchārya. The Sacred Books of the East*, Vols. 34, 38. Oxford: The Clarendon Press, 1890, 1896.

Tripati, M. S., A *Sketch of the Vedānta Philosophy*. Bombay: N.T.M. and Co., 1901.

Urquhart, W. S., *The Vedānta and Modern Thought*. London: Humphrey Milford, Oxford University Press, 1928.

Upadhyaya, Veerdmani Prasad, *Lights on Vedānta*. Varanasi: Chowkhamba Sanskrit Series Office, 1959.

Vaswani, T. L., *Atmagran*. Madras: Ganesh and Co., 1922.
Venkatarama Iyer, M. K., *Advaita Vedānta According to Śaṁkara*. Bombay: Asia Publishing House, 1964.
Venkataramanan, S. (translator), *Select Works of Śrī Śaṅkarāchārya*. Madras: G. A. Natesan and Co., n.d.
Verma, Prem Mohanlal, *Role of Vedānta as Universal Religion and Science of Self-realization*. Allahabad: Indian National Renaissance Society, 1959.
Vidyabhusana, Satis Chandra, *A History of Indian Logic*. Calcutta: University of Calcutta, 1921.
Vidyaratna, K., *Advaita Philosophy*. Calcutta: Calcutta University, 1924.
Vivekananda, Swami, *Addresses on the Vedānta Philosophy*. Luzac and Co., 1896.
Vivekananda, Swami, *Vedānta Philosophy. Jñāna Yoga*. London: Luzac and Co., 1907.
Viveswarananda, Swami, *Brahmasūtras*. Calcutta: Advaita Ashrama, 1936.

Wadiyar, Jaya Chamaraja, *Dattātreya*. London: George Allen and Unwin, 1957.
Warrier, A. G. Krishna, *The Concept of Mukti in Advaita Vedānta*. Madras: University of Madras, 1961.

Yale, John, *What Vedānta Means to Me: A Symposium*. London: Rider and Co., 1961.
Yateswarananda, Swami, *Adventures in Vedānta*. London: Rider and Co., 1961.

KARMA MĀRGA

Aiyar, V. V. S. (translator), *Kural*, or *Maxims of Tiruvalluvar*. Madras: Amudha Nilayam, 1961.
Altekar, A. S., *Education in Ancient India*. Banaras: Indian Book Shop, 1934.
Altekar, Anant S., *The Position of Women in Hindu Civilization*. Benares: The Culture Publication House, Benares Hindu University, 1938.
Altekar, A. S., *Sources of Hindu Dharma in its Socio-religious Aspects*. Sholapur: Institute of Public Administration, 1952.
Altekar, Ananta Sadasiva, *State and Government in Ancient India*. Banaras: Motilal Banarasidass, 1955.
Ambedkar, B. R., *Annihilation of Caste*. Bombay: Bharat Bhushan Publishing Press, 1937.
Ambedkar, B. R., *Mr. Gandhi and the Emancipation of the Untouchables*. Bombay: Thacker and Co., 1943.
Ambedkar, B. R., *Untouchables—Who were they and why they became Untouchables*. New Delhi: Amrit Book Co., 1948.
Ambedkar, B. R., *What Congress and Gandhi have done to the Untouchables*. Bombay: Thacker and Co., 1945.
Ambedkar, B. R., *Who were the Sudras?* Bombay: Thacker and Co., 1946.
Andrews, C. F., *Mahatma Gandhi's Ideas*. London: George Allen and Unwin, 1929.
Appasamy, Paul, *Legal Aspects of Social Reform*. Madras: The Christian Literature Society for India, 1929.
Apte, V. M., *Social and Religious Life in the Gṛhya-Sūtras*. Bombay: Popular Book Depot, 1954.

Aranganatha Mudaliar, A. (translator), *Thirukkural*. Madras: Swarna Vilas, 1949.
Auboyer, Jeannine, *Daily Life in Ancient India*. Translated by S. W. Taylor. London: Asia Publishing House, 1965.
Aurobindo, *Bankim-Tilak-Dayānanda*. Calcutta: Arya Publishing House, 1947.
Aurobindo, *Essays on the Gītā*. New York: Sri Aurobindo Library, 1950.

Bader, Clarisse, *Women in Ancient India*. Translated by Mary E. R. Martin. London: Kegan Paul and Co., 1925.
Baig, Tara Ali (editor), *Women of India*. Delhi: Ministry of Information and Broadcasting, Government of India, 1958.
Bailey, F. G., *Caste and the Economic Frontier*. Manchester: Manchester University Press, 1957.
Bain, F. W. (translator), *The Ashes of a God*. London: Methuen and Co., 1911.
Bal, Upendranath, *Rammohun Roy*. Calcutta: U. Ray and Sons, 1935.
Banerjea, A. C., *Studies in the Brāhmaṇas*. Delhi: Motilal Banarsidass, 1963.
Banerji, G. C. (compiler), *Keshub Chunder Sen, Testimonies in Memoriam*. Allahabad: publisher not given, 1934.
Banerji, G. C., *Keshub Chundra and Ramakrishna*. Allahabad: Gyan Kutir, 1931.
Banerji, G. C., *Keshub as Seen by his Opponents*. Allahabad: The Indian Press, 1940.
Banerji, Suras Chandra, *Dharma-Sūtras: A Study in their Origin and Development*. Calcutta: Punthi Pustak, 1962.
Baroda, Her Highness the Maharani of, and Mitra, S. M., *The Position of Women in Indian Life*. New York: Longmans, Green and Co., 1911.
Basu, Srisa Chandra, *Daily Practice of the Hindus. Sacred Books of the Hindus*, Vol. 20. Allahabad: The Panini Office, 1918.
Benton, A. H., *Indian Moral Instruction and Caste Problems*. London: Longmans, Green and Co., 1917.
Bhagavan Das, *Science of Social Organization or the Laws of Manu in the Light of Ātmanvidyā*, Vol. 1. Adyar: Theosophical Publishing Society, 1932. Vol. 2, Adyar: Theosophical Publishing Society, 1935. Vol. 3, Banaras: Ananda Publishing House, 1948.
Bhandarkar, R. D., *Some Aspects of Ancient Hindu Polity*. Calcutta: Calcutta University Press, 1929.
Bharadwaja, Chiranjiva, *Light of Truth, or An English Translation of the Satyarth Prakash of Swami Dayananda Saraswati*. Allahabad: The Star Press, 1882.
Bharati, Swami Agehananda, *A Functional Analysis of Indian Thought and its Social Margins*. Varanasi: Chowkhamba Sanskrit, 1964.
Bhattacharya, Jogendra Nath, *Hindu Castes and Sects*. Calcutta: Thacker, Spink and Co., 1896.
Bhattacharyya, Bhabatosh, *Studies in Dharmaśāstra*. Calcutta: Ramakrishna Maitra, 1964.
Bhattacharyya, Panchanan, *Ideals of Indian Womanhood*. Calcutta: Goldguin and Co., 1921.
Bhatty, E. C., "Religious Minorities and the Secular State," in *Religious Freedom*. Bangalore: Committee for Literature on Social Concerns, 1956.

Bhave, Vinoba, *Talks on the Gita*. London: George Allen and Unwin, 1960.
Bloomfield, Maurice, *The Atharva-Veda*. Strassburg, 1899.
Bloomfield, Maurice (translator), *Hymns of the Atharva-Veda. Together with Extracts from the Ritual Books and the Commentaries. The Sacred Books of the East*, Vol. 42. Oxford: Clarendon Press, 1897.
Blunt, E. A. H., *The Caste System of Northern India*. London: Oxford University Press, 1931.
Bon, Tridandi Swami B. H., *The Geeta: as a Chaitanyite Reads It*. Bombay: Popular Book Depot, 1938.
Bondurant, J. V., *Conquest of Violence: The Gandhian Philosophy of Conflict*. London: Oxford University Press, 1959. Berkeley: University of California Press, 1966.
Bose, R. C., *Brahmoism;* or *History of Reformed Hinduism*. New York: Funk and Wagnalls, 1884.
Bose, Rajnarain, *The Adi Brahmo Samaj as a Church*. Calcutta: Valmiki Press, 1873.
Briggs, G. W., "The Harijan and Hinduism." *Review of Religion*, Vol. 2, No. 1, November 1937, pp. 33–59.
Brown, D. Mackenzie, *The White Umbrella: Indian Political Thought from Manu to Gandhi*. Berkeley: University of California Press, 1953.
Brown, W. Norman, *The Indian and Christian Miracles of Walking on the Water*. Chicago: Open Court Publishing Co., 1928.
Brown, W. Norman, *Man in the Universe. Some Cultural Continuities in India*. Berkeley and Los Angeles: University of California Press, 1966.
Buhler, Georg (translator), *The Laws of Manu with Extracts from Seven Commentaries. The Sacred Books of the East*, Vol. 25. Oxford: Clarendon Press, 1886.
Buhler, Georg (translator), *The Sacred Laws of the Aryas as Taught in the Schools of Apastamba, Gautama, and Baudhāyana. The Sacred Books of the East*, Nos. 2, 14. Oxford: Clarendon Press, 1897.
van Buitenen, J. A. B., "Dharma and Mokṣa." *Philosophy East and West*, Vol. 7, Nos. 1 and 2, April-July 1957, pp. 33–40.

Chakladar, Haran Chandra, *Social Life in Ancient India*. Calcutta: Susil Gupta, 1954.
Chakravarti, A., *Religion of Ahimsa*. Bombay: Ratan Chand Hirachand, 1959.
Chakravarti, A. (translator), *Tirukkural*. Madras: Diocesan Press, 1953.
Chakravarti, C., *A Study in Hindu Social Polity*. Calcutta: Ram Chandra Chakraberty, 1923.
Chakravarti, Satishchandra (editor), *Rammohun Roy: The Father of Modern India*. Calcutta: Rammohun Roy Centenary Committee, 1935.
Chandra, Ramaprasad and Majumdar, Jatindra Kumar, *Selections from Official Letters and Documents Relating to the Life of Raja Rammohun Roy*. Calcutta: Calcutta Oriental Book Agency, 1938.
Chatterjee, Heramba, *Studies in Some Aspects of Hindu Samskaras in Ancient India*. Calcutta: Sanskrit Pustak Bhandar, 1965.
Chatterji, Hiralal, *International Law and Inter-State Relations in Ancient India*. Calcutta: Firma K. L. Mukhopadhyay, 1958.
Chattopadhyaya, Basanta Kumar, "The Caste System." *The Mother*, Vol. 7, No. 4, December 1964, pp. 165–176.

Chattopadhyaya, Basanta Kumar, "Sahamaran or Sati." *The Mother,* Vol. 8, No. 8, April 1966, pp. 317–320.
Chattopadhyaya, Kamaladevi, *The Awakening of Indian Women.* Madras: Everyman's Press, 1939.
Chitale, Mahadeo Parashuram, *Bhagavad-Gītā and Hindu Dharma.* Poona: Continental Booksellers and Publishers, 1953.
Colebrooke, H. T. (translator), *The Law of Inheritance according to Mitākṣarā.* Calcutta: Hindusthanee Press, 1869.
Colebrooke, H. T. (translator), *Two Treatises on the Hindu Law of Inheritance.* Calcutta: Hindustanee Press, 1810.
Committee on Religious and Moral Instruction. *Report of the Committee on Religious and Moral Instruction.* New Delhi: Government of India Press, 1960.
Coomaraswamy, Ananda K., *Am I My Brother's Keeper?* New York: John Day, 1947.
Coomaraswamy, A. K., *The Religious Basis of the Forms of Indian Society.* New York: Orientalea, 1946.
Copeland, E. Luther, "Neo-Hinduism and Secularism." *A Journal of Church and State,* Vol. 9, No. 2, Spring 1967, pp. 200–210.
Cormack, Margaret, *The Hindu Woman.* Bombay: Asia Publishing House, 1961.
Cox, Oliver Cromwell, *Caste, Class, and Race.* New York: Monthly Review Press, 1959.

Dange, S. A., *India from Primitive Communism to Slavery.* Bombay: People's Publishing House, 1949.
Das, Adhar Chandra, "Christian and Indian Spiritual Ethics." *Visvabharati Quarterly,* Vol. 18, Part 4, 1953, pp. 307–320.
Das, Anivasa-Chandra, *The Vaisya Caste.* Calcutta: A. K. Roy and Co., 1903.
Dasgupta, Ramaprasad, *Crime and Punishment in Ancient India.* Calcutta: Calcutta Book Co., 1930.
Dasgupta, Surama, *Development of Moral Philosophy in India.* Bombay: Orient Longmans, 1961.
Datta, Bhupendra Nath, *Dialectics of Hindu Rituals.* Calcutta: Gupta Press, 1950.
Datta, D. M., *The Philosophy of Mahatma Gandhi.* Madison: University of Wisconsin Press, 1953.
Dayananda, Saraswati, *Light of Truth* (*Satyārtha Prakāśa*). Translated by G. P. Upadhyaya. Allahabad: Kal Press, 1947.
Desai, Mahadev, *The Gospel of Selfless Action,* or *the Gita According to Gandhi.* Ahmedabad: Navajivan Publishing House, 1946.
Devaraja, N. K., "Some Reflections on the Dearth of Ethical Thought in Indian Philosophy," in *Proceedings of the 36th session of the Indian Philosophical Congress,* Vol. 3, pp. 234–241.
Dhawan, G. N., *The Political Philosophy of Mahatma Gandhi.* Ahmedabad: Narajivan Publishing House, 1957.
Diehl, C. G., *Instrument and Purpose: Studies on Rites and Rituals in South India.* Lund: C. W. K. Gleerup, 1956.
Dimock, Edward C. and Gupta, Pratul Chandra (editors), *The Maharashta Purana.* Vol. 12 of A.A.S. Monographs, 1965.

Divatia, H. V., *The Art of Life in the Bhagavad Gita*. Bombay: Bhanan, 1953.
Diwakar, R. R., *Satyagraha, Its Technique and History*. Bombay: Hind Kitabs, 1946.
Drew, W. H. and Lazarus, John (translators), *Thirukkural*. Madras: Teacher's Publishing House, 1956.
Dubois, J. A., *Description of the Characters, Manners, and Customs of the People of India*. Madras: Higginbotham and Co., 1879.
Dubois, J. A., *Hindu Manners, Customs, and Ceremonies*. Third edition. Oxford: Clarendon Press, 1943.
Durrany, K. S., "The Humanistic Tradition and Tagore." *Darshana*, Vol. 7, No. 3, July 1967, pp. 42–48.
Dutt, B. N., *Studies in Indian Social Polity*. Calcutta: Purabi Publishers, 1944.
Dutt, M. N. (translator), *Dharma-śāstra*. Calcutta: Elysium Press, 1906–08.
Dutt, Manmatha Nath (translator), *A Prose English Translation of the Mahābhārata*, 8 vols. Calcutta: H. C. Dass, 1895–1905. Reprint, New Delhi, 1960.
Dutt, Nripendra Kumar, *Origin and Growth of Caste in India*. Vol. 1. London: Kegan Paul, Trench, Trubner and Co., 1931. Vol. 2, Calcutta: Firma F. L. Mukhopadhyay, 1965.
Dutt, Romesh C., *The Mahabharata Epic of the Bharatas*. Allahabad: Kitabistan, 1944.
Dutt, Romesh C., *The Ramayana and Mahabharata*. New York: E. P. Dutton and Co., 1898.
Dutt, Romesh C., *The Ramayana Epic of Rama, Prince of India*. Allahabad: Kitabistan, 1944.

Edgerton, Franklin, *The Bhagavad Gītā Translated and Interpreted. Harvard Oriental Series*, Vols. 38, 39. Cambridge: Harvard University Press, 1944.
Edgerton, Franklin, *The Mīmāṁsā Nyāya Prakāśa of Āpadevī: A Treatise on the Mīmāṁsā System of Apadeva*. New Haven: Yale University Press, 1929.
Edgerton, Franklin, "The Philosophic Materials of the Atharva Veda," in *Studies in Honor of Maurice Bloomfield*. New Haven: Yale University Press, 1920, pp. 117–135.
Edgerton, William Franklin (translator), *The Panchatantra Reconstructed*. New Haven: Yale University Press, 1924.
Ellis, F. W., *Thirukkural*. Madras: University of Madras, 1955.

Fischer, Louis, *The Life of Mahatma Gandhi*. London: Jonathan Cape, 1951.

Gaer, Joseph, *The Adventures of Rama*. Boston: Little, Brown, 1954.
Gandhi, M. K., *Autobiography, The Story of My Experiments with Truth*. Ahmedabad: Navajivan Press, 1940. Washington, D.C.: Public Affairs Press, 1948.
Gandhi, M. K., *Constructive Programme, Its Meaning and Practice*. Ahmedabad: Navajivan Press, 1938.
Gandhi, M. K., *The Gandhi Sutras*. New York: Devon-Adair Co., 1949.
Gandhi, M. K., *Hindu Dharma*. Edited by Bharatan Kumarappa. Ahmedabad: The Navajivan Publishing House, 1950.

Gandhi, M. K., *Rāmanāma, The Infallible Remedy*. Karachi: Anand T. Hingorani, 1947.
Ghosh, Batakrishna, *The Hindu Ideal of Life*. Calcutta: Bharati Mahavidyalaya, 1947.
Ghosha, K. C., *Keshab Chunder Sen and the New Reformation*. Allahabad: G. C. Banerjee, 1937.
Ghoshal, Upendra Nath, *A History of Hindu Political Theories*. London: Oxford University Press, Humphrey Milford, 1923.
Ghoshal, Upendra Nath, *History of Hindu Public Life*, Part 1. Calcutta: Ramesh Ghoshal, 1945.
Ghurye, G. S., *Caste and Race in India*. Bombay: Popular Book Depot, 1957.
Ghurye, G. S., *Caste, Class and Occupation*. Bombay: Popular Book Depot, 1961.
Gonda, Jan, *Ancient Indian Kingship From the Religious Point of View*. Leiden: E. J. Brill, 1966.
Govinda, Das, *Hindu Ethics*. Madras: G. A. Natesan, 1927.
Govinda, Dasa Kaunsal, *Mahatma Gandhi, The Great Rogue of India?* Delhi: 'Garcon,' 1939.
Graham, J. Reid, *The Arya Samaj as a Reformation in Hinduism with Special Reference to Caste*. Unpublished doctoral dissertation. New Haven: Yale University, 1942.
Griffith, R. T. H. (translator), *The Rāmāyana of Valmiki*, 5 vols. London: Trubner and Co., 1870.
Growse, F. S. (translator), *The Ramayana of Tulsi Das*. Allahabad: N.W. Provinces and Oudh Government Press, 1883.

Hamsa Yogi, *Samskaras: the Genius behind Sacramental Rites*. Madras: Suddha Dharma Office, 1951.
Held, G. I., *The Mahābhārata: an Ethnological Study*. London: Kegan Paul, 1935.
Hill, W. D. P. (translator), *Bhagavad-Gītā*. London: Oxford University Press, 1928.
Hill, W. D. P., *The Holy Lake of the Acts of Rāma*. Translation of *Ramacaritamanasa* of Tulsi Das. London: Oxford University Press, 1952.
Hogg, A. G., *Karma and Redemption*. Madras: Christian Literature Society for India, 1910.
Hopkins, Edward Washburn, *Ethics of India*. New Haven: Yale University Press, 1924.
Hopkins, Edward Washburn, *The Great Epic of India*. New York: Charles Scribner's Sons, 1901.
Hopkins, Edward Washburn, "Modification of the Karma Doctrine." *Journal of the Royal Asiatic Society of Great Britain and Ireland*. 1906. pp. 581–593.
Hopkins, Edward Washburn, *The Mutual Relations of the Four Castes*. Leipzig: publishing house not given, 1881.
Houghton, G. C. (editor), *Manava-Dharma-śāstra*, or *The Institutes of Manu*, Vol. 1, Sanskrit text. Vol. 2, English translation. London: publishing house not given, 1825.
Humphreys, Christmas, *Karma and Rebirth*. London: John Murray, 1959.
Hutton, J. H., *Caste in India*. Cambridge: Cambridge University Press, 1946.

Ingalls, Daniel H. H., "Dharma and Mokṣa." *Philosophy East and West*, Vol. 7, Nos. 1 and 2, April-July 1957, pp. 41–48.

Isaacs, Harold, *India's Ex-Untouchables*. New York: John Day and Co., 1965.

Jagirdar, P. J., *India's Major Problems*. Bombay: Hind Kitabs, 1945.

Jast, J. S., *Reincarnation and Karma*. New York: Castle Books, 1956.

Jayaswal, Kasi Prasad, *Hindu Polity*. Bangalore: Bangalore Printing and Publishing Co., 1955.

Jayaswal, K. P., *Manu and Yājñavalkya—A Basic History of Hindu Law*. Calcutta: Butterworth, 1930.

Jha, Ganganatha (translator), *Manu Smṛti, The Laws of Manu with the Bhasya of Medhatithi*, 5 vols. Calcutta: Calcutta University, 1920–1926.

Jha, Ganganatha, *Prabhākara School of Pūrva Mīmāṁsa*. Benares: Benares Hindu University, 1918.

Jha, Ganganatha, *Pūrva Mīmāṁsa in its Sources: with a Critical Bibliography by Umesha Mishra*. Benares: Benares Hindu University, 1942.

Jha, Ganganatha (translator), *The Pūrva Mīmāṁsa Sūtras of Jaimini*, Ch. 1–3, in *Sacred Books of the Hindus*, Vol. 10. Oxford: Clarendon Press, 1916.

Jolly, Julius, *Hindu Law and Custom*. Translated by B. K. Ghosh. Calcutta: Greater India Society, 1928.

Jolly, Julius (translator), *The Institutes of Viṣṇu. The Sacred Books of the East*, Vol. 7. Oxford: Clarendon Press, 1880.

Jolly, Julius (translator), *The Minor Law-books* (Part I); *Nārada Bṛhaspati. The Sacred Books of the East*, Vol. 33. Oxford: Clarendon Press, 1889.

Jolly, Julius (translator), *Naradiva Dharmaśāstra*, or *The Institutes of Nārada*. London: Trubner and Co., 1876.

Jolly, Julius, *Outlines of a History of the Hindu Law of Partition, Inheritance, and Adoption, as Contained in the Original Sanskrit Treatises*. Calcutta: Thacker, Spink and Co., 1885.

Jones, William (translator), *Institutes of Hindu Law*; or *the Ordinances of Manu*. Calcutta: Indian Government, 1794.

Judge, William Q. and Crosbie, Robert, *Notes on the Bhagavad Gītā*. Los Angeles: The Theosophy Co., 1928.

Kane, Pandurang Vanam, *A Brief Sketch of the Pūrva-Mīmāṁsā System*. Poona: printed for the author by A. B. Patvardham at the Aryabhushan Press, 1924.

Kane, Pandurang Vaman, *History of Dharmashastra*, 5 vols. Poona: Bhandarkar Oriental Research Institute, 1932–1958.

Kannan, C. T., *Intercaste and Intercommunity Marriages in India*. Bombay: Allied Publishers, 1963.

Kapadia, K. M., *Hindu Kinship; an Important Chapter in Hindu Social History*, Bombay: Popular Book Depot, 1947.

Kapadia, K. M., *Marriage and Family in India*. Bombay: Oxford University Press, 1955.

Karambelkar, V. M., *The Atharva-Veda and the Ayur-Veda*. Nagpur: Vidarbha Samshodhana Mandala, 1961.

Karandikar, S. V., *Hindu Exogamy*. Bombay: D. B. Taraporevala Sons and Co., 1929.

Karim, Nazmul, *Changing Society in India and Pakistan*. London: Oxford University Press, 1956.
Karve, Irawati, *Changing India: Aspects of Caste Society*. Bombay: Asia Publishing House, 1961.
Karve, Irawati, *Hindu Society: An Interpretation*. Poona: Deccan College, 1961.
Karve, Irawati, *Kinship Organization in India*. Poona: Deccan College, 1953.
Keer, Dhananjay, *Dr. Ambedkar, Life and Mission*. Bombay: A. V. Keer, 1954.
Keith, A. B., *Karma Mimamsa*. Calcutta: Association Press, 1921.
Keith, A. B., *The Sanskrit Dharma in its Origin, Development, Theory, and Practice*. Oxford: Clarendon Press, 1924.
Kellock, James, *Mahadev Govind Ranade, Patriot and Social Servant*. Calcutta: Association Press, 1926.
Ketkar, Shridhar V., *The History of Caste in India*. Ithaca: Taylor and Carpenter, 1909.
Kitts, Eustace John, *A Compendium of the Castes and Tribes found in India*. Bombay: Education Society's Press, 1885.
Kripalani, Krishna R., *Rabindranath Tagore: A Biography*. London: Oxford University Press, 1962.

Lacy, Creighton, *The Conscience of India: Moral Traditions in the Modern World*. New York: Holt, Rinehart and Winston, 1965.
Lal, P. (translator), *The Bhagavad Gita*. Calcutta: Writers Workshop, 1965.
Lararas, J. (translator), *The Kural of Tiruvalluvar*. Madras: W. Pushparatha Chettiar, 1885.
Law, Narendra Nath, *Aspects of Ancient Indian Polity*. Oxford: Clarendon Press, 1921.
Law, Narendra Nath, *Studies in Ancient Hindu Polity, based on the Arthaśāstra of Kartilya*. London: Longmans and Co., 1914.
Leonard, G. S., *A History of the Brahmo Samaj from its Rise to 1878*. Calcutta: Adi Brahmo Samaj Press, 1879.
Lillingston, F., *The Brahmo Samaj and Arya Samaj in Their Bearing upon Christianity*. London: Macmillan and Co., 1901.

McCulloch, Leonard Arden, *The Teachings of the Bhagavad Gītā and the Teachings of the Fourth Gospel Compared and Contrasted*. Kharar: Masha'l Printing Press, n.d.
Macdougall, William Charles, *The Way of Salvation in the Ramayan of Tulsi Das*. Chicago: University of Chicago Libraries, 1926.
Macfie, J. M., *Myths and Legends of India*. Edinburgh: T. and T. Clark, 1924.
Macfie, J. M., *The Ramayan of Tulsī Dās, or the Bible of Northern India*. Edinburgh: T. and T. Clark, 1930.
Macfie, J. M., *The Vishnu Purāna*. Madras: Christian Literature Society for India, 1926.
McKenzie, John, *Hindu Ethics: a Historical and Critical Essay*. London, New York: Oxford University Press, Humphrey Milford, 1922.
Maine, Henry James Sumner, *Dissertations on Early Law and Custom*. London: John Murray, 1883.
Maitra, S. K., *The Ethics of the Hindus*. Calcutta: Calcutta University Press, 1925.

Majumdar, D. N., *Caste and Communication in an Indian Village*. Bombay: Asia Publishing House, 1959.

Majumdar, D. N., *Races and Cultures of India*. Bombay: Asia Publishing House, 1961.

Majumdar, Jatindrakumar, *Raja Rammohun Roy and Progressive Movements in India. A Selection from Records.* (1775–1845). Calcutta: Art Press, 1941.

Majumdar, Jatindra Kumar (editor), *Raja Rammohun Roy and the Last Moghuls*. Calcutta: Art Press, 1939.

Majumdar, R. C., *Corporate Life in Ancient India*. Calcutta: publishing house not given, 1918.

Majumder, J. C., *Ethics of the Mahābhārata*. Calcutta: the author, 1953.

Mal, Lala Kannoo (translator), *The Aphorisms of Narada*. Madras: S. Ganeson, 1923.

Mallick, Promatha Natha, *The Mahabharata as It Was, Is and Ever Shall Be; A Critical Study*. Calcutta: The Pioneer Press, 1934.

Mascaro, Juan (translator), *The Bhagavad Gītā*. Harmondsworth, Middlesex: Penguin Books, 1962.

Mayer, Adrian Curtis, *Caste and Kinship in Central India*. London: Routledge and Kegan Paul, 1960.

Mayne, John Dawson, *A Treatise on Hindu Law and Usage*. Tenth edition. Madras: Higginbothams, 1938.

Mazumdar, B. C., "Durga: Her Origin and History." *Journal of the Royal Asiatic Society of Great Britain and Ireland*, 1906, pp. 355–362.

Mees, Gualterus M., *Dharma and Society*. Holland: 'S-Gravenhage, 1935.

Meyer, Johann Jacob, *Sexual Life in Ancient India: A Study in the Comparative History of Indian Culture*. London: Routledge and Kegan Paul, 1930.

Mitra, S. K., *Ethics of the Hindus*. Calcutta: Calcutta University Press, 1925.

Motwani, Kewal, *Manu, A Study in Hindu Social Theory*. Madras: Ganesh and Co., 1937.

Motwani, Kewal, *Manu Dharma Śāstra*. Madras: Ganesh and Co., 1958.

Motwani, Kewal, *Science and Society in India*. Bombay: Hind Kitabs, 1945.

Mozoomdar, P. C., *The Faith and Progress of the Brahmo Samaj*. Calcutta: Calcutta Central Press Co., 1882. Second edition, Calcutta: Navavidhan Publication Committee, 1934.

Mozoomdar, P. C., *Keshub Chunder Sen and His Times*. Calcutta: The Brotherhood, 1917.

Mozoomdar, P. C., *The Life and Teachings of Keshub Chunder Sen*. Calcutta: Baptist Mission Press, 1887. Calcutta: Nababidhan Trust, 1931.

Mukerji, S. N., *Education in India—Today and Tomorrow*. Baroda: Acharya Book Depot, 1950.

Mukharji, Dhan Gopal, *Caste and Outcast*. London: J. M. Dent and Sons, 1923.

Mukharji, Dhan Gopal (translator), *The Song of God*. London: J. M. Dent and Sons, 1932.

Müller, F. Max, *Ram Mohan to Ramakrishna*. Calcutta: Susil Gupta, 1952.

Müller, F. Max, *Ramakrishna: His Life and Sayings*. New York: Charles Scribner's Sons, 1899. Calcutta: Advaita Ashrama, 1951.

Murdock, John (translator), *The Laws of Manu*, or *Manava-dharma-sastras*. London and Madras: The Christian Literature Society for India, 1898.

Myrdal, Gunnar, *Asian Drama*. 3 vols. New York: Random House, Pantheon Books, 1968.

Naik, Ramaro N., *Brahmanism without Casteism with Scientific Reasons Justifying Hindu Philosophy*. Bombay: Naik Brothers, 1961.
Nair, Kusum, *Blossoms in the Dust*. London: Gerald Duckworth and Co., 1961.
Nanda, B. R., *Mahatma Gandhi*. Boston: Beacon Press, 1958.
Nārada, *Nārada Sūtra: An Inquiry into Love-Bhaktijyansa*. London, Bombay, 1896. Second edition, London: John M. Watkins, 1904.
Nārada, *Naradiya dharmaśāstras*, or *the Institutes of Nārada*. London: Trubner and Co., 1896.
Narasimhan, Cakravarthi V. (translator), *The Mahabharata*. Calcutta: Oxford Book Company, 1965.
Naravane, V. S., *Rabindranath Tagore: A Philosophical Study*. Allahabad: Central Book Depot, n.d.
Narayana, Bhagavan Sri, *Sanātana Dharma Sootras*. Madras: The Suddha Dharma Office, 1958.
Narayanaswami Aiyar, K., *The Purāṇas in the Light of Modern Science*. Adyar, Madras: the author, 1914.
Navlekar, N. R., *A New Approach to the Rāmāyaṇa*. Jabalpur: the author, 1947.
Nigama, M. Zorawar Singh, *The Vedic Religion and its Expounder Swami Dayananda Saraswati*. Allahabad: Leader Press, 1914.
Nikhilananda, Swami (translator), *The Bhagavad Gītā*. New York: Ramakrishna-Vivekananda Center, 1944.
Nikhilananda, Swami (translator), *The Gospel of Sri Ramakrishna*. New York, Melbourne: Rider and Co., 1942.
Nikhilananda, Swami, *Ramakrishna: Prophet of New India*. New York: Harper and Brothers, 1942.
Noble, Margaret Elizabeth, *Religion and Dharma*. Calcutta: Advaita Ashrama, 1952.

Oldenberg, Hermann (translator), *The Gṛhya-Sūtras: Rules of Vedic Domestic Ceremonies. The Sacred Books of the East*, Vols. 29, 30. Oxford: Clarendon Press, 1886, 1892.
O'Malley, L. S. S., *Indian Caste Customs*. Cambridge: Cambridge University Press, 1932.
O'Malley, Lewis Sydney Steward, *India's Social Heritage*. Oxford: Clarendon Press, 1934.
Oman, J. C., *The Great Indian Epics: The Stories of the Rāmāyaṇa and the Mahābhārata*. London: G. Bell and Sons, 1894.
Otto, Rudolf, *The Original Gītā*. Edited and translated by J. E. Turner. London: George Allen and Unwin, 1939.
Ouwerkerk, Louise, *The Untouchables of India*. Oxford: Oxford University Press, 1945.

Pal, Bipinchandra, *The Brahmo Samaj and the Battle for Swaraj in India*. Calcutta: Sadharan Brahmo Samaj, 1945.
Pal, B. C., *The Spirit of Indian Nationalism*. London: Hind Nationalist Agency, 1910.

Pal, Radhabinod, *The Hindu Philosophy of Law in the Vedic and Post-Vedic Times Prior to the Institutes of Manu*. Calcutta: Bishwabhander Press, 1927.
Pal, Radhabinod, *The History of Hindu Law in the Post-Vedic Times Down to the Institutes of Manu*. Calcutta: Calcutta University, 1958.
Pande, Raj Bali, *Hindu Saṁskāras, a Socio-religious Study of the Hindu Sacraments*. Banaras: Vikrama, 1949.
Panikkar, K. M., *Caste and Democracy*. London: Hogarth Press, 1933.
Panikkar, K. M., *Hindu Society at Cross Roads*. Bombay: Asia Publishing House, 1955.
Parekh, Manilal C., *The Brahma Samaj*. Rajkot: Manilal C. Parekh, 1929.
Parekh, Manilal C., *Rajarshi Ram Mohan Roy*. Rajkot: Oriental Christ House, 1927.
Pargiter, Frederick Eden (translator), *The Mārkaṇḍeya Purāna*. Calcutta: Asiatic Society of Bengal, 1888.
Pillai, G. K., *Origin and Development of Caste*. Allahabad: Kitab Mahal, 1959.
Pinkham, M. W., *Women in the Sacred Scriptures of Hinduism*. New York: Columbia University Press, 1941.
Pope, G. U. (translator), *The "Sacred" Kural of Tiruvaḷḷuva Nāyanār*. London: W. H. Allen and Co., 1886.
Pope, G. U. (translator), *Thirukkural*. Tirunelvelli, Madras: South India Saiva Siddhanta Works Publishing Society, 1958.
Popley, H. A. (translator), *The Sacred Kural*, or *The Tamil Veda of Tiruvaḷḷuvar*. Calcutta: YMCA Publishing House, 1958.
Potdar, K. R., *Sacrifice in the Ṛgveda*. Bombay: Bharatiya Vidya Bhavan, 1953.
Prabhu, P. N., *Hindu Social Organization*. Bombay: Popular Book Depot, 1954.
Prasad, Beni, *Theory of Government in Ancient India—Post-Vedic*. Allahabad: Indian Press, 1927.
Prasad, Mahadeva, *Social Philosophy of Mahatma Gandhi*. Gorakpur: Vishwavidyalaya Prakashan, 1958.
Prasad, Narmadeshwar, *The Myth of the Caste System*. Patna: Samjna Prakashan, 1957.
Pratapachandra Ghosha, *Durga Puja*. Calcutta: Hindoo Patriot Press, 1871.
Pratapachandra Ghosha, *Origin of the Durga Puja*. Calcutta: Hindoo Patriot Press, 1874.
Prem, Sri Krishna, *The Yoga of the Bhagavat Gītā*. London: John M. Watkins, 1951.
Purnalingam Pillai, M. S., *Critical Studies in Kural*. Munnirpallam: publishing house not given, 1927.
Purnalingam Pillai, M. S. (translator), *Kural in English*. Tirunelveli, Madras: South India Saiva Siddhanta Works Publishing Society, 1942.
Pusalker, A. D., *Studies in the Epics and Purānas*. Bombay: Bharatiya Vidyabhavan, 1951.
Pyarelal, *Mahatma Gandhi, The Last Phase*. Ahmedabad: Navajivan Publishing House. Vol. 1, 1956; Vol. 2, 1958.

Radhakrishnan, Sarvepalli, *Education, Politics and War*. Poona: International Book Service, 1944.

Radhakrishnan, Sarvepalli, *Introduction to Mahatma Gandhi.* London: George Allen and Unwin, 1939.

Radhakrishnan, Sarvepalli, *The Philosophy of Rabindranath Tagore.* London: Macmillan and Co., 1918.

Radhakrishnan, Sarvepalli, *Religion and Society.* London: George Allen and Unwin, 1948.

Rai, Lala Lajput, *The Arya Samaj.* London: Longmans, Green and Co., 1915.

Rajagopala Aiyangar, M. R. (translator), *Thirukkural.* Madras: S. Viswanathan, 1950.

Rajagopalachari, C. (translator), *Kural.* Madras: Rochouse and Sons, 1950.

Rajagopalachari, C., *The Mahābhārata.* Fifth edition. Bombay: Bharatiya Vidya Bhavan, 1958.

Raju, P. T., "Activism in Indian Thought." *Annuals of the Bhandarker Oriental Institute,* Vol. 31, Parts 3–4, October 1958.

Ram Gopal, *India of Vedic Kalpa-Sutras.* Delhi: National Publishing House, 1959.

Rama-Chandra Aiyar, G., *The Hindu Ideal.* Madras: Madras Law Journal Press, 1933.

Ramachandra Dikshitar, V. R. (translator), *Thirukkural in Roman Transliteration.* Madras: Adyar Library, 1949.

Ramakrishna, *The Disciples of Sri Ramakrishna.* Almore: Published by Swami Pavitrananda, 1943. Calcutta: Advaita Ashrama, 1955.

Ramakrishna, *The Gospel of Ramakrishna.* Edited by Swami Abhedananda. New York: Vedanta Society, 1907.

Ramakrishna, *The Life of Sri Ramakrishna.* Calcutta: Advaita Ashrama, 1955.

Ramakrishna, *The Sayings of Sri Ramakrishna.* Mylapore, Madras: Sri Ramakrishna Math, 1925.

Ramakrishna, *Tales and Parables of Sri Ramakrishna.* Madras: Sri Ramakrishna Math, 1943.

Ramakrishna, *The Teachings of Sri Ramakrishna.* Almora: published by Swami Pavitrananda, 1943.

Ramakrishna, *Works.* Mylapore, Madras: Sri Ramakrishna Math, 1922.

Ramaswami, Sastri, K., *Studies in the Rāmāyana.* Baroda: Department of Education, 1944.

Ranade, Mahadeva Govinda, *Religious and Social Reform.* Collected and compiled by M. B. Kolasker. Bombay: G. Claridge and Co., 1902.

Ranade, R. D., *Bhagvadgītā as the Philosophy of God-Realization.* Nagpur: Nagpur University, 1959.

Rangacharya, Malur Rao Bahadur, *The Hindu Philosophy of Conduct.* Vol. 1, Madras: The Law Printing House, 1915; Vol. 2, Madras: G. A. Natesan, 1936; Vol. 3, Madras: G. A. Natesan, 1939.

Rangaswami Aiyanger, K. V., *Aspects of Ancient Indian Economic Thought.* Benares: Benares Hindu University, 1934.

Rangaswami Aiyanger, K. V., *Aspects of the Social and Political System of Manusmrti.* Lucknow: Lucknow University, 1949.

Rangaswami Aiyanger, K. V., *Some Aspects of the Hindu View of Life According to Dharmaśāstra.* Baroda: Baroda University, 1952.

Rao, P. Nagaraja, *The Bhagavad Gītā and the Changing World.* Ahmedabad: Sri Ramakrishna Seva Samiti, 1953.

Rao, Shakuntala Sastri, *Women in the Sacred Laws*. Bombay: Bhavan's Book, 1953.

Rao, Shakuntala Sastri, *Women in the Vedic Age*. Bombay: Bharatiya Vidyabhavan, 1954.

Rice, Stanley, *Hindu Customs and their Origins*. London: George Allen and Unwin, 1937.

Rolland, Romain, *The Life of Ramakrishna*. Mayavati, Almora: Advaita Ashrama, 1930.

Rolland, Romain, *The Life of Vivekananda and the Universal Gospel*. Calcutta: Advaita Ashrama, 1953.

Roy, Anilbaran, "Gita, the World Scripture," in *The Integral Philosophy of Śri Aurobindo*. Edited by Haridas Chaudhuri and Frederick Spiegelberg. London: George Allen and Unwin, 1960, pp. 231–238.

Roy, Anilbaran (editor) *The Message of the Gita as Interpreted by Sri Aurobindo*. London: George Allen and Unwin, 1938.

Roy, Pratapa Chandra (editor), *The Mahābhārata*. 12 vols. Calcutta: Oriental Publishing Co., 1884–1894.

Roy, Rammohun, *The English Works of Raja Ram Mohun Roy*. Edited by Jugendra Chunder Ghose. Calcutta: Eshan Chunder Bose, Vol. 1, 1885; Vol. 2, 1887.

Roy, Rammohun, *The English Works of Raja Rammohun Roy*. Edited by Kalidas Nag and Debajyoti Burman. Calcutta: Sadharan Brahmo Samaj, 1945.

Roy, Rammohun, *The Life and Letters of Raja Rammohun Roy*. Third edition. Edited by Dilip Kumar Biswas and Prabhat Chandra Ganguli. Calcutta: Sadharan Brahmo Samaj, 1962.

Roy Rammohun, *Raja Ram Mohun Roy, His Writings and Speeches*. Madras: Nathesan, 1925.

Roy, Rammohun, *Tuhfatul Muwahhiddin*, or *A Gift to the Deists*. Translated by Moulari Obaidullah el Obaide. Calcutta: Adi Brahmo Samaj, 1884.

Roy, Sarat Chandra, "Caste, Race, and Religion in India." *Man in India* (Ranchi), Vol. 14, 1934, pp. 39–63, 75–220, 271–311.

Roy, Satish Chandra, *The Bhagavad-Gītā and Modern Scholarship*. London: Luzac, 1941.

Ryder, Arthur W. (translator), *The Panachatantra*, Chicago: Chicago University Press, 1925.

Sampat Kumaran, M. R., "Hindu Social Ideals." *Triveni*, Vol. 10, May 1938, pp. 17–27.

Sandal, Pandit Mohan Lal (translator), *The Mīmāṁsā Sūtras of Jaimini. Sacred Books of the Hindus*, Vols. 27, 28, 1925.

Sarkar, B. K., *Positive Background of Hindu Sociology*. Allahabad: Panini Office, 1937.

Sarkar, Hem Chandra, *Brahmo Prayer Book*. Calcutta: the author, n.d.

Sarkar, Jadunath, "Indian Renaissance of the Nineteenth Century," in *Prabhuddha Bharata* (Calcutta), September 1928.

Sarkar, Kisarilala, *The Mīmāṁsā Rules of Interpretation as Applied to Hindu Law*. Calcutta: University of Calcutta, 1909.

Sarkar, Kishori Lal, *The Hindu System of Moral Science*. Calcutta: S. C. Majumder, 1912.

Sarkar, Mahendranath, *Mysticism in the Bhagavad Gītā*. Calcutta: Longmans, Green, and Co., 1929.
Sarkar, Subimal Chandra, *Some Aspects of the Earliest Social History of India*. London: Oxford University Press, 1920.
Sastri, Sivanath, *History of the Brahmo Samaj*. Calcutta: R. Chatterjee, 1911–1912.
Scott, Roland W., *Social Ethics in Modern Hinduism*. Calcutta: YMCA Publishing House, 1953.
Seal, Brajendranath, *Rammohun, The Universal Man*. Calcutta: Sadharan Brahmo Samaj, n.d.
Sen, Keshub Chunder, *Keshub Chunder Sen in England: Diary, Sermons, Addresses and Epistles*. Third edition. Calcutta: Navavidhan Publication Committee, 1938.
Sen, Keshub Chunder, *Keshub Chunder Sen's Lectures in India*. London: Cassell and Co., Vol. 1, 1901; Vol. 2, 1904.
Sen, Keshub Chunder, *Lectures and Tracts*. Edited by Sophia Dobson Collet. London: Strahan and Co., 1870.
Sen, Makhan Lal (translator), *The Ramayana*. Calcutta: Oriental Publishing Co., 1927.
Sen, Prosanto Kumar, *Biography of a New Faith*. Calcutta: Thacker, Spink and Co., Vol. 1, 1950; Vol. 2, 1954.
Sen, P. K., *Keshub Chunder Sen*. Calcutta: The Art Press, 1938.
Sen, Rajendra Nath (translator), *The Brahma Vaivarta Puranam, Brahma and Prakriti Khandas. Sacred Books of the Hindus*, Vol. 24, Part 1. Allahabad: The Panini Office, 1920.
Senart, Emile, *Caste in India*. Translated by B. Denison Ross. London: Methuen and Co., 1930.
Sengupta, N. C., *Evolution of Ancient Indian Law*. Calcutta: Eastern Law House, 1953.
Sengupta, Nares Chandra, *Outlines of a History of Hindu Law from the Vedic Times down to Manu*. Calcutta: Nares C. Sen Gupta, 1930.
Sengupta, N. C., *Sources of Law and Society in Ancient India*. Calcutta: Art Press, 1914.
Sharma, I. C., *Ethical Philosophies of India*. London: George Allen and Unwin, 1965.
Sharma, I. C., *India's Democracy and the Communist Challenge*. Lincoln, Nebraska: Johnsen Publishing Co., 1967.
Sharma, Ramsharan, *Śūdras in Ancient India*. Delhi: Motilal Banarsidass, 1958.
Shastri, Dakshinaranjan, *Origin and Development of the Rituals of Ancestor Worship in India*. Calcutta: Bookland Private Limited, 1963.
Shastri, H. P., *The Rāmāyana*. 3 vols. London: Shanti Sadan, 1952–1959.
Shastri, Pashupatinath, *Introduction to the Pūrva Mīmāṁsa*. Calcutta: A. N. Bhattacharya, 1923.
Sherring, M. A., *Hindu Tribes and Castes*. Calcutta: Thacker, Spink and Co., 1881.
Singh, Iqbal, *Rammohun Roy*. Bombay: Asia Publishing House, 1958.
Sitaramdas Omkarnath *et al*, "The Caste System," *The Mother*, Vol. 7, No. 4, December 1964, pp. 165–176.

Sivaswamy Aiyar, P. S., *Evolution of Hindu Moral Ideals*. Calcutta: University of Calcutta, 1935.
Smith, William Roy, *Nationalism and Reform in India*. New Haven: Yale University Press, 1938.
Srinivas, M. N. (editor), *Caste in Modern India and Other Essays*. Bombay: Asia Publishing House, 1962.
Srinivas, M. N., "Social Structure," in *The Gazetteer of India*, Vol. 1. The Government of India, 1965, pp. 501–577.
Srinivasachari, C. S., *Social and Religious Movements in the Nineteenth Century*. Bombay: National Information and Publications, 1947.
Srisa Chandra Vasu, *A Catechism of Hindu Dharma. The Sacred Books of the Hindus*, Extra III. Allahabad: The Panini Office, 1919.
Srisa Chandra Vasu (translator), *Yajñavalkya Smṛti*. Allahabad: The Panini Office, 1918.
Stevenson, Mrs. Sinclair, *The Rites of the Twice-Born*. London: Oxford University Press, 1920.
Stevenson, Mrs. Sinclair, *Without the Pale. The Life Story of an Outcaste*. Calcutta: Association Press, 1930.
Subba Rao, T., *The Philosophy of the Bhagavad Gita*. Madras: The Theosophical Society, 1912.
Sukthankar, Vishnu Sistam, *On the Meaning of the Mahabharata*. Bombay: Asiatic Society of Bombay, 1957.
Sundara-Rama Aiyar, *The Hindu Ideal and Practice of Duty*. Madras: Srinivan and Co., 1892.
Sundararama Aiyar, K, *Dharma and Life*. Srirangam: Vani Valas Press, 1924.
Sundarama Aiyar, K., *The Vedānta: Its Ethical Aspect*. Srirangam: Sri Vani Valas Press, 1923.

Tagore, Devendranath, *The Autobiography of Maharshi Devendranath Tagore*. Translated by Satyendra Nath Tagore and Indira Tagore. Calcutta: S. K. Lahiri and Co., 1909.
Tagore Rabindranath, *Creative Unity*. London: Macmillan and Co., 1922.
Tagore, Rabindranath, *Personality*. London: Macmillan and Co., 1959.
Tagore, Rabindranath, *The Religion of Man*. London: George Allen and Unwin, 1931.
Tagore, Rabindranath, *Sādhanā*. London: Macmillan and Co., 1913.
Tagore, Rabindranath, *Towards Universal Man*. Bombay: Asia Publishing House, 1961.
Tattvabhushan Sitanath, *A Manual of Brahma Ritual and Devotions*. Calcutta: Executive Committee, Sabharan Brahma Samaj, 1924.
Tennyson, Hallam, *India's Walking Saint: the Story of Vinoba Bhava*. New York: Doubleday, 1955.
Thadani, Nanikram Vasanmal, *The Mīmāmsā: The Secret of the Sacred Books of the Hindus*. Delhi: The Bharati Research Institute, 1952.
Thandani, N. V., *The Mystery of the Mahabharata*. 5 vols. Karachi: Bharat Publishing House, 1933.
Thirumalaimuthuswami, A., *A Bibliography on Thirukkural*. Madurai: Meenakshi Puththaka Nilayam, 1962.
Thomas, P., *Hindu Religion, Customs, and Manners*. Bombay: D. B. Taraporevala and Sons, 1948.

Thompson, Edward, *Ethical Ideals in India Today*. London: Watts and Co., 1942.
Thompson, Edward, *Suttee: A Historical and Philosophical Inquiry into the Hindu Rite of Widow-Burning*. London: George Allen and Unwin, 1928.
Tilak, Bal Gangadhar, *Bal Gangadhar Tilak, His Writings and Speeches*. Madras: Ganesh and Co., 1919.
Tilak, Bal Gangadhar, *Gita Rahasya*, or *The Science of Karma Yoga*. Poona: R. B. Tilak, 1935.
Tiwari, Chitra, *Śūdras in Manu*. Delhi: Motilal Banarsidass, 1963.

Underhill, Muriel Marion, *The Hindu Religious Year*. Calcutta: Association Press, 1921.

Vaidya, Chintaman V., *Epic India*. Bombay: Mrs. Radhabai Atmaram Sagoon, 1907.
Valavalkar, P. H., *Hindu Social Organization*. Bombay: Popular Book Depot, 1954.
Varadachari, K., *Aspects of Bhakti*. Mysore: Mysore University, 1956.
Varadachariar, S., *The Hindu Judicial System*. Lucknow: Lucknow University, 1946.
Vidyarnava, Rai Bahadur Srisa Chandra, *The Daily Practice of the Hindus*. Allahabad: The Panini Office, 1918.
Vidyarthi, L. P. (editor), *Aspects of Religion in Indian Society*. Meerut: Kedar Nath Ram Nath, 1962.
Visvanatha Aiyar, S. V., *International Law in Ancient India*. London: Longmans, Green and Co., 1925.
Visvanatha Aiyar, S. V., *Racial Synthesis in Hindu Culture*. London: Kegan Paul, 1928.
Vivekananda, Swami, *The Complete Works of Swami Vivekananda*. 8 vols. Mayavati, Almora, Himalayas: Advaita Ashrama, 1931.
Vivekananda, Swami, *The Life of Swami Vivekananda*. Calcutta: Advaita Ashrama, 1955.

Wadiyar, Jaya Chamaraja, *The Gītā and Indian Culture*. Calcutta: Orient Longmans, 1963.
Weber, Max, *The Religion of India: The Sociology of Hinduism and Buddhism*. Translated and edited by Hans H. Gerth and Don Martindale. Glencoe, Ill.: Free Press, 1958.
Whitehead, Henry, *Indian Problems in Religion, Education, Politics*. London: Constable and Co., 1924.
Whitney, W. D. and Lanman, C. R., *Atharva-veda Saṁhitā. Harvard Oriental Series*, Vols. 7, 8. Cambridge, Mass.: Harvard University, 1905.
Wood, Ernest, *The Bhagavad Gītā Explained*. San Francisco: American Academy of Asian Studies Graduate School, 1961.

Young, Miriam, *Among the Women of the Punjab: A Camping Record*. London: Carey Press, 1916.
Young, Miriam, *Seen and Heard in a Punjab Village*. London: Student Christian Movement Press, 1931.

Young, Miriam, *Storm Tossed. A Story of Indian Life*. London: Edinburgh House Press, 1934.

Zacharias, Hans Conrad Ernst, *Renascent India. From Rammohan Roy to Mohandas Gandhi*. London: George Allen and Unwin, 1933.

BHAKTI MĀRGA

Abadhut, Nityapadanda, *Philosophy of Union by Devotion*. Nabadip, West Bengal: Mahanirban Math, 1953.

Abhedananda, Swami, *Sayings of Sri Ramakrishna*. New York: Vedanta Society, 1903.

Ahmad Shah and Ormerad, S. W., *Hindi Religious Poetry*. Cawnpore: publishing house not given, 1925.

Allchin, F. R. (translator), *Kavitāvalī*. London: George Allen and Unwin, 1964.

Allison, W. L., *The Sadhs*. Calcutta: YMCA Publishing House, 1935.

Archer, William George, *Love Songs of Vidyapati*. London: Allen and Unwin, 1963.

Archer, William George, *The Loves of Krishna in Indian Painting and Poetry*. London: George Allen and Unwin, 1957.

Arnold, Edwin (translator), *Indian Idylls*. London: Trubner and Co., 1883.

Atkins, A. G., *The Ramayana of Tulsidas*. New Delhi: The Hindustan Times, 1954.

Aurobindo, *Hymns to the Mystic Fire*. London: Luzac and Co., 1952.

Ayyar, A. S. P., *Sri Krishna, the Darling of Humanity*. Madras: Madras Law Journal Office, 1957.

Baij Nath, Lala (translator), *Bradmanda Purana. The Adhyatma Ramayana. Sacred Books of the Hindus*, Extra I. Allahabad: The Panini Office, 1913.

Barnett, L. D., *Hindu Gods and Heroes*. London: Orient Press, 1922.

Barthwal, P. D., *The Nirguṇa School of Hindi Poetry*. Banaras: Indian Book Shop, 1936.

Basham, A. L., *History and Doctrines of the Ājīvikas: A Vanished Indian Religion*. London: Luzac and Co., 1951.

Basu, Anath Nath, *Mirabai*. London: George Allen and Unwin, 1934.

Basu, Manindramohan, *The Post-Caitanya Sahajiyā Cult of Bengal*. Calcutta: Calcutta University, 1930.

Basu, Srisa Chandra (translator), *Shiva Saṃhitā*. Calcutta: Heeralal Dhole, 1893. *Sacred Books of the Hindus*, Vol. 5, 1910; Vol. 15, Part I, 1914.

Baumer, Sybil, *An Introduction to Rabindranath Tagore's Mysticism*. London: H. R. Allenson, n.d.

Belvalkar, S. K. (translator), *Śrīmad Bhagavad-Gītā*. Varanasi. Hindu Visvavidyalaya, 1959.

Besant, Annie (translator), *The Bhagavad-Gītā*, or *The Lord's Song*. Wheaton, Illinois: The Theosophical Press, 1929.

Bhaktivinode, Thakur, *Sri Chaitanya Mahaprabhu: His Life and Precepts*. Seventh edition. Calcutta: Gaudiya Mission, 1946.

Bhandarkar, Prabhakar Ramakrishna, *Two Masters: Jesus and Tukārām*. Bombay: Tatvavivechaka Press, 1903.

Bhandarkar, Ramkrishna Gopal, *Vaiṣṇavism, Śaivism and Minor Religious Systems*. Strasbourg: K. J. Trubner, 1913.

Bharadwaj, Krishna Datta, *The Philosophy of Ramanuja*. New Delhi: Sir Shankar Lall Charitable Trust Society, 1958.

Bhattacarya, Siddhesvara, *The Philosophy of the Śrimad-Bhāgavata*. Santiniketan: Visva-Bharati Research Publication. Vol. 1, 1960; Vol. 2, 1962.

Bhattacharyya, Tarapada, *The Cult of Brahma*. Patna: C. Bhattacharya, 1957.

Bhave, Vinoba, *Talks on the Gita*. Kashi: Akhil Bharat Sarva Seva Prakashan, 1959.

Bon, Bhakti Hrdaya (translator), *Śrī Rūpa Gosvamī's Bhakti-Rasāmṛta-Sindhuh*. Vrindaban: Institute of Oriental Philosophy, 1965.

van Buitenen, J. A. B., *Ramanuja on the Bhagavad-Gītā, a Condensed Rendering of his Gitabhasya*. Leiden: 'S Gravenhage, 1954.

van Buitenen, J. A. B. (editor and translator), *Rāmānuja's Vedārthasamgraha*. Poona: Deccan College, 1956.

Carpenter, James Nelson, *The Theology of Tulasī Dās*. Madras: Christian Literature Society for India, 1918.

Carpenter, Joseph Estlin, *Theism in Medieval India*. London: Williams and Norgate, 1921.

Carstairs, G. Morris, *The Twice Born*. London: Hogarth Press, 1961.

Cave, Sydney, *Redemption, Hindu and Christian*. London: Oxford University Press, 1919.

Chakrabarti, Sandananda, *Our Master, Sri Sri Sitaramdas Onkarnath*. Calcutta: Srikumar Banerjee, 1957.

Chakravarti, Prabhatchandra, "Analysis of Bhakti." *Journal of Department of Letters*, Calcutta University, Vol. 28, 1935, pp. 1–13.

Chakravarti, P. C., *Doctrine of Śakti in Indian Literature*. Calcutta: General Printers and Publishers, 1940.

Chapman, J. A., *Religious Lyrics of Bengal*. Calcutta: The Book Co., 1926.

Chari, S. M. Shrinivasa, *Advaita and Viśiṣṭādvaita*. Bombay: Asia Publishing Co., 1961.

Chatterjee, S. C., *Classical Indian Philosophies, Their Synthesis in the Philosophy of Shri Rama Krishna*. Calcutta: University of Calcutta, 1963.

Chatterji, J. C., *Kashmir Śaivism*. Srinagar: Jammu and Kashmir State Research Department, 1914.

Chattopadhyaya, Narendra-Nath, *The Universal Religion of Sri Chaitanya*. Panihati: the author, 1926.

Chattopadhyaya, Nisikanta, *The Yātras*, or *The Popular Dramas of Bengal*. London: Trubner and Co., 1882.

Chattopadhyaya, Sudhakar, *The Evolution of Theistic Cults in Ancient India up to the Time of Saṁkarāchārya*. Calcutta: Progressive Publishers, 1962.

Chaudhuri, Niraja Kanta, "The Major Puranas." *The Mother*, Vol. 9, No. 8, April 1967, pp. 341–352.

Chaudhuri, Roma, *Sufism and Vedānta*. Calcutta: J. B. Chaudhuri, 1945–1948.

Coomaraswamy, Ananda K., *The Darker Side of the Dawn*. Washington, D.C.: Smithsonian Institute, 1935.

Coomaraswamy, Ananda K., *History of Indian and Indonesian Art*. London: Edward Goldston, 1927.

Coomarswamy, Ananda K., *The Transformation of Nature in Art*. Cambridge, Mass.: Harvard University Press, 1934.

Crooke, William, *An Introduction to the Popular Religion and Folklore of Northern India*. Westminister: Archibald Constable, 1896.

Crooke, William, *Religion and Folklore of Northern India*. London: Oxford University Press, 1926.

Crooke, William, "Secret Messages and Symbols Used in India." *Journal of the Bihar and Orissa Research Society* (Bankipore), Vol. 5, 1919, pp. 451–462.

Crowell, E. B. (translator), *The Aphorisms of Sandilya with the Commentary of Swapneswara*, or *The Hindu Doctrine of Faith*. Calcutta: Asiatic Society of Bengal, 1878.

Danielou, Alain, *Hindu Polytheism*. London: Routledge and Kegan Paul, 1964.

Das, A. C., *A Modern Incarnation of God*. Calcutta: General Printers and Publishers, 1958.

Das, Sudhendukumar, *Śakti* or *Divine Power*. Calcutta: Calcutta University, 1934.

Dasgupta, Alokeranjan, *The Lyric in Indian Poetry*. Calcutta: Firma K. L. Mukhopadhyay, 1962.

Dasgupta, B. V., *Some Aspects of Bengal Vaishnavism*. Dacca: S. N. Dasgupta, 1937.

Dasgupta, Shashi Bhusan, *Obscure Religious Cults*. Calcutta: Firma K. L. Mukhopadhyay, 1962.

Datta, Dhirendra Mohan, "Does Rāmānuja admit Identity-in-Difference?" Nineteenth Indian Philosophical Congress (Lucknow), 1944, pp. 139–142.

Datta, Santosha, *The Sacred Flame*. Chinsurah: Sudhir Dutta, 1940.

De, Sishil Kumar, *Ancient Indian Erotics and Erotic Literature*. Calcutta: Firma K. L. Mukhopadhyay, 1959.

De, Sushil Kumar, *Bengali Literature in the Nineteenth Century*. Calcutta: Firma K. L. Mukhopadhyaya, 1962.

De, Sushil Kumar, *Bengal's Contribution to Sanskrit Literature and Studies in Bengal Vaiṣṇavism*. Calcutta: Firma K. L. Mukhopadhyay, 1960.

De, Sushil Kumar, "The Bhakti-Rasa-Śāstra of Bengal Vaiṣṇavism." *Indian Historical Quarterly*, Vol. 8, No. 4, 1932, pp. 643–688.

De, Sushil Kumar, "Caitanya as an Author." *Indian Historical Quarterly*, Vol. 10, 1934, pp. 301–320.

De, Sushil Kumar, *Early History of the Vaiṣṇava Faith and Movement in Bengal*. Calcutta: General Printers and Publishers, 1942.

De, Sushil Kumar, *History of Sanskrit Poetics*. Calcutta: Firma K. L. Mukhopadhyaya, 1960.

De, Sushil Kumar, *Sanskrit Poetics as a Study of Aesthetics*. Berkeley: University of California Press, 1963.

Deming, Wilbur, *Rāmdās and the Rāmdāsīs*. Calcutta: Association Press, 1928.

Deutsch, Eliot S., "Śakti in Medieval Hindu Sculpture." *The Journal of Aesthetics and Art Criticism*, Fall 1965, pp. 81–89.

Dimock, Edward C., *The Place of the Hidden Moon*. Chicago: University of Chicago Press, 1966.

Dutt, Kanai Lal and Purkayastha, Kshetra M., *The Bengal Vaishnavism and Modern Life*. Calcutta: Sribhumi Publishing Co., 1963.
Dutt, M. C. (translator), *The Poems of Kalidasa*. Allahabad: Kitabistan, n.d.

Eidlite, Walther, *Bhakta, eine Indische Odyssee*. Hamburg: Choosen Verlag, 1951.
Elmore, Wilbur Theodore, *Dravidian Gods in Modern Hinduism*. Madras: Christian Literature Society for India, 1925.

Farquhar, J. N., *Modern Religious Movements in India*. New York: The Macmillan Co., 1915.
Foulkes, Thomas (translator), *A Catechism of the Śaiva Religion*. Madras: Williams and Norgate, 1863.
Fraser, J. N. and Edwards, J. F., *Life and Teaching of Tukārām*. Madras: Christian Literature Society for India, 1922.
Fraser, J. N., and Marathe, K. B. (translators), *The Poems of Tukārām*. 3 vols. London: The Christian Literature Society, 1909–1915.
Fuchs, Stephen, *Rebellious Prophets: A Study of Messianic Movements in Indian Religions*. New York: Asia Publishing House, 1966.

Gairola, Tara Dutt, *Psalms of Dadu*. Benares: Indian Book Shop, 1929.
Getty, Alice, *Gaṇeśa, A Monograph on the Elephant-Faced God*. Oxford: Clarendon Press, 1936.
Ghose, Shishir Kumar, *Lord Gauranga, or Salvation for All*. Calcutta: Golap Lal Ghose, 1897.
Ghosh, Atal Behari, *Śiva and Śakti*. Rajshahi, Bengal: Varendra Research Society, 1935, pp. 12–16.
Ghosha, Pratapachandra, *Durgā Pūjā*. Calcutta: publisher not given, 1841.
Ghurye, G. S., *Gods and Man*. Bombay: Popular Book Depot, 1962.
Ghurye, G. S., *The Indian Sadhus*. Bombay: Popular Prakashan, 1964.
Gonda, Jan, *Aspects of Early Viṣṇuism*. Utrecht: N.V.A. Oosthoek's Uitgevers Mij, 1954.
Gopinatha Rau, T. A., *Sir Subrahmanya Ayyar Lectures on the History of Śrī Vaiṣṇavas*. Madras: Madras University, 1923.
Goswami, B. K., *The Bhakti Cult in Ancient India*. Calcutta: B. Banerjee and Co., 1925.
Goswami, K. G., *A Study of Vaiṣṇavism*. Calcutta: Oriental Book Association, 1956.
Gover, Charles E. (translator), *The Folk-songs of Southern India*. Tirenelveli, Madras: The South India Śaiva Saddhanta Works Publishing Society, 1959.
Govindāchārya Alkondavilli (translator), *Bhagavadgītā, with Śrī Rāmānujāchārya's Viśishtādvaita Commentary*. Madras: Vaijayanti Press, 1898.
Govindāchārya, Alkondavilli (translator), *The Divine Wisdom of the Dravida Saints*. Madras: C. N. Press, 1902.
Govindacharya Alkondavilli, *The Holy Lives of the Āzhvārs or the Drāvida Saints*. Mysore: G.T.A. Press, 1902.
Govindāchārya, Alkondavilli, *The Life of Rāmānujāchārya*. Madras: S. Murthy and Co., 1906.
Greenlees, Duncan (translator), *The Gospel of Nārada*. Adyar: Theosophical

Publishing House, 1951. Translations of *Nārada Pancarata, Nārada Bhakti Sūtras,* and *Nārada Gītā.*

Grierson, George A., "Notes on Tulsi Das." *The Indian Antiquary,* Vol. 22, 1893, pp. 89–98, 122–129, 197–206, 225–236, 253–274.

Gupte, B. A., *Hindu Holidays and Ceremonials.* Calcutta: Thacker, Spink and Co., 1916.

Hall, Manly P., *The Guru. A Study of the Mystic Life of India.* London: Vision Press, 1959.

Handoo, Chandra Kumari, *Tulasīdāsa.* Bombay: Orient Longmans, 1964.

Hawkridge, Emma, *Indian Gods and Kings: The Story of a Living Past.* Boston: Houghton Mifflin Co., 1935.

Herbert, Jean, *Spiritualite Hindoue.* Paris: Editions Albin Michel, 1947.

Hiriyanna, Mysore, *Art Experience.* Mysore: Kavyalaya Publishers, 1954.

Hoernle, A. F. R. (editor and translator), *Uvāsagadasāo,* or *The Religious Professions of an Uvāsaga. Bibliotheca Indica,* Vol. 105. Calcutta: Asiatic Society of Bengal, 1885–1890.

Hoisington, Henry R. (translator), "Śiva-Gnāna-Pātham." *Journal of the American Oriental Society,* Vol. 4, 1854, pp. 31–102.

Hoisington, Henry R. (translator), "Śiva-Pirakāsam." *Journal of the American Oriental Society,* Vol. 4, 1854, pp. 125–244.

Hooper, J. S. M., *Hymns of the Ālvars.* Calcutta: Association Press, 1929.

Hopkins, Thomas, *The Vaiṣṇava Movement in the Bhāgavata Puraṇa.* An unpublished doctoral dissertation. Yale University, 1959.

Hoyland, John S. (translator), *Village Songs of Western India: Translations from Tukārām.* London: Allenson and Co., 1935.

Isherwood, Christopher, *Ramakrishna and His Disciples.* New York: Simon and Schuster, 1965.

Jhabvala, S. H. (translator), *Kabir.* Bombay: the author, n.d.

Jhala, G. C., *Kalidāsa. A Study.* Bombay: Padma Publications, 1943.

Johnson, J. (translator), *The Vedāntatattvasāra ascribed to Rāmānujāchārya.* Benares: E. J. Lazarus and Co., 1898.

Jones, W. (translator), *Gitagovinda or Songs of Jayadeva.* Calcutta: Asiatick Researches, 1792.

Jung, C. G., "The Psychology of Eastern Meditation," in *Psychology and Religion; West and East. The Collected Works of C. G. Jung,* Vol. 2, pp. 558–575. Translated by R. F. C. Hull. London: Routledge and Kegan Paul, 1958.

Kapali Sastri, T. V., *Further Lights: the Veda and the Tantra.* Madras: Sri Aurobindo Library, 1951.

Keay, F. E., *Kabīr and His Followers.* Calcutta: Association Press, 1931.

Kennedy, Melville T., *The Chaitanya Movement.* Calcutta: Association Press, 1925.

Keyt, G. (translator), *Sri Jayadeva's Gita Govinda.* Bombay: Kutub Publishers, 1947.

Kingsbury, F. and Phillips, G. E., *Hymns of the Tamil Śaivite Saints.* Calcutta: Association Press, 1921.

Kittel, F. and Oldham, C. F., *Phallism and Serpent Worship in India*. London: Susil Gupta, 1966.
Krishnadas (editor and translator), *Krishna of Vrindabana*. Calcutta: Charuchandra Guha, 1927.
Krishnaswami Aiyangar, S., *Early History of Vaiṣṇavism in South India*. London: Oxford University Press, 1920.
Krishnaswami Aiyangar, S., "Sri Ramanujacharya: His Life and Times," in *Three Great Acharyas: Sankara, Ramanuja, Madwa*, pp. 113–151. Madras: G. A. Natesan, 1923.
Kumarappa, Bharatan, *The Hindu Conception of the Deity as Culminating in Rāmānuja*. London: Luzac and Co., 1934.
Kumaraswamiji, Shree, *The Vīraśaiva Philosophy and Mysticism*. Dharwar: V. R. Koppal, 1949.
Kundu, Nundo Lall, *Non-dualism in Śaiva and Śākta Philosophy*. Calcutta: Sri Sri Bhairabi Jogeswari Math, n.d.

Law, Narendra Nath, "Śrī Kṛṣṇa and Śrī Caitanya." *Indian Historical Quarterly*, Vol. 23, 1947, pp. 261–299; Vol. 24, 1948, pp. 19–66.

Macauliffe, Max Arthur, *The Sikh Religion*. 6 vols. Oxford: Clarendon Press, 1909.
McCullough, Jay R., "Indian Theism and the Importance of Moral Acts." *Review of Religion*, Vol. 21, pp. 5–16.
Macmunn, George, *The Religions and Hidden Cults of India*. London: Sampson, Low, Marston and Co., 1932.
Macnicol, Nicol, *Indian Theism from the Vedic to the Mohammedan Period*. London: Oxford University Press, 1915.
Macnicol, Nicol, *The Living Religions of the Indian People*. London: Student Christian Movement Press, 1934.
Macnicol, N., *Psalms of Marāṭha Saints*. London: Oxford University Press, 1919. Calcutta: Association Press, 1919.
Madhavananda, Swami, *Life of Sri Ramakrishna*. Mayavati, Almora: Advaita Ashrama, 1925.
Madhavananda, Swami (translator), *Visvanatha Nyayapancanana, Bhasaparic-cheda with Siddhantamuktavali*. Calcutta: Advaita Ashrama, 1940.
Mal, Bahadur, *Shri Krishna: His Philosophy and His Spiritual Path*. Hoshiarpur: Vishreshvaranand V. R. Institute, 1960.
Mal, Lala Kannoo, *The Sayings of Kabir*. Madras: S. Ganesan, 1923.
Mal, Lala Kannoo, *The Sayings of Tulsidas*. Madras: S. Ganesan, 1923.
Mallik, G. N., *The Philosophy of Vaiṣṇava Religion*. Lahore: Motilal Banarsi Das, 1927.
Mallika, Balarama, *Krishna and Krishnaism*. Calcutta: S. K. Lahiri and Co., 1898.
Mathers, E. Powys (translator), *Eastern Love*. London: John Rodker, 1927.
Mathers, E. Powys (translator), *Love Songs of Asia*. London: Pushkin Press, 1944.
Matthews, Gordon (translator), *Śiva-Nāna-Bōdham*. Oxford: University Press, 1948.
Meht, S. S., *A Monograph on Mirabai*. Bombay: S. S. Mehta, n.d.

Mohan Singh, *Kabir and Bhakti Movement*. Lahore: Atma Ram and Sons, 1934.

Mohana Simha, M. A., *Mysticism, Philosophy, Religion—Mainly Oriental*. Amritsar: Mohan Singh, 1953.

Mozoomdar, Jadunath (translator), *Religion of Love*, or *Hundred Aphorisms of Śāṇḍilya*. Calcutta: Baptist Mission Press, 1898.

Mukerjee, Prabhat, *The History of Mediaeval Vaiṣṇavism in Orissa*. Calcutta: R. Chatterjee, 1940.

Mukerjee, Radhakamal, *The Lord of the Autumn Moons*. Bombay: Asia Publishing House, 1957.

Mukerjee, Radhakamal, *The Theory of Art in Mysticism*. Bombay: Asia Publishing House, 1960.

Mukharji, Dhan Gopal, *Devotional Passages from the Hindu Bible*. New York: E. P. Dutton Co., 1929.

Mukherji, S. C., *A Study of Vaiṣṇavism in Ancient and Medieval Bengal*. Calcutta: Punthi Pustak, 1966.

Munge, P. R., *Inspirations of Saint Tukaram*. Bombay: the author, 1930.

Nallaswami Pillai, J. M., *Śivajñāna Siddhiyār of Arunandi Śivācharya*. Madras: Meykandan Press, 1913.

Nallaswami Pillai, J. M., *Studies in Śaiva Siddhānta*. Madras: J. N. Ramanathan, 1911.

Nandimath, S. C., *Handbook of Viraśaivism*. Dharwar: L. E. Association, 1942.

Narain, K., *A Critique of Madhva Refutation of the Śaṁkara School of Vedānta*. Allahabad: Udayana Publications, 1964.

Narayan, R. K., *Gods, Demons, and Others*. London: Heinemann, 1965.

Narayana Aiyar, C. V., *The Origin and Early History of Śaivism in South India*. Madras: Madras University, 1936.

Noble, Margaret Elizabeth, *Kali, the Mother*. London: Swam Sonnenschein and Co., 1900.

Oman, J. C., *The Brāhmans, Theists, and Muslims of India*. London: T. Fisher Unwin, 1907.

Oman, J. C., *Cults, Customs, and Superstitions of India*. London: T. Fisher Unwin, 1908.

Oman, J. C., *The Mystics, Ascetics, and Saints of India*. London: T. Fisher Unwin, 1903.

Orr, W. G., *A Sixteenth-Century Indian Mystic*. London: Lutterworth Press, 1947.

Otto, Rudolf, *India's Religion of Grace and Christianity Compared and Contrasted*. London: Student Christian Movement, 1930.

Otto, Rudolf, *Mysticism East and West*. Translated by Bertha L. Bracey and Richenda C. Payne. New York: The Macmillan Co., 1932.

Pal, Bipin Chandra, *Bengal Vaishnavism*. Calcutta: Modern Book Agency, 1933.

Pal, Dhirendra Nath, *Śiva and Śakti: An Elaborate Discourse on Hindu Religion and Mythology*. Calcutta: S. C. Gupta, 1910.

Pandey, Kanti Chandra, *Comparative Aesthetics*, Vol. 1. *Indian Aesthetics*. Banaras: Chowkhamba Sanskrit Series Office, 1950.

Pandey, S. M., "Mirabai and Her Contributions to the Bhakti Movement." *History of Religions*. Vol. 5, No. 1, Summer 1965, pp. 54–73.
Paranjoti, V., *Śaiva Siddhānta in the Meykaṇḍa Śāstra*. London: Luzac and Co., 1938.
Payne, Ernest Alexander, *The Śāktas*. Calcutta: YMCA Publishing House, 1933.
Pillai, Tiru G. S., *Introduction and History of Śaiva Siddhānta*. Annamalainagar, Chidambaram: Annamalai University, 1948.
Poddar, Hanumanprasad, *The Philosophy of Love*. (Bhakti Sutras of Devarshi Narada) Gorakhpur: Ghanshyamdas Jalan, 1940.
Pope, G. U. (translator), *The Tiruvāśagam*, or *Sacred Utterances of the Tamil Poet, Saint and Sage Māṇikka-*Vāçacar. Oxford: Clarendon Press, 1900.
Premanand Bharati, *Sree Krishna: The Lord of Love*. London: William Rider and Son, 1904.

Raghavan, Venkata-rama, *The Number of Rasas*. Adyar, Madras: Adyar Library, 1940.
Raghavan, V. (translator), *Śrīmad Bhāgavata*. Madras: G. A. Natesan, 1947.
Raghavendracharya, H. N., "Caitanya (Knowledge) in Advaita." *Mysore University Journal*, Vol. 2, 1928, pp. 1–24.
Raghavendrachar, H. N., *Conception of Svatantra*. Mysore: Mysore University, 1943.
Rajagopalachariar, T., *The Vaishnavite Reformers of India*. Madras: G. A. Natesan and Co., 1909.
Ramachandra Dikshitar, V. R., "Early Tamil Religious Literature." *Indian Historical Quarterly*, Vol. 18, 1942, pp. 1–19.
Ramaiah, A. S., *Sri Krishna, the Soul of Humanity*. Madras: Kanara Press, 1918.
Rangacharya, M., *Rāmānuja and Vaishṇavism*. Madras: Brahmavadin Press, 1909.
Rangacharya, M., "Rāmānuja and Vaishṇavism," in *Three Great Acharyas: Sankara, Ramanuja, Madwa*, pp. 168–224. Madras: G. A. Natesan, 1923.
Rangacharya, M. and Varadaraja Iyengar, M. B. (translators), *The Vedānta-Sūtras with the Śri-Bhāshya of Rāmānujāchārya*. Madras: The Educational Publishing Co. Vol. 1, 1961; Vol. 2, 1964; Vol. 3, 1965.
Ray, Nagendra Kumar (translator), *Sri Sri Chaitanya Charitamrita*. 6 vols. Calcutta: Radharani Ashram, 1959.
Raychoudhuri, Hemchandra, *Materials for the Study of the Early History of the Vaishṇava Sect*. Calcutta: University of Calcutta, 1920.
Reichelt, Karl Ludvig, *Meditation and Piety in the Far East*. Translated by Sverre Holth. London: Lutterworth Press, 1953.

Sakhare, M. R., *History and Philosophy of Lingāyata Religion*. Belgaum: M. R. Sakhare, 1942.
Sampat Kumaran, M. R., *The Life and Teachings of Sri Krishna*. Madras: G. A. Natesan and Co., 1941.
Sanyal, J. M. (translator), *The Srimad-Bhagavatam*. 5 vols. Calcutta: Oriental Publishing Co., 1936.
Sanyal, Nisi Kanta, *The Erotic Principle and Unalloyed Devotion*. Calcutta: Gaudiya Mission, 1941.

Saradananda, Swami, *Sri Ramakrishna, The Great Master*. Madras: Sri Ramakrishna Math, 1952.

Saraswati, Swami Sadananda, *Nārada Bhakti Sūtras*. Rishikesh: Yoga Vedānta Forest University, 1952.

Sarkar, Jadunath, *Caitanya's Pilgrimages and Teachings*. Calcutta: M. C. Sarkar and Sons, 1913.

Sarkar, Mahendranath, *Hindu Mysticism; Studies in Vaiṣṇavism and Tantricism*. Calcutta: Satis Chandra Seal, 1943.

Sarma, D. S., *Krishna and His Song*. Bombay: International Book House, 1940.

Sastri, K. A. Nilakanta, *Development of Religion in South India*. Bombay: Orient Longmans, 1963.

Sastri, R. Anantakrishna, *Śakti-Sūtra*. Madras: The Adyar Library, 1896.

Schrader, F. O., *Introduction to the Pāñcarātra and the Ahirbudhnya Saṁhitā*. Madras: The Adyar Library, 1916.

Seal, Brajendranath, *Comparative Studies in Vaishṇavism and Christianity*. Calcutta: Hare Press, 1897.

Sen, Dinesh Chandra, *Chaitanya and His Age*. Calcutta: Calcutta University, 1922.

Sen, Dinesh Chandra, *Chaitanya and His Companions*. Calcutta: University of Calcutta, 1917.

Sen, Dinesh Chandra, *History of Bengali Language and Literature*. Second edition. Calcutta: University of Calcutta, 1954.

Sen, Dinesh Chandra, *Opinions on Banga Sahitya Parichava, or Typical Selections from Old Bengali Literature*. Calcutta: University of Calcutta, 1914.

Sen, Dinesh Chandra, *The Vaiṣṇava Literature of Mediaeval Bengal*. Calcutta: Calcutta University, 1917.

Sen, Kshitimohan, *Mediaeval Mysticism of India*. Tr. by Manomohan Ghosh. London: Luzac and Co., 1936.

Sen, Makhan Lal, *Lord Sree Krishna: His Life and Teachings*. Calcutta: Oriental Publishing Co., 1954.

Shastri, B. K., *The Bhakti Cult in Ancient India*. Varanasi: Chowkhamba Sanskrit Series Office, 1965.

Shastri, Hari Prasad (translator), *Nārada Sūtras: The Philosophy of Love*. London: Shanti Sadan, 1963.

Shivapadasundaram, S., *The Śaiva School of Hinduism*. London: George Allen and Unwin, 1934.

Simpson, Alicia, *Bhakti Mārga*, or *The Religion of Divine Love*. London: Luzac and Co., 1910.

Singh, Mohan, *Kabir and Bhakti Movement*. Lahore: Atma Ram and Sons, 1934.

Sinha, Nandalal, *Bhakti Śāstra. Sacred Books of the Hindus*, Vol. 7. Allahabad: The Panini Office, 1911–1912.

Sinha, Purendu Narayan, *A Study of the Bhāgavata Puraṇa*, or *Esoteric Hinduism*. Benares: Freeman and Co., 1901.

Sivananda, Swami (translator), *Practice of Bhakti-Yoga*. Amritsar: Airi, 1937.

Srinivasa Aiyangar, M., *Tamil Studies*. Madras: Guardian Press, 1914.

Srinivasa Aiyangar, T. R. (translator), *Śaiva Upaniṣads*. Madras: The Adyar Library, 1953.

Srinivasa Aiyangar, T. R. (translator), *Vaiṣṇava Upaniṣads*. Madras: The Adyar Library, 1945.

Srinivasa Aiyengar, C. R., *The Life and Teachings of Sri Ramanujacharya*. Madras: R. Venkateshwar and Co., n.d.

Srinivasa Iyengar, P. T., *Yatindra-Mata-Dipikā*, or *The Light of the School of Sri Ramanuja*. Madras: The Meykandan Press, 1912.

Srinivasachari, P. N., *The Philosophy of Bhedābheda*. Adyar: The Adyar Library, 1950.

Srinivasachari, P. N., *The Philosophy of Viśiṣṭādvaita*. Adyar: The Adyar Library, 1943.

Srinivasachari, P. N., *Rāmānuja's Idea of the Finite Self*. Calcutta: Longmans Green and Co., 1928.

Srisa Chandra Vasu, *The Śiva Samhitā*. *Sacred Books of the Hindus*, Vol. 15. Allahabad: The Panini Office, 1923.

Srisa Chandra Vasu, *Studies in the Vedānta Sūtras of Bādārayaṇa*. *Sacred Books of the Hindus*, Vol. 22. Allahabad: The Panini Office, 1918.

Srisa Chandra Vasu, *The Vedānta-Sūtras of Bādārayaṇa with the Commentary of Baladeva*. *Sacred Books of the Hindus*, Vol. 5. Allahabad: The Panini Office, 1912.

Streeter, W. B. and Appasamy, A. S., *The Sadhu, A Study in Mysticism and Practical Religion*. London: Macmillan and Co., 1922.

Sturdy, E. T. (translator), *Nārada Sūtra: An Inquiry into Love—Bhaktijyansa*. London: John M. Watkins, 1904.

Subba Rau, Sedambi (translator), *Śrīmad Bhāgavata Purāṇam*. Tirupati, 1928.

Subramanian, K. R., *Origin of Śaivism and Its History in the Tamil Land*. Madras: Madras University, 1927.

Sukthankar, Vasudev Anant, *The Teachings of Vedānta According to Rāmānuja*. Vienna, 1908.

Sundararama Iyer, K., *Place of Rāmānuja in the Story of India*. Bangalore: Higginbotham and Co., 1911.

Swarupananda, Swami (translator), *Śrīmad-Bhāgavad-Gītā*. Fifth edition. Mayavati, Almora: Advaita Ashrama, 1933.

Tagore, Rabindranath, *One Hundred Poems of Kabir*. Calcutta: Macmillan and Co., 1943.

Tambyah, T. Isaac, *Psalms of a Saiva Saint*. London: Luzac and Co., 1925.

Tattvabhushan, Sitanath, *Krishna and the Gītā*. Calcutta: Sarkar, 1900.

Tattwananda, Swami, *Vaiṣṇava Sects, Śaiva Sects and Mother Worship*. Calcutta: Nirmalendu Bikach Sen Gupta, 1962.

Thibaut, George (translator), *The Vedānta Sūtras with the Commentary of Rāmānuga*. *The Sacred Books of the East*, Vol. 48. Oxford: The Clarendon Press, 1904.

Thomas, P., *Kāma Kalpa*, or *The Hindu Ritual of Love*. Bombay: D. B. Taraporevala Sons, 1959.

Thompson, E. J. and Spencer, A. M., *Bengali Religious Lyrics, Śākta*. Calcutta: Association Press, 1923.

Thompson, Edward, *Rabindranath Tagore, Poet and Dramatist*. London: Oxford University Press, 1948.

Tirtha, Bhakti Pradip, *Chaitanya Mahaprabhu*. Calcutta: Gaudiya Mission, 1947.

Tirtha, Bhakti Vilas, *Sri Chaitanya's Concept of Theistic Vedānta*. Madras· Sree Gaudiya Math, 1964.

Tygisananda, Swami (translator), *Nārada Bhakti-Sūtras*. Madras: Ramakrishna Math, 1952.

Varadachari, K. C., *Sri Ramanuja's Theory of Knowledge*. Sri Venkatesvara Oriental Institute Studies, No. 1. Tirupati: Tirumalai-Tirupati Devasthanams Press, 1943.
Varadachari, K. C., *Viśiṣṭādvaita*. Travancore University Lectures, 1954.
Vaswami, T. L., *Sri Krishna: The Saviour of Humanity*. Madras: Ganesh and Co., 1921.

Westcott, W. H., *Kabir and the Kabir Panth*. Cawnpore: Christ Church Mission Press, 1907.
Whitehead, Henry, *The Village Gods of South India*. London: Oxford University Press, 1921.
Wood, Ernest (translator), *Song of Praise to the Dancing Shiva*. London: Luzac and Co., 1931.

Zaehner, R. C., *Hindu and Muslim Mysticism*. London: Athlone Press, 1960.
Zimmer, Heinrich, *The Art of Indian Asia*. New York: Pantheon Books, 1955.
Zimmer, Heinrich, *Myths and Symbols in Indian Art and Civilization*. New York: Pantheon Books, 1951.

YOGA MĀRGA

Abhedananda, Swami, *How to be a Yogi*. New York: The Vedanta Society, 1902.
Abhedananda, Swami, *Yoga Psychology*. Calcutta: Ramakrishna Vedanta Math, 1960.
Aiyanger, K. V. Rangaswami, *Rājdharma*. Madras: Adyar Library, 1941.
Aprabuddha, *The Science of Yoga*. Nagpur: V. K. Palekar, 1949.
Arundale, George Sydney, *Kundalini: An Occult Experience*. Adyar, Madras: Theosophical Publishing House, 1962.
Athalya, D. V., *Quintessence of Yoga Philosophy*. Bombay: Taraporevala, 1954.
Atkinson, William Walker, *Hatha Yoga*. London: L. N. Fowler and Co., 1931.
Atkinson, William Walker, *The Hindu-Yoga Science of Breath*. London: L. N. Fowler and Co., n.d.
Atkinson, William Walker, *The Inner Teachings of the Philosophies and Religions of India*. London: L. N. Fowler and Co., 1918.
Atkinson, William Walker, *The Life Beyond Death*. Chicago: Yogi Publishing Society, c. 1940.
Atkinson, William Walker, *A Series of Lessons in Gnan Yoga*. Chicago: Yogi Publishing Society, 1907.
Atkinson, William Walker, *A Series of Lessons in Raja Yoga*. London: L. N. Fowler and Co., 1917.
Atreya, B. L., "The Yoga We Need Today," *Darshana International*, Vol. 5, No. 3, July 1965, pp. I–X.
Aundh, The Raja of, *The Ten-Point Way to Health*. London: Dent, 1951.
Aurobindo, *Bases of Yoga*. Calcutta: Arya Publishing House, 1949.
Aurobindo, *Elements of Yoga*. Pondicherry: Sri Aurobindo Ashram, 1953.

Aurobindo, "The Indian Conception of Life," in *The Indian Philosophical Congress Silver Jubilee Commemoration Volume*, 1950, pp. 73–84.
Aurobindo, *The Life Divine*. Calcutta: Arya Publishing House, 1947. New York: The Greystone Press, 1949.
Aurobindo, *Lights on Yoga*. Calcutta: Arya Publishing House, 1948.
Aurobindo, *The Mind of Light*. New York: Dutton, 1953.
Aurobindo, *More Lights on Yoga*. Pondicherry: Sri Aurobindo Ashram, 1948.
Aurobindo, *The Problems of Rebirth*. Pondicherry: Sri Aurobindo Ashram, 1952.
Aurobindo, *The Synthesis of Yoga*. Madras: Sri Aurobindo Library, 1948.
Aurobindo, *The Yoga and Its Objects*. Calcutta: Arya Publishing House, 1949.

Bagchi, P. C., *Studies in the Tantras*. Calcutta: Calcutta University, 1939.
Bailey, Alice A., *The Light of the Soul*. New York: Lucis Publishing Co., 1927.
Bala Sanyasi, *Rājā-Yoga with Nava Kalpa*. Bangalore: Parashakti Ashram, n.d.
Ballantyne, J. R. (editor), *A Lecture on the Sāṅkhya Philosophy Embracing the Text of "Tattwa Samasa" of Kapila*. Mirzapore: Orphan School Press, 1850.
Ballantyne, J. R. and Sastri Deva, Govind (translators), *Yoga Sutras of Patañjali*. Calcutta: Susil Gupta, 1882.
Banerji, Satish Chandra (translator), *Sāṅkhya Philosophy with Gaudapada's Scholia and Narayana's Gloss*. Calcutta: Hare and Co., 1898.
Basu, Sri Chandra, *Esoteric Science and Philosophy of the Tantras*. Calcutta: Heeralal Dhole, 1893. Allahabad: Dharma Press, 1914.
Basu, Srischandra (translator), *Haṭhayoga-pradīpikā*. Allahabad: The Panini Office, n.d.
Basu, Srisa Chandra (editor), *The Philosophy and Science of Vedanta and Raja Yoga*. Lahore: New Lyall Press, 1895.
Behanan, Kovoor Thomas, *Yoga, A Scientific Evaluation*. London: Martin Secker and Warburg, 1937.
Bernard, Theos, *Hatha Yoga*. New York: Columbia University Press, 1944.
Bernard, Theos, *Heaven Lies Within Us*. New York: Rider and Co., 1941.
Besant, Annie, *An Introduction to Yoga*. Madras: Theosophical Publishing House, 1920.
Bhagavan Das, *Ancient Psycho-synthesis Vs. Modern Psychoanalysis*. Adyar: Theosophical Publishing House, 1949.
Bhandarkar, R. G., "The Sāṅkhya Philosophy," *The Indian Philosophical Review*, January 1919.
Bharati, Agehananda, *The Tantric Tradition*. London: Rider, 1965.
Bharati, Yogi Shuddhananda, *Secret of Yoga*. Madras: Ganesh and Co., 1956.
Bhatnagar, K. N., *Nidāna-Sūtra of Patañjali*. Lahore: Das Publishing House, 1939.
Bhattacharya, Kalipada, "Some Problems of Sāṅkhya Philosophy and Sāṅkhya Literature." *Indian Historical Quarterly* (Calcutta), Vol. 8, No. 3, 1932, pp. 509–520.
Bhattacharyya, Benoytosh (translator), *Śaktisaṇgama Tantra. Gaekwad's Oriental Series*, Vols. 61, 91, 104. Baroda: Oriental Institute, 1932, 1941, 1947.
Bloomfield, Maurice, "On False Ascetics and Nuns in Hindu Fiction." *Journal of the American Oriental Society*, Vol. 44, 1924, pp. 202–242.

Bolle, Kees W., "Tantric Elements in Sri Aurobindo." *Numen*, IX/2, pp. 128–142.

Bose, D. N. and Haldar, Hiralal, *Tantras: Their Philosophy and Occult Secrets*. Third edition. Calcutta: Orient Publishing Co., 1956.

Bragdon, Claude, *An Introduction to Yoga*. New York: Alfred A. Knopf, 1949.

Bragdon, Claude, *Yoga for You*. New York: Alfred A. Knopf, 1953.

Briggs, George Weston, *Gorakhnāth and the Kānphaṭa Yogis*. London: Oxford University Press, 1938.

Brunton, Paul, *Discover Yourself*. New York: E. P. Dutton and Co., 1939.

Brunton, Paul, *The Hidden Teaching Beyond Yoga*. London: Rider and Co., 1941.

Brunton, Paul, *The Inner Reality*. London: Rider and Co., 1939.

Brunton, Paul, *A Message from Arunachala*. London: Rider and Co., 1936.

Brunton, Paul, *The Quest of the Over Self*. London: Rider and Co., 1937.

Brunton, Paul, *A Search in Secret India*. London: Rider and Co., 1934.

Brunton, Paul, *The Secret Path*. London: Rider and Co., 1935.

Brunton, Paul, *The Wisdom of the Over Self*. London: Rider and Co., 1943.

van Buitenen, J. A. B., "Studies in Sāṁkhya." *Journal of the American Oriental Society* (New Haven), Vol. 76, 1956, pp. 153–157; Vol. 77, 1957, pp. 15–25, 88–107.

Carrington, Hereward, *Higher Psychical Development—Yoga Philosophy*. London: Kegan Paul, 1920.

Chakravarti, Chintaharan, "Ideals of Tantra Rites," *The Indian Historical Quarterly*, Vol. 10, pp. 486–492.

Chakravarti, Chintaharan, *The Tantras: Studies on their Religion and Literature*. Calcutta: Punthi Pustak, 1963.

Chakravarti, Kshetrapala, *Lectures on Hindu Religion, Philosophy and Yoga*. Calcutta: U. C. Shome, 1893.

Chakravarti, P. C., "Philosophy of the Tantras," in *Jha Commemoration Volume*. Poona: Oriental Book Agency, 1937, pp. 93–100.

Chakravarti, Pulinbhari, *Origin and Development of the Sāṁkhya System of Thought*. Calcutta: Metropolitan Printing and Publishing House, 1951.

Chatterjee, T. D., *A Handbook of Sri Aurobindo's Yoga*. Calcutta: Sri Aurobindo Pathamandir, 1961.

Chattopadhyaya, S. K., "In Defense of Sāṁkhya Dualism," in *34th Session of the Indian Philosophical Congress* (Cuttack), 1959, pp. 25–36.

Chaudhuri, Haridas and Spiegelberg, Frederic (editors), *The Integral Philosophy of Sri Aurobindo*. London: George Allen and Unwin, 1960.

Chaudhuri, Haridas, *Integral Yoga*. London: George Allen and Unwin, 1965.

Chaudhuri, Haridas, *The Philosophy of Integralism*, or *The Metaphysical Synthesis Inherent in the Teaching of Sri Aurobindo*. Calcutta: Sri Aurobindo Pathamandir, 1954.

Chaudhuri, Haridas, *Sri Aurobindo: The Prophet of Life Divine*. Calcutta: Sri Aurobindo Pathamandir, 1951.

Colebrooke, Henry Thomas (translator), *The Sāṅkhya Kārika of Īśvarakṛṣṇa*. Bombay: Tookaram Tatya, 1887.

Conger, G. P., "A Naturalistic Approach to Sāṁkhya-Yoga." *Philosophy East and West*, Vol. 3, October 1953.

Coomaraswamy, A. K., "The Tantric Doctrine of Divine Biunity." *Annals of the Bhandarkar Oriental Research Institute*, Vol. 19, 1938, pp. 173–183.
Coster, Geraldine, *Yoga and Western Psychology: A Comparison*. London: Oxford University Press, 1934.

Dahlman, Joseph, Sāṁkhya-Philosophie. Berlin: F. L. Dames, 1902.
Danielou, Alain, *Yoga, The Method of Re-integration*. London: Christopher Johnson, 1949.
Dasgupta, Surendranath, *The Study of Patañjali*. Calcutta: University of Calcutta, 1920.
Dasgupta, Surendranath, *Yoga as Philosophy and Religion*. London: Kegan Paul, Trench, Trubner and Co., 1924.
Dasgupta, Surendra Nath, *Yoga Philosophy in Relation to other Indian Systems of Thought*. Calcutta: University of Calcutta, 1930.
Datta, D. M., "Some Difficulties of the Sāṅkhya System." *The Philosophical Quarterly*. Calcutta, Vol. 11, July 1935, pp. 146–151.
Davies, John (editor), *Hindu Philosophy: The Sāṅkhya Kārikā of Īśwara Krishna, an Exposition of the System of Kapila with an Appendix on the Nyāya and Vaiśeshika Systems*. London: Kegan Paul, Trench, Trubner and Co., 1890.
Davies, John, *The Sāṅkhya Kārikā of Īśwara Krishna*. London: Trubner and Co., 1881.
Day, Harvey, *About Yoga, The Complete Philosophy*. London: Thorsons Publishers, 1951.
Day, Harvey, *The Study and Practice of Yoga*. London: Thorsons Publishers, 1957.
Demaitre, Edmond, *The Yogis of India*. Translated by Henry Dawson Beaumont. London: Geoffrey Bles, 1937.
Deutsch, Eliot, "Sri Aurobindo's Interpretation of Spiritual Experience: A Critique." *International Philosophical Quarterly*, Vol. 4, No. 4, December 1964, pp. 581–594.
Dhopeshwarkar, A. D., *Krishnamurti and the Experience of the Silent Mind*. Bombay: Chetana, 1956.
Dikshit, S. K., *The Mother Goddess*. New Delhi: the author, n.d.
Donnelly, Morwenna, *Founding the Life Divine: An Introduction to the Integral Yoga of Sri Aurobindo*. London: Rider and Co., 1955.
Dunne, Desmond, *The Manual of Yoga*. London: W. Foulsham and Co., 1956.
Dunne, Desmond, *Yoga: The Way to Long Life and Happiness*. New York: Wilfred Funk, 1953.
Dürckheim, Karlfried Graf von, *Hara, the Vital Centre of Man*. Translated by Sylvia-Monica von Kospoth. London: George Allen and Unwin, 1962.
Dvivedi, M. N., *The Yoga Sūtras of Patañjali*. Madras: Theosophical Publishing House, 1934.

Edgerton, Franklin, "The Meaning of Sāṅkhya and Yoga." *American Journal of Philology*, Vol. 45, 1924, pp. 1–46.
Eliade, Mircea, *Techniques du Yoga*. Paris: Gallimard, 1948.
Eliade, Mircea, *Yoga: Immortality and Freedom*. Translated by Willard R. Trask. New York: Pantheon Books, 1958.

Flagg, William J., *Yoga or Transformation*. London: G. Redway, 1898.
Francis, Philip Garry, *Yoga: The Amazing Life Science*. London: Thorsons Publishers, 1958.
Fuller, John Frederic Charles, *Yoga*. London: William Rider and Son, 1931.

Garbe, Richard, *Aniruddha's Commentary and the Original Parts of Vedāntin Mahādeva's Commentary on the Sāṁkhya Sūtras*. Calcutta: Baptist Mission Press, 1892.
Garbe, Richard, *Sāṁkhya and Yoga*. Strasbourg: K. J. Trubner, 1896.
Garbe, Richard, *Die Sāṁkhya Philosophie*. Leipzig, 1894.
Garbe, Richard (editor), *The Sāṅkhya-pravacana-bhāṣya*, or *Commentary on the Exposition of the Sāṅkhya Philosophy*. Cambridge, Mass.: Harvard University Press, 1895.
Garbe, Richard, "Yoga," in *Encyclopaedia of Religion and Ethics*. Edited by Hastings. Vol. 12, pp. 831–833.
Garrison, Omar, *Tantra. The Yoga of Sex*. New York: Julian Press, 1964.
Gervis, Pearce, *Naked They Pray*. London: Cassell and Co., 1956.
Ghosh, Jajneswar, *Sāṁkhya and Modern Thought*. Calcutta: The Book Co., 1930.
Ghosh, Jajneswar, *A Study of Yoga*. Hooghly: Sanatkuman Ghosh, 1933.
Gilmore, George W., "Tantrism—the Newest Hinduism." *American Journal of Theology*, Vol. 23, 1919, pp. 440–457.
Gongulee, Kumudini Kant, *Self-control and Self-realization*. Dacca: Nagendra Kumar Ray, 1916.
Guenther, Herbert V., *Yuganaddha, The Tantric View of Life*. Banaras: Chowkhamba Sanskrit Series Office, 1952.
Gupta, Nalini Kanta, *The Yoga of Sri Aurobindo*. Pondicherry: the author, 1943.
Guyot, Felix, *Yoga for the West*. Translated by W. Bosman. London: Rider and Co., 1934.
Guyot, Felix, *Yoga, The Art and Science of Self-mastery for Success*. Chicago: Nelson-Hall Co., 1951.

Hauer, J. W., *Der Yoga*. Stuttgart: W. Kohlhammer, 1958.
Hiriyanna, Mysore, "The Sāṁkhya System," in *The Cultural Heritage of India*, Vol. 3. Calcutta: Belur Math, 1953, pp. 41–52.
Hittleman, Richard L., *Be Young with Yoga*. Preston: A. Thomas, 1963.
Hopkins, Edward Washburn, "Yoga-Technique in the Great Epic." *Journal of the American Oriental Society*, Vol. 22, 1901, pp. 333–379.

Indra Devi, *Forever Young, Forever Healthy*. Blackpool: A. Thomas, 1955.
Iyangar, Shrinavas, *The Hatha-Yoga Pradipika of Swatmaram Swami*. Bombay: Bombay Theosophical Publication Fund, 1893.
Iyengar, K. R. Srinivasa, *Sri Aurobindo*. Calcutta: Arya Publishing House, 1945.

Jha, Ganganatha, *The Study of Patañjali*. Calcutta: University of Calcutta, 1920.
Jha, Ganganatha (translator), *The Yoga-Darśana*. Bombay: Bombay Theosophical Publication Fund, 1907.

Jha, Ganganatha, *The Yogasārasangraha of Vijñāna Bhikshu*. Bombay: Bombay Theosophical Publication Fund, 1894.
Jha, Mahamahopadhyaya Ganganath (translator), *The Tattva-Kaumudī. Vācaspati Miśra's Commentary on the Sāṁkhya-Kārikā*. Poona: Oriental Book Agency, 1965.
Johnston, Charles (translator), *The Yoga Sūtras of Patañjali*. New York: Quarterly Book Department, 1912.
Johnston, Edward Hamilton, *Early Sāṁkhya: An Essay on its Historical Development according to the Texts*. London: Royal Asiatic Society, 1937.
Johnston, Edward Hamilton, "Some Sāṁkhya and Yoga Conceptions of the *Śvetāśvatara Upaniṣad*." *Journal of the Royal Asiatic Society*, London, 1930, pp. 855–878.
Judge, W. Q. (translator), *The Yoga Aphorisms of Patañjali*. New York: Theosophical Publishing Co. of New York, 1912.
Jung, C. G., "Yoga and the West," in *Psychology and Religion: West and East. The Collected Works of C. G. Jung*, Vol. 2. Tr. by R. F. C. Hull. London: Routledge and Kegan Paul, 1958, pp. 529–537.

Keith, A. Berriedale, *The Sāṁkhya System*. Calcutta: Association Press, 1918.
Krishna Pres, *The Yoga of the Bhagavat Gita*. London: John M. Watkins, 1948.

Langley, G. H., *Sri Aurobindo*. London: David Marlowe, 1949.
Lawl, Jag Mohan (translator), *The Sāṁkhya Philosophy of Kapila*. Edinburgh: Orpheus Publishing House, 1921.
Lindquist, Sigurd, *Die Methoden des Yoga*. Lund, 1932.
Lindquist, Sigurd, *Siddhi und Abhiññā: eine Studie uber die klassischen Wunder des Yoga*. Upsala, 1935.
Louis-Frederic, *Yoga Āsanas*. London: Thorsons, 1959.

Maharaj, Swami Dharma, *Yoga for all*, or *The Religion of the Gītā*. Lahore: Har Bhagnan, 1941.
Maitra, Surya Kanta, *An Introduction to the Philosophy of Sri Aurobindo*. Benares: Benares Hindu University, 1941.
Maitra, Surya Kanta, *The Meeting of the East and the West in Sri Aurobindo's Philosophy*. Pondicherry: Sri Aurobindo Ashram, 1956.
Maitra, Surya Kanta, *Studies in Sri Aurobindo's Philosophy*. Benares: Benares Hindu University, 1945.
Majumdar, Abhay Kumar, *The Sāṅkhya Conception of Personality*. Calcutta: Calcutta University Press, 1930.
Majumdar, S., *Healthy Middle-Age through Yoga*. Bombay: Jaico Publishing House, 1960.
Marqués-Rivière, Jean, *Tantrik Yoga*. Translated by H. E. Kennedy. London: Rider, 1940.
Marshall, Anne, *Hunting the Guru in India*. London: Victor Gollancz, 1963.
Mischkowski, Agnes A. M., *Soul-Culture and Yoga*. London: Luzac, 1933.
Mishra, Rammurti S., *The Textbook of Yoga Psychology*. New York: Julian Press, 1963.
Mitra, Rajendra Lal, (translator), *The Yoga Aphorisms of Patañjali with the*

Commentary of Bhoja Rāja. Bibliotheca Indica, Vol. 93. Calcutta, 1881–1883.
Mitra, Sisirkumar, *The Liberator: Sri Aurobindo, India and the World.* Delhi: Jaico Publishing House, 1954.
Mohanty, J. N., *Modern Philosophical Anthropology and the Concept of Man in Sri Aurobindo's Philosophy.* Bombay: Sri Aurobindo Circle Annual, 1956.
Mouni Sadhu, *Concentration.* London: George Allen and Unwin, 1959.
Mouni Sadhu, *In Days of Great Peace.* London: George Allen and Unwin, 1957.
Mouni Sadhu, *Samadhi.* London: George Allen and Unwin, 1962.
Mouni Sadhu, *Theurgy.* London: George Allen and Unwin, 1965.
Mouni Sadhu, *Ways of Self-realization.* London: George Allen and Unwin, 1963.
Mujumdar, S., *Yogic Exercises for the Fit and the Ailing.* Bombay: Orient Longmans, 1949.
Mukerji, J. N., *Sāṁkhya or the Theory of Reality.* Calcutta: S. N. Mukerji, 1930.
Mulbagala, K. V., *Popular Practice of Yoga.* London: Kegan Paul, 1935.
Mumford, John, *Psychosomatic Yoga.* London: Thorsons Publishers, 1962.
Murlidhar, Pandit, *Yoga for Self Culture.* New Delhi: Amrit Book Co., 1944.

Narasimha, Swami B. V., *Self-Realization, Life and Teachings of Ramana Maharshi.* Tiruvannamalai, 1936.
Narayananda, Swami, *The Primal Power in Man.* Rishikesh: N. K. Prasad, 1960.
Narayananda, Swami, *Secrets of Mind Control.* Rishikesh: N. K. Prasad, 1954.
Narayanaswami Aiyar, K., *Yoga; Lower and Higher.* Adyar: the author, 1916.
Nath, Radha Govinda, *The Yogis of Bengal.* Calcutta: Mani Bhasan Nath, 1909.
Noyes, Humphrey F., "Meditation: the Doorway to Wholeness." *Main Currents in Modern Thought,* Vol. 22, No. 2, November–December, 1965, pp. 35–40.

Osborne, Arthur (editor), *The Collected Works of Ramana Maharshi.* Tiruvannamalai: T. N. Venkataraman, 1959.
Osborne, Arthur W., *The Expansion of Awareness; One Man's Search for Meaning in Living.* Madras: Theosophical Publishing House, 1961.
Osborne, Arthur, *The Incredible Sai Baba.* Bombay: Orient Longmans, 1957.
Osborne, Arthur, *Ramana Maharshi and the Path of Self-Knowledge.* Bombay: Jaico Publishing House, 1957.
Osborne, Arthur (editor), *The Teachings of Bhagavan Sri Ramana Maharshi in His Own Words.* Tiruvannamalai: Sri Ramanasramam, 1960.

Palekar, V. R., *Science of Yoga.* Nagpur: V. K. Palekar, 1959.
Pancham Sinh (translator), *Hatha Yoga Pradīpikā. Sacred Books of the Hindus,* Vol. 15, Part 3. Allahabad: The Panini Office, 1915.
Pandit, M. P., *Lights on the Tantra.* Madras: Ganesh and Co., 1957.
Pandit, M. P., *Sadhana in Sri Aurobindo's Yoga.* Pondicherry: the author, 1963.
Paul, Nabin Chandra, *A Treatise on the Yoga Philosophy.* Calcutta: Indian Echo Press, 1883.

Pearson, Nathaniel, *Sri Aurobindo and the Soul Quest of Man*. London: George Allen and Unwin, 1952.
Pott, P. H., *Yoga en Yantra*. Leiden, 1946.
Prabhavananda, Swami and Isherwood, Christopher, *How to Know God: The "Yoga Aphorisms" of Patanjali*. New York: Harper, 1953.
Prakash, Buddha, "The Decadence of Hindu Culture: A Study of Tantrikism." *Bharat Vidya*, Vol. 16, pp. 52–64.
Prasada, Rama (translator), *The Yoga Sūtras of Patañjali*. *Sacred Books of the Hindus*, Vol. 4. Allahabad: The Panini Office, 1910.
Purnananda, Swami, *Yoga and Perfection*. Barisal: Motilal Sen, 1927.
Purohit, Swami (translator), *Aphorisms of Yoga*. London: Faber and Faber, 1938.

Rama Prasada, F. T. S., *Breath and the Philosophy of the Science of Tatwas with Explanatory Essays on Nature's Finer Forces*. London: Theosophical Publishing Society, 1890.
Rama-Prasada (translator), *Patañjali's Yoga Sūtras with the Commentary of Vyāsa and the Gloss of Vāchapati Misra*. *Sacred Books of the Hindus*, Vol. 4. Allahabad: The Panini Office, 1924.
Rao, K. B. Ramakrishna, "The Gunas of Prakṛti According to the Sāṁkhya Philosophy." *Philosophy East and West*, Vol. 13, April 1963, pp. 61–71.
Rele, Vasant G., *The Mysterious Kundalini*. Bombay: D. B. Taraporevala Sons, 1927.
Rele, V. G., *Yogic Āsanas*. Bombay: Taraporevala Sons, 1939.
Rhys Davids, C. A. F., "Sāṅkhya and Original Buddhism." *Indian Historical Quarterly*, Vol. 9, 1933, pp. 585–587.
Richmond, Sonya, *Yoga and Your Health*. London: Arco Publications, 1962.
Roy, S. N., "The Problem of Error in Sāṁkhya." *The Philosophical Quarterly* (Calcutta), Vol. 11, April 1936.
Rukmini Devi, *Yoga: Art of Science*. Adyar, Madras: Theosophical Publishing House, n.d.
Rutledge, Dom Denys, *In Search of a Yogi*. London: Routledge and Kegan Paul, 1962.

Sarkar, Kishori Lal, *The Hindu System of Self Culture*, or *The Patañjala Yoga-Shāstra*. Calcutta: Sarasi Lal Sarkar, 1902.
Sastri, S. S. Suryanarayana (translator), *The Sāṅkhyakārikā of Īśvara Kṛṣṇa*. Madras: University of Madras, 1930.
Sastry, T. V. Kapali, *Further Lights: the Veda and the Tantra*. Madras: Sri Aurobindo Library, 1951.
Satprem, *Sri Aurobindo*, or *The Adventure of Consciousness*. New York: India Library Society, 1964.
Schwendimann, Max Allain, *Yoga for Perfect Health*. London: Thorsons Publishers, 1957.
Sen, Keshub Chunder, *Yoga*, or *Communion with God*. Calcutta: Brahmo Tract Society, 1899.
Sen Gupta, Anima, *Essays on Sāṁkhya and Other Systems of Indian Philosophy*. Patna: United Press, 1964.
Sen Gupta, Anima, *The Evolution of the Sāṁkhya School of Thought*. Lucknow: The Pioneer Press, 1959.

Shankaracharya, A *Compendium of Raja Yoga Philosophy*. Bombay: Bombay Theosophical Publication Fund, 1888.

Sharma, H. D., *The Sāṁkhya-Kārikā*. Poona: Bhandarkar Oriental Research Institute, 1933.

Sharma, Vidyasudhakara Har Dutta (translator), *The Tattvakaumudi (Vacaspati Miśra's Commentary on the Sāṁkhya-Karika)*. Poona: Oriental Book Agency, 1934.

Shastri, Hari Prasad, *Yoga*. London: W. and G. Foyle, 1957.

Sivananda, Swami, *Concentration and Meditation*. Sivanandanagar: Yoga-Vedanta Forest Academy, 1964.

Sivananda, Swami, *Kundalini Yoga*. Sivanandanagar: Yoga-Vedanta Forest Academy, 1963.

Sivananda, Swami, *Practical Lessons in Yoga*. Lahore: Hotalal Banarsi Dass, 1938.

Sivananda, Swami, *Tantra Yoga, Nada Yoga, and Kriya Yoga*. Rishkesh: Yoga-Vedanta Forest University, 1955.

Snellgrove, D. L. (editor), *Hevajra Tantra*. New York: Oxford University Press, 1961.

Spring, Clara and Goss, Madeleine, *Yoga for Today*. New York: Henry Holt, 1959.

Srinivasa Aiyengar (translator), *Hatha-Yoga Pradīpikā*. Bombay: Bombay Theosophical Publication Fund, 1893.

Srinivasa Aiyangar, T. R. (translator), *The Yoga Upaniṣads*. Adyar: The Adyar Library, 1938.

Srisa Chandra Vasu, *An Introduction to the Yoga Philosophy. Sacred Books of the Hindus*, Vol. 15, Part 4. Allahabad: The Panini Office, 1915.

Strakaty, E., *Yoga for Americans*. New York: Prentice-Hall, 1959.

Strakaty, Eugene, *Yoga: The Technique of Health and Happiness*. Allahabad: Kitabistan, 1948.

Sukul, Deva Ram, *Yoga and Self-culture*. New York: Yoga Institute of America, 1947.

Sundaram, S., *Yogic Physical Culture*. Bangalore: The Brahmcharya Publishing House, 1931.

Svatmarama Svamin, *Haṭayogaprakīpikā with the Commentary of Brahmānanda and Glosses of Śrīdhara*. Bombay: publishing house not given, 1889.

Taimni, J. K., *The Science of Yoga*. Adyar: Theosophical Publishing House, 1961.

Tattvabushan, Hemchandra (translator), *Kamaratna Tantra*. Shillong, 1928.

Tuxen, P., *Yoga*. Copenhagen, 1911.

Vadekar, D. D., "The Sāṁkhya Arguments for the Puruṣa." 34th Indian Philosophical Congress, Cuttack, 1959, pp. 37–40.

Vijayatunga, Jinadasa, *Yoga, the Way of Self-Fulfilment*. London: Casement Publications, 1953.

Vishnudevanda, Swami, *The Complete Illustrated Book of Yoga*. New York: Julian Press, 1960.

Vithaldas, Yogi, *The Yoga System of Health*. London: Faber and Faber, 1939.

Vivekananda, Swami, *Raja-Yoga*, or *Conquering the Internal Nature*. Calcutta: Advaita Ashram, 1955.

Vivekananda, Swami, The *Yogas and Other Works*. New York: Ramakrishna-Vivekananda Center, 1953.
Volin, Michael and Phelan, Nancy, *Yoga Over Forty*. London: Pelham, 1965.

Wase, Charles, *The Inner Teachings and Yoga*. London: William Rider and Son, 1921.
Widutis, Florence, *Yours is the Power*. Somerville, New Jersey: The Pilgrims, 1957.
Wood, Ernest, *Concentration*. Adyar: Theosophical Publishing Co., 1955.
Wood, Ernest, *Great Systems of Yoga*. New York: Philosophical Library, 1954.
Wood, Ernest, *The Intuition of the Will*. Adyar: Theosophical Publishing House, 1926.
Wood, Ernest, *The Occult Training of the Hindus*. Madras: Ganesh and Co., 1931.
Wood, Ernest, *Practical Yoga: Ancient and Modern*. New York: E. P. Dutton, 1948.
Wood, Ernest, *Yoga*. Baltimore and Harmondsworth: Penguin Books, 1959.
Wood, Ernest, *Yoga Dictionary*. New York: Philosophical Library, 1955.
Woodroffe, John, *The Garland of Letters: Studies in Mantra Shāstra*. Madras: Ganesh and Co., 1922.
Woodroffe, John, *The Great Liberation*. Madras: Ganesh and Co., 1963.
Woodroffe, John, *Introduction to Tantra Śāstra*. Madras: Ganesh and Co., 1956.
Woodroffe, John and Mukhyaopadhyaya, P. N., *Mahāmāyā: The World as Power*. Madras: Ganesh and Co., 1954.
Woodroffe, John, *Principles of Tantra*. Madras: Ganesh and Co., 1960.
Woodroffe, John, *The Serpent Power*. London: Luzac, 1919.
Woodroffe, John, *Shakti and Shākta*. Madras: Ganesh and Co., 1929.
Woodroffe, John, *The Tantra of the Great Liberation*. Madras: Ganesh and Co., 1913.
Woodroffe, John, *Tantrarāja Tantra*. Madras: Ganesh and Co., 1954.
Woodroffe, John and Pratyagatmananda, Swami, *The World as Power*. 5 volumes. Madras: Ganesh and Co., 1957.
Woods, James Naughton (translator), *The Yoga System of Patañjali*, or *The Ancient Hindu Doctrine of Concentration of Mind. Harvard Oriental Series*, Vol. 17. Cambridge, Mass.: Harvard University Press, 1914.

Yeats-Brown, F., *Yoga Explained*. Calcutta: Susil Gupta, 1937.
Yesudian, Selvarajan and Haich, Elizabeth, *Yoga and Health*. London: George Allen and Unwin, 1953.
Yesudian, Selvarajan, *A Yoga Miscellany*. London: George Allen and Unwin, 1963.
Yesudian, Selvarajan and Haich, Elizabeth, *Yoga Uniting East and West*. London: George Allen and Unwin, 1956.
Yogananda, Paramahamsa, *The Autobiography of a Yogi*. London: Rider and Co., 1950.
Yogananda, Paramahamsa, *The Science of Religion*. Los Angeles: Self-Realization Publishing House, 1953.
Yogendra, Shri, *Yoga Personal Hygiene*. Bombay: The Yoga Institute, 1940.

Sanskrit Index

Name Index

Abadhut, Nityapadanda, 283n, 295n.
Abid Husain, S., 6, 71n.
Acharya, Ananda, 151.
Adhedānanda, Swami, 5.
Allchin, Raymond, 164n, 278n.
Ambedkar, B. R., 16, 159, 210, 229, 230.
Anaximander, 101.
Andrews, C. F., 25.
Apparsvāmi, 288.
Archer, William, 177, 275, 276n.
Aristotle, 20, 71, 108, 122, 213, 217, 307.
Arrian, Flavius, 224.
Aśoka, 74, 78, 216.
Atkins, A. G., 278n.
Atreya, B. L., 193, 194n.
Atri, 294.
Augustine, 91.
Aurobindo, Sri, 32, 37, 53, 59, 60, 85, 115, 116, 154, 165, 168, 171, 173, 174, 223, 255, 317, 335, 344.
Avalon, Arthur. See John Woodroffe.

Bādarāyaṇa, 18, 43, 181, 182.
Baldeva, 182.
Bānabhaṭṭa, 322n.
Barnes, Hazel E., 66n.
Barth, A., 248, 264.
Barth, Karl, 103, 340.
de Bary, William Theodore, 161.
Basham, A. L., 233n, 346n.
Beauchamp, Henry K., 224n.
de Beauvoir, Simone, 67.
Besant, Annie, 25.
Bhagavan Das, 211.
Bhandarkar, Ramakrishna Gopal, 264, 265.
Bhartrihari, 127.
Bhattacharya, Deben, 276n.
Bhattacharyya, K. C., 45n.
Bhattacharyya, Kalidas, 40n, 341n.
Bhave, Vinoba, 125.
Bhedabheda, 18.
Bhutattar, 296.
Blackham, H. J., 336n.
Blakney, Raymond Bernard, 109n.
Bloomfield, Maurice, 249n.
Bonhoeffer, Dietrich, 17, 341n.
Bose, D. N., 321.
Bose, Jagadish Chandra, 64.
Bose, R. C., 170.
Bose, Subhas Chandra, 79.
Boss, Medard, 23n.
Boswell, James, 111.
Bradley, F. H., 113.
Brahma, Nalini Kanta, 21, 22, 209, 257n, 292n, 343.

General Index